"Everyone aspiring to expound ~~book, Old Testament. One of t~~ neglect of adequate preparation ~~boun in perso~~ Bible with accuracy. Such neglect leads to a denial of biblical unity and continuity. Greg Harris instructs the expositor by exemplifying the process and explaining the foundation for each step. He studiously ties exposition to the text by means of a sound hermeneutic.

Throughout *The Bible Expositor's Handbook, New Testament,* readers will experience the care and compassion of their guide and intuitively understand that he is interceding with the Father on their behalf as they read, study, and apply biblical truth to their lives. Recommend this resource to every Christian—it will richly reward their time within its pages and along its trails."

—*William D. Barrick, professor emeritus of Old Testament, The Master's Seminary*

"I am absolutely thrilled that this volume has been written! *The Bible Expositor's Handbook, Old & New Testaments* is not your ordinary textbook. Greg Harris has written an easy-to-read masterpiece that exposes readers to the glory and wonder of Christ in both Old and New Testaments. *The Bible Expositor's Handbook* is worthy of recognition, time and attention. Anyone interested in the Bible should be interested in this excellent work. I have already begun to use this book to teach at our theological institute in the South Pacific because it is relentlessly biblical, and I liked its straightforward exegesis. The study questions at the end of each chapter are well thought out and ready to be used in a classroom setting. It is a must read because of its Bible-centered approach. Highly Recommended!"

—*Premend Choy, executive vice-president, College of Theology and Evangelism, Fiji*

"Greg Harris is known for his God-given ability to open the Scriptures to his audience, as well as his faithfulness to the inspiration, inerrancy and infallibility of the Bible. His deep commitment to the Word of God, along with his experience as a teacher of Bible Exposition classes for over three decades, culminates in *The Bible Expositor's Handbook, Old & New Testaments* where he, with the Bible as the only source, shows the unity and incredible works of our Lord Jesus Christ. This is not a book about the Bible—this is a worshipful read and an incredibly valuable tool. For the serious student of the Scriptures, *The Bible Expositor's Handbook, Old & New Testaments* contains an unparalleled wealth of wisdom. It will be a book that you will never stop using with others."

—*Georg Huber, national director, Precept Ministries, German-speaking Europe*

"*The Bible Expositor's Handbook* is a helpful guide to understanding the overall message of Scripture. Greg Harris demonstrates what it means to have a consistent, literal-grammatical-historical hermeneutic all the way from Genesis to Revelation. This is a rare resource that does not shy away from difficult passages that are often raised against interpreting the Bible according to the plain sense. I highly recommend this resource to every faithful expositor."

—*John McArthur, pastor-teacher, Grace Community Church, Sun Valley, CA, and chancellor emeritus, The Master's Seminary*

"In *The Bible Expositor's Handbook, Old & New Testaments*, Harris uses clear and attractive language to explain deep biblical truths. The approach is didactic, emphasizing each step of the exegetical process. The deliberate use of the Bible only as the textbook is a great feature of this book; it allows Scripture to interpret Scripture. Every chapter contributes to a clearer understanding of the sovereignty of God in history and sets the text studied within God's overarching plan for humanity. This combined edition offers an overview of the key messages of Scripture, and provides a pattern for expositional study. This is an essential work in the library of any Bible teacher and Bible lover."

—*Faly Ravoahangy, ministry partner, Madagascar 3M*

"*The Bible Expositor's Handbook: Old & New Testaments* summarizes Greg Harris' best thinking on various themes of both the Old and New Testaments. With his commitment to the inspiration, inerrancy and authority of Scripture, Harris calls for a return to the priority of reading and expositing the Bible itself, via a historical-grammatical hermeneutic. The book provides crucial keys needed to unlock specific portions of Scripture. I am so thankful for this *Handbook* that is a gift to the church, and consider it an honor to give endorsement to a work by my life-long friend who has greatly enriched my life beyond words."

—*Imad N. Shehadeh, president, professor of theology, Jordan Evangelical Theological Seminary*

THE BIBLE
EXPOSITOR'S
HANDBOOK

THE BIBLE
EXPOSITOR'S
HANDBOOK

OLD & NEW TESTAMENTS

GREG HARRIS

ACADEMIC
NASHVILLE, TENNESSEE

Contents

Dedication

To the Master's Academies International, and to all such lovers of God's Word, especially to such students as those whom I taught at Washington Bible College (1989–95), Southeastern College at Wake Forest/Southeastern Baptist Theological Seminary (1997–2006), and The Master's Seminary (2006–present).

And He said to them, "O foolish men and slow of heart to believe in all that the prophets have spoken! Was it not necessary for the Christ to suffer these things and to enter into His glory?" Then beginning with Moses and with all the prophets, He explained to them the things concerning Himself in all the Scriptures. —Luke 24:25–27

Now He said to them, "These are My words which I spoke to you while I was still with you, that all things which are written about Me in the Law of Moses and the Prophets and the Psalms must be fulfilled." —Luke 24:44

Acknowledgments

Dr. Greg Harris's personal editor: Rebecca R. Howard.

Dr. Greg Harris's website www.glorybooks.org.

An eternal gratitude for the godly input and expertise put into this book by Dr. William Barrick—and for his friendship and brotherhood. God will show you in heaven the fruits of your labors.

The Master's Seminary consulting class, Fall 2015: Abera Ajula, David Highfield, Daniel MtPleasant, Andy Ramanahyake, Andre Randolph, Curtis Tyler, Daniel Wilson, and, those untimely born and grafted in, Chazz Anderson, Kevin Laymon, Faly Ravoahangy, and Michael Butler.

The Master's Seminary consulting class, Spring 2017: Hans Kaufman, Bruce Alvord, Faly Ravoahangy, and Andre Randolph. Untimely born and grafted in: Chazz Anderson, Kevin Laymon, and Jamie Jackson.

The Master's Seminary consulting class, Spring 2019 (We didn't actually have a TMS consulting class this time around, but I went ahead and used the term anyway): Bob and Julie Fanciullacci, Becky Howard, Nancy Anderson—and those untimely born and grafted in: Kevin Laymon, Jim Rouse, Rob Thurman, Aaron Filburn, Faly Ravoahangy, Chad Tucker, Sandra Laymon, Chris Fowler, and Bill Barber.

Thanks for the men's retreat, Spring 2017, for Grace Chapel, Indio, California, for being my "guinea pig" group for "In Christ Alone."

PART 1

THE OLD TESTAMENT

CHAPTER I

So You Want to Be an Expositor?

To become a seasoned expositor of God's Word requires a method, or a series of specific steps. Equally important, however, is one's starting point, which is, sadly, quite often lacking. One's starting point is important not only for learning how to become a better expositor, but also as a means of attaining reverence for God, another aspect of biblical exposition that is often overlooked. In this chapter, we will discuss the starting point for becoming a Bible expositor before we look at the process. In short, we start—and stay—with God.

I have had the high privilege and calling of teaching Bible Exposition classes for more than thirty years. Very often, when I finish a class on a book such as Isaiah or Hebrews, students will sigh and say, "Oh, if we could only go back to the beginning of the Bible and do what we are doing now, it would be so tremendously rewarding!"

I agree—such is the richness of God's Word. However, I remind them that if we were to do that, they would be in seminary for twenty or more years and never leave our campus or go to minister to churches or institutions. Yet it is in response to this desire, and through God's sovereignty, that *The Bible Expositor's Handbook: Old Testament Edition*, has come into existence.

What most intrigued me about writing this series was the vision of B&H Academic to make the Bible the primary text. It is not that Bible research and commentaries are unimportant; there are wonderful resources available with which God has blessed His church throughout the centuries. But unfortunately too often, the more students progress in theological training, the less they use their Bibles. As my current and former students know, I do not permit computers in my classes. This is not punishment; it is intended as part of the process of hiding God's Word in their hearts—not their hard drives. And there are no quick solutions for accomplishing this. We all learn throughout our entire lives. I tell students to bring a Bible they can mark as we follow some of God's biblical trails. I hope that it will be a Bible they can take into the hospital room of someone facing death, use to comfort people in mourning or grief, or pull out as they witness to someone in the seat next to them on a bus or plane. What's more, I fear a time will come when around the world, even in America, the Bible may be the only resource available to God's people. Yet even then, owning a Bible could prove to be dangerous.

Of course, no single biblical resource could cover everything needed to be an expositor of God's Word or deal with every theological issue or current hotly debated topic. And such is not my intent. The purpose of this book is to establish some biblical boundaries based upon several divine, and immovable, truths for understanding and expositing God's Word. There are times, most would agree, when assistance is needed from a more seasoned believer in helping others better understand biblical truths. Acts 18:24–26 shows such an example, in Priscilla and Aquila:

> Now a certain Jew named Apollos, an Alexandrian by birth, an eloquent man, came to Ephesus; and he was mighty in the Scriptures. This man had been instructed in the way of the Lord; and being fervent in spirit, he was speaking and teaching accurately the things concerning Jesus, being acquainted only with the baptism of John; and he began to speak out boldly in the synagogue. But when Priscilla and Aquila heard him, they took him aside and explained to him the way of God more accurately.

My desire is that *The Bible Expositor's Handbook* will be used in the same way. And while no book can cover every issue, it will be shown that there are some issues you must be aware of if you are going to understand God's Word.

The Irreplaceable Point of Beginning

The discipline of hermeneutics can be defined as the rules by which the Bible is interpreted. With this in mind, hermeneutics serves an indispensable role in the formation of one's methodology. While a sound methodology is utterly important and cannot be overlooked, true, God-honoring lovers of God's Word need an even more fundamental starting point. Simply expressed, before the methodology (the how-to), we need to focus on—and prayerfully worship in Spirit and truth—the God to whom the Bible belongs.

Below are just a few examples (to which many more could be added) of some of the core biblical truths from which we can establish the irreplaceable point of beginning for biblical exposition. That beginning point entails knowing how to approach God and His Word. First, one must be humble before God, contrite in spirit, and trembling at His Word. Isaiah 66:1–2 reads:

> *Thus says the LORD,*
>
> *"Heaven is My throne, and the earth is My footstool.*
>
> *Where then is a house you could build for Me?*
>
> *And where is a place that I may rest ?*
>
> *For My hand made all these things,*
>
> *Thus all these things came into being," declares the LORD.*
>
> *"But to this one I will look,*
>
> *To him who is humble and contrite of spirit, and who trembles at My word."*

Note the three divine requirements for approaching God and His Word: being humble, being contrite of spirit, and being one who trembles (in fear or excitement) at His Word. All of these spiritual dispositions, it should be observed, are mocked by the world and by many who are considered to be part of "the Christian world."

Second, one must be a learner. In Matt 11:28–29, Jesus says, "Come . . . learn of Me" (KJV), with the word learn serving, in the Greek, as the base word for disciple. A disciple, then, is a learner, and that is just what God calls us to be. He did not say, come and I will teach you a method. He says, come and learn of—and from—Me.

Third, one must hunger for the pure milk of God's Word. First Peter 2:1–3 states, "Therefore, putting aside all malice and all deceit and hypocrisy and envy and all slander, like newborn babes, long for the pure milk of the word, so that by it you may grow in respect to salvation, if you have tasted the kindness of the Lord." The biblical command here entails longing "for the pure milk of the word"—not theological studies (although that has its place), not coffee-table debates, and not philosophy. God wants us, even commands us, to long for the pure milk of His Word as a newborn baby would for his mother's milk. Sadly, often as we grow in our faith, we get "weaned away" from the pure milk of the Word, and we replace it with something else, wrongly concluding, "we can take it from here."

Fourth, one should strive to grow in grace and knowledge. In 2 Pet 3:18 the author exhorts us to "grow in the grace and knowledge of our Lord and Savior Jesus Christ. To Him be the glory, both now and to the day of eternity. Amen." Both grace and knowledge are required for spiritual growth. To grow in grace only, and not have that bound to true biblical knowledge, has no boundaries or basis for evaluation. Since the beginning of the church, many people have called—and still call today—virtually anything "growing in grace," even if what is done is contrary to Scripture. Simply put, growing in grace must have solid biblical evidence for it, otherwise, it is not truly growing in God's grace, no matter how well meaning it may be. Paul thus warned the church in Col 2:18, "Let no one keep defrauding you of your prize by delighting in self-abasement and the worship of the angels, taking his stand on visions he has seen, inflated without cause by his fleshly mind." Paul concluded Colossians 2 this way: "These are matters which have, to be sure, the appearance of wisdom in self-made religion and self-abasement and severe treatment of the body, but are of no value against fleshly indulgence" (v. 23). Many at the church in Colossae would have considered most or all of these components to be wonderful aspects of their Christian spiritual growth. Yet God—by means of the apostle Paul—did not find them to be acceptable to Him.

So to grow only in grace has no biblical boundaries for how that is accomplished or measured, or even if it has occurred at all. In a similar manner, the other extreme is valid to consider: to grow only in knowledge without grace not only treats God's Word as a mere textbook, but also removes God Himself from the hermeneutical task. God does not permit either extreme in true biblical exposition.

> **CORE TRUTH:** Never go to God's Word merely for a sermon or Bible lesson; go to God's Word for truth; the preaching or teaching comes from those truths.

Fifth, one must receive the Word with great eagerness. Acts 17:11 describes the Jews at the synagogue of Berea: "Now these were more noble-minded than those in Thessalonica, for they received the word with great eagerness, examining the Scriptures daily to see whether these things were so." The prayer of the "Berean Christian" might be best summed up by Ps 119:18, "Open my eyes, that I may behold wonderful things from Your law." From this psalm about the truthfulness and treasure of God's Word comes this prayer that God would open our eyes to behold wonderful truths in His Word. God is the ultimate teacher; God is the ultimate author; and God is the ultimate illuminator of His Word. And, while I do not want to sound overly mystical, there will always be a spiritual component to true biblical exposition that the world will never understand. Being a "Berean Christian," then, is not only recommended, it is required for those delving into this book and for any other book that presents itself as teaching biblical truths. A "Berean Christian," then, will carefully search the Scriptures to see whether what is being presented is true or not.

In summary, the fundamental starting point of true biblical exposition, that is, the irreplaceable point of beginning and staying, is to come humbly before God, contrite in spirit, and trembling at His Word (Isa 66:1–2); to come as learners, as His disciples (Matt 11:29); to hunger for the pure milk of God's Word (1 Pet 2:1–3); to strive to grow in grace (from the inside out while walking with Him) and knowledge (true, biblical knowledge, not our mere emotion); and to receive the Word with great eagerness. For those who find these core biblical truths unimportant or overly simplistic, read—and fear—Jesus's rebuke of the Ephesian church in Rev 2:1–7, who after doing so many things right "had left their first love."

Why Do We Need a Bible Exposition Handbook?

One might ask why we need another book about Bible exposition. To answer this question, it is important to explain a few terms. This book will assume a clear distinction between Bible exposition and expository preaching or teaching. While these two tasks are related, they are not identical. I will use Bible exposition to refer to the expositional method and the expositional preparation. Expository preaching and teaching, however, are outlets for the truths you have found in God's Word in your expositional studies. Therefore, this handbook will focus primarily on the content part and secondarily on the methodology undergirding that content. In other words, we are not seeking to sermonize the text but to grow in our understanding of biblical truth. Undergirding this approach are two important convictions:

> **CORE TRUTH:** Your expository preaching or teaching will only be as good as your expository study—or lack thereof.

> **CORE TRUTH:** Expository preaching is much more than "expository calendaring."

It is important not to reverse this process. You can set up your calendar to ensure that all biblical texts are addressed in a particular order (e.g., week 1, Phil 1:1–4; week 2, Phil 1:5–7, etc.). To be sure, many would consider this approach to be expository preaching. But without solid Bible exposition (expository preparation), it is possible to use this method for years without ever addressing what the book is actually about. For instance, if you did not know that virtually everything Paul wrote to the Corinthians in his first epistle was extremely corrective in nature for what they were doing wrong, you could "calendar preach" through 1 Corinthians and ignorantly encourage your listeners to follow the same example of this multifacetedly sinful church. That is why this handbook will focus more on the study of the content than on the delivery of that content. One way we hope to achieve this goal is by implementing the hermeneutical methods you may have already been taught and applying them to key biblical texts. This approach will not only help readers grow in the understanding of God's Word, but also make readers become more aware of some of the obstacles to learning.

A brief example might help illustrate the importance of moving from Bible exposition to expository preaching and teaching. While conceding that there are different ways to approach the text, we will confine our method to the oft-used trifold approach of Howard Hendricks's *Living by the Book*, which includes (1) observation—what the text says, (2) interpretation—what the text means, and (3) application—what we can apply to our lives. This hermeneutical approach will be applied to Job 8:3–7, a discourse spoken by Eliphaz:

> *Does God pervert justice*
>
> *Or does the Almighty pervert what is right?*
>
> *If your sons sinned against Him,*
>
> *Then He delivered them into the power of their transgression.*
>
> *If you would seek God*
>
> *And implore the compassion of the Almighty,*
>
> *If you are pure and upright,*
>
> *Surely now He would rouse Himself for you*
>
> *And restore your righteous estate.*
>
> *Though your beginning was insignificant,*
>
> *Yet your end will increase greatly.*

Although one could make a number of observations about this text, we will limit ourselves to one, namely that it begins with a rhetorical question that asks if Almighty God would pervert justice. Assuming a negative answer, a reader might draw several interpretive conclusions related to God delivering sinners into the power of the transgressions committed and then related to imploring one to seek God and His compassion. Further, the overarching meaning of the text might even be connected to Jesus and His work in the Gospels. Finally, an application might ask if anyone would like to partake of the same offer from God.

The problem with this interpretation, however, is that it is all wrong. You might reply, "This cannot be wrong! How could this possibly be wrong or contrary to Scripture?" Here we need to note a major truth: Scripture references are not fortune cookies or one-liners. One must consider whether there is other divine revelation that God has given earlier or later that gives clarification. In this case He has. The dialogue in Job 8:3–7 comes from the lips of Eliphaz, one of Job's friends. Yet when we come to the end of the book, God warns Eliphaz and others:

> It came about after the Lord had spoken these words to Job, that the Lord said to Eliphaz the Temanite, "My wrath is kindled against you and against your two friends, because you have not spoken of Me what is right as My servant Job has. Now therefore, take for yourselves seven bulls and seven rams, and go to My servant Job, and offer up a burnt offering for yourselves, and My servant Job will pray for you. For I will accept him so that I may not do with you according to your folly, because you have not spoken of Me what is right, as My servant Job has." So Eliphaz the Temanite and Bildad the Shuhite and Zophar the Naamathite went and did as the Lord told them; and the Lord accepted Job. (Job 42:7–9)

Twice in this section God declares that Eliphaz and his two friends did not speak the truth concerning Him, and God strongly warned that I may "not deal with you as your folly deserves." People who cite or quote from the book of Job often refer unwittingly to various passages from Job's three friends whom God says do not speak accurately concerning him. Granted, some of these same concepts or truths may be found elsewhere in Scripture; that is not the point here. The point is that you can follow a time-honored hermeneutical procedure with an expositional calendaring of the texts and unintentionally fail to do either sound Bible exposition or the solid biblical expository teaching or preaching that would follow.

What is frequently omitted in such ill-advised approaches, then, is the continuity, cohesiveness, and unity of Scripture as a whole, which will be one of the primary emphases of *The Bible Expositor's Handbook*. Where does a verse occur in Scripture? Who is being addressed or written about? What information has God already given? What does He give later to clarify or expand? This is a lifetime of learning for all of us, and no one ever learns all of it. Although we cannot cover everything in the Bible, there certainly are things we must cover.

That Bible exposition should give special attention to the continuity and assimilation of a given text is a focus of the present study; undergirding this effort is a literal-grammatical hermeneutic. More and more people are abandoning this hermeneutic as being outdated and out of fashion. Yet I will argue that the biblical writers themselves do not hold such a position. To clarify what I mean by literal-grammatical, let us consider the example above of the Bereans in Acts 17 who (1) were more noble-minded than those at Thessalonica, (2) received the word with great eagerness, (3) examined the Scriptures daily to see whether those things were so. It is evident from this text that those so described received God's Word, studied it carefully, and examined it daily to see whether these things were true. For them to study, compare, and make conclusions, they would have had to have employed the literal-grammatical hermeneutic, because that was the only way by which any of the claims could have been evaluated.

A literal-grammatical approach, then, takes the biblical text at face value, rather than an approach that spiritualizes much of the historical elements of a given text. Such spiritualizing approaches, however, often differ wildly from one interpreter to the next. Before abandoning the literal-grammatical hermeneutic, one ought to consider if such an approach fits within the unfolding message of Scripture. And while we cannot consider all the verses of the Bible, we can apply this approach to key verses. We will begin the next chapter with Jesus's own understanding of the Scriptures, that is, the Old Testament.

One Final Prayer for Us

We note one final item for this first chapter, and we do so by going to the Luke 24 account of Jesus with His two disciples on the road to Emmaus on the day He arose from the dead. Before Jesus revealed to them who He was and is, He mildly rebuked and admonished them in Luke 24:25–27:

> *And He said to them, "O foolish men and slow of heart to believe in all that the prophets have spoken! Was it not necessary for the Christ to suffer these things and to enter into His glory?" And beginning with Moses and with all the prophets, He explained to them the things concerning Himself in all the Scriptures.*

We note the following verses as well:

And they approached the village where they were going, and He acted as
though He were going farther. But they urged Him, saying, "Stay with us,
for it is getting toward evening, and the day is now nearly over." So He went
in to stay with them. When He had reclined at the table with them, He took
the bread and blessed it, and breaking it, He began giving it to them. Then
their eyes were opened and they recognized Him; and He vanished from
their sight. (Luke 24:28–31)

Following this grand encounter with the risen Christ, these two lovers of God's Word responded in true worship, as recorded in Luke 24:32:
"They said to one another, 'Were not our hearts burning within us while
He was speaking to us on the road, while He was explaining the Scriptures
to us?'" May this hold true for you and for me—that our hearts would burn
within us as we go through God's Word, and that it would be multiplied
and used many times over to the glory of God, as people feed on the Word
of God and grow in true grace and knowledge of Him.

Conclusion

In this chapter we learned, first, that the starting point for becoming an
expositor of God's Word is God Himself, and there are no shortcuts. It
takes time and effort to "grow in the grace and knowledge of our Lord and
Savior Jesus Christ" (2 Pet 3:18). And if you think you will ever outgrow
this initial core concept that being a disciple means being a person who
is ultimately taught by God, you will not have any true ministry resulting
from your walk with Him. Second, we learned that one should not go to
God's Word for a sermon or a teaching outline; we go to God's Word for
truth. From these truths emerge expository sermons and teachings. Third,
two additional truths from this initial chapter are interconnected: (1) Your
expository preaching or teaching will only be as good as your expository
study, or lack thereof. (2) Expository preaching is much more than "expository calendaring." You can go through the text of a biblical book in se-
quential order and still not necessarily be handling God's Word accurately.
So even employing the "tried-and-true" process of (1) observation of a

text, (2) interpretation of the text, and (3) application from the text will not necessarily involve rightly dividing the Word of God.

Part of the purpose of the Old Testament part of this book is to assist with the lifelong process of expositing God's Word. While we cannot cover all of the Old Testament, we will highlight some incredibly essential texts and learn as we go by doing. Also, we will implement a literal-grammatical hermeneutic to see if this is indeed a logical means of biblical interpretation, and we will do so as we follow the biblical trail that God has set before us.

Deeper Walk Study Questions

1. From the texts given, list and summarize all the spiritual qualifications of being an expositor. Why are these verses important to understand at the beginning of becoming an expositor? What are some of the disasters (spiritually speaking) if one does not start with or keep these in mind throughout one's entire life? What are you going to do to keep them from happening to you? Explain and be specific.

2. List and discuss five substantial truths regarding what the Ephesian church did that prompted rebuke by Jesus in Rev 2:1–7. List and discuss five disastrous truths if people do not heed the example of the Berean church in Acts 17:11.

3. Name five specific ways "going to the Bible for truth" differs from going to the Bible for a sermon or a teaching. Why is this so important to your overall Christian walk? Explain.

4. Make five sound deductions from the following sentence: "Expository preaching is much more than expository calendaring." Why is this true? List some of this truth's consequences.

5. List six deductions from Job 42:7–9 that help us better understand the book of Job. Make four deductions about how this relates to studying the rest of the Bible.

CHAPTER 2

The Old Testament Is the Story of Jesus

I have written *The Bible Expositor's Handbook* for those who believe the Bible.

I do not argue for the Bible's God-breathed origin and uniqueness; God does (2 Tim 3:16). Others have the God-given mandate/assignment to argue against those who reject God's Word.

Many people expositing the Old Testament assume what I did for years, namely that the Old Testament contains many examples for us to use in our own Christian lives. Paul himself wrote concerning the wilderness generation, "Now these things happened as examples for us, so that we would not crave evil things, as they also craved" (1 Cor 10:6), and then a few verses later, "Now these things happened to them as an example, and they were written for our instruction, upon whom the ends of the ages have come" (1 Cor 10:11). This is an example of a direct application of Old Testament texts. While applying them directly to our lives has its place, it becomes problematic when the entire Old Testament is treated in such a way. In this chapter we will explore the ways in which God has revealed just how He wants His Old Testament to be interpreted. We find these foundational truths in the New Testament and, by understanding these verses, we are able to look at the Old Testament with better clarity.

CORE TRUTH: A pitfall for many expositors is either to ignore the Old Testament as a text containing God-breathed doctrine, or to take a doctrinal truth set forth by God and turn this into "life lessons."

Foundational Truths for Studying the Old Testament

God chose to disclose truths about the Old Testament so that when these texts are viewed accordingly, they make the Scriptures open up before our very eyes. However, one must, first, note what those truths are, and, second, apply them to the interpretation of the Old Testament accordingly. Let's look at three foundational truths critical to our interpreting the Old Testament.

First, just like the New Testament, the Old Testament contains God-inspired doctrine. As a matter of fact, it is the Old Testament that serves as the scriptural context for the New Testament authors' claim that "all Scripture is given by inspiration of God." Consider 2 Tim 3:14–17:

> *You, however, continue in the things you have learned and become con-vinced of, knowing from whom you have learned them, and that from child-hood you have known the sacred writings which are able to give you the wisdom that leads to salvation through faith which is in Christ Jesus.*

> *All Scripture is inspired by God and profitable for teaching, for reproof, for correction, for training in righteousness; so that the man of God may be adequate, equipped for every good work.*

Many expositors are oblivious to or ignore the Old Testament as a text containing God-breathed doctrine, or they take a doctrinal truth set forth by God in the Old Testament and turn this into "life lessons." However, 2 Tim 3:16 does not say, "All [Old Testament] Scripture is profitable for application or life lessons." Not everything necessarily carries over from the Old Testament into the New. Nevertheless, if the God-inspired doctrine of the Old Testament is ignored, there remains a vast gap in "the man of God" being complete, "equipped for every good work."

I will sometimes jokingly say to my classes, "Let's turn to the first verses of Scripture." While the students are turning to Genesis 1, I start reading out loud from John 1. Even though written many centuries after Moses wrote Genesis, John 1:1–3 contains Scripture references that refer to the earliest time in all the Bible: "In the beginning was the Word, and the Word was with God, and the Word was God. He was in the beginning with God. All things came into being through Him, and apart from Him nothing came into being that has come into being." These verses refer to eternity past, long before Genesis 1. However, the creator aspect of the second Member of the Godhead is found not only in John 1:3 but also in John 1:10, "He was in the world, and the world was made through Him, and the world did not know Him."

> **CORE TRUTH:** John 1 is a great section of Scripture to present to people in cults, such as Jehovah's Witnesses and Mormons, who teach the false doctrine that Jesus was a created being and is lower in status than God the Father.

Second, according to the New Testament, the Pentateuch is the story of Jesus. Accordingly, it is doctrinal or, more specifically, Christological truth, not merely life lessons or application. Consider John 5:45–47:

> *Do not think that I will accuse you before the Father; the one who accuses you is Moses, in whom you have set your hope. For if you believed Moses, you would believe Me, for he wrote about Me. But if you do not believe his writings, how will you believe My words?*

These important verses changed my perspective on the Old Testament. I had no doubt read these verses many times before, but I had failed to notice their hermeneutical significance. What's more, I had read many books on the Pentateuch. I had even taught a class on the topic a few times before considering and implementing what Jesus revealed to the Jews who opposed Him in John 5:45–47. If you had asked me then about the Old Testament, I would have answered as most people do, that it is the story of creation, Adam and Eve, the fall, the flood, Moses's birth, and so forth. But Jesus specifically said, "Moses wrote about Me," and linked His teaching about Himself to properly understanding this biblical doctrine. So while the first five books of the Bible contain the creation account and Adam and Eve and such, Jesus specifically sets forth that the Pentateuch is His story—the story of Jesus. If you are looking for Him, you will clearly see Him in these first five books; if you are not looking for Him, you most likely will miss Him, as I did. Once I started factoring John 5:45–47 into my studies, the name of the class unofficially became "Jesus in the Pentateuch."

> **FOUNDATIONAL TRUTH:** John 5:45–47 clearly states that the Pentateuch is the story of Jesus and is doctrinal truth—not life lessons or application.

> **FOUNDATIONAL TRUTH:** Watch out for the other extreme—instead of ignoring the teaching of Jesus in John 5:45–47, trying to make everything in the Pentateuch a picture of or a reference to Jesus.

A third truth: not only the Pentateuch, but all of the Old Testament is the story of Jesus. If you were like me, you may have started reading your Bible in Luke 2, the birth of Jesus, or in Gabriel's pronouncement to Mary in Luke 1. Or perhaps you began with the cross of Jesus as the initial place to begin to understand the gospel. Yet in light of John 5, cited above, the first five books of the Bible are just as much a part of His story as the New Testament. I have taught these verses at various churches and Bible conferences, and it makes those who love God and His Word say, "Let's go find Jesus in the Pentateuch!" instead of avoiding it. But there is more, for the story of Jesus expands well beyond the Pentateuch.

Luke 24 contains the account of the resurrected Jesus and the women at the empty tomb. It also contains the account of His special visit with two of His disciples later on that same day:

> *And behold, two of them were going that very day to a village named Emmaus, which was about seven miles from Jerusalem. And they were talking with each other about all these things which had taken place. While they were talking and discussing, Jesus Himself approached and began travelling with them. But their eyes were prevented from recognizing Him. And He said to them, "What are these words that you are exchanging with one another as you are walking?" And they stood still, looking sad. One of them, named Cleopas, answered and said to Him, "Are You the only one visiting Jerusalem and unaware of the things which have happened here in these days?" And He said to them, "What things?" And they said to Him, "The things about Jesus the Nazarene, who was a prophet mighty in deed and word in the sight of God and all the people, and how the chief priests and our rulers delivered Him to the sentence of death, and crucified Him. But we were hoping that it was He who was going to redeem Israel. Indeed, besides all this,*

it is the third day since these things happened. But also some women among us amazed us. When they were at the tomb early in the morning, and did not find His body, they came, saying that they had also seen a vision of angels, who said that He was alive. Some of those who were with us went to the tomb and found it just exactly as the women also had said; but Him they did not see." And He said to them, "O foolish men and slow of heart to believe in all that the prophets have spoken! Was it not necessary for the Christ to suffer these things and to enter into His glory?" And beginning with Moses and with all the prophets, He explained to them the things concerning Himself in all the Scriptures. (Luke 24:13–27)

Note especially the importance of the last sentence above: "And beginning with Moses and with all the prophets . . ." Jesus used a twofold division of the Old Testament to broaden it from John 5 and the Pentateuch to "all the Scriptures." So beginning with Moses and then all the way through to the end, "He explained . . . concerning Himself"—eternal doctrine, not life lessons—"in all the Scriptures." Of course, the reference to "all the Scriptures" at this time meant the Old Testament. So from this encounter, we should look for and expect Jesus not only in the books of Moses but all the way through Scripture.

But the story does not end there.

Later, on the same day, after Jesus had dined with the two disciples on the road to Emmaus, after which He instantaneously vanished from their sight, they ran to report it to the eleven apostles, as Luke 24:36–47 explains:

And while they were telling these things, He Himself stood in their midst. But they were startled and frightened and thought that they were seeing a spirit. And He said to them, "Why are you troubled, and why do doubts arise in your hearts? See My hands and My feet, that it is I Myself; touch Me and see, for a spirit does not have flesh and bones as you see that I have." And when He had said this, He showed them His hands and His feet. While they still could not believe it for joy and were marveling, He said to them,

"Have you anything here to eat?" They gave Him a piece of a broiled fish; and He took it and ate it before them.

Now He said to them, "These are My words which I spoke to you while I was still with you, that all things which are written about Me in the Law of Moses and the Prophets and the Psalms must be fulfilled." Then He opened their minds to understand the Scriptures, and He said to them, "Thus it is written, that the Christ would suffer and rise again from the dead the third day; and that repentance for forgiveness of sins would be proclaimed in His name to all the nations, beginning from Jerusalem."

In Luke 24:44, Jesus chose to use the threefold division of the Old Testament. But as with the earlier use in the same chapter, Jesus specifically established the biblical doctrine "that all things which are written about Me in the Law of Moses and the Prophets and the Psalms must be fulfilled." So although not every individual Scripture verse given at the time alludes to Jesus, they most certainly collectively and definitively point to Jesus as the promised Messiah, Son of God. As mentioned previously, these are not "life application lessons," this is the Life (John 14:6) teaching biblical doctrine in reference to Himself. One more item to note—the original need in Luke 24:45, namely that "He opened their minds [literally, "mind" singular] to understand the Scriptures."

From Jesus's twofold examples in Luke 24, we should not overlook a very important point: Jesus began—and stayed—in God's written Word to point to eternal doctrines about Himself.

FOUNDATIONAL TRUTH: On the day He was resurrected, twice in instructing His disciples, Jesus began "with [the books of] Moses," not with any theoretical or presumed covenant of grace or covenant of works, to which many Christians hold. Everything Jesus taught that day was taken solely from Scripture.

Jesus began—and stayed—in God's written Word to point to eternal doctrines about Himself.

A final foundational truth about interpreting the Old Testament is evident in Peter's sermon in Acts 2: the death of Jesus was "the predetermined plan"—singular, not "plans"—"and foreknowledge of God." Consider Peter's words in Acts 2:22–23:

Men of Israel, listen to these words: Jesus the Nazarene, a man attested to you by God with miracles and wonders and signs which God performed through Him in your midst, just as you yourselves know—this Man, delivered over by the predetermined plan and foreknowledge of God, you nailed to a cross by the hands of godless men and put Him to death.

These verses give both the human and the divine side of the death of Jesus; they also contain two tremendously important truths that help our understanding of the Old Testament. First, the death of Jesus was "the predetermined plan and foreknowledge [where we get our word prognosis] of God."

> **FOUNDATIONAL TRUTH:** Acts 2:23 is good to cite to counter liberal critics who claim that events got out of control and that Jesus never intended to be crucified, an aspect of "open theology," which teaches that God did not know how things would turn out; God was "learning" as events unfolded from Genesis onward.

Second, these verses also reveal that there was and never is any "Plan B" with God—only one plan. What's more, this plan was set in motion long before the events of Genesis 1 and all that followed. That this plan would center on the person and work of Jesus who was "foreknown before the foundation of the world" is evident from 1 Pet 1:17–21:

If you address as Father the One who impartially judges according to each one's work, conduct yourselves in fear during the time of your stay on earth; knowing that you were not redeemed with perishable things like silver or gold from your futile way of life inherited from your forefathers, but with precious blood, as of a lamb unblemished and spotless, the blood of Christ. For He was foreknown before the foundation of the world, but has appeared in these last times for the sake of you who through Him are believers in God, who raised Him from the dead and gave Him glory, so that your faith and hope are in God.

> **FOUNDATIONAL TRUTH:** Before there was the first sin, the Godhead had already determined the divine plan—singular—of salvation.

> **FOUNDATIONAL TRUTH:** Before the first sinners in Genesis 3, there was already a Savior—singular—in the mind of God.

Before creation and the subsequent fall of Adam and Eve, the Trinity had determined what Paul would so beautifully articulate in Phil 2:5–8:

> *Have this attitude in yourselves which was also in Christ Jesus, who, although He existed in the form of God, did not regard equality with God a thing to be grasped, but emptied Himself, taking the form of a bond-servant, and being made in the likeness of men. Being found in appearance as a man, He humbled Himself by becoming obedient to the point of death, even death on a cross.*

Even prior to the first sin, according to Paul, the Godhead had already determined the divine plan—singular—of salvation through Jesus Christ.

Yet this is a unified plan that begins to unfold in Genesis and is subsequently written about and prophesied from Genesis all the way through Revelation. As such, it is all part of the overall love story of God, all part of the Old Testament being the story of Jesus. While space precludes an analysis of every aspect of the story of Jesus within the Old Testament, some treatment of its early development in the Genesis account is warranted here.

After the pristine beauty of God's perfect creation in Genesis 1–2, an enemy approached unannounced and led God's two children into sinful defilement in Genesis 3. Once the first sins occurred, the following took place in Gen 3:6–7:

> *When the woman saw that the tree was good for food, and that it was a delight to the eyes, and that the tree was desirable to make one wise, she took from its fruit and ate; and she gave also to her husband with her, and he ate. Then the eyes of both of them were opened, and they knew that they were naked; and they sewed fig leaves together and made themselves loin coverings.*

> **FOUNDATIONAL TRUTHS:** Sin kills; it always kills. Sin separates; it always separates. Also, it was Adam and Eve's first sin—not their millionth—that made them unholy, defiled, and lost before the Holy God.

Subsequent to this failure of the first couple was the initial impulse to hide from their Creator. Genesis 3:8 explains, "They heard the sound of the LORD God walking in the garden in the cool of the day, and the man and his wife hid themselves from the presence of the LORD God among the trees of the garden."

In addition to shame and separation, the ramifications of their sin were manifest in God's curse against Adam and Eve and their offspring, the physical serpent, and ultimately "the serpent of old," Satan (Rev 12:9). Yet God also gave a revelatory promise in Gen 3:15:

And I will put enmity

Between you and the woman,

And between your seed and her seed;

He shall bruise you on the head,

And you shall bruise him on the heel.

The operative question from this point forward is, who is this One who will crush the head of the serpent? God knew the answer, long ago determined in history past; we who live this side of the cross know the answer as well. Those present at the time did not know, because it was not yet revealed to them. The Old Testament begins telling the story of the One who will not only crush the head of the serpent at the Savior's death, but, far beyond this, it tells of His return in and reign in glory.

FOUNDATIONAL TRUTH: The Old Testament is the story of Jesus—not "was the story"—because so much of it remains unfulfilled. If the Old Testament "was" the story of Jesus, every prophecy about Him would have already been fulfilled, but as we will clearly see, more prophecies remain unfulfilled about Him at the present time than have already been fulfilled.

We could add more, but one final grace gift in Genesis 3 should be noted. Genesis 3:7 states that after their sin Adam and Eve "sewed fig leaves together and made themselves loin coverings." But God in His holiness and grace did not accept their man-made attempt to cover their own sin. Genesis 3:21 reveals that God took "garments of skin for Adam and his wife, and clothed them." While not stated explicitly, it is implied that this divine act represents the first blood sacrifice in history, the first "substitutionary atonement."

This is not fair. Adam and Eve sinned, not this animal. This animal was holy, innocent, and undefiled. The text does not say what animal shed its blood as a temporary covering for the sins of the first couple, but a lamb would fit beautifully here. We will have to wait to get to heaven to see if it was indeed a lamb. Regardless of the animal's species, its death must have been horribly sad for Adam and Eve. This was an animal they had named; this was an animal known to them; this is the first death recorded in Scripture—and it was done so that others might live by that death.

It is true that this is not fair—this is the grace of God.

Whether or not it was a lamb who died in Genesis 3, it most certainly will later be the Lamb who will indeed redeem "with precious blood, as of a lamb unblemished and spotless, the blood of Christ. For He was foreknown before the foundation of the world, but has appeared in these last times for the sake of you" (1 Pet 1:19–20); and "if you believe Moses you would believe" Him, for Moses wrote about Him (John 5:45–47). The Old Testament is the beginning of God unfolding His story.

Conclusion

In this chapter we learned the core essential truths for how God wants His Old Testament to be read. First, it is clear from passages such as John 5:45–47; Luke 24:27, 44; Acts 2:22–23; and 1 Pet 1:17–21 that the Old Testament presents many eternally doctrinal truths—not merely life-lesson applications. Second, and more specifically, it was shown that long before there was the first sin, the Godhead had already determined the divine plan—singular—of salvation; before the first sinners in Genesis 3, there was already a Savior—singular—in the mind of God. Genesis 3:15 promised that One will come and crush the head of Satan, and the Old Testament is the beginning of that blessed, unfolding story. Third, we learned that the Old Testament is the story of Jesus—not "was the story"—because so much of it remains yet to be fulfilled by the same God who already fulfilled the first part.

Deeper Walk Study Questions

1. What are the biblical significances of how Paul referred to the Old Testament in 1 Cor 10:6 and 11? As related to Bible exposition, name six pitfalls for taking these verses beyond Paul's intentions.

2. List five theological problems that arise if one ignores the doctrinal parts of the Old Testament.

3. List five observations each about the importance of John 5:45–47; Luke 24:13–27; and Luke 24:36–47. Name three truths that would be missing if we tried to turn these into "life lessons" rather than receiving them as sound biblical doctrine.

4. What is the theological significance of Jesus starting in Genesis to explain Himself? How does this argue against so-called covenantal theology? Explain.

5. What is the theological significance of Acts 2:22–23 and of 1 Pet 1:17–21? List five truths found in each passage.

CHAPTER 3

Why Are There So Many Different Interpretations of the Bible?

B efore I left for seminary, two dear friends asked me almost identical questions, summarized as, how can people who love God and His Word end up with such vastly different interpretations of it? I said I did not know but would see what I could find out. It took me years to determine that the answer comes down to two simple questions: (1) what is the first covenant of God in the Bible, and what are the hermeneutics used to interpret it?, and (2) what is the second covenant of God in the Bible, and what are the hermeneutics used to interpret it? How one answers these questions will set a governing trajectory for how the rest of Scripture—rightly or wrongly—will be interpreted. We will start by answering the first of these questions.

The First Covenant of God in The Bible Is the Noahic Covenant

As we know, Adam and Eve's sin had a far-reaching impact. By the time Genesis 6 occurs, no longer could God call His creation good:

> Then the LORD saw that the wickedness of man was great on the earth, and that every intent of the thoughts of his heart was only evil contin-ually. The LORD was sorry that He had made man on the earth, and He was grieved in His heart. The LORD said, "I will blot out man whom I have created from the face of the land, from man to animals to creeping things and to birds of the sky; for I am sorry that I have made them." (Gen 6:5–7)

After God informed Noah that God was about to destroy His earth and further instructed Noah to build an ark, God used a word that does not occur previously in Genesis—the word covenant in Gen 6:17–18:

> Behold, I, even I am bringing the flood of water upon the earth, to destroy all flesh in which is the breath of life, from under heaven; everything that is on the earth shall perish. But I will establish My covenant with you; and you shall enter the ark—you and your sons and your wife, and your sons' wives with you.

God Himself said that He would establish "My covenant with you." We note two important points about this covenant, called the Noahic, or Noachian, covenant. First, God called it "My covenant," not a covenant, your covenant, or our covenant. Second, God used the future tense, stating, "I will establish My covenant with you." So whatever God was going to do, He announced it here first in Gen 6:18 but chose not to reveal exactly what that entailed until a later time.

Before going any further, it is important to establish a working definition for the word covenant and consider a biblical example that will help us understand the concept. In simplest terms, a covenant is a legally recognized and legally binding agreement between two or more parties. Covenants can apply to individuals or groups of people, such as countries signing a war treaty or entering into trade agreements.

Biblical covenants can also vary depending on the context, but perhaps the prophet Malachi best captures the nature of biblical covenants. Malachi 2:14 states, "Yet you say, 'For what reason [is God mad at us]?' Because the LORD has been a witness between you and the wife of your youth, against whom you have dealt treacherously, though she is your companion and your wife by covenant."

By this point in Israel's history, the Jewish people had gone into the Babylonian exile because of their sins and had returned to their land because of God's faithfulness. When they returned to the land, they started setting aside their older wives for purportedly "new and improved" Gentile wives. God rebuked His wayward people for their sins and in doing so set a clear example of what a covenant is. In short, whenever a couple gets married, they enter into a covenant agreement, being a legally recognized and legally binding agreement between two or more parties. There are, in general, terms of the covenant for one or both parties, which in contemporary society take the form of wedding vows. Covenants often have signs that they are in force, such as the exchanging of rings. More important, the covenant must have an official ratification or starting point. It is not until the one performing the wedding says "I now pronounce you husband and wife" that the marriage covenant is ratified; that is, it is now official in all its respects.

With this definition of covenant in mind, we can now resume our discussion of the Noahic covenant. Although the first explicit reference to a "covenant" occurs in Gen 6:18, God did not give the details of His covenant until after the flood in Gen 9:8–17:

> *Then God spoke to Noah and to his sons with him, saying, "Now behold, I Myself do establish My covenant with you, and with your descendants after you; and with every living creature that is with you, the birds, the cattle, and every beast of the earth with you; of all that comes out of the ark, even every beast of the earth. I establish My covenant with you; and all flesh shall never again be cut off by the water of the flood, neither shall there again be a flood to destroy the earth." God said, "This is the sign of the covenant which I am making between Me and you and every living creature that is with you, for all successive generations; I set My bow in the cloud, and it shall be for a sign of a covenant between Me and the earth. It shall come about, when I bring a cloud over the earth, that the bow will be seen in the cloud, and I will remember My covenant, which is between Me and you and every living creature of all flesh; and never again shall the water become a flood to destroy all flesh. When the bow is in the cloud, then I will look upon it, to remember the everlasting covenant between God and every living creature of all flesh that is on the earth." And God said to Noah, "This is the sign of the covenant which I have established between Me and all flesh that is on the earth."*

Several observations should be noted from this text. First, God referred to what He is doing as "My covenant" three times in this text (Gen 9:9, 11, 15). Second, He no longer used a future tense as He had earlier in Genesis 6:18, for His covenant was now being ratified. Third, as with other covenants, this covenant has a sign, namely God's rainbow (Gen 9:12–13). Fourth, God viewed this agreement as an everlasting covenant (Gen 9:16). Fifth, this covenant is "between God and every living creature of all flesh that is on the earth" (Gen 9:16). Sixth, God stipulated that He will never again destroy the earth by means of flood.

> **CORE TRUTH:** Whoever makes the covenant is the one who has the responsibility of doing his or her part. In the Noahic covenant, it is God alone making a covenant with Noah and the earth's living beings from that time forward.

This sixth point deserves special treatment. Whoever makes the covenant is the one who has the responsibility of doing his or her part. This agreement does not entail both God and Noah making a bilateral covenant with each other. It is God alone making a covenant with Noah and the earth's living beings from that time forward.

In this particular covenant, God binds Himself under His own word to accomplish certain future actions, but He does not bind Noah and his descendants under any obligation. They—and we—simply enjoy the benefits of the covenant that God alone ratified.

Thus God calls it "My covenant" throughout, not our covenant, although we are the beneficiaries of His good grace. God is the One who has the stipulations in this part, namely, never to destroy His earth by means of flood. God is the One who creates the sign of this covenant in the sky. So after it rains, and you look and see God's rainbow in the sky, you are looking at God's rainbow of the covenant He ratified, as described in Genesis 9.

Some of you may be thinking, Well, that's all fine and good, but what's the big deal about the Noahic covenant? What does this first biblical covenant have to do with there being so many different interpretations of Scripture? Here comes our first "parting of the ways" biblically in how one answers this critical question that must be answered:

> **THE FIRST KEY INTERPRETATIONAL QUESTION:** What is the first covenant of God, and what are the hermeneutics used to interpret it?

Again, we are not addressing liberal "Christians" who deny the inspiration and infallibility of Scripture. Their hermeneutic is irrelevant, because they have not even properly identified the source from which they are reading. Most of them view Genesis 1–11 as fairy-tale material, certainly not literal truths explaining events from the creation through the flood.

But for those who love God's Word, this question must be answered, and how it is answered affects their interpretation of so much else of the Bible. Is the Noahic covenant the first covenant of God?

Many teach as doctrine one or two covenants that are not in the Bible and are not used by Jesus in either of the Luke 24 accounts when He teaches doctrinal truths about Himself. What is their hermeneutic? Also with this, what is the hermeneutic used to understand the Noahic covenant for those who accept the Bible as God's Word? Do they take this biblical account to be an application or life lessons, akin to 1 Cor 10:6, 11? For instance, is the point taught in this section along the line of "God wants you to make rainbows out of your rainstorms"? As you can see, it is extremely important how one interprets—or misinterprets—this Scripture.

To reiterate: I hold that the Noahic covenant of Genesis 6–9 was the first covenant of God and that God intended a literal-grammatical hermeneutic. Noah and his sons were real people. There really was a worldwide flood sent by God. People outside of the ark perished when God sent the flood. God preserved Noah and seven other humans and different animals on the ark through the midst of the flood. After the floodwaters subsided, God Himself entered into His first covenant with Noah and his descendants "and every living creature of all flesh." God alone ratified this covenant; God called it an everlasting covenant; God gave His rainbow in the sky as the visible sign of His covenant. Further, bound now under His own word, God will never again destroy the world by means of a flood.

All of these details about the Noahic covenant make sense with a normal understanding of language, a normative literal-grammatical interpretation. Nothing is wild and bizarre; nothing has to be pounded into an interpretation, for instance, if someone were to propose that Noah's ark was actually a space capsule that orbited Earth. We accept God's Word for what it is, and in this case, a normative understanding of this Scripture passage makes good sense.

The Second Theological Divide for Bible Believers

I'll put this out for us to consider:

> **THE SECOND KEY INTERPRETATIONAL QUESTION:** What is the second covenant of God, and what are the hermeneutics used to interpret it?

Although it may be hard for some people to accept it as such, how these two questions are answered affects how one approaches and interprets the rest of the Bible, all the way up to the book of Revelation. Someone will do very well when measured against the warnings in Jas 3:1, that God holds those who teach His Word to a stricter judgment, and some of us are not going to do so well when we stand before the LORD at the Bema Seat Judgment. We saw in Job 42 how seriously God takes those who inaccurately present Him and His Word.

The second covenant of God occurs relatively shortly after Genesis 9, in Gen 12:1–3:

Now the LORD said to Abram,

"Go forth from your country,

And from your relatives

And from your father's house,

To the land which I will show you;

And I will make you a great nation,

And I will bless you,

And make your name great;

And so you shall be a blessing;

And I will bless those who bless you,

And the one who curses you I will curse.

And in you all the families of the earth will be blessed."

Although the word covenant is not stated here, it is used elsewhere. In Gen 12:1–3 God promised three particular elements that He would give: a land (not described yet), a seed (or lineage), and a blessing for all the families of the earth. From an observation point, note that God used future tenses in promising the land, the seed, and the blessing. This is therefore not the ratification of what would eventually be called the Abrahamic covenant.

After nephew Lot departed from Abram to go to more pleasant (at that time) Sodom and Gomorrah (Gen 13:8-13), Gen 13:14–18 continues the account, picking up where the author left off in Genesis 12:

> And the LORD said to Abram, after Lot had separated from him, "Now lift up your eyes and look from the place where you are, northward and southward and eastward and westward; for all the land which you see, I will give it to you and to your descendants forever. I will make your descendants as the dust of the earth, so that if anyone can number the dust of the earth, then your descendants can also be numbered. Arise, walk about the land through its length and breadth; for I will give it to you." Then Abram moved his tent and came and dwelt by the oaks of Mamre, which are in Hebron, and there he built an altar to the LORD.

In this account, not only did God have Abram look at the four compass points of the land Abram could see; God also said, "I will give it to you and to your descendants forever" (Gen 13:15). Notice once more that God employed future tenses; this is not the ratification of the covenant at this point. Abram responded to God's commands by moving to a particular place in the land, the oaks of Mamre in Hebron and building an altar there. There is nothing so far in the account that indicates that the fulfillment of such promises was anything but literal and physical. God really did mean the land of which He spoke.

Genesis 15 is a major development in the unfolding of God's revelation. Genesis 15:1–11 shows Abram's dilemma and God's answer and actions:

> After these things the word of the LORD came to Abram in a vision, saying,
>
> "Do not fear, Abram.
>
> I am a shield to you;
>
> Your reward shall be very great."
>
> Abram said, "O Lord God, what will You give me, since I am childless, and the heir of my house is Eliezer of Damascus?" And Abram said, "Since

You have given no offspring to me, one born in my house is my heir." Then behold, the word of the LORD came to him, saying, "This man will not be your heir; but one who will come forth from your own body, he shall be your heir." And He took him outside and said, "Now look toward the heavens, and count the stars, if you are able to count them." And He said to him, "So shall your descendants be." Then he believed in the LORD; and He reckoned it to him as righteousness. And He said to him, "I am the LORD who brought you out of Ur of the Chaldeans, to give you this land to possess it." He said, "O Lord GOD, how may I know that I will possess it?" So He said to him, "Bring Me a three year old heifer, and a three year old female goat, and a three year old ram, and a turtledove, and a young pigeon." Then he brought all these to Him and cut them in two, and laid each half opposite the other; but he did not cut the birds. The birds of prey came down upon the carcasses, and Abram drove them away.

In light of this backdrop, God ratified what would be known as the Abrahamic covenant in Gen 15:12–21:

Now when the sun was going down, a deep sleep fell upon Abram; and behold, terror and great darkness fell upon him. God said to Abram, "Know for certain that your descendants will be strangers in a land that is not theirs, where they will be enslaved and oppressed four hundred years. But I will also judge the nation whom they will serve, and afterward they will come out with many possessions. As for you, you shall go to your fathers in peace; you shall be buried at a good old age. Then in the fourth generation they will return here, for the iniquity of the Amorite is not yet complete."

It came about when the sun had set, that it was very dark, and behold, there appeared a smoking oven and a flaming torch which passed between these pieces. On that day the LORD made a covenant with Abram, saying,

"To your descendants I have given this land,

From the river of Egypt as far as the great river, the river Euphrates: the Kenite and the Kenizzite and the Kadmonite and the Hittite and the Perizzite and the Rephaim and the Amorite and the Canaanite and the Girgashite and the Jebusite."

It is important to remember that, just as with Noah, the one who ratifies the covenant has the responsibility of bringing about his part. Abram slept through the whole thing—just as God intended. God alone ratified this covenant; God alone has the responsibility to fulfill what He had covenanted. In this ratification of the Abrahamic covenant, no more future tenses are used: "On that day the Lord made a covenant with Abram, saying, 'To your descendants I have given this land, / From the river of Egypt as far as the great river, the river Euphrates'" (Gen 15:18). Just to show by other means that God intended for these promises to be fulfilled literally and physically, God listed people groups who then had or would inhabit the land; these were real people with whom Abraham and his descendants had to deal.

Years later, after Lot and his family had departed for Sodom and Gomorrah, God reminded Abraham of His promise once again, in Gen 17:7–8.

> *"I will establish My covenant between Me and you and your descendants after you throughout their generations for an everlasting covenant, to be God to you and to your descendants after you. I will give to you and to your descendants after you, the land of your sojournings, all the land of Canaan, for an everlasting possession; and I will be their God."*

In this section, God is the One who described this as "My covenant" and "for an everlasting covenant," and for the land that He gave Abram and his descendants "for an everlasting possession," along with God's own special relationship with them, "and I will be their God."

Those who love God's Word and accept the literal-grammatical interpretation of the flood account and accept that the Noahic covenant is in effect must explain this important question:

KEY THEOLOGICAL CONSIDERATION: The burden of proof is on those who will accept and interpret God's first covenant in Genesis 9 (i.e., the Noahic covenant) in a literal fashion for everything about it and then switch the hermeneutic so that some or much of the next covenant of God is allegorical. This second covenant is from the same God, the same author, the same book, and the same genre. How, other than a predisposition to bring something to the text, could one arrive at and thrust into the text this new hermeneutic?

The remainder of the Old Testament section of this book will implement a literal-grammatical hermeneutic in key passages and see if it fits as a reasonable hermeneutic to be used in understanding God's Word.

Important Biblical Linkage of the Abrahamic Covenant

Those who think that the covenants of God are not important should consider their role in the announcements regarding the birth of the promised Messiah. After Gabriel informed Mary that she would be the mother of God's Messiah, she responded in appropriate praise, in Luke 1:46–53:

"My soul exalts the Lord,

And my spirit has rejoiced in God my Savior.

For He has had regard for the humble state of His bondslave;

For behold, from this time on all generations will count me blessed.

For the Mighty One has done great things for me;

And holy is His name.

AND HIS MERCY IS UPON GENERATION AFTER GENERATION

TOWARD THOSE WHO FEAR HIM.
He has done mighty deeds with His arm;

He has scattered those who were proud in the thoughts of their heart. He has brought down rulers from their thrones,

And has exalted those who were humble.

HE HAS FILLED THE HUNGRY WITH GOOD THINGS;
And sent away the rich empty-handed."

And then in the midst of Mary's praise comes this ending—and reminder—that this work is part of promises that God gave long ago: "He has given help to Israel His servant, / In remembrance of His mercy, / As He spoke to our fathers, / To Abraham and his descendants forever" (Luke 1:54–55).

Likewise, when the father of John the Baptist finally had his tongue loosed, here is what happened, as recorded in Luke 1:67–71:

And his father Zacharias was filled with the Holy Spirit, and prophesied, saying:

"Blessed be the Lord God of Israel,

For He has visited us and accomplished redemption for His people,

And has raised up a horn of salvation for us In the house of David His servant—As He spoke by the mouth of His holy prophets from of old—Salvation FROM OUR ENEMIES,

AND FROM THE HAND OF ALL WHO HATE US."

As Mary had previously done, so Zacharias, now much wiser and filled with the Holy Spirit, directly pointed to the Abrahamic covenant as part of his praise unto God:

"To show mercy toward our fathers,

And to remember His holy covenant,

The oath which He swore to Abraham our father,

To grant us that we, being delivered from the hand of our enemies,

Might serve Him without fear,

In holiness and righteousness before Him all our days." (Luke 1:72–75)

> **KEY TRUTH:** There is no Luke 2—the Christmas story—without Luke 1, and Luke 1 contains two direct references to the Abrahamic covenant. In both chapters the prophetic promises given and their fulfillment were in a literal-grammatical hermeneutic.

You cannot accurately do Bible exposition without understanding God's covenants and how they factor in to God's revelatory Word. Those who say they will preach or teach out of the New Testament only cannot do this very long without going back to God's promises in the Old Testament, which, after all, is the story of Jesus, as we will repeatedly see.

Conclusion

How one answers the two following questions will set a governing trajectory for how the rest of Scripture will be interpreted: (1) What is the first covenant of God in the Bible? and, What are the hermeneutics used to interpret it?; and (2) what is the second covenant of God in the Bible, and what are the hermeneutics used to interpret it? In this chapter we proposed that the burden of proof is on those who accept and interpret God's first covenant in Genesis 9 (i.e., the Noahic covenant) in a literal fashion for everything contained in it, and yet switch the hermeneutic for the next covenant of God, so that much of it is to be understood as fulfilled spiritually. Following the biblical trail of the unfolding story line of the Old Testament, it is the literal-grammatical hermeneutic that makes the most logical sense. This approach is manifest, not least, in Luke 1–2. Here both chapters refer to the Abrahamic promises the fulfillment of which are best understood in light of a literal-grammatical hermeneutic.

Deeper Walk Study Questions

1. Explain what a covenant is, how it functions, and why it is important in understanding the Bible. Then list the specific items God promised in Gen 6:18 and 9:8–17. Did God mean these to be literal promises as He gave them? How do you know? Give six supports for your answer.

2. Why are the first key interpretational questions so important to understanding Scripture? How does the literal-grammatical hermeneutic make sense with (1) God's promise regarding the sinful world, (2) God's promise to Noah and his family, and (3) God's covenant promises after Noah's family came out of the ark?

3. List each specific item that God promised in the Abrahamic covenant in Gen 12:1–3; 13:14–18; 15; and 17:7–8. Are these literal promises or allegorized life lessons? How do you know? Give at least five supports for your answer.

4. Explain the importance of Luke 1 as the basis for the events that will unfold in Luke 2. What is promised in Luke 1? (Be specific.) Do these promises seem in any way an allegorical interpretation of what God previously promised many centuries before, or are these to be understood as literal promises from God? Give ten supports for your answer.

5. Why is it impossible to do a proper interpretation—even of the Christmas story—without Luke 1? What would you be missing if you started with Luke 1? Explain.

CHAPTER 4

Four Biblical Examples of Moses Writing about Jesus

A s we have previously seen, Jesus is the One who linked Himself and His teachings directly to the writings of Moses in John 5:46–47, "For if you believed Moses, you would believe Me, for he wrote about Me. But if you do not believe his writings, how will you believe My words?" We have already seen beautiful examples of Jesus showing up in Genesis 3. This chapter addresses the questions: How do we know when the Old Testament is revealing an aspect of Jesus and when it is not?

Are there safeguards to use to ensure that we are accurate and that we do not go to extremes by concluding that there are references to the future Messiah where God did not intend?

Regarding safeguards, two observations have served me well over the years. First, note any direct New Testament texts that clearly show that the Holy Spirit intended a reference to the Messiah. Second, in the event that no New Testament parallel exists, take note of anyone who appears in the text who displays (1) the attributes of God and/or (2) the activities of God. We will consider four examples of Old Testament texts that link to the person and work of Christ, three of which have clear connections with a New Testament text and one that has no explicit New Testament parallel reference. We will address this latter exception first.

The Angel of the Lord

We previously saw the ratification of the Abrahamic covenant in Genesis 15. The next chapter, Genesis 16, is likewise extremely important in understanding Scripture and the ministry of Jesus. Genesis 16:1–6 gives the context:

> *Now Sarai, Abram's wife had borne him no children, and she had an Egyptian maid whose name was Hagar. So Sarai said to Abram, "Now behold, the LORD has prevented me from bearing children. Please go in to my maid; perhaps I shall obtain children through her." And Abram listened to the voice of Sarai. After Abram had lived ten years in the land of Canaan, Abram's wife Sarai took Hagar the Egyptian, her maid, and gave her to her husband Abram as his wife. He went in to Hagar, and she conceived; and when she saw that she had conceived, her mistress was despised in her sight. And Sarai said to Abram, "May the wrong done me be upon you. I gave my maid into your arms, but when she saw that she had conceived, I was despised in her sight. May the LORD judge between you and me." But Abram said to Sarai, "Behold, your maid is in your power; do to her what is good in your sight." So Sarai treated her harshly, and she fled from her presence.*

Genesis 16:7 continues the story, introducing a new character, namely the "angel of the Lord." Consider Gen 16:7–12:

> *Now the angel of the LORD found her by a spring of water in the wilderness, by the spring on the way to Shur. He said, "Hagar, Sarai's maid, where have you come from and where are you going?" And she said, "I am fleeing from the presence of my mistress Sarai." Then the angel of the LORD said to her, "Return to your mistress, and submit yourself to her authority." Moreover, the angel of the LORD said to her, "I will greatly multiply your descendants so that they shall be too many to count." The angel of the LORD said to her further,*
>
> *"Behold, you are with child,*
>
> *And you shall bear a son;*
>
> *And you shall call his name Ishmael,*
>
> *Because the LORD has given heed to your affliction.*
>
> *He will be a wild donkey of a man,*

His hand will be against everyone,

And everyone's hand will be against him;

And he will live to the east of all his brothers."

The text is clear that this is no ordinary angel from God. The angel's unique role is evident not only by the repetition of the phrase "the angel of the Lord" four times, but also in his manifestation of the attributes and activities of God. In Gen 16:10, for example, the angel of the Lord says that he—I—"will greatly multiply" the descendants of her offspring. This is not an announcement that God would do this, similar to Luke 1 where the angel Gabriel speaks on behalf of God. In Genesis 16 the "angel of the Lord" speaks as and for God. Note also Hagar's eventual wonderment of whom she actually saw. Genesis 16:13 states, "Then she called the name of the Lord who spoke to her, 'You are a God who sees;' for she said, 'Have I even remained alive here after seeing Him?'"

Most Arab peoples trace their history to Genesis 16. Consider a few very important biblical nuggets in this regard:

> **CORE TRUTH:** While God has designated that Jews have a special place in God's working and future plans, Genesis 16 shows that God has likewise prophesied things in regard to the Arab peoples. Genesis 16 is a great chapter to use with Arabic evangelism.

> **CONSIDER ALSO:** Hagar does something no one else does in the entire Bible: she gives God a name, and He accepts it! She calls Him El Roi, the God Who Sees. This is very loving on God's part and also great to use with Arabic evangelism—especially to the women.

But let us consider Hagar's question in Gen 16:13: did she really see God, or was it only a high-ranking angel? The account of God's commissioning of Moses clearly gives the answer. Consider Exod 3:1–2:

Now Moses was pasturing the flock of Jethro his father-in-law, the priest of Midian; and he led the flock to the west side of the wilderness, and came to Horeb, the mountain of God. The angel of the Lord appeared to him in a blazing fire from the midst of a bush; and he looked, and behold, the bush was burning with fire, yet the bush was not consumed.

The angel of the Lord who appeared to Moses here is the same angel of the Lord who appeared to Hagar in Genesis 16. Further, the angel of the Lord in Exodus 3 is directly linked with God Himself. That these two divine characters are one and the same is evident from the context. Exodus 3:3–6 states,

So Moses said, "I must turn aside now, and see this marvelous sight, why the bush is not burned up." When the LORD saw that he turned aside to look, God called to him from the midst of the bush, and said, "Moses, Moses!" And he said, "Here I am." Then He said, "Do not come near here; remove your sandals from your feet, for the place on which you are standing is holy ground." He said also, "I am the God of your father, the God of Abraham, the God of Isaac, and the God of Jacob." Then Moses hid his face, for he was afraid to look at God.

Many years later, as recorded in Exodus 33, following the golden-calf rebellion of Exodus 32 and as a personal object lesson to the wayward nation, God removed His presence from the midst of Israel's camp. Exodus 33:11 states, "Thus the LORD used to speak to Moses face to face, just as a man speaks to his friend." Yet in the same chapter, after Moses pleaded with God to show him His glory, God responded with this seemingly contradictory statement: "But He said, 'You cannot see My face, for no man can see Me and live!'" (Exod 33:20).

So which is right, that Moses used to speak with God face to face, just as a man speaks to his friend or that Moses could not see God and live?

They are both right, and they set the stage for revelatory gold given us by God:

IMPORTANT NOTE: Exodus 33 requires at least a two-member Godhead. The Trinity is not fully revealed yet in Scripture, but at least by Exodus 33, in order for Scripture to be correct, it requires a Godhead member who can be seen and also a Godhead member who cannot be seen.

The Angel of the Lord is the preincarnate Jesus, the second Member of the Godhead who would, from time to time as He desired, step into the world He created and interact as He saw fit. Along with the previous statement, note this:

KEY CONSIDERATION: In this case, the Angel of the Lord not appearing in the New Testament is a good thing. Think of it in these terms: once the incarnation of Jesus occurred, the Angel of the Lord never showed Himself that way again in the remainder of the Bible.

After Genesis 16, the angel of Lord appears next in Genesis 22:

Now it came about after these things, that God tested Abraham, and said to him, "Abraham!" And he said, "Here I am." He said, "Take now your son, your only son, whom you love, Isaac, and go to the land of Moriah, and offer him there as a burnt offering on one of the mountains of which I will tell you." So Abraham rose early in the morning and saddled his donkey, and took two of his young men with him and Isaac his son; and he split wood for the burnt offering, and arose and went to the place of which God had told him. On the third day Abraham raised his eyes and saw the place from a distance. Abraham said to his young men, "Stay here with the donkey, and I and the lad will go over there; and we will worship and return to you." Abraham took the wood of the burnt offering and laid it on Isaac his son, and he took in his hand the fire and the knife. So the two of them walked on together. Isaac spoke to Abraham his father and said, "My father!" And he said, "Here I am, my son." And he said, "Behold, the fire and the wood, but where is the lamb for the burnt offering?" Abraham said, "God will provide for Himself the lamb for the burnt offering, my son." So the two of them walked on together. (Gen 22:1-8)

And then, just before Abraham was to sacrifice his own son, God intervened.

Note again the form that God chose for Himself to interact with and further instruct Abraham:

Then they came to the place of which God had told him; and Abraham built the altar there and arranged the wood, and bound his son Isaac and laid him on the altar, on top of the wood. Abraham stretched out his hand and took the knife to slay his son. But the angel of the LORD called to him from heaven and said, "Abraham, Abraham!" And he said, "Here I am." He said, "Do not stretch out your hand against the lad, and do nothing to him; for now I know that you fear God, since you have not withheld your son, your only son, from Me." Then Abraham raised his eyes and looked, and behold, behind him a ram caught in the thicket by his horns; and Abraham went and took the ram and offered him up for a burnt offering in the place of his son. Abraham called the name of that place The LORD Will Provide, as it is said to this day, "In the mount of the LORD it will be provided."

Then the angel of the LORD called to Abraham a second time from heaven, and said, "By Myself I have sworn, declares the LORD, because you have done this thing and have not withheld your son, your only son, indeed I will greatly bless you, and I will greatly multiply your seed as the stars of the heavens and as the sand which is on the seashore; and your seed shall possess the gate of their enemies. In your seed all the nations of the earth shall be blessed, because you have obeyed My voice." So Abraham returned to his young men, and they arose and went together to Beersheba; and Abraham lived at Beersheba. (Gen 22:9-19)

KEY CONSIDERATION: We who are parents think how impossibly hard it would be for us to sacrifice our own child if we were in the same situation as Abraham, but that is not the main point. We are not Abraham in this example; we are Isaac, bound and laid on God's altar with a death sentence upon us unless someone intervenes and takes our place. In the predetermined plan and foreknowledge of God, determined long before the foundation of the world, One would indeed eventually become flesh and do just that for us.

Genesis 22 would definitely be part of the John 5:46 reference, "Moses wrote about Me," and we would have great confidence that this would be part of Jesus giving the twofold "beginning at Moses" teaching concerning Himself in Luke 24. Accordingly, we should note a couple of critical doctrinal truths. First, Jesus would eventually take our place on the altar of God, but no voice would call out from heaven to stop the Father, as it did for Abraham: "Take now your son, your only son, whom you love" and sacrifice him (Gen 22:2; cf. John 3:16). Second, much in the same way that God provided a temporary sacrifice and covering for Adam and Eve (Genesis 3), in Gen 22:13 He provided for Abraham a ram—but not a lamb—until the Lamb He had prepared before the foundation of the world would appear.

God's Passover Lamb

Having addressed an Old Testament text that links to Christ even without an explicit New Testament parallel, we turn now to the first of three Old Testament texts that do have a New Testament parallel. If you are saved, believe in the authority of God's Word, and read your Bible, you would have to wear spiritual blinders to miss Jesus as being the ultimate Lamb of God foreshadowed in Exodus 12. In conjunction with the tenth and final plague upon Egypt, God instructed Moses in Exodus 12:2–3, 5–7, 12–13:

> *Speak to all the congregation of Israel, saying, "On the tenth day of this month they are each one to take a lamb for themselves, according to their fathers' households, a lamb for each household. . . .*
>
> *Your lamb shall be an unblemished male a year old; you may take it from the sheep or from the goats.*
>
> *You shall keep it until the fourteenth day of the same month, then the whole assembly of the congregation of Israel is to kill it at twilight. Moreover, they shall take some of the blood and put it on the two doorposts and on the lintel of the houses in which they eat it. . . . For I will go through the land of Egypt on that night, and will strike down all the firstborn in the land of Egypt, both man and beast; and against all the gods of Egypt I will execute judgments—I am the Lord. The blood shall be a sign for you on the houses where you live; and when I see the blood, I will pass over you, and no plague will begall you to destroy you when I strike the land of Egypt."*

That Jesus is to be identified with this Passover lamb is evident in John 1:29–34:

> *The next day he saw Jesus coming to him, and said, "Behold, the Lamb of God who takes away the sin of the world! This is He on behalf of whom I said, 'After me comes a Man who has a higher rank than I, for He existed before me.' I did not recognize Him, but in order that He might be*

manifested to Israel, I came baptizing in water." John testified saying, "I have seen the Spirit descending as a dove out of heaven, and He remained upon Him. And I did not recognize Him, but He who sent me to baptize in water said to me, 'He upon whom you see the Spirit descending and remaining upon Him, this is the One who baptizes in the Holy Spirit.' I myself have seen, and have testified that this is the Son of God."

And then, once more in John 1:35–37, just to make sure we do not miss the connection, "Again the next day John was standing with two of his disciples, and he looked at Jesus as He walked, and said, 'Behold, the Lamb of God!' The two disciples heard him speak, and they followed Jesus."

Decades later, the apostle Paul uses this same Old Testament example as a means of addressing a sinful situation in the church at Corinth. Given that Israel was to prepare themselves spiritually by removing sin from their lives before, not after, the Passover, Paul reasons in 1 Cor 5:7, "For Christ our Passover also has been sacrificed." Paul's point is that this sin within the Corinthian church should not be going on, if for no other reason than it was out of step with God's chronology whenever Passover was obediently observed in Israel. Considering the twofold account in John 1 and Paul's specific designation of "Christ our Passover," there are many biblical texts supporting Jesus as the true Passover Lamb given by God to the world. If you were to leave this truth out of your understanding of Jesus and the gospel, you would be lacking significant, essential truths regarding the person and work of the Messiah.

The Lion From the Tribe of Judah

As in the previous example, so also here we look at scriptural references in the Old Testament that find their fulfillment in Jesus. These connections are not based in personal presumption, but on verses that have New Testament biblical support for having been fulfilled in Jesus. Genesis 49, a chapter we will come back to later, contains such a prophecy that no doubt applies to Jesus in the New Testament. Genesis 49:9–12 prophesies about a coming ruler over all the peoples:

Judah is a lion's whelp;

From the prey, my son, you have gone up.

He couches, he lies down as a lion,

And as a lion, who dares rouse him up?

The scepter shall not depart from Judah,

Nor the ruler's staff from between his feet,

Until Shiloh comes,

And to him shall be the obedience of the peoples.

He ties his foal to the vine,

And his donkey's colt to the choice vine;

He washes his garments in wine

And his robes in the blood of grapes.

His eyes are dull from wine,

And his teeth white from milk.

Scripture will develop this prophecy in much more detail in subsequent biblical books. Yet as early as Genesis 49 comes One from the tribe of Judah described in strength ("lion") and reigning ("scepter"). This reign is described as, in some way, God's peace ("Shiloh") and not just over the Jews, but "to Him shall be the obedience of the peoples." I note one other crucial truth in this prophecy: nothing in this text indicates this One as being meek and mild, rejected by His people, and ultimately killed by them. Such characteristics of the Messiah were not the emphasis at this point but would emerge in greater detail in later divine prophecies that God would give as a reflection of His progressive revelation.

New Testament recognition of this connection between Genesis 49 and Jesus is evident in the book of Revelation. The aged apostle John, probably more than ninety years old, the last living apostle, and a prisoner on the island of Patmos presents this account:

After these things I looked, and behold, a door standing open in heaven, and the first voice which I had heard, like the sound of a trumpet speaking with me, said, "Come up here, and I will show you what must take place after these things." Immediately I was in the Spirit; and behold, a throne was standing in heaven, and One sitting on the throne. (Rev 4:1–2)

In this vision, God brought John into His very own throne room, where the following takes place:

I saw in the right hand of Him who sat on the throne a book written inside and on the back, sealed up with seven seals. And I saw a strong angel proclaiming with a loud voice, "Who is worthy to open the book and to break its seals?" And no one in heaven or on the earth or under the earth was able to open the book or to look into it. Then I began to weep greatly, because no one was found worthy to open the book, or to look into it. (Rev 5:1–4)

John somehow knew in this vision that as long as the scroll remained sealed, the fullness of the Messiah's reign and Satan's judgment would never occur—and he responded by weeping greatly.

This tension set the stage for the following divine proclamation: "And one of the elders said to me, 'Stop weeping; behold, the Lion that is from the tribe of Judah, the Root of David, has overcome so as to open the book and its seven seals'" (Rev 5:5). The description of Jesus as "the Lion that is from the tribe of Judah" uses a title taken straight from the Messianic promises of Gen 49:9–12. As with the other examples, so also here is a clear, direct biblical reference that this prophecy must be about Jesus.

CORE TRUTH: A divine promise can be made hundreds or even thousands of years before it is fulfilled. Unless He so dictates, God is not limited in time by His promises, and every promise God makes must come true, because God's character, holiness, and omnipotence are at stake; plus, Scripture cannot be broken (John 10:35).

The Rock

Finally, that the "the rock" of Exodus 17 would be a designation and title for the Lord Jesus Christ is an association you may not have made, but it is referenced many times throughout Scripture.

The original usage occurs after God brought Israel out of slavery. Exodus 17:1–7 records:

Then all the congregation of the sons of Israel journeyed by stages from the wilderness of Sin, according to the command of the LORD, and camped at Rephidim, and there was no water for the people to drink. Therefore the people quarreled with Moses and said, "Give us water that we may drink." And Moses said to them, "Why do you quarrel with me? Why do you test the LORD?" But the people thirsted there for water; and they grumbled against Moses and said, "Why, now, have you brought us up from Egypt, to kill us and our children and our livestock with thirst?" So Moses cried out to the LORD, saying, "What shall I do to this people? A little more and they will stone me." Then the LORD said to Moses, "Pass before the people and take with you some of the elders of Israel; and take in your hand your staff with which you struck the Nile, and go. Behold, I will stand before you there on the rock at Horeb; and you shall strike the rock, and water will come out of it, that the people may drink." And Moses did so in the sight of the elders of Israel. He named the place Massah and Meribah because of the quarrel of the sons of Israel, and because they tested the LORD, saying, "Is the LORD among us, or not?"

It may come as a surprise, but many centuries later the Holy Spirit used Paul to disclose the following revelation:

For I do not want you to be unaware, brethren, that our fathers were all under the cloud and all passed through the sea; and all were baptized into Moses in the cloud and in the sea; and all ate the same spiritual food; and all drank the same spiritual drink, for they were drinking from a spiritual rock which followed them; and the rock was Christ. (1 Cor 10:1–4)

In this text Paul uses the wilderness generation as an example of those who had many spiritual privileges granted to them and yet remained unfaithful.

One might wonder why God would specifically refer to the rock as being the Messiah. God specifically promised in Exod 17:6, "Behold, I will stand before you there on the rock at Horeb; and you shall strike the rock, and water will come out of it, that the people may drink.' And Moses did so in the sight of the elders of Israel." The most important thing is not that the rock gave water but that God Himself said that He would stand before them on the rock. In addition, He commanded that the rock be struck with Him standing on it. This is a beautiful picture of "the predetermined plan and foreknowledge of God" (Acts 2:23) in reference to the Lamb whom God one day would send and have struck down, as future prophecies would show.

But note that God would allow His Messiah-Rock to be struck only once, in accordance with His sovereign grace and divine will. In Num 20:8, for example, God commanded Moses to speak to the rock. Moses disobeyed and struck the rock. Although God graciously allowed water to flow forth, because of his disobedience Moses received God's strong judgment, with God refusing Moses permission to lead Israel into the Promised Land. Not only was Moses disobedient to God's command, then, but he unknowingly upset God's picture of the Messiah to be struck—but only once and never again.

> **CORE TRUTH:** This does not mean that every rock reference in the Old Testament is automatically a picture of Jesus. But it does mean this: whenever the Rock is used as a designation for God, it is also a designation for the preincarnate second Member of the Godhead.

A few examples from Scripture will suffice to show some of the other designations of God the Rock, the Messiah. Just before Moses was to die, God told him that Israel would not be obedient in the future. God had him compose the song found in Deuteronomy 32, often called the Song of Moses. The four opening verses contain multiple references to God as the Rock:

Give ear, O heavens, and let me speak;
And let the earth hear the words of my mouth.
Let my teaching drop as the rain,
My speech distill as the dew,
As the droplets on the fresh grass
And as the showers on the herb.
For I proclaim the name of the LORD;
Ascribe greatness to our God!
The Rock! His work is perfect,

For all His ways are just;

A God of faithfulness and without injustice,

Righteous and upright is He. (Deut 32:1–4)

Consider also Deut 32:15: "But Jeshurun [Israel] grew fat and kicked—/ You are grown fat, thick, and sleek—/ Then he forsook God who made him, / And scorned the Rock of his salvation." Likewise, Deut 32:18 states, "You neglected the Rock who begot you, / And forgot the God who gave you birth."

In the same song, Deut 32:30–31 contrasts the true Rock, the Messiah God, with their enemies' "rock" to which they cling:

How could one chase a thousand,

And two put ten thousand to flight,

Unless their Rock had sold them,

And the LORD had given them up?

Indeed their rock is not like our Rock,

Even our enemies themselves judge this.

Just as Deuteronomy 32 was the last song of Moses, so also 2 Samuel 23 is called David's Last Song, and he definitely knew who the Rock was, as the opening verses show:

Now these are the last words of David.

David the son of Jesse declares,

The man who was raised on high declares,

The anointed of the God of Jacob,

And the sweet psalmist of Israel,

"The Spirit of the LORD spoke by me,

And His Word was on my tongue.

"The God of Israel said,

The Rock of Israel spoke to me,

'He who rules over men righteously,

Who rules in the fear of God. . . ." (2 Sam 23:1–3)

Although one could find many more examples in Scripture, two more references in Isaiah will suffice. Isaiah 26:4 counsels Israel to "Trust in the LORD forever, / For in God the LORD, we have an everlasting Rock." In Isa 44:6–8, when contrasting Himself with any false god, God says in reference to Himself:

Thus says the LORD, the King of Israel and his Redeemer, the LORD of hosts:

"I am the first and I am the last,

And there is no God besides Me.

Who is like Me? Let him proclaim and declare it;

Yes, let him recount it to Me in order,

From the time that I established the ancient nation.

And let them declare to them the things that are coming

And the events that are going to take place.

Do not tremble and do not be afraid;

Have I not long since announced it to you and declared it?

And you are My witnesses.

Is there any God besides Me,

Or is there any other Rock?

I know of none."

Nor then should we.

In my classes, when we go through these or related topics, very often people will say, "It's all here in the Bible. Why didn't I ever see this before?" Part of the answer is—if you were like me—I never looked for Jesus in the Pentateuch (John 5:46) or looked for Him elsewhere throughout the Old Testament, as we saw twice described in Luke 24. Yet we should expect to find Jesus in the Old Testament, because, as we are more clearly seeing, the Old Testament truly is the story of Jesus.

Conclusion

In this chapter we discussed two important safeguards for studying Old Testament texts to see if they correctly apply to the Messiah: (1) There is a direct New Testament text that clearly shows that the Holy Spirit intended this to be in reference to the Messiah? (2) If no New Testament parallels exist, who appears exhibiting the attributes of God or doing the activities of God? Considering these safeguards, we saw that the "angel of the LORD" spoke as God, acted as God, was worshiped as God. In addition, we looked at three examples that have New Testament verification, God's Passover Lamb (John 1:29–36; 1 Cor 5:7), the Lion from the tribe of Judah (Rev 5:1–5) and, finally, the Rock, in 1 Cor 10:1–4 ("and the Rock was Christ").

Deeper Walk Study Questions

1. How do Genesis 16 and Exodus 3 and 33 support the claim that the "angel of the LORD" is God? List ten items from each text that support this.

2. How does the God who cannot be seen (Exod 33:20) harmonize with Exod 33:11, which refers to God speaking face to face with Moses? Based on the answers given in question 1 (above), explain how the person of Jesus is the only correct, fitting answer.

3. Explain how noting the appearance of the angel of the Lord in Genesis 22 gives new appreciation for Jesus.

4. Give five supports from John 1:29–36 and 1 Cor 5:7 that Jesus truly is God's Passover Lamb. Why is this important? Explain.

5. What does Gen 49:9–12 promise regarding "the Lion from the tribe of Judah" (Rev 5:5)? List five items. How does Revelation 4–5 give biblical proof that this uniquely points to the person of Jesus? Explain. Why is this important to understanding the book of Revelation?

6. "The Rock" as a designation for the Messiah may be a concept new to you. How do we know "the Rock" refers to Jesus? Give five supports from Exodus 17 and 1 Cor 10:1–4, and five each from Deut 32:1–31; 2 Samuel 23; and Isa 44:6–8.

CHAPTER 5

The Mosaic Covenant and Its Biblical Relevance

To Christians the Mosaic covenant is perhaps the most familiar Old Testament covenant, because it is referenced so many times in Scripture. The Bible presents the Mosaic covenant by various synonyms, such as "the law of Moses," "Moses wrote," or just "the law." This covenant will play an important part in understanding the Bible, especially as it relates to important events in the life of Jesus. In this chapter, we will present the view that the significance of the Mosaic covenant is directly related to its roles as a continuation of the truth that God had previously given in Genesis as part of the Abrahamic covenant, and other promises that Yahweh made.

Background for the Mosaic Covenant

As important as the Mosaic covenant is, one cannot start with that covenant in Exodus as a study by itself. It is the continuation of truth that God had previously given in Genesis as part of the Abrahamic covenant. You must know what God has previously promised—and to whom—and make the appropriate connections. We previously saw in the ratification of the Abrahamic covenant in Gen 15:12–14 that God revealed prophetic truths regarding what would eventually become the nation of Israel:

Now when the sun was going down, a deep sleep fell upon Abram; and behold, terror and great darkness fell upon him. God said to Abram, "Know for certain that your descendants will be strangers in a land that is not

theirs, where they will be enslaved and oppressed four hundred years. But
I will also judge the nation whom they will serve, and afterward they will
come out with many possessions."

These verses set the stage for the book of Exodus in three distinct
ways: (1) The Jewish people would be enslaved and oppressed for four
hundred years. (2) God promised that He Himself will judge that nation.
(3) Israel would come out (of Egypt) with many possessions. So in Genesis 15, God binds Himself by His own word; if He does not perform what
He had promised, then He is not God. So nothing in Exodus happens coin-
cidently; everything happens just as God said it would, and God acted just
as He said He would act. Exodus 1 shows the nation of Israel enslaved in
Egypt. Exodus 2 ends with God acting in full accordance with His Word,
"So God heard their groaning; and God remembered His covenant with
Abraham, Isaac, and Jacob. And God saw the sons of Israel, and God took
notice of them" (Exod 2:24–25).

CORE TRUTH: To study God's Word accurately, you cannot start with
Exodus as a study by itself. It is the continuation of truth that God
had previously given throughout Genesis. You must know what God
has previously promised—and to whom—and make the appropriate
biblical connections.

Yet the book of Exodus is not just about an enslaved people gaining their physical redemption from the enslaving country. It continues the
story of God and His faithfulness, and it ultimately continues the story of
Jesus.

The Ratification of the Mosaic Covenant—And Beyond

After God brought the newly redeemed people to Mount Sinai (Exodus
19), He further brought the people to Himself. Exodus 24:1–8 gives the
account:

Then He said to Moses, "Come up to the LORD, you and Aaron, Nadab and
Abihu and seventy of the elders of Israel, and you shall worship at a dis-

tance. Moses alone, however, shall come near to the LORD, but they shall not come near, nor shall the people come up with him."

Then Moses came and recounted to the people all the words of the LORD and all the ordinances; and all the people answered with one voice and said, "All the words which the LORD has spoken we will do!" Moses wrote down all the words of the LORD. Then he arose early in the morning, and built an altar at the foot of the mountain with twelve pillars for the twelve tribes of Israel. He sent young men of the sons of Israel, and they offered burnt offerings and sacrificed young bulls as peace offerings to the LORD. Moses took half of the blood and put it in basins, and the other half of the blood he sprinkled on the altar. Then he took the book of the covenant and read it in the hearing of the people; and they said, "All that the LORD has spoken we will do, and we will be obedient!" So Moses took the blood and sprinkled it on the people, and said, "Behold the blood of the covenant, which the LORD has made with you in accordance with all these words."

A few matters stand out as extremely important in this account. First, the Mosaic covenant is the only covenant of God so far where somebody else was present and active. Previously in the Noahic covenant (Genesis 9) and the Abrahamic covenant (Genesis 15), God alone ratified the covenant. Remember: those who ratify the covenant have a responsibility to do their part. So in the Mosaic covenant, God has a part and the nation of Israel has a part. Second, unlike the previous two covenants, the Mosaic covenant is not stated as being everlasting. Third, twice the people claim, "All that the LORD has spoken we will do, and we will be obedient!" Yet, as the Bible clearly shows, rare are the times when the people are in covenant obedience to Yahweh. Fourth, from Exodus 24 onward, as long as the Mosaic covenant is in effect, national Israel is under covenant obligation to do what God tells them to do. So this covenant relationship goes far beyond the events of Exodus 24 into Joshua, Judges, 1 Samuel, and so forth. Fifth, all Jewish people were as much under the Mosaic covenant obligations as any of their ancestors on the day the covenant was ratified in Exodus 24, as long as that covenant was operative. Sixth, Exod 24:4 reveals that Moses "arose early in the morning, and built an altar at the foot of the mountain with twelve pillars for the twelve tribes of Israel." Thus, the Mosaic covenant was made only with the nation of Israel, not with all the nations of the world, and has items specifically for them alone.

> **KEY TRUTH:** As we will repeatedly see in upcoming verses, the Bible presents the Mosaic covenant by various synonyms such as "the law of Moses," "Moses wrote," or just "the law."

Among other matters, the Mosaic covenant establishes the basis for the tabernacle (and later the temple), the Levitical priesthood, the holy of holies, and the ark of the covenant. Right after the Mosaic covenant was ratified, God made these wonderful and personal promises. In Exod 25:8 God commanded, "Let them construct a sanctuary for Me, that I may dwell among them." Exodus 25:20–22 adds:

> *The cherubim shall have their wings spread upward, covering the mercy seat with their wings and facing one another; the faces of the cherubim are to be turned toward the mercy seat. You shall put the mercy seat on top of the ark, and in the ark you shall put the testimony which I will give to you. There I will meet with you; and from above the mercy seat, from between the two cherubim which are upon the ark of the testimony, I will speak to you about all that I will give you in commandment for the sons of Israel.*

Later in the same context, God made a promise to do something that He had never done since Genesis 3: He consecrated a specific place with His own glory.

> *I will meet there with the sons of Israel, and it shall be consecrated by My glory. I will consecrate the tent of meeting and the altar; I will also conse-crate Aaron and his sons to minister as priests to Me. I will dwell among the sons of Israel and will be their God. They shall know that I am the LORD their God who brought them out of the land of Egypt, that I might dwell among them; I am the LORD their God. (Exod 29:43–46)*

> **FOUNDATIONAL TRUTH:** For the first time since Genesis 3, God condescended to dwell among humanity. In Genesis 3, God expelled Adam and Eve from His presence. In Exodus 25, immediately after

the ratification of the Mosaic covenant, God promised His very presence among the people. This is not an Old Testament God of hate (as many claim); these are aspects of God's love and grace—and faithfulness.

Such was God's original plan—and joy and delight: to have fellowship with His people whom He had recently brought to Himself in a special, covenant relationship with Himself.

But Exod 32:1–6 describes the desert scene only a few days after the ratification of the Mosaic covenant:

> *Now when the people saw that Moses delayed to come down from the mountain, the people assembled about Aaron and said to him, "Come, make us a god who will go before us; as for this Moses, the man who brought us up from the land of Egypt, we do not know what has become of him." Aaron said to them, "Tear off the gold rings which are in the ears of your wives, your sons, and your daughters, and bring them to me. Then all the people tore off the gold rings which were in their ears, and brought them to Aaron. He took this from their hand, and fashioned it with a graving tool and made it into a molten calf; and they said, "This is your god, O Israel, who brought you up from the land of Egypt." Now when Aaron saw this, he built an altar before it; and Aaron made a proclamation and said, "Tomorrow shall be a feast to the LORD." So the next day they rose early and offered burnt offerings, and brought peace offerings; and the people sat down to eat and to drink, and rose up to play.*

Exodus 32 shows several high-handed sins of covenant disobedience and rebellion under the Mosaic covenant. God, being fully aware of Israel's sins, informed Moses accordingly:

> *Then the LORD spoke to Moses, "Go down at once, for your people, whom you brought up from the land of Egypt, have corrupted themselves. They have quickly turned aside from the way which I commanded them.*
>
> *They have made for themselves a molten calf, and have worshiped it and have sacrificed to it, and said, 'This is your god, O Israel, who brought you up from the land of Egypt!'" The LORD said to Moses, "I have seen this people, and behold, they are an obstinate people. Now then let Me alone, that*

*My anger may burn against them and that I may destroy them; and I will
make of you a great nation." (Exod 32:7–10)*

Moses responded by interceding for the sinful nation:

*Then Moses entreated the LORD his God, and said, "O LORD, why does Your
anger burn against Your people whom You have brought out from the land
of Egypt with great power and with a mighty hand? Why should the Egyptians speak, saying, 'With evil intent He brought them out to kill them in the
mountains and to destroy them from the face of the earth'? Turn from Your
burning anger and change Your mind about doing harm to Your people.
Remember Abraham, Isaac, and Israel, Your servants to whom You swore by
Yourself, and said to them, 'I will multiply your descendants as the stars of
the heavens, and all this land of which I have spoken I will give to your descendants, and they shall inherit it forever.'" So the LORD changed His mind
about the harm which He said He would do to His people. (Exod 32:11–14)*

CORE TRUTH: Moses pleaded with God based on His faithfulness to the
Abrahamic covenant not the nation's sin under the Mosaic covenant.

When God offered to destroy the nation of Israel and start over with
him, Moses said in essence and reverently, "You cannot do that, God!"
God knew about His covenant with Abraham and that, in spite of Israel's
heinous sins, He would remain faithful and true to what He had promised.
Moses did not instruct God in this account; this is very much like Jesus's
asking Philip where they would get enough to feed the multitudes (John
6:1–6), with Jesus fully knowing ahead of time what He would do. In both
cases, Jesus led Philip and God led Moses into the deductions that both
should have.

FOUNDATIONAL TRUTH: Evident in Moses's—and God's—understanding
of the promises God had previously made under the Abrahamic
covenant is a literal-grammatical hermeneutic. God did not respond to
Moses's interpretation by saying, "You have that all wrong! These are
allegorical truths only."

> **FOUNDATIONAL TRUTH:** If God had acted as He said, destroying Israel and starting over with Moses, making him a great nation, then the twelve tribes of Israel would have been destroyed—other than Moses, who was from the tribe of Levi—and thus there would be no Lion from the tribe of Judah, whom God had already promised in Gen 49:8–12. We who are saved should be extremely thankful to God for being true to all His promises!

Even though Moses had made a successful intervention for the people, as an object lesson, God removed His visible presence outside the camp because of this high-handed sin of the nation (Exodus 33). Sin kills; it always kills. Sin separates; it always separates. Exodus 34–39 gives instructions for the building of God's tabernacle and the start of the Levitical priesthood. In keeping His Word, God ultimately did consecrate His tabernacle with His glory, as seen in Exod 40:34–38:

> *Then the cloud covered the tent of meeting, and the glory of the LORD filled the tabernacle. Moses was not able to enter the tent of meeting because the cloud had settled on it, and the glory of the LORD filled the tabernacle. Throughout all their journeys whenever the cloud was taken up from over the tabernacle, the sons of Israel would set out; but if the cloud was not taken up, then they did not set out until the day when it was taken up. For throughout all their journeys, the cloud of the LORD was on the tabernacle by day, and there was fire in it by night, in the sight of all the house of Israel.*

Thus, the book of Exodus ends on both a positive and a negative note. Positively, God is present, and He exhibits an aspect of His glory to the nation of Israel. Negatively, access to God is significantly limited given that His presence resides in the holy of holies, a place even Moses was not permitted to enter.

> **CORE TRUTH:** What began in Exodus 40—God being in the holy of holies with very limited access to Him—will stay that same way through Matt 27:50–51: "And Jesus cried out again with a loud voice, and yielded up His spirit. And behold, the veil of the temple

was torn in two from top to bottom; and the earth shook and the rocks were split." Much more about this eternally life-altering biblical truth later.

The Blessing and the Curse

When the people of Israel said twice in Exodus 24, "All that Yahweh says to do we will do," the people were bound to anything Yahweh said for them to do as long as they were under the Mosaic covenant. So when God established the sacrifices, the Day of Atonement, and other matters, He was adding these to the long list of things He would have national Israel observe or do. Once these commands—not suggestions—were given by God, the outcome depended on whether national Israel would be obedient. Usually the nation was far from being faithfully obedient.

Leviticus 26 is the first detailed issuing of the "blessing and the curse" as part of the Mosaic covenant. God promised national Israel tremendous blessings if they obeyed him:

> *You shall not make for yourselves idols, nor shall you set up for your-selves an image or a sacred pillar, nor shall you place a figured stone in your land to bow down to it; for I am the LORD your God. You shall keep My sabbaths and reverence My sanctuary; I am the LORD. If you walk in My statutes and keep My commandments so as to carry them out, then I shall give you rains in their season, so that the land will yield its produce and the trees of the field will bear their fruit. Indeed, your threshing will last for you until grape gathering, and grape gathering will last until sowing time. You will thus eat your food to the full and live securely in your land. I shall also grant peace in the land, so that you may lie down with no one making you tremble. I shall also eliminate harmful beasts from the land, and no sword will pass through your land. But you will chase your ene-mies and they will fall before you by the sword; five of you will chase a hundred, and a hundred of you will chase ten thousand, and your enemies will fall before you by the sword. So I will turn toward you and make you fruitful and multiply you, and I will confirm My covenant with you. You will eat the old supply and clear out the old because of the new. Moreover, I will make My dwelling among you, and My soul will not reject you. I will*

also walk among you and be your God, and you shall be My people. I am the LORD your God, who brought you out of the land of Egypt so that you would not be their slaves, and I broke the bars of your yoke and made you walk erect. (Lev 26:1-13)

This blessing section specifically given by God for national Israel included bountiful crops, abundant rains, peace in the land, victories over their enemies. And beyond all these important but subsidiary blessings, God promises to dwell in their midst in rich fellowship.

But none of these blessings were automatic. Leviticus 26:14–39 contains the items pertaining to "the curse" section under the Mosaic covenant.

But if you do not obey Me and do not carry out all these commandments, if, instead, you reject My statutes, and if your soul abhors My ordinances so as not to carry out all My commandments, and so break My covenant, I, in turn, will do this to you: I will appoint over you a sudden terror, consumption and fever that will waste away the eyes and cause the soul to pine away; also, you will sow your seed uselessly, for your enemies will eat it up. I will set My face against you so that you will be struck down before your enemies; and those who hate you will rule over you, and you will flee when no one is pursuing you. (Lev 26:14–17)

God foretold that enemies would rule over the nation of Israel if they disobeyed Him; if His strong punishment did not draw the sinful people back to Him in repentance and obedience, He promised an intensification of His cursing on them, including severe drought and falling into the hands of their enemies:

If also after these things you do not obey Me, then I will punish you seven times more for your sins. I will also break down your pride of power; I will also make your sky like iron and your earth like bronze. Your strength will be spent uselessly, for your land will not yield its produce and the trees of the land will not yield their fruit.

If then, you act with hostility against Me and are unwilling to obey Me, I will increase the plague on you seven times according to your sins. I will let loose among you the beasts of the field, which will bereave you of your children and destroy your cattle and reduce your number so that your roads lie deserted.

*And if by these things you are not turned to Me, but act with hostility
against Me, then I will act with hostility against you; and I, even I, will
strike you seven times for your sins. I will also bring upon you a sword
which will execute vengeance for the covenant; and when you gather together into your cities, I will send pestilence among you, so that you shall
be delivered into enemy hands. When I break your staff of bread, ten women
will bake your bread in one oven, and they will bring back your bread in
rationed amounts, so that you will eat and not be satisfied.*

*Yet if in spite of this you do not obey Me, but act with hostility against
Me, then I will act with wrathful hostility against you, and I, even I, will
punish you seven times for your sins. (Lev 26:18–28)*

God even promised cannibalism of their own children as part of His
curse in Lev 26:29–31:

*Further, you will eat the flesh of your sons and the flesh of your daughters
you will eat. I then will destroy your high places, and cut down your incense
altars, and heap your remains on the remains of your idols, for My soul
shall abhor you. I will lay waste your cities as well and will make your sanc-
tuaries desolate, and I will not smell your soothing aromas.*

Although the nation of Israel was not yet in the land God had promised
them, God pointed to exile from that land as part of the curse for national
Israel if they did not obey him:

*I will make the land desolate so that your enemies who settle in it will be
appalled over it. You, however, I will scatter among the nations and will
draw out a sword after you, as your land becomes desolate and your cities
become waste.*

*Then the land will enjoy its sabbaths all the days of the desolation, while
you are in your enemies' land; then the land will rest and enjoy its sabbaths. All the days of its desolation it will observe the rest which it did not
observe on your sabbaths, while you were living on it. As for those of you
who may be left, I will also bring weakness into their hearts in the lands
of their enemies. And the sound of a driven leaf will chase them, and even
when no one is pursuing they will flee as though from the sword, and they
will fall. They will therefore stumble over each other as if running from
the sword, although no one is pursuing; and you will have no strength to
stand up before your enemies. But you will perish among the nations, and*

your enemies' land will consume you. So those of you who may be left will rot away because of their iniquity in the lands of your enemies; and also because of the iniquities of their forefathers they will rot away with them. (Lev 26:32–39)

The blessing-or-the-curse section was an either/or for national Israel; God proposed no additional options: obey Me—Jewish people—and I will bless you; disobey Me, and these are the curses that will certainly come upon you.

> **FOUNDATIONAL TRUTHS:** The blessing or the curse becomes a spiritual barometer for national Israel as long as they were under the Mosaic covenant. Nothing merely happened; God remains true to His Word. If the nation was under famine, such as in Ruth 1:1 ("Now it came about in the days when the judges governed, that there was a famine in the land"), the problem was not a weather problem. The true problem was lack of obedience to Yahweh. In the same way, whenever Israel was defeated in battle (such as at Ai, in Joshua 7), the problem was not a military problem; the problem was a lack of covenant obedience to Yahweh under the Mosaic covenant.

> **NOTE AS WELL:** Since "the blessing and the curse" is under the Mosaic covenant and limited to national Israel, famines or military defeats anywhere else or at any other time are totally unrelated. For instance, a famine in Egypt or Ethiopia in biblical times or a famine in the United States or elsewhere has nothing to do with the Mosaic covenant promises that God had made to national Israel.

As you read through the Old Testament, virtually every item of God's promised curse is shown in the Bible's account of sinful national Israel, especially in books such as Judges and 1 and 2 Kings. What's more, these promises make perfect sense within a literal-grammatical hermeneutic—not with an allegorical interpretation.

However, the blessing section of Lev 26:1–13 and the curse section of 26:14–39 are not the only parts of what God promised. In Lev 26:40–46

God looked many centuries beyond and made additional promises to this same Jewish people, even after He had sent them into exile:

> *"If they confess their iniquity and the iniquity of their forefathers, in their unfaithfulness which they committed against Me, and also in their acting with hostility against Me—I also was acting with hostility against them, to bring them into the land of their enemies—or if their uncircumcised heart becomes humbled so that they then make amends for their iniquity, then I will remember My covenant with Jacob, and I will remember also My covenant with Isaac, and My covenant with Abraham as well, and I will remember the land. For the land will be abandoned by them, and will make up for its sabbaths while it is made desolate without them. They, meanwhile, will be making amends for their iniquity, because they rejected My ordinances and their soul abhorred My statutes. Yet in spite of this, when they are in the land of their enemies, I will not reject them, nor will I so abhor them as to destroy them, breaking My covenant with them; for I am the L<small>ORD</small> their God. But I will remember for them the covenant with their ancestors, whom I brought out of the land of Egypt in the sight of the nations, that I might be their God. I am the L<small>ORD</small>."*

> *These are the statutes and ordinances and laws which the L<small>ORD</small> established between Himself and the sons of Israel through Moses at Mount Sinai.*

CORE FOUNDATIONAL TRUTHS: Just as in the account of Moses in Exodus 32, God based His future actions on His faithfulness in keeping His part of the Abrahamic covenant, not national Israel's failure under the Mosaic covenant.

CORE FOUNDATIONAL TRUTHS: If God intended the blessing and the curse sections of Leviticus 26 for national Israel to be understood with a literal-grammatical hermeneutic, those who want to allegorize God's future promises to the same national Israel must answer why God would switch midstream and intend an allegorical interpretation regarding the very same Jewish people. Simply explained, there is no good biblical reason to switch any of Leviticus 26—the blessing and

> the curse and the promise of a future regathering of the nation—to an allegorical interpretation.

The Essential Chronological Marker in Galatians 4

Before closing this chapter, we note one crucial time marker for our reading and understanding of God's Word, namely Gal 4:4–5, "But when the fullness of the time came, God sent forth His Son, born of a woman, born under the Law, so that He might redeem those who were under the Law, that we might receive the adoption as sons."

The ramifications of this passage are tremendously important. Jesus being "born of a woman, born under the Law" is another way of saying that Jesus was born under the Mosaic covenant. This means that the Mosaic covenant, which was ratified in Exodus 24, stayed in existence for national Israel until the death of Jesus—not His birth. If Jesus was "born of a woman, born under the Law," then His earthly parents were also born under the Mosaic covenant. Accordingly, they were as much under covenant obligation as any other Jew was from Exodus 24 to that time. Luke 2:21–22 offers one demonstration that Joseph and Mary faithfully kept God's commands under the Mosaic covenant:

> *And when eight days had passed, before His circumcision, His name was then called Jesus, the name given by the angel before He was conceived in the womb.*
>
> *And when the days for their purification according to the law of Moses [the Mosaic covenant] were completed, they brought Him up to Jerusalem to present Him to the Lord.*

In addition, that Jesus was "born of a woman, born under the Law" means His cousin John the Baptist, the promised forerunner of the Messiah, was also under the Mosaic covenant. He is, therefore, the last of the Old Testament prophets, not the first of the New Testament prophets. The Mosaic covenant, then, had a definitive beginning with Moses (Exodus 24) and—as we will see later in the book—a definitive ending with the death of Jesus, all part of the Godhead's predetermined plan and foreknowledge, decided by the Godhead before the foundation of the world, precisely when God wanted this "in the fullness of the time" (Gal 4:4).

Conclusion

This chapter shows that we cannot start a study of Scripture with the Mosaic covenant. By this time God had revealed many other truths, such as the continuation of the Abrahamic covenant, given in Genesis. We saw, for example, that when God ratified the Abrahamic covenant in Gen 15:12–14, He foretold events that would occur later in Exodus. Accordingly, while Exodus 1 shows the nation of Israel enslaved in Egypt, Exodus 2 ends with God acting in full accordance with His Word, remembering His covenantal promises to Abraham.

Regarding the Mosaic covenant: First, it is the only covenant of God so far where somebody else was present and active. Second, as long as the Mosaic covenant was in effect, the nation of Israel was under covenant obligation to do what God told them to do. Third, the Mosaic covenant includes the "blessing-and-curse" section of Leviticus 26, where God promised to bless national Israel if they walked in covenant obedience with Him and enumerated specific curses if they did not. Fourth, we noted the eschatological importance of Leviticus 26 ending with hope given by God to the Jewish people. Just as in the account of Moses in Exodus 32, God based His future actions on His faithful keeping of the Abrahamic covenant, not on national Israel's failure under the Mosaic covenant. Finally, we learned of one crucial time marker for our reading and understanding of God's Word, namely Gal 4:4–5. Jesus being "born of a woman, born under the Law" is another way of saying that Jesus was born under the Mosaic covenant. Ratified in Exodus 24, this covenant stayed in existence for national Israel until the death of Jesus and was just as binding for Jesus in His lifetime as it was for Moses or David or any other Jew.

Deeper Walk Study Questions

1. How do God's promises in the Abrahamic covenant in Gen 15:12–14 set the stage for the events in Exodus? Explain.

2. Explain how Exod 2:23–25 gives support to a literal-grammatical hermeneutic.

3. What is the difference between the Mosaic covenant and the previous covenants that we have studied? Why is this important, and how does it help us understand Scripture from Exodus 24 onward?

4. How do God's actions in Exodus 25 differ from what He did at the end of Genesis 3? Why is this important? Be specific. Explain how this demonstrates God's grace.

5. How does the interaction between God and Moses demonstrate that both employed a literal-grammatical hermeneutic when speaking with each other? Why is this important? If God destroyed Israel, would God be breaking previous promises He had made? Explain. What does this say about God's character? Explain.

6. Explain the significance of "the blessing and the curse" in understanding the Old Testament. Who is it for? Who is it not for? Why is this important? Explain how the blessing and the curse becomes a spiritual barometer for the spiritual condition of the nation of Israel under the Mosaic covenant. Explain and give examples.

7. What does God promise in Lev 26:40–45, and why is this so important? Explain and
   be specific.

8. What is the biblical time marker found in Gal 4:4–5? Why is this so important for
   understanding where you are biblically?

CHAPTER 6

A Star! A Star! Shining in the Night!

Anyone who has ever preached about the spectacular events associated with the birth of Jesus, has participated in a nativity scene or has been in a Christmas pageant is aware of the account of the wise men who followed a revelatory star. Matthew 2:1–2 states, "Now after Jesus was born in Bethlehem of Judea in the days of Herod the king, magi from the east arrived in Jerusalem, saying, 'Where is He who has been born King of the Jews? For we saw His star in the east, and have come to worship Him.'" Those who check biblical cross-references or read commentaries will see that most scholars link this verse with one in the Old Testament, Num 24:17, "I see him, but not now; / I behold him, but not near; / A star shall come forth from Jacob, / A scepter shall rise from Israel." To preach about the wise men and the star they followed and to cross-reference it to Num 24:17 is certainly valid. But one should not overlook other prophetic Scriptures that likewise point to the person and work of Jesus Christ. Numbers 24:17 comes toward the end of a section of promises; we risk leaving out so much God-given gold if we start and end with that one verse. In this chapter we will explore the ways in which Scripture progressively builds upon itself by harmonizing with, and expanding upon, previous promises that God has given. This broader view of Scripture, then, will expand our understanding of the fulfillment of God's promises through Christ.

Biblical Rationale From Our Previous Studies

Numbers 24:17 is a good place for us to briefly pause and think through—and apply—pertinent previously discussed biblical truths. Here are a few that are significant:

1. In the unfolding revelation of God, Scripture builds upon itself; we cannot hope to be biblically accurate if we begin our understanding of God and His work at Num 24:17 without viewing it through the biblical lens (i.e., not adding to the text, not taking anything away from the text).
2. Numbers 24 (and related passages) would most definitely be part of what Jesus meant in John 5:46–47 ("Moses wrote about Me") and twice in Luke 24, where Jesus referred to Moses in teaching about Himself.
3. This section is part of the "predetermined plan [singular] and foreknowledge of God" (Acts 2:23) before the foundation of the world (1 Pet 1:20).
4. But—and this is important to note—the predetermined plan (still singular) and foreknowledge of God includes the reign of God's holy Messiah, not just His death. "Star" and "scepter" (associated with reigning) are both contained in Num 24:17.
5. The Noahic, Abrahamic, and Mosaic covenants have been ratified, and all are operative.

The immediate context of Num 24:17 points the reader to earlier prophetic texts. Note, for example, Num 24:14, "And now, behold, I am going to my people; come, and I will advise you what this people will do to your people in the days to come." The phrase "in the days to come," similar in meaning to phrases such as "the end of the days," and "last days," is used here for the second time in Scripture.

> **KEY TRUTH:** I recommend searching to find whether some word or phrase is used previously in Scripture. Where is it used for the first time in Scripture? Note its background (rather than just picking a verse out of context) and see if there is any relevance for better

> understanding God's Word or for preparing you to teach or preach. As we will see, in this case, the first and second use of "the end of the days" or "the last days" are intricately bound together.

The first occurrence of "the end or the days" or "last days" is in Gen 49:1, when Jacob gathered his sons before his death. "Then Jacob summoned his sons and said, 'Assemble yourselves that I may tell you what shall befall you in the days to come.'" This is the same section that contains several beautiful prophecies of the Messiah:

Judah, your brothers shall praise you;

Your hand shall be on the neck of your enemies;

Your father's sons shall bow down to you.

Judah is a lion's whelp;

From the prey, my son, you have gone up.

He couches, he lies down as a lion,

And as a lion, who dares rouse him up?

The scepter shall not depart from Judah,

Nor the ruler's staff from between his feet,

Until Shiloh comes,

And to him shall be the obedience of the peoples.

He ties his foal to the vine,

And his donkey's colt to the choice vine;

He washes his garments in wine,

And his robes in the blood of grapes.

His eyes are dull from wine,

And his teeth white from milk. (Gen 49:8–12)

As was noted in a previous chapter, there is clear biblical evidence that the reference to Judah as a lion refers specifically to Jesus Christ. In Revelation 5, after the apostle John has been transported in a vision to heaven, he sees a sealed scroll and somehow knows that until that scroll is opened and completed, Satan will still work his work and the Messiah's reign will never come. John is instructed by one of the twenty-four elders in this vision in Rev 5:5, "Stop weeping; behold, the Lion that is from the tribe of Judah, the Root of David, has overcome so as to open the book and its seven seals." Those of us who accept the inerrancy of God's Word know that this description of Jesus comes directly from the prophetic truths in Genesis 49, and these things must come to pass in the end of the days or the last days.

The Theological Significance of Numbers 22–24

We started in Num 24:17, but Numbers 22–24 is one section of Scripture that contains four separate prophetic sections. Taken together these chapters record the attempt of a Gentile king Balak to hire a "somewhat-of-a-prophet," named Balaam, to curse Israel for him. Within this context, God chose to reveal sublime prophecies of the coming Messiah. While we cannot here deal with all the particulars of Numbers 22–24, certain significant matters must be noted. (1) The oracles in Numbers 22–24 are God's word, not Balaam's word. (2) The text repeatedly refers to national Israel as a people. (3) The blessing or cursing of Numbers 22–24 is the heart of the Abrahamic covenant promises. (4) The unfolding revelatory light concerning the promised Messiah expands and harmonizes with God's previous promises.

The Oracles in Numbers 22–24 Are Yahweh's Word—Not Balaam's Word

Although it is common to label these chapters as "Balaam's Oracles" or "the Oracles of Balaam," this is not how God viewed these prophecies. The wonderful promises and revelation that occur in these chapters are neither Balaam's thoughts nor his opinions, nor do they transpire by means of any learned technique on his part; he was simply a mouthpiece for God to communicate these holy truths. Repeatedly the text emphasizes that these are the very words of God. For instance, God told Balaam to go with the king's emissaries, "but only the word which I speak to you shall you do" (Num 22:20). After Balaam's terrifying experience with the Angel of the Lord (the same Angel of the Lord we have previously seen in Genesis 16 and 22 and Exodus 3), God warned Balaam, "Go with the men, but you shall speak only the word which I tell you" (Num 22:35). Numbers 23:5 states, "The LORD put a word in Balaam's mouth and said . . ." concurring with Num 23:16, "The LORD met Balaam and put [an oracle] in his mouth," again instructing him precisely what he must speak to Balak. In Num 24:2 the text states that "the Spirit of God came upon [Balaam]," so when Balaam spoke the word of God, he spoke just what the text says: the word of God. Consequently, any attempts to downplay the importance of what is revealed in these chapters should not be accepted; they are the very words of God Himself. The word of God given by means of Balaam in Numbers 22–24 should be received as you would receive any other part of the word of God elsewhere in Scripture.

> **KEY TRUTH:** God is not limited by the frail and sinful human containers in the giving and receiving of God's word. Paul wrote in 2 Cor 4:7, "But we have this treasure in earthen vessels, so that the surpassing greatness of the power will be of God and not from ourselves." No matter who the best holy prophet or apostle of God was, it would still require divine inspiration to bring into being God's word, because His Word would never originate in the hearts or minds of fallen humanity.

> **CONSIDER ALSO:** When giving His revelation, neither is God limited by fallen humans who oppose Him and are lost and dead in their sins. Anyone who thinks it is impossible for God to use someone such as Balaam as a means of receiving and expressing His divine revelation should consider the account given in John 11:47–52:
>
> Therefore the chief priests and the Pharisees convened a council, and were saying, "What are we doing? For this man is performing many signs.
>
> If we let Him go on like this, all men will believe in Him, and the Romans will come and take away both our place and our nation." But one of them, Caiaphas, who was high priest that year, said to them, "You know nothing at all, nor do you take into account that it is

> expedient for you that one man die for the people, and that the whole
> nation not perish." Now he did not say this on his own initiative; but
> being high priest that year, he prophesied that Jesus was going to die
> for the nation, and not for the nation only, but in order that He might
> also gather together into one the children of God who are scattered
> abroad.

National Israel As a People Occurs Repeatedly Within the Text

Many believe there is no indication in the text of Gen 12:1–3 that the
promise to bless the ones who blessed Abraham and the warning about
those who cursed him was ever intended to extend beyond Abraham. However, this is a presupposition forced on the text and certainly not one derived from it. The designation of the nation of Israel as a people occurs
frequently in Numbers 22–24. For instance, in the immediate context there
was a "great fear because of the people" [of Israel] (Num 22:3). Numbers
22:5 gives this description by King Balak: "a people came out of Egypt;
behold, they cover the surface of the land, and they are living opposite
me," following this request for Balaam to "come, curse this people" (Num
22:6, 17). Before beginning one of the God-given oracles, Balaam saw "a
portion of the people" (Num 22:41). Elsewhere God by means of Balaam
describes Israel as "a people who dwells apart" (Num 23:9) and "a people
[that] rises like a lioness" (Num 23:24).

Of infinitely more importance was Yahweh's own statement in Num
22:12 as He instructed Balaam concerning the nation of Israel's present
status before Him. When Balak's messengers first approached Balaam,
Yahweh warned him, "Do not go with them; you shall not curse the people, for they are blessed." God considered the blessing that He had given
Abraham as still operative for the Jewish nation at this time and certainly
not restricted only to the original promise He had made with Abraham.
The nation of Israel's current status was that "they are blessed" before Him
because of the unfailing love and the covenant promises given by Yahweh.

Finally, beyond the present, God, by means of Balaam, informed
Balak and others what would transpire in the future: "And now, behold, I

am going to my people; come, and I will advise you what this people will do to your people in the days to come" (Num 24:14). The significance of this verse will be developed in chapter 10. Suffice it to say, the burden of proof is on those who would want to remove any of the references made to the people of Israel instead of understanding the verse in its normative way.

The Blessing or Cursing of Numbers 22–24 Is the Heart of the Abrahamic Covenant Promises

Balak's request to have Balaam curse Israel is more than just an inappropriate choice of words: this story would reveal the very heart of whether God's promises to national Israel were still in force. Based on the three victories found in Numbers 21, Numbers 22–24 is one unit that develops in more detail the same theology with the repeated emphasis throughout this account of either blessing or cursing.

While the immediate context for Numbers 22–24 is the three military victories that God granted in Numbers 21, the earlier context from the exodus onward has not spoken well of Israel as a whole and includes such things as the evil reporting by the spies and God's subsequent judging of that generation (Numbers 13–14), Korah's rebellion (Numbers 16), and Moses's sinning by striking the rock the second time (Numbers 20). Thus, this important theological issue should not be overlooked: in spite of Israel's sins, Yahweh still would honor His Word. Even more to the point, Gen 12:3 ("And I will bless those who bless you, / And the one who curses you I will curse. / And in you all the families of the earth shall be blessed") becomes the basis for the Balak-Balaam encounter and an indicator of whether God considered the promises He had previously made to be understood in a literal or spiritual fashion.

Numbers 22:1–3 explains Moab's fear, after the victories Yahweh had recently given Israel:

> *Then the sons of Israel journeyed, and camped in the plains of Moab beyond the Jordan opposite Jericho.*

Now Balak the son of Zippor saw all that Israel had done to the Amorites.
So Moab was in great fear because of the people, for they were numerous;
and Moab was in dread of the sons of Israel.

Balak's invitation to Balaam came with a specific purpose: "Now, therefore, please come, curse this people for me since they are too mighty for me; perhaps I may be able to defeat them and drive them out of the land. For I know that he whom you bless is blessed, and he whom you curse is cursed" (Num 22:6). This statement cannot be true, for Gen 12:3 has already indicated that blessing and cursing are exclusively reserved to be pronounced by Yahweh, especially as it relates to national Israel.

God appeared to Balaam warning him, "Do not go with them; you shall not curse the people; for they are blessed" (Num 22:12). Notice that Yahweh considered the Jewish people then currently blessed, with the basis of this blessing originating from the Abrahamic covenant, not the people's repeated failure at keeping the Mosaic covenant. So Balak's second plea for Balaam to curse the people was met by Balaam's response in Num 22:18: "I could not do anything, either small or great, contrary to the command of the LORD my God" which, as subsequent events will show, was not a true indication of Balaam's spiritual status. Nonetheless, Balaam was accurate in his statement about not being able to speak contrary to God's word or God's will.

Balak's second attempt to have Balaam curse Israel follows the episode of Balaam, his donkey, and the terrifying presence of the Angel of the Lord, with drawn sword in hand (Num 22:22–34), who sent Balaam to Balak but who strongly warned him to speak only what God revealed to him (Num 22:35–41). Thus, Balaam pronounced a discourse directly from the Lord (Num 23:5). When Balak requested, "Come curse Jacob for me" (Num 23:7), Balaam had no response other than "How shall I curse whom God has not cursed? / And how can I denounce whom the LORD has not denounced?" (Num 23:8).

Consequently, Numbers 22–24 should not be considered as some minor offense against Yahweh, but rather as Balaam attempting to encroach on the domain and territory—and attributes—of God.

Another attempt at cursing Israel was just as futile as the others (Num 23:11–30). Again, "the LORD met Balaam and put a word in his mouth"

(Num 23:16). Within the discourse that follows, the famous verse Num 23:19 occurs: "God is not a man, that He should lie, / Nor a son of man, that He should repent; / Has He said, and will He not do it? / Or has He spoken, and will He not make it good?" From Gen 1:1 through Num 23:19, other than items yet to be fulfilled (e.g., Lev 26:40–45), God has done all that He has promised and has made good every bit of His Word. Not only has Yahweh repeatedly done what He said He would do, but He Himself is the One who said, "You shall not curse the people, for they are blessed" (Num 22:12), based on His own previous blessing of them.

The Unfolding Revelatory Light Concerning the Promised Messiah Expands and Harmonizes with God's Previous Promises

Time and space limitations do not permit a fuller treatment of all pertinent texts up through Numbers 24 regarding God's promises. However, three texts in particular relate to God's promises in Numbers 24: Genesis 22, 27, and 49.

First, Gen 22:16–18 recounts the additional revelation from God regarding the promised seed, after the Angel of the Lord abruptly stopped Abraham from sacrificing his own son:

> *"By Myself I have sworn," declares the* Lord, *"because you have done this thing, and have not withheld your son, your only son, indeed I will greatly bless you, and I will greatly multiply your seed as the stars of the heavens and as the sand which is on the seashore; and your seed shall possess the gate of their enemies. In your seed all the nations of the earth shall be blessed, because you have obeyed My voice."*

Years later Yahweh appeared to Abraham's son Isaac and made further promises in Gen 26:24: "The Lord appeared to him the same night and said, 'I am the God of your father Abraham; / Do not fear, for I am with you. / I will bless you, and multiply your descendants, / For the sake of My servant Abraham.'" Isaac later reaffirmed to his son Jacob what God previously had promised:

Now may God give you of the dew of heaven,

And of the fatness of the earth,

And an abundance of grain and new wine;

May peoples serve you,

And nations bow down to you;

Be master of your brothers,

And may your mother's sons bow down to you.

Cursed be those who curse you,

And blessed be those who bless you. (Gen 27:28–29)

By the time of the events of Numbers, God has already revealed much more definitive information regarding His promised Messiah. For instance, as we saw, Genesis 49 adds additional revelation not only regarding Israel, but also regarding specific prophecies related to the future promised Messiah who will reign over the nations. These same truths are found and expanded in Numbers. Within these oracles that God gave came a developing clarity about the identity of the One to come. Numbers 23:21 states, "The LORD his God is with him, / And the shout of a king is among them." We should note the significance of this extremely important prophecy: centuries before Saul reigned as Israel's first king, God had already revealed in Numbers the future King Messiah who would have an extremely close relationship with the Lord. Of course, God revealed more and more biblical truths about exactly how close that relationship was in eternity past and into eternity future.

With a glimpse into the future, God also explained how He currently viewed national Israel in spite of their multiple high-handed sins: "For there is no omen against Jacob, / Nor is there any divination against Israel; / At the proper time it shall be said to Jacob / And to Israel, what God has done!" (Num 23:23). Ever the slow learner, King Balak hoped that perhaps another change in location would render a different result (Num 23:25–30). This sets the stage for the magnificent divine revelation of Numbers 24, the emphasis again being that this is ultimately God's word—not Balaam's—as "the Spirit of God came upon him" (Num 24:2).

Among other things, God through Balaam promised:

He will devour the nations [Gentiles] who are his adversaries,

And will crush their bones in pieces,

And shatter them with his arrows.

He couches, he lies down as a lion,

And as a lion, who dares rouse him? (Num 24:8–9)

Immediately after a pronouncement of what the Messiah will eventually do to His adversaries, we see the reiteration of God's earlier promise in Gen 12:3, now stated in Num 24:9: "Blessed is everyone who blesses you, / And cursed is everyone who curses you." In Numbers 24 the focus turns to God's promise to deliver Israel in the future, especially by means of His own deliverer (see Num 24:8).

Within this same passage another marvelous messianic preview occurs:

I see him, but not now;

I behold him, but not near.

A star shall come forth from Jacob,

A scepter shall rise from Israel,

And shall crush through the forehead of Moab,

And tear down all the sons of Sheth.

Edom shall be a possession,

Seir, its enemies, also will be a possession,

While Israel performs valiantly.

One from Jacob shall have dominion,

And will destroy the remnant from the city. (Num 24:17–19)

The tremendous significance of these verses should not be understated, as it relates to the future work of the One of whom the prophecy speaks. Again, the future aspect reveals not only that the Messiah will fight, but also of the enemies against whom He and His descendants will fight.

If we keep the promises made by God from Genesis through Numbers 24 in mind, a composite sketch of the promised Messiah emerges. The future King will have the service of an obedient Israel (Gen 27:29; 49:8) whom He has brought back into the land in accordance with His covenant faithfulness (Lev 26:40–45). This King will ultimately rule over the nations as well (Gen 49:10; Num 24:17–19), will possess the gates of His enemies (Gen 22:17), will have His hand on the neck of His enemies (Gen 49:8), and will exercise dominion over them (Num 24:19). Both Genesis 49 and Numbers 24 depict the promised King as fierce, crouching and lying down like a lion whom no one will dare to rouse (Gen 49:9; Num 24:9), and—most significantly—it is through this promised individual King that both the blessing and the cursing will come in its fullness (Gen 12:3; 27:29; Num 24:9).

It is difficult to argue that God considered His promise to curse those who curse Israel as having been completed during Abraham's lifetime, since the core issue to bless or curse national Israel repeatedly occurs in Numbers 22–24 and is part of the rationale for God's instruction to Balaam and the revelation about the nation, the coming Messiah, and His future reign as King. Not only is the Gen 12:3 promise to bless or curse still present and operative, but also God expands His previous revelation to include the Messiah as both a beneficiary of the promise and the ultimate means by which these prophetic promises will be fulfilled. Those who would spiritualize these promises would have to answer the following questions: (1) Should all, any, or only some of the promises that God gave in Numbers 22–24 be taken as literal promises? (2) On what basis should they be considered as either literal or spiritual? (3) Most important, if the promises that God made and expanded in these chapters are not literal truths regarding the nation of Israel and the Messiah, exactly what did God mean by reaffirming and expanding the promises in these passages, using language very similar or identical to that used previously?

KEY CONSIDERATION: Those who take Num 24:17 to be a reference to Jesus the Messiah and the star announcing His birth must give a good biblical reason not to understand the other elements of this prophecy through a literal-grammatical hermeneutic as well.

These wonderful chapters of Numbers 22–24, although unknown to most Christians, would have been a significant part of John 5:46, "Moses wrote about Me," and part of the teaching mentioned twice in Luke 24: Jesus "beginning with Moses" and speaking of things concerning Himself.

Conclusion

In this chapter we explored the ways in which Scripture progressively builds upon itself by harmonizing with, and expanding upon, previous God-given promises. We saw that (1) Numbers 22–24 is God's word, not Balaam's word; (2) this text repeatedly refers to national Israel as a people; and (3) the blessing or cursing that Balak wants Balaam to perform is at the heart of the Abrahamic covenant promises and a direct challenge to Yahweh's authority and domain (e.g., Gen 12:3; Num 24:9). So (4) the character of God is at stake if Balaam is allowed to curse whom God has not cursed. Finally, (5) Numbers 22–24 adds additional revelatory light that expands and harmonizes with God's previous promises about His Messiah, such as the promise of a king in Num 23:21: "The LORD his God is with him, / And the shout of a king is among them." Accordingly, the Christmas account featuring the wise men is not based upon one isolated prophecy but a series of prophecies, most of which have yet to be fulfilled, many of them awaiting the second coming of the Messiah. And since God fulfilled the star promise of Num 24:17, we can have confidence that He will do so with the remaining promises.

Deeper Walk Study Questions

1. Since Scripture builds on Scripture, list the details from the pertinent truths given in the chapter's initial review section (before continuing with our consideration of Num 24:17). How do these truths help direct our studies so far? Explain.

2. What is the significance of Gen 49:1, 8–12 and Rev 5:1–5 as these texts pertain to Jesus? List five important truths from these verses. Explain and be specific.

3. How does Numbers 22–24 repeatedly and specifically refer to the nation of Israel? Be specific. Why is this important? Explain.

4. If someone began at Num 24:17 to preach or teach without knowing what God had promised up to that point from Gen 49:1, 8–12 and Num 22:1–24:16, how limited would that person's understanding be? List ten important truths from these passages that one would need to know in order to understand accurately Num 24:17.

5. Why was King Balak's desire to have Balaam curse Israel an infringement on God's domain? Explain.

6. List and explain the verses in Numbers 22–24 that show that this is truly God's word and not Balaam's idea. Is this truly God's word? Explain. Describe a valuable New Testament parallel passage that shows someone unsaved and in opposition to God still receiving a divine revelation from God.

7. Considering Numbers 22–24 as being one unit in Scripture that deals with the nation of Israel, why are the biblical prophecies about the Messiah given in these chapters so important? Develop a composite sketch of what God has promised so far for His Messiah.

CHAPTER 7

The Biblical Logic of Joshua 1–6[1]

The book of Joshua is a wonderful book for Christians to read and from which they can learn life lessons in keeping with Paul's "Now these things happened as examples for us" (1 Cor 10:6) and "were written for our instruction" (1 Cor 10:11). Wonderful truths can be gleaned from this specific part of God's Word as it relates to living the Christian life. From a methodological perspective, this would encompass the application of biblical truths to our lives. In applying these truths to our world, however, we must carefully follow the biblical trail to see the truths and doctrines that God has firmly placed within them. Good, solid biblical applications are important, but they will be more easily adaptable and more biblically accurate if we first engage in a close study of the book to see how they fit with other truths that God has revealed.

Perhaps there's no better place to see this than in Joshua 6, which recounts the "battle of Jericho." This is one of the most famous sections in Scripture. Some who have never read much or any of the Bible are still familiar with the battle of Jericho. But as with so many other places in Scripture, there is no "battle of Jericho" without the spiritual realities inherent in the context leading up to Joshua 6. As in the previous chapter, we will explore how this epic battle is related to the promises that God had already given in His Word.

---

[1] I spoke at The Master's Seminary chapel on many of the biblical truths in this chapter. Titled "Prep for Spiritual Victory" (Joshua 5), the audio can be accessed: http://www.sermonaudio.com/sermoninfo.asp?SID=1029111151394

The Biblical Background for the Events Leading to Joshua 5

Before the Jewish people were ever a nation, in fact, before "Father Abraham" had his first child, when God ratified the Abrahamic covenant, He also made these promises in Genesis 15:12–16:

> *Now when the sun was going down, a deep sleep fell upon Abram; and behold, terror and great darkness fell upon him. And God said to Abram,*
>
> *"Know for certain that your descendants will be strangers in a land that is not theirs, where they will be enslaved and oppressed four hundred years. But I will also judge the nation whom they will serve; and afterward they will come out with many possessions. As for you, you shall go to your fathers in peace; you shall be buried at a good old age. Then in the fourth generation they shall return here, for the iniquity of the Amorite is not yet complete."*

By the time Joshua 1 begins, God had already fulfilled many of the promises He had previously made, the fulfillment of which would significantly affect the nation of Israel. Since God promised He would bless the ones who bless Israel and curse those who curse Israel (Gen 12:3), after Egypt had enslaved and oppressed the Jewish people for four hundred years, God judged Egypt and redeemed the Jewish people out of slavery. He ratified the Mosaic covenant with Israel (Exodus 24), making the Jewish people into a nation. However, as we know, the Jewish people quickly rebelled against Yahweh, and God sentenced those who were more than twenty years of age to die in the wilderness (Numbers 13–14), with the exception of Joshua and Caleb. By the time Joshua 1 opens, Moses has been replaced by Joshua as the leader of God's people.

But one of the things God also revealed in Gen 15:16 was that "in the fourth generation they will return here"—not maybe or might return here. Simply put, God was ready to fulfill the last part of these particular promises made centuries earlier. The book of Joshua opens with the nation of Israel outside of the land God had given them and on the verge of crossing over into it—just as God had said. If God does not fulfill what He has promised, then He is not holy, true, almighty—and His character is at stake.

There are a few verses in Joshua 1–5 that we should note as we work our way to Joshua 6. God's promise in Josh 1:1–4, for example, includes a reference to the land promises of the Abrahamic covenant:

Now it came about after the death of Moses the servant of the LORD that the LORD spoke to Joshua the son of Nun, Moses' servant, saying, "Moses My servant is dead; now therefore arise, cross this Jordan, you and all this people, to the land which I am giving to them, to the sons of Israel. Every place on which the sole of your foot treads, I have given it to you, just as I spoke to Moses. From the wilderness and this Lebanon, even as far as the great river, the river Euphrates, all the land of the Hittites, and as far as the Great Sea toward the setting of the sun will be your territory."

God continues in Josh 1:5–9, promising to bless Joshua and again noting the land promises He had sworn to give Israel under the Abrahamic covenant:

"No man will be able to stand before you all the days of your life. Just as I have been with Moses, I will be with you; I will not fail you or forsake you. Be strong and courageous, for you shall give this people possession of the land which I swore to their fathers to give them. Only be strong and very courageous; be careful to do according to all the law which Moses My servant commanded you; do not turn from it to the right or to the left, so that you may have success wherever you go. This book of the law shall not depart from your mouth, but you shall meditate on it day and night, so that you may be careful to do according to all that is written in it; for then you will make your way prosperous, and then you will have success. Have I not commanded you? Be strong and courageous! Do not tremble or be dismayed, for the LORD your God is with you wherever you go."

According to these introductory verses, God began His instruction to Joshua not by outlining administrative techniques or even military strategy; Yahweh began—and continued—Joshua's training by instructing him to be careful to study and keep "the book of the law" and to live in faithful obedience to Him. Other lessons and instructions would be important, but none ever overrode this core component.

> **CONSIDER ALSO:** If the liberal critics of the Bible are right, and the Pentateuch was not yet written when the story of Joshua took place, then one also has to throw away the book of Joshua, because there God gave Joshua commands to carefully cling to the Law that wouldn't yet have been fully given to him. Everyone will believe someone or something. If these critics are right, the Bible is wrong, and if the Bible is right, they are wrong. There is no middle ground for this. I hope you have already staked your claim on the Word of the Living God.

Another contextually important text for understanding Joshua 6 is Josh 1:10, where God's instruction broadens from Joshua to include the nation of Israel:

> *Then Joshua commanded the officers of the people, saying, "Pass through the midst of the camp and command the people, saying, 'Prepare provisions for yourselves, for within three days you are to cross this Jordan, to go in to possess the land which the Lord your God is giving you, to possess it.'"*

Joshua 2, then, presents the account of how Rahab the harlot housed and protected the two Jewish spies sent out by Joshua to view the land, especially Jericho.

In Josh 2:8–11 Rahab gave this account of how the people of Jericho viewed what had happened. She included an accurate description of what was yet to come:

> *Now before they [the two spies] lay down, she came up to them on the roof, and said to the men, "I know that the Lord has given you the land, and that the terror of you has fallen on us, and that all the inhabitants of the land have melted away before you. For we have heard how the Lord dried up the water of the Red Sea before you when you came out of Egypt, and what you did to the two kings of the Amorites who were beyond the Jordan, to Sihon and Og, whom you utterly destroyed. When we heard it, our hearts melted and no courage remained in any man any longer because of you; for the Lord your God, He is God in heaven above and on earth beneath."*

Following the account of Rahab, Josh 3:7–8 records God's direct intervention when the nation of Israel came to the brink of the Promised Land at the Jordan River but were unable to cross due to flooding:

Now the LORD said to Joshua, "This day I will begin to exalt you in the sight of all Israel, that they may know that just as I have been with Moses, I will be with you. You shall, moreover, command the priests who are carrying the ark of the covenant, saying, 'When you come to the edge of the waters of the Jordan, you shall stand still in the Jordan.'"

As in Exodus, God then provided yet another miraculous crossing:

So when the people set out from their tents to cross the Jordan with the priests carrying the ark of the covenant before the people, and when those who carried the ark came into the Jordan, and the feet of the priests carrying the ark were dipped in the edge of the water (for the Jordan overflows all its banks all the days of harvest), the waters which were flowing down from above stood and rose up in one heap, a great distance away at Adam, the city that is beside Zarethan; and those which were flowing down toward the sea of the Arabah, the Salt Sea, were completely cut off. So the people crossed opposite Jericho. And the priests who carried the ark of the covenant of the LORD stood firm on dry ground in the middle of the Jordan while all Israel crossed on dry ground, until all the nation had finished crossing the Jordan. (Josh 3:14–17)

Appropriately, God wanted such a miraculous crossing to be used as a teaching tool for later generations, commanding that each of the twelve tribes was to put a stone marker in the middle of the dried Jordan (Josh 4:1–9). After God brought all of the people safely across the Jordan, the following account took place, as recorded in Josh 4:15–18:

Now the LORD said to Joshua, "Command the priests who carry the ark of the testimony that they come up from the Jordan." So Joshua commanded the priests, saying, "Come up from the Jordan." It came about when the priests who carried the ark of the covenant of the LORD had come up from the middle of the Jordan, and the soles of the priests' feet were lifted up to the dry ground, that the waters of the Jordan returned to their place, and went over all its banks as before.

Joshua the leader then explained:

*Now the people came up from the Jordan on the tenth of the first month
and camped at Gilgal on the eastern edge of Jericho. Those twelve stones
which they had taken from the Jordan, Joshua set up at Gilgal. He said to
the sons of Israel, "When your children ask their fathers in time to come,
saying, 'What are these stones?' then you shall inform your children, saying,
'Israel crossed this Jordan on dry ground.' For the LORD your God dried up
the waters of the Jordan before you until you had crossed, just as the LORD
your God had done to the Red Sea, which He dried up before us until we
had crossed; that all the peoples of the earth may know that the hand of
the LORD is mighty, so that you may fear the LORD your God forever." (Josh
4:19–24)*

The entire young nation was now officially in—but not yet in possession of—the land that God had promised them. After reporting how the
Gentile kings' "hearts melted" and they were spiritless when they heard
what God had done, Joshua 5 gives what probably seemed like a strange
but clear command from God. "At that time the LORD said to Joshua,
'Make for yourself flint knives and circumcise again the sons of Israel the
second time.' So Joshua made himself flint knives and circumcised the
sons of Israel at Gibeath-haaraloth" (Josh 5:2–3).

From a human standpoint, this appears to be an incredibly foolish
command and response: (1) You are in the midst of enemy territory. (2)
The formidable enemy peoples are in front of you, and the flooded Jordan
River is at your back, blocking any attempt to escape that way. (3) The
entire nation is open and exposed and in plain sight of the enemy. (4) To
make the situation even worse, it is not good military strategy to take the
only strong warriors you have and physically disable them for about a two-
to three-week period.

So let's consider a pertinent question: why was circumcision of the
males of this people so important to God? The answers are found previously in Scripture. When God gave the original instruction for the nation
to follow, He did that as part of the blessings inherent in the Abrahamic
covenant, as Gen 17:7–14 shows:

*"I will establish My covenant between Me and you and your descendants
after you throughout their generations for an everlasting covenant, to be
God to you and to your descendants after you. I will give to you and to your*

descendants after you, the land of your sojournings, all the land of Canaan, for an everlasting possession; and I will be their God."

God said further to Abraham, "Now as for you, you shall keep My covenant, you and your descendants after you throughout their generations. This is My covenant, which you shall keep, between Me and you and your descendants after you: every male among you shall be circumcised. And you shall be circumcised in the flesh of your foreskin; and it shall be the sign of the covenant between Me and you. And every male among you who is eight days old shall be circumcised throughout your generations, a servant who is born in the house or who is bought with money from any foreigner, who is not of your descendants. A servant who is born in your house or who is bought with your money shall surely be circumcised; thus shall My covenant be in your flesh for an everlasting covenant. But an uncircumcised male who is not circumcised in the flesh of his foreskin, that person shall be cut off from his people; he has broken My covenant."

That one "shall be cut off from his people" often meant being put to death. And just to show that God actually meant this, long after He had commissioned Moses and sent him to Egypt, God showed His intense anger with Moses in Exod 4:24–26:

Now it came about at the lodging place on the way that the LORD met him [Moses] and sought to put him to death. Then Zipporah [the wife of Moses] took a flint and cut off her son's foreskin and threw it at Moses' feet, and she said, "You are indeed a bridegroom of blood to me." So He let him alone. At that time she said, "You are a bridegroom of blood"—because of the circumcision.

CORE TRUTH: Moses had been commissioned by God to lead Israel out of Egypt, and yet Moses was in covenant disobedience by not having circumcised his own son. Here is a good biblical example of the truth that the human leader is never above God's requirements.

Exodus 12:42–49 likewise reflects the importance of circumcision, given God's clear instructions concerning His Passover:

It is a night to be observed for the LORD for having brought them out from the land of Egypt; this night is for the LORD, to be observed by all the sons of Israel throughout their generations.

The LORD said to Moses and Aaron, "This is the ordinance of the Passover: no foreigner is to eat of it; but every man's slave purchased with money, after you have circumcised him, then he may eat of it. A sojourner or a hired servant shall not eat of it. It is to be eaten in a single house; you are not to bring forth any of the flesh outside of the house, nor are you to break any bone of it. All the congregation of Israel are to celebrate this. But if a stranger sojourns with you, and celebrates the Passover to the LORD, let all his males be circumcised, and then let him come near to celebrate it; and he shall be like a native of the land. But no uncircumcised person may eat of it. The same law shall apply to the native as to the stranger who sojourns among you."

With this background in mind, then, we return to Joshua 5 for the explanation that God gave, which makes perfect sense with the previous commands:

This is the reason why Joshua circumcised them: all the people who came out of Egypt who were males, all the men of war, died in the wilderness along the way, after they came out of Egypt. For all the people who came out were circumcised, but all the people who were born in the wilderness along the way as they came out of Egypt had not been circumcised. For the sons of Israel walked forty years in the wilderness, until all the nation, that is, the men of war who came out of Egypt, perished because they did not listen to the voice of the LORD, to whom the LORD had sworn that He would not let them see the land which the LORD had sworn to their fathers to give us, a land flowing with milk and honey. Their children whom He raised up in their place, Joshua circumcised; for they were uncircumcised, because they had not circumcised them along the way. (Josh 5:4–7)

This account reflects yet other examples of wickedness committed by the wilderness generation, namely their failure to circumcise their male children at birth. So when the nation crossed the Jordan into the land that Yahweh had sworn to give, circumcision was the first order of business. Joshua 5:8–9 adds additional details from God's perspective:

> *Now when they had finished circumcising all the nation, they remained
> in their places in the camp until they were healed. Then the LORD said to
> Joshua, "Today I have rolled away the reproach of Egypt from you." So the
> name of that place is called Gilgal to this day.*

With the nation prepared spiritually, they again enjoyed the fellowship
meal of the Lord's Passover, which was only the third Passover recorded
in Scripture:

> *While the sons of Israel camped at Gilgal they observed the Passover on the
> evening of the fourteenth day of the month on the desert plains of Jericho.
> On the day after the Passover, on that very day, they ate some of the produce
> of the land, unleavened cakes and parched grain. (Josh 5:10–11)*

One more item to note in Josh 5:12: "The manna ceased on the day
after they had eaten some of the produce of the land, so that the sons of
Israel no longer had manna, but they ate some of the yield of the land of
Canaan during that year."

FOUNDATIONAL TRUTH: Every bit of Scripture that we have covered to
this point makes perfect sense by employing the literal-grammatical
hermeneutic. Absolutely no part of it needs to be spiritualized to
make it fit scripturally. God repeatedly has been, currently is, and in
the future will be completely faithful to His Word.

God had prepared Israel for an attack on Jericho; now He intervened
to prepare the leader of the people and to remind him who the true Leader
was. Consider Josh 5:13–14:

> *Now it came about when Joshua was by Jericho, that he lifted up his eyes
> and looked, and behold, a man was standing opposite him with his sword
> drawn in his hand, and Joshua went to him and said to him, "Are you for
> us or for our adversaries?" He said, "No; rather I indeed come now as cap-
> tain of the host of the LORD." And Joshua fell on his face to the earth, and
> bowed down, and said to him, "What has my lord to say to his servant?"*

Joshua's simple response of immediate obedience is also noteworthy
and should be emulated: "The captain of the LORD's host said to Joshua,

'Remove your sandals from your feet, for the place where you are standing is holy.' And Joshua did so" (Josh 5:15).

Godly scholars debate whether the captain of the host of the Lord speaking here was the preincarnate Jesus, because the text does not contain, for instance, the specific designation that this was the "angel of the LORD." This is one of those pick-your-battles-carefully texts where you would not (I hope!) sever fellowship with someone who takes a different position.

Here is what I believe and why I believe it. The incident about Joshua standing on holy ground is purposely parallel to the encounter that Moses had with God, in Exod 3:4–6:

> When the LORD saw that he turned aside to look, God called to him from the midst of the bush, and said, "Moses, Moses!" And he said, "Here I am." Then He said, "Do not come near here; remove your sandals from your feet, for the place on which you are standing is holy ground." He said also, "I am the God of your father, the God of Abraham, the God of Isaac, and the God of Jacob." Then Moses hid his face, for he was afraid to look at God.

God had promised to be with Joshua just as He had been with Moses. It would be very unlikely that the disciple-in-training leader who would eventually take the leadership position after the death of Moses would not know about the special encounter Moses had with God in Exodus 3. In both Exodus 3 and Joshua 5, it should be noted, the ground was holy because Moses and Joshua were in the very special presence of God. That the divine figure in Joshua 5 is more than merely an angelic being is perhaps supported by later divine encounters. In Luke 1, for example, the high-ranking angel Gabriel encountered Zacharias and then Mary, neither of whom was told to remove shoes or that the ground on which each stood was holy. If Joshua had stood before a mere angelic being, it would seem that his experience would be more similar to Zacharias's and Mary's encounters with God's angel, as presented in Luke. But since the Joshua 5 encounter was more similar to Moses's encounter with God (Exodus 3), it seems that the preincarnate Jesus appeared here also.

Viewing the Fall of Jericho Through a Biblical Lens

With the previous spiritual realities established, we can now consider the significance of the fall of Jericho in Joshua 6. The people had been brought into the land—and, even more important—back into covenant fellowship with God, enjoying the Passover with Him. Thus, the people put themselves into the blessing part of "the blessing and the curse." Leviticus 26:7–8 states that when Israel was obedient to Yahweh, this would happen: "But you will chase your enemies, and they will fall before you by the sword; five of you will chase a hundred, and a hundred of you will chase ten thousand, and your enemies will fall before you by the sword."

Deuteronomy 28:7 reinforces this, saying, "The LORD shall cause your enemies who rise up against you to be defeated before you; they will come out against you one way and will flee before you seven ways."

Now read the Joshua 6 account of the fall of Jericho and do so with (perhaps) "new biblical eyes." There is no recorded battle of Jericho. It is, accordingly, a clear demonstration of God being—again—completely faithful to what He had promised under "the blessing and the curse." The only thing that might surprise us is the manner by which God destroyed this city; but it was an already forgone conclusion that Jericho would fall, in spite of all its fortifications.

Joshua 1–6 makes perfect sense with a literal-grammatical hermeneutic. You have God's word on it—and none of that word needs to be allegorized.

Conclusion

In this chapter we have seen that one cannot start with the battle of Jericho (Joshua 6) and hope to be remotely accurate in one's understanding of Scripture. The significance of this epic battle is understood only in light of (1) the land promises that God had made under the Abrahamic covenant (Gen 13:14–17; 15:12–21; 17:7–8) and (2) the reality that national Israel was under the Mosaic covenant, and in this covenant, as part of the blessing and the curses, God promised military victories if they were obedient to Him (Lev 26:7–8; Deut 28:7). Accordingly, God responded exactly as He had promised, bringing national Israel back into covenant fellowship with Him. Yet in Josh 5:13–15, it is clear that God not only prepared the nation, He also prepared the individual leader Joshua, and this is a text Jesus would most likely have pointed to in Luke 24, when speaking of things that concerned Him from all the Scriptures.

Deeper Walk Study Questions

1. From what we have studied in the previous chapters of this book, review and list ten biblical truths that would have been left out of your understanding if you began your studies in Joshua 1. For instance, any of the truths we saw from John 5:46; Luke 24 (twice); Acts 2:23; 1 Pet 1:17–20; etc. This is for you not only to review and refresh, but also to remember to implement these truths when approaching any Old Testament book.

2. Some claim that Joshua 1 equals "prosperity gospel," in which God promises to make you rich, healthy, and happy. Give five reasons why Josh 1:8 is not promoting a prosperity gospel.

3. Why was circumcision so important to God? Why should it have been important to the people? What does this add to your understanding of the wickedness of the wilderness generation? Explain.

4. Why, in the same way that there is no Luke 2 without Luke 1, is there no Joshua 6 without the spiritual realities of Joshua 5? List five reasons.

5. How did God prepare the leader in Joshua 5? List four important spiritual life lessons that you can learn from this and apply them to your life.

6. Why is it incorrect to say or sing "Joshua fought/fit the battle of Jericho"? Explain your answer with biblical support.

CHAPTER 8

But Doesn't Joshua 21:43–45 Show That God Has Fulfilled His Land Promises?

S everal years ago I was asked by The Master's Seminary to present an academic paper for a professors' conference and submit it to its journal for possible publication. I complied by writing about Josh 21:43–45, because many Bible readers use this passage as a proof text to show that God had in the time of Joshua fulfilled the land promises given to the Jewish people in the Abrahamic covenant. Consequently, it is argued, one should not expect any future fulfillment for either the land or the nation of Israel. Joshua 21:43–45 reads as follows:

> *So the LORD gave Israel all the land which He had sworn to give to their fathers, and they possessed it and lived in it. And the LORD gave them rest on every side, according to all that He had sworn to their fathers, and not one of all their enemies stood before them; the LORD gave all their enemies into their hand. Not one of the good promises which the LORD had made to the house of Israel failed; all came to pass.*

Everyone who studies God's Word must study this text because (1) the word *land* is the fourth most common substantive in the Old Testament, (2) so many of the biblical interpretive controversies directly relate to this passage, and (3) from an initial reading, it certainly looks as though Josh 21:43–45 shows that God has fulfilled all of His land promises to Israel and nothing else should be expected.

When I started the research and writing process, I had no idea how controversial Josh 21:43–45 was or still is; entire denominations are based on what these verses purportedly teach us. Also, in the sovereignty of God, I did not write only one journal article; I wrote two journal articles. For those who want the full academic setting and documentation, the first article, "Did God Fulfill Every Good Promise?: Toward a Biblical Understanding of Joshua 21:43–45 (Part 1),"[1] dated July 26, 2012, deals with Scripture verses up to Joshua 21. The second article, "Did God Fulfill Every Good Promise?: Toward a Biblical Understanding of Joshua 21:43–45 (Part 2)"[2], dated May 15, 2013, deals with relevant verses after Joshua 21.

A Brief Overview of Relevant Verses Up to Joshua 21

In the first journal article, I laid out the following purpose: to examine the validity of the claims that Josh 21:43–45 inarguably proves that all the land promises given by God to Israel have already been fulfilled and consequently have no future eschatological significance. The paper was outlined as follows: (1) a brief overview of the covenants of God up to Joshua 21, (2) an examination of the original geographic boundaries of the Abrahamic covenant, with special note of the importance of the Euphrates River, (3) a survey of the eschatological significance of Lev 26:40–45, (4) an examination of strategic passages from the book of Joshua, (5) a critique of a popular proponent who argues for the complete fulfillment of the Josh 21:43–45 text, and finally (6) a proposed interpretation of Josh 21:43–45. We will be able to address some—but not all—of these subheadings in this chapter. Those of you who want the fuller biblical reasoning may read the previously mentioned articles.

Having already addressed the biblical covenants leading up to Joshua 21 in previous chapters, after we note one pertinent section from the Mosaic covenant that factors into the argument, we can begin our discussion with the immediate context of the book of Joshua.

---

[1] "Did God Fulfill Every Good Promise?: Toward a Biblical Understanding of Joshua 21:43–45," The Master's Seminary, July 26, 2012, https://www.tms.edu/msj/msj23-1-4/.
[2] "Did God Fulfill Every Good Promise?: Toward a Biblical Understanding of Joshua 21:43–45 (Part 2)," The Master's Seminary, May 15, 2013, https://www.tms.edu/msj/msj24-1-4/.

The Mosaic Covenant

As we have seen, the Mosaic covenant was ratified in Joshua's lifetime (Exod 24:1–8). He and the Jewish nation lived under its mandates. As before, time does not permit a full treatment of all the elements of this covenant of Yahweh. However, among other things, one tremendously relevant and important point should be marked, namely that on three different occasions within the Mosaic covenant, Yahweh Himself referred to the Euphrates River as part of the land boundaries for the Abrahamic covenant after He ratified it in Gen 15:18. (1) Exodus 23:31: "I will fix your boundary from the Red Sea to the sea of the Philistines, and from the wilderness to the River Euphrates; for I will deliver the inhabitants of the land into your hand, and you will drive them out before you." (2) To the nation Joshua would soon lead into the Promised Land, Yahweh instructed in Deut 1:7, "Turn and set your journey, and go to the hill country of the Amorites, and to all their neighbors in the Arabah, in the hill country and in the lowland and in the Negev and by the seacoast, the land of the Canaanites, and Lebanon, as far as the great river, the river Euphrates." (3) Deuteronomy 11:24: "Every place on which the sole of your foot treads shall be yours; your border will be from the wilderness to Lebanon, and from the river, the river Euphrates, as far as the western sea."

As we have previously seen concerning other promises to which Yahweh bound Himself, one should take the same approach to what He had promised and how these relate to Josh 21:43–45. For instance, for Yahweh already to have fulfilled "every good promise" by the end of Joshua 21 means that He would have had to fulfill "the good promise" He had made in Lev 26:40–45:

> *If they confess their iniquity and the iniquity of their forefathers, in their unfaithfulness which they committed against Me, and also in their acting with hostility against Me—I also was acting with hostility against them, to bring them into the land of their enemies—or if their uncircumcised heart becomes humbled so that they then make amends for their iniquity, then I will remember My covenant with Jacob, and I will remember also My covenant with Isaac, and My covenant with Abraham as well, and I will remember the land. For the land will be abandoned by them, and will make up for its sabbaths while it is made desolate without them. They, meanwhile, will*

be making amends for their iniquity, because they rejected My ordinances
and their soul abhorred My statutes. Yet in spite of this, when they are in
the land of their enemies, I will not reject them, nor will I so abhor them as
to destroy them, breaking My covenant with them; for I am the LORD their
God. But I will remember for them the covenant with their ancestors, whom
I brought out of the land of Egypt in the sight of the nations, that I might be
their God. I am the LORD.

For these to have been fulfilled by the time Josh 21:45 occurred, the
following elements must have transpired historically, and we must have
proof that these things did indeed occur: (1) a national confession of the
nation's sin and the iniquity of their forefathers (Lev 26:40); (2) Yahweh
acting with hostility to exile the Jewish nation into the land of their enemies (Lev 26:41); (3) after the national confession of Israel's sin in the
exile, Yahweh remembering His covenant with Jacob, Isaac, and Abraham
(Lev 26:42); (4) the land being abandoned until all its sabbaths were made
up (Lev 26:43); (5) the Jewish nation making amends for iniquity once in
exile (Lev 26:43); (6) Yahweh not abhorring them or breaking His covenant even when the people are in the land of their enemies (Lev 26:44);
and (7) God remembering His covenant made with the Jewish people (Lev
26:45).

KEY TRUTH: By no stretch of the imagination can any of these elements
have transpired historically, especially since the people were in the
land in Joshua 21 and had not yet been exiled. Consequently, the
burden of proof is on those who make sweeping claims that Yahweh
had indeed fulfilled all His "good promises." Also, as before, one
would have to determine what Yahweh in fact had attempted to
communicate about the future by the promises in Lev 26:40–45 if He
did not mean to exile and to regather the Jewish nation.

These are just as much "the good promises" of Yahweh as is anything
else promised elsewhere by Yahweh from Gen 3:15 onward. And by the
time of Joshua, they are yet unfulfilled.

Significant Passages From the Book of Joshua

Three particular texts within the book of Joshua will help set a proper context for our interpretation of Josh 21:43–45. (1) God's opening charge to Joshua in 1:1–4, (2) Joshua 13–21 considered as one unit within the book that presents the dividing of the land among the Jewish people, and (3) the opening summary statement God made in Josh 13:1–7.

First, God's opening charge to Joshua in Josh 1:1–4 begins with specific boundaries markers that would have been very familiar to Joshua:

> *Now it came about after the death of Moses the servant of the LORD that the LORD spoke to Joshua the son of Nun, Moses' servant, saying, "Moses My servant is dead; now therefore arise, cross this Jordan, you and all this people, to the land which I am giving to them, to the sons of Israel. Every place on which the sole of your foot treads, I have given it to you, just as I spoke to Moses. From the wilderness and this Lebanon, even as far as the great river, the river Euphrates, all the land of the Hittites, and as far as the Great Sea toward the setting of the sun, will be your territory.*

The mention of the Euphrates River in Josh 1:4 is significant for several reasons. First, God had previously included it as part of the boundaries of the land promise on four different occasions, beginning with the ratification of the Abrahamic covenant (Gen 15:18), at Sinai in the chapter before the ratification of the Mosaic covenant (Exod 23:31), and twice in Deuteronomy (1:7; 11:24). Second, Josh 1:4 is the only reference to the Euphrates River in the entire book of Joshua; not one other reference exists to the Euphrates, such as decades earlier when Joshua had been part of the spies sent out to survey the land (Numbers 13). In addition, there are no references indicating that it was portioned out as part of the land divisions in the book and gained as a rightful Promised Land possession. It should also be noted that Joshua would have been very familiar with the promises and warnings from Leviticus 26 and Deuteronomy 28–30, as well as with the ultimate future hope for both the land and the Jewish nation as revealed in Lev 26:40–45.

Second, regarding the division of the land given in Joshua 13–21, these chapters represent just one segment within the book as a whole, and these individual chapters must be viewed within this broader context. Actually,

Josh 21:43–45 are the last three verses in this section and offer a "glorious summary" of the land division. The opening verse of this section, Josh 13:1, is extremely important in that God Himself evaluated what He had accomplished thus far as well as what remained yet to be accomplished: "Now Joshua was old and advanced in years when the LORD said to him, 'You are old and advanced in years, and very much of the land remains to be possessed.'" Yahweh then delineated groups within the "very much" unpossessed land:

> This is the land that remains: all the regions of the Philistines and all those of the Geshurites; from the Shihor which is east of Egypt, even as far as the border of Ekron to the north (it is counted as Canaanite); the five lords of the Philistines: the Gazite, the Ashdodite, the Ashkelonite, the Gittite, the Ekronite; and the Avvite to the south, all the land of the Canaanite, and Mearah that belongs to the Sidonians, as far as Aphek, to the border of the Amorite; and the land of the Gebalite, and all of Lebanon, toward the east, from Baal-gad below Mount Hermon as far as Lebo-hamath. All the inhabitants of the hill country from Lebanon as far as Misrephoth-maim, all the Sidonians, I will drive them out from before the sons of Israel; only allot it to Israel for an inheritance as I have commanded you. Now therefore, apportion this land for an inheritance to the nine tribes and the half-tribe of Manasseh. (Josh 13:2–7)

Considering Josh 13:1–7, which deals with particulars related to the land of Canaan, with the added reference in Josh 1:4 to the territory associated with the Euphrates that lies outside of the then-occupied land, it is beyond argument that Israel never possessed the land as stipulated in the Abrahamic covenant during the days of Joshua. Israel's failure to occupy all the land that God promised is a significant point observed by both nondispensational and dispensational camps. Regarding the land promises given to Israel, several amillennial scholars acknowledge the clear teaching that the Israelites never came into undisputed possession of the whole Promised Land, to the full extent of the boundaries God had given.

Finally, regarding a proposed interpretation of Josh 21:43–45, at first glance Joshua 21:45 does seem to be all encompassing: "Not one of the good promises which the LORD had made to the house of Israel failed; all came to pass." But as has been shown, these verses do not sit isolated, away from the previous revelation from God. Those who cite Josh 21:43–45 as having fulfilled God's land promises of the Abrahamic covenant are, admittedly, not completely taking verses out of context, because Joshua 21 does indeed refer to portions of the land promised to Israel by God. Nevertheless, such an interpretation of Josh 21:43–45 is built upon a reading of the text in isolation and exclusion from previous revelation given by God regarding the specific land boundaries, eschatological promises from the Pentateuch, and even passages within the book of Joshua, namely Josh 1:1–4 and 13:1–7. Simply put, those who cite Josh 21:43–45 as indication that God had fulfilled all of His land promises to Israel disregard some very significant problem passages for this position.

It is no wonder that John Calvin and many others avoided the claim that all of God's land promises had been fulfilled by God by the time of Josh 21:43–45; this interpretation is inherently weak and laden with massive—and ultimately unexplainable—theological problems for those who accept the Bible as God's divine revelation, if for no other reason than how God Himself appraised the land situation in Josh 13:1–7.

It is better to understand Josh 21:43–45 in a much more restricted manner: Yahweh had indeed fulfilled all His good promises up to that time, but Josh 21:43–45 is just a historical marker in God's faithfulness and not the pinnacle or completion of His covenant faithfulness. Such an understanding is found elsewhere in Scripture. For instance, Paul's benediction in Rom 16:25–27 makes a far-reaching statement regarding how far the gospel had gone forth by the time Paul authored the epistle:

> *Now to Him who is able to establish you according to my gospel and the preaching of Jesus Christ, according to the revelation of the mystery which has been kept secret for long ages past, but now is manifested, and by the Scriptures of the prophets, according to the commandment of the eternal God, has been made known to all the nations, leading to obedience of faith; to the only wise God, through Jesus Christ, be the glory forever. Amen.*

Likewise, in Col 1:23 Paul wrote regarding the gospel that the Colossians should not be "moved away from the hope of the gospel that you have heard, which was proclaimed in all creation under heaven." One would be hard-pressed to argue that the Lord meant that the gospel indeed "has been made known to all the nations" (Rom 16:26) or that Col

1:23—"proclaimed in all creation under heaven"—had been fulfilled by the time Paul wrote these verses, or even almost two thousand years later that no unreached people groups remain. One day all nations under heaven will be reached, as Jesus declared, "This gospel of the kingdom shall be preached in the whole world for a witness to all the nations, and then the end shall come" (Matt 24:14), as God will one day fulfill every good promise He has made down to the last smallest part, culminating with the full blessings of Jesus the Messiah, whose first advent had not arrived by Joshua 21 and whose Second Advent yet awaits us.

A Brief Overview of Relevant Verses After Joshua 21

While the first article on Josh 21:43–45 summarized above used verses only from Genesis through Joshua, the second paper addressed select verses from Joshua 21 onward, some of which are cited as evidence by those who believe that all of God's land promises for the nation of Israel have already been fulfilled. Yet we'll here see that other texts subsequent to Joshua 21 reflect a future dimension to the fulfillment to these promises.

First Kings 4:20–21, for example, is often levied as support for the view that the land promises have no future relevance in prophecy. It states,

> Judah and Israel were as numerous as the sand that is on the seashore in abundance; they were eating and drinking and rejoicing.
>
> Now Solomon ruled over all the kingdoms from the River to the land of the Philistines and to the border of Egypt; they brought tribute and served Solomon all the days of his life.

I note that this passage specifically names the Euphrates River as the northern boundary that God first gave in Gen 15:18. Consequently, it is held that God has more than fulfilled His promises to national Israel.

It could seem on an initial reading that 1 Kgs 4:20–21 does indeed add support to the fulfillment of the Abrahamic covenant land promises also found in Josh 21:43–45, although this interpretation is not without its problems. It is my position that just the opposite occurs: including both passages to show the fulfillment of all the land promises of God does not strengthen these scholars' position, but weakens it. As a point of logic, if Josh 21:43–45 totally fulfilled the land promises given by God to the

Jewish nation, then 1 Kgs 4:20–21 becomes irrelevant to their argument: both passages cannot prove the same fulfillment of the same event centuries removed from each other. In the same way, if 1 Kgs 4:20–21 is the fulfillment of all of the land promises, then Josh 21:43–45 becomes irrelevant to their argument. Each passage must stand or fall on the weight of its own merits (or lack thereof).

Subsequent verses should be studied because, after all, if either Josh 21:43–45 or 1 Kgs 4:20–21 demonstrates that God has already fulfilled all the land promises for the nation of Israel, then no additional land promises from God would be expected past these two sections of Scripture, especially past 1 Kings 4. However, if subsequent Scripture does indeed contain the same promises that God made before Joshua 21 or 1 Kings 4, the theological position that all the land promises have already been fulfilled comes into question. In addition, such passages' bearing on the interpretation of other prophecies must be considered as well.

If God had fulfilled all the land promises from the Abrahamic covenant by Joshua 21 or 1 Kings 4, one would expect to find no more divine prophecies or statements from God about the future land promises. Instead, multiple references show the opposite. Consider, for example, several texts from the book of Jeremiah. Centuries after Joshua, after God had exiled the northern kingdom, and while God's promised exile of Judah by means of the Babylonians rapidly approached, Yahweh still gave many indications of the permanency of the land promises as still being in effect. For instance, in calling the nation to repent, part of the blessing God promised in Jer 7:7 was "then I will let you dwell in this place, in the land that I gave to your fathers forever and ever." This again points not only to the future regathering, but also, as becomes clearer, to the promised advent and reign of the Messiah in Jer 23:1–5:

> *"Woe to the shepherds who are destroying and scattering the sheep of My pasture!" declares the LORD. Therefore thus says the LORD God of Israel concerning the shepherds who are tending My people: "You have scattered My flock and driven them away, and have not attended to them; behold, I am about to attend to you for the evil of your deeds," declares the LORD. "Then I Myself will gather the remnant of My flock out of all the countries where I have driven them and bring them back to their pasture; and they will be fruitful and multiply. I will also raise up shepherds over them and*

they will tend them; and they will not be afraid any longer, nor be terrified, nor will any be missing," declares the LORD.

"Behold, the days are coming," declares the LORD, "When I shall raise up for David a righteous Branch; / And He will reign as king and act wisely/ And do justice and righteousness in the land."

In keeping with God's previous promises, Jer 25:4–5 once more presents similar promises from God and again demonstrates how God viewed the land He had given to the Jewish people:

And the LORD has sent to you all His servants the prophets again and again, but you have not listened nor inclined your ear to hear, saying, "Turn now everyone from his evil way and from the evil of your deeds, and dwell on the land which the LORD has given to you and your forefathers forever and ever."

These texts give no indication that Yahweh considered His previous promises concerning the land no longer to be in effect or to have been fulfilled in Joshua 21 or 1 Kings 4. In fact, God Himself acknowledged the land He has previously given "to your fathers forever and ever" (Jer 7:7; 25:5). If this promise is not taken literally, it would cast suspicion on multiple uses of "forever and ever," because this phrase frequently relates to the attributes and activities of God.

KEY CONSIDERATION: All of the following have "forever and ever" as part of their description, and those who accept the Word of God as true would never reduce or eradicate any of these doctrinally important verses: God to be blessed forever and ever (1 Chron 29:10; Neh 9:5; Ps 145:1–2, 21; Dan 2:20); God blotted out the name of the lost forever and ever (Ps 9:5); the Lord shall reign forever and ever (Exod 15:18; Rev 11:15); the Lord is King forever and ever (Ps 10:16); the Lord's throne is forever and ever (Ps 45:6); the Lord is to be blessed by the peoples forever and ever (Ps 45:17); God's own existence/who lives forever and ever (Ps 48:14; Rev 4:9; 10:6; 15:7); God's lovingkindness (Ps 52:8), precepts (Ps 111:8), and decrees (Ps 148:6) are forever and ever; the Lord established the earth on its foundations so that it will not totter forever and ever (Ps 104:5); the length of time for those in hell (Isa 34:10; Rev 14:11; 20:10); commanded to walk in the name of the Lord forever and ever (Mic 4:5); the shining brightness of the redeemed (Dan 12:3); glory to God in the church (Eph 3:21; 1 Pet 4:11) and glory to our God/Father/ Jesus forever and ever (Phil 4:20; 1 Tim 1:17; 2 Tim 4:18; Heb 13:21); God's glory and dominion/to be worshiped forever and ever (1 Pet 5:11; Rev 1:6; 4:10; 5:13; 7:12); the reign of the redeemed is forever and ever (Rev 22:5). Only Ps 21:4 ("He asked life of You, / You did give it to him, / Length of days forever and ever") at first may seem questionable as truly "forever and ever," yet with its listing as part of the royal psalms, this too points ultimately to the reign of the Messiah, so it also should be understood in a literal fashion. The only two remaining uses of "forever and ever" are the two land promises given by God in Jer 7:7 and 25:5. From all of the previous uses, I would be extremely careful in reducing or erasing any of God's "forever and ever" promises—including the two uses of the land promises that God still saw as being "forever and ever."

None of the verses cited in the box, which represent only a small sampling, gives any indication that God considered His multiple promises for the land and for the Jewish people to have been fulfilled by Josh 21:43–45 or 1 Kgs 4:20. None of these verses gives any indication that Yahweh no longer considered the land to be the land that He had sworn to give to the nation of Israel and their forefathers to possess "forever and ever" (Jer 7:7; 25:5). Not only that, but all of these verses are in harmony with God's previous promises that He would bring the Jewish people back to their Promised Land at some undisclosed time in the future (e.g., Lev 26:40–45).

Two other texts subsequent to Joshua 21 should be noted, namely Psalm 72 and Zech 9:9–10. Before assessing those texts, we must briefly address the significance of the Euphrates River in the land promises. The Euphrates in the Bible is called by other name designations, including "the great river, the river Euphrates" or simply "the River" (Exod 23:31; Deut 11:24). The Bible uses the word Euphrates thirty times, first naming it as one of the four rivers recorded in the garden of Eden (Gen 2:14). Of the thirty occurrences of the word Euphrates, five use the designation "the great river, the river Euphrates," with each such usage in the Old Testament specifically detailing the northern land boundaries of the Abrahamic covenant (Gen 15:18; Deut 1:7; Josh 1:4). Joshua would have known about the Genesis 15:18 reference, and he directly heard the other two designations, especially God's opening charge to him where again God refers to a land boundary being the Euphrates River (Josh 1:1–4). The remaining two references of "the great river Euphrates" occur in the New Testament, both in the book of Revelation (9:14; 16:12). In the Old Testament instances, the Euphrates River is virtually universally accepted as being the actual Euphrates River. Even those who cite 1 Kgs 4:21 as their proof text for the fulfillment ("Now Solomon ruled over all the kingdoms from the River to the land of the Philistines and to the border of Egypt") recognize that the designation "the River" clearly refers to the Euphrates and understand it to be the literal river, thus fulfilling the Abrahamic land boundary promises. The accepted universal understanding of "the River" being the literal Euphrates River is important for two prophecies in particular about the promised reign and rule of the Messiah, namely Psalm 72 and Zech 9:9–10.

Psalm 72 is a royal psalm, in similar fashion to Psalm 2, celebrating the coronation of the king of Israel, at the time of his inauguration or at the annual festival in which his coronation was celebrated. Although the language could apply to any of Israel's kings, both Jewish and Christian teachers interpret this psalm as messianic, although surprisingly the New Testament never cites Psalm 72 in messianic terms. Of significance also is that the subscript of Psalm 72 presents Solomon as the author. In reflecting upon the righteous rule of the king, the psalmist states in Ps 72:1–7:

Give the king Your judgments, O God,

And Your righteousness to the king's son.

May he judge Your people with righteousness

And Your afflicted with justice.

Let the mountains bring peace to the people,

And the hills, in righteousness.

May he vindicate the afflicted of the people,

Save the children of the needy,

And crush the oppressor.

Let them fear You while the sun endures,

And as long as the moon, throughout all generations.

May he come down like rain upon the mown grass,

Like showers that water the earth.

In his days may the righteous flourish,

And abundance of peace till the moon is no more.

Solomon then at the conclusion prays for these divine blessings:

May there be abundance of grain in the earth on top of the mountains;

Its fruit will wave like the cedars of Lebanon;

And may those from the city flourish like vegetation of the earth.

May his name endure forever;

May his name increase as long as the sun shines;

And let men bless themselves by him;

Let all nations call him blessed.

Blessed be the LORD God, the God of Israel,

Who alone works wonders.

And blessed be His glorious name forever;

And may the whole earth be filled with His glory.

Amen, and Amen. (Ps 72:16–19)

Included in Solomon's understanding and expectation for the future comes this important designation in Ps 72:8: "May he also rule from sea to sea, / And from the River to the ends of the earth." This is not a prayer for the author himself to reign from those designated boundaries; this well-known designation for the Euphrates River emerges from the original land promises made to the nation of Israel, and they will be fully enjoyed when Messiah reigns. Psalm 72 concludes with the worshipful prayer, "And may the whole earth be filled with His glory. Amen, and Amen." Such divine attributes are fitting only for the Godhead, not for Solomon.

Obviously Solomon looked well past his own present reign to some future descendant of David who would fulfill these promises, including those found in verse 8; it would be hard to argue that he would apply all of these prophecies to his own life, such as in the last part of verse 8, where he prayed that this one's reign would be—in keeping with Psalm 2 and other messianic psalms—"to the ends of the earth." The Euphrates River will be the northern boundary of Israel over which Messiah will reign, but ultimately His reign will extend far beyond this to the very ends of the earth.

In similar fashion, Zech 9:9–10 offers one final significant promise of the Messiah's reign, in addition to other promises made regarding both the people and the land. It should be noted that these promises came long after Solomon's reign and the writing of Psalm 72, long after the exile and regathering, and in the midst of "the times of the Gentiles" (Luke 21:24) when no one reigned on David's throne and all were once more in harmony with what God had previously promised. For instance, after promising that the coming Messiah would hold offices of both priest and king (Zech 6:12–13), God once more made land promises in Zech 8:1–8 that are in perfect agreement with previous promises made by God in passages such as Ezekiel 20, 28, and 34:

> Then the word of the LORD of hosts came, saying, "Thus says the LORD of hosts, 'I am exceedingly jealous for Zion, yes, with great wrath I am jealous for her.' Thus says the LORD, 'I will return to Zion and will dwell in the midst of Jerusalem. Then Jerusalem will be called the City of Truth, and the mountain of the LORD of hosts will be called the Holy Mountain.' Thus says the LORD of hosts, 'Old men and old women will again sit in the streets of Jerusalem, each man with his staff in his hand because of age. And the streets of the city will be filled with boys and girls playing in its streets.' Thus says the LORD of hosts, 'If it is too difficult in the sight of the remnant of this people in those days, will it also be too difficult in My sight?' declares the LORD of hosts. Thus says the LORD of hosts, 'Behold, I am going to save My people from the land of the east and from the land of the west; and I will bring them back and they will live in the midst of Jerusalem; and they shall be My people, and I will be their God in truth and righteousness.'"

Zechariah 9:9 then presents this prophecy that the Bible so obviously connects with the First Advent prophecy of Jesus as He entered into Jerusalem a few days before His crucifixion (Matt 21:5; John 12:15–16):

Rejoice greatly, O daughter of Zion!

Shout in triumph, O daughter of Jerusalem!

Behold, your king is coming to you;

He is just and endowed with salvation,

Humble, and mounted on a donkey,

Even on a colt, the foal of a donkey.

The verse that immediately follows Zech 9:9 relates to the second coming of this same Messiah, is nearly identical to the promise made long before in Ps 72:8 and currently remains unfulfilled prophecy:

And I will cut off the chariot from Ephraim,

And the horse from Jerusalem;

And the bow of war will be cut off.

And He will speak peace to the nations;

And His dominion will be from sea to sea,

And from the River to the ends of the earth. (Zech 9:10)

Note the promised activities of Messiah at His Second Advent: He will cut off the implements of war; He will speak peace to the nations; His dominion will be from sea to sea and from the Euphrates River to the ends of the earth. Just as with the original promises related to the Euphrates River being the northern boundary of the land promises for national Israel, and in keeping with Ps 72:8, the Euphrates River marks the boundary within which the Messiah will reign on David's throne and fulfill the promises of God regarding both the land and His people Israel. As stated before, in every Old Testament passage where the Euphrates River is designated, a literal interpretation makes perfect sense.

CORE TRUTH: Zechariah 9:9 had a literal fulfillment for and by Jesus, down to the smallest part. We would expect God to be just as faithful in completing and fulfilling the next part of Zech 9:10, when Jesus returns to earth to reign.

Conclusion

Instead of all the land promises being fulfilled by Josh 21:41–43 and/or 1 Kgs 4:20–21, the Bible clearly, repeatedly, and persistently presents just the opposite, and it does so in a way that beautifully harmonizes with previous God-given prophecies (cf. Lev 26:40–45; Deut 30:1–10). In fact, nothing indicates that these prophecies had been fulfilled by the time of Solomon's life or even up to our present time. Not only are these land boundary promises originally given in the Abrahamic covenant and reiterated in the Mosaic covenant and in the opening of the book of Joshua, but the Bible again presents the Euphrates River as the northern boundary for the nation of Israel long after 1 Kings 4. More important, twice the Euphrates River also specifically relates to the Messiah's reign, first in Ps 72:8, and then centuries afterward in the midst of "the times of the Gentiles" in Zech 9:10. In both cases the Euphrates River will be the northern boundary of Israel for His worldwide rule.

So harmonious are God's prophecies regarding the land promises that if one did not know of an existing interpretational controversy regarding whether the land promises had been completely fulfilled by the time of Josh 21:41–43 and/ or 1 Kgs 4:20–21, one would never surmise this from the text. Why? Because the promises made by God after Joshua 21 and 1 Kings 4 harmonize perfectly with—and in some case even mirror—the multiple promises God had previously made. If anything, the Bible gives even more support past Joshua 21 and 1 Kings 4 regarding the future promises of God and His Messiah who will reign over the entire world (Ps 2:8), which includes the Euphrates River as part of the boundary for the northern part of the nation of Israel. When His reign does occur, as prophecy is fulfilled in the future, indeed the "plans formed long ago, with perfect faithfulness" (Isa 25:1) likewise will be fulfilled.

Deeper Walk Study Questions

1. Why is Josh 21:43–45 so hotly debated? What does it matter whether God has fulfilled all the land promises to Israel by this time? Explain by listing five ways this factors into interpreting other Scriptures.

2. Why is the hermeneutic employed in the Noahic covenant so important to understanding God's promises given in Genesis 15 in the Abrahamic covenant, especially concerning the land promises? How would our understanding of Scripture be somewhat limited if those who say God has fulfilled the land promises applied this same hermeneutic to the Noahic covenant? Explain and list five ways it would be weakened.

3. Why is Josh 13:1–7 so important in understanding Josh 21:43–45? List and explain four relevant truths from Josh 13:1–7. Why would those citing only Josh 21:43–45 as a proof text be using this text in isolation or exclusion from other verses? Explain.

4. How do Rom 16:25–27 and Col 1:23 give biblical examples of how Josh 21:43–45 should be viewed? List five truths from these verses that show their connection.

5. What is the problem for those who cite 1 Kgs 4:20–21 as part of the fulfilment of the land promises? Explain why this actually weakens—not strengthens—the case for those who say that the land promises are already fulfilled.

6. List five ways the Euphrates River plays a role in Messiah's future role from Psalm 72 and Zech 9:9–10. Why is this important? Explain.

7. How blessed are the "forever and evers" God has given in Scripture! List five biblical truths that would be weakened if these were interpreted the way some people interpret the land promises that were given to the Jewish people "forever and ever."

CHAPTER 9

Choose You This Day Whom You Will Serve; as for Me and My House, We Will Serve the Lord

G od literally and eternally changed my life about thirty years ago. I was preaching through Joshua and came to the most well-known, most quoted, and most cited verse out of that book, Josh 24:15: "Choose you this day whom ye will serve . . . but as for me and my house, we will serve the LORD" (KJV).[1] Actually, Josh 24:15 is a much fuller verse:

> *If it is disagreeable in your sight to serve the LORD, choose for yourselves today whom you will serve: whether the gods which your fathers served which were beyond the River, or the gods of the Amorites in whose land you are living; but as for me and my house, we will serve the LORD.*

IMPORTANT NOTE: Most people who quote or display Josh 24:15 verse have no idea that they are quoting phrases derived from a longer verse. This is good reminder to be careful when using or citing a text, and to be sure to accurately present what the text states. From a study standpoint, you would be removing much of the original verse that God put there, and that is not at all a safe practice to follow. German higher criticism followed—and follows—the same pattern with disastrous effects.

---

[1] The sermon on Josh 24:15 that I preached at The Master's Seminary chapel, posted October 5, 2015, is available at https://vimeo.com/141424030.

What was so life changing to me that Sunday in College Park, Maryland, was that God "cut the lights on" for me, spiritually speaking. Before, I had consistently used the Word to preach. Joshua 24:15 was the first time I truly "preached the Word"—and I got to see God use His Word in my life first, then in the life of my church, and in many places where I have since preached or taught—never has God not used this.

A major part of "preaching the Word" is to drop down into the world of whatever chapter we are in, as much as is possible, to see with the characters' eyes and hear with their ears. You will see this done in this chapter, and you will also see God's Word open and unfold before you. Many of these things were written for our example and instruction (see 1 Cor 10:6, 11) and are pertinent to living the Christian life, but even more so, this is biblically accurate. When we follow the biblical trail in Joshua 24 to see what God had set before the people, we will also see what God has set before us as well.

Dropping Down into the Setting of Joshua 24

My scriptural quest started when I read the initial charge given by Joshua and then the people's response. Joshua commanded the Jewish nation (Josh 24:15), and the people responded thusly, in Josh 24:16–18:

> *Far be it from us that we should forsake the LORD to serve other gods; for the LORD our God is He who brought us and our fathers up out of the land of Egypt, from the house of bondage, and who did these great signs in our sight and preserved us through all the way in which we went and among all the peoples through whose midst we passed. The LORD drove out from before us all the peoples, even the Amorites who lived in the land. We also will serve the LORD, for He is our God.*

Now notice the surprising response of Joshua. Instead of rejoicing in Israel's desire to follow the Lord, he said, "You will not be able to serve the LORD, for he is a holy God. He is a jealous God; He will not forgive your transgression or your sins" (Josh 24:19). Why did Joshua give the invitation, have the people respond exactly the way he had implored them to, and then not accept the response he had asked them for? The answer can be found in a careful analysis of the surrounding context.

Looking back to the beginning of the chapter, for example, Josh 24:1 says, "Then Joshua gathered all the tribes of Israel to Shechem, and called for the elders of Israel and for their heads and their judges and their officers; and they presented themselves before God." We will come back to this verse later, but for now we note that the Jewish people assembled at Shechem. I checked the concordance to see if Shechem had played any significant role previously in Scripture; in fact, it had. In Genesis 12 after God called Abram out of the land of Ur to another land and gave the elements of what would become the Abrahamic covenant (the land, the seed, the blessing), we read the following:

> *So Abram went forth as the Lord had spoken to him; and Lot went with him. Now Abram was seventy-five years old when he departed from Haran. And Abram took Sarai his wife and Lot his nephew, and all their possessions which they had accumulated, and the persons which they had acquired in Haran, and they set out for the land of Canaan; thus they came to the land of Canaan. And Abram passed through the land as far as the site of Shechem, to the oak of Moreh. Now the Canaanite was then in the land. (Gen 12:4–6)*

Shechem was the place where Abraham dwelt when he entered the land that would be promised to him and his descendants. God gathered the Jewish people to Shechem in Joshua 24 in the same way He had brought their forefather there centuries earlier.

The map in the back of your Bible would likely show Shechem as a town a mile or so removed from Mount Gerizim and Mount Ebal. The significance of Shechem, however, may not be readily apparent unless one knows the role of these two mountains in the Pentateuch.

Deuteronomy 27:1–8, for example, states,

> *Then Moses and the elders of Israel charged the people, saying, "Keep all the commandments which I command you today. So it shall be on the day when you cross the Jordan to the land which the Lord your God gives you, that you shall set up for yourself large stones and coat them with lime and write on them all the words of this law, when you cross over, so that you may enter the land which the Lord your God gives you, a land flowing with milk and honey, as the Lord, the God of your fathers, promised you. So it shall be when you cross the Jordan, you shall set up on Mount Ebal, these stones, as*

I am commanding you today, and you shall coat them with lime. Moreover,
you shall build there an altar to the LORD your God, an altar of stones; you
shall not wield an iron tool on them. You shall build the altar of the LORD
your God of uncut stones; and you shall offer on it burnt offerings to the
LORD your God; and you shall sacrifice peace offerings and eat there, and
you rejoice before the LORD your God. You shall write on the stones all the
words of this law very distinctly.

Moses had received the command from Yahweh and then passed this
on with the following instruction:

Then Moses and the Levitical priests spoke to all Israel, saying, "Be silent
and listen, O Israel! This day you have become a people for the LORD your
God. You shall therefore obey the LORD your God, and do His command-
ments and His statutes which I command you today." (Deut 27:9–10)

Then came this very specific command from God once the people entered the land that God had given them:

Moses also charged the people on that day, saying, "When you cross the
Jordan, these shall stand on Mount Gerizim to bless the people: Simeon,
Levi, Judah, Issachar, Joseph, and Benjamin. For the curse, these shall
stand on Mount Ebal: Reuben, Gad, Asher, Zebulun, Dan, and Naphtali."
(Deut 27:11–13)

God used His own creation as a divine object lesson. He used His flood
to formulate two of His mountains to be side-by-side gracefully rounded
mountains that look virtually identical; you might call them twin mountains. Half of the people were told to stand on Mount Gerizim to show the
blessing of God, and half the people were to stand on Mount Ebal, where
God had previously instructed them to take large stones, coat them with
lime, write God's law on them, and build an altar to Him. If you were to
stand in ancient Shechem, then, you could look out at these two mountains
not far removed from the village.

So was Moses's command ever followed? Yes, under the godly leadership of Joshua and after the spiritual preparation of the people and the
leader (Joshua 5), the fall of Jericho (Joshua 6), the sin of Achan in breaking the ban that God had given (Joshua 7), and the initial military defeat

because of the covenant violations (Joshua 8) followed by the eventual victory over Ai, Josh 8:30–35 records that the following took place:

> *Then Joshua built an altar to the LORD, the God of Israel, in Mount Ebal, just as Moses the servant of the LORD had commanded the sons of Israel, as it is written in the book of the law of Moses [Deuteronomy 27], an altar of uncut stones, on which no man had wielded an iron tool; and they offered burnt offerings on it to the LORD, and sacrificed peace offerings. He wrote there on the stones a copy of the law of Moses, which he had written, in the presence of the sons of Israel. All Israel with their elders and officers and their judges were standing on both sides of the ark before the Levitical priests who carried the ark of the covenant of the LORD, the stranger as well as the native. Half of them stood in front of Mount Gerizim and half of them in front of Mount Ebal, just as Moses the servant of the LORD had given command at first to bless the people of Israel. Then afterward he read all the words of the law, the blessing and the curse [from Leviticus 26 and Deuteronomy 27–28], according to all that is written in the book of the law. There was not a word of all that Moses had commanded which Joshua did not read before all the assembly of Israel with the women and the little ones and the strangers who were living among them.*

NOTE: As so many times before, God offered two options and only two options—the blessing or the curse—but no middle ground. Note as well that in the Joshua 8 passage the people were used only as an illustration. It did not mean that these people were automatically cursed (or the others automatically blessed) because of the two mountains on which they were commanded to stand.

With this background in mind, let's return to Josh 24:1 and note three very important items: First, "Then Joshua gathered all the tribes of Israel to Shechem, and called for the elders of Israel and for their heads and their judges and their officers; and they presented themselves before God." In Joshua 8, the people stood at the base of each of the two mountains; in Joshua 24 they stood on flat ground at Shechem looking out on the two mountains. Second, they did not present themselves before Joshua, they "presented themselves before God." Joshua could not see into everyone's heart, or know of everyone's sinful activity—but God could, and God still can. Third, the people had been at Mount Gerizim and Mount Ebal before; the law would still be on Mount Ebal. So in Joshua 24, God called the nation back to a place where they had collectively gathered before.

The next part of Joshua 24 presents very specific acts of covenant faithfulness on God's part. Notice the repeated use of the first-person pronoun "I" in Josh 24:2–8:

> And Joshua said to all the people, "Thus says the LORD, the God of Israel, 'From ancient times your fathers lived beyond the River, namely, Terah, the father of Abraham and the father of Nahor, and they served other gods. Then I took your father Abraham from beyond the River, and led him through all the land of Canaan, and multiplied his descendants and gave him Isaac. To Isaac I gave Jacob and Esau, and to Esau I gave Mount Seir, to possess it; but Jacob and his sons went down to Egypt. Then I sent Moses and Aaron, and I plagued Egypt by what I did in its midst; and afterward I brought you out. I brought your fathers out of Egypt, and you came to the sea; and Egypt pursued your fathers with chariots and horsemen to the Red Sea. But when they cried out to the LORD, He put darkness between you and the Egyptians, and brought the sea upon them and covered them; and your own eyes saw what I did in Egypt. And you lived in the wilderness for a long time. Then I brought you into the land of the Amorites who lived beyond the Jordan, and they fought with you; and I gave them into your hand, and you took possession of their land when I destroyed them before you."

Joshua 24:9–10 continues, with God recounting the attempt by Balaam to curse Israel, a narrative we discussed in a previous chapter:

> Then Balak the son of Zippor, king of Moab, arose and fought against Israel, and he sent and summoned Balaam the son of Beor to curse you. But I was not willing to listen to Balaam. So he had to bless you, and I delivered you from his hand.

God concluded this section:

> You crossed the Jordan and came to Jericho; and the citizens of Jericho fought against you, and the Amorite and the Perizzite and the Canaanite and the Hittite and the Girgashite, the Hivite and the Jebusite. Thus I gave them into your hand. Then I sent the hornet before you and it drove out the two kings of the Amorites from before you, but not by your sword or your

bow. I gave you a land on which you had not labored, and cities which you had not built, and you have lived in them; you are eating of vineyards and olive groves which you did not plant. (Josh 24:11–13)

The nation was gathered there that day only because God had faithfully kept His Word and repeatedly intervened to rescue, deliver, and provide for them.

Joshua 24:14–23 in Light of the Context

With this background we can now come to the verses presented at the beginning of the chapter. Israel was gathered before the Lord (Josh 24:1). At Shechem they could look out and see the two mountains. They have before them two options only: the blessing and the curse, with the outcome determined by whether or not they were living in covenant obedience to Yahweh.

> **CORE TRUTH:** You cannot stand on Mount Gerizim and Mount Ebal at the same time; it is a physical impossibility. Similarly, you cannot stand spiritually on the Mount of Blessing and the Mount of Cursing at the same time. God has so decreed that no one straddle both of His mountains by living simultaneously in covenant obedience and disobedience.

That is why Josh 24:15 is not an evangelistic "come-forward-and-meet-the-unknown-God" invitation, as it is sometimes used. The people of Israel were already in national covenant fellowship with Him, under the Mosaic covenant. Following the author's account of God's history with Israel, Josh 24:14–15 states,

Now, therefore, fear the LORD and serve Him in sincerity and truth; and put away the gods which your fathers served beyond the River and in Egypt, and serve the LORD. If it is disagreeable in your sight to serve the LORD, choose for yourselves today whom you will serve: whether the gods which your fathers served which were beyond the River, or the gods of the

Amorites in whose land you are living; but as for me and my house, we will
serve the LORD.

Joshua, under God's leading, commands the people to do specific
things: (1) fear the Lord, (2) serve Him in sincerity and truth, (3) put away
the gods of their past, and (4) keep themselves from the gods of the present
in whose land they were living.

CONSIDER: If all of the people assembled that day were asked whether
they wanted to be blessed by God or cursed by Him, in all likelihood
they all would say they wanted the blessing. Joshua 24:14–15 shows
that there are definitive steps that must be taken regarding turning
from sin and actively following God; nothing just happened in and of
itself.

KEY TRUTH: As a means of application, the same remains true today.
John ended his first epistle with this short command, "Little children,
guard yourselves from idols" (1 John 5:21). It may not involve
physical items (although I have had many students who came from
idolatrous countries and cultures), and we are not Jews gathered
before God at Shechem. But anything that takes the place of fully
following God is an idol—thus John's warning, and thus we can learn
much from Joshua 24.

KEY ALSO: When God saved us, many of us came out of decadent
lifestyles. We have a long list of "gods of the past." We have to watch
and see that a god of the past has not reappeared and taken a place
in our hearts. The "gods of the present" can be much subtler because
they are not as brazen (usually) as the gods of the past: materialism,
busyness, envy of what God is doing in someone else's life—and on
and on the list goes.

Following Joshua's commands, the people collectively responded:

The people answered and said, "Far be it from us that we should forsake the LORD to serve other gods; for the LORD our God is He who brought us and our fathers up out of the land of Egypt, from the house of bondage, and who did these great signs in our sight and preserved us through all the way in which we went and among all the peoples through whose midst we passed. The LORD drove out from before us all the peoples, even the Amorites who lived in the land. We also will serve the LORD, for He is our God." (Josh 24:16–18)

Joshua 24:19–22 continues the interaction:

Then Joshua said to the people, "You will not be able to serve the LORD, for He is a holy God. He is a jealous God; He will not forgive your transgression or your sins. If you forsake the LORD and serve foreign gods, then He will turn and do you harm and consume you after He has done good to you." The people said to Joshua, "No, but we will serve the LORD." Joshua said to the people, "You are witnesses against yourselves that you have chosen for yourselves the LORD, to serve Him." And they said, "We are witnesses."

This is followed by Josh 24:23–24:

"Now therefore, put away the foreign gods which are in your midst, and incline your hearts to the LORD, the God of Israel." The people said to Joshua, "We will serve the LORD our God and we will obey His voice."

With this narrowed context in mind, we are now in a position to make some observations as to why Joshua responded the way he did. First, Joshua had repeatedly called the nation to put away their idols. Yet not one time in the people's response did they ever even acknowledge that they had idols, let alone that they had put them away.

Second, when the people repeatedly declared that they would serve the Lord, they did so by their own definition—not God's definition—of how they would do that, and it was not accepted by God, then or now. By doing so, they did not fear the Lord and serve Him in sincerity and truth (Josh 24:14); neither did they put away the gods of the past or of the present (Josh 24:14–15). By their own reasoning, this was not necessary, yet by God's command, it was and it still is. What was true then is true today; nothing has changed on this side of the cross of Jesus.

Third, four times in this dialogue the people used the future tense as opposed to the present tense: "We also will serve the LORD, for He is our God" (Josh 24:18); "The people said to Joshua, 'No, but we will serve the LORD'" (Josh 24:21); and twice in Josh 24:24, "The people said to Joshua, 'We will serve the LORD our God and we will obey His voice.'"

CORE TRUTH: A future tense is nonthreatening. A future tense is "I am in full agreement with what you say, and I have every intention of doing this." Simply put, a future tense in regard to neglecting the commands of God is nonetheless a present sin, and a future tense stays a future tense until you do what God commands you to do— from Adam and Eve up through Joshua's time, up to the present and into eternity.

Joshua 24:23 helps round out the picture: "Now therefore, put away the foreign gods which are in your midst, and incline your hearts to the LORD, the God of Israel." First, notice the present tense, "the foreign gods which are in your midst"—not "if the foreign gods are there" and not in the future tense. Second, to "incline your hearts to the LORD" is not legalism; it is a relationship to the holy God. You can put away your idols without the heart being even remotely inclined to God. Collectively, then, the commands were (1) fear God, (2) serve Him in sincerity and truth, (3) put away the gods of the past, (4) keep yourselves from the gods of the present, and (5) incline your hearts to the Lord. This remains true for all Christians as well. We live this side of the cross, but we still have a great capacity to sin, to seek idols, to self-worship, to lust—and the list goes on. This is a call to humble yourself before God and walk with Him in holiness.

Finally, still within the context and truths we have seen in Joshua 24, this application can also be used as an evangelistic sermon or teaching or as an additional invitation to the lost to repent, to turn from their idols to the living God (1 Thess 1:9). But make sure that you inform people that turning away from every idol they ever had or would have—if that were possible—in itself is not enough for someone to be saved. It does not address the forgiveness and atonement needed for sins committed. The eternal problem of unforgiven sins before a holy God still must be addressed.

This forgiveness requires a reception of the person and work of the blood of the Lamb of God, the Lord Jesus Christ. The multiple encounters of Jesus with the Pharisees in the Gospels is a clear picture of what happens when people attempt to put away the gods of the past and kept themselves from the gods of the present, but never did incline their hearts to the Lord.

Conclusion

We have demonstrated in this chapter how the governing context of Josh 24:15 moves the interpreter beyond a merely evangelistic application. It was not, then, an invitation for national Israel to come and meet the unknown God, but rather a call for national repentance, especially since they were already under the Mosaic covenant. We noted the importance of tracing a line back to Shechem (Josh 24:1), an event that is even more significant when viewed in light of Deut 27:1–13. So when one comes to Joshua 24, the nation has been there before. Yet this time, instead of having the nation divided with half of them on Mount Gerizim and half on Mount Ebal, they are gathered at Shechem looking out at the Mount of Blessing and the Mount of Cursing and faced, yet again, with the decision to choose whom they would serve: the gods of their past and their present false gods or Yahweh. If the people were to serve Yahweh, they must put away their false gods. Tragically, while they came there that day in a sinful state, they left in yet a worse state, since they did not respond to God's call through Joshua. By applying the text only after one has dropped down into the biblical world, it becomes evident that the primary application is for Christians to put away their idols (1 John 5:21).

Deeper Walk Study Questions

1. From a study standpoint, and with a full understanding of the text, what is wrong with starting with Josh 24:15 as "Choose you this day whom ye will serve. . . . As for me and my house, we will serve the LORD" (KJV)? Why is this important? Explain.

2. What is the biblical significance of Shechem (Josh 24:1) as it relates to Abraham and the Jewish people? How does this factor in to Deut 27:1–13?

3. Name five lessons you can learn from national Israel's obedience to God in Josh 8:30–35. Why is what they did important? What does it tell you about the nation's spiritual condition at that time, especially in view of all of them being under the Mosaic covenant? Explain.

4. Name five significant aspects of the people appearing before God and not just Joshua (Josh 24:1). Why is this important? Explain.

5. List ten truths from the verses we studied in this chapter that show the people were not coming forward to meet a God they had never heard of before. (I note that the text studied in this chapter is often used today for evangelistic sermons "to come forward and meet the unknown God.")

6. Name five specific commands out of Joshua 24. How can you apply these to your life personally? Explain in detail. How can you use Joshua 24 when discipling someone? Explain and be specific.

7. List any biblical truths from this chapter that you cannot wait to tell someone about. Why are they important? Explain and be specific.

CHAPTER 10

This Just In: David's Victory over Goliath Was Not an Upset!

T he term David versus Goliath has become commonplace in the realm of sports and politics to describe a contest where the heavily favored is defeated by a considerably lesser opponent. It seems practically everyone is familiar with this biblical account of David, the brave young shepherd, going to battle against Goliath, the giant and seasoned warrior. The odds were so overwhelmingly against David that his victory would seem extremely unlikely. So when the weaker participant defeats the heavily favored, stronger opponent, this is considered a David-versus-Goliath upset.

Only one major problem exists with this line of reasoning: it is totally opposite from how the Bible portrays the event. Scripture makes it clear that David's victory over Goliath was anything but a one-in-a-million type of upset. As we will see, God had announced the outcome multiple times before David ever went out to fight the Philistine. And we will also see that instead of the David-versus-Goliath scenario being only a historical note of interest, how one understands—or misunderstands—this biblical account will factor in to the interpretation of other texts subsequent to this event.

As in previous chapters, it is important to set the context for our study of this epic story, noting any divine promises in pertinent biblical texts that lead up to David's victory over Goliath.[1]

---

[1] For access to the *Master's Seminary Journal* article on this text: https://www.tms.edu/msj/just-davids-victory-goliath-not-upset/.

Consideration of Pertinent Promises
God Made to National Israel

Part of the ratification of the Abrahamic covenant, where God told Abram, "Know for certain that your descendants will be strangers in a land that is not theirs, where they will be enslaved and oppressed four hundred years" (Gen 15:13), includes an implementation of the Gen 12:3 pronouncement, "The one who curses you I will curse." This link would be expected if God were to keep His promise made in Gen 15:14, "But I will also judge the nation whom they will serve," which would turn out to be Egypt. Exodus 2:24–25 and 3:8 reiterate that God brought about the exodus in keeping with His covenant faithfulness to the Abrahamic covenant. Exodus 2 concludes, "So God heard their groaning; and God remembered His covenant with Abraham, Isaac, and Jacob. God saw the sons of Israel, and God took notice of them" (Exod 2:24–25). In the commissioning of Moses comes this clear reminder that God is the true Redeemer: "So I have come down to deliver them from the power of the Egyptians, and to bring them up from that land to a good and spacious land, to a land flowing with milk and honey, to the place of the Canaanite and the Hittite and the Amorite and the Perizzite and the Hivite and the Jebusite" (Exod 3:8). The clear reference to the Abrahamic covenant promise indicates that the events in Exodus did not merely happen. God acted because of His covenant vow and in keeping with what He had previously promised the descendants of Abraham.

Yet it was not only the Egyptians whom Yahweh cursed in judgment for cursing national Israel. Another such response by God occurred when the people grumbled against Moses and put God to the test shortly after God had punished Egypt and the nationally redeemed Jewish people had been brought out of Egypt. In the immediate context, God had instructed Moses:

> *"Behold, I will stand before you there on the rock at Horeb; and you shall strike the rock, and water will come out of it, that the people may drink." And Moses did so in the sight of the elders of Israel. He named the place Massah and Meribah because of the quarrel of the sons of Israel, and because they tested the LORD, saying, "Is the LORD among us, or not?" (Exod 17:6–7)*

The unique presence of God should not be overlooked in this passage. It is not only that God had performed a miracle, but rather that God's special presence was there that day as God had explicitly promised Moses, saying, "I will stand there before you by the rock at Horeb."

> **KEY TRUTH:** Here is another use of what we saw in a previous chapter of this handbook, where Paul later revealed the messianic significance of this event: "For I do not want you to be unaware, brethren, that our fathers were all under the cloud and all passed through the sea; and all were baptized into Moses in the cloud and in the sea; and all ate the same spiritual food; and all drank the same spiritual drink, for they were drinking from a spiritual rock which followed them; and the rock was Christ" (1 Cor 10:1–4). In answer to the question, "Is the LORD among us or not?," the Lord certainly was at Rephidim in Exod 17 with the preincarnate Messiah present. It is also another example of John 5:46, where Jesus taught, "If you believed Moses, you would believe Me, for he wrote about Me."

After the special presence of God had been revealed, the Gentile king Amalek and his people warred against Israel (Exod 17:8–13). In that battle Aaron and Hur held up Moses's arms as God gave Israel the victory over the Amalekites. Following the defeat of one Gentile king and his people who had attacked national Israel, and in keeping with Gen 12:3, Yahweh also issued this far-reaching divine pronouncement in Exod 17:14–16:

> Then the LORD said to Moses, "Write this in a book as a memorial and recite it to Joshua, that I will utterly blot out the memory of Amalek from under heaven." Moses built an altar and named it The LORD is My Banner; and he said, "The LORD has sworn; the LORD will have war against Amalek from generation to generation."

It is important to note that the ramifications resulting from the battle with Amalek in Exodus 17 went far beyond the immediate situation, as is clear from Exod 17:16: "The LORD will have war with Amalek from generation to generation." Taken literally this phrase could be rendered "war for Yahweh against Amalek from generation [to] generation," which is another way of saying that Yahweh had declared holy war on the Amalekites. Therefore, God's declaration, "I will utterly blot out the memory of Amalek from under heaven," constitutes a very early oracle against a Gentile nation, a common form of oracle found later in the prophetic books. These oracles predict the destruction or suppression of an enemy of Israel—who is thus automatically an enemy of God—at some future time of God's choosing.

This account represents biblical evidence of Yahweh cursing an enemy of Israel who had cursed them, just as He had promised. In addition, it is an account that went well beyond Abraham's life. If God's declaration in Exod 17:14–16 is to be understood as a literal promise, then one would expect (1) for God eventually to blot out the memory of Amalek under heaven, and (2) that the Lord would have war against Amalek from generation to generation. Yahweh, though sometimes delayed, determines by His sovereign counsel the time when such divine retribution will occur—as well as the means of that retribution. Even more striking in the Exodus 17 account is that this military victory for Israel was directly due to the presence of God and His divine intervention. The key issue is not who won this initial battle; the key issue is that Yahweh was utterly faithful to His promise of Gen 12:3 to "curse the one who curses you." Simply expressed, the "I will curse the one" promise goes beyond the immediate military victory and points to divine action by God at some point(s) in the future.

We saw in chapter 6, "A Star! A Star! Shining in the Night!," that Numbers 22–24 is one scriptural unit that contains four separate prophetic sections. You will also recall the attempt of a Gentile king Balak to hire a somewhat-of-a-prophet Balaam to come and curse Israel for him. Within this context God chose to reveal sublime prophecies of the coming Messiah. The importance of Numbers 22–24 in detailing more precisely the unfolding revelation from God, then, should not be underestimated. By way of review, included below are several points that are important for setting the context for the account of David and Goliath: (1) The oracles in Numbers 22–24 are God's word not Balaam's word. (2) National Israel as a people is repeatedly referred to within the text. (3) The blessing or cursing of Numbers 22–24 is the heart of the Abrahamic covenant promises. (4) The unfolding revelatory light concerning the promised Messiah harmonizes with and expands God's previous promises. Go back for more information or a refresher, if you need to do so, but these are foundational truths that cannot be ignored if you want to follow the biblical trail that God has left for us.

The Importance of Amalek As a Past and Future Enemy

The last part of Numbers 22–24 includes not only the promise of the ultimate victory and reign of the One who will have the scepter of Israel, but also God's remembrance of what He had previously promised by means of Balaam: "And he looked at Amalek and took up his discourse and said, Amalek was the first of the nations / But his end shall be destruction'" (Num 24:20). That the Amalekites were "the first of the nations" is interpreted in various ways, having varying degrees of merit. For instance, some say that the Amalekites considered themselves among the preeminent nations; in a much more generalized way, they were first among the nations in the sense that their ancestry could be traced back to Esau, making them an ancient people (cf. Gen 36:16). It is more likely, however, that Amalek was first among the nations in that it was the first Gentile nation after the exodus to open the conflict of the heathen nations against national Israel.

That the Amalekites were the earliest of the nations to be hostile to national Israel after the exodus implies not only that there have been many more such hostilities from other nations throughout history, but also that there will be more in the future. Furthermore, as previously shown, several eschatological prophecies occur in Num 24:7–8 regarding the king who shall devour the nations. These prophecies are in harmony with the "end of the days" prophecies introduced in Gen 49:1, featuring the Lion who is from the tribe of Judah and His scepter (Gen 49:8–12; Num 24:9). In this context of the Messiah's future presence in national Israel, Yahweh reiterates His promise: "Blessed is everyone who blesses you, And cursed is everyone who curses you" (Num 24:9). Even more to the point, the section that contains the reference to Amalek begins with "Come, and I will advise you what this people will do to your people in the days to come" [end of the days] (Num 24:14).

To summarize thus far, the Bible contains many references demonstrating that God literally and repeatedly fulfilled His promise to curse the ones who cursed national Israel up through Numbers 24. In fact, not one of the enemies that Israel encountered was exempt from the promised cursing; every enemy that attacked Israel received judgment, sometimes immediate, and sometimes (as with Amalek) God also promised future punishment.

> **CORE TRUTH:** Once the Mosaic covenant was ratified in Exodus 24, the blessing and the curse in Leviticus 26 and Deuteronomy 27–28 by no means guaranteed Israel automatic military victories over their enemies. Such victories would come only if national Israel was in covenant obedience to Yahweh.

For those who maintain that the blessings and curses of Genesis 12 were never intended to extend beyond Abraham, the Numbers 22–24 reference to national Israel as those who are "blessed" (Num 22:12), as well as subsequent promises God gave about Israel's future, suggest otherwise. Those who hold that a future for national Israel is only some new prophetic trend of the twentieth century not found in Scripture also err, because God alone is the author of the prophecies made about the Messiah and the people from whom He would emerge—and I assure you that God does not think this to be new or a trend.

In fact, not only is the promise to bless those who bless and curse those who curse national Israel still operative up through Numbers 24, but also this promise is added to and expanded by God so that it begins to show more frequent and profound glimpses of this coming King who will emerge from that nation. Well beyond the original promise of Gen 12:3 and Num 24:9 comes God's reiterated and expanded promise to include the future Messiah not only as a participant in this promise as a Jew, but also to fulfill this promise to the fullest degree when Messiah will reign (Num 24:8). Incredibly, some of the most precise messianic prophecies come in this section, as well as another promise of the future destruction of Amalek (Num 24:20).

> **IMPORTANT NOTE:** Replacement theologians (who teach that God has replaced Israel with the church) would have to explain what God meant by these additional promises given through Numbers 24, if they were not presented and received with a literal-grammatical hermeneutic. Also, they must answer why anyone should ever believe God's first revelation given in Genesis 12, because centuries later the same God would make the same (and expanded) promises to Abraham's descendants. If God did not intend to keep His subsequent promises in Numbers 22–24, why should anyone believe them when He first gave them in Gen 12:3? These promises harmonize perfectly with what He has previously promised, including matters related to "the end of the days" (Gen 49:1; Num 24:14), yet we are told that these verses have no reference to national Israel in eschatological matters. Numbers 24 concludes with the "I will bless or I will curse" promise fully in place, as Num 24:9 clearly shows: "He couches, he lies down as a lion, / And as a lion, who dares rouse him? / Blessed is everyone who blesses you, / And cursed is everyone who curses you."

God's Further Instruction in the Pentateuch Regarding Amalek

Written to the children of the mostly wicked wilderness generation, Deuteronomy reveals additional details that are not disclosed elsewhere as Yahweh repeatedly reviewed His covenant faithfulness to Israel. For instance, in reviewing the three victories over the Gentiles recorded in Numbers 21, Yahweh disclosed this new revelation concerning what He had performed for national Israel: "This day I will begin to put the dread and fear of you upon the peoples everywhere under the heavens, who, when they hear the report of you, will tremble and be in anguish because of you" (Deut 2:25). In a sovereignty-of-God passage, which would be completely behind the scenes unless God had revealed it, came this truth: "But Sihon king of Heshbon was not willing for us to pass through his land; for the LORD your God hardened his spirit and made his heart obstinate, in order to deliver him into your hand, as he is today" (Deut 2:30). Note also that Moses in Deuteronomy 3 reviewed the military victories of Numbers 21, which was the historical setting for Balak imploring Balaam to curse Israel

(Numbers 22–24). Yet Moses in Deuteronomy completely omits the Balak narrative and goes to the sin at Baal-peor (Num 25:1–3; Deut 4:1–4). It may be that at least Balak the king had enough fear of God that he himself would not curse the people, for instead he departed and "went his way" (Num 24:25). Technically speaking, Balak did not specifically curse Israel and fight against them, and thus he did not receive the explicitly promised cursing from Yahweh.

As previously mentioned, God declared holy war on Amalek in Exodus 17 "from generation to generation," and the foretelling of his future demise occurs again in Num 24:20: "And he looked at Amalek and took up his discourse and said, 'Amalek was the first of the nations, / But his end shall be destruction.'" Elsewhere Deuteronomy clearly shows that Yahweh had not forgotten Amalek's sin (Exodus 17) or His own divine word by means of Balaam regarding their future destruction as the first of the Gentile nations (*goyim*) to fight against the nation of Israel after the exodus. Consequently, it should not be surprising that Yahweh fully intended to carry out His decree as He gave this explanation, command, and warning in Deut 25:17–19:

> *Remember what Amalek did to you along the way when you came out from Egypt, how he met you along the way and attacked among you all the strag- glers at your rear when you were faint and weary; and he did not fear God. Therefore it shall come about when the LORD your God has given you rest from all your surrounding enemies, in the land which the LORD your God gives you as an inheritance to possess, you shall blot out the memory of Amalek from under heaven; you must not forget.*

Three points are of special importance. First, the core problem with Amalek was that "he did not fear God" (Deut 25:18); his subsequent actions against Israel proved this. Because of Amalek's cowardly actions, the Lord placed the Amalekites under His judgment (Exod 17:14), promising to bring them to utter ruin (Num 24:20). Such prophecies are to be understood as literal promises fulfilled in the judgment upon the Amalekites once the nation of Israel had entered their land promised to them by Yahweh. And yet these promises are also tied in eschatologically with Messiah's reign at "the end of the days" (Num 24:14). Second, God revealed the means by which He would accomplish His judgment on the Amalekites, namely by using the Jewish people: "You shall blot out the memory of

Amalek from under heaven" (Deut 25:19). Third, God concludes this section by emphasizing the seriousness of what He had just instructed Israel to do regarding Amalek. He ended His instruction to Israel, for example, saying, "You must not forget" (Deut 25:19). As an emphatic enforcement of the word remember, it could be literally rendered as "remember this!" This strong "do not forget!" is the last of nine such commands in Deuteronomy and was to be taken most seriously by the Jewish people.

God's Judgment on Amalek in 1 Samuel 15

In spite of God's specific instruction to the Jewish people in Deuteronomy 25, they did forget about Amalek and did not carry out God's commands against the descendants of Amalek. First Samuel is one of the books that clearly reveals that God indeed carries out His Word (see Num 23:19), that Yahweh had not forgotten His previous declarations, and that He was about to act. First Samuel 15:1–3 is the account of God remembering His previous prophecies regarding Amalek:

> *Then Samuel said to Saul, "The LORD sent me to anoint you as king over His people, over Israel; now therefore, listen to the words of the LORD. Thus says the LORD of hosts, 'I will punish Amalek for what he did to Israel, how he set himself against him on the way while he was coming up from Egypt. Now go and strike Amalek and utterly destroy all that he has, and do not spare him; but put to death both man and woman, child and infant, ox and sheep, camel and donkey.'"*

If one did not know that this command was centuries removed from the previous ones, it would seem as if it were given only a short time after God's previous commands in Deut 25:19: "Therefore it shall come about when the LORD your God has given you rest from all your surrounding enemies, in the land which the LORD your God gives you as an inheritance to possess, you shall blot out the memory of Amalek from under heaven; you must not forget." Obviously, nothing can be shown to say at this time in history that Gen 12:3 and Num 24:9 had ended or been fulfilled. God based His command entirely on His promise in Gen 12:3 and Num 24:9 to curse those who curse Israel and on the holy war promise God had made regarding Amalek (Exod 17:14–16).

Saul, however, carried out only partial obedience to Yahweh's command:

> *He captured Agag the king of the Amalekites alive, and utterly destroyed all the people with the edge of the sword. But Saul and the people spared Agag and the best of the sheep, the oxen, the fatlings, the lambs, and all that was good, and were not willing to destroy them utterly; but everything despised and worthless, that they utterly destroyed. (1 Sam 15:8–9)*

Partial obedience to God's command seemed to Saul to be only a minor offense, for which he ultimately blamed the people as he repeatedly protested to Samuel that he had been obedient to Yahweh's command (1 Sam 15:13–21). Saul's disobedience impugns both God and His character, because God had promised that His eradicating judgment would come to Amalek, and King Saul failed to completely fulfill the requirements of God's command.

Because Saul had rejected God's word, Yahweh had rejected Saul from being king over Israel (1 Sam 15:22–28). God's far-reaching punishment of Saul for his sins serves as an object lesson of how seriously God reacts to willful disobedience. In spite of Saul's eventual repentance and his attempt to cling to Samuel's robe, the following certainties were revealed:

> *But Samuel said to Saul, "I will not return with you; for you have rejected the word of the LORD, and the LORD has rejected you from being king over Israel." As Samuel turned to go, Saul seized the edge of his robe, and it tore. So Samuel said to him, "The LORD has torn the kingdom of Israel from you today and has given it to your neighbor, who is better than you." (1 Sam 15:26–28)*

As was previously shown, part of God's prophecies by means of Balaam was the destruction of Amalek and his descendants since they were the first of the nations (*goyim*) to fight against the redeemed people of Israel after the exodus (Num 24:20).

In this section the divine revelation of Num 23:19 was also given: "God is not a man, that He should lie, / Nor a son of man, that He should repent; / Has He said, and will He not do it? / Or has He spoken, and will He not make it good?" This previous pronouncement of the utter and absolute faithfulness of God to His Word becomes the basis for Samuel's strong rebuke and renunciation of Saul, and it connects with the divine prophecies in Numbers 22–24: "Also the Glory of Israel will not lie or change His mind; for He is not a man that He should change His mind" (1 Sam 15:29). To emphasize the finality of the judgment against Saul, Samuel—under the inspiration of the Holy Spirit—created a new title for Yahweh: "the Everlasting One" ("the Glory") and attached it to an indirect quotation from the Torah (cf. Num 23:19). Thus, the words of judgment spoken against Saul by an eternal God would stand unchanged forever.

Ultimately the prophet Samuel—not the previously anointed King Saul—accomplished Yahweh's stated will before the very presence of Yahweh:

> Then Samuel said, "Bring me Agag, the king of the Amalekites." And Agag came to him cheerfully. And Agag said, "Surely the bitterness of death is past." But Samuel said, "As your sword has made women childless, so shall your mother be childless among women." And Samuel hewed Agag to pieces before the LORD at Gilgal. (1 Sam 15:32–33)

At the very least, then, Yahweh's promise to curse the ones who curse Israel is still operative up to 1 Samuel 15. Nothing in the text makes sense otherwise; all of the subsequent actions are based entirely on God's stated word and promises. In addition to this, several key considerations up to this point in Scripture should be marked: (1) Yahweh clearly meant what He had said in Exodus 17, Numbers 24, and Deuteronomy 25 concerning the destruction and annihilation of Amalek due to the holy war that Yahweh had pronounced against him and his descendants. (2) A literal-grammatical hermeneutic is evident in both the prophecy and its fulfillment. (3) The temporal gap between the pronouncement and ultimate fulfillment in no way nullifies the clearly stated decrees and promises of God. (4) Because Amalek was the first of the nations to wage war against Israel after the exodus (Exodus 17), his destruction was based entirely on the "I will curse the ones who curse you" promises of God in Gen 12:3 and Num 24:9. Accordingly, similar fates should be expected for other Gentile nations who would wage the same kind of war against Israel not only in the biblical account but also throughout history unless God has indeed abrogated His promise to national Israel. (5) The "replacement" of replacement theology definitely has not occurred by 1 Samuel 15.

The David Versus Goliath Account in
View of God's Previous Promises

In light of this context, we can now assess the account of David versus Goliath. As shown previously, Yahweh rejected Saul as being king of Israel. God then instructed Samuel to go to Jesse of Bethlehem and anoint the new king (1 Sam 16:1–11), with God's emphasis not on the outer appearance but on the man's heart (1 Sam 16:7). God by His sovereign election chose the shepherd youth David as the next king of Israel. After Samuel anointed the future king, "the Spirit of the LORD came mightily upon David from that day forward" (1 Sam 16:13), but the Spirit of the Lord departed from Saul, and an evil spirit was sent to terrorize him (1 Sam 16:14). With God's anointing of the next king, the Spirit of the Lord came upon David (as the Spirit had often come upon some of the judges before him), thus enabling him to fulfill the specific tasks God assigned to him.

Therefore, the account of David and Goliath in 1 Samuel 17 is much more than a good example of a wonderful lesson to teach in children's church; it is another example of Yahweh being completely faithful to His revealed word in what He had previously promised. First Samuel 17 records the Philistines going to war against the nation of Israel by using Goliath, their Philistine champion. And this battle became the perfect background for God to demonstrate His covenant faithfulness to His people. The fact that the Philistines stood in battle against disobedient, unbelieving King Saul shows the poor spiritual condition of the king and his people (1 Sam 17:1–18). As was the case before, the problem for Israel was not a military one; Saul and the people had a deep spiritual problem.

The Philistine champion Goliath defied "the ranks of Israel" (1 Sam 17:10, 25) and did so morning and evening for forty days (1 Sam 17:16). Consequently, the Gen 12:3 and Num 24:9 promise of "I will curse the one who curses you" ultimately applies to Goliath and to the Philistines as well. However, since the ratification of the Mosaic covenant (Exodus 24), "the blessing or the curse" also applied to the nation of Israel; Yahweh promised military victory against the enemies of Israel only if the nation was in covenant obedience to Him (Lev 26:6–8; Deut 28:7), but certain military defeat if the Jewish nation lived in covenant disobedience before Him (Lev 26:23–25; Deut 28:25). Yahweh offered no middle ground; it was an either/

or proposition for the nation of Israel based on their spiritual condition; their only hope for victory was in obedience to Yahweh. Saul and the nation were living in covenant disobedience before Yahweh when they encountered Goliath and the Philistines. David, however, was living in covenant obedience before Yahweh and had confidence in Yahweh, correctly appraising the situation based on the faithfulness of God to His Word.

In 1 Sam 17:26 David asked, as more of a challenge than a mere question, "For who is this uncircumcised Philistine, that he should taunt the armies of the living God?" By not being circumcised, Goliath stood outside of the covenant promises of Yahweh. Throughout the remainder of the chapter, David's basis for the victory he knew would come was that this Philistine had taunted the armies of the living God (1 Sam 17:36–37).

As a sad indication of the spiritual condition of Saul and the nation, 1 Sam 17:26 contains the first reference to God in the entire chapter: "Then David spoke to the men who were standing by him, saying, 'What will be done for the man who kills this Philistine and takes away the reproach from Israel? For who is this uncircumcised Philistine, that he should taunt the armies of the living God?'" This is in keeping with the vastly different spiritual conditions of David (1 Sam 16:12–13) and Saul (1 Sam 16:14), as is also seen in their subsequent actions. Once David rightly referred to God's name, the name Goliath does not occur in the remainder of the chapter. "Goliath" occurs only in 1 Sam 17:4 and 23. After this, he is repeatedly referred to as, for example, "this uncircumcised Philistine" (1 Sam 17:26), "this Philistine" (1 Sam 17:26), or merely "the Philistine" (17:41ff.). He is, as such, just another in the long line of Gentile enemies of God and His people, but nothing more. God's promise in Gen 12:3 and Num 24:9 and Leviticus 26 and Deuteronomy 28 (as an enemy of national Israel) applied just as much to this uncircumcised Philistine as it did to all other enemies of Yahweh and His people.

Goliath cursed David by his—the uncircumcised Philistine's—gods (1 Sam 17:43). It is not by accident that the word cursed used here is the same used in Gen 12:3. Without knowing it, nor would he have believed it if it had been told him ahead of time, Goliath was bringing down God's curse on himself, and thus the outcome was already given by God in Scripture.

David repeatedly referred to Yahweh as the basis for his victory, as shown in 1 Sam 17:45–47:

> *Then David said to the Philistine, "You come to me with a sword, a spear, and a javelin, but I come to you in the name of the LORD of hosts, the God of the armies of Israel, whom you have taunted. This day the LORD will deliver you up into my hands, and I will strike you down and remove your head from you. And I will give the dead bodies of the army of the Philistines this day to the birds of the sky and the wild beasts of the earth, that all the earth may know that there is a God in Israel, and that all this assembly may know that the LORD does not deliver by sword or by spear; for the battle is the LORD's and He will give you into our hands."*

The character and reputation of God was at stake here. If Yahweh does not respond as He had promised He would, then He is not holy, true, powerful, and worthy of worship.

The core truth of this encounter should not be overlooked: contrary to virtually universal modern usage, David defeating Goliath was not an upset of the underdog against seemingly overwhelming odds. David's victory is yet another example of Yahweh being true to His Word, especially the Gen 12:3 and Num 24:9 promise to curse the ones who curse Israel and the promise to grant military victory to national Israel when they were in covenant obedience to Him (Leviticus 26; Deuteronomy 28). This is also another affirmation of Num 23:19: "Has He said, and will He not do it? / Or has He spoken, and will He not make it good?" God responds in 1 Samuel 17 exactly as we would expect Him to do with a literal-grammatical hermeneutic employed in what God promised and in what God did.

Conclusion

Although many would not deem it so, David's victory over Goliath clearly was not an upset. In David's victory over Goliath, God had not established "the odds"; God had previously revealed and announced this outcome long before the 1 Samuel account. It should also be noted that nothing that God has promised, or its ultimate fulfillment, should be taken in any way other than the normative, literal-grammatical hermeneutic. God's initial promise to "curse the ones who curse" Israel (Gen 12:3), His promise to curse

Amalek for attacking Israel (Exodus 17), His reiteration of these promises in Numbers 22–24, and His additional warnings for national Israel not to forget to fulfill the promised destruction of the Amalekites up through 1 Samuel 13 all make perfect sense with the normative use of language.

When Goliath cursed Israel by his gods in 1 Sam 17:43, the Gen 12:3 and Num 24:9 curse rested on him as well. With David walking in covenant obedience to Yahweh under Mosaic covenant, the military outcome was already determined before the two warriors ever faced each other. Not only was David's victory not an upset under the circumstances, but the outcome would have been the same each time. Let one thousand Goliaths or more appear under these same circumstances, and they all would have been defeated—every time—just as God's Word has repeatedly promised. When this same Spirit, who had also come upon some of the judges, came mightily upon David (1 Sam 16:13), would one expect any less of a striking victory, all in keeping with God keeping His covenant promises? In addition, with God's pinpoint precision of both His pronouncement and fulfillment, one should confidently expect Him to continue fulfilling His Word in the normative, literal-grammatical hermeneutic as it relates to future prophecies and their fulfillment. With the faithfulness of Yahweh to honor His Word up to 1 Samuel 17, the burden of proof is on those who would spiritualize the fulfillment of the related prophecies before or after David's victory over Goliath and with those who would curse national Israel today.

Deeper Walk Study Questions

1. What is the biblical significance of what God promised in Gen 12:3 and Gen 15:13–14 concerning what God would do in Exodus? How does this support the literal-grammatical hermeneutic? Explain.

2. What is the biblical significance of Exodus 17 concerning what God promised to the Amalekites? How does this support the literal-grammatical hermeneutic? Explain.

3. List ten ways the truths in Numbers 22–24 support a literal-grammatical understanding of the text. Why is this important? Explain.

4. How does Deut 25:17–19 support the literal-grammatical hermeneutic? Explain.

5. How does 1 Samuel 15 support the literal-grammatical hermeneutic used with Gen 12:3; Exodus 17; and Deut 25:17–19? Why is this important theologically? Explain.

6. How does 1 Samuel 17 support the literal-grammatical hermeneutic used in Gen 12:3; Exodus 17; Deut 25:17–19; and 1 Samuel 15? Why is this important theologically? Explain.

7. Did God really mean that He intended to war against Amalek "from generation to generation"? How do you know? List four reasons for your answer. Also, how does this help strengthen your understanding of the text? How does this help strengthen your understanding of God? Explain.

CHAPTER 11

The Davidic Covenant and Its Theological Relevance

W hen Peter preached his sermon on Pentecost, hours after the Spirit had been sent by Jesus, he spoke these familiar verses:

> *Men of Israel, listen to these words: Jesus the Nazarene, a man attested to you by God with miracles and wonders and signs which God performed through Him in your midst, just as you yourselves know—this Man, delivered over by the predetermined plan and foreknowledge of God, you nailed to a cross by the hands of godless men and put Him to death. (Acts 2:22–23)*

As previously noted, God's predetermined plan (singular) was for Jesus not just to die, but to be resurrected and eventually to reign. So the predetermined plan of God goes from Genesis 1 all the way to Revelation 22 and beyond into eternity.

Some individuals never teach or preach on prophecy from Scripture because of uncertainty concerning a given prophecy and its fulfillment or perhaps because they believe it is not important. Such an approach, however, is precarious, given that approximately one-third of God's written revelation is prophetic in nature. Although such caution may sound reasonable initially, it is not what God intended, as we can see from the biblical example left by Paul. Paul addressed the Ephesian elders in his farewell by reminding them that he "did not shrink from declaring to you anything that was profitable, and teaching you publicly and from house to house" (Acts 20:20). And again in Acts 20:27, Paul reminded them, "For I did not shrink from declaring to you the whole purpose of God." As will become evident below, this "whole purpose of God" included the prophetic part of Scripture, including the holy Scriptures that God revealed through Paul His apostle (2 Pet 3:14–16). It would be foolish, then, to claim to preach the full counsel of God and yet by default remove the one-third of Scripture that is prophetic for fear of what people will think or because prophecy is a controversial topic.

> **WARNING:** God takes seriously the failure to use prophetic Scripture. James 3:1 ("Let not many of you become teachers, my brethren, knowing that as such we will incur a stricter judgment") is not only warning against false doctrine, but also referring to those who remove about one-third of the Bible by avoiding verses that God Himself gave as part of the scriptural canon and part of His predetermined plan. Many preachers glibly avoid prophetic Scripture; when they do, they do not declare to those who hear them "the whole purpose of God," and they need to start formulating the answer they will give to Jesus when he asks them why they did not preach "the whole purpose of God."

In this chapter we will see extensive evidence of God's predetermined plan and foreknowledge, as we see more divine revelation about God's Messiah, who not only would be born and dwell among us, but who also one day will rule. God started giving more revelatory light with the promises that He gave in His next covenant, the Davidic covenant.

The Biblical Basis for the Davidic Covenant

By the time we come to David's reign in Scripture, centuries have passed since the exodus under Moses and the appointment of his successor, Joshua. Those intervening years included the following: (1) Joshua brought the Jewish people into the land God had promised them. (2) The nation spiraled downward spiritually, as is repeatedly shown in the book of Judges. (3) Samuel was the last judge and began a new part of the prophetic ministry of God's prophets to the wayward Jewish people. (4) National Israel asked Samuel for a king, so they could be like the other nations, and God gave them Saul, who was not at all a good king. (5) God promised that the next king would be a man after God's own heart. (6) In accordance with His Word, God removed Saul and placed David as king over all of Israel.

With this background in mind, we come to 2 Samuel where David is securely established as king in Jerusalem. He looked around at his opulent surroundings and viewed these in contrast with the rather austere tabernacle where Yahweh dwelt with His special presence. David decided to build a house (a building) for God. Instead, God informed David that God Himself would build David a house, by which God meant a dynastic lineage. The setting for such a promise is described in 2 Sam 7:1–17:

> *Now it came about when the king lived in his house, and the* LORD *had given him rest on every side from all his enemies, that the king said to Nathan the prophet, "See now, I dwell in a house of cedar, but the ark of God dwells within tent curtains." Nathan said to the king, "Go, do all that is in your mind, for the* LORD *is with you."*
>
> *But in the same night the word of the* LORD *came to Nathan, saying, "Go and say to My servant David, 'Thus says the* LORD, *"Are you the one who should build Me a house to dwell in? For I have not dwelt in a house since the day I brought up the sons of Israel from Egypt, even to this day; but I have been moving about in a tent, even in a tabernacle. Wherever I have gone with all the sons of Israel, did I speak a word with one of the tribes of Israel, which I commanded to shepherd My people Israel, saying, 'Why have you not built Me a house of cedar?'"'*
>
> *"Now therefore, thus you shall say to My servant David, 'Thus says the* LORD *of hosts, "I took you from the pasture, from following the sheep, to be ruler over My people Israel. I have been with you wherever you have gone and have cut off all your enemies from before you; and I will make you a great name, like the names of the great men who are on the earth. I will also appoint a place for My people Israel and will plant them, that they may live in their own place and not be disturbed again, nor will the wicked afflict them any more as formerly, even from the day that I commanded judges to be over My people Israel; and I will give you rest from all your enemies. The* LORD *also declares to you that the* LORD *will make a house for you. When your days are complete and you lie down with your fathers, I will raise up your descendant after you, who will come forth from you, and I will establish his kingdom. He shall build a house for My name, and I will*

establish the throne of his kingdom forever. I will be a father to him and he will be a son to Me; when he commits iniquity, I will correct him with the rod of men and the strokes of the sons of men, but My lovingkindness shall not depart from him, as I took it away from Saul, whom I removed from before you. Your house and your kingdom shall endure before Me forever; your throne shall be established forever."'" In accordance with all these words and all this vision, so Nathan spoke to David.

Among other things, Yahweh established three important promises: (1) the permanency of David's throne, "I will establish the throne of his kingdom forever" (2 Sam 7:13), and "Your house and your kingdom shall endure before Me forever, and your throne shall be established forever" (2 Sam 7:16); (2) that God would enter into a Father-son relationship with each of David's descendants who would sit on his throne: "I will be his father and he will be My son" (2 Sam 7:14); and (3) that Yahweh's covenant-keeping lovingkindness would not depart from him (2 Sam 7:15). Second Samuel 7 follows a pattern much like Gen 12:1–3, where details are given of what would become the Abrahamic covenant in Genesis 15. Although it is neither described as such nor ratified in that chapter, God here promised foundational and eternal truths in what will be called the Davidic covenant.

David responded in overwhelming amazement at God's grace and at his understanding that God's promises would extend far beyond his lifetime. Consider 2 Sam 7:18–29:

Then David the king went in and sat before the Lord, and he said, "Who am I, O Lord God, and what is my house, that You have brought me this far? And yet this was insignificant in Your eyes, O Lord God, for You have spoken also of the house of Your servant concerning the distant future. And this is the custom of man, O Lord God. Again what more can David say to You? For You know Your servant, O Lord God! For the sake of Your word, and according to Your own heart, You have done all this greatness to let Your servant know. For this reason You are great, O Lord God; for there is none like You, and there is no God besides You, according to all that we have heard with our ears. And what one nation on the earth is like Your people Israel, whom God went to redeem for Himself as a people and to make a name for Himself, and to do a great thing for You and awesome things for Your land, before Your people whom You have redeemed for

Yourself from Egypt, from nations and their gods? For You have estab-
lished for Yourself Your people Israel as Your own people forever, and You,
O LORD, have become their God. Now therefore, O Lord GOD, the word that
You have spoken concerning Your servant and his house, confirm it forever,
and do as You have spoken, that Your name may be magnified forever, by
saying, 'The LORD of hosts is God over Israel'; and may the house of Your
servant David be established before You. For You, O LORD of hosts, the God
of Israel, have made a revelation to Your servant, saying, 'I will build you
a house'; therefore Your servant has found courage to pray this prayer to
You. Now, O LORD GOD, You are God, and Your words are truth, and You
have promised this good thing to Your servant. Now therefore, may it please
You to bless the house of Your servant, that it may continue forever before
You. For You, O LORD GOD, have spoken; and with Your blessing may the
house of Your servant be blessed forever."

KEY TRUTH: Genesis 49:8–12 speaks of the Lion of the tribe of Judah and His worldwide rule that will eventually come. From 2 Samuel 7 onward, this lineage will be narrowed down from the tribe of Judah to the household of David. Whoever the Messiah would be must prove that His lineage went back to David. Also, whenever someone in the Gospels cried out to Jesus, "Have mercy on me, Son of David!" he or she recognized Him as the rightful heir to the Davidic covenant promises of Yahweh.

Important Biblical Passages Giving the Details of the Davidic Covenant

Skipping ahead chronologically, long past David's life and death, Psalm 89 gives some of the details of this everlasting covenant that God had made with David and his lineage:

I will sing of the lovingkindness of the LORD forever;

To all generations I will make known Your faithfulness with my mouth.

For I have said, "Lovingkindness will be built up forever;

In the heavens You will establish Your faithfulness."

"I have made a covenant with My chosen;

I have sworn to David My servant,

I will establish your seed forever

And build up your throne to all generations." (Ps 89:1–4)

The everlasting nature of this covenant shows that God views His covenant—and its promises—to be everlasting and forever. Consider Ps 89:17–37:

For You are the glory of their strength,

And by Your favor our horn is exalted.

For our shield belongs to the LORD,

And our king to the Holy One of Israel.

Once You spoke in vision to Your godly ones,

And said, "I have given help to one who is mighty;

I have exalted one chosen from the people.

"I have found David My servant;

With My holy oil I have anointed him,

With whom My hand will be established;

My arm also will strengthen him.

"The enemy will not deceive him,

Nor the son of wickedness afflict him.

"But I shall crush his adversaries before him,

And strike those who hate him.

"My faithfulness and My lovingkindness will be with him,

And in My name his horn will be exalted.

I shall also set his hand on the sea

And his right hand on the rivers.

"He will cry to Me, 'You are my Father,

My God, and the rock of my salvation.'

"I also shall make him My firstborn,

The highest of the kings of the earth.

"My lovingkindness I will keep for him forever,

And My covenant shall be confirmed to him.

So I will establish his descendants forever

And his throne as the days of heaven.

"If his sons forsake My law and do not walk in My judgments,

If they violate My statutes

And do not keep My commandments,

Then I will punish their transgression with the rod

And their iniquity with stripes.

"But I will not break off My lovingkindness from him,

Nor deal falsely in My faithfulness.

My covenant I will not violate,

nor will I alter the utterance of My lips.

"Once I have sworn by My holiness;

I will not lie to David.

"His descendants shall endure forever

And his throne as the sun before Me.

"It shall be established forever like the moon,

And the witness in the sky is faithful." Selah.

Every verse in this psalm includes scriptural gold mines. Suffice it to say that Psalm 89 bears repeated witness to the everlasting nature of God's covenant with David and his lineage. Nothing within this psalm would give any indication that God saw it as temporary in nature.

KEY TRUTH: The Davidic covenant has nothing to do with the death of Jesus, His atonement, and His propitiation for sin, which is one reason John the Baptist and others would have a hard time understanding whether Jesus was the promised One. Many other Scriptures point to the sacrificial death of Jesus.

The emphasis of the Davidic covenant is instead on the reigning and ruling. The death, resurrection, and ascension of Jesus is eternally important, but it is not the end of the story.

Psalm 2, considered a messianic psalm by orthodox Jews and Christians, shows the reigning aspect of Messiah's work. While Psalm 2 does not name the Davidic covenant as such, the contents of this psalm clearly show that it is based on the Davidic covenant promises:

> *Why are the nations in an uproar*
>
> *And the peoples devising a vain thing?*
>
> *The kings of the earth take their stand*
>
> *And the rulers take counsel together*
>
> *Against the LORD and against His Anointed, saying,*
>
> *"Let us tear their fetters apart*
>
> *And cast away their cords from us!"*
>
> *He who sits in the heavens laughs,*
>
> *The Lord scoffs at them.*
>
> *Then He will speak to them in His anger*
>
> *And terrify them in His fury, saying,*
>
> *"But as for Me, I have installed My King*
>
> *Upon Zion, My holy mountain."*
>
> *"I will surely tell of the decree of the LORD:*
>
> *He said to Me, 'You are My Son,*
>
> *Today I have begotten You.*
>
> *Ask of Me, and I will surely give the nations as Your inheritance,*
>
> *And the very ends of the earth as Your possession.*
>
> *You shall break them with a rod of iron,*
>
> *You shall shatter them like earthenware.'"*
>
> *Now therefore, O kings, show discernment;*
>
> *Take warning, O judges of the earth.*
>
> *Worship the LORD with reverence*
>
> *And rejoice with trembling.*

Do homage to the Son, that He not become angry, and you perish in the way,

For His wrath may soon be kindled.

How blessed are all who take refuge in Him! (Ps 2:1–12)

According to this psalm, the eventual worldwide reign of the Messiah is part of the predetermined plan and foreknowledge of God that harmonizes with many prophecies we have seen, such as Genesis 49 and Numbers 22–24.

The permanency of the Davidic covenant is an important characteristic as well. In 2 Samuel 11, we find the multiple, high-handed sins of David pertaining to the adultery with Bathsheba and the murder of her husband, Uriah the Hittite. Yet in spite of these capital crimes, God still viewed the Davidic covenant as being functional and permanent. How do we know? Second Chronicles 21:4–7 is just one of several examples that describe a sinful grandson of David contrasted with the covenant-keeping God:

Now when Jehoram had taken over the kingdom of his father and made himself secure, he killed all his brothers with the sword, and some of the rulers of Israel also. Jehoram was thirty-two years old when he became king, and he reigned eight years in Jerusalem. He walked in the way of the kings of Israel, just as the house of Ahab did (for Ahab's daughter was his wife), and he did evil in the sight of the LORD. Yet the LORD was not willing to destroy the house of David because of the covenant which He had made with David, and since He had promised to give a lamp to him and his sons forever.

Isaiah 9:6–7, which is read so often on Christmas Eve or at Christmas services, also relates to the Davidic covenant promises:

For a child will be born to us, a son will be given to us;

And the government will rest on His shoulders;

And His name will be called Wonderful Counselor, Mighty God, Eternal Father, Prince of Peace.

There will be no end to the increase of His government or of peace.

On the throne of David and over his kingdom,

To establish it and to uphold it with justice and righteousness

From then on and forevermore.

The zeal of the LORD of hosts will accomplish this.

The next time you preach or teach from Isa 9:6–7 or hear it used with some aspect of Christmas, remember this doctrinal truth: the only part of this prophecy that already has been fulfilled with the incarnation of Jesus is the first part: a child born to us, a son given to us. Much remains yet to be fulfilled by Jesus, such as that the government will rest on His shoulders, and that there will be no end to the increase of His government or of His peace—and on it goes.

KEY TRUTH: You cannot go very far in the New Testament without encountering a reference to the Davidic covenant.

The Importance of the Davidic Covenant in The New Testament

Without treading too far into the contents of the New Testament edition of this handbook, it is important to note briefly how the Davidic covenant formulates the theology of the New Testament. You will not get very far in the New Testament without encountering a reference to the Davidic covenant. Matthew 1:1, for example, begins, "The record of the genealogy of Jesus the Messiah, the son of David, the son of Abraham." This is not only a reference to the Davidic covenant as being the basis for Jesus's genealogy. Note also that this verse is written out of chronological order. The Abrahamic covenant occurred centuries before the Davidic covenant, yet the Holy Spirit switched the order to emphasize the Davidic covenant. This same focus, then, is evident throughout the entire book, as Matthew sets forth repeated evidence that Jesus alone qualifies as the heir of the Davidic covenant and the Messiah sent by God. In Matthew 2, for example, the wise men ask the location of the one who was born King of the Jews. King Herod was a temporary usurper of the throne, not a king born in David's lineage. His murderous response shows his futile attempt to keep the One whom God had sent from eventually reigning on His rightful throne.

As noted in a previous chapter, there is no Luke 2 (the Christmas story) without Luke 1, and the Davidic covenant is part of the interaction between Gabriel and Mary and later evident in Zacharias's Spirit-filled praise:

> *Now in the sixth month the angel Gabriel was sent from God to a city in Galilee, called Nazareth, to a virgin engaged to a man whose name was Joseph, of the descendants of David; and the virgin's name was Mary.*
>
> *And coming in, he said to her, "Greetings, favored one! The Lord is with you." But she was very perplexed at this statement, and kept pondering what kind of salutation this was.*
>
> *The angel said to her, "Do not be afraid, Mary; for you have found favor with God. And behold, you will conceive in your womb, and bear a son, and you shall name Him Jesus. He will be great and will be called the Son of the Most High; and the Lord God will give Him the throne of His father David; and He will reign over the house of Jacob forever, and His kingdom will have no end." (Luke 1:26–33)*

Later, after Gabriel slapped Zacharias with a nine-month silence, the Spirit-filled priest presented the following praise to God and the holy assessment of what God was doing in Luke 1:67–73:

> *And [John's] father Zacharias was filled with the Holy Spirit, and prophesied, saying:*
>
> *Blessed be the Lord God of Israel,*
>
> *For He has visited us and accomplished redemption for His people,*
>
> *And has raised up a horn of salvation for us*
>
> *In the house of David His servant—As He spoke by the mouth of His holy prophets from of old—SALVATION FROM OUR ENEMIES,*
>
> *AND FROM THE HAND OF ALL WHO HATE US;*
>
> *To show mercy toward our fathers,*
>
> *And to remember His holy covenant,*
>
> *The oath which He swore to Abraham our father.*

God's work was based largely on keeping His promises in both the Abrahamic and Davidic covenants.

Moving beyond the Gospels, Paul began his tremendously important epistle of Romans with the following introduction: "Paul, a bond-servant of Christ Jesus, called as an apostle, set apart for the gospel of God, which He promised beforehand through His prophets in the holy Scriptures, concerning His Son, who was born of a descendant of David according to the flesh" (Rom 1:1–3).

"The gospel of God" for which Paul was set apart contains the Davidic covenant. We need to emphasize that most of the Davidic covenant remains unfulfilled prophecy at the present time. Accordingly, Paul did not write only that Jesus was "born of a descendant of David according to the flesh," as in the genealogy of Matthew 1, but wrote even more about His return and ruling to fulfill the God-given covenant promises.

CONSIDER: If you are not preaching or teaching about matters related to the Davidic covenant when they are found in the book of Romans (e.g., Romans 9–11), your gospel does not match the gospel of God for which Paul was set apart and with which he was entrusted.

In addition, Paul taught the same truths in his death-row epistle, 2 Timothy. Some of the last words Paul ever penned help explain and expand what he meant by his introduction to Romans:

You therefore, my son, be strong in the grace that is in Christ Jesus.

The things which you have heard from me in the presence of many witnesses, entrust these to faithful men who will be able to teach others also. Suffer hardship with me, as a good soldier of Christ Jesus. No soldier in active service entangles himself in the affairs of everyday life, so that he may please the one who enlisted him as a soldier. Also if anyone competes as an athlete, he does not win the prize unless he competes according to the rules. The hard-working farmer ought to be the first to receive his share of the crops. Consider what I say, for the Lord will give you understanding in everything.

Remember Jesus Christ, risen from the dead, descendant of David, according to my gospel. (2 Tim 2:1–8)

Let us quickly consider a few points. First, Messiah and Christ are interchangeable terms, with Messiah being a Hebrew term and Christ a Greek one. When Andrew found Peter, he said to him, "'We have found the Messiah' (which translated means Christ)" (John 1:41). Jesus is His name, and Messiah or Christ is His title or office. Second, whenever Paul uses the designation Christ Jesus, such as he repeatedly does in 2 Timothy, you could appropriately translate this as "King Jesus," with the focus on the reigning aspects yet to be fulfilled by Messiah Jesus under the Davidic covenant. Third, Paul states in 2 Tim 2:8, "Remember Jesus Christ, risen from the dead, descendant of David, according to my gospel"—note the order; this refers to the second coming of Jesus (after the resurrection), not to His initial incarnation.

In addition to the Pauline Epistles, the book of Revelation supports the importance of the Davidic covenant. When the apostle John, for example, was transported in the Spirit, by a vision, to heaven, before the prophetic events were about to be unfolded before him, he saw a scroll in the hand of God the Father. John understood the problem, and in Rev 5:1–5 one of the heavenly beings in this vision gave him—and the human and angelic world, both the holy and the evil ones—God's answer:

> *I saw in the right hand of Him who sat on the throne a book written inside and on the back, sealed up with seven seals. And I saw a strong angel proclaiming with a loud voice, "Who is worthy to open the book and to break its seals?" And no one in heaven or on the earth or under the earth was able to open the book or to look into it. Then I began to weep greatly because no one was found worthy to open the book or to look into it; and one of the elders said to me, "Stop weeping; behold, the Lion that is from the tribe of Judah [Gen 49], the Root of David [Davidic covenant material], has overcome so as to open the book and its seven seals."*

Everything that will occur from Revelation 5 through Revelation 20 ultimately and directly ties in with the future fulfillment of the Davidic covenant and the worldwide rule of Jesus the Messiah on earth.

In addition, Rev 22:16 records the penultimate words Jesus spoke in Scripture: "I, Jesus, have sent My angel to testify to you these things for the churches. I am the root [originator] and the offspring [descendant] of David, the bright morning star." Those who say they will not preach on

prophecy need to consider this: Jesus wants the churches—His churches—
to know that He is both the root and offspring of David. If this does not
factor into your theology and preaching and teaching, you are leaving out
important truths that Jesus wants preached and taught.

Finally, the Davidic covenant bookends the New Testament. Matthew
1:1 begins with a reference to the Davidic covenant, and Rev 22:16, in
the final six verses of the New Testament, is likewise a Davidic covenant
reference. No other covenant of God has that distinction, so it must be
tremendously important to the Trinity that we know, mark, understand,
preach, and teach these important biblical truths that are such an integral
part in the unfinished work of Jesus the Messiah.

Conclusion

This chapter explored the far-reaching theological significance of the
Davidic covenant and its prophetic implications for the coming of God's
Messiah. First, God used the historical account of David wanting to build
God a house (a physical structure) (2 Sam 7:1–7) to instead promise David that God would build him a house (a lineage of descendants) in what
would eventually become the Davidic covenant (2 Sam 7:8–17). Second,
the promises inherent in the Davidic covenant were "concerning the distant future" (2 Sam 7:19). Third, God promised that He would establish
the throne of His kingdom forever (2 Sam 7:13). Fourth, Psalm 89 reaffirms "the forever promises" of the Davidic covenant (Ps 89:1–2, 28–29,
30–37), even though no one sat on David's throne when the psalm was
written (Ps 89:38–52), Fifth, the Davidic covenant secures the Messiah's
right to rule over all the world, as Psalm 2 shows. Sixth, Matthew's Gospel
uniquely emphasizes the ways in which Jesus Christ meets and fulfills the
requirements of the Davidic covenant. Seventh, Luke's Gospel reinforces
the ways in which the eternal promises God made in the Davidic covenant
apply to Jesus. Eighth, Paul's introduction to Romans (1:1–4) and 2 Tim
2:1–8 point to God's promises made to the Davidic covenant heir, Jesus
Christ. Ninth, the Davidic covenant promises most certainly would have
been something that Jesus taught concerning Himself in Luke 24. Finally,

Matt 1:1 and Rev 5:1–5 and 22:16 bookend the New Testament with Davidic covenant references and reminders of who and what is to come.

Deeper Walk Study Questions

1. What is the context for 2 Samuel 7? How does God use this as the backdrop for the Davidic covenant? What does God promise David and his descendants in 2 Samuel 7:8–17? Name the items and be specific.

2. How does David's response in 2 Sam 7:18–29 support the literal-grammatical hermeneutic? Explain. List five important truths from this section.

3. List ten biblical truths from Psalm 89 regarding the Davidic covenant. Why are these important? Explain.

4. List and explain the messianic truths presented in Psalm 2. Why is this important biblically? Explain.

5. What is the significance of the first verse of Matthew's Gospel? Why does this matter theologically? Explain.

6. What is meant by "There is no Luke 2 (the Christmas story) without Luke 1"? What do Luke 1:26–33 and 1:67–73 have to do with God's faithfulness and the birth of Jesus? Explain and be specific.

7. What does Rom 1:1–3 teach in regard to Paul's gospel and the Davidic covenant? Why is this important? Explain and be specific.

8. List the biblical truths found in 2 Tim 2:1–8. Why are these important? Explain and be specific.

9. List the biblical truths found in Rev 5:1–5 and 22:16. Why are these important? Explain and be specific.

CHAPTER 12

Worship and Wisdom

For some time now I have had the privilege of teaching a one-week class in the master of arts in biblical studies program at The Master's College. I must admit, I was at first overwhelmed when I saw what we were assigned to cover in five class sessions: Job, Psalms, Proverbs, and Ecclesiastes! During class we focused on Proverbs and branched out from there. But even before that, we had to decide on a working definition of both worship and wisdom. And, as you would expect, they had to be defined from biblical truths. After all, if we were going to study these two concepts from a biblical perspective, it would make sense to define them biblically. Also, given the frivolity and pretense that exists in much of the "Christian world" about these two topics, I had hoped that a biblical definition would help clarify not only what these terms mean, but also how they should affect our lives and our churches. This chapter will explore the biblical concepts of both worship and wisdom.

A Biblical Definition of Worship

Worship is one of the most—if not the most—misused and erroneously defined words in many churches and denominations today. Throughout the years we have somehow morphed into seeing singing unto the Lord—which I love to do—as the only time we collectively worship in the church service. Many churches will have a "worship leader" and/or "worship team" whose purpose is to lead the congregation in singing. While we should thank God for such godly leaders in this aspect of worship, congregational singing by no means encompasses the totality of what God's Word says about worship. Alternatively, I suggest the following biblical definition of true worship: a response to the attributes and/or the activities of God in spirit (Spirit) and truth. What follows are several biblical texts that support this definition.

We will start with what Jesus told the "woman at the well," in John 4:23–24: "But an hour is coming, and now is, when the true worshipers will worship the Father in spirit and truth; for such people the Father seeks to be His worshipers. God is spirit, and those who worship Him must worship in spirit and truth."

There are at least two observations about biblical worship that emerge from this text. First, that there is such a thing as "true worship" indicates that there is also false worship. In other words, not everything that is presented as worship of God is what God would consider true worship.

Second, true worship of God must be in spirit and truth. If both components are not there and functioning, it is not true worship, regardless of the grand scope of the church gathering. For true worship of God, then, you must have the spiritual component. You can sing a wonderfully accurate hymn such as "Holy, Holy, Holy" yet have your mind wandering, be living in sin, be refusing to forgive someone who has asked you to, or be lusting in your heart for someone at church or work. God does not accept this as true worship of Him because the spiritual element is not there. When "dead" churches sing such songs, it is not true worship either because there is no spirit/Spirit present. The second component of worship—truth—is equally important. Simply expressed, regardless of one's intentions, if it is not done in truth, it is not worship. Cults who deny the deity of Jesus can sing the "Hallelujah Chorus" in lavish surroundings (humanly speaking), yet because their theology is not based on truth, their singing does not meet the requirement that Jesus revealed and established in John 4.

The messianic Psalm 2 gives us another component of true biblical worship: "Worship the LORD with reverence, / And rejoice with trembling" (Ps 2:11). Sadly, reverence for God is lacking at many churches or Christian gatherings. So if worship does not possess or promote reverence for God, it is not true biblical worship as God intends.

Romans 12:1–2 presents yet another aspect of worship that most Christians might not readily identify:

> *Therefore I urge you, brethren, by the mercies of God, to present your bodies a living and holy sacrifice, acceptable to God, which is your spiritual service of worship. And do not be conformed to this world, but be transformed by the renewing of your mind, so that you may prove what the will of God is, that which is good and acceptable and perfect.*

Many worship leaders do not think in terms of presenting their bodies as a living sacrifice to be their "spiritual service of worship." Nonetheless, it is true that this is also an aspect of worship but not the totality of worship—any more than singing songs unto the Lord is the totality of worship.

Again, here is my proposed biblical definition of true worship of God: a response to the attributes and/or the activities of God in spirit (Spirit) and truth. I think I can convince you biblically. Let's look at a couple of examples out of Revelation 4 and 5. From the heavenly throne room comes this praise in Rev 4:8–11:

> *And the four living creatures, each one of them having six wings, are full of eyes around and within; and day and night they do not cease to say,*
>
> *"HOLY, HOLY, HOLY [ATTRIBUTE] IS THE LORD GOD, THE ALMIGHTY [ATTRIBUTE], WHO WAS AND WHO IS AND WHO IS TO COME." [ATTRIBUTE/ACTIVITY]*
>
> *And when the living creatures give glory and honor and thanks to Him who sits on the throne, to Him who lives forever and ever, the twenty-four elders will fall down before Him who sits on the throne [RESPONSE], and will worship Him who lives forever and ever [RESPONSE], and will cast their crowns before the throne [RESPONSE], saying,*
>
> *"Worthy are You, our Lord and our God [ATTRIBUTE], to receive glory and honor and power; for You created all things [ACTIVITY], and because of Your will they existed, and were created" [ACTIVITY].*

Also Rev 5:9–10 as a similar example:

> *And they sang a new song, saying [RESPONSE],*
>
> *"Worthy are You [ATTRIBUTE] to take the book and to break its seals [ACTIVITY]; for You were slain, and purchased for God with Your blood men from every tribe and tongue and people and nation [ACTIVITY].*

*"You have made them to be a kingdom and priests to our God [ACTIVITY];
and they will reign upon the earth."*

CONSIDER: For those who want a worship-evoking prolonged quiet time
with God, go through each psalm (or even selected psalms) and write
and record (and keep somewhere where you can often review these)
the attributes and/or activities of God. For instance, Ps 19:1: "The
heavens are telling the glory of God [attribute]; / And their expanse
is declaring the work of His hands" [activity]. This is a rich, life-
changing study and very much worth the effort.

Such texts reflect the character of worship as, fundamentally, a response to the attributes and/or activities of God. Accordingly, the same
standard of a response to the attributes and activities of God in spirit/Spirit
and truth should be evident in godly Christian songs.

WARNING: If what we sing is not true, even though it is well intended,
it is not true worship. One popular song includes a line, "In all I do,
I honor you" (Billy James Foote, "You Are My King [Amazing Love],"
2003). I ask people, "Is that true? Who taught you that?" If that is
true, we no longer for the rest of our lives need to confess our sin to
God (1 John 1:9) or to each other (Jas 5:16). We can collectively sing
this, and it may have been written with the best of intentions, but it
contradicts the clear teaching of Scripture. I wish that "in all I do, I
honor you" were true for me, but it is not and will not be until I get
to heaven. I hum that part of such songs or remain silent. At best, for
the present time, that is a solo line reserved for Jesus.

Let's look at one more biblical example and make some noteworthy
observations. Matthew 14:22–31 says,

*Immediately He made the disciples get into the boat, and go ahead of Him
to the other side, while He sent the crowds away. After He had sent the
crowds away, He went up on the mountain by Himself to pray; and when it*

was evening, He was there alone. But the boat was already a long distance [literally, "many stadia"; a stadia was 600 feet] away from the land, battered by the waves; for the wind was contrary. And in the fourth watch of the night He came to them, walking on the sea [activity].

When the disciples saw Him walking on the sea, they were terrified, and said, "It is a ghost!" And they cried out in fear. But immediately Jesus spoke to them, saying, "Take courage, it is I; do not be afraid."

Peter said to Him, "Lord, if it is You, command me to come to You on the water." And He said, "Come!" [activity]. And Peter got out of the boat, and walked on the water and came toward Jesus. But seeing the wind, he became frightened, and beginning to sink, he cried out, "Lord, save me!" Immediately Jesus stretched out His hand and took hold of him [activity], and said to him [activity], "You of little faith, why did you doubt?"

Notice what immediately follows in Matt 14:32–33: "When they got into the boat, the wind stopped [activity]. And those who were in the boat worshiped Him, saying [response], 'You are certainly God's Son!'" [attribute].

Note that this is the first time the disciples collectively worshiped Jesus. This draws us to two profound observations.

KEY TRUTH: All the men in the boat were Jewish; they all were born "under the Law" (Gal 4:4). For them to worship Jesus clearly breaks the Mosaic covenant ("no other gods/no other worship than the true God") unless Jesus is God. That Jesus did not rebuke them for worshiping Him and that He received worship is good to use when talking with those who say that Jesus never claimed to be God. There is no middle ground or third option: Jesus either is the incarnate God worthy to receive worship or not—and how one responds to this will literally be shown throughout eternity, whether saved or lost.

KEY CONSIDERATION: Judas Iscariot was there, saw Jesus walk on water, saw the wind stop, and responded in worship. (The text does not say, "And they worshiped Him, except Judas.") Judas worshiped Jesus, yet Judas was never saved (John 6:70–71). No one present at that time knew this other than Jesus—which includes Judas. Judas had truth in properly assessing what Jesus did, but he did not have the spirit/Spirit. We need to note this: the basis of our salvation is the finished work of Jesus on the cross, not our worship. Unsaved people can worship God for a time, but unless they are saved in this lifetime, they are headed for hell, such as the people Jesus identified in Matt 7:21–23.

More can be done with this, but I will leave you with one thought. Over the years I have observed and taught and preached many times, "We are at our best—ministry-wise—when we escort people into the presence of God." This is done in many ways, including evangelism, pastoring, biblically accurate expository preaching and teaching, the gift of mercy, the gift of helps. However, the next part is even more important: "We are at our best when we truly worship God in spirit/Spirit and truth." The above ministries are types of activities, and rightfully so; true worship is a response to the attributes and/or activities of God in Spirit and truth born from a close walk and relationship to God. This means we must be walking in the Spirit, having the word of Christ dwell in us richly, thinking on the things of God instead of the world, not letting the sun go down on our anger, being at peace with one another as much as it is possible—and all of these can be accomplished only if we are currently walking with God in obedience.

A Biblical Definition of Wisdom

I realize this sounds trite, but a biblical definition should have the Bible as its main source (which, sadly, is not always the case). Let me add one disclaimer: The biblical definition I am about to use I found written in notes for my studies done almost thirty years earlier. I do not know if they are my words or someone else's. I have looked and looked but cannot find this anywhere. If someone finds that it did come from someone else, I will gladly cite it.

We build our biblical definition for wisdom, then, from the book of Proverbs, beginning with its opening verses:

The proverbs of Solomon the son of David, king of Israel:

To know wisdom and instruction,

To discern the sayings of understanding,

To receive instruction in wise behavior,

Righteousness, justice and equity;

To give prudence to the naive,

To the youth knowledge and discretion,

A wise man will hear and increase in learning,

And a man of understanding will acquire wise counsel,

To understand a proverb and a figure,

The words of the wise and their riddles.

The fear of the LORD is the beginning of knowledge;

Fools despise wisdom and instruction. (Prov 1:1–7)

From these verses, here is our proposed biblical definition of the word wisdom: a skilled and sensible approach to life, by God's definition and standard, beginning with the fear of the Lord, and always showing up in one's behavior. The component parts of this definition can be further defined as follows:

1. A skilled (wisdom is presented as a skill to be acquired in Prov 4:4, 7)
2. and sensible (wisdom is not random, erratic thoughts; this is a systematic approach)
3. approach to life (true wisdom applies to all areas of our lives, not just to certain parts; to leave wisdom out of areas of one's life is sinful activity)
4. by God's definition and standard (which implies a separation from society; see Matt 16:26 "For what will it profit a man if he gains the whole world and forfeits his soul?")
5. beginning with the fear of the Lord (which also implies separation, see Prov 1:7; 9:10: "The fear of the LORD is the beginning of wisdom")

6. and always showing up in one's behavior (Prov 1:3: wisdom will ultimately include something to do, something to put into practice; if the right behavior is not brought about, it is not true biblical wisdom)

CONSIDER: Knowledge is an important component of wisdom, but the two are not interchangeable. With knowledge, you can know the right answer, and yet your knowledge may have nothing to do with your behavior or any appropriate actions. A good example of this is found in Matt 2:3–5, where Herod called in his chief priest and all his scribes and asked them where the Messiah was to be born. They appropriately answered Bethlehem. They had knowledge on this, but no wisdom, as far as we can tell, because they never traveled down the road about six miles to find out if He had been born. So privately or in church gatherings, whenever anyone is praying for wisdom (Jas 1:5, "If any of you lacks wisdom, let him ask of God"), in essence that person is saying, "I do not know what to do"—because true biblical wisdom always shows up in one's behavior, and if behavior is not in play, it is not true biblical wisdom, regardless of the claims made.

So to summarize, true biblical wisdom is:

A skilled and sensible approach to life
By God's definition and standard
Beginning with the fear of the Lord
And always showing up in one's behavior.

Proverbs is clear that wisdom is available to whomever desires wisdom. Wisdom is not hidden; she cries out in the street with her invitation for those to come to her (Prov 1:20–23). But acquiring wisdom is not automatic. The introductory verses of Proverbs have two options only: "a wise man" or "fools." Proverbs 1:29 describes fools as those who "hated knowledge / And did not choose the fear of the LORD."

> **CONSIDER:** Another rich study is to go through the book of Proverbs and implement the parts of the biblical definition for wisdom at the appropriate places. It will really make the book "come alive."

That the concept of wisdom finds its ultimate fulfillment in Jesus Christ is evident in several New Testament texts, two of which come from Paul's letter to Corinth. First Corinthians 1:18–24 states:

> For the word of the cross is foolishness to those who are perishing, but to us who are being saved it is the power of God. For it is written,

> "I WILL DESTROY THE WISDOM OF THE WISE,

> AND THE CLEVERNESS OF THE CLEVER I WILL SET ASIDE."

> Where is the wise man? Where is the scribe? Where is the debater of this age? Has not God made foolish the wisdom of the world? For since in the wisdom of God the world through its wisdom did not come to know God, God was well-pleased through the foolishness of the message preached to save those who believe. For indeed Jews ask for signs, and Greeks search for wisdom; but we preach Christ crucified, to Jews a stumbling block and to Gentiles foolishness, but to those who are the called, both Jews and Greeks, Christ the power of God and the wisdom of God.

Jesus Christ is God's wisdom to us—in what He said and in what He did. First Corinthians 1:25–31 continues:

> . . . Because the foolishness of God is wiser than men, and the weakness of God is stronger than men.

> For consider your calling, brethren, that there were not many wise according to the flesh, not many mighty, not many noble; but God has chosen the foolish things of the world to shame the wise, and God has chosen the weak things of the world to shame the things which are strong, and the base things of the world and the despised God has chosen, the things that are not, that He may nullify the things that are, so that no man may boast before God. But by His doing you are in Christ Jesus, who became to us wisdom from God, and righteousness and sanctification, and redemption, so that, just as it is written, "LET HIM WHO BOASTS, BOAST IN THE LORD."

The phrase "who became to us wisdom from God" explicitly presents Jesus as the Wisdom of God. Consider also Jas 3:13–18:

> *Who among you is wise and understanding? Let him show by his good behavior his deeds in the gentleness of wisdom. But if you have bitter jealousy and selfish ambition in your heart, do not be arrogant and so lie against the truth. This wisdom is not that which comes down from above, but is earthly, natural, demonic. For where jealousy and selfish ambition exist, there is disorder and every evil thing. But the wisdom from above is first pure, then peaceable, gentle, reasonable, full of mercy and good fruits, unwavering, without hypocrisy. And the seed whose fruit is righteousness is sown in peace by those who make peace.*

With Paul's understanding of Jesus as Wisdom incarnate, and James's understanding of Jesus as "the wisdom from above," one could go through the Gospels and see how Jesus exhibited as wisdom

A skilled and sensible approach to life

By God's definition and standard

Beginning with the fear of the Lord

And always showing up in one's behavior.

Looking back on Proverbs where we began our discussion of biblical wisdom, every instance of "Wisdom" represents a personified description of Jesus in what He thought, what He said, and what He did.

NOTE: Proverbs 1–9 presents Wisdom as a woman crying out in the streets, and since 1 Corinthians 1 twice shows Jesus to be the wisdom of God, does that mean that this is revealing "the feminine side of Jesus," as some claim? No, this personification is used to contrast "the woman of folly" who also shows up in these Proverbs chapters. This is not a biblical problem any more than the fact that the Holy Spirit manifested Himself once as a dove, which does not mean that He is white, with feathers and a beak, and is always gentle.

It was a representation that the Godhead chose for that particular usage.

Knowing that Jesus is the true Wisdom of God, it is another great study to take "the wisdom from above" and the attributes that God gives in this section of James and go through the Gospels to find multiple examples of how Jesus embodied true wisdom. I think you will be quite proud of your Savior and your Lord by the time you have finished.

Conclusion

This chapter explored the biblical concepts of worship and wisdom. Regarding biblical worship: (1) John 4:23–24 presents God as actively seeking people to be true worshippers of Him in spirit and truth. (2) Part of God's requirement for true worship is reverence before Him. Remove reverence from worship and it does not qualify as true worship that God accepts. (3) We proposed a working definition for true, biblically defined worship of God: a response to the attributes and/or activities of God in spirit and truth. (4) That New Testament writers presented Jesus as receiving worship supports the doctrine that Jesus presented Himself as God. (5) Judas Iscariot responded as did the other apostles did, yet he never offered worship in spirit and truth, although no one there except Jesus would have known this.

Regarding biblical wisdom: (1) Biblical wisdom is a skill that can be learned. It is a sensible and systematic approach to all areas of life, as opposed to random thoughts or a compartmentalized area that is off-limits to God. True biblical wisdom is solely by God's definition and standard; it always begins with the fear of the Lord, and it will always show up in someone's behavior. (2) Knowledge is important to wisdom, but the two are not interchangeable. (3) We proposed a working definition for true, biblically defined wisdom: a skilled and sensible approach to life, by God's definition and standard, beginning with the fear of the Lord, and always showing up in one's behavior. (4) The New Testament presents Jesus as the embodiment of true biblical wisdom (1 Cor 1:24, 30). (5) Proverbs 1-9 is a good place to look for where Jesus would have pointed to Himself as being the true Wisdom of God (see Luke 24). (6) The New Testament presents a great contrast between God's wisdom and earthly and/ or demonic wisdom (Jas 3:13–18). (7) Jesus as the true Wisdom of God is clearly portrayed in Jas 3:13–18.

Deeper Walk Study Questions

1. What is the proposed definition of true biblical worship? Do you agree with this? If so, why, and if not, why not? List ten examples to support your position.

2. How does John 4:23–24 help you understand how God views worship? Give five biblical truths you can learn from these verses.

3. What is the biblical mandate of worship from Ps 2:11? How does this show up in practical application to your own life and the lives of others? Explain by giving five examples.

4. How does Revelation 4–5 show the proposed biblical definition of worship? Explain by giving ten examples.

5. What is the difference between "We are at our best—ministry-wise—when we escort people into the presence of God" and "We are at our best when we worship God in spirit and truth"? What are the ramifications of these statements? List five for each one.

6. What is the proposed biblical definition of wisdom? How does this show up in Proverbs 1? Give five examples. How does this show up in the life of Jesus? Cite ten examples.

7. How does this chapter change anything you understood about yourself? Explain and cite examples. How does this chapter help you better understand the Godhead? Explain and give ten examples.

CHAPTER 13

I Know the Plans I Have for You

J eremiah 29:11 is a well-known verse that many people often claim as their "life verse" or as a "special promise from God." It reads, "'For I know the plans that I have for you,' declares the Lord . . . 'to give you a future and a hope.'" Yet as we saw above with Josh 24:15, this quotation is only part of the whole verse: "'For I know the plans that I have for you,' declares the Lord, 'plans for welfare and not for calamity to give you a future and a hope.'" By understanding this verse as a whole, and within its larger context, we will encounter yet another rich section of Scripture in which God's predetermined plan unfolds.

The Setting of Jeremiah 29

Under the Mosaic covenant, part of "the curse" section of Leviticus 26 featured Yahweh's promise of eventual exile if the nation of Israel stayed in its brazenly sinful condition and covenant disobedience to Him. Yahweh promised in Lev 26:31–33:

> I will lay waste your cities as well and will make your sanctuaries desolate, and I will not smell your soothing aromas. I will make the land desolate so that your enemies who settle in it will be appalled over it. You, however, I will scatter among the nations and will draw out a sword after you, as your land becomes desolate and your cities become waste.

In addition to the promised future exile of national Israel, however, Yahweh also promised eventual return and restoration in Lev 26:40–45.

Fast-forward about a thousand years to Jeremiah's time when God's promised exile was about to occur. The setting appropriately revolves around Jerusalem. The prophets Daniel, Ezekiel, and Jeremiah all lived in Jerusalem for a period and, as part of the righteous remnant, they almost certainly knew one another. All of these prophets were greatly affected by the fast-approaching Babylonian exile. Although they walked in covenant obedience and holiness before Yahweh, they were the rare exceptions; the vast majority of their contemporaries lived in sexual sin, practiced idolatry and child sacrifices to foreign gods, and in other ways disobeyed God's law.

The Babylonian exile unfolded in three phases, beginning with the initial deportation of Daniel and others to Babylon in 605 BC. Daniel 1:1–2 describes the besiegement of Jerusalem and the initial deportation of the people. Jerusalem and God's temple still stood and functioned as they had in the past, but the end was drawing near. In the second deportation in 597 BC, Ezekiel was deported to Babylon. Ezekiel 1, for example, begins with Ezekiel in Babylon with the exiles. God required Jeremiah, however, to remain in Jerusalem; this weeping prophet had much to weep about as he witnessed firsthand the rape and pillage of the people and temple in 586 BC. Part of Jeremiah's writing occurs before Jerusalem falls, part during the fall of Jerusalem, and the last part after the fall when he deals with the "spiritual riffraff" left behind.

When Jeremiah 29 was written, then, Jerusalem had not yet fallen to the Babylonians. After God calls His prophet and gives an overall negative report on the spiritual condition of the people (Jeremiah 1), Jeremiah 2–29 records (with only a few glimpses of future restoration) fourteen messages of condemnation and warning to the people to repent and submit to God, given the approaching divine judgment. After decades of such messages, there was no national revival in Jerusalem; collective Israel and their king stood in covenant disobedience to Yahweh.

Jeremiah 29 begins with Jeremiah still in Jerusalem, writing to the exiles already in Babylon:

Now these are the words of the letter which Jeremiah the prophet sent from Jerusalem to the rest of the elders of the exile, the priests, the prophets, and all the people whom Nebuchadnezzar had taken into exile from Jerusalem to Babylon. (This was after King Jeconiah and the queen mother, the court officials, the princes of Judah and Jerusalem, the craftsmen and the smiths had departed from Jerusalem.) (Jer 29:1–2)

In Jer 29:4–7 God twice referred to the fact that *He*—not the Babylonians—sent Israel into exile:

Thus says the LORD of hosts, the God of Israel, to all the exiles whom I have sent into exile from Jerusalem to Babylon, "Build houses and live in them; and plant gardens, and eat their produce. Take wives and become the fathers of sons and daughters, and take wives for your sons and give your daughters to husbands, that they may bear sons and daughters; and multiply there and do not decrease. Seek the welfare of the city where I have sent you into exile, and pray to the LORD on its behalf; for in its welfare you will have welfare."

Some of the false prophets in Babylon, on the other hand, were telling the people that God was not mad (He was), and that they should not unpack because they would soon be going back to Jerusalem (they would not be), and that God did not really mean what He said by the promised exile (which He did mean). With this as the backdrop, Jer 29:8–10 makes perfect sense:

For thus says the LORD of hosts, the God of Israel, "Do not let your prophets who are in your midst and your diviners deceive you, and do not listen to the dreams which they dream. For they prophesy falsely to you in My name; I have not sent them," declares the LORD.

For thus says the LORD, "When seventy years have been completed for Babylon, I will visit you and fulfill My good word to you, to bring you back to this place."

God then reinforced what He had already promised about the length of the exile:

"This whole land will be a desolation and a horror, and these nations will serve the king of Babylon seventy years.

"Then it will be when seventy years are completed I will punish the king of Babylon and that nation," declares the LORD, "for their iniquity, and the land of the Chaldeans; and I will make it an everlasting desolation." (Jer 25:11–12)

In this context we come to Jer 29:10–11, in which God promised what He would do for Jerusalem and the Jewish people immediately after the seventy-year exile:

> *For thus says the LORD, "When seventy years have been completed for Babylon, I will visit you and fulfill My good word to you, to bring you back to this place. For I know the plans that I have for you," declares the LORD, "plans for welfare and not for calamity to give you a future and a hope."*

This is God's promise to the Jewish people: the same God who exiled them into Babylon will visit them again and fulfill His Word by bringing them back to their land after seventy years. While I have heard people quote part of Jer 29:11 as their "life verse," I have yet to meet anyone who uses 29:10 as a "life verse."

CONSIDER: While everything about Jer 29:11 is Jewish in nature, God does offer very similar verses in the New Testament that are true for us, if we are saved. Romans 8:28 promises, "And we know that God causes all things to work together for good to those who love God, to those who are called according to His purpose." Likewise, Phil 1:6 is another good promise of God: "For I am confident of this very thing, that He who began a good work in you will perfect it until the day of Christ Jesus."

Jeremiah 30–33

When we read through the first twenty-nine chapters of Jeremiah, it becomes apparent that God's wrathful judgment is building for Judah and Jerusalem. Yet before the destruction of Jerusalem and the beginning of the exile, Jeremiah 30 begins a section of four chapters of incredible prophetic promises concerning the future of Israel and the world. Such divine promises would be amazing anywhere in Scripture, but in the context of Jeremiah 1–29, in the midst of some of the most brazen wickedness by the Jewish people, they are even more striking. In short, Jeremiah 30–33 gives a detailed description that expands and explains "the good plans" of Jer 29:11.

Space will allow us to address only a few salient aspects of these "good plans." First, Jer 30:3 begins with a phrase that frequently occurs in this section, "'For, behold, days are coming,' declares the LORD, 'when I will restore the fortunes of My people Israel and Judah.' The LORD says, 'I will also bring them back to the land that I gave to their forefathers and they shall possess it.'" At this time in history, Israel was made up of the ten northern tribes that had separated to become their own country and had taken the name Israel. The Assyrians took them into exile in 722 BC, and they ceased being a functional, independent nation at that time. Judah and Benjamin, the two southern tribes, who were called Judah, had the temple in Jerusalem and were ruled by the Davidic covenant heir. Some of the godly of the ten tribes of Israel migrated to Judah before the Assyrian exile, and thus the twelve tribes stayed intact. Both Israel and Judah received promises from God about the future, but they did so as one people; never again would the northern tribes serve as an independent nation removed from Judah.

Second, after promising a cleansing type of judgment in the future of Israel, God promises in Jer 31:1 that "At that time,' declares the LORD, 'I will be the God of all the families of Israel, and they shall be My people.'" In subsequent verses of this chapter (Jer 31:2–22), God promises future blessings on the ten northern tribes to bring them back into covenant fellowship with Yahweh. Further, God promises the two southern tribes, in Jer 31:23–25:

> *Thus says the LORD of hosts, the God of Israel, "Once again they will speak this Word in the land of Judah and in its cities, when I restore their fortunes,*
>
> *'The LORD bless you, O abode of righteousness,*
>
> *O holy hill!'*
>
> *"Judah and all its cities will dwell together in it, the farmer and they who go about with flocks. For I satisfy the weary ones and refresh everyone who languishes."*

Third, having addressed the two divisions separately, Yahweh followed with additional blessings in Jeremiah 31 each of which begins with a phrase we previously mentioned, "Behold, days are coming" (Jer 31:27, 31, 38). In Jer 31:27–30 Yahweh promised this:

> *"Behold, days are coming," declares the* LORD, *"when I will sow the house of Israel and the house of Judah with the seed of man and with the seed of beast. As I have watched over them to pluck up, to break down, to overthrow, to destroy, and to bring disaster, so I will watch over them to build and to plant," declares the* LORD.
>
> *"In those days they will not say again,*
>
> *'The fathers have eaten sour grapes,*
>
> *And the children's teeth are set on edge.'*
>
> *"But everyone will die for his own iniquity; each man who eats the sour grapes, his teeth will be set on edge."*

The same God who will have by that time previously devastated the land by His strong and severe judgment will once more repopulate the land with humans and animals. Also, the verse about "sour grapes," seems to be a proverb among the people that in essence claimed that all judgments of God were poured out because of their ancestors' sins. When this prophecy is fulfilled, everyone will take ownership of his or her own sins.

Fourth, Jer 31:31–34 features the first occurrence of the words new covenant in Scripture:

> *"Behold, days are coming," declares the* LORD, *"when I will make a new covenant with the house of Israel and with the house of Judah, not like the covenant which I made with their fathers in the day I took them by the hand to bring them out of the land of Egypt [the Mosaic covenant], My covenant which they broke, although I was a husband to them," declares the* LORD. *"But this is the covenant which I will make with the house of Israel after those days," declares the* LORD, *"I will put My law within them and on their heart I will write it; and I will be their God, and they shall be My people. They will not teach again, each man his neighbor and each man his brother, saying, 'Know the* LORD,' *for they shall all know Me, from the least of them to the greatest of them," declares the* LORD, *"for I will forgive their iniquity, and their sin I will remember no more."*

Although there had been hints that this type of covenant was coming (see Deut 30:1–10), there had yet been nothing this specific. Note as well that the original participants are Jewish in nature, "the house of Judah and the house of Israel," just as we saw in Jeremiah 30. This covenant has to do with the forgiveness of sins. Note also that the future tense is used throughout; this is not the ratification of the new covenant, this is the descriptive prophecy telling what the new covenant will involve once it is ratified.

Fifth, before the final section of Jeremiah 31, Yahweh pauses to interject that even with the nation poised to go into exile, with utter certainty His promises would eventually come true—in spite of the great sins that Israel would commit. In Jer 31:35–37 God promises:

Thus says the LORD,

Who gives the sun for light by day

And the fixed order of the moon and the stars for light by night,

Who stirs up the sea so that its waves roar;

The LORD of hosts is His name:

"If this fixed order departs

From before Me," declares the LORD,

"Then the offspring of Israel also shall cease

From being a nation before Me forever."

Thus says the LORD,

"If the heavens above can be measured,

And the foundations of the earth searched out below,

Then I will also cast off all the offspring of Israel

For all that they have done," declares the LORD.

CORE TRUTH: Based on these promises and with God comparing His keeping of His creation with the keeping of what He has promised national Israel, I would be very fearful about removing these promises from God and His Word—but many people do so.

The final part of this section, with the third "Behold, days are coming," is equally a part of God's previous promises for the future—although it is neglected by many who see no hope for Israel's future. In Jer 31:38–40 God promises:

> *"Behold, days are coming," declares the LORD, "when the city will be rebuilt for the LORD from the Tower of Hananel to the Corner Gate. The measuring line will go out farther straight ahead to the hill Gareb; then it will turn to Goah. And the whole valley of the dead bodies and of the ashes, and all the fields as far as the brook Kidron, to the corner of the Horse Gate toward the east, shall be holy to the LORD; it will not be plucked up or overthrown anymore forever."*

When the fullness of the new covenant comes, not only will sins be forgiven, but also the land will be reclaimed by Yahweh. Many of the places mentioned above are physical places that we know about, such as the brook Kidron. Also there is the promise that not only will Jerusalem be rebuilt, but it will be rebuilt for the Lord. This is the same Jerusalem that then was the capital of Judah; this is the same Jerusalem where Jesus would be crucified.

Sixth, while the prophetic glories of these promises by God would be more than enough, God is not finished. Remember that Jeremiah 30–33 is one unit in the book; other promises connected with this are in Jer 32:36–40, where God pronounces the everlasting nature of what He is about to do:

> *Now therefore thus says the LORD God of Israel concerning this city of which you say, "It is given into the hand of the king of Babylon by sword, by famine, and by pestilence." Behold, I will gather them out of all the lands to which I have driven them in My anger, in My wrath, and in great indignation; and I will bring them back to this place and make them dwell in safety. They shall be My people, and I will be their God; and I will give them one heart and one way, that they may fear Me always, for their own good, and for the good of their children after them. I will make an everlasting covenant with them that I will not turn away from them, to do them good; and I will put the fear of Me in their hearts so that they will not turn away from Me.*

The promises of Yahweh for Israel include Jer 33:14–18, which begins with another "Behold, days are coming":

*"Behold, days are coming," declares the L*ORD*, "when I will fulfill the good word which I have spoken concerning the house of Israel and the house of Judah. In those days and at that time I will cause a righteous Branch of David to spring forth; and He shall execute justice and righteousness on the earth. In those days Judah will be saved and Jerusalem will dwell in safety; and this is the name by which she shall be called: the L*ORD* is our righteousness." For thus says the L*ORD*, "David shall never lack a man to sit on the throne of the house of Israel; and the Levitical priests shall never lack a man before Me to offer burnt offerings, to burn grain offerings and to prepare sacrifices continually."*

When the fullness of the new covenant blessings occur, God promises that the fullness of the Davidic covenant blessings will also occur. From this point onward—although always in the mind of God as part of the predetermined plan of God—the Davidic covenant and the new covenant must be functioning in full force at that time; you cannot biblically have one of these covenants without the other. Further, one of the God-given mandates for the Messiah is found in Jer 33:15: "He shall execute justice and righteousness on the earth."

Finally, God concludes this glorious section of Jeremiah 30–33 with these prophetic pronouncements in Jer 33:19–22 with the utter certainty that He will fulfill all of His good word. God spoke to Jeremiah saying,

*Thus says the L*ORD*, "If you can break My covenant for the day, and My covenant for the night, so that day and night will not be at their appointed time, then My covenant may also be broken with David My servant that he will not have a son to reign on his throne, and with the Levitical priests, My ministers. As the host of heaven cannot be counted and the sand of the sea cannot be measured, so I will multiply the descendants of David My servant and the Levites who minister to Me."*

This section ends with one more challenge to those who want to remove, ignore, or spiritualize the fulfillment of the future promises that God has made to Israel and to the world.

Jeremiah 33:23–26 states:

*And the word of the L*ORD* came to Jeremiah, saying, "Have you not observed what this people have spoken, saying, 'The two families which the L*ORD* chose [Judah and Israel], He has rejected them'? Thus they despise*

My people, no longer are they as a nation in their sight. Thus says the
LORD, 'If My covenant for day and night stand not, and the fixed patterns of
heaven and earth I have not established, then I would reject the descendants
of Jacob and David My servant, not taking from his descendants rulers
over the descendants of Abraham, Isaac, and Jacob. But I will restore their
fortunes and will have mercy on them.'"

I do not know how God could have said this any more clearly regarding those who want to remove His future covenant keeping as part of His being faithful to the promises, which will extend through the time when His Messiah will reign in the kingdom on earth and ultimately in the eternal state. For those who want to spiritualize these promises, the burden is on them to answer the question, if God did not intend to be faithful to future Israel, what did God mean to convey by the repeated and precise promises He made? Also, would they apply that same hermeneutic to other Scriptures? After all, maybe God did not really mean that He would send His Messiah to reign or that He would forgive sins forever. I personally would be very hesitant to go down this road, but many, many people do. Yet Scripture undeniably and repeatedly proclaim that God—in His predetermined plan before the foundation of the world—did send His Messiah, who ultimately keeps all of His promises and will one day reign over the whole world.

The New Covenant in the New Testament

While we will say more about this when we get to the New Testament section of this book, we need to note two important matters here. First, when John the Baptist appeared and proclaimed to national Israel, "Repent, for the kingdom of heaven is at hand" (Matt 3:2), he did so to people under the Mosaic covenant. But what he pronounced is tied in with the fullness of the —not as much to the new covenant. For instance, he never proclaimed, "Repent, for the new covenant is at hand."

Jesus also never referred to the new covenant until the incredibly important time of Luke 22:14–20:

And when the hour had come He reclined at the table, and the apostles with
Him. And He said to them, "I have earnestly desired to eat this Passover

> *with you before I suffer; for I say to you, I shall never again eat it until it is*
> *fulfilled in the kingdom of God." And when He had taken a cup and given*
> *thanks, He said, "Take this and share it among yourselves; for I say to you,*
> *I will not drink of the fruit of the vine from now on until the kingdom of God*
> *comes." And when He had taken some bread and given thanks, He broke it,*
> *and gave it to them, saying, "This is My body which is given for you; do this*
> *in remembrance of Me." And in the same way He took the cup after they had*
> *eaten, saying, "This cup which is poured out for you is the new covenant in*
> *My blood."*

We have to note that the new covenant would be ratified not that night, but the next day when the Lamb of God, foreknown before the foundation of the world, would take away the sins of the world (John 1:29), and He would do that in the ratification of the new covenant in His own body and blood.

Conclusion

In this chapter we have shown how Jer 29:11 as a whole, and indeed its entire context, is important for understanding what God intended by this particular promise. First, the setting of the book of Jeremiah shows national Israel living in brazen covenant disobedience to Yahweh. Exile was looming for the Jewish people (Lev 26:31–33), yet God promises an eventual return at some undisclosed point in the future (Lev 26:40–45). Second, Jeremiah 2–29 contains fourteen messages of mostly condemnation of national Israel for their wickedness as well as a repeated call for them to return and repent. Third, Jer 29:1–10 reminds the exiles that God had sent them there; that they should unpack and live there, given that the exile would last seventy years, after which time He would return "and fulfill My good word to you." Fourth, with this background in mind, Jer 29:11 makes sense only for the Jewish people, not as a "life verse" for a new covenant believer. Fifth, more significant for the new covenant believer is the next section of Jeremiah (30–33), where the same God looks to the future and promises wonderful messianic eschatological blessings. Sixth, Jeremiah 31 unfolds some of the fullness of the new covenant in which Jerusalem will be rebuilt for the Lord, holy to Him, and forevermore protected by

Him. Seventh, when all of the new covenant blessings become operative, they will all be everlasting (Jer 32:36–40), and also will be interwoven with the fullness of the blessings of the Messiah as part of the Davidic covenant (Jer 33:14–26). Eighth, while the new covenant is utterly ir-replaceable for anyone born ever to be saved, Jesus never taught regarding this last of the covenants of God until the Last Supper (Luke 22:14–20). Finally, the ratification of the new covenant began the next day at the death of Jesus—not at the birth of Jesus or as any part of His earthly ministry before His crucifixion.

Deeper Walk Study Questions

1. What does Lev 26:31–33 indicate about Israel's spiritual condition before God as the promised Babylonian exile approached? How do you know? What does Lev 26:40–45 teach? Is this true? Explain and support your answer.

2. How did the Babylonian exile affect the prophets Daniel, Ezekiel, and Jeremiah? What specifically was Jeremiah's role in remaining behind in Jerusalem, and how did that set the stage for what he would write in Jeremiah 29?

3. What is the background for Jeremiah 29? What is the specific content for Jer 29:1–10? List the content and be specific.

4. How long was the Babylonian exile to last? How do you know? What does this tell you about the literal-grammatical hermeneutic? Explain and support your answer.

●

5. Why is Jer 29:11 not a good "life verse" for someone to use? Explain and be specific. Why is Rom 8:28 or Phil 1:6 more appropriate for people in the church than Jer 29:11? Explain and support your answer.

6. What is the importance of Jeremiah 30–33 being one unit? How does it stand in stark contrast to the Jewish people's sins and the rapidly approaching Babylonian exile? Why does that matter? Explain and give five truths from this.

7. What does God specifically promise with the threefold use of "Behold, days are coming" in Jer 31:27, 31, 38? List what God promised all the way through. Did God really mean what He promised? How do you know?

8. What does God promise in Jer 33:14–18? Did God actually mean what He promised? How do you know? Be specific.

9. In Jer 33:19–22, how certain is God about the events yet to be fulfilled in the future? How do you know? Be specific. Consider the same questions for Jer 33:23–26. What does God say here? Did He really mean it? Explain and be specific.

10. What is the significance of Jesus's first mention of the new covenant in Luke
    22:14–20? What did He teach in this passage? Why is that important? Also, what is
    the significance of the new covenant being ratified, not during the Last Supper, but the
    next day, with the death of Jesus. Explain and defend your answer.

CHAPTER 14

Great Is Thy Faithfulness

M any Christians have been comforted by the great hymn of the faith "Great Is Thy Faithfulness." Perhaps some could cite the reference of the Bible verse on which the song is based, Lam 3:23. Fewer could tell you the amazing background and context that led to this verse or the promises of God that go with it. As we have seen above, one cannot start with Lamentations 3; we must "get there" biblically by studying the background and context.

Biblical Background and Context

When God redeemed the Jewish people out Egypt, He brought them to Mount Sinai (Exodus 19) and ratified the Mosaic covenant in Exodus 24. Israel's response, "All that Yahweh said, we will do," would include any subsequent divine revelation, from Exodus 24 onward. As part of "the curse" of "the blessing and the curse" of Leviticus 26, Yahweh warned what would happen to national Israel if they continually disobeyed him: "I will set My face against you so that you shall be struck down before your enemies; and those who hate you will rule over you, and you will flee when no one is pursuing you" (Lev 26:17). Further, in Lev 26:26–29, God warned of the extremely serious consequences if the nation did not obey Him, namely the cannibalism of their own children because of the famine He would send:

When I break your staff of bread, ten women will bake your bread in one oven, and they will bring back your bread in rationed amounts, so that you will eat and not be satisfied.

Yet if in spite of this you do not obey Me, but act with hostility against Me, then I will act with wrathful hostility against you, and I, even I, will punish you seven times for your sins. Further, you will eat the flesh of your sons and the flesh of your daughters you will eat.

After the famine, if Israel did not repent, exile would follow. Leviticus 26:32–33 states, "I will make the land desolate so that your enemies who settle in it shall be appalled over it. You, however, I will scatter among the nations and will draw out a sword after you, as your land becomes desolate and your cities become waste." However, it is important to recall from the chapter above on the Mosaic covenant that the blessing and the curse of Leviticus 26 ends with God's promise to gather the nation and bring them back to the land at some undisclosed future time, based on His faithfulness to the Abrahamic covenant:

If they confess their iniquity and the iniquity of their forefathers, in their unfaithfulness which they committed against Me, and also in their acting with hostility against Me—I also was acting with hostility against them, to bring them into the land of their enemies—or if their uncircumcised heart becomes humbled so that they then make amends for their iniquity, then I will remember My covenant with Jacob, and I will remember also My covenant with Isaac, and My covenant with Abraham as well, and I will remember the land. For the land will be abandoned by them, and will make up for its sabbaths while it is made desolate without them. They, meanwhile, will be making amends for their iniquity, because they rejected My ordinances and their soul abhorred My statutes. Yet in spite of this, when they are in the land of their enemies, I will not reject them, nor will I so abhor them as to destroy them, breaking My covenant with them; for I am the LORD their God. But I will remember for them the covenant with their ancestors, whom I brought out of the land of Egypt in the sight of the nations, that I might be their God. I am the LORD. (Lev 26:40–45)

As we have seen, in response to the negative report of the spies in Numbers 13–14, God sentenced that original generation of the exodus to become the "wilderness generation," with only Joshua and Caleb going into the land that God had given for the Jewish people. As would become evident from the book of Deuteronomy, this new generation was likewise under the blessings and curse of the Mosaic covenant. Accordingly, in the blessing and the curse given to this generation that was poised to enter the land under the leadership of Joshua, God forewarned of the severity of what national disobedience to Him would entail. In Deut 28:25, for example, God promised that He would be the source of their military defeats: "The LORD shall cause you to be defeated before your enemies; you will go out one way against them, but you shall flee seven ways before them, and you will be an example of terror to all the kingdoms of the earth." As before, if Israel did not respond properly by repentance from sin, the curses would increase until, ultimately, the pagan nations would besiege their cities. Consider Deut 28:49–52:

> The LORD will bring a nation against you from afar, from the end of the earth, as the eagle swoops down, a nation whose language you shall not understand, a nation of fierce countenance who will have no respect for the old, nor show favor to the young. Moreover, it shall eat the offspring of your herd and the produce of your ground until you are destroyed, who also leaves you no grain, new wine, or oil, nor the increase of your herd or the young of your flock until they have caused you to perish. It shall besiege you in all your towns until your high and fortified walls in which you trusted come down throughout your land, and it shall besiege you in all your towns throughout your land which the Lord your God has given you.

What's more, God promised the cannibalism of children by their own mothers in Deut 28:53–55:

> Then you shall eat the offspring of your own body, the flesh of your sons and of your daughters whom the LORD your God has given you, during the siege and the distress by which your enemy will oppress you. The man who is refined and very delicate among you shall be hostile toward his brother and toward the wife he cherishes and toward the rest of his children who remain, so that he will not give even one of them any of the flesh of his children which he will eat, since he has nothing else left, during the siege and the distress by which your enemy will oppress you in all your towns.

Such warnings, then, account for the numerous examples of national Israel being repeatedly held accountable when they collectively sinned against Yahweh from Joshua through Chronicles.

> **CORE TRUTH:** If God presented these warnings to be understood with the literal—grammatical hermeneutic, we would expect numerous biblical examples of national Israel being repeatedly held accountable when they collectively sinned against Yahweh—which is exactly what happens from Joshua through Chronicles.

The Immediate Context for Lamentations

Fast-forward more than eight hundred years to the time of the ministries of Jeremiah, Ezekiel, and Daniel. That which God had promised was about to occur, as Babylonian soldiers surrounded and besieged Jerusalem. In two deportations, Daniel and others are taken first into exile in Babylon in 605 BC, followed later by Ezekiel in 597 BC. For decades, Jeremiah had the hard ministry of warning Israel of the pending severe judgment of God due to the perpetuation and depth of their sins. Jeremiah also had the sad fate of watching Jerusalem fall, God's temple being destroyed, and all the savagery against the people that accompanied the destruction. Jeremiah 39:1–10 records the short version of Jerusalem's fall:

> *Now when Jerusalem was captured in the ninth year of Zedekiah king of Judah, in the tenth month, Nebuchadnezzar king of Babylon and all his army came to Jerusalem and laid siege to it; in the eleventh year of Zedekiah, in the fourth month, in the ninth day of the month, the city wall was breached. Then all the officials of the king of Babylon came in and sat down at the Middle Gate: Nergal-sar-ezer, Samgar-nebu, Sarsekim the Rab-saris, Nergal-sar-ezer the Rab-mag, and all the rest of the officials of the king of Babylon. When Zedekiah the king of Judah and all the men of war saw them, they fled and went out of the city at night by way of the king's garden through the gate between the two walls; and he went out toward the Arabah. But the army of the Chaldeans pursued them and overtook Zedekiah in the plains of Jericho; and they seized him and brought*

him up to Nebuchadnezzar king of Babylon at Riblah in the land of Hamath, and he passed sentence on him. Then the king of Babylon slew the sons of Zedekiah before his eyes at Riblah; the king of Babylon also slew all the nobles of Judah. He then blinded Zedekiah's eyes and bound him in fetters of bronze to bring him to Babylon. The Chaldeans also burned with fire the king's palace and the houses of the people, and they broke down the walls of Jerusalem. As for the rest of the people who were left in the city, the deserters who had gone over to him and the rest of the people who remained, Nebuzaradan the captain of the bodyguard carried them into exile in Babylon. But some of the poorest people who had nothing, Nebuzaradan the captain of the bodyguard left behind in the land of Judah, and gave them vineyards and fields at that time.

The subsequent account includes the kind treatment that Jeremiah received from the Gentile king Nebuchadnezzar, in Jer 39:11–12: "Now Nebuchadnezzar king of Babylon gave orders about Jeremiah through Nebuzaradan the captain of the bodyguard, saying, 'Take him and look after him, and do nothing harmful to him, but rather deal with him just as he tells you.'"

Such is the background for the book of Lamentations, which gives the longer—but by no means the complete—account of the fall of Jerusalem, the rape and slaughter of the people, and the destruction of the city. Lamentations is the Holy Spirit-inspired "lamenting" of these events, and it offers a biblical assessment of the overall situation.

God chose to arrange the book with certain unique characteristics. First, four of the five chapters have twenty-two verses with only Lamentations 3, at the center, featuring sixty-six verses. Such a structure draws attention to the core of the author's lament in chapter 3. Second, the first four chapters are each an acrostic, with the first letter of each verse corresponding to the letters of the Hebrew alphabet. Such a literary technique would foster the memory of such texts among the wayward people and later generations. Third, Hebrew scholars describe Lamentations 1–4 as written in a "limping meter" or funeral-dirge cadence. Finally, Lamentations 5 is set apart as a prayer, differing from the acrostic pattern and limping meter of the first four chapters.

Lamentations 1 gives the general description of the fall of Jerusalem and what that meant to the city and the people. The book of Lamentations begins:

How lonely sits the city

That was full of people!

She has become like a widow

Who was once great among the nations!

She who was a princess among the provinces

Has become a forced laborer!

She weeps bitterly in the night,

And her tears are on her cheeks;

She has none to comfort her

Among all her lovers.

All her friends have dealt treacherously with her;

They have become her enemies.

Judah has gone into exile under affliction,

And under harsh servitude;

She dwells among the nations,

But she has found no rest;

All her pursuers have overtaken her

In the midst of distress.

The roads of Zion are in mourning

Because no one comes to the appointed feasts.

All her gates are desolate;

Her priests are groaning,

Her virgins are afflicted,

And she herself is bitter. (Lam 1:1–4)

Lamentations 1:5 shows that God Himself has caused judgment as the result of Israel's great and constant sinning:

Her adversaries have become her masters,

Her enemies prosper;

For the Lord *has caused her grief*

Because of the multitude of her transgressions;

Her little ones have gone away

As captives before the adversary.

Thus, these horrible events did not occur of their own accord: "The Lord has caused her grief / Because of the multitude of her transgressions."

Lamentations 2 gives more details of the fall of Jerusalem, beginning with the first two verses, which show God's wrathful judgment as the source for what has happened:

How the Lord has covered the daughter of Zion

With a cloud in His anger!

He has cast from heaven to earth

The glory of Israel,

And has not remembered His footstool

In the day of His anger.

The Lord has swallowed up; He has not spared

All the habitations of Jacob.

In His wrath He has thrown down

The strongholds of the daughter of Judah;

He has brought them down to the ground;

He has profaned the kingdom and its princes.

Lamentations 2:17–20, then, shows in sad yet striking terms what God had promised:

The Lord *has done what He purposed;*

He has accomplished His Word

Which He commanded from days of old.

He has thrown down without sparing,

And He has caused the enemy to rejoice over you;

He has exalted the might of your adversaries.

Their heart cried out to the Lord,

"O wall of the daughter of Zion,

Let your tears run down like a river day and night;

Give yourself no relief;

Let your eyes have no rest.

"Arise, cry aloud in the night

At the beginning of the night watches;

Pour out your heart like water

Before the presence of the Lord;

Lift up your hands to Him

For the life of your little ones

Who are faint because of hunger

At the head of every street."

See, O Lord, and look!

With whom have You dealt thus?

Should women eat their offspring,

The little ones who were born healthy?

Should priest and prophet be slain

In the sanctuary of the Lord?

Sadly, as noted above, the reference to those women who "eat their offspring, / The little ones who were born healthy" is exactly what God promised He would cause to happen in the blessing and the curse if national Israel did not repent of her sins.

On the other side of chapter 3, to which we will return momentarily, Lamentations 4:6 offers an evaluation of how heinous the sins of the people were: "For the iniquity of the daughter of my people / Is greater than the sin of Sodom, / Which was overthrown as in a moment, / And no hands were turned toward her." Lamentations 4:9–11 records the consequences of their depravity:

Better are those slain with the sword

Than those slain with hunger;

For they pine away, being stricken

For lack of the fruits of the field.

The hands of compassionate women

Boiled their own children;

They became food for them

Because of the destruction of the daughter of my people.

The Lord has accomplished His wrath,

He has poured out His fierce anger;

And He has kindled a fire in Zion

Which has consumed its foundations.

In light of this surrounding context, we return to Lamentations 3. As was noted above, chapters 1–2 and 4–5 bookend this middle chapter. Chapters 2 and 4, for example, each contain a reference to the cannibalism performed by mothers of their own children. So it is in this setting that Lam 3:19–23 stands out so strikingly:

Remember my affliction and my wandering, the wormwood and

bitterness.

Surely my soul remembers

And is bowed down within me.

This I recall to my mind,

Therefore I have hope.

The Lord's lovingkindnesses indeed never cease,

For His compassions never fail.

They are new every morning;

Great is Your faithfulness.

Lamentations 3:24–25 continues, "'The Lord is my portion,' says my soul, / 'Therefore I have hope in Him.' / The Lord is good to those who wait for Him, / To the person who seeks Him."

Several important observations emerge. First, the last line of Lam 3:23, "Great is Your faithfulness," is stated in the very midst of God's promised and severe judgment, not His promised blessing. When we sing "Great Is Thy Faithfulness," we generally sing it while looking back over our lives and finding God faithful, which certainly is appropriate. However, in Lamentations 3, these are more declarations of faith, similar to Habakkuk's prayer in his closing chapter, where in spite of the promised judgment coming by means of the Babylonians, Habakkuk placed his trust totally in the Lord.

Second, both the promised judgment and its fulfillment are understood with the literal-grammatical hermeneutic. Yahweh fulfilled exactly what He said He would do if national Israel persisted in their sin. They could have read the text and known what was coming, if they had chosen to do so.

Third, if God was so precise in fulfilling His promised judgment, the burden of proof lies with those who would spiritualize future blessings that God has promised for the people whom He has judged. We would expect the same pinpoint precision in God fulfilling all the promises He has given in His Word, such as the future regathering of national Israel back to the land God had given them (Lev 26:40–45).

Fourth, as much as we abhor watching the unfolding of such severe judgment of God, we who live on this side of the cross can look back on that event as proof that God is absolutely true to His Word. How do we know Rom 5:1 is correct ("Therefore, having been justified by faith, we have peace with God through our Lord Jesus Christ")? We know so because God has definitively proven His utter truthfulness in fulfilling judgments that were not His desire to send. We can trust God's Word with utter confidence knowing that He who has shown Himself faithful throughout history will do so into eternity. The certainty of God fulfilling His Word goes beyond our spiritual highs and lows, different moods, or anything else. Romans 5:1 and all of God's other statements are true based on who He is, not on our feelings at a particular time.

Finally, the fall of Jerusalem and the accompanying horrible circumstances are not the only judgments God has promised. For those of us who live on this side of the cross, God has promised a future judgment. Paul wrote in 2 Cor 5:9–10:

> *Therefore we also have as our ambition, whether at home or absent, to be pleasing to Him. For we must all appear before the judgment seat of Christ,*

*so that each one may be recompensed for his deeds in the body, according
to what he has done, whether good or bad.*

Furthermore, in Rev 20:11–15, God promises the following judgment
to the lost of all ages:

*Then I saw a great white throne and Him who sat upon it, from whose pres-
ence earth and heaven fled away, and no place was found for them. And I
saw the dead, the great and the small, standing before the throne, and books
were opened; and another book was opened, which is the book of life; and
the dead were judged from the things which were written in the books, according to their deeds. And the sea gave up the dead which were in it,
and death and Hades gave up the dead which were in them; and they were
judged, every one of them according to their deeds. Then death and Hades were thrown into the lake of fire. This is the second death, the lake of
fire. And if anyone's name was not found written in the book of life, he was
thrown into the lake of fire.*

How do we know that God will perform these judgments and that
this is a literal judgment of the damned who will be cast into literal hell?
One important reason emerges among many: approximately eight hundred years before the actual events occurred, God had raised up the Babylonians, who would besiege Jerusalem in the future, setting the stage
for the literal fulfillment of His Word. In doing so, God emphasized His
great faithfulness, as Lamentations 3 so clearly proclaims: "Great is Your
faithfulness!"

Conclusion

In this chapter we continued to learn more specific biblical truths and see
in an ever-expanding way the interwoven connections and cohesions of
the Word of God. First, the promised and prophesied fall and destruction
of Jerusalem and the burning of God's temple in Jer 39:1–10 provides
the background for Lam 3:23 as Jeremiah laments with tears the terrible
atrocities he had just witnessed. Second, structurally Lamentations is a
V-shape, with everything on both sides pointing to chapter 3. Third, in
context, Lam 3:23, "Great is Your faithfulness," is stated in the very midst
of God's promised and severe judgment—not God's promised blessing.

These statements, then, are more declarations of faith. Fourth, given the precision with which God fulfilled His promised judgment, the burden of proof lies with those who would spiritualize future blessings that God has promised for the people He has thus judged. We should expect the same pinpoint precision in God eventually fulfilling all the promises He has given in His Word, such as the future regathering of national Israel back to the land God had given them that concludes this section of the blessing and the curse (Lev 26:40–45). Finally, the same God who promised judgment on national Israel under the Mosaic covenant, as we saw in Lamentations, likewise promises future judgments. For those of us saved this side of the cross, we are promised that we must all appear before the judgment seat of Christ to give an account for all that we have done (2 Cor 5:9–10). Finally, in Rev 20:11–15, Jesus will render His judgment on the eternally damned who will stand before Him.

Deeper Walk Study Questions

1. To get biblical truths, why would it not be good to begin with Lam 3:20–23? What would be omitted biblically? In keeping with this, why must the greater context and meaning of Israel being under the Mosaic covenant be considered in studying Lamentations? How would that help keep you from doing sheer application of the text?

2. Specifically, what were the pertinent warnings God gave in Leviticus 26 and Deuteronomy 28 as they relate to Lamentations? How do these support the literal-grammatical hermeneutic? Explain. List five important truths from this section.

3. How did God use the formatting of the book of Lamentations to convey spiritual truths? Why is this important in how He arranged the book? Explain and be specific.

4. How do chapters 2 and 4 support the literal-grammatical hermeneutic from what was promised by God in the blessing and the curse? Be specific.

5. Considering the greater context and the near context, how do the truths found in Lam 3:20–23 stand out even more? Why is this important? Explain.

6. What do God's precise warning and literal fulfillment tell you about other judgments that God has promised? How is this helpful? Explain, giving five reasons.

CHAPTER 15

As I Live, I Shall Be King over You[1]

As we have previously seen, when Nebuchadnezzar and the Babylonians surrounded Jerusalem, but before the city fell, two partial deportations had transpired, allowed by God in His sovereignty. The first group deported in 605 BC included the young prophet Daniel; the second deportation in 597 BC included Ezekiel the prophet. Both men would play important roles not only in ministering to the exiles in Babylon, but also as vessels through whom God would reveal great biblical truths and prophecies about the future of Israel, the future of the entire world, and, even greater, the future advent and reign of Messiah. This last chapter will, due to space limitations, limit itself to the prophetic ministry of Ezekiel.

God's Revelation About His Glory Given to Ezekiel

As was true for the prophets Jeremiah and Daniel, part of Ezekiel's ministry occurred before Jerusalem and God's temple were destroyed and part of it occurred after Jerusalem fell and "the times of the Gentiles" (Luke 21:24) began. To the small faithful remnant of Israel, and to the world at large, because of what would take place in the future with God's holy city and the Jewish people, it must have seemed that God had abandoned Israel. Yet the prophecies God reveals amid the pending slaughter and destruction show not only that He is far from finished with the Jews or the

---

[1] For free audio downloads of matters associated with this chapter: http://www.glorybooks.org/weve-been-expecting-you-part-1/.

Gentiles, but also that He supremely remained in sovereign control over all things. The book of Ezekiel opens with this backdrop:

> *Now it came about in the thirtieth year, on the fifth day of the fourth month, while I was by the river Chebar among the exiles, the heavens were opened and I saw visions of God.*
>
> *(On the fifth of the month in the fifth year of King Jehoiachin's exile, the word of the LORD came expressly to Ezekiel the priest, son of Buzi, in the land of the Chaldeans by the river Chebar; and there the hand of the LORD came upon him.) (Ezek 1:1–3)*

We see from this passage that (1) Ezekiel was "among the exiles"; (2) also in exile in Babylon was a Davidic covenant king, Jehoiachin, whom God would use to preserve the Davidic covenant lineage, even during "the times of the Gentiles"; and (3) God's revelation came to "Ezekiel the priest" (1:3). This last part is important. Ezekiel would have been trained all of his life to serve as a priest in God's temple. As such, he would be completely familiar with all the matters pertaining to the layout of the temple, the sacrifices, and the priestly services. He would have an understanding of these priestly matters that an average person would not have.

The remainder of Ezekiel 1 is a vision from God, in which God appears with some of His angels (Ezek 1:4–21), accompanied by a description in more detail as they appear closer to Ezekiel (Ezek 1:22–27). Repeatedly throughout this chapter, the words "like" or "something like" are used, because human words were inadequate to accurately describe this revelation. The explanation of what God showed Ezekiel is given in Ezek 1:28: "As the appearance of the rainbow in the clouds on a rainy day, so was the appearance of the surrounding radiance. Such was the appearance of the likeness of the glory of the LORD. And when I saw it, I fell on my face and heard a voice speaking."

Ezekiel 1 will also serve as the backdrop for another section of revelatory visions in Ezek 8–11. Beginning in Ezek 8:1–4 the prophet made the appropriate connection with what God previously had permitted him to witness:

> *And it came about in the sixth year, on the fifth day of the sixth month, as I was sitting in my house with the elders of Judah sitting before me, that*

> *the hand of the Lord GOD fell on me there. Then I looked, and behold, a*
> *likeness as the appearance of a man; from His loins and downward there*
> *was the appearance of fire, and from His loins and upward the appearance*
> *of brightness, like the appearance of glowing metal. And He stretched out*
> *the form of a hand and caught me by a lock of my head; and the Spirit lifted*
> *me up between earth and heaven and brought me in the visions of God to*
> *Jerusalem, to the entrance of the north gate of the inner court, where the*
> *seat of the idol of jealousy, which provokes to jealousy, was located. And*
> *behold, the glory of the God of Israel was there, like the appearance which I*
> *saw in the plain.*

Several important matters should be noted. First, marking the time of
the opening verse by using our calendar would place this vision in the year
592 BC, six years before the actual destruction of Jerusalem and God's
temple. Second, remember that Ezekiel was a priest, so when God took
him in a vision from Babylon into God's temple, Ezekiel needed no explanation from God about what he saw. Third, Ezekiel saw and marked the
importance of his vision in Ezek 8:4: "And behold, the glory of the God of
Israel was there, like the appearance which I saw in the plain."

Before progressing further we note how the glory of God had first
played an important part with God's tabernacle and centuries later at the
dedication of God's temple. Exodus 40:34–38 shows what took place
when all was completed for God's tabernacle:

> *Then the cloud covered the tent of meeting, and the glory of the LORD filled*
> *the tabernacle. Moses was not able to enter the tent of meeting because*
> *the cloud had settled on it, and the glory of the LORD filled the tabernacle.*
> *Throughout all their journeys whenever the cloud was taken up from over*
> *the tabernacle, the sons of Israel would set out; but if the cloud was not*
> *taken up, then they did not set out until the day when it was taken up. For*
> *throughout all their journeys, the cloud of the LORD was on the taberna-*
> *cle by day, and there was fire in it by night, in the sight of all the house of*
> *Israel.*

Even Moses, who spoke to God face-to-face as one would speak to a
friend (Exod 33:11), could not enter into the tabernacle once God filled it
with His glory. Similarly, the same event and same restrictions occurred
with the dedication of God's temple, as 2 Chr 7:1–3 shows:

*Now when Solomon had finished praying, fire came down from heaven
and consumed the burnt offering and the sacrifices, and the glory of the
Lord filled the house. The priests could not enter into the house of the Lord
because the glory of the Lord filled the Lord's house. All the sons of Israel,
seeing the fire come down and the glory of the Lord upon the house, bowed
down on the pavement with their faces to the ground, and they worshiped
and gave praise to the Lord, saying, "Truly He is good, truly His lovingkindness is everlasting."*

Beginning with Moses and later with God's priests, who were Ezekiel's predecessors, no one could enter God's tabernacle as long as His
glory resided there. The reference to God's glory in His temple in the
opening verses of Ezekiel 8, then, becomes important because in Ezekiel
8–11 God was prepared to remove His glory from His temple in a somber
three-part removal.

After showing Ezekiel the horrible sins occurring in His very own
house, God then showed in the vision what was to happen, all ultimately
relating to His glory. In this part of the vision in Ezek 9:1–3, God called for
divine angelic executioners who would come, but this also marks the first
stage of God removing His glory from the holy of holies:

*Then He cried out in my hearing with a loud voice saying, "Draw near, O
executioners of the city, each with his destroying weapon in his hand." Behold, six men came from the direction of the upper gate which faces north,
each with his shattering weapon in his hand; and among them was a certain
man clothed in linen with a writing case at his loins. And they went in and
stood beside the bronze altar.*

*Then the glory of the God of Israel went up from the cherub on which it had
been, to the threshold of the temple. And He called to the man clothed in
linen at whose loins was the writing case.*

As a divine preview of what would soon occur, as we saw in Jeremiah
and Lamentations, in Ezek 9:4–7 God revealed what He was going to do:

*The Lord said to him, "Go through the midst of the city, even through the
midst of Jerusalem, and put a mark on the foreheads of the men who sigh
and groan over all the abominations which are being committed in its
midst." But to the others He said in my hearing, "Go through the city after
him and strike; do not let your eye have pity, and do not spare. Utterly slay*

old men, young men, maidens, little children, and women, but do not touch
any man on whom is the mark; and you shall start from My sanctuary."
So they started with the elders who were before the temple. And He said to
them, "Defile the temple and fill the courts with the slain. Go out!" Thus
they went out and struck down the people in the city.

Ezekiel's reaction is recorded in Ezek 9:8: "As they were striking the
people and I alone was left, I fell on my face and cried out saying, Alas,
Lord GOD! Are You destroying the whole remnant of Israel by pouring out
Your wrath on Jerusalem?'"

God's response then comes in Ezek 9:9–10:

Then He said to me, "The iniquity of the house of Israel and Judah is very,
very great, and the land is filled with blood, and the city is full of perver-
sion; for they say, 'The LORD has forsaken the land, and the LORD does not
see!' But as for Me, My eye will have no pity nor will I spare, but I will
bring their conduct upon their heads."

Continuing in this vision, God showed Ezekiel the second stage of the
removal of His glory:

Now the cherubim were standing on the right side of the temple when the
man entered, and the cloud filled the inner court. Then the glory of the LORD
went up from the cherub to the threshold of the temple, and the temple was
filled with the cloud and the court was filled with the brightness of the glory
of the LORD. (Ezek 10:3–4)

In Ezek 11:1–12 God previewed His pending annihilating judgment
on the wicked Jewish leaders. This revelation caused Ezekiel to cry out for
the second time for fear that God would destroy the entire remnant. Consider Ezek 11:13: "Now it came about as I prophesied, that Pelatiah son of
Benaiah died. Then I fell on my face and cried out with a loud voice and
said, 'Alas, Lord GOD! Will You bring the remnant of Israel to a complete
end?'"

Ezekiel's cry and concern that God would destroy the entire Jewish
remnant became the basis for God's answer for what He would do in the
future. With judgment just a few years away and His wrath ready to be
poured out, instead of destroying the Jewish remnant, as Ezekiel feared,
God spoke about a future grace and the benefits that would come to them.

In what is clearly stated using the same spiritual benefits of the eventual new covenant that God has also revealed in Jeremiah 30–33, Ezek 11:14–21 promises:

> Then the word of the LORD came to me, saying, "Son of man, your broth-ers, your relatives, your fellow exiles and the whole house of Israel, all of them, are those to whom the inhabitants of Jerusalem have said, 'Go far from the LORD; this land has been given us as a possession.' Therefore say, 'Thus says the Lord GOD, "Though I had removed them far away among the nations and though I had scattered them among the countries, yet I was a sanctuary for them a little while in the countries where they had gone."' Therefore say, 'Thus says the Lord GOD, "I will gather you from the peoples and assemble you out of the countries among which you have been scattered, and I will give you the land of Israel."' When they come there, they will remove all its detestable things and all its abominations from it. And I will give them one heart, and put a new spirit within them. And I will take the heart of stone out of their flesh and give them a heart of flesh, that they may walk in My statutes and keep My ordinances and do them. Then they will be My people, and I shall be their God. But as for those whose hearts go after their detestable things and abominations, I will bring their conduct down on their heads," declares the Lord GOD.

CORE TRUTH: Those who maintain that God is completely finished with the Jewish people and that they have no hope and play no role in God's future plans have to explain exactly what God meant by the Ezek 11:14–21 promise if He did not fully intend to keep every word of His promises made here. Those whose interpretation is contrary to the plain teaching of this text must explain what God intended to convey to Ezekiel and to others—and why—by using language that clearly shows future hope. If God intended no future hope for national Israel, how will they determine if any of God's promises are to be understood in a literal manner?

On the heels of the previous God-given promises and with no more fanfare, the following takes place in Ezek 11:22–25:

*Then the cherubim lifted up their wings with the wheels beside them, and the glory of the God of Israel hovered over them. The glory of the L*ORD *went up from the midst of the city and stood over the mountain which is east of the city. And the Spirit lifted me up and brought me in a vision by the Spirit of God to the exiles in Chaldea. So the vision that I had seen left me. Then I told the exiles all the things that the L*ORD *had shown me.*

I note a few crucial matters from Ezekiel 11. First, this is the last time that the glory of God appears in the Old Testament. Second, the removal of God's glory was necessary. If Moses and later God's priests could not enter the temple because of God's glory, it would have been impossible for the Gentile invaders to have entered. That God removed His glory meant that the Gentile invaders could destroy His temple, if He allowed them to. Third, God's temple functioned for about six years without His glory being present, but the people and much of the priesthood were so consumed with their sins that they neither noticed nor cared that such consequential events had transpired. Fourth, the story is by no means over. The glory of God will play an eternal part in the person and work of Jesus the Messiah, but we will have to wait for a chapter in the New Testament section of this book to address this issue.

God's Additional Revelation Given to Ezekiel After God Removed His Glory

Before the news that Jerusalem had fallen, God gave the following vision to Ezekiel that has incredibly far-reaching consequences. God is sure of both His and national Israel's destiny, proclaiming in Ezek 20:33–40 His declarative will for the rebellious Jewish people:

*"As I live," declares the Lord G*OD, *"surely with a mighty hand and with an outstretched arm and with wrath poured out, I shall be king over you. I will bring you out from the peoples and gather you from the lands where you are scattered, with a mighty hand and with an outstretched arm and with wrath poured out; and I will bring you into the wilderness of the peoples, and there I will enter into judgment with you face to face. As I entered into judgment with your fathers in the wilderness of the land of Egypt, so I will enter into judgment with you," declares the Lord G*OD. *"I will make you pass*

*under the rod, and I will bring you into the bond of the covenant; and I will
purge from you the rebels and those who transgress against Me; I will bring
them out of the land where they sojourn, but they will not enter the land of
Israel. Thus you will know that I am the LORD.*

*"As for you, O house of Israel," thus says the Lord GOD, "Go, serve every-
one his idols; but later, you will surely listen to Me, and My holy name you
will profane no longer with your gifts and with your idols. For on My holy
mountain, on the high mountain of Israel," declares the Lord GOD, "there
the whole house of Israel, all of them, will serve Me in the land; there I shall
accept them, and there I will seek your contributions and the choicest of
your gifts, with all your holy things."*

At some future time, if God's Word is true, the following must take
place as part of the Davidic covenant promises and other prophecies, as
God emphatically stated in Ezek 20:33: "'As I live,' declares the Lord
GOD, "surely with a mighty hand and with an outstretched arm and with
wrath poured out, I shall be king over you.'" Also, all the other prophecies
that God previously made must come true, and those from Ezek 20:33–40
harmonize with God bringing the people back into the land (Lev 26:40–
45) and back to Himself in the effects seen in the new covenant (Deut
30:1–10; Jer 31:31–34). If God does not make these happen, He is not
God; He is therefore bound by His own word to accomplish what He said
He would do.

Ezekiel 33 is of special importance, and we should mark it accordingly. News finally arrived in Babylon of Jerusalem's downfall, which
we have seen in Jeremiah 39 and Lamentations. Ezekiel 33:21 reports the
following: "Now in the twelfth year of our exile, on the fifth of the tenth
month, the refugees from Jerusalem came to me, saying, 'The city has
been taken.'" However, the next verse, revealed what God had done the
night before, "Now the hand of the LORD had been upon me in the evening, before the refugees came. And He opened my mouth at the time they
came to me in the morning; so my mouth was opened, and I was no longer
speechless." What follows is another set of prophecies in Ezekiel 34–39,
which should be viewed as one section of the book. Far from abandoning
the Jewish people forever because of the sins that they had committed,
God instead made promises for their future restoration, in Ezek 36:22–32:

*"Therefore say to the house of Israel, 'Thus says the Lord G*OD*, "It is not for your sake, O house of Israel, that I am about to act, but for My holy name, which you have profaned among the nations where you went. I will vindicate the holiness of My great name which has been profaned among the nations, which you have profaned in their midst. Then the nations will know that I am the L*ORD*," declares the Lord G*OD*, "when I prove Myself holy among you in their sight. For I will take you from the nations, gather you from all the lands and bring you into your own land. Then I will sprinkle clean water on you, and you will be clean; I will cleanse you from all your filthiness and from all your idols. Moreover, I will give you a new heart and put a new spirit within you; and I will remove the heart of stone from your flesh and give you a heart of flesh. I will put My Spirit within you and cause you to walk in My statutes, and you will be careful to observe My ordinances. You will live in the land that I gave to your forefathers; so you will be My people, and I will be your God. Moreover, I will save you from all your uncleanness; and I will call for the grain and multiply it, and I will not bring a famine on you. I will multiply the fruit of the tree and the produce of the field, so that you will not receive again the disgrace of famine among the nations. Then you will remember your evil ways and your deeds that were not good, and you will loathe yourselves in your own sight for your iniquities and your abominations. I am not doing this for your sake," declares the Lord G*OD*, "let it be known to you. Be ashamed and confounded for your ways, O house of Israel!"*

God continued with additional connective prophecies in Ezek 36:33–38:

*'Thus says the Lord G*OD*, "On the day that I cleanse you from all your iniquities, I will cause the cities to be inhabited, and the waste places will be rebuilt. The desolate land will be cultivated instead of being a desolation in the sight of everyone who passes by. They will say, 'This desolate land has become like the garden of Eden; and the waste, desolate and ruined cities are fortified and inhabited.' Then the nations that are left round about you will know that I, the Lord, have rebuilt the ruined places and planted that which was desolate; I, the L*ORD*, have spoken and will do it."*

*'Thus says the Lord G*OD*, "This also I will let the house of Israel ask Me to do for them: I will increase their men like a flock. Like the flock for sacrifices, like the flock at Jerusalem during her appointed feasts, so will the waste cities be filled with flocks of men. Then they will know that I am the L*ORD*."'*

In Ezek 39:17–29, God also promised a future restoration in part of the same section of the visions (Ezekiel 34–39) that God gave before Jerusalem fell:

"As for you, son of man, thus says the Lord God, 'Speak to every kind of bird and to every beast of the field, "Assemble and come, gather from every side to My sacrifice which I am going to sacrifice for you, as a great sacrifice on the mountains of Israel, that you may eat flesh and drink blood. You will eat the flesh of mighty men and drink the blood of the princes of the earth, as though they were rams, lambs, goats and bulls, all of them fatlings of Bashan. So you will eat fat until you are glutted, and drink blood until you are drunk, from My sacrifice which I have sacrificed for you. You will be glutted at My table with horses and charioteers, with mighty men and all the men of war," declares the Lord God.

"And I will set My glory among the nations; and all the nations will see My judgment which I have executed and My hand which I have laid on them. And the house of Israel will know that I am the Lord their God from that day onward. The nations will know that the house of Israel went into exile for their iniquity because they acted treacherously against Me, and I hid My face from them; so I gave them into the hand of their adversaries, and all of them fell by the sword. According to their uncleanness and according to their transgressions I dealt with them, and I hid My face from them."'"

Therefore thus says the Lord God, "Now I will restore the fortunes of Jacob and have mercy on the whole house of Israel; and I will be jealous for My holy name. They will forget their disgrace and all their treachery which they perpetrated against Me, when they live securely on their own land with no one to make them afraid. When I bring them back from the peoples and gather them from the lands of their enemies, then I shall be sanctified through them in the sight of the many nations. Then they will know that I am the Lord their God because I made them go into exile among the nations, and then gathered them again to their own land; and I will leave none of them there any longer. I will not hide My face from them any longer, for I will have poured out My Spirit on the house of Israel," declares the Lord God.

Conclusion and Transition

With all of the prophecies that God has given thus far in our study, plus the many others we did not address, God has chosen to bind Himself by His own word to show Himself holy, powerful, and strong among the Jewish people, and ultimately to all of the Gentile nations. As we have seen in these prophecies in Ezekiel, God repeatedly draws attention to the truth that the Gentiles will know that He did this when He shows Himself as Yahweh, as God Almighty by fulfilling every word of all the promises and prophecies He has made. Failure to do so on God's part shows Him to be, in essence, evil, because if He does not do what He said He would do, He is a liar, and thus not holy—and thus not God. The character of God is at stake; His story is by no means over—and He takes this very seriously.

So as we pause at this portion of Scripture, it would be inconclusive to say that we have come to the end of anything biblical concerning the Lord and His Messiah, national Israel, and ultimately the entire world. Yahweh clearly promises that He will eventually vindicate His holy name that the Jewish people have defiled among all the Gentiles. After all, as Jesus would ultimately say of Himself, in a very real sense of the word, we are progressing to "the Beginning." So we end here scripturally, to ponder on what we have seen in even a small portion of God's promises up to this chapter in the *Handbook*, and we look ahead to the New Testament text.

The best connective one-sentence description between the ending of the Old Testament and the beginning of the New Testament will also be the name of the first chapter in the New Testament section of this book:

We've Been Expecting You

Deeper Walk Study Questions

1. What is the significance of the time marker given in Ezek 8:1 as it relates to that immediate setting? Why is this important? Give five biblical truths related to this as it relates to what had happened historically and what was about to happen.

2. What can we learn about God's glory with His tabernacle and later with His temple? List eight biblical truths from this and explain why each is important.

3. Instead of God destroying the entire Jewish remnant, He promised future blessing in Ezek 11:14–21. Itemize each blessing given by God and summarize all the blessings collectively. Did God actually mean what the text says? How do you know? Support your answer biblically.

4. Why did God have to remove His glory from His temple before Jerusalem fell? Why is this important biblically? Explain.

5. What did God mean by what He said in Ezek 20:33–40? List each item individually and then formulate a summary of these promises. Did Yahweh actually mean what He said? How do you know this? Explain and support you answer.

6. What is the importance of the two historical time markers in Ezek 33:21–22? Why are these important for understanding Ezekiel 34–39? Explain and be specific.

7. What did Yahweh specifically promise in Ezek 36:22–32? List each item and give a summary description of what God promised. Is there any biblical reason not to understand these promises using a literal-grammatical hermeneutic? Explain and support your answer.

8. What did Yahweh specifically promise in Ezek 36:33–38? List each item and give a summary description of what God promised. Is there any biblical reason not to understand these promises using a literal-grammatical hermeneutic? Explain and support your answer.

9. Itemize the promises Yahweh gave in Ezek 39:17–29. How does God say that He will use these promises for the Jewish people and for all the Gentiles to know about him? Did He really mean what He promised? How do you know? Support your answer biblically.

10. Considering what you have studied in the Old Testament section of this book, why is "We've Been Expecting You" the best summary and transition statement between the two testaments? From what you have learned in these fifteen chapters, list at least fifty biblical truths that God has given in reference to His Messiah.

PART 2
THE NEW TESTAMENT

CHAPTER 16

We've Been Expecting You[1]

A bout forty years ago, when I was in my early twenties, I taught eighth grade English in a public school for four years in Garner, North Carolina. I had either just gotten saved or else was saved earlier and then did the prodigal son route throughout college. I will find out when I get to heaven exactly when I was saved. Still, even at this early part of my Christian walk, I had a keen desire to know what the Bible said and what it meant. In a time before the Internet existed and without many other resources that are available now, two other teachers and I sat in a circle, started in Matt 1:1, and made our way through a few verses. With each verse, we told the others, "This is what this verse means to me." We were the blind leading the blind, and fortunately no recordings were made of our well-intended folly. We each had the King James Version for our Bible and had to work through all the "begats" in Matthew 1 (e.g., v. 2 "Abraham begat Isaac"). We only met a few times. As before, our motives were good, but our methodology was woefully lacking. We will tie this in with another example in a moment, but let's consider one core truth for our study: "This is what this verse means to me" is totally irrelevant to biblical truth; however, "This is what God means by this verse"—if understood accurately (2 Tim 2:15)—is eternally important.

Fast-forward two decades later to a time when I was blessed to teach three years at a pastors' conference in Kenya that included more than two hundred attendees. Many of the pastors had walked for days to come and

---

[1] Free audio downloads of matters associated with this chapter: http://www.glorybooks.org/weve-been-expecting-you-part-1/.

study the Bible; for most of them, it was the only training they would receive that year. Also, many of the pastors only had a pocketsize Gideons New Testament. The conference provided Bibles for the pastors who needed them, and what a delight to watch some of the pastors read Genesis 1 for the first time.

We three well-intended teachers who did their Bible study starting in Matthew 1 actually—by default—did what many of the Kenyan pastors did and many well-meaning Christians today still do: anyone who begins a study of the Bible in Matthew 1 will be just as lacking as we were because of three irreplaceable doctrinal truths. First, if we begin in Matthew 1, we do not begin where Jesus did previously in John 5:46 ("For if you believed Moses, you would believe Me, because he wrote about Me"). Second, later on the day of His resurrection, Jesus revealed to the two road-to-Emmaus disciples, in Luke 24:25–27, the importance of the Old Testament in its witness of Him:

> And He said to them, "O foolish men and slow of heart to believe in all that the prophets have spoken! Was it not necessary for the Christ to suffer these things and to enter into His glory?" Then beginning with Moses and with all the prophets, He explained to them the things concerning Himself in all the Scriptures.

And He would likewise do this with the assembled apostles, in Luke 24:44–47:

> Now He said to them, "These are My words which I spoke to you while I was still with you, that all things which are written about Me in the Law of Moses and the Prophets and the Psalms must be fulfilled." Then He opened their minds to understand the Scriptures, and He said to them, "Thus it is written, that the Christ would suffer and rise again from the dead the third day, and that repentance for forgiveness of sins would be proclaimed in His name to all the nations, beginning from Jerusalem."

If we begin studying the Bible in Matthew 1, (1) we do not start where Jesus started, and (2) we do not know or mark any of the tremendously important Old Testament prophetic truths in reference to the Person and work of who the Messiah would be or the scriptural qualifications and requirements that the Messiah must fulfill if He is to truly qualify as God's

Messiah. So, our final irreplaceable doctrinal truth connects with this: (3) we do not know of any previous promises and prophecies that God had given for the Jewish people and ultimately that they effect the entire world—as well as anyone ever born. If we begin our study in Matthew 1, we do not know that we are starting—at the very least—in mid-story, oblivious to many of the doctrinal truths God has already revealed, especially as seen in His covenants that He made and many divine prophecies contained within and beyond these verses.

Further, the noble Berean believers are often cited—for good reason—as using the proper mode of investigating the teaching of others. In Acts 17:11, "Now these [people of Berea] were more noble-minded than those in Thessalonica, for they received the word with great eagerness, examining the Scriptures daily to see whether these things were so." The Scriptures they were examining were the Old Testament Scriptures, which began setting forth the story of Jesus and the covenant faithfulness of God. The New Testament would flesh out and fulfill much of the story of Jesus and—and, as we will clearly see in Scripture—so many more precise promises and prophecies still remain to be fulfilled on this side of the cross.

The Stirring Up by Way or Reminder and Transitioning to the New Testament

When Peter was just about to die, he wrote 2 Peter, using a large part of it to counter the teachings of false teachers. Peter protectively wrote to certain churches in Asia Minor in 2 Pet 1:12–15:

> *Therefore, I will always be ready to remind you of these things, even though you already know them, and have been established in the truth which is present with you. I consider it right, as long as I am in this earthly dwelling, to stir you up by way of reminder, knowing that the laying aside of my earthly dwelling is imminent, as also our Lord Jesus Christ has made clear to me. And I will also be diligent that at any time after my departure you will be able to call these things to mind.*

The same will be true for us.

Ideally, before we start the next part of our study, everyone has read the Old Testament section of this book where—in the space of only fifteen chapters—I tried to set forth a logical progression that feeds into the New Testament and this initial chapter in this section. I know, however, this is not the case. So, if you are able, read the Old Testament edition first, and if you are not able to do that, at least read the Scripture verses we covered. Ideally you should do this first because, as we saw, starting your study of the Bible anywhere in the New Testament is starting mid-story and is removed from many of the promises and prophecies of God, especially as He showed in His covenants.

Does Anybody Really Know What Time It Is?

I must note two crucial time markers for our reading and understanding God's Word as we approach our study of the New Testament. One time marker we have seen already (or you can find) in the Old Testament section in the chapter about the Mosaic covenant, namely, Gal 4:4–5: "But when the fullness of the time came, God sent forth His Son, born of a woman, born under the Law, so that He might redeem those who were under the Law, that we might receive the adoption as sons." The ramifications from these verses are tremendously important. For Jesus to be "born of a woman, born under the Law" is another way of saying that Jesus was born under the benefits and obligations of the Mosaic covenant, as all of the Jewish people were of His day. That meant the Mosaic covenant, which was ratified in Exodus 24, was fully functional and mandatory for national Israel from the birth of Jesus all the way through the remainder of His life in the incarnation.

CORE TRUTH: I have seen some people have a difficult time grasping this biblical truth initially, but when you open your Bible to Matthew 1, even though on that page or one before it says "the New Testament," technically speaking Matthew is not yet the New Testament as it relates to time. The book of Matthew opens on Old Testament times; that is, the Mosaic covenant was fully operative and binding for the Jewish people. As we saw earlier in our studies and will see later in much more detail, at the death of Jesus, God will change this.

Let's consider a few ways in which we will clearly see the importance of the Gal 4:4–5 time marker. When you open your Bible to the New Testament at Matthew 1, Jesus was born of a woman, born under the Law; that means His earthly parents were born under the Mosaic covenant, and, consequently, they were as much under covenant obligation as any other Jew was from Exodus 24 to that time. Luke 2:21–22 gives one demonstration that Joseph and Mary faithfully kept God's commands under the Mosaic covenant:

> *And when eight days had passed, before His circumcision, His name was then called Jesus, the name given by the angel before He was conceived in the womb. And when the days for their purification according to the law of Moses [the Mosaic covenant] were completed, they brought Him up to Jerusalem to present Him to the Lord.*

Also, if Jesus was born of a woman, born under the Law, then that meant His cousin, John the Baptist, the promised forerunner of the Messiah, was also born under the Mosaic covenant. Thus, John is the last of the Old Testament prophets—not the first of the New Testament prophets.

So, the Mosaic covenant had a definitive beginning with Moses (Exodus 24) and a definitive ending with the death of Jesus. This was all part of the Godhead's predetermined plan and the foreknowledge of God, decided by them before the foundation of the world. The precise time when God wanted this was "in the fullness of time" (Gal 4:4).

The second crucial time marker comes from Jesus toward the end of His incarnation. In the latter part of Luke 21:24, Jesus declared, "Jerusalem will be trampled under foot by the Gentiles until the times of the Gentiles are fulfilled." The times of the Gentiles goes all the way back to 586 BC to the destruction of Jerusalem and God's temple by the Babylonians. King Zedekiah was the last "son of David" to sit on David's throne as part of the Davidic covenant. Simply put, Israel has not had a Davidic covenant heir sit on David's throne from then to the present time and, as you will see later in our studies, all the way into the tribulation, the reign of the Antichrist, and the return of Jesus to earth. So, during the lifetime of Jesus, He was born under the Mosaic covenant, but He was also born during the times of the Gentiles, with Israel having no Davidic covenant king reigning. The king reigning when the New Testament opens was King Herod, who was a usurper, not of the Davidic covenant lineage.

Once you drop down into the world of Scripture, as much as you can, verses that you have read many times often take on new importance. For instance, the opening verse in the Christmas story, Luke 2:1 states, "Now in those days a decree went out from Caesar Augustus [the Gentile ruler during the times of the Gentiles], that a census be taken of all the inhabited earth," that is, of the entire Roman Empire. The Jewish people had no recourse but to follow what they were commanded to do because even though they did not refer to it this way, this is part of the hardships of living under Gentile power and domination. However, God in His sovereignty used worldwide events so that Joseph and Mary would travel to Bethlehem because this was the small city where the Messiah was to be born (Mic 5:2), and thus a messianic promise—and requirement—would be fulfilled.

So, the times of the Gentiles specifically refers not only to the Jewish people but also to Jerusalem, which will be "trampled under foot by the Gentiles until the times of the Gentiles are fulfilled." This revelation by Jesus gives us this crucial time marker that Jerusalem will not always be trampled by the Gentiles. The Bible clearly and repeatedly shows that this will one day end, as you will see in much more detail in this edition of the *Handbook*.

Second, you can look to the city of Jerusalem—especially up to current worldwide events—and mark this in our biblical doctrine: Jerusalem will play an incredibly important role in the fulfillment of God-ordained eschatological events, from the reign of the Antichrist up to the return of Jesus Christ to earth. You will clearly see this in upcoming chapters in this edition of *The Bible Expositor's Handbook*.

KEY TRUTH: As long as you see Jerusalem trampled underfoot by the nations, you can be certain that the times of the Gentiles still exist. So when we look at the news, we are not surprised about all of the turmoil in the Middle East—especially concerning Jerusalem. There is currently a pagan mosque on the Temple Mount. You will see more about such matters later in our studies and why this is so important in the life and ministry—and reign—of King Jesus.

Summary and Conclusion

Chapter 1 in this edition of the *Handbook* is a broad review of the content from what was covered in *The Bible Expositor's Handbook—Old Testament* edition. While this is a stirring up by way of reminder for some, it is new information for many. Whichever the case, this initial chapter in the book is a transition into our studying the New Testament. (1) With even what we broadly reviewed from the Old Testament in this opening chapter, I hope you see without any hesitation how woefully lacking our understanding of God and His Word and works would be if we start our Bible studies in Matthew 1, we do not know we are starting—at the very least—in mid-story, and (2) we are oblivious to many of the doctrinal truths God has already revealed, especially as seen in His covenants that He made and divine prophecies contained within and beyond these verses. (3) The irreplaceable starting point for becoming an expositor of God's Word is God Himself, and there are no shortcuts to becoming a seasoned expositor. It takes time and effort to "grow in the grace and knowledge of our Lord and Savior Jesus Christ" (2 Pet 3:18). Without being overtly mystical about this, if you think you will ever outgrow this initial core concept that being a disciple means being a person who is ultimately taught by God, you will not have any true ministry resulting from your walk with Him. (4) The Old Testament is—rather than was—the story of Jesus because so much of it remains yet to be fulfilled by the same God who has already fulfilled the first part with His holy precision. (5) In asking how there can be so many different interpretations of the Bible, the way someone answers the two following simple questions gives a clear indication for how the rest of Scripture will be interpreted by them. First, what is the first covenant of God in the Bible, and what are the hermeneutics used to interpret it? And second, what is the second covenant of God in the Bible, and what are the hermeneutics used to interpret it? (6) The two important safeguards for studying Old Testament texts to see if they correctly apply to the Messiah are two questions. First, is there a direct New Testament text(s) that clearly shows the Holy Spirit intended this to be in reference to the Messiah? Second, if no New Testament parallel texts exist, who appears that is exhibiting the attributes of God or doing the activities of God? (7) With regard to the Mosaic covenant, it is first the first and only covenant of God so far for which somebody else was present and active at its ratification. Second, as long as the Mosaic covenant was in effect, the Jewish people of national Israel were under covenant obligation to do all that Yahweh commanded them to do. Third, the Mosaic covenant included the "blessing-and-curse" section of Leviticus 26 (and Deuteronomy 27–28), where God promised to bless national Israel if they walked in covenant obedience with Him and enumerated specific curses that would surely come upon them if they did rebel against Him. Fourth, we noted the eschatological importance of Lev 26:40–45, which ended with hope given by God to the Jewish people, especially in reference to a future regathering of national Israel to the land, based throughout this section on the land promises God had made—and would keep—under the Abrahamic covenant. (8) We explored the ways in which Scripture progressively builds on itself by harmonizing with, and expanding on, previous God-given promises. We saw that first, Numbers 22–24 is God's word, not Balaam's word; second, this text repeatedly refers to national Israel as a people; and third, the blessing or cursing that the Gentile king Balak wanted Balaam to perform is at the heart of the Abrahamic covenant promises and is a direct challenge to Yahweh's authority and domain (e.g., Gen 12:3; Num 24:9). So, fourth, the character of God is at stake if Balaam is allowed to curse those whom God has not cursed. Finally, fifth, Numbers 22–24 adds additional revelatory light that expands and harmonizes with God's previous promises about His Messiah. Accordingly, the Christmas account featuring the wise men is not based on one isolated prophecy but a series of prophecies, most of which have yet to be fulfilled; many of them await the second coming of the Messiah. And because God fulfilled the star promise of Num 24:17, we can have confidence that He will do so with the remaining promises.

In this chapter we also saw that (9) we cannot start with the battle of Jericho (Joshua 6) and hope to be remotely accurate in interpreting Scripture. The significance of this epic battle is understood only in light of, first, the land promises that God had made under the Abrahamic covenant (Gen 13:14–17; 15:12–21; 17:7–8), and second, the reality that national Israel was under the Mosaic covenant, and in this covenant, as part of the blessing and the curse, God promised national Israel military victories if they were obedient to Him (Lev 26:7–8; Deut 28:7). Accordingly, God responded exactly as He had promised, bringing national Israel back into covenant fellowship with Him, as seen in Joshua 5—before God's actions against Jericho began. (10) Instead of all the land promises being fulfilled by Josh 21:41–43 and/or 1 Kgs 4:20–21, the Bible clearly, repeatedly, and persistently presents just the opposite. It does so in a way that beautifully harmonizes with previous God-given prophecies (see Lev 26:40–45; Deut 30:1–10). In fact, nothing indicates that these prophecies had been fulfilled by the time of Solomon's life or even up to our present time. Not only are these land boundary promises originally given in the Abrahamic covenant and reiterated in the Mosaic covenant and in the opening of the book of Joshua, but the Bible again presents the Euphrates River as the northern boundary for the nation of Israel long after 1 Kings 4. More important, twice the Euphrates River also specifically relates to the Messiah's reign, first in Ps 72:8, and then centuries afterward in the midst of the times of the Gentiles in Zech 9:10. In both cases the Euphrates River will be the northern boundary of Israel for His worldwide rule. So harmonious are God's prophecies regarding the land promise to national Israel under the Abrahamic covenant, that if one did not know of an existing interpretational controversy regarding whether the land promises had been completely fulfilled by the time of Josh 21:41–43 and/or 1 Kgs 4:20–21, one would never surmise this from the text. Also, (11) Josh 24:15 is often used as an evangelistic sermon: "Choose for yourselves today whom you will serve . . . as for me and my house, we will serve the LORD." However, the context clearly moves the interpreter beyond a merely evangelistic application. This passage was not, then, an invitation for national Israel to come and meet the unknown God; rather, it was a call for national Israel of Joshua's generation to repent and walk in covenant obedience with Yahweh, especially because they were already under the Mosaic covenant. We noted the importance of tracing a line back to Shechem (Josh 24:1), an event that is even more significant when viewed in light of Deut 27:1–13. So, when one comes to Joshua 24, the nation has been there before. Yet this time, instead of having the nation divided with half of the people standing on Mount Gerizim and half on Mount Ebal, they were gathered at Shechem and looked out at the Mount of Blessing and the Mount of Cursing and were faced, yet again, with the decision to choose whom they would serve:

the gods of their past and their present false gods or Yahweh. If the people were to serve Yahweh, they had to take definitive actions to do so, such as putting away their false gods.

In this chapter we also saw (12) that although many would not deem it so, David's victory over Goliath clearly was not an upset. In David's victory over Goliath, God had not established the odds; God had previously revealed and announced this outcome long before the 1 Samuel account. It should also be noted that nothing that God has promised, or its ultimate fulfillment, should be taken in any way other than the normative, literal-grammatical hermeneutic. God's initial promise to curse the ones who curse Israel (Gen 12:3), His promise to curse Amalek for attacking Israel (Exodus 17), His reiteration of these promises in Numbers 22–24, and His additional warnings for national Israel not to forget to fulfill the promised destruction of the Amalekites up through 1 Samuel 13 all make perfect sense with the normative use of language. Further, when Goliath cursed Israel by his gods in 1 Sam 17:43, the Gen 12:3 and Num 24:9 curse rested on him as well. With David walking in covenant obedience to Yahweh under the Mosaic covenant, the military outcome was already determined before the two warriors ever faced each other. Additionally, with God's pinpoint precision of both his pronouncement and fulfillment, we can confidently expect Him to continue fulfilling His Word in the normative, literal-grammatical hermeneutic as it relates to future prophecies and their fulfillment. Also, with the faithfulness of Yahweh to honor His Word up to 1 Samuel 17, "the Replacement" of Replacement Theology has not happened by this point in Scripture, and the burden of proof is on those who would spiritualize the fulfillment of the related prophecies before or after David's victory over Goliath and with those who would curse national Israel today.

In this chapter we also were shown (13) that the Davidic covenant has far-reaching theological significance and prophetic implications for the coming of God's promised Messiah. First, God used the historical account of David wanting to build God a house (a physical structure; 2 Sam 7:1–7) to promise David that God would instead build him a house (a lineage of descendants) in what would eventually become the Davidic covenant (vv. 8–17). Second, the promises inherent in the Davidic covenant were "concerning the distant future" (v. 19). Third, God promised that He would establish the throne of His kingdom forever (v. 13). Fourth, Psalm 89 reaffirms "the forever promises" of the Davidic covenant (vv. 1–2, 28–29, 30–37), even though no one sat on David's throne when the psalm was written (vv. 38–52). Fifth, the Davidic covenant secures the Messiah's right to rule over all the world, as Psalm 2 shows. Sixth, Matthew's Gospel uniquely emphasizes the ways in which Jesus Christ meets and fulfills the requirements of the Davidic covenant. Seventh, Luke's Gospel reinforces the ways in which the eternal promises God made in the Davidic covenant apply to Jesus. Eighth, Paul's introduction to Romans (1:1–4), and later his death-row epistle of 2 Timothy 2 (vv. 1–8), point to God's promises made to the Davidic covenant heir, Jesus Christ. Ninth, the Davidic covenant promises most certainly would have been something that Jesus taught concerning Himself in Luke 24. Tenth and finally, Matt 1:1 begins and Rev 5:1–5 and 22:16 end the New Testament with Davidic covenant references and reminders, thus bookending the New Testament with Davidic covenant promises of Who and what is to come.

We reviewed in this chapter (14) the biblical concepts of true worship and true biblical wisdom and showed the importance of building a biblical definition from the text versus imposing on it a definition not taken from Scripture—which many people do, still referring to their definitions as "this is what the Bible teaches." (15) While many Christians consider a paraphrasing of Jer 29:11 to be a personal life-verse ("I know the plans that I have for you," declares the LORD, ". . . to give you a future and a hope"), we saw how verse 11 as a whole, and indeed its entire context, is important for understanding what God intended by this particular promise. First, the setting of the book of Jeremiah shows national Israel living in brazen covenant disobedience to Yahweh. Exile was looming for the Jewish people, as God had previously warned (Lev 26:31–33). Yet God promised an eventual return at some undisclosed point in the future (vv. 40–45). Second, Jeremiah 2–29 contains fourteen messages of mostly condemnation of national Israel for their wickedness as well as repeated calls for them to return and repent. Third, Jer 29:1–10 reminds the exiles in Babylon that God Himself had sent them there; that they should unpack and live there, given that the exile would last seventy years, after which time He would return "and fulfill [His] good word to [them]." Fourth, with this background in mind, verse 11 makes sense only for the Jewish people; it is not meant as a life verse for a New Testament believer. In addition to this, we also studied (16) how dropping down into the world of the passage from which the beautiful hymn "Great Is Thy Faithfulness" is based shows an entirely different background to the concept than most people realize. First, the promised and prophesied fall and destruction of Jerusalem and the burning of God's temple in Jer 39:1–10 provide the background for Lam 3:23 as Jeremiah laments with tears the terrible atrocities that he had just witnessed. Second, Lamentations is a V-shape structurally, with everything on both sides pointing to chapter 3. Third, in context, Lam 3:23, "Great is Your faithfulness," is stated in the very midst of God's promised and severe judgment—not during a joyous time of receiving God's blessings. These statements, then, are more declarations of faith in the midst of horrid devastation. Fourth, given the precision with which God fulfilled His promised judgment, the burden of proof lies with those who would spiritualize future blessings that God has promised for the same Jewish people He has thus judged.

We saw with all of the prophecies that God has given thus far in our study—plus the many others I did not address—that (17) God has chosen to bind Himself by His own word to show Himself holy, powerful, and strong not only among the Jewish people but ultimately to all of the Gentile nations. In Ezek 20:33, Yahweh promised the Jewish people, "As I live . . . surely with a mighty hand and with an outstretched arm and with wrath poured out, I shall be king over you." He further informed the Jewish people—and the world—in Ezek 36:22–23,

> Therefore say to the house of Israel, "Thus says the Lord GOD, 'It is not for your sake, O house of Israel, that I am about to act, but for My holy name, which you have profaned among the nations where you went. I will vindicate the holiness of My great name which has been profaned among the nations, which you have profaned in their midst. Then the nations will know that I am the Lord,' declares the Lord GOD, 'when I prove Myself holy among you in their sight.'"

In these and other prophecies in Ezekiel, God repeatedly draws attention to the truth that the Gentiles will know that He did this when He shows

Himself as Yahweh, and thus as God Almighty, by fulfilling every word of all the promises and prophecies He has made, thus vindicating His holy name that national Israel had profaned among the nations. Failure to do so on God's part would show Him to be, in essence, evil, because if He does not do what He said He would do, He is a liar, and thus not holy—and thus not God. The character of God is at stake; His story is by no means over—and He takes this quite seriously.

Finally, we saw (19) two very important time indicators that will greatly help our understanding of where we are scripturally. The first one is Gal 4:4–5: "But when the fullness of the time came, God sent forth His Son, born of a woman, born under the Law, so that He might redeem those who were under the Law, that we might receive the adoption as sons." The ramifications of these verses are tremendously important. For Jesus to be "born of a woman, born under the Law" is another way of saying that Jesus was born under the benefits and obligations of the Mosaic covenant, as all of the Jewish people were. That meant that the Mosaic covenant, which was ratified in Exodus 24, was fully functional and mandatory for national Israel from the birth of Jesus all the way through the remainder of His life in the incarnation. The second crucial time marker comes from Jesus toward the end of His incarnation. In the latter part of Luke 21:24, Jesus declared, "Jerusalem will be trampled underfoot by the Gentiles until the times of the Gentiles are fulfilled." The times of the Gentiles go all the way back to 586 BC to the destruction of Jerusalem and God's temple by the Babylonians. King Zedekiah was the last "son of David" to sit on David's throne as part of the Davidic covenant. National Israel has not had a Davidic covenant heir who could sit on David's throne all the way up to the present time, and as you will see later in our studies, this absence extends all the way into the tribulation, the reign of the Antichrist, and the return of Jesus to earth. So during the earthly life of Jesus, He was born under the Mosaic covenant, but He was also born during the times of the Gentiles, with Israel having no Davidic covenant king reigning. The king reigning when the New Testament opens is King Herod, who was a usurper; he was not of the Davidic covenant lineage.

Deeper Walk Study Questions

1. Name five theological hazards facing anyone who does Bible study by saying, "This is what this verse means to me."

2. From just what we have seen in John 5:45–46 and twice in Luke 24, list five ways that whoever begins his studies in Matthew 1 is starting mid-story in the story of Jesus. Why are these important? Explain.

3. What is the meaning and significance of the statement, "The Old Testament is—not was—the story of Jesus"? List four reasons why knowing this is important.

4. Explain why there are so many different interpretations of the Bible. Does it really come down to just two questions? Support your answer with five biblical points.

5. How is understanding the Mosaic covenant important to understanding other places in the Bible? Show ways it helps explain other passages.

6. Why is going only to Numbers 24 for the star at the Christmas story such an incomplete understanding of the text? List five substantial truths from Numbers 22–24.

7. List eight ways that Josh 21:43–44 and 1 Kgs 4:20–21 do not show that God has fulfilled the land promises of the Abrahamic covenant. Also, why is it wrong biblically to point to both passages together as proof of God's fulfillment?

8. List seven ways that we know that Josh 24:15, "Choose for yourselves today whom you will serve . . . as for me and my house, we will serve the LORD," was not originally used as an evangelistic sermon.

9. Give six biblical reasons why David's victory over Goliath was not an upset.

10. List eight biblical reasons why the Davidic covenant is so important to understanding the Bible.

11. How does Jeremiah 29 ("I know the plans I have for you . . .") look entirely different when studied in its context as opposed to the way it is often applied today? Show six reasons biblically and explain why each one is important.

12. How different is the hymn "Great Is Thy Faithfulness" when viewed with the text it was taken out of in Lamentations? How does the context for the book show this? Give six ways and tell why these are important.

13. Why is the promise by God in Ezek 20:33 and 36:22 so important in understanding what God has promised? List six items God promised and tell why each of these are important.

14. What is the biblical significance of the two time markers that we saw in Gal 4:4–5 and Luke 21:24? Give three biblical reasons for each one with regard to why knowing this is so important to understanding the Bible.

CHAPTER 17

The Gospel According to Isaiah

One of the hardest things about writing *The Bible Expositor's Handbook—Old Testament Edition* was to decide what to put in and what to leave out. I was limited to fifteen chapters; I think I could have written two-hundred-plus chapters, given the space and the time to do it—such is the richness of God's Word. Even the book of Isaiah did not make the Old Testament version of the *Handbook*, but I properly reserved a place for this in the New Testament edition because so much of God's revelation from Isaiah factors into many places in the New Testament. Also, the study of Isaiah by itself could be a three-to-four-volume book. It is not my purpose to attempt to cover every verse in Isaiah, nor even every Isaiah verse that is cited in the New Testament, but we will glean crucial verses that contribute to our understanding of God's progressive revelation in the New Testament. You will see in this chapter that (1) your understanding of the Bible would be seriously deficient were you to omit some of the key prophecies from Isaiah, (2) how Jesus quoted Isaiah or how the Gospel writers quoted Isaiah at crucial places about Jesus in Scripture, and that (3) these prophecies in Isaiah were some of the prophecies Jesus used to point to Himself in Luke 24:27, as we saw previously, when beginning with Moses and referring to all the prophets, "He explained to them the things concerning Himself."

A Broad Walk through the Book of Isaiah

The book of Isaiah was written approximately seven hundred years before the birth of Jesus Christ. Thus, when God set forth His Word by means of Isaiah, the Jewish people had Davidic covenant heirs sitting on David's throne; consequently, "the times of the Gentiles" had not begun, which means the temple had not yet been destroyed. Also, the Jewish people were under the Mosaic covenant blessings, restrictions, and warnings, but most of the Jewish people—including most of their kings—were not in covenant obedience to Yahweh and, thus, had experienced different parts of the curse section of the Mosaic covenant (Leviticus 26; Deuteronomy 27–28) but not the exile yet.

When we go through Isaiah in our class, we follow the natural layout of the book by noting that chapters 36–39 have a historical interlude that was written in the same genre as is true for Bible books such as Joshua and Judges. This section is a good divider for us, so broadly speaking,

Isaiah 1–35
- The section has an Assyrian world power vantage point.
- Nineveh, where Jonah had been sent by God, was Assyria's capital.
- This section of Isaiah is primarily judgment based on the Jewish people's sins under the Mosaic covenant, yet it is interspersed with glimpses of future blessings by God.

Isaiah 36–39
The historical interlude starts from the Assyrian vantage point but switches to a Babylonian vantage point. Babylon was not then the dominant Gentile world power, but it would become that power.

Isaiah 40–66
- The Babylonian perspective would primarily be future events when Isaiah wrote this.
- Where Isaiah 1–35 was mostly judgment with glimpses of future blessing, chapters 40–66 are the opposite: *primarily blessing,* with some judgment interwoven, but blessing that is not automatic.
- The last section of Isaiah divides beautifully and symmetrically:

- Isaiah 40–48 *Theology Proper*—the doctrine of God; the utter truthfulness of God and His Word, especially when contrasted with idols.
- Isaiah 49–57 *Soteriology*—the doctrine of salvation; Isaiah 53 is included in this section, which is familiar to many Christians.
- Isaiah 58–66 *Eschatology*—the doctrine of end times, both judgments and blessings.

CONSIDER: It is a worthwhile study in the New Testament to mark quotes from Isaiah 40–66, noting which of the three sections they are under: theology proper, soteriology, or eschatology. We will see this at appropriate places in our study.

A few other boundary markers remain that we need to note. Isaiah 1–5 is the panoramic overview of the book of Isaiah. Everything within the book of Isaiah can be found in chapters 1–5 and will be expounded in more detail in the remaining chapters of the book. Also, Isaiah 6 is the commissioning of Isaiah, which we will study in another chapter of the *Handbook*.

Studying Isaiah 7–12 will serve us well because it is frequently referred to as the "Book of Immanuel." Each chapter contains at least one messianic promise. These chapters will be our launching pad into the New Testament because the prophecies in these chapters clearly point to God's promised Messiah, Jesus Christ.

KEY: Whenever you encounter a New Testament quote from Isaiah 7–12, look for specific messianic promises to be cited, fulfilled, etc. These will play an important part in our present study. However, do not wrongly conclude that Isaiah 7–12 contains all the messianic prophecies; many other messianic prophecies that Jesus either has already fulfilled or will fulfill in the future are found throughout much of the entire book.

Initial Uses of Isaiah in the Gospels

With this background, we can now examine pertinent uses of Isaiah in the Gospels. We will start in Matthew 1. We need to note how Matthew begins his Gospel in 1:1: "The record of the genealogy of Jesus the Messiah, the son of David, the son of Abraham." Two important points occur here. First, there is a switching of the normal flow of what occurred historically. If he were to be chronologically accurate, Matthew would have written, the son of Abraham (Abrahamic covenant first), the son of David (the Davidic covenant second). So, second, switching of the order of the two covenant references is intentional. What this chronological altering of alignment signifies is that the Gospel of Matthew puts the emphasis primarily on Jesus as the One who alone qualifies to be the true Son of David, the Messiah; everything in Matthew presents God's attestation regarding His Messiah whom He sent. Matthew 1 has, for example, the genealogy that establishes the lineage of Jesus traced through the Davidic covenant heirs. From a human standpoint, Jesus's lineage qualifies Him to be the Davidic covenant heir.

Now we get to see our first usage of Isaiah in Matthew's Gospel, namely Matt 1:18–21:

> Now the birth of Jesus Christ was as follows: when His mother Mary had been betrothed to Joseph, before they came together she was found to be with child by the Holy Spirit. And Joseph her husband, being a righteous man and not wanting to disgrace her, planned to send her away secretly. But when he had considered this, behold, an angel of the Lord appeared to him in a dream, saying, "Joseph, son of David [Davidic covenant lineage], do not be afraid to take Mary as your wife; for the Child who has been conceived in her is of the Holy Spirit. She will bear a Son; and you shall call His name Jesus, for He will save His people from their sins."

CONSIDER: Even with Matthew's Gospel presenting Jesus as the promised King/Messiah of Israel, part of His God-ordained mission is also to be the One who "will save His people from their sins." Most of the Jewish people would not expect this part for the Messiah. We know, living well past the original giving of Acts 2:22–23, that in the

> predetermined plan and foreknowledge of God, the Messiah must be a Savior first. However, the Savior must also reign as King and Messiah. Many people ignore this last part, but they should not. The promised reign of Jesus Messiah is as much a biblical doctrine from God as that He did all that was necessary for the forgiveness of sins to take place.

Now mark carefully the explanation of the significance of what just occurred as seen in Matt 1:22–23: "Now all this took place to fulfill what was spoken by the Lord through the prophet: ' BEHOLD, THE VIRGIN SHALL BE WITH CHILD AND SHALL BEAR A SON, AND THEY SHALL CALL HIS NAME IMMANUEL,' which translated means, 'GOD WITH US.'"

Note several relevant truths from this Scripture. Initially, the quote is from Isa 7:14, appropriately taken from the Book of Immanuel (Isaiah 7–12), and this verse is one of the reasons this section is called that. Second, this explains biblically that Immanuel signifies the incredible truth about the grace gift of God being with us. Third, this shows the divine process. As seen in the Old Testament edition of the *Handbook,* it was not Balaam's word in Numbers 22–24; it was God's word by means of Balaam. The same is true for Isa 7:14 (and for other such uses): they "fulfill what was spoken by the Lord [the true source] through the prophet [the human instrument]." So we will see that these will not be Isaiah's prophecies; these will be God's prophecies through His faithful servant Isaiah. The prophet did not generate any of this on his own—neither prophecies nor reasons; God alone did.

Our second use of Isaiah is found in Matt 3:1–3, which quotes from Isa 40:3:

> *Now in those days John the Baptist came, preaching in the wilderness of Judea, saying, "Repent, for the kingdom of heaven is at hand."*
>
> *For this is the one referred to by Isaiah the prophet, when he said, "THE VOICE OF ONE CRYING IN THE WILDERNESS, 'MAKE READY THE WAY OF THE LORD.'"*

Before looking more at the particulars, we need to note one more important item out of Isaiah. I did not do this earlier for fear of information overload. Now is the right time to note that Isa 40:3 occurs in the chapters

40–48 section on theology proper, the doctrine of God, but in the same way that we saw that Isaiah 1–5 was a panoramic overview of the remainder of the book, 40:1–11 is a panoramic overview of the remainder of chapters 40–66. The first eleven verses of Isaiah 40 contain truths that the remaining chapters will enlarge, including soteriology (the doctrine of salvation) as well as eschatology (the doctrine of last things).

All four Gospels contain a reference to Isa 40:3 to explain who John the Baptist was, what he was doing, and why he was doing it (Mark 1:3; Luke 1:76; Luke 3:3–6 cites Isa 40:3–5). In John 1:22–23, John the Baptist Himself used Isa 40:3 to establish his identity and ministry:

> Then they said to him, "Who are you, so that we may give an answer to those who sent us? What do you say about yourself?" He said, "I am A VOICE OF ONE CRYING IN THE WILDERNESS, 'MAKE STRAIGHT THE WAY OF THE LORD,' as Isaiah the prophet said."

All four of the Gospels use Isa 40:3 directly to refer to John the Baptist, authenticating both his identity and his ministry. But here is an observation to consider: if all four Gospels use Isa 40:3, why do none of them use verses 1–2? In other words, neither John the Baptist nor any of the four Gospel writers cite Isa 40:1–2 to indicate that part of John the Baptist's God-ordained ministry consisted of any of the following:

> "Comfort, O comfort My people," says your God.
>
> "Speak kindly to Jerusalem;
>
> And call out to her, that her warfare has ended,
>
> That her iniquity has been removed,
>
> That she has received of the LORD's hand,
>
> Double for all her sins."

We can answer this question biblically; it is a question that often is not asked but should be. From what we have studied in the previous chapter, when John the Baptist proclaimed that the kingdom of heaven/God is at hand, that would mean (1) the Davidic covenant heir is at hand, (2) as well as the pending kingdom of God's Messiah who will sit on David's throne, (3) whose ruling will end the times of the Gentiles, which had begun about six hundred years earlier (Luke 24:21), resulting in (4) Jerusalem never again being trampled underfoot by the Gentiles (Jer 31:38–40). However, Isa 40:1–2 was not cited by John the Baptist, nor by the Gospel writers, about himself and his mission because these events had not occurred before nor at the time of the arrival of the Messiah's forerunner. These prophecies continue to remain unfulfilled and must take place at some point in the future: (1) speak kindly to Jerusalem (2) because her warfare has ended [it has not yet ended], (3) her iniquity has been removed [it has not been removed], and (4) she has received from the Lord's hand double for her sins [this has not yet happened]. These truths will take place in the eschatological section of Isaiah (chaps. 58–66), and as we will see, God gives many more details later in other biblical books, ending with the book of Revelation.

> **CRUCIAL:** Liberal scholars do not believe in divine revelation. Many of them do not believe only one prophet wrote Isaiah 1–35, and other scholars believe, especially because the tone changes to the future, that other authors wrote this section and all of the alleged authors put this together into one prophecy that they named "Isaiah." They claim some of the prophecies—such as the naming of Cyrus in Isaiah 44–45—is so precise that it must have been written *after* the fact but made to appear as a prophecy, and is thus a lie. By the time we come to Matt 3:1–3, both sections of Isaiah have been presented: Matt 1:22–23 from Isa 7:14 and Matt 3:3 from Isaiah 40. Beware! Everyone will believe some one or some thing (like an oracle). God has set His truths before the world, and both quotes so far are attributed to Isaiah the prophet—singular. This is either 100 percent true or 100 percent false. God is either lying or telling the truth, but no other option exists. I hope you have already eternally set your foundation on the holy and true Word of the holy and true God. Never are these prophecies presented as "Isaiah the Committee." This is another one of the either/or scenarios in the Bible. There is no middle ground, and whether you believe or not will affect your theology—and in varying degrees, your eternity as well.

Our third use of Isaiah is found in Matt 4:12–17, with the citation of Isaiah taken from the Book of Immanuel section, namely Isa 9:1–2:

> *Now when Jesus heard that John had been taken into custody, He withdrew into Galilee; and leaving Nazareth, He came and settled in Capernaum, which is by the sea, in the region of Zebulun and Naphtali. This was to fulfill what was spoken through Isaiah the prophet:*

> "THE LAND OF ZEBULUN AND THE LAND OF NAPHTALI
>
> BY THE WAY OF THE SEA, BEYOND THE JORDAN, GALILEE OF THE GEN-
>
> TILES—"THE PEOPLE WHO WERE SITTING IN DARKNESS SAW A GREAT LIGHT,
>
> AND THOSE WHO WERE SITTING IN THE LAND AND SHADOW OF DEATH,
>
> UPON THEM A LIGHT DAWNED."

> *From that time Jesus began to preach and say, "Repent, for the kingdom of heaven is at hand."*

Let us think through some pertinent factors about where these verses go in our understanding of God and His Word. We just saw Isa 9:1–2 cited in Matt 4:12–17. But here is something interesting: Isa 9:6–7—which is often read during Christmas Eve or Christmas Day services, and appropriately so—is never cited in the New Testament.

> *For a child will be born to us, a son will be given to us;*
>
> *And the government will rest on His shoulders;*
>
> *And His name will be called Wonderful Counselor, Mighty God,*
>
> *Eternal Father, Prince of Peace.*
>
> *There will be no end to the increase of His government or of peace,*
>
> *On the throne of David and over his kingdom,*
>
> *To establish it and to uphold it with justice and righteousness*
>
> *From then on and forevermore.*
>
> *The zeal of the LORD of hosts will accomplish this.*

The answer as to why these verses are not cited in the New Testament is that the only thing that has come true historically is the first line: "For a child will be born to us, a son will be given to us." The last part is a prophecy that directly relates some of the specifics of the Davidic covenant.

When these verses will be fulfilled, "there will be no end to the increase of His government or of peace"; "on the throne of David and over his kingdom," He will establish it (because it has not yet been established). When the Davidic covenant King establishes His kingdom, it will be eternal: "from then on and forevermore." Finally, God declares with certainty that not only will these events occur, but that He Himself will bring them about: "The zeal of the LORD of hosts will accomplish this." None of these wonderful promises from God occurred on the night Jesus was born, nor even in any of the remaining days of His incarnation. Every one of these messianic prophecies must be fulfilled—literally—or God is not God and the Bible is not His Word. Because Isa 9:6–7 remains presently unfulfilled, these prophecies must be fulfilled at the second coming of Jesus the Messiah.

> **CONSIDER:** For Orthodox Jews—from the Pharisees who lived when Jesus lived, such as the rich young ruler to Saul of Tarsus, before he became Paul the Christian and apostle, up to the present time—one of the greatest stumbling blocks is their conclusion that the Messiah is to be the Son of David (the human part) only and not the Son of God, and certainly not God in the flesh. Isaiah 9:6–7 are appropriate verses to use with Jewish evangelism because these verses so clearly set forth matters relating to the Messiah who will sit on David's throne and establish His kingdom. This same section describes the Messiah as "mighty God" and "eternal Father"—both descriptions are Godhead designations. Whoever will have these names and attributes of deity must in the same manner become "a child . . . born to us, a son . . . given to us"—and this has already taken place—and His name is Jesus.

But we need to address one other important item: who is the "us" implied in "a child will be born to us" and "a son will be given to us"? This cannot refer to the Gentiles/nations because they have already been addressed earlier in Matt 4:15: "BY THE WAY OF THE SEA, BEYOND THE JORDAN, GALILEE OF THE GENTILES—THE PEOPLE WHO WERE SITTING

IN DARKNESS SAW A GREAT LIGHT" (see Isa 9:1–2). This is a major point to consider not only for properly understanding the book of Isaiah but for properly interpreting much of the Bible.

God clearly sets out by means of Isaiah, who is identified in 1:1, "The vision of Isaiah the son of Amoz concerning Judah and Jerusalem which he saw during the reigns of [the Davidic covenant heirs and Jesus' forefathers] Uzziah, Jotham, Ahaz, and Hezekiah, kings of Judah." It does not mean that other people cannot benefit from this wonderful book of the Bible, including the other tribes of the twelve tribes of Israel, and ultimately Gentiles as well. But Isa 1:1 clearly states that the prophet is writing concerning Judah—the tribe that God designated to give birth to the Messiah under the Davidic covenant—and Jerusalem, which will play such an important part in both His first and second comings, as seen in 2:1–4:

> *The word which Isaiah the son of Amoz saw concerning Judah and Jerusalem [almost identical to the wording of Isa 1:1].*
>
> *Now it will come about that*
>
> *In the last days,*
>
> *The mountain of the house of the LORD*
>
> *Will be established as the chief of the mountains,*
>
> *And will be raised above the hills;*
>
> *And all the nations will stream to it.*
>
> *And many peoples will come and say,*
>
> *"Come, let us go up to the mountain of the LORD,*
>
> *To the house of the God of Jacob;*
>
> *That He may teach us concerning His ways,*
>
> *And that we may walk in His paths."*
>
> *For the law will go forth from Zion,*
>
> *And the word of the LORD from Jerusalem.*
>
> *And He will judge between the nations,*
>
> *And will render decisions for many peoples;*
>
> *And they will hammer their swords into plowshares*
>
> *and their spears into pruning hooks.*

Nation will not lift up sword against nation,

And never again will they learn war.

None of Isaiah's prophecies in 2:1–4 came true during the lifetime of Jesus, nor have they yet been fulfilled, and it must be "concerning Judah and Jerusalem" and "in the last days." The nations certainly will still "learn war" during the tribulation, as we will see in our chapters on Revelation. But if you literally accept the prophecies, such as a virgin birth (Isa 7:14; Matt 1:22–23), the ministry of John the Baptist (Isa 40:3–4), and that the Gentiles will see a great light (9:2), why would you switch your hermeneutics to understand 1:1 and 2:1–4 as figurative language or subject them to an allegorical interpretation only? How would you decide whether or not the part from 7:14 was only figurative as well, and that God never intended to convey the virgin birth as one of the characteristics—and requirements—of the Messiah, thus trying to make Jesus anyone other than the One as the Bible presents Him, if you started allegorizing certain specific promises of God? This is precisely how the early Gnostics attacked many churches in the first century as well as how many liberal theologians over the centuries have incorrectly interpreted this Scripture, who removed much about the person and work of Jesus in a normative use of the language.

Another important use of Isaiah is found in Luke 4. Verses 1–13 are the account of Satan's temptation of Jesus, in which Satan utterly failed. So, after this initial segment of satanic temptation ended, the following took place in verses 14–21:

And Jesus returned to Galilee in the power of the Spirit, and news about Him spread through all the surrounding district. And He began teaching in their synagogues and was praised by all. And He came to Nazareth, where He had been brought up; and as was His custom, He entered the synagogue on the Sabbath, and stood up to read. And the book of the prophet Isaiah was handed to Him. And He opened the book and found the place where it was written,

"THE SPIRIT OF THE LORD IS UPON ME,

BECAUSE HE ANOINTED ME TO PREACH THE GOSPEL TO THE POOR.

HE HAS SENT ME TO PROCLAIM RELEASE TO THE CAPTIVES,

AND RECOVERY OF SIGHT TO THE BLIND,

TO SET FREE THOSE WHO ARE OPPRESSED,

TO PROCLAIM THE FAVORABLE YEAR OF THE LORD."

And He closed the book, gave it back to the attendant and sat down; and the eyes of all in the synagogue were fixed on Him. And He began to say to them, "Today this Scripture has been fulfilled in your hearing."

We need to see specifically where Jesus turned in the book of Isaiah the prophet: "He opened the book and found the place where it was written"—what Jesus did was purposeful and not a random reading of the scroll in a synagogue on the Sabbath. Jesus turned to 61:1–2:

The Spirit of the Lord GOD is upon me,

Because the LORD has anointed me

To bring good news to the afflicted;

He has sent me to bind up the brokenhearted,

To proclaim liberty to captives,

And freedom to prisoners;

To proclaim the favorable year of the LORD,

And the day of vengeance of our God;

To comfort all who mourn.

Notice specifically what Jesus did not do. He read only the first part of Isa 61:2 but not beyond that. The Spirit of the Lord God was surely upon Him, having anointed Him at His baptism. Part of the ministry of Jesus was to bring good news to the afflicted, to bind up the brokenhearted, to proclaim liberty to captives, to set free prisoners free, and to proclaim the favorable year of the Lord in sending His promised Messiah to earth to accomplish this part of God's plan and program.

But mark well precisely where Jesus stopped reading and that He refused to read further from the scroll that day past the middle part of Isa 61:2. He did this because during the incarnation, when He came as the Servant of Yahweh, offering Himself and His gospel, it was not then—and still is not yet—"the day of vengeance of our God," nor time "to comfort all [who are truly His] who mourn." These will occur with events that will most certainly come true one day, but they will all be directly tied to the second coming of Jesus Christ to earth—not to events that happened during His First Advent.

I end this chapter with one more use of Isaiah in Matthew 12. By this time, Jesus had presented Himself as authoritatively speaking God's Word (Matthew 5–7), showing His power over the realms of sickness, demons, and death. While many people rejoiced to see His day, many others grew in hostility against Him—especially the religious leaders of Jesus's time. In Matthew 12, Jesus had to address a controversy about what could be done on the Sabbath. He concluded that section with a verse that will be key with what follows in the account: "For the Son of Man is Lord of the Sabbath" (v. 8) With that background, the following took place in verses 9–21:

> *Departing from there, He went into their synagogue. And a man was there whose hand was withered. And they questioned Jesus, asking, "Is it lawful to heal on the Sabbath?"—so that they might accuse Him. And He said to them, "What man is there among you who has a sheep, and if it falls into a pit on the Sabbath, will he not take hold of it and lift it out? How much more valuable then is a man than a sheep! So then, it is lawful to do good on the Sabbath." Then He said to the man, "Stretch out your hand!" He stretched it out, and it was restored to normal, like the other. But the Pharisees went out and conspired against Him, as to how they might destroy Him. But Jesus, aware of this, withdrew from there. Many followed Him, and He healed them all, and warned them not to tell who He was. This was to fulfill what was spoken through Isaiah the prophet:*

> "BEHOLD, MY SERVANT WHOM I HAVE CHOSEN;

> MY BELOVED IN WHOM MY SOUL IS WELL-PLEASED;

> I WILL PUT MY SPIRIT UPON HIM,

> AND HE SHALL PROCLAIM JUSTICE TO THE GENTILES.

> HE WILL NOT QUARREL, NOR CRY OUT;

> NOR WILL ANYONE HEAR HIS VOICE IN THE STREETS.

> A BATTERED REED HE WILL NOT BREAK OFF,

> AND A SMOLDERING WICK HE WILL NOT PUT OUT,

> UNTIL HE LEADS JUSTICE TO VICTORY.

> AND IN HIS NAME THE GENTILES WILL HOPE."

The Isaiah quote is from Isa 42:1–4 and is taken from the first of four sections that are called "The Servant of Yahweh Songs," or simply "The Servant Songs" (Isa 42:1–9), although they are not really songs. Isaiah 53 is part of these Servant Songs and is probably the most recognizable for many people.

I hope that you can see why this chapter was entitled "The Gospel According to Isaiah." Although we have completed this chapter, the book of Isaiah will continue to play a major role in many other chapters of our study in *The Bible Expositor's Handbook—New Testament*.

Summary and Conclusion

Among other matters in this chapter, we have seen (1) how inadequate our understanding of the New Testament would be without at least some understanding of the book of Isaiah. (2) The broad divisions of Isaiah include chapters 1–35, primarily judgment due to sins with some promised blessings mixed in, and the historical interlude of chapters 36–39, and the third major division, which consists of primarily blessings with some judgment passages within this section as well. (3) Isaiah 7–12 is often referred to as the Book of Immanuel because every chapter contains at least one reference to God's promised Messiah. We also noted that while chapters 7–12 are quite important to understanding much of the New Testament, quotes from Isaiah show up beyond these chapters. (4) The first use of Isaiah in the New Testament occurs appropriately in the first chapter in the New Testament. Matthew 1:22–23 cites the virgin conception as the fulfillment of Isa 7:14. We also saw the means that God used: God was the source of the truth and the human prophet was the mouthpiece God used to communicate His truth. (5) The second use of Isaiah occurs in Matt 3:1–3 (and appropriate parallel passages), with either John the Baptist answering regarding himself or else the other Gospel writers attesting to his God-ordained ministry by citing at least Isa 40:3 (Luke cited Isa 40:3–5). (6) Not one of the Gospels cites Isa 40:1–2 as tied in with the ministry of John the Baptist, nor the lifetime of Jesus. These are matters connected with the return and reign of King Jesus on earth. (7) Matthew 4:12–17 cites from the Book of Immanuel portion of Isaiah (9:1–2), acknowledging prophecies of Jesus and the Gentiles. (8) Although often read at Christmas Eve services, Isa 9:6–7 is never cited in the New Testament because other than "a child will be born to us, a son will be given to us," nothing else in this passage has been fulfilled but will be at the second coming of Jesus Messiah to earth. (9) We saw that because Isa 9:1–2 clearly refers to the Gentiles, the "us" in verses 6–7 must be the Jewish people. We also saw how twice, in Isa 1:1 and 2:1, the Scripture specifically names things written about Judah (and by extension, the other tribes of Israel) and Jerusalem, while Isa 2:2 says these things will come about "in the last days." (10) After Satan's failed temptation of Jesus (Luke 4:1–13), verses 14–21 showed Jesus specifically taking the scroll of Isaiah and turning to what would eventually be marked in the chapter divisions of the Bible, 61:1–2. But we also saw that Jesus stopped reading in the middle part of verse 2 because "the day of vengeance of our God" was not fulfilled at that time, and even up to today it has not been fulfilled. These are matters connected with the second coming of Jesus, and we will see this in much more detail in the portion of the *Handbook* that is based on Revelation. (11) Matthew 12:9–21 quotes from Isa 42:1–9, which is the first of four so-called Servant Songs of Isaiah, with Isaiah 53 being perhaps the most familiar to many people. And finally, indeed just from this limited portion we have already seen that (12) truly it is the Gospel according to Isaiah—and we will see many more important citations from Isaiah elsewhere in our study of the New Testament in this *Handbook*.

Deeper Walk Study Questions

1. Why is the Book of Immanuel so named? Where is it, and why is it important in understanding the New Testament? Also, name one safeguard against studying only from Isaiah 7–12.

2. Give the broad divisions of Isaiah. List three ways knowing how the book divides is important.

3. Matthew 1:22–23 quotes from Isa 7:14. Just knowing where this verse occurs, why
    would we consider this important? Also, what is the process God shows in His
    manner of communicating this beautiful truth? Why does this matter? Explain and be
    specific.

4. The second use of Isaiah is found in Matt 3:1–3, where here, and in the parallel
    passages, either John the Baptist or the writers of the Gospels use Isa 40:3 as showing
    John the Baptist to be the Messiah's foreordained forerunner. Why is this important to
    know? Give three reasons.

5. What is the theological significance that neither John the Baptist nor any of the
    Gospel writers cited the first two verses of Isaiah 40? Give four reasons why this
    matters, from an interpretational standpoint.

6. Matthew 4:12–17 cites from the Book of Immanuel section in Isa 9:1–2. What
    do these verses say, and why is that important? Be specific. How is this useful in
    evangelism to the nations? Explain by giving three reasons.

7. Although read at many Christmas Eve services, Isa 9:6–7, unlike the first two verses
    in this same chapter, is never cited as fulfilled in the New Testament. What part has
    come true? What parts have not come true? Why is that important? Explain and give
    four supports for your answers.

8. Isaiah 9:1–2 specifically refers to the Gentiles, but to whom does the "us" in "a child will be born to us, a son will be given to us" refer? How specifically does not only the context of Isaiah 9 but also 1:1 and 2:1–2a help show to whom this was written? Why is this important? Explain and give four supports for your answer.

9. How are attributes of who the Messiah will be useful for evangelism—to either Jews or Gentiles who see the Messiah as being only an elevated human? Give three reasons and tell why knowing these truths is important.

10. Luke 4:14–21 showed Jesus specifically looking in the scroll of Isaiah to what would eventually be called Isa 61:1–2, once chapter and verse divisions were added to Scripture. Where did Jesus read up to? What did He leave out? Give three reasons why this is important.

11. Matthew 12:9–21 quotes from Isa 42:1–9, which is the first of the so-called Servant Songs of Isaiah. Write six different ways the Messiah is presented in this section. What does this tell you about Jesus? Explain.

12. Why would this chapter of this *Handbook* be called "The Gospel According to Isaiah"? List five favorite things that you learned from this small portion of the New Testament citations from Isaiah.

CHAPTER 18

Why Do You Speak to Them in Parables?

As we see in Matthew 13 and parallel passages, Jesus began using parables in both the content and the method of delivery in His public ministry. The reason and the significance of Jesus speaking in parables make sense biblically, but to understand this, we must go back to our beloved friend, the book of Isaiah. Jesus's teaching by means of parables occurred for specific reasons, as we will see in this chapter.

The Gospel According to Isaiah

Often when teaching a class on Isaiah, I inform the students that we have "to ski over goldmines" that we do not have time to stop and enjoy in class. This present chapter is that way also, but we can at least note some of the theologically significant truths pertinent for this chapter.

Isaiah 6 is God's commissioning of Isaiah the prophet. You may not have thought about this, but this is an unusual place in Scripture to commission the prophet because it occurs in the sixth chapter. Usually, the commissioning occurs in the first chapter, as was true for Jeremiah (1:1–4) and Ezekiel (1:1–3)—but not for Isaiah. Why did God choose to put the commissioning of Isaiah in chapter 6? Does this mean that Isaiah 1–5 is uninspired? No, Isaiah 1–5 is definitely part of God-breathed Scripture and is important in understanding the book of Isaiah. As we saw in the previous chapter of the *Handbook,* Isaiah 1–5 is the panoramic overview of the entire book of Isaiah. Everything that occurs in the overview also will be found in the remaining chapters of Isaiah giving specific details and the development of these details.

Isaiah 1 itself is the panoramic overview of the panoramic overview. We saw that 1:1 presents Isaiah's prophecy as specifically given "concerning Judah and Jerusalem." It does broaden to include the remainder of the twelve tribes of Israel and, ultimately, the entire world, eventually including all of the Gentile nations. But Judah receives special attention because it is from its lineage that the Messiah will be born, and Jerusalem will play an important place in the life, death—and reign—of Jesus. Isaiah 1–35 is the main section that presents primarily denouncement and judgment on most of the Jewish people because of the extent of their wickedness, especially as seen in their Mosaic covenant violations before Yahweh, such as seen in Isa 1:4:

> *Alas, sinful nation,*
>
> *People weighed down with iniquity,*
>
> *Offspring of evildoers,*
>
> *Sons who act corruptly!*
>
> *They have abandoned the Lord,*
>
> *They have despised the Holy One of Israel,*
>
> *They have turned away from Him.*

The Jewish people's sin was incredibly deep, comparable to other wickedness found earlier in Genesis:

> *Unless the LORD of hosts*
>
> *Had left us a few survivors,*
>
> *We would be like Sodom,*
>
> *We would be like Gomorrah. (Isa 1:9)*

Isaiah 1:18 is a familiar Scripture to many and is often used for an evangelistic sermon:

> *"Come now, and let us reason together,"*
>
> *Says the LORD,*
>
> *"Though your sins are as scarlet,*
>
> *They will be as white as snow;*

Though they are red like crimson,
They will be like wool."

As we saw in the last chapter, in answering the question who is the "us" of Isa 9:6–7 and finding this to be a reference to the Jewish people, so it is in 1:18; the "us" in the "come now, and let us reason together" in its context specifically denotes the Jewish people, most of whom were not obedient to Yahweh. This was not an invitation for the Jewish nation to come forward and meet their unknown God; this invitation was for the Jewish people—already under the Mosaic covenant—to turn from their sin and return to walking in obedience with Yahweh so that they could receive the blessing part of the blessing and curse. But if the Jewish people refused to repent and failed to heed God's warnings, they would receive the curse part, as seen in Isa 1:19–20:

"If you consent and obey,
You will eat the best of the land;
"But if you refuse and rebel,
You will be devoured by the sword."
Truly, the mouth of the LORD has spoken.

Isaiah 2:1–4 refers again to Judah and Jerusalem, as part of the panoramic overview of Isaiah, and includes a description of the reign of the Messiah as part of the Davidic covenant promises that will come true "in the last days:"

The word which Isaiah the son of Amoz saw concerning Judah and
Jerusalem.
Now it will come about that
In the last days
The mountain of the house of the LORD
Will be established as the chief of the mountains,
And will be raised above the hills;
And all the nations will stream to it.
And many peoples will come and say,

"Come, let us go up to the mountain of the LORD,

To the house of the God of Jacob;

That He may teach us concerning His ways

And that we may walk in His paths."

For the law will go forth from Zion

And the word of the Lord from Jerusalem.

And He will judge between the nations,

And will render decisions for many peoples;

And they will hammer their swords into plowshares and their spears into pruning hooks.

Nation will not lift up sword against nation,

And never again will they learn war.

But rather than living in obedience to Yahweh and enjoying the accompanying blessings that He had promised—especially those that would occur during His Messiah's future kingdom—the people to whom Isaiah spoke were living in sinful wickedness, as 5:24–25 reveals:

Therefore, as a tongue of fire consumes stubble

And dry grass collapses into the flame,

So their root will become like rot and their blossom will blow away as dust;

For they have rejected the law of the LORD *of hosts*

And they despised the word of the Holy One of Israel.

On this account the anger of the LORD *has burned against His people,*

And He has stretched out His hand against them and struck them down.

And the mountains quaked, and their corpses lay like refuse in the middle of the streets.

For all this His anger is not spent,

But His hand is still stretched out.

The core of national Israel's brazen sins listed above could be summarized as "they have rejected the instruction of the LORD of Armies, and they have despised the word of the Holy One of Israel" (v. 24).

With this background and in this context, we come to Isaiah 6, which includes God's commissioning of His prophet, beginning in verse 1: "In the year of King Uzziah's death I saw the Lord sitting on a throne, lofty and exalted, with the train of His robe filling the temple."

> **REMEMBER:** In Exod 33:11 God revealed, "Thus the LORD used to speak to Moses face to face, just as a man speaks to his friend." Later, Moses beseeched God to show him His glory (Exod 33:18), to which Yahweh answered in Exod 33:20, "You cannot see My face, for no man can see Me and live." As in Exodus 33, and now in Isaiah 6, in the progressive revelation of God, there *must* be at least a two-member Godhead: One who can be seen, and One who cannot be seen. That it is actually a three-member Godhead—the Trinity—will become apparent in additional biblical revelation that God will give.

The commissioning of Isaiah continues in Isa 6:2–7:

> *Seraphim stood above Him, each having six wings: with two he covered his face, and with two he covered his feet, and with two he flew. And one called out to another and said,*
>
> *"Holy, Holy, Holy is the LORD of hosts.*
>
> *The whole earth is full of His glory."*
>
> *And the foundations of the thresholds trembled at the voice of him who called out, while the temple was filling with smoke. Then I said,*
>
> *"Woe is me, for I am ruined!*
>
> *Because I am a man of unclean lips,*
>
> *And I live among a people of unclean lips;*
>
> *For my eyes have seen the King, the LORD of hosts."*
>
> *Then one of the seraphim flew to me with a burning coal in his hand, which he had taken from the altar with tongs. He touched my mouth with it and said, "Behold, this has touched your lips; and your iniquity is taken away and your sin is forgiven."*

Isaiah 6:8 is used at many commissioning services for missionaries or for pastors: "Then I heard the voice of the Lord, saying: 'Whom shall I send, and who will go for Us?' Then I said, 'Here am I. Send me.'" Most people do not include verses 9–13 as part of their commissioning service for obvious reasons, as we see in the accompanying bewilderment that these verses produced in the prophet Isaiah. In Isa 6:9–13 God continues:

> *Go, and tell this people:*
>
> *'Keep on listening, but do not perceive;*
>
> *Keep on looking, but do not understand.'*
>
> *"Render the hearts of this people insensitive,*
>
> *Their ears dull,*
>
> *And their eyes dim,*
>
> *Otherwise they might see with their eyes,*
>
> *Hear with their ears,*
>
> *Understand with their hearts,*
>
> *And return and be healed."*
>
> *Then I said, "Lord, how long?" And He answered,*
>
> *"Until cities are devastated and without inhabitant,*
>
> *Houses are without people*
>
> *And the land is utterly desolate,*
>
> *"The Lord has removed men far away,*
>
> *And the forsaken places are many in the midst of the land.*
>
> *"Yet there will be a tenth portion in it,*
>
> *And it will again be subject to burning,*
>
> *Like a terebinth or an oak*
>
> *Whose stump remains when it is felled.*
>
> *The holy seed is its stump."*

In summarizing this chapter so far, we have seen: (1) Yahweh had presented His Word repeatedly to the Jewish people, (2) but other than the righteous remnant, the people had brazenly rejected God's Word. (3) God promised to give them additional revelation (in this context by means of Isaiah the prophet), (4) which the sinful nation will not understand. (5) Yahweh would hold the people responsible for this new revelation because

(6) Yahweh will divinely work to blind them and harden them in their own sinful spiritual condition (7) they have already chosen for themselves by living in brazen covenant disobedience before Yahweh.

Simply stated, it is a dangerous thing to reject and turn away from the Word of God.

Jesus Switches to Parables in Matthew's Gospel

Fast-forward from Isaiah's time to many centuries later in Matthew's Gospel. In 3:1–2 comes, initially from John the Baptist and then later from Jesus in 4:17, this Davidic covenant pronouncement and invitation to the Jewish people: "Repent, for the kingdom of heaven is at hand." As Matthew's Gospel unfolds, Jesus has spoken authoritatively as King, for instance in the Sermon on the Mount (chaps. 5–7), and has shown His authority over sickness, demons, and death and has performed numerous other miracles that verified His identity and mission in the subsequent account of that Gospel. At the commissioning of His twelve apostles, Jesus gave them quite restrictive instructions in 10:5–7: "Do not go in the way of the Gentiles, and do not enter any city of the Samaritans; but rather go to the lost sheep of the house of Israel. And as you go, preach, saying, 'The kingdom of heaven is at hand.'" At that time, this was the easiest commandment that Jesus had ever given to the apostles; they had no desire—at that point—to go to the Gentile nations or to a Samaritan town.

> **CONSIDER:** We who are Gentiles familiar with the Gospels rejoice that (1) Matthew 10 is not the end of the Gospel and that (2) Matthew 28 will end with exactly the opposite instructions, as the disciples were then instructed to take the gospel to the farthest reaches of the earth.

Throughout the Gospels, leading up to Matthew 12, there has been growing opposition to Jesus—especially by the Jewish religious establishment. Many Jews received and believed Jesus; many more did not. By verses 22–24 a dividing line had been reached:

Then a demon-possessed man who was blind and mute was brought to Jesus, and He healed him, so that the mute man spoke and saw. All the crowds were amazed, and were saying, "This man cannot be the Son of David, can he?" But when the Pharisees heard this, they said, "This man casts out demons only by Beelzebul the ruler of the demons."

> **NOTE:** The religious leaders did not deny that Jesus actually had performed miracles simply because they could not. What they did deny was the source of those miracles. The denial of the miracles of Jesus did not come until later, and they still are disdained as myths or fairy tales by liberal theological scholars.

> **KEY:** Such denying of the source of the miracles of Jesus and what follows is the "unpardonable sin," that in the original context is national Israel, led by their religious leaders, sinning by not receiving Jesus as sent from God. Instead, they concluded that His work—and He Himself—was an agent from Satan.

As Matt 13:1–3a shows, Jesus changed His method of public teaching and preaching and began using parables: "That day Jesus went out of the house and was sitting by the sea. And large crowds gathered to Him, so He got into a boat and sat down, and the whole crowd was standing on the beach. And He spoke many things to them in parables."

Not only did the method of the preaching change but also the content of the message changed, as seen in Matt 13:3b–8. Jesus said,

Behold, the sower went out to sow; and as he sowed, some seeds fell beside the road, and the birds came and ate them up. Others fell on the rocky places, where they did not have much soil; and immediately they sprang up, because they had no depth of soil. But when the sun had risen, they were scorched; and because they had no root, they withered away. Others fell among the thorns, and the thorns came up and choked them out. And others fell on the good soil and yielded a crop, some a hundredfold, some sixty, and some thirty.

In verse 9, Jesus concluded with this eternally serious admonition to respond to what He has just taught: "He who has ears, let him hear."

After Jesus had finished preaching, His disciples came to Him in private, asking, "Why do You speak to them in parables?" (Matt 13:10). They probably added to this such things as, "We've been with You for years. We have never heard You teach only in parables before. Why do You do so now?" Remember that this is immediately following chapter 12, which mentions the unpardonable sin of rejecting God's Word, especially in what Jesus had preached and taught, and so He responded in Matt 13:11–12:

> *To you it has been granted to know the mysteries of the kingdom of heaven, but to them it has not been granted. For whoever has, to him shall more be given, and he will have an abundance; but whoever does not have, even what he has shall be taken away from him.*

There are three things to note here. First, Jesus is revealing something that He never had revealed before, namely that now He is instructing regarding "the mysteries of the kingdom of heaven." A mystery—biblically speaking—is something that God had not previously revealed at all, or it is something that He had revealed only in small detail but now has more revelatory disclosure. In Matthew 3, John the Baptist did not say, nor did Jesus say later in chapter 4, "Repent, for the mysteries of the kingdom of heaven are at hand." So, what is now being revealed specifically relates to the kingdom of heaven, but there remained mystery information that Jesus had yet to reveal. Second, "For whoever has, to him shall more be given" does not refer to material wealth. Only to those who have received, accepted, and acted on God's Word does Jesus promise to give more and more. However, third, "whoever does not have"—an understanding of God's Word—"even that will be taken away from him."

Jesus explained further in Matt 13:13–15 why He took such action, and in doing so He quoted from Isa 6:9–10:

> *Therefore I speak to them in parables; because while seeing they do not see, and while hearing they do not hear, nor do they understand. In their case the prophecy of Isaiah is being fulfilled, which says,*
>
> "YOU WILL KEEP ON HEARING, BUT WILL NOT UNDERSTAND;
>
> YOU WILL KEEP ON SEEING, BUT WILL NOT PERCEIVE;
>
> FOR THE HEART OF THIS PEOPLE HAS BECOME DULL,
>
> WITH THEIR EARS THEY SCARCELY HEAR,

AND THEY HAVE CLOSED THEIR EYES,

OTHERWISE THEY WOULD SEE WITH THEIR EYES,

HEAR WITH THEIR EARS,

AND UNDERSTAND WITH THEIR HEART AND RETURN,

AND I WOULD HEAL THEM."

CORE TRUTH: Jesus quoted from Isaiah 6 because the identical sinful condition existed at this time. To those up to Matthew 12, God had given His Word—repeatedly—His written and incarnate Word. Those who rejected Him sinned against the Light that God had sent them, and these people were even more guilty than their forefathers had been in Isaiah's time. God promises that He will reveal more biblical truths—in this case by means of parables—that He knows they will not understand; nevertheless, He will still hold them accountable. In keeping with the Isaiah 6 background, God will harden such ones in the sinful spiritual condition that they have chosen for themselves

---

KEY TRUTH: It is a dangerous thing—from the time of Cain in Genesis through Isaiah's time through the Incarnation time and to the present time—to reject the Word of God. Such a rejection can have eternal consequences, especially if God chooses to harden those in the spiritual condition that they have brought upon themselves.

Look at the contrast between the rejection of Jesus and His Word by most people versus the reception of Him by the apostles as Jesus described in Matt 13:16–17: "But blessed are your eyes, because they see; and your ears, because they hear. For truly I say to you that many prophets and righteous men desired to see what you see, and did not see it; and to hear what you hear, and did not hear it." And from what we read earlier, we now recognize that Jesus was beginning to explain some of the mysteries of the kingdom of God that the people had not received before. Notice specifically how He started in verses 18–19a, which calls our attention to the Word of God as being a major element of this parable: "Hear then the parable of the sower. When anyone hears the word of the kingdom..." So, including the previous verses, here in Matt 13:18–23 is Jesus's first teaching of the mysteries of the kingdom of God:

> *Hear then the parable of the sower. When anyone hears the word of the kingdom and does not understand it, the evil one comes and snatches away what has been sown in his heart. This is the one on whom seed was sown beside the road. The one on whom seed was sown on the rocky places, this is the man who hears the word and immediately receives it with joy; yet he has no firm root in himself, but is only temporary, and when affliction or persecution arises because of the word, immediately he falls away. And the one on whom seed was sown among the thorns, this is the man who hears the word, and the worry of the world, and the deceitfulness of wealth choke the word, and it becomes unfruitful. And the one on whom seed was sown on the good soil, this is the man who hears the word and understands it; who indeed bears fruit and brings forth, some a hundredfold, some sixty, and some thirty.*

Mark well, beloved, that all of the parables in Matthew 13 are mysteries of the kingdom of God/heaven parables. In verse 24, "Jesus presented another parable to them, saying, 'The kingdom of heaven,'" and He does so each time in verses 31 and 33. Matthew 13:34 shows the new normal that Jesus is beginning to use in His public ministry: "All these things Jesus spoke to the crowds in parables, and He did not speak to them without a parable." Verses 44, 45, and 47 are kingdom parables as well. So these parables will not be about business practices, self-worth, or the prosperity gospel; instead, they will be specifically about the kingdom of God, which will not come yet but most assuredly will come at some future undesignated time.

Parables became the method by which Jesus revealed new mysteries of the kingdom truth to those receptive to the Word and concealed truth from those who had rejected His Word already.

KEY: From this point onward, no longer will the message be "[t]he kingdom of heaven is at hand." The kingdom of heaven is still going to come eventually but no longer at this point—but all under God's sovereignty. Matthew 13 gives divine revelation of some of what will occur from that point onward until the return of the King to establish His kingdom, including the worldwide nature of the end of this time and the worldwide judgment.

CONSIDER ALSO: These new directives from Jesus would be much harder for the apostles to preach than the wonderful message they had previously shared with the lost sheep of the house of Israel. As you will see in another chapter, this message becomes even more difficult for them to live out.

One Further Sobering Usage

Fast-forward approximately a year to John 12 to a time after Jesus had entered Jerusalem in what is often misnamed "The Triumphal Entry" (vv. 12–19). In some of His last public words before His trial began, Jesus said in verse 27, "Now My soul is troubled. What should I say, Father, save Me from this hour? But that is why I came to this hour." The account continues in John 12:28–36a:

> "Father, glorify Your name." Then a voice came out of heaven: "I have both glorified it, and will glorify it again." So the crowd of people who stood by and heard it were saying that it had thundered; others were saying, "An angel has spoken to Him." Jesus answered and said, "This voice has not come for My sake, but for your sakes. Now judgment is upon this world; now the ruler of this world will be cast out. And I, if I am lifted up from the earth, will draw all men to Myself." But He was saying this to indicate the kind of death by which He was to die. The crowd then answered Him, "We have heard out of the Law that the Christ is to remain forever; and how can You say, 'The Son of Man must be lifted up'? Who is this Son of Man?" So Jesus said to them, "For a little while longer the Light is among you. Walk while you have the Light, so that darkness will not overtake you; he who walks in the darkness does not know where he goes. While you have the Light, believe in the Light, so that you may become sons of Light."

This incredibly crucial account continues in John 12:36b–40:

These things Jesus spoke, and He went away and hid Himself from them. But though He had performed so many signs before them, yet they were not believing in Him. This was to fulfill the word of Isaiah the prophet which he spoke: "LORD, WHO HAS BELIEVED OUR REPORT? AND TO WHOM HAS THE ARM OF THE LORD BEEN REVEALED?" For this reason they could not believe, for Isaiah said again, "HE HAS BLINDED THEIR EYES AND HE HARDENED THEIR HEART; SO THAT THEY WOULD NOT SEE WITH THEIR EYES AND PERCEIVE WITH THEIR HEART, AND BE CONVERTED AND I HEAL THEM."

Note well this additional use of Isaiah 6, just as we saw in Matthew 13, and the digression that occurs. "But though He had performed so many signs before them, yet they were not believing in Him" (John 12:37); this notes the same core issues—only worse—that were true for those of Isaiah 6 and Matthew 13. John used the imperfect tense in the Greek to show their actions: they were not believing—imperfect tense, repeated action; over and over they were not believing. But note how the digression downward ends: "For this reason they could not believe" (John 12:39). This coincides with another use of Isaiah 6 in another judgmental capacity given to them by God.

KEY: These verses include sections from the two major divisions of Isaiah, where liberal scholars claim that multiple authors wrote the book, namely 53:1 for the first reference and 6:10 for the second usage. You *must* decide how you interpret this. This is either God Himself speaking by means of Isaiah the prophet—singular—or it is written by Isaiah the committee over a period of centuries by unknown authors. Everyone will believe some one or some thing. You must either believe and accept that God is the source for the prophecies, or you will believe the critics of the Bible and accept them—but you cannot do both. As before, your choice as to which source you will accept as being truthful will have eternal consequences, one way or the other.

Mark well, beloved, that John 12:41 reveals exactly the One whom Isaiah saw in Isaiah 6: "These things Isaiah said because he saw His glory, and he spoke of Him." That was the preincarnate, second member of the Godhead whom Isaiah saw. He was clearly the Godhead member who could be seen, the One of whom the apostle Paul would so beautifully write in Phil 2:5–8:

> *Have this attitude in yourselves which was also in Christ Jesus, who, although He existed in the form of God, did not regard equality with God a thing to be grasped, but emptied Himself, taking the form of a bond-servant, and being made in the likeness of men. Being found in appearance as a man, He humbled Himself by becoming obedient to the point of death, even death on a cross.*

CORE ADMONITION: Such truths as we have seen in these biblical passages and the following truths need to be part of your ministry, part of your messages, part of your witnessing to others. Many people naively think that they can repeatedly reject God and His Word and that the rejections will have no consequence in their lives. God, by His grace, does bring about deathbed conversions, and praise Him for that. But from what we have seen in Isaiah 6, Matthew 13, and John 12, He may also choose to confirm those in the sinful rebellion that they have chosen for themselves. It is most assuredly a dangerous thing to reject and turn away from the Word of God.

One Final Usage

I conclude this chapter with one final related passage, Acts 28:16–23, which describes events after the apostle Paul had arrived at Rome:

> *When we entered Rome, Paul was allowed to stay by himself, with the soldier who was guarding him.*
>
> *After three days Paul called together those who were the leading men of the Jews, and when they came together, he began saying to them, "Brethren, though I had done nothing against our people or the customs of our fathers, yet I was delivered as a prisoner from Jerusalem into the hands of the Romans. And when they had examined me, they were willing to release me because there was no ground for putting me to death. But when the*

Jews objected, I was forced to appeal to Caesar, not that I had any accu-
sation against my nation. For this reason, therefore, I requested to see you
and to speak with you, for I am wearing this chain for the sake of the hope
of Israel." They said to him, "We have neither received letters from Judea
concerning you, nor have any of the brethren come here and reported or
spoken anything bad about you. But we desire to hear from you what your
views are; for concerning this sect, it is known to us that it is spoken against
everywhere."

When they had set a day for Paul, they came to him at his lodging in large
numbers; and he was explaining to them by solemnly testifying about the
kingdom of God and trying to persuade them concerning Jesus, from both
the Law of Moses and from the Prophets, from morning until evening.

We should mark this well: Paul also taught about the kingdom of God.
He tried to persuade the Jewish representatives concerning Jesus from the
Law of Moses and the Prophets—just as Jesus did twice in Luke 24, and
just as we (I hope) did with the Old Testament edition of *The Bible Exposi-*
tor's Handbook. So we have seen how the Luke 24 truths about Jesus and
how the Old Testament played such an important part in Paul's ministry
and presentation of the gospel all the way up through Acts 28.

The account in Acts 28:24–28 continues with one final use of Isaiah 6:

Some were being persuaded by the things spoken, but others would not
believe. And when they did not agree with one another, they began leaving
after Paul had spoken one parting word, "The Holy Spirit rightly spoke
through Isaiah the prophet to your fathers, saying,

'GO TO THIS PEOPLE AND SAY,

"You will keep on hearing, but will not understand;

And you will keep on seeing, but will not perceive;

For the heart of this people has become dull,

And with their ears they scarcely hear,

And they have closed their eyes;

Otherwise they might see with their eyes,

And hear with their ears,

And understand with their heart and return,

And I would heal them."'

Therefore let it be known to you that this salvation of God has been sent to the Gentiles; they will also listen."

This is the third biblical use of Isaiah 6 in the New Testament; twice it was used by or about Jesus and once by the apostle Paul. Note—and be encouraged—that Paul saw the ultimate author of Scripture who was speaking through Isaiah the prophet: "The Holy Spirit rightly spoke through Isaiah the prophet to your fathers" (Acts 28:25).

After all, and in keeping with what we previously saw, it is a dangerous thing to reject the Word of God, and those who do—unless they repent and receive the grace of God through Jesus the Messiah—may become entrenched in that sinful rebellion of rejection of God's Word and, tragically, experience the damning eternal consequences that they have brought upon themselves.

Summary and Conclusion

In this chapter we initially learned (1) the commissioning of Isaiah (chap. 6) came after the panoramic overview of the entire book of Isaiah (chaps. 1–5), which gave some preview of blessings for the faithful but mostly showed the nation of Israel living in severe covenant disobedience before Yahweh. (2) We have seen previously that Isa 1:1 and 2:1 both point to these prophecies being for Judah and Jerusalem. Others will be addressed at various places, but the core of the book directly ties in with Judah and Jerusalem. Even the famous "come now, and let us reason together" phrase (1:18) comes in the context of God delineating many of the sins of national Israel and Yahweh's offer for the nation to repent and be in fellowship with Him. (3) As people being under the Mosaic covenant, the blessing and curse of Leviticus 26 and Deuteronomy 27–28 was true for them. If the nation did not repent, God would send His promised judgments. Isaiah 1:19–20 follows the offer, "Come now, and let us reason together," with God declaring, "'If you consent and obey, You will eat the best of the land; But if you refuse and rebel, You will be devoured by the sword.' Truly, the mouth of the LORD has spoken." (4) The core of national Israel's brazen sins listed above could be summarized as "they have rejected the instruction of the LORD of hosts. And despised the word of the Holy One of Israel" (Isa 5:24).

It is with this background that God commissions Isaiah (chap. 6), which begins with Isaiah seeing the Lord. We saw in Exod 33:11 God's revelation, "Thus the LORD used to speak to Moses face to face, just as a man speaks to his friend." Later, Moses beseeched God to show him His glory(v. 18), to which Yahweh answered in verse 20, "You cannot see My face, for no man can see Me and live." This requires at least a two-member Godhead: One who can be seen and One who cannot be seen. God reveals more information about the Trinity later in His progressive revelation. God commissioned Isaiah to go to a disobedient Jewish people who were living in sin. In summarizing the content of the commissioning of Isaiah, Yahweh had presented His Word repeatedly to the Jewish people; other than the righteous remnant, however, the people had brazenly rejected God's Word. God promised to give them additional revelation (in this context by means of Isaiah the prophet), which the sinful nation will not understand. Yahweh would hold the people responsible for this new revelation because Yahweh will divinely work to blind them and harden them in their own sinful spiritual condition that they have already chosen for themselves by living in brazen covenant disobedience before Yahweh. Simply stated, it is a dangerous matter to reject and turn away from the Word of God—which in this context, the Jewish people had done.

In Matthew's Gospel, John the Baptist (3:1–2), Jesus (4:17), and then the Twelve (10:5–7) were originally sent only to national Israel, with the message for the Jewish people to repent, for the kingdom of God was at hand. However, as the ministry of Jesus progressed, the religious leaders in Matthew 12 commit the unpardonable sin when shown a demon-possessed man whom Jesus healed; they horribly conclude that Jesus cast out demons only by "Beelzebul the ruler of the demons," namely by means of Satan (vv. 22–24). It was because of this national rejection of Jesus by the religious leaders that Jesus switched to parables as His means of public teaching, beginning in Matthew 13, and every parable in this section is part of "the mysteries of the kingdom of heaven" (v. 11). No longer will the message be "repent for the kingdom of God is at hand." Jesus is still King, and He will most certainly bring in His kingdom, but it was no longer being offered to national Israel at that time. In answering the disciples' question as to "Why do You speak to them in parables?" (v. 10), Jesus quoted from Isa 6:9–10 as the reason He switched both the content and the means by which He spoke. The same core sinful condition existed at this time, as it had with their ancestors during Isaiah's lifetime. To those up to Matthew 12, God had given His Word—repeatedly—his written and incarnate Word. Those who rejected Him sinned against the Light whom God had sent them, and these people were even more guilty than their forefathers in Isaiah's time. Jesus promised to reveal more biblical truths—in this case by means of parables—that He knows they will not understand, but for which He will still hold them accountable. In keeping with the Isaiah 6 background, God will harden such ones in the sinful spiritual condition that they have chosen for themselves.

Fast-forward approximately a year to John 12, to a time after Jesus had entered Jerusalem in what is often misnamed the Triumphal Entry (vv. 12–19). In verses 36b–40, after Jesus spoke some of His last public words before the events leading to His crucifixion, the two passages of Isaiah are quoted to explain what had happened, one being 53:1 and the other being an additional use of Isaiah 6—and, as before, in a most negative way. John 12:37 revealed, "Though He had performed so many signs before them, yet they were not believing in Him," noting the same core issues—only worse—that were true for those of Isaiah 6 and Matthew 13. John used the imperfect tense in the Greek to show their actions: they were not believing—imperfect tense, repeated action; over and over they were not believing. We noted how the digression downward ends: "For this reason they could not believe" (John 12:39). This coincides with another use of Isaiah 6 in another judgmental capacity God had given to them. John 12:41 reveals the crucial biblical doctrine of exactly whom the prophet Isaiah saw in Isaiah 6: "These things Isaiah said because he saw His glory, and he spoke of Him." Isaiah beheld the preincarnate, second member of the Godhead in Isaiah 6—the Godhead member who could be seen.

One final use of Isaiah 6 occurs in Acts 28:24–28. As before, it references the same core heart condition of not receiving the Word of God, even after the apostle Paul had spoken to the Jewish people who came to hear him from sunrise to sunset, giving multiple proofs from the Old Testament text that Jesus was the promised Messiah sent by God. This final usage of Isaiah 6 becomes the basis for Paul turning his ministry primarily to the Gentiles (Acts 28:28).

Deeper Walk Study Questions

1. Name some aspects of the sinful condition God revealed in the panoramic overview (Isaiah 1–5) that show the wicked actions of the present Jewish generation to whom Isaiah would minister.

2. List eight facts about Isaiah's commissioning from God in Isaiah 6, including whom the prophet saw and specific truths about the people to whom he would be sent.

3. What was the original message of John the Baptist, Jesus, and the Twelve for national Israel? Why is this important?

4. What was the core, unpardonable sin of the religious leaders in Matthew 12? How does this fit with the change in both method and content of Jesus publicly teaching national Israel from this point forward by means of parables?

5. How does Jesus use Isa 6:9–10 to explain the same core sin problems for national Israel? Be specific about His explanation that He gives in Matthew 13.

6. List fifteen truths that come from John 12:28–40. Why is this such an important designation for those who had rejected the Word of God? How does the Isaiah 6 usage fit with Isaiah's generation and Jesus's previous use in Matthew 13? What core sins did they share? Explain.

7. How does John 12:41 tie things together with Isaiah 6? Explain what this means and give four reasons why this is important.

8. Whom did the apostle Paul address in Acts 28:16–23? Identify specifically the occasion concerning whom was being addressed and why. How does this other use of Isaiah 6 in Acts 28:24–28 harmonize with Isaiah 6, Matthew 13, and John 12? Explain by giving five supports.

9. How did God use this final use of Isaiah 6 to direct the apostle Paul in his ministry? Give three reasons why this is important to note at this point in Acts.

CHAPTER 19

Five Theological Bombshells from Matthew 16

S ome chapters in the Bible are hinge chapters because they include so
much of God's revelation, some or all of it entirely new—and in some
cases, eternally significant. Matthew 16 is such a chapter and contains
five theological bombshells, one right after another. It is not too broad
a statement to say that if you miss or do not understand the theological
revelation of this chapter you will misinterpret much of the remainder of
God's Word.

This chapter is purposely a shorter chapter in this edition of *The Bible
Expositor's Handbook*, but I wanted to have Matthew 16 (1) as part of the
unfolding story of Jesus in the New Testament and (2) I will repeatedly
refer to these theological bombshells in upcoming chapters of this edition.

Setting for Matthew 16

When Jesus brought the Twelve to what will transpire in Matthew 16,
much had taken place already. He had about a year left to live, and He still
had so much to teach His disciples. Jesus had restricted His public ministry and had chosen to have the private ministry in training the Twelve for
what He had determined for them already, after He had returned to heaven.

Even the location to which Jesus brought the Twelve is important.
They came to Caesarea Philippi, in northern Israel, where the mythological god Pan, who was considered by many to be a half man and half goat,
was worshipped. (Many are familiar with the children's story of Peter Pan,

which is based on this half man—or boy—and half goat.) Later the city's name was changed to Panias (or Banias), still associated with the patron god Pan. Furthermore, the city had carved into its mountain other mythological gods; each supposedly was endowed with various attributes and interacted with humanity in varying degrees. It is this backdrop of false gods that Jesus chose to use for His disclosure concerning His person and His work.

Jesus led the Twelve into what He wanted to teach them by asking, "Who do people say that the Son of Man is?" (Matt 16:13). The term "Son of Man" is innocent enough and somewhat generic in its usage. For instance, God repeatedly addressed the prophet Ezekiel in this same way: "Then He said to me, 'Son of man, stand on your feet that I may speak with you'" (Ezek 2:1). The title "Son of Man" used to refer to Jesus was not offensive by itself, which is probably one reason Jesus often referred to Himself by this designation. Being designated as the Son of Man for this One who came to dwell among us is fitting for Him during His incarnation. Also appropriate is the designation "Son of David," as we have seen referring to Jesus's earthly lineage as the Davidic covenant heir, for instance, in Matt 1:1: "The record of the genealogy of Jesus the Messiah, the son of David, the son of Abraham." Being called either Son of Man or Son of David was not considered a blasphemous title that would cause someone to be killed for using those titles.

But in Matthew 16, what God discloses about Jesus changes everything. God does this by revealing five theological bombshells. Each one presents monumental, eternal, "shake-the-world" doctrinal truths.

Five Theological Bombshells of Matthew 16

The first theological bombshell of Matthew 16 regards the true identity of Jesus the Messiah, as seen in verses 13–17:

> *Now when Jesus came into the district of Caesarea Philippi, He was asking His disciples, "Who do people say that the Son of Man is?" And they said, "Some say John the Baptist; and others, Elijah; but still others, Jeremiah, or one of the prophets." He said to them, "But who do you say that I am?" Simon Peter answered, "You are the Christ, the Son of the*

living God." And Jesus said to him, "Blessed are you, Simon Barjona,
because flesh and blood did not reveal this to you, but My Father who is in
heaven."

The significance of this first theological bombshell is multifaceted. To begin with, this is quite specific in the Greek where four definite articles ("the") are used: "You are the Messiah, the Son of the God the living One." Jesus is not a Messiah; He is the Messiah. The God who sent Him is not a god, a point that is especially pertinent considering the false gods we saw that were associated with Caesarea Philippi. Rather, He is the God, the living One. Also, Peter did not say, "You were the Messiah, but the religious leaders rejected you [as we saw in Matthew 12], so you no longer qualify." Jesus did—and still does—uniquely qualify as the Christ. The people who rejected Him in Matthew 12 (or at any other time), do so to their own peril—not His. Also, not only is He a son of David (human lineage), Jesus is uniquely the Son of God (deity). Finally, what Peter stated declaratively was something he could not reason out on his own. God the Father was actively at work to reveal this key doctrine to Peter, and He will reveal that doctrine to anyone else who will receive Him.

> **REMEMBER:** *Christ* and *Messiah* are interchangeable words that mean the same thing. John 1:41 states that Andrew first found "his own brother Simon and said to him, 'We have found the Messiah' (which translated means Christ)." Remember also that Jesus is His name and Christ or Messiah is His title. As we previously saw, the word *King* comes close to the meaning of Christ or Messiah, and all of these titles emerge from the Davidic covenant promises God has given.

The second theological bombshell of Matthew 16 is that this is the first time the word church occurs in the Bible, and it is used with a future tense. Verses 18–20 state:

"I also say to you that you are Peter, and upon this rock I will build My
church; and the gates of Hades will not overpower it. I will give you the
keys of the kingdom of heaven; and whatever you bind on earth shall have
been bound in heaven, and whatever you loose on earth shall have been

loosed in heaven." Then He warned the disciples that they should tell no one that He was the Christ.

The Godhead will disclose much more about His church in Acts and the Epistles, but this proclamation would have been a totally new doctrine for the Twelve. Jesus and His disciples did not go to church—none existed. They went to either a synagogue or the temple in Jerusalem. Also, the men would not fully have understood what Jesus meant until after Luke 24 and with the events of Acts 1–2.

The third theological bombshell of Matthew 16 is that this is the first time that Jesus specifically tells of His death and resurrection, as disclosed in verses 21–23:

> *From that time Jesus began to show His disciples that He must go to Jeru-salem, and suffer many things from the elders and chief priests and scribes, and be killed, and be raised up on the third day. Peter took Him aside and began to rebuke Him, saying, "God forbid it, Lord! This shall never happen to You." But He turned and said to Peter, "Get behind Me, Satan! You are a stumbling block to Me; for you are not setting your mind on God's interests, but man's."*

CORE TRUTH: Jesus never told of His death without also telling of His resurrection. The death of Jesus without His resurrection is only a sad story—for Him and for us. Later, Paul will write in detail (1 Corinthians 15) about the significance of what having no resurrection would mean for the redeemed. Without the resurrection of Jesus, there could be no salvation for anyone.

We live on this side of the cross and the grave of Jesus, but initially the Twelve did not. We know that Jesus's life, death, and resurrection were all in the predetermined plan and foreknowledge of God before the world be-gan (Acts 2:22–23; 1 Pet 1:17–20). Though written later than Matthew 16, verses in Luke 18 give additional insight into why the Twelve did not un-derstand what Jesus said about His pending death and resurrection, which was first given in Matthew 16.

*Then He took the twelve aside and said to them, "Behold, we are going up
to Jerusalem, and all things which are written through the prophets about
the Son of Man will be accomplished. For He will be handed over to the
Gentiles, and will be mocked and mistreated and spit upon, and after they
have scourged Him, they will kill Him; and the third day He will rise again."
But the disciples understood none of these things, and the meaning of this
statement was hidden from them, and they did not comprehend the things
that were said. (Luke 18:31–34)*

The statement "was hidden from them" does not directly identify who
hid these things, but obviously God was the One who hid these core biblical truths from the Twelve until after the resurrection of Jesus.

I will add one more item here, but more detailed information comes
later about the following subject. It is evident that Satan had an active
interest in and a knowledge of what was taking place and that he actively
worked in the midst of Matthew 16 to keep Jesus from ever going to His
cross. In both cases, Jesus was the One who identified God the Father as
the source of divine revelation, and Jesus was the One who in the same
manner identified and revealed the satanic nature of Peter's words. It did
not mean that Peter was "Satan possessed," but it did mean that he was
an unwitting—and ignorant—means of Satan's communication. Also, just
because God the Father had revealed divine revelation to Peter, it did not
mean that everything else Peter said or did automatically originated with
God.

The fourth theological bombshell of Matthew 16 is that Jesus now
gives the cost of being His disciple:

*If anyone wishes to come after Me, he must deny himself, and take up his
cross and follow Me. For whoever wishes to save his life will lose it; but
whoever loses his life for My sake will find it. For what will it profit a man if
he gains the whole world and forfeits his soul? Or what will a man give in
exchange for his soul? (vv. 24–26)*

The cost of discipleship is an ongoing, threefold ordeal: deny yourself,
take up your cross (Luke 9:23 adds the word daily), and follow Him. For
the Twelve who were previously sent out with instructions to announce that
the kingdom of heaven/God was at hand, this was a much more difficult

message to preach, and, as they will learn experientially, this was a much harder message to live daily.

> **KEY:** Notice the broadening of this requirement to be a disciple of Jesus to "anyone" who wants to be His disciple—not just to any Jewish person. The Jews will still play an important part in God's program and in receiving the gospel first (e.g., Rom 1:16). But now there is a broader widening that goes beyond the previous limitations that Jesus placed on the Twelve in Matthew 10, that they could not go to the Samaritans or to the Gentiles.

The fifth theological bombshell of Matthew 16 is that this is the first time that Jesus teaches on the glory of God, and He connects the glory of God directly to His Second Coming—not to His First Advent, the incarnation, as verses 27–28 reveal:

> *For the Son of Man is going to come in the glory of His Father with His angels, and WILL THEN REPAY EVERY MAN ACCORDING TO HIS DEEDS. Truly I say to you, there are some of those who are standing here who will not taste death until they see the Son of Man coming in His kingdom.*

I will expand this subject in the upcoming chapters, but it is not happenstance that the transfiguration account immediately follows this last theological bombshell. Matthew 17:1–2 states, "Six days later Jesus took with Him Peter and James and John his brother, and led them up on a high mountain by themselves. And He was transfigured before them; and His face shone like the sun, and His garments became as white as light." The transfiguration was a brief preview and unveiling of what the King and His kingdom will look like when he comes back with His angels and in the glory of God His Father and will also appropriately reward His faithful ones.

One Final Item to Note

At the end of the digital version of *The Bible Expositor's Handbook— Old Testament* and included in chapter 1 of this *New Testament Edition*, I provided a link for a series of free download messages God allowed me to preach. They are based on many of the prophecies that we have seen about the arrival of the Messiah and matters of biblical importance connected with His arrival, such as the covenants of God. Because the core truth was based on whom God would send and what He would do, I entitled this series "We've Been Expecting You." Based on the reception of and belief in God's Word, godly ones, such as Simeon in Luke 2, should have been expecting the arrival of God's Messiah. But now—still based on the promises of the Word of God—Matthew 16 has given us two more additional components for the series "We've Been Expecting You." From Matthew 16 we pick up two new parts, which you can listen to as free downloads. "We've Been Expecting You, II"[1] is taken from the third theological bombshell, so that we are now expecting Him to go to Jerusalem, to be turned over to the Gentiles, to be killed, and to be raised again on the third day. Most of Matthew 16 onward (plus the appropriate parallel passages) tell the story of events leading up to the arrest, trial, torture, death—and resurrection—of the Messiah. "We've Been Expecting You, III"[2] is based on the fifth theological bombshell from Matthew 16; it deals with matters related to the second coming of our Lord Jesus Christ to earth, in the glory of God and with His angels. These free audio downloads often cover material that I did not have room to address in this *Handbook*.

As a reminder, you must note this: in order for Scripture to be fulfilled, these additional revelations from God must come true just as He has promised. However, both the death of Jesus (the third bombshell) and His return in glory and His reign (the fifth theological bombshell) cannot occur at the same time. Even as early as Acts 1:9–11 the disciples were instructed to look for the last of the five theological bombshells from Matthew 16:

And after He had said these things, He was lifted up while they were looking on, and a cloud received Him out of their sight. And as they were gazing intently into the sky while He was going, behold, two men in white clothing

---

[1] https://www.sermonaudio.com/search.asp?subsetitem=We%27ve+Expecting+You%2C+II&subsetcat=series&keyword=gregharris&SourceOnly=true&includekeywords=&ExactVerse=.

[2] https://www.sermonaudio.com/search.asp?subsetitem=We%27ve+Been+Expecting+You%2C+III&subsetcat=series&keyword=gregharris&SourceOnly=true&includekeywords=&ExactVerse.=

stood beside them. They also said, "Men of Galilee, why do you stand look-
ing into the sky? This Jesus, who has been taken up from you into heaven,
will come in just the same way as you have watched Him go into heaven."

So now, much of the rest of Scripture, in various degrees, reveals more
details and culminates with the many details that will eventually be fulfilled in the book of Revelation, at the second coming of Jesus—many
years past the revealing of the five theological bombshells of Matthew 16.

Summary and Conclusion

We saw in this chapter the importance of knowing Matthew 16 as a hinge
chapter because so much doctrine is revealed in this place. We saw that
even the location to which Jesus brought the Twelve is important. He
brought them to Caesarea Philippi, in northern Israel, where the mythological god Pan, who was considered by many to be a half man and half
goat, was worshipped. It is a fitting place for Jesus to ask who the people
say that He is. God used this background to give us five theological bombshells in the remaining verses of Matthew 16.

The first theological bombshell of Matthew 16 regards the true identity
of Jesus the Messiah (vv. 13–17) and is multifaceted. We saw this is quite
specific in the Greek where four definite articles ("the") are used: "You are
the Messiah, the Son of the God the living One." Jesus is not a Messiah;
He is the Messiah. The God who sent Him is not a god, like the false gods
we saw that were associated with Caesarea Philippi; rather, He is the God,
the living One. Also, Peter did not say, "You were the Messiah, but the
religious leaders rejected you [as we saw in Matthew 12], so you no longer
qualify." Jesus did—and still does—uniquely qualify as the Messiah.

The second theological bombshell of Matthew 16 is that this is the first
time the word church occurs in the Bible, and it is used with a future tense
(vv. 18–20). In Acts and in the Epistles, God gives much more revelation
concerning the wonderful ministry of His church, but the fact that Jesus
used a future tense—not the present tense—in Matthew 16 shows that the
church was not in existence at this time.

The third theological bombshell of Matthew 16 is that this is the first
time that Jesus specifically tells of His death and resurrection (v. 21). We

saw that Jesus never told of His death without also telling of His resurrection. The death of Jesus without His resurrection is only a sad story—for Him and for us. Luke 18:31–34 informs us that God hid this truth from the Twelve until after the resurrection of Jesus.

The fourth theological bombshell of Matthew 16 is that Jesus now gives the cost of being His disciple (vv. 24–26) by beginning with, "If anyone wants to come with Me, he must deny himself, take up his cross, and follow Me." The cost of discipleship is threefold: deny yourself, take up your cross (Luke 9:23 adds the word daily), and follow Him. For the Twelve who were previously sent out with instructions to announce that the kingdom of heaven/God was at hand, this is a much more difficult message to preach, and, as they will learn experientially, this was a much harder message to live out daily.

The fifth theological bombshell of Matthew 16 is that this is the first time that Jesus teaches on the glory of God, and He connects the glory of God directly to His Second Coming—not to His First Advent, the incarnation (vv. 27–28). The transfiguration (Matthew 17) is a preview of the glory of God on the face of the Messiah; it is a foretaste of how He will look in His return to earth to set up His kingdom.

Finally, we saw that the five theological bombshells from Matthew 16 now give us two new items of expansion as part of "the predetermined plan and foreknowledge of God" that were not known before Matthew 16. These are specifically the suffering, death, and resurrection of Jesus but also at some point in the future, His return in the glory of His Father with His angels (the fifth theological bombshell). They must occur, and they must occur in order. The rest of Matthew and parallel passages from the other Gospels record many of the events leading up to the death and resurrection of Jesus. We also saw that as early as the ascension of Jesus in Acts 1:9–11, the faithful were asked, "Men of Galilee, why do you stand looking into the sky? This Jesus, who has been taken up from you into heaven, will come in just the same way as you have watched Him go into heaven." So now, much of the remainder of Scripture, in various degrees, fills in many details and culminates with the book of Revelation. Especially important to note is from Matthew 16, "We've Been Expecting You" now expands beyond the earlier part of the incarnation of Jesus to include two new sections: "We've Been Expecting You" (Part 2) to go to the cross and die and be resurrected, and "We've Been Expecting You" (Part 3) to return in the glory of the Father and with His holy angels—just as Jesus so clearly revealed, in the fifth theological bombshell of Matthew 16.

Deeper Walk Study Questions

1. What made the setting of Caesarea Philippi a wonderful place for Jesus to ask who people said that He was? Give five reasons this is so.

2. What are five significant truths that we can learn about Jesus from the first theological bombshell of Matthew 16, "You are the Christ, the Son of the living God"? Be specific and support your answers biblically.

3. What are three significant truths that we can learn about Jesus from the second theological bombshell of Matthew 16, that He will build His church? Be specific.

4. What are three significant truths that we can learn about Jesus from the third theological bombshell of Matthew 16 that Jesus would be tortured and killed in Jerusalem but also that He would be raised on the third day? Why is the death of Jesus without His resurrection just a sad story—for Him and for us? Explain and be specific. Also, what does Luke 18:31–34 reveal about why the disciples failed to comprehend what Jesus said by means of this truth?

5. Name five specific truths from the fourth theological bombshell of Matthew 16—that Jesus now gives the cost of being His disciple (vv. 24–26) beginning with, "If anyone wishes to come after Me, he must deny himself, take up his cross and follow Me."

6. Name three biblical truths from the fifth theological bombshell of Matthew 16—that this is the first time Jesus teaches on the glory of God and connects the glory of God directly to His Second Coming, not to His First Advent, the incarnation (vv. 27–28). Why is this so important? Explain.

CHAPTER 20

The Glory of God Changes Everything

A fter more than thirty-five years of studying and teaching Bible Exposition classes, I am fully convinced the best six-word encapsulation and summary of the entire Bible is this: The Glory of God Changes Everything.

I think I can convince you that this is true biblically.

It is hard to know exactly how many "glory of God" passages are in the Bible. For instance, a verse many are familiar with, Ps 19:1, contains such a usage: "The heavens are telling of the glory of God; / And their expanse is declaring the work of His hands." Yet this is the only time in Psalm 19 that the actual phrase "glory of God" occurs; the remainder of the verses help explain or elaborate on what Ps 19:1 states. So, our dilemma is this: how many verses in Psalm 19 are "glory of God" references, only the first verse or the remaining thirteen verses of that psalm? I believe that all fourteen verses are "glory of God" verses. You could use that method of reckoning with many such examples throughout the entire Bible. If you add to this the appropriate verses containing "glorify/glorified/glorifying" that refer to God, this gives us more than a thousand references to His glory. Just from the mammoth number of occurrences in Scripture, you could make a strong case for the theological importance of the glory of God. You will be lacking in your overall understanding of much of the Bible unless you understand some of the incredible biblical truths about the glory of God.

Mark 10:35–37 is where I first began my study on the glory of God. This is the account of when James and John approached Jesus and made the following request of Him, and you can see why the glory of God is of great interest to me:

> James and John, the two sons of Zebedee, came up to Jesus, saying, "Teacher, we want You to do for us whatever we ask of You." And He said to them, "What do you want Me to do for you?" They said to Him, "Grant that we may sit, one on Your right and one on Your left, in Your glory."

But as you have probably figured out, we cannot begin in Mark 10:35 and understand what these verses teach and why they—and so many other verses linked to them—are so crucial for us to know. We must walk there biblically on the appropriate biblical trail.

A Few Biblical Presuppositions on the Glory of God

If you have read your Bible for an extended time and are like I was, you may know very little about the glory of God—other than it certainly does occur frequently in Scripture and it is mentioned in some of the songs that we sing. Establishing some biblical presuppositions about the glory of God will help frame our studies.

Biblical Presupposition 1: *God's glory is vastly beyond what we can comprehend.*

Returning to the verse I began with in this chapter, Ps 19:1 states incredible truths about the glory of God: "The heavens are telling of the glory of God; / And their expanse is declaring the work of His hands." Scientists and astronomers around the world, such as those associated with our NASA program, are not sure exactly how many solar systems exist, nor even how many stars exist in our galaxy. In Gen 15:5a, "He [God] took [Abram] outside and said, 'Now look toward the heavens, and count the stars, if you are able to count them.'" Modern estimates, which will likely expand as new equipment gives us better and newer peeks into aspects of God's creation, even now project that approximately 200 billion galaxies exist, each containing—give or take—200 billion stars. So when God asks Abram to count the stars, God knows that man could never count them.

But there is another truth connected with this. "The heavens declare the glory of God," but the heavens do not contain the glory of God. Instead, the glory of God contains or encompasses the heavens. However many galaxies, however many stars, or however many other creations God has created elsewhere and in eternity past, these do not contain His glory—His glory contains these and anything else that He has made.

> **IMPORTANT:** Connected with the above biblical presupposition, anytime God's glory is manifested in Scripture—such as in Exod 16:10: "As Aaron spoke to the whole congregation of the sons of Israel, . . . they looked toward the wilderness, and behold, the glory of the LORD appeared in the cloud"—it is only a miniscule sliver of God's glory. It is enough for people to know of its presence without grasping the full extent of what God's glory encompasses.

Biblical Presupposition 2: *Although currently veiled and not fully disclosed, God's glory extends to every place God is—but not to one unique place where He chooses not to disclose it: hell.*

In Matt 25:41 Jesus revealed the place that those who had rejected Him would eternally inhabit after His return to earth: "Depart from me, accursed ones, into the eternal fire which has been prepared for the devil and his angels." Hell was originally prepared—not created—for the devil and his angels. Those who are eternally lost will certainly go there as well, but that was not the original design or purpose of hell. Later, in 2 Thess 1:9–10 comes this aspect of what hell will consist of for the lost:

> *These will pay the penalty of eternal destruction, away from the presence of the Lord and from the glory of His power, when He comes to be glorified in His saints on that day, and to be marveled at among all who have believed—for our testimony to you was believed.*

This hell is the only place in God's entire creation where He has purposely chosen to remove any display of "the glory of His power." Revelation 14:9–10 clearly states that those who will be tormented in hell will do so in the presence of the Lord Jesus and His angels:

> *Then another angel, a third one, followed them, saying with a loud voice, "If anyone worships the beast and his image, and receives a mark on his*

forehead or on his hand, he also will drink of the wine of the wrath of God,
which is mixed in full strength in the cup of His anger; and he will be tor-
mented with fire and brimstone in the presence of the holy angels and in the
presence of the Lamb.

Not to downplay in any way the eternal torment in the flames of hell, but another part of hell's torment will be being eternally "away from the presence of the Lord and from the glory of His power." While that may not seem like anything of importance, we must consider that the Bible elsewhere often describes heaven with the glory of God playing an indescribable part. So, if being in the presence of God and His glory best describes (in our currently restricted view) an important aspect of what heaven is. Hell is just the opposite; the removal of any trace of God's glory being manifested is one of the aspects that comprises hell. Fire most certainly will be there, but any display of the glory of God will not.

Biblical Presupposition 3: *(This one is connected with the previous truth).*
A major component of Satan's active works involves the glory of God.
In 2 Cor 4:3–4, God through the apostle Paul informs us,

And even if our gospel is veiled, it is veiled to those who are perishing, in
whose case the god of this world has blinded the minds of the unbelieving so
that they might not see the light of the gospel of the glory of Christ, who is
the image of God.

Satan could be (and is) involved with many other things, but one thing he will not neglect is blinding people's minds to the glory of God. Also, wherever there is evangelism based on the Word of God, there is spiritual warfare—and you need to be aware of that. God still works and people are saved, but Satan still actively works also. Part of God's answer, as well as another "glory of God" reference, continues in 2 Cor 4:5–6:

For we do not preach ourselves but Christ Jesus as Lord, and ourselves as
your bond-servants for Jesus' sake. For God, who said, "Light shall shine
out of darkness," is the One who has shone in our hearts to give the Light of
the knowledge of the glory of God in the face of Christ.

Biblical Presupposition 4: *(This one is connected with previous truths.) The present and future spiritual warfare battlefield ultimately and directly relates to the glory of God.*

In Ps 96:1–9 God commands the redeemed to do the following acts for and to him:

> *Sing to the Lord a new song;*
>
> *Sing to the Lord, all the earth.*
>
> *Sing to the Lord, bless His name;*
>
> *Proclaim good tidings of His salvation from day to day.*
>
> *Tell of His glory among the nations,*
>
> *His wonderful deeds among all the peoples.*
>
> *For great is the Lord and greatly to be praised;*
>
> *He is to be feared above all gods.*
>
> *For all the gods of the peoples are idols,*
>
> *But the Lord made the heavens.*
>
> *Splendor and majesty are before Him,*
>
> *Strength and beauty are in His sanctuary.*
>
> *Ascribe to the Lord, O families of the peoples,*
>
> *Ascribe to the Lord glory and strength.*
>
> *Ascribe to the Lord the glory of His name;*
>
> *Bring an offering and come into His courts.*
>
> *Worship the Lord in holy attire;*
>
> *Tremble before Him, all the earth*

Twice, the glory of God is specifically set forth in this psalm. In verse 3, part of what we are to do in evangelism and missions is to "[d]eclare His glory among the nations [that is, among Gentiles], His wondrous works among all peoples." Then in verses 7–8a, "Ascribe [give credit] to the Lord, you families of the peoples, ascribe to the Lord glory and strength. Ascribe to the Lord the glory of His name." As we saw in 2 Cor 4:3–4, Satan actively works to do just the opposite of what God calls for in Psalm 96, specifically by blinding the minds of the unbelievers so they cannot see the light of the gospel of the glory of Christ. This is the basis for most of the present spiritual warfare, and it will not go away; this battle will intensify the closer we come to the return of the Lord Jesus Christ and will not end until His return.

> **CRUCIAL COMPONENT:** In order to tell the nations of God's glory, you need to understand some of what the glory of God entails. There is much more to it than saying, "God has glory!" The glory of God is best defined as any of the attributes and/or activities of God, and that succinctly covers everything. The details—and full disclosure of God's glory—will take an eternity to behold and embrace.

Biblical Presupposition 5: *God not only brings the redeemed to be with Him in heaven, but a major component of that heaven is the glory of God.*

In Heb 2:9–10 we see the following truths for both Jesus the Messiah and for those He saves:

> *But we do see Him who was made for a little while lower than the angels, namely, Jesus, because of the suffering of death crowned with glory and honor, so that by the grace of God He might taste death for everyone. For it was fitting for Him, for whom are all things, and through whom are all things, in bringing many sons to glory, to perfect the author of their salvation through sufferings.*

From the moment you were saved, God started a process of walking you to heaven. For some, that walk is a relatively long one; for others, it is a much shorter walk. But Heb 2:10 is quite specific in revealing that He is "bringing many sons [in this usage, "people"] to glory," which is heaven. We may not define heaven by that description, but God does, and that is all that matters.

To prove that this truly is what God has revealed in His Word, He gives us even more specifics in what for me is one of the top five most amazing verses in all the Bible, 2 Thess 2:14: "It was for this He called you through our gospel, that you may gain [literally, "to the gaining of"] the glory of our Lord Jesus Christ." If we had written on our own what this verse teaches, it would be blasphemy. But God put it in His Word, and we can have confidence that this is eternally true. If you ever wondered why God called you through His gospel, it is so that you may gain the glory of our Lord Jesus Christ.

> **CONSIDER:** God will not give us His full glory, for that would mean our being worshipped, and Scripture does not teach that. But *any* of the glory of God that He will give us is part of what makes heaven what it is and allows us to have the fullest enjoyment with Him in eternity. Not everyone will receive the same amount of God's glory, for there will be degrees of reward for the redeemed.

> **CONSIDER ALSO:** The ongoing battle and attack concerning the glory of God is specifically for unbelievers, as we saw in 2 Cor 4:3–6. But there is another logical deduction that is for you personally, or maybe for you to use to encourage faithful servants of His who are walking with the Lord but who are battered in the spiritual warfare battle. They may be despondent or just losing hope. To such persons please send Heb 2:9–10 and especially 2 Thess 2:14 for encouragement. I fully believe that, while it does not specifically say this in Scripture, it reasons that while Satan cannot blind the minds of the redeemed to the gospel of the glory of Jesus Christ, he does actively work to keep the minds and focus of the redeemed away from those Scriptures and on other distractions—especially as evil progresses.

Biblical Presupposition 6: *If you are saved and walking in obedience to Him, God is in the process of presently developing His glory within you.*

From previous verses that we have seen, it would seem that other than the current spiritual battle most of the references are either associated with the return of the Lord Jesus Christ in glory or with the glory of God for us in heaven as a major aspect of our eternity. We will study two passages that reveal doctrinal truths about the glory of God in this lifetime.

When I was going through the worst of times in my life as a Christian, I erroneously—and sinfully—concluded that God was doing nothing in my life at that time other than keeping me alive and providing food and shelter. In Rom 8:18, God gives the following encouragement for those Christians who are enduring whatever form of suffering they were/are enduring: "For I consider that the sufferings of this present time are not worthy to be compared with the glory that is to be revealed to us." And to those who are like I was, this is biblically what God is doing, if you are walking with Him in the midst of your trials.

> *Therefore we do not lose heart, but though our outer man is decaying, yet our inner man is being renewed day by day. For momentary, light affliction is producing for us an eternal weight of glory far beyond all comparison, while we look not at the things which are seen, but at the things which are not seen; for the things which are seen are temporal, but the things which are not seen are eternal. (2 Cor 4:16–18)*

Often in this lifetime, our afflictions and sufferings seem neither momentary nor light, but they are—especially when viewed with the glories that await us in eternity with the Godhead. When I thought God was doing nothing, He was using my afflictions and sufferings in "producing for [me] an eternal weight of glory far beyond all comparison." I could spend the rest of the book writing only about the cascading truths revealed in this one passage, but I will limit this to two crucial doctrinal truths. (1) God's glory has weight to it—most of us would never view this truth in reference to the glory of God. (2) The Holy Spirit says that such is the contrast between the present sufferings and afflictions now for the redeemed and the glory of God yet to be revealed to us. There is no language on earth that properly expresses it so that we can comprehend it.

We who are saved should learn from just these two truths from the previous paragraph to "[p]repare [our] minds for action, keep sober in spirit, fix [our] hope completely on the grace to be brought to [us] at the revelation of Jesus Christ" (1 Pet 1:13). After all, when our Lord Jesus Christ returns, not only will He come back in the Father's glory and with His holy angels (Matt 16:27), but He will do what He promises in Phil 3:20–21, another "glory of God" passage:

> *For our citizenship is in heaven, from which also we eagerly wait for a Savior, the Lord Jesus Christ; who will transform the body of our humble state*

into conformity with the body of His glory, by the exertion of the power that He has even to subject all things to Himself.

Come soon, Lord Jesus!

Biblical Presupposition 7: (This is connected with the previous biblical presupposition.) *We know now, if we did not know before, that if we are walking with God, He uses our sufferings and afflictions to produce in us an eternal weight of glory beyond all comparison. Many of us did not, or do not, recognize or appreciate that this is a process that God uses, and that the Godhead has decided the degree of the length and the depth to which it goes for each individual.*

God patiently and faithfully works in us who walk with Him with eternity in view and, as we now know, prepares us during our lifetime for eternity with Him. Not only is this true for us, but it was true for James and John who asked Jesus that they might sit in His glory. To this Jesus replied in Mark 10:38, "You do not know what you are asking. Are you able to drink the cup that I drink?"

The Biblical Trail to Mark 10:35–41: "We Want to Sit in Your Glory"

> **NOTE:** For those who want to follow the biblical trail in the much fuller measure, there is a free audio download of *The Cup and the Glory* available online.[1] It is also available on Amazon.[2]

We could not begin in Mark 10:35–38 and interpret this passage correctly. We must go back in the biblical trail, and, in doing so, we will see a good example of a parallel passage of Scripture that often gives us more information and helps us to view other passages in light of other

---

[1] https://www.sermonaudio.com/search.asp?sourceonly=true&currSection=sermons source&keyword=gregharris&subsetcat=series&subsetitem=The+Cup+and+the+Glory+-+Book

[2] Greg Harris, *The Cup and the Glory: Lessons on Suffering and the Glory of God* (The Woodlands, TX: Kress Biblical Resources, 2006).

Scriptures. As we saw in the parallel passage of Matthew 16, this was the first time that Jesus taught concerning the glory of God and linked that demonstration of God's glory with His own return to earth. The transfiguration follows immediately and connects to the glory of God, as seen in Matt 17:1–2: "Six days later Jesus took with Him Peter and James and John his brother, and led them up on a high mountain by themselves. And He was transfigured before them; and His face shone like the sun, and His garments became as white as light." The transfiguration was a brief preview—a snapshot—of the fifth theological bombshell of what the coming King and His kingdom will look like when He returns in the glory of God. What Peter, James, and John were permitted to see—quite briefly—was "the glory of God in the face of Christ" (2 Cor 4:6).

We who were not present and who read the biblical account generally note that the glory of God is mentioned, but often do not see it as all that important—but God does. The Holy Spirit reveals more about this decades later by recalling the transfiguration to Peter's mind and by having him record it in the holy and eternal Word of God. As Peter was only days—or hours—away from his own crucifixion in Rome, he went back—or better still, the Holy Spirit took him back—in his memory to that one day that was above every other day with Jesus (other than the day Peter was saved). He recalled the transfiguration, as seen in 2 Pet 1:16–18:

> For we did not follow cleverly devised tales when we made known to you the power and coming of our Lord Jesus Christ [the fifth theological bombshell of Matthew 16], but we were eyewitnesses of His majesty. For when He received honor and glory from God the Father, such an utterance as this was made to Him by the Majestic Glory, "This is My beloved Son with whom I am well-pleased"—and we ourselves heard this utterance made from heaven when we were with Him on the holy mountain.

Do not worry that you were not at the transfiguration. That was a snapshot only; we will get to partake freely and eternally of the ongoing "movie" of what God has us do with Him in glory.

With this background, we start the path to the Mark 10 passage by means of Mark 8. We will note the parallel passage to the Matthew 16 account we have used in Mark 8:27–28. You can read that on your own, but note that it does not have as much detail as the Matthew 16 account. So to show the parallel, here is the fourth theological bombshell of Matthew 16 in Mark 8:34–37; it is the cost for the disciple following Jesus.

And He summoned the crowd with His disciples, and said to them, "If anyone wishes to come after Me, he must deny himself, and take up his cross and follow Me. For whoever wishes to save his life will lose it, but whoever loses his life for My sake and the gospel's will save it. For what does it profit a man to gain the whole world, and forfeit his soul? For what will a man give in exchange for his soul?"

Here is Mark's statement for the fifth theological bombshell: "For whoever is ashamed of Me and My words in this adulterous and sinful generation, the Son of Man will also be ashamed of him when He comes in the glory of His Father with the holy angels." (Mark 8:38)

> **CRUCIAL:** Mark 8:38 is a good verse to use with people who try to remove the person of Jesus from the words of Jesus—which cannot be done. Whenever God tolerates, He does so only temporarily. Ultimately, Phil 2:9–11 will be wonderfully and appropriately fulfilled and tied in with the glory of God: "For this reason also, God highly exalted Him, and bestowed on Him the name which is above every name, so that at the name of Jesus every knee will bow—of those who are in heaven and on earth and under the earth, and that every tongue will confess that Jesus Christ is Lord, to the glory of God the Father."

As with Matthew 16, the Mark 8 account is followed by the transfiguration account in Mark 9:1–8:

And Jesus was saying to them, "Truly I say to you, there are some of those who are standing here who will not taste death until they see the kingdom of God after it has come with power."

Six days later, Jesus took with Him Peter and James and John, and brought them up on a high mountain by themselves. And He was transfigured before them; and His garments became radiant and exceedingly white, as no launderer on earth can whiten them. Elijah appeared to them along with Moses; and they were talking with Jesus. Peter said to Jesus, "Rabbi, it is good for us to be here; let us make three tabernacles, one for You, and one for Moses,

*and one for Elijah." For he did not know what to answer; for they became
terrified. Then a cloud formed, overshadowing them, and a voice came
out of the cloud, "This is My beloved Son, listen to Him!" All at once they
looked around and saw no one with them anymore, except Jesus alone.*

Also beneficial in better understanding the Mark 10 passage is 9:9–10:
"As they were coming down from the mountain, He gave them orders not
to relate to anyone what they had seen, until the Son of Man rose from the
dead. They seized upon that statement, discussing with one another what
rising from the dead meant."

Note one very important biblical truth from these passages: until the
resurrection and appearance of Jesus to His disciples, three of His apostles—Peter, James, and John—witnessed and knew incredible truths that
God blessed them with, but they were not permitted to talk with anyone
else about what they had seen.

With this background we come to Mark 10:35–41, and I think from
our walk up to this point, we will have the passage open up before us:

*James and John, the two sons of Zebedee, came up to Jesus, saying, "Teacher,
we want You to do for us whatever we ask of You." And He said to them,
"What do you want Me to do for you?" They said to Him, "Grant that we
may sit, one on Your right and one on Your left, in Your glory." But Jesus
said to them, "You do not know what you are asking. Are you able to drink
the cup that I drink, or to be baptized with the baptism with which I am baptized?" They said to Him, "We are able." And Jesus said to them, "The cup
that I drink you shall drink; and you shall be baptized with the baptism with
which I am baptized. But to sit on My right or on My left, this is not Mine
to give; but it is for those for whom it has been prepared." Hearing this, the
ten began to feel indignant with James and John.*

Note some major points in this account. First, look who asked Jesus—James and John—and look who was left out—Peter. In Mark 10:41,
when the ten became indignant, no one would have been more indignant
than Peter, the one James and John left out of what they asked Jesus. Peter
alone knew what they knew, but the three had been instructed not to tell
anyone what they had seen. In other words, Peter would have been more
infuriated than the remaining ten apostles were, but he was restricted from
saying much.

Second, when James and John asked Jesus about sitting in His glory, this would be based on the fifth theological bombshell of Matthew 16/Mark 9, the return of Jesus in glory, and in light of all that they had been privileged to witness at His transfiguration. They would have been stunned by His response that they did not know what they were asking for when they asked to be allowed to sit in His glory. To them it would seem from the answer that Jesus gave them He must not have considered the eternal significance of His transfiguration.

Third, in harmony with other scriptural verses the Godhead will reveal later, sitting in the glory of Jesus is not only a simple gift from God. In this case, it is a process largely determined by their actions as His disciples.

Fourth, coupled with the above truth, the answer that Jesus gave to James and John about sitting in His glory has two parts. One is an active voice—in which you do the action (for example, "I kick the ball"); one is a passive voice—in which you receive the action (for example, "I was kicked").

When Jesus asked them if they were able to drink the cup that He drank, He used the active voice—they were to do the action. So, in view of this, what does drinking the cup of Jesus entail? It is taken from the fourth theological bombshell of Matthew 16: whatever you do to deny yourself, take up your cross daily and follow Jesus as His disciple. These are the matters that you control, whether you do them or not; these are the choices you make to follow Jesus. As the general course of life, you decide to read the Bible or not; you decide how much prayer will play a part of your Christian life; you decide whether or not to attend a Bible-believing church. You decide whether you will use your computer to consume porn or to share His truth—and on and on the list goes.

The second part of the answer from Jesus regarded whether James and John—or you and I—can "be baptized with the baptism with which [Jesus is] baptized" (Mark 10:38). In drinking His cup, we do the action; in being baptized in His baptism, we receive the action—which goes beyond the choices we actively make. In this context, being baptized with His baptism is not the baptism in water after someone is saved; rather, it refers to the things that God in His sovereignty brings into your life that you have no control over but that are part of walking by faith with the Lord. These include, but are not limited to, persecution, family rejection, your twins dying at birth, and anything else that God in His sovereignty permits—such as attacks by Satan, as we see in Job 1–2—but will not give us full disclosure about until we are with Him in glory.

Fifth, not only did Jesus use the passive voice in reference to His disciples ("be baptized"); He used the passive voice in reference to what God had for His Son the Servant, "with the baptism with which I am baptized?" He would drink His cup—voluntary action—and He would be baptized—voluntary submission. Jesus would say later in Luke 12:50, as He prepared for the cross, that the Trinity had foreordained for Him before the world existed: "But I have a baptism to undergo, and how distressed I am until it is accomplished!" We will see in much more detail some of what His cup and His baptism entailed in upcoming chapters of this book.

Summary and Conclusion

We saw in this chapter that it is difficult to tell how many references the Bible contains on the glory of God. We did see some presuppositions on the glory of God that help us establish some biblical parameters. First, God's glory is vastly beyond what we can comprehend. Psalm 19:1 tells that "[t]he heavens are telling of the glory of God; / And their expanse is declaring the work of His hands." "The heavens are telling of the glory of God," but the heavens do not contain the glory of God. Second, although currently veiled and not fully disclosed, God's glory extends to every place God is—but not to one unique place: hell (Matt 25:41; 2 Thess 1:9–10). Third, connected with the previous truth, a major component of Satan's active works involves the glory of God (2 Cor 4:3–4). Satan could be (and is) involved with many other things, but one thing he will *not* neglect is blinding people's minds to the glory of God.

The fourth presupposition, which is connected with all that we have seen so far in this chapter, is that the present and future spiritual warfare battlefield ultimately and directly relates to the glory of God. In Ps 96:1–9 God says twice to tell the nations of His glory. As we saw in 2 Cor 4:3–4, Satan actively works to do just the opposite of what God calls for in Psalm 96; specifically, he blinds the minds of the unbelievers so they cannot see the light of the gospel of the glory of Christ. This at the core is the basis for most of the present spiritual warfare, and it will not go away until the Lord Jesus Christ returns in glory. We also learned that in order to tell the nations of God's glory we need to understand some of what the glory of God entails. There is much more to it than saying, "God has glory!" The glory of God is best defined as any of the attributes and/or activities of God, and that succinctly covers everything about the Godhead. The de-tails—and full disclosure of God's glory—will take an eternity to behold and embrace.

The fifth presupposition is that God not only brings the redeemed to be with Him in heaven, but a major component of that heaven is the glory of God (Heb 2:9–10). From the moment you were saved, God started a pro-cess of walking you to heaven. He shows this in one of the most amazing verses in the entire Bible, 2 Thess 2:14: "And it was for this He called you through our gospel, that you may gain [literally, "to the gaining of"] the glory of our Lord Jesus Christ." If we humans had written on our own what this verse teaches, it would be blasphemy. But God put it in His Word, and we can have confidence that this is eternally true. If you ever wondered why God called you through His gospel, it is so "you may gain the glory of our Lord Jesus Christ." We also saw with this that God will not give us His full glory, for that would mean our being worshipped, and that is not in Scripture. But any of the glory of God that He will give us is part of what makes heaven be heaven and allows us to have the fullest enjoyment with Him in eternity. Not everyone will receive the same amount of God's glory, for there will be degrees of reward for the redeemed.

The sixth presupposition is that if you are saved and walking in obe-dience to Him, God is in the process of presently developing His glory within you (Rom 8:18; 2 Cor 4:16–18). While I could spend the rest of the book writing only about the cascading truths revealed in this one passage, I will limit this to two crucial doctrinal truths: (1) God's glory has weight to it—most of us would never view this truth in reference to the glory of God; and (2) the Holy Spirit says that such is the contrast between the present sufferings and afflictions now for the redeemed and the glory of God yet to be revealed to us. There is no language on earth that could properly ex-press it so that we could comprehend it.

The seventh presupposition (connected with the previous biblical presupposition) is that we know now, if we did not know before, that if we are walking with God, He uses our sufferings and afflictions to produce in us an eternal weight of glory beyond all comparison. Many of us did not, or do not, recognize or appreciate that this is a process God uses, and the Godhead has decided how long and to what degree of depth this goes for each individual.

In addition to these things, we also saw in Mark 9:1–9 the transfiguration, in which for a short time, the glory of God showed on the face of Christ. When we came to the Mark 10:35–41 account, we saw that (1) James and John left out Peter when they went to ask Jesus about sitting in His glory. (2) In Mark 10:41, when the ten became indignant, no one would have been more indignant than Peter, the one James and John left out of what they asked Jesus. Peter alone also knew what they knew, but they were instructed not to tell anyone what they had seen. (3) When James and John asked Jesus about sitting in His glory, this would be based on the fifth theological bombshell of Matthew 16/Mark 9, with Jesus returning in the glory of God, and in light of all that they had been privileged to witness at His transfiguration. They would have been stunned by His response that they did not know what they were asking for when they asked to be allowed to sit in His glory. (4) In harmony with other scriptural verses the Godhead will reveal later, sitting in the glory of Jesus is not only a simple gift from God. In this case, it is a process largely determined by their actions as His disciples. And (5), coupled with the previous truth, the answer that Jesus gave to James and John in Mark 10:38 about what was required to sit in His glory has two parts: one is an active voice ("drink of My cup"—you do the action); one is a passive voice ("be baptized with the baptism with which I am baptized"—you receive the action). In drinking His cup, you do the action; in being baptized in His baptism, you submit to the sovereign choices that God has made for your life.

Deeper Walk Study Questions

1. Why is it hard to tell how many instances of "the glory of God" occur in the Bible? Give four examples.

2. What is the significance of the truth (based on verses such as Ps 19:1) that the heavens do not contain the glory of God, but that the glory of God surrounds the heavens? Tell truths we know about God from this biblical doctrine.

3. What can we learn about hell and God's glory from Matt 25:41 and 2 Thess 1:9–10? Give four biblical truths from these and explain why they are important theologically.

4. What is the theological significance from 2 Cor 4:3–4? Carefully list six truths from these verses and tell why they are important.

5. How do Psalm 96 and 2 Cor 4:3–4 explain the basis for most of the true spiritual warfare that exists? List five biblical truths from these passages and explain why they are important to living the Christian life or how they relate to ministry.

6. List seven truths from Heb 2:9–10 and 2 Thess 2:14. Why are these important to know? Explain.

7. Name eight biblical truths that can be learned from Rom 8:18 and 2 Cor 4:16–18. How do these help you live the Christian life better? Explain.

8. Why would we not know the full story of Mark 10:35–41 if we stayed only in these verses? From the previous contexts, name four important matters we would not have known if we did not back up a few chapters to pick up some pertinent information. Explain.

9. Why would James and John be so surprised at how Jesus responded to their questions in Mark 10:35–40?

10. What is the difference between the active voice "drink the cup" and the passive voice "be baptized"? How does this help us view the Christian life better? Explain.

11. Why would Peter be the most upset of the other apostles who were indignant at what James and John asked Jesus?

CHAPTER 21

This Is the Day That the Lord Has Made

M any people are familiar with the title of this chapter because, if for no other reason, they may have sung the song by that name or have heard it used in different calls to worship in churches or other Christian gatherings: "This is the day which the LORD has made; / Let us rejoice and be glad in it." Many who have used this verse may not have realized it is Ps 118:24 which as we will soon see, is important to know.

As common as Ps 118:24 is in many circles, it is surprising that the New Testament never quotes or cites this particular verse. But as we will see in this chapter (1) the New Testament repeatedly quotes verses from Psalm 118 (2) that show up in tremendously important or strategic places and ways (3) as part of the unfolding story of God's promised Messiah and (4) does so in worship-evoking biblical truths.

Most will never look at Psalm 118 again in the same way—as God fully intends that you will not.

My Initial Encounter with Psalm 118
Used in the New Testament

I had no idea initially how God would use these eternity-changing verses in my life and in many other lives as well. My first encounter with this psalm—other than the normal, casual reading of the Bible through which I learned enough to know that the passage exists without necessarily understanding its significance—began for me when I was preaching through

First Peter at Berwyn Baptist Church in College Park, Maryland. We came to 1 Pet 2:4–8:

> And coming to Him as to a living stone which has been rejected by men, but is choice and precious in the sight of God, you also, as living stones, are being built up as a spiritual house for a holy priesthood, to offer up spiritual sacrifices acceptable to God through Jesus Christ. For this is contained in Scripture:
>
> "BEHOLD, I LAY IN ZION A CHOICE STONE, A PRECIOUS CORNER STONE,
>
> AND HE WHO BELIEVES IN HIM WILL NOT BE DISAPPOINTED."
>
> THIS PRECIOUS VALUE, THEN, IS FOR YOU WHO BELIEVE; BUT FOR THOSE WHO DISBELIEVE,
>
> "THE STONE WHICH THE BUILDERS REJECTED,
>
> THIS BECAME THE VERY CORNER STONE,"
>
> AND,
>
> "A STONE OF STUMBLING AND A ROCK OF OFFENSE";
>
> for they stumble because they are disobedient to the word, and to this doom they were also appointed.

As I was studying to prepare to preach through this passage, what struck me initially is the repeated use of "stone" as a description of Jesus the Messiah: "coming to Him as to a living stone," "a choice stone," "a precious corner stone," "the stone which the builders rejected," became "the very corner stone," and "a stone of stumbling and a rock of offense." In only a few verses, a sixfold usage of "stone" to describe the Messiah is significant. The number of uses should alert the careful reader that the Holy Spirit intends for us not only to mark that these verses exist but also desires that we pay careful attention to each one. The second thing that struck me was the threefold citing of Old Testament verses to show their original source. First Peter 2:6 begins, "For this is contained in Scripture" and follows with three Old Testament citations: two from Isa 28:16 and from the Book of Immanuel section of Isaiah (Isaiah 7–12; 8:14) and one from Ps 118:22.

We should note/emphasize three important truths. (1) These verses are "Stone Prophecies" or declarations about the qualifications/characteristics/

description of God's Messiah that must be true for Him, especially to the smallest detail. (2) The most frequently used word-picture title or description of the Messiah in the Bible is that of "the Lamb." Perhaps you can think of many such uses. What many people do not realize is that "the Stone" is the second most used designation from God's Word about His Messiah, such as in the six uses in 1 Pet 2:4–8. As I previously wrote, I had no idea this was true until I was studying to preach on 1 Peter 2. From my interactions with many people over the years, I started to entitle this chapter accordingly: "Those Magnificent 'Stone Prophecies' about God's Messiah That Remain Totally Hidden to So Many."

And (3) because the Stone is the second most used designation of the Messiah in Scripture, it would be a worthwhile study to go through the Bible to note each time it is used accordingly. In doing this you could concoct a remarkably broad and inclusive biblical theology about who the Messiah is, plus what He must do in His life, death, resurrection, return in the glory of God, and reign. You would find that not only do such Stone Prophecies repeatedly occur, but they are cited at some of the most incredibly strategic places in the New Testament. I think you will see such occurrences in this chapter of *The Bible Expositor's Handbook* and be convinced that not only should you know about these verses, but that your biblical theology would be woefully lacking unless you increase your understanding about God's Messiah accordingly. Some will respond, as other people do, "I cannot believe that I missed these verses all these years. They are right here before me in Scripture."

We must consider that although there is some debate among scholars, I have found Psalm 110 and Psalm 118 to be the two most frequently cited/ quoted psalms in the New Testament, such as we saw 118:22 quoted in 1 Pet 2:7. Psalm 110 has verses many are familiar with, including "The LORD says to my Lord: / 'Sit at My right hand / Until I make Your enemies a footstool for Your feet'" (v. 1), and verse 4 says, "You are a priest forever / According to the order of Melchizedek." But we limit our study in this chapter to Psalm 118—if for no other reason than the Holy Spirit sees fit to repeatedly cite this psalm as having such an important role in describing the life and work of Jesus the Messiah. We would do well to track this biblical trail.

> **CONSIDER:** The study that I did by following the biblical trail of
> the Stone Prophecies about the Messiah became a "Glory Book,"
> entitled, appropriately enough, *The Stone and the Glory.* So for those
> who want to begin earlier in the Bible to follow along the biblical trail
> in much more detail—as well as focusing on many more such Stone
> Prophecies specifically about Jesus Christ—*The Stone and the Glory*
> is available on Amazon.[1]

Psalm 118 and the Final Days of the Incarnation of Jesus Christ

With Psalm 118 being one of the two most cited and strategically used
psalms in the New Testament, we should not be surprised to see this psalm
used in the days of the life of Jesus. The context for this is the Triumphal
Entry.

> **MARK WELL:** I do not know who first decided that this entry of Jesus
> into Jerusalem should be called the Triumphal Entry, but this is *not*
> an accurate name for what Jesus was about to do. Human titles or
> designations are just that—human titles or designations—and are not
> inspired by the Holy Spirit. Some titles/designations are accurate,
> and others, such as calling this the Triumphal Entry, are woefully
> inaccurate; nevertheless, they become entrenched in people's minds
> as biblical truth or doctrine. This account in Matthew 21 is not
> the Triumphal Entry, though some translations use that phrase as a
> subheading. If you want to read about the real Triumphal Entry, read
> Zechariah 14 or Revelation 19. While I acknowledge that this is a
> rather long title, the Matthew 21 account (and parallel passages)
> could best be entitled, "The Prophetic Fulfillment of Israel's Humble
> Messiah Who Rides on in Silence to Redeem—Not to Rule."

---

[1] Greg Harris, *The Stone and the Glory: Lessons on the Temple Presence and the Glory of God* (The Woodlands, TX: Kress Biblical Resources, 2010).

Matthew 21:1–8 gives this account of Jesus entering Jerusalem with only a few days remaining before His atoning death:

When they had approached Jerusalem and had come to Bethphage, at the Mount of Olives, then Jesus sent two disciples, saying to them, "Go into the village opposite you, and immediately you will find a donkey tied there and a colt with her; untie them and bring them to Me. If anyone says anything to you, you shall say, 'The Lord has need of them,' and immediately he will send them." This took place to fulfill what was spoken through the prophet:

"SAY TO THE DAUGHTER OF ZION,

'BEHOLD YOUR KING [THE DAVIDIC COVENANT HEIR] IS COMING TO YOU,

GENTLE, AND MOUNTED ON A DONKEY,

EVEN ON A COLT, THE FOAL OF A BEAST OF BURDEN.'"

The disciples went and did just as Jesus had instructed them, and brought the donkey and the colt, and laid their coats on them; and He sat on the coats. Most of the crowd spread their coats in the road, and others were cutting branches from the trees and spreading them in the road.

Many are familiar with this part in Matt 21:9:

The crowds going ahead of Him, and those who followed, were shouting,

Hosanna to the Son of David;

BLESSED IS HE WHO COMES IN THE NAME OF THE LORD;

Hosanna in the highest!"

The people shouted verses taken from Ps 118:25–26 and did so in recognition that Jesus is God's Messiah sent to them. All of the parallel passages specifically, in varying and sometimes additional detail, use Psalm 118 with the arrival of God's Messiah, the Davidic covenant King and His kingdom. Mark 11:10 states, "Blessed is the coming kingdom of our father David; Hosanna in the highest!" and Luke 19:38 adds, "BLESSED IS THE KING WHO COMES IN THE NAME OF THE LORD; Peace in heaven and glory in the highest!" John 12:12–13 offers,

On the next day the large crowd who had come to the feast, when they heard that Jesus was coming to Jerusalem, took the branches of the palm trees and went out to meet Him, and began to shout, "Hosanna! BLESSED IS HE WHO COMES IN THE NAME OF THE LORD, even the King of Israel."

We will stay in Matthew's account. Jesus cleansed His temple (Matt 21:12–17) and left and spent the night in nearby Bethany. The next day He returned and taught in His temple, which gave an opportunity for the religious leaders to come and accost Jesus, asking by whose authority He did such things (vv. 23–27). I will go into more detail about this passage in another chapter of this *Handbook,* but note for the time being that the question about Jesus's authority and His answer were based on whether the source of the ministry of John the Baptist was from God or man (vv. 24–27). Jesus instructed the Twelve in Matthew 13 that He would only speak to His enemies about Himself by means of parables. Thus, He spoke of Himself in the subsequent parable in Matt 21:28–32; it is about two sons, one who acted faithfully and one who did not.

With this background, we continue with verse 33, and remember that Jesus is speaking in the public courts of the Temple Mount, and not in private. Many others would be hearing what Jesus said:

> *Listen to another parable. There was a landowner who* PLANTED A VINEYARD *AND PUT A WALL AROUND IT AND DUG A WINEPRESS IN IT, AND BUILT A TOWER* [cited from Isa 5:2—the panoramic overview section of the book of Isaiah], *and rented it out to vine-growers and went on a journey.*

With the Isaiah quote noted as the basis for the Messiah's next teaching, here is His parable in full:

> *"Listen to another parable. There was a landowner who* PLANTED A VINEYARD *AND PUT A WALL AROUND IT AND DUG A WINEPRESS IN IT, AND BUILT A TOWER, and rented it out to vine-growers and went on a journey. When the harvest time approached, he sent his slaves to the vine-growers to receive his produce. The vine-growers took his slaves and beat one, and killed another, and stoned a third. Again he sent another group of slaves larger than the first; and they did the same thing to them. But afterward he sent his son to them, saying, 'They will respect my son.' But when the vine-growers saw the son, they said among themselves, 'This is the heir; come, let us kill him and seize his inheritance.' They took him, and threw him out of the vineyard and killed him. Therefore when the owner of the vineyard comes, what will he do to those vine-growers?" (Matt 21:33-40)*

The religious leaders themselves—and not the crowds at the temple—answered Jesus's question in verse 41, which would be easy for them to answer: "He will bring those wretches to a wretched end," they told Him, "and will rent out the vineyard to other vine-growers who will pay him the proceeds at the proper seasons."

It is in this specific context that Jesus appropriately quoted Ps 118:22–23 to the religious leaders in Matt 21:42:

Jesus said to them, "Did you never read in the Scriptures,

'THE STONE WHICH THE BUILDERS REJECTED,

THIS BECAME THE CHIEF CORNER STONE;

THIS CAME ABOUT FROM THE LORD,

AND IT IS MARVELOUS IN OUR EYES'?

Jesus continued in verses 43–44: "Therefore I say to you, the kingdom of God will be taken away from you and given to a people, producing the fruit of it. And he who falls on this stone will be broken to pieces; but on whomever it falls, it will scatter him like dust."

The religious leaders who had gathered that day finally understood what Jesus had said, and they wanted to respond appropriately: "When the chief priests and the Pharisees heard His parables, they understood that He was speaking about them. When they sought to seize Him, they feared the people, because they considered Him to be a prophet" (vv. 45–46).

I continue the story with the account in *The Stone and the Glory* (pp. 109–10), and because I am quoting my own writing, I will make this part of the body of this text rather than using the usual citation method:

Jesus had mentioned no names in His parables. Why then did the chief priests and Pharisees react so violently? Simply put, the opponents of Jesus responded in wrath because they clearly understood what Jesus was claiming: He Himself was the cornerstone placed by God. This concerned Jesus's origin and mission and answered their initial question of, "By what authority are you doing these things?" (Matt 21:23)—"by My Father who placed Me here."

Consider what Jesus said to them, "Did you never read in the Scriptures, 'The stone which the builders rejected, this became the chief corner stone?'" This question by Jesus contained many subsidiary implications that struck at the core of the Jewish leaders' tragically misguided and self-exalting theology.

Maybe the religious leaders did not know the psalm as did God's true worshippers who had shouted Psalm 118 two days before at the advent of Israel's Messiah.

Maybe they had read it, but it was merely a repeated ritual, a routine of no unusual significance: similar to having the right answer about where the Messiah would be born but not by walking a few miles down the road to Bethlehem to investigate for themselves the heralded birth (Matt 2:1–6).

Maybe Psalm 118 was merely an academic exercise without any personal relevance to them and, for some, certainly not the inspired holy Word of God.

Maybe the religious leaders had mixed their tradition with the Word of God so that the composite blend had become merely a form of godliness devoid of any true spiritual life.

But beyond these additional condemnations, one essential truth emerged above all the rest: Psalm 118 strongly supports the messianic claims of Jesus of who the Messiah of Israel is. Whoever the Messiah was, He had to be initially rejected before He would reign in order for Scripture to be fulfilled. Not only was the Messiah to be rejected, but also this rejection must come from those in places of religious authority and responsibility. This prophecy was being fulfilled from the very ones repudiating Jesus at that very moment. That hour was the Trinity-ordained time of Jesus's rejection—not His reign—as the Godhead had mandated in eternity past. Nevertheless, it still made those who rejected Him responsible for their actions (Matt 21:44).

The chief priests and elders were not only the builders who rejected the Stone, but they were also the ones who opposed God the Father because God Himself had placed the Stone. They—not the Stone—were the ones standing in direct opposition and hostility to God, and they collectively stood condemned by Scripture. Ironically, the rejection of the Stone by the religious leaders did not diminish the claims of Jesus: the stronger the hostile reaction by the leaders, the greater the messianic substantiation. God's own Word predicted this would—and must—happen, just as it did, and predicted or not, they intended to add their intensified hostility against the Lamb of God who takes away the sins of the world (John 1:29).

To further document the importance of what was taking place in Matthew 21, let us fast-forward a few months to events recorded in the book of Acts for a crucial substantiation of part of Psalm 118 having been fulfilled.

By Acts 2, Jesus had sent forth the Holy Spirit, and His church was born. This sound of a strong rushing wind—with no actual wind blowing—in such a dusty place as Jerusalem (since any wind would put dust into the air and in people's faces) could not be explained away. This sound of the rushing wind gave the masses at the temple a reason to gather and hear Peter's first sermon that we are just noting because this is not our focus here. He concluded this way, in Acts 2:36–41:

> *"Therefore let all the house of Israel know for certain that God has made Him both Lord and Christ—this Jesus whom you crucified."*
>
> *Now when they heard this, they were pierced to the heart, and said to Peter and the rest of the apostles, "Brethren, what shall we do?" Peter said to them, "Repent, and each of you be baptized in the name of Jesus Christ for the forgiveness of your sins; and you will receive the gift of the Holy Spirit. For the promise is for you and your children and for all who are far off, as many as the Lord our God will call to Himself." And with many other words he solemnly testified and kept on exhorting them, saying, "Be saved from this perverse generation!" So then, those who had received His Word were baptized; and that day there were added about three thousand souls.*

Acts 2 set the stage for what would occur in 3:1–10:

> *Now Peter and John were going up to the temple at the ninth hour, the hour of prayer. And a man who had been lame from his mother's womb was being carried along, whom they used to set down every day at the gate of the temple which is called Beautiful, in order to beg alms of those who were entering the temple. When he saw Peter and John about to go into the temple, he began asking to receive alms. But Peter, along with John, fixed his gaze on him and said, "Look at us!" And he began to give them his attention, expecting to receive something from them. But Peter said, "I do not possess silver and gold, but what I do have I give to you: In the name of Jesus Christ the Nazarene—walk!" And seizing him by the right hand, he raised him up; and immediately his feet and his ankles were strengthened. With a leap he stood upright and began to walk; and he entered the temple with them, walking and leaping and praising God. And all the people saw him walking and praising God; and they were taking note of him as being the one who*

used to sit at the Beautiful Gate of the temple to beg alms, and they were
filled with wonder and amazement at what had happened to him.

The miracle that was performed and the surrounding excitement gathered people together to hear Peter's second sermon, recorded in verses
11–26, which you can read on your own.

Acts 4:1–4 picks up the account and gives a progress report:

As they were speaking to the people, the priests and the captain of the
temple guard and the Sadducees came up to them, being greatly disturbed
because they were teaching the people and proclaiming in Jesus the res-
urrection from the dead. And they laid hands on them and put them in jail
until the next day, for it was already evening. But many of those who had
heard the message believed; and the number of the men came to be about
five thousand.

Acts 4:5–6 marks the gathering of the religious officials: *"On the next day,*
their rulers and elders and scribes were gathered together in Jerusalem;
and Annas the high priest was there, and Caiaphas and John and Alexander,
and all who were of high-priestly descent."

The account continues in *The Stone and the Glory* (pp. 149–50):

With Annas presiding over the Sanhedrin, a reenactment of the Passover week was about to play out again. The issue at hand was identical to
what this same group had asked Jesus, only weeks before, after He had
cleansed the Temple: "By what authority are You doing these things, and
who gave You this authority?" (Matt 21:23). Now the same people would
ask Jesus's followers the same thing: "By what power, or in what name,
have you done this?" (Acts 4:7), in reference to the healing of the man who
had been born lame (3:1–10).

Although Jesus was not physically present, the Holy Spirit manifested
Himself by filling Peter and bringing about once more the exact words that
God intended for the renewing of His lesson (Acts 4:8a). The disciple re-
peated to the same people what they collectively had heard from the Lord
Jesus only a few months earlier. Acts 4 continues the account:

"Rulers and elders of the people, if we are on trial today for a benefit done
to a sick man, as to how this man has been made well, let it be known to
all of you, and to all the people of Israel, that by the name of Jesus Christ

the Nazarene, whom you crucified, whom God raised from the dead—by this name this man stands here before you in good health. He is the STONE WHICH WAS REJECTED by you, THE BUILDERS, but WHICH BECAME THE CHIEF CORNER stone And there is salvation in no one else; for there is no other name given among men, by which we must be saved" (vv. 8–12).

> **VERY IMPORTANT:** Many people are familiar with or can quote Acts
> 4:12: "And there is salvation in no one else; for there is no other
> name under heaven that has been given among men by which we
> must be saved." What most people do not recognize is the immediate
> context of the verse before this and the recognition of the fulfillment
> of a portion of one of the Stone Prophecies about the Messiah, as
> seen in verse 11: "He is the STONE WHICH WAS REJECTED by you, THE
> BUILDERS, but WHICH BECAME THE CHIEF CORNER stone."

The following verse describes the reaction of those who were once more confronted face-to-face with this message that they long assumed had died. Luke noted the shocked reaction of the gathered religious leaders, reporting that "they were marveling, and began to recognize that they had been with Jesus" (4:13). Their amazement probably resulted as much as anything from hearing afresh the quotation of Ps 118:22. Their heads must have snapped up in unison when they heard this messianic psalm for at least the sixth time. Try as they might, the rejecters could not rid themselves of the Stone. Though absent from view, the Stone continually encountered them. Everywhere they went—both physically and spiritually—the Foundation Stone awaited them. Everywhere they went, they still stumbled over the Stumbling Stone.

Having seen in Acts that the Holy Spirit wants us to know that the Stone prophecy about the religious leaders rejecting the Messiah has been fulfilled, we can return to Matthew's Gospel to mark another crucial doctrinal truth. We will skip over to the remaining accounts leading up to Matthew 23 in *The Stone and Glory* (pp. 111–12):

Having shut the mouths of the stonehearted, Jesus then took the offensive. In Matthew 23 Jesus instructed the multitudes by rebuking the ways of the scribes and Pharisees. In concluding His denouncement of the religious leaders, Jesus promised pending judgment on that generation and other generations who had rejected or who would reject Him (vv. 34–36). Yet, even in the midst of His reproof, the deep love of the heartsick Messiah showed forth: "Jerusalem, Jerusalem, who kills the prophets and stones those who are sent to her! How often I wanted to gather your children together, the way a hen gathers her chicks under her wings, and you were unwilling. Behold, your house is being left to you desolate" (vv. 37–38).

Then Jesus said something totally unexpected—to the disciples, to the masses, and to His opponents. He quoted the exact phrase from Psalm 118 that many within the multitude had shouted only two days before at His unforgettable entry into Jerusalem: "For I say to you, from now on you shall not see Me until you say, 'Blessed is He who comes in the name of the LORD!'" (Matt 23:39).

When we consider them, what Jesus declared must have greatly confused the vast majority of those who heard Him. His statements were made on the same day as the discourses of Matthew 21 and 22—and somewhere close to forty-eight hours after His "Triumphal Entry" into Jerusalem. His reasoning seems disjointed, as though two distinct conversations occurred simultaneously, each incongruous with the other. Jesus demanded future praise from Israel, praise that had previously been given Him only a few days earlier. The people had already publicly proclaimed what Jesus had told them was necessary for the nation to see Him, namely, "Blessed is He who comes in the name of the LORD" (Matt 21:9; Ps 118:26). One thing is certain; the answer that Jesus gave indicated that He did not view Ps 118:25–26 as having had its fulfillment at the Triumphal Entry.

Why did Jesus not accept Israel's praise at the advent of her Messiah? Simply put, He could not have received the praise of Israel at that time because Ps 118:22 ("the stone which the builders rejected") had not yet transpired, but would culminate in His crucifixion. The people sang and desired Ps 118:25–26: "O LORD, do save [Hosanna!], we beseech You; / O LORD, we beseech You, do send prosperity! / Blessed is the one who comes in the name of the LORD." But such prophesied days of blessing could not come without the builders first rejecting the Stone placed there by God Himself. The times of blessing could not come unless the Lamb of God made proper atonement for the sin of the world (John 1:29). Most of the people in Israel—especially the various religious groups—saw no need for such atonement; after all, they had the functioning temple sacrifices. Jesus never permitted these basest of needs to leave His thoughts.

Reading Psalm 118:22–29 in a New Light

Sometimes it is best to return to the passage's actual usage in its own context. This helps in two ways. (1) As we have seen in other places, sometimes there is more to a verse than people may know, such as Josh 24:15: "Choose you this day whom you will serve . . . as for me and my house, we will serve the LORD," which is only a partial quote from a larger verse. (2) Sometimes there are other truths connected with the passage that are very rich and that greatly add to our understanding.

And from such a vantage point, let us appreciate—and worship in spirit/Spirit and truth—as we read Ps 118:22–29 in its context and in its chronological significance:

The stone which the builders rejected

Has become the chief corner stone.

This is the LORD's doing;

It is marvelous in our eyes.

This is the day which the LORD has made;

Let us rejoice and be glad in it.

O LORD, do save, we beseech You;

O LORD, we beseech You, do send prosperity!

Blessed is the one who comes in the name of the LORD;

We have blessed you from the house of the LORD.

The LORD is God, and He has given us light;

Bind the festival sacrifice with cords to the horns of the altar.

You are my God, and I give thanks to You;

You are my God, I extol You.

Give thanks to the LORD, for He is good;

For His lovingkindness is everlasting.

CRUCIAL TRUTHS: "This is the day that the Lord has made / Let us rejoice and be glad in it" (Ps 118:24) is the specific day determined by Yahweh (v. 23) where He presents His Messiah before Israel's religious leaders ("the builders"), who will reject "the Stone, the Messiah," sent to them. And in spite of the rejection at this point, the Messiah will eventually become "the chief corner stone." Furthermore, verses 25–26 ("O Lord, do save, we beseech You; / O Lord, we beseech You, do send prosperity! / Blessed is the one who comes in the name of the Lord.") used by the multitudes in Matthew 21 and the other Gospels' accounts is not, as we know, the true Triumphal Entry at the First Advent of Jesus, but it will be true— and truly done—by national Israel when Jesus the Messiah returns to reign, and He will accept that praise and those people when He returns. Long before those future events occurred, they were already included—"This is the day that the Lord has made/ Let us rejoice and be glad in it"—and go beyond the rejection of the Messiah by the religious leaders. Psalm 118:27 shows very fittingly, in this Old Testament messianic depiction of Jesus, His sacrificial death as well: "The Lord is God, and He has given us light; / Bind the festival sacrifice with cords to the horns of the altar." Binding the Lamb of God to the horns of the sacrificial altar they most assuredly intended to do—and they did do—to the Lamb of God, who takes away the sins of the world (John 1:29). While this was not His official Triumphal Entry, it was His triumphal, willful submission to the Father to do everything necessary to secure our salvation—and we eternally praise Him for it.

IMPORTANT ALSO: The following reasonings from Scripture are very appropriate to use in Jewish evangelism, especially with orthodox Jews or rabbis who believe God's Word in the Hebrew Bible (what we would call the Old Testament). Ask them if it would be possible for God to have sent His Messiah already. Could He have been presented to the nation and rejected by the majority of the Jews but especially by the religious leaders at the time? Most likely, the only answer they will give is "No! That would be impossible. We would never miss the Messiah when He comes." In response, don't use Matthew 21 but, rather, use the same Psalm 118 account from which Jesus asked— as you can ask—"Have you never read in the Scriptures, 'The stone which the builders rejected has become the chief corner stone? This came about from the Lᴏʀᴅ and is marvelous in our sight. This rejected one will ultimately be bound to the horns of the altar for sacrifice.'" Remember, these items are not optional; this is a messianic truth— and requirement—because whoever the Messiah is must fulfill these things.

How reverently appropriate that the Bible chapter with which we began this chapter of the *Handbook*—1 Peter 2—ends this way in verses 21–25:

> *For you have been called for this purpose, since Christ also suffered for you, leaving you an example for you to follow in His steps,* WHO COMMITTED NO SIN, NOR WAS ANY DECEIT FOUND IN HIS MOUTH; *and while being reviled, He did not revile in return; while suffering, He uttered no threats, but kept entrusting Himself to Him who judges righteously; and He Himself bore our sins in His body on the cross, so that we might die to sin and live to righteousness; for by His wounds you were healed. For you were continually straying like sheep, but now you have returned to the Shepherd and Guardian of your souls.*

Summary and Conclusion

So many important biblical truths are in this chapter, including (1) 1 Pet 2:4–8 having a sixfold use of "stone," referring to the Messiah, cited as Old Testament quotes from Isaiah (28:26 and 8:14) and one from Ps 118:22. (2) Though not universally acknowledged, the two most cited psalms in the New Testament are Psalm 110 and 118. Most times—if not all—Psalm 118 is used to cite some type of Stone Prophecy about the Messiah, which is how Peter used it in 1 Pet 2:7. (3) Although it is virtually universally called this, the Triumphal Entry is not a good name at all for what Jesus was about to do upon entering Jerusalem. We noted that you can read about the real Triumphal Entry in Zechariah 14 or Revelation 19. (4) In the so-called Triumphal Entry passages, when the multitudes kept shouting at the arrival of Jesus, "Hosanna to the Son of David! BLESSED IS HE WHO COMES IN THE NAME OF THE LORD" (Matt 21:9), the people shouted verses taken from Ps 118:25–26 and did so in recognition that Jesus is God's Messiah sent to them. (5) After Jesus had cleansed His temple, answered multiple questions, used a parable of the vineyard owner (who would eventually send even his own son), and the religious leaders rightly concluded that those who killed the son deserved the full wrath of the father (Matt 21:33–40), Jesus then quoted Ps 118:22–32 in reference to them (Matt 21:42)—and this is important—but also in reference to Himself: "THE STONE [the Messiah sent from God] WHICH THE BUILDERS [the Jewish religious establishment] REJECTED, THIS BECAME THE CHIEF CORNER STONE." (6) Jesus had mentioned no names in His parables, but finally the chief priests and Pharisees understood what Jesus was claiming: *He Himself* was the cornerstone *placed by God.* This concerned the origin and mission of Jesus and answered their initial question, "By what authority are You doing these things?" (Matt 21:23). His answer was essentially, "By My Father who placed Me here." (7) One essential truth emerged above all the rest: Psalm 118 strongly supports the messianic claims of Jesus regarding who the Messiah of Israel is. Whoever the Messiah is, He *had to be initially rejected* before He would reign in order for Scripture to be fulfilled. Not only was the Messiah to be rejected, but this rejection must come from those in places of religious authority and responsibility. This prophecy was being fulfilled by the very leaders repudiating Jesus. (8) That hour was the Trinity-ordained time of the Messiah's rejection—not His reign—as the Godhead had mandated in eternity past. (9) We know the events in Acts lead up to the apostles being brought before the same religious leaders who had rejected Jesus only a few months before. Just in case any doubt existed as to the Stone and the builders who rejected Him, Acts 4:11–12 clarifies: "He is the STONE WHICH WAS REJECTED by you, THE BUILDERS, but WHICH BECAME THE CHIEF CORNER STONE. And there is salvation in no one else; for there is no other name under heaven that has been given among men by which we must be saved."

(10) We also learned in this chapter that His last recorded public words to national Israel before events leading to His crucifixion included something totally unexpected—to the disciples, to the masses, and to His opponents. He quoted the exact phrase from Psalm 118 that many within the multitude had shouted only two days before at His unforgettable entry into Jerusalem: "For I say to you, from now on you will not see Me until you say, 'BLESSED IS HE WHO COMES IN THE NAME OF THE LORD!'" (Matt 23:39). When we consider them, Jesus's predictions must have greatly confused the vast majority of those who heard Him. These statements were made on the same day as the discourses of Matthew 21 and 22— and were given somewhere close to forty-eight hours after His entry into Jerusalem. His reasoning seems disjointed, as though two distinct conversations occurred simultaneously, each incongruous with the other. Jesus demanded future praise from Israel, praise that had previously been given Him only a few days earlier. The people had already publicly proclaimed what Jesus had told them was necessary for the nation to see Him, namely "BLESSED IS HE WHO COMES IN THE NAME OF THE LORD" (Matt 21:9; Ps 118:26). We marked how the answer that Jesus gave indicated that He did not view Ps 118:25–26 as having had its fulfillment at the "Triumphal Entry." (11) We saw that Jesus did not accept Israel's praise during the last part of His incarnation because Ps 118:22 ("the stone which the builders rejected") had not yet transpired but would culminate in His crucifixion. The people sang and desired Ps 118:25–26: "O LORD, do save [Hosanna!], we beseech You; / O LORD, we beseech You, do send prosperity! / Blessed is the one who comes in the name of the LORD!" But such prophesied days of blessing could not come without the builders first rejecting the Stone placed there by God Himself. (12) The times of blessing could not come unless the Lamb of God made proper atonement for the sin of the world (John 1:29). Most of the people in Israel—especially the various religious groups—saw no need for such atonement; after all, they had the functioning temple sacrifices. Jesus, however, never permitted this basest of needs to leave His thoughts.

When we read Ps 118:22–29 in light of what we have studied in this chapter, we learned that (13) "This is the day which the LORD had made / Let us rejoice and be glad in it" (v. 24) is the specific day determined by Yahweh (v. 23) when He presented His Messiah before Israel's religious leaders ("the builders"), who would reject "the Stone, the Messiah," sent to them. And in spite of the rejection at this point, the Messiah will eventually become "the chief corner stone." Furthermore, verses 25–26 ("O LORD, do save, we beseech You; / O LORD, we beseech You, do send prosperity! / Blessed is the one who comes in the name of the LORD; / We have blessed you from the house of the LORD"), used by the multitudes in Matthew 21 and the other Gospels' accounts are not, as we know, the true Triumphal Entry. Such will be true—and truly done—by national Israel when Jesus the Messiah returns to reign, and He will accept that praise and those people when He returns. But before such events occur in the future, and in keeping with the Passover season during which these events occurred in the earthly life of Jesus, the sacrificial Lamb of God had to be slain. Also included in "this is the day which the LORD has made / Let us rejoice and be glad in it" is not just the rejection of the Messiah by the religious leaders; it ultimately includes all unbelievers, as we saw in 1 Peter 2. Psalm 118:27 shows quite fittingly, in this Old Testament messianic depiction of Jesus, His sacrificial death as well: "The LORD is God, and He has given us light; / Bind the festival sacrifice with cords to the horns of the altar." Binding the Lamb of God to the horns of the sacrificial altar most certainly did happen to the Lamb of God, who takes away the sins of the world (John 1:29). We noted that while this was not His Triumphal Entry, it was His triumphal, willful submission to the Father to do everything necessary to secure our salvation.

And finally, we learned (14) that Ps 118:22–29 is very appropriate to use in Jewish evangelism, especially with orthodox Jews or rabbis who believe the Hebrew Scriptures, our Old Testament, to be God's Word. If asked whether it were possible that God already had sent His Messiah and the religious leaders rejected Him, they would answer this would be impossible; they—and everyone else—will clearly know when the Messiah is present. We also saw how you should not use Matthew 21 but, rather, Psalm 118 in reaching such people. Jesus quoted from it when He asked— as you can ask—"Did you never read in the Scriptures, / 'The stone which builders; / this became the chief cornerstone? / This came about from the LORD, / and it marvelous in our eyes.'" Whoever this rejected One is, He must ultimately be bound to the horns of the altar for sacrifice—and, this must come about from the Lord Himself. Remember, these items are not optional; they are messianic truths—and requirements—because whoever the Messiah is must fulfill these things. No one can answer this any further than did the silenced religious leaders when Jesus asked them about it many centuries ago.

Deeper Walk Study Questions

1. Name six important doctrinal truths we can see in the Stone Prophecies about the Messiah in 1 Pet 2:4–8. Why is it important that these are taken from three quotes from the Old Testament? Give three reasons.

2. What is the significance of Psalm 118 not only being one of the most cited psalms in the New Testament, but that it is always used as part of God's prophecies about His Messiah, in either who He is or actions He will take? Make five sound biblical deductions because of these truths. Be specific.

3. Why is the Triumphal Entry not a good name to use to describe what Jesus was about to do when entering Jerusalem? What was the suggested title offered in the *Handbook?* Do you agree with the suggestion or not? Give three supports for your answer.

4. What is the significance of Jesus using Psalm 118 to answer the religious leaders in Matt 21:33–42? Give special attention to the significance of how Jesus used verses 22–23 in reference to both Himself and the religious leaders. Name six important truths.

5. Somewhat connected with the question above, from what we have seen in our studies in this chapter, one of the God-given requirements for the Messiah is that He must be rejected by the Jewish religious leaders. Why is this good for who the Messiah is? How is this good to use to identify false messiahs? Write five biblical truths for your answer and explain why each one is important.

6. How does additional revelation later in Acts 4:8–12 help authenticate that the prophecy of "the Stone" being rejected by "the builders" had already been fulfilled by that time? Give four supports. Also, how does the familiar verse 12 ("And there is salvation in no one else; for there is no other name under heaven that has been given among men by which we must be saved") make even more sense when you read this in verse 11 ("He is the STONE WHICH WAS REJECTED by you, THE BUILDERS, but WHICH BECAME THE CHIEF CORNER")? Write four significant biblical truths that we can learn from this.

7. How do we know that Jesus did not accept national Israel's praise of Ps 118:25–26 during His First Advent? Why is this important? List five reasons.

8. How do we know with biblical certainty that one day Jesus will rightly receive—and accept this time—the Ps 118:25–26 praise from national Israel? Why is this important to understanding the Bible? Give four reasons plus the biblical support for this.

9. How does reading Ps 118:22–29 in view of other truths we have seen in this chapter make it so much richer in meaning? Write fifteen biblical truths from this passage that we can thank God for, focusing on how these verses relate solely to Jesus the Messiah.

10. In light of Ps 118:22–29, what does "[t]his is the day which the LORD has made. / Let us rejoice and be glad in it" mean? Why is this so important to understand? Give five reasons and supports for your answers.

11. Why is Ps 118:22–29 such a good passage to use when evangelizing Jews, especially when asking an orthodox Jew whether it would be possible for God to have sent His Messiah already though the nation did not receive him? Although such a person would answer that such could never be possible, we know biblically that whoever the Messiah is, He *must* be rejected first by the Jewish religious elders before He is received. Write ten important biblical deductions we can learn from this and can use in witnessing.

CHAPTER 22

The Wager and Why the Darkness
Was over the Cross

Few things have led to as much wonder among those who love the
Lord Jesus Christ as the wonders of what took place when He was
crucified. We have read about them many times, and, because the scene
is so familiar, we think we have an understanding about what occurred
during that time. In this chapter you will study and appreciate truths that
God has given us in His Word, and you can worship deeply the One who so
lovingly endured for us what we could never endure for ourselves.

Setting Up the Biblical Trail

In *The Cup and the Glory*, I wrote about our cups as disciples of Jesus.
I had no intention of writing more glory books. Through unexpected circumstances, I was led into the deepening study and story of God's glory
during the events surrounding the crucifixion of Jesus. As a result of that
study, I wrote *The Darkness and the Glory*.[1] In that book you will find
much more detail about the crucifixion as you begin with the foreword and
read through the book.

As we have seen in a previous chapter in this *Handbook,* when James
and John asked Jesus to allow them to sit in His glory, He responded this
way: "You do not know what you are asking. Are you able to drink the

---

[1] Greg Harris, *The Darkness and the Glory: His Cup and the Glory from Gethsemane to
the Ascension* (The Woodlands, TX: Kress Biblical Resources, 2008).

cup that I drink, or to be baptized with the baptism with which I am baptized?" (Mark 10:38). Jesus referred to His drinking this cup in the present progressive tense, and it could be translated, "the cup that I am drinking." Everything that He endured was absolutely necessary were He to fulfill His perfect life so He could die His perfect death.

Yet there was a pending future aspect of the cup that Jesus drank that was beyond what He already had endured, as Matt 20:20–22 reveals:

Then the mother of the sons of Zebedee came to Jesus with her sons, bowing down and making a request of Him. And He said to her, "What do you wish?" She said to Him, "Command that in Your kingdom these two sons of mine may sit, one on Your right and one on Your left." But Jesus answered, "You do not know what you are asking. Are you able to drink the cup that I am about to drink?" They said to Him, "We are able."

Here Jesus fully specified a future tense in "the cup that I am about to drink," which would be part of His overall cup, but this last part of His cup differed significantly from all of the combined previous aspects of His cup.

Fast-forward to the Upper Room Discourse (John 13–17), during which Jesus has what many call "the Last Supper." John 13:1–2 reveals this scene to be a deep love story—as well as also one of incredible hatred:

Now before the Feast of the Passover, Jesus knowing that His hour had come that He would depart out of this world to the Father, having loved His own who were in the world, He loved them to the end. During supper, the devil having already put into the heart of Judas Iscariot, the son of Simon, to betray Him . . .

Jesus answered the question as to who would betray Him and then dismissed His betrayer, as recounted in John 13:26–30:

Jesus then answered, "That is the one for whom I shall dip the morsel and give it to him." So when He had dipped the morsel, He took and gave it to Judas, the son of Simon Iscariot. After the morsel, Satan then entered into him. Therefore Jesus said to him, "What you do, do quickly." Now no one of those reclining at the table knew for what purpose He had said this to him. For some were supposing, because Judas had the money box, that Jesus was saying to him, "Buy the things we have need of for the feast"; or else, that he should give something to the poor. So after receiving the morsel he went out immediately; and it was night.

Immediately after Jesus dismissed both Judas and Satan, He proclaimed the following joyous—yet totally stunning to those present—revelation in verses 31–38:

"Now is the Son of Man glorified, and God is glorified in Him; if God is glorified in Him, God will also glorify Him in Himself, and will glorify Him immediately. Little children, I am with you a little while longer. You will seek Me; and as I said to the Jews, now I also say to you, 'Where I am going, you cannot [are not able to] come.' A new commandment I give to you, that you love one another, even as I have loved you, that you also love one another. By this all men will know that you are My disciples, if you have love for one another."

Simon Peter said to Him, "Lord, where are You going?" Jesus answered, "Where I go, you cannot [are not able to] follow Me now; but you will follow later." Peter said to Him, "Lord, why can I not [am I not able to] follow You right now? I will lay down my life for You." Jesus answered, "Will you lay down your life for Me? Truly, truly, I say to you, a rooster will not crow until you deny Me three times."

Each detail of the interactions between Jesus and His disciples—especially with Peter—emerged from Jesus telling them that they were not able to go where He was going. This is not a lack of permission; this is the utter lack of qualifications among the eleven who were with Jesus that night. Where Jesus was going, He alone was able to go.

Some people reason that because Jesus was God in the flesh what He endured would have been relatively easy for Him and would have been done as if He were functioning on automatic pilot. Actually, the reverse is true, and we can understand this from the intense agony of His threefold crying out prayer in Gethsemane:

They came to a place named Gethsemane; and He said to His disciples, "Sit here until I have prayed." And He took with Him Peter and James and John, and began to be very distressed and troubled. And He said to them, "My soul is deeply grieved to the point of death; remain here and keep watch." And He went a little beyond them, and fell to the ground, and began to pray that if it were possible, the hour might pass Him by. And He was saying, "Abba! Father! All things are possible for You; remove this cup from Me; yet not what I will, but what You will." And He came and found them sleeping, and said to Peter, "Simon, are you asleep? Could you not keep watch for one hour? Keep watching and praying that you may not come into temptation; the spirit is willing, but the flesh is weak." Again He went away and prayed, saying the same words. And again He came and found them sleeping, for their eyes were very heavy; and they did not know what to answer Him. And He came the third time, and said to them, "Are you still sleeping and resting? It is enough; the hour has come; behold, the Son of Man is being betrayed into the hands of sinners." (Mark 14:32–41).

This prayer was regarding the same cup that Jesus had referenced in Matt 20:22 that He was about to drink.

> **MARK THIS:** Although movies and books often depict Satan tempting Jesus in Gethsemane, this is not possible biblically. Nothing in the prayers of Jesus indicated that Satan tempted Him. Satan was not there because he had entered into Judas, and when Judas left, Satan left in him. Satan cannot be in two places at one time.

After His threefold prayer, Jesus left Gethsemane. Notice that after this prayer, His perspective had changed concerning His cup. John 18:10–11 reveals that at the arrest of Jesus,

Simon Peter then, having a sword, drew it and struck the high priest's slave, and cut off his right ear; and the slave's name was Malchus. So Jesus said to Peter, "Put the sword into the sheath; the cup which the Father has given Me, shall I not drink it?"

"The cup" that was uniquely His was what the Father had given Him (perfect tense verb: completed action, on-going results). The future tense "will give Me" was not used. The Father had already given the cup to Jesus, and Jesus had submitted to the Father's will.

Is there any way to see biblically what made the cup that Jesus drank so different from ours that explains why we were not able to drink it?

The Greatly Perplexing Biblical Quandary

Before answering the questions about His cup, we need to go back to the beginning of this study. During a time of four to six weeks, I wrestled with this question from two different texts in Scriptures. The first text was the third theological bombshell in Matt 16:21–23. In it the following takes place:

> *From that time Jesus began to show His disciples that He must go to Jerusalem, and suffer many things from the elders and chief priests and scribes, and be killed, and be raised up on the third day. Peter took Him aside and began to rebuke Him, saying, "God forbid it, Lord! This shall never happen to You." But He turned and said to Peter, "Get behind Me, Satan! You are a stumbling block to Me; for you are not setting your mind on God's interests, but man's."*

Everything about this account makes sense biblically. If Jesus goes to the cross, He is the victor—which Satan knew; therefore, Satan attempted to use the apostle Peter in an effort to make Jesus avoid the cross.

So here then is the perplexing biblical quandary: Why would Satan then switch his strategy to the one that took place in Luke 22:3–4? ("And Satan entered into Judas who was called Iscariot, belonging to the number of the twelve. And he went away and discussed with the chief priests and officers how he might betray Him to them.")

This question weighed heavily on me and was ever in my first thoughts upon waking and until I went to bed at night.

Matthew 16—Satan actively worked to keep Jesus from going to the cross.

Luke 22—Satan actively worked to make Jesus go to the cross.

It would seem that the absolute last thing that Satan would want was for Jesus to go to His cross. So why this drastic change in tactics? What result did Satan desire?

Part of the answer is found in Isaiah 53, which is familiar to many.

The following is taken from *The Darkness and the Glory* (pp. 20–23):

Beyond such detailed prophecies, Isaiah 53 presents a description of the Messiah's sacrificial role. Isaiah 53 is actually wonderful New Testament theology, as the Trinity so intended. Isaiah prophesied, "He has no stately form or majesty that we should look upon Him, nor appearance that we should be attracted to Him. He was despised and forsaken of men, a man of sorrows, and acquainted with grief; and like one from whom men hide their face, He was despised, and we did not esteem Him" (53:2–3). In summation of the sacrificial ministry of atonement the Servant of Yahweh alone could bring, Isaiah concluded, "By His knowledge the Righteous One, My Servant, will justify the many, as He will bear their iniquities. . . . He poured out Himself to death, and was numbered with the transgressors; yet He Himself bore the sin of many, and interceded for the transgressors" (53:11b–12).

But there is more. While often not realized by many readers of the Bible, Isaiah 53 actually begins with the three previous verses, namely Isa 52:13–15. Remember, chapter and verse divisions are manmade inventions placed for our convenience. These last three verses of Isaiah 52 contain a summary of what follows in Isaiah 53:

> *Behold, My servant will prosper,*
>
> *He will be high and lifted up, and greatly exalted.*
>
> *Just as many were astonished at you, My people,*
>
> *So His appearance was marred more than any man,*
>
> *And His form more than the sons of men.*
>
> *Thus He will sprinkle many nations,*
>
> *Kings will shut their mouths on account of Him;*
>
> *For what had not been told them they will see,*
>
> *And what they had not heard they will understand.*

Here is another example of a prophet of God predicting the sufferings of Christ and the glories that follow (1 Pet 1:10–11). Once more we see the atoning benefits of His sacrifice in that "He will sprinkle many nations," using Old Testament terminology particularly associated with the high priest and the Day of Atonement.

But consider this question for a moment. Is Isa 52:14 a true statement, or is it a hyperbole—that is, is it merely an exaggeration for the sake of effect? Was the appearance of Jesus actually "marred more than any man, and His form more than the sons of men"? To begin with, we should hope that this description is not an overstatement by God because if it is the effects of His sprinkling and accepted sacrifice might be exaggerated for the sake of effect as well—and consequently we who are saved might not be truly cleansed. We also should note Isa 52:15 begins with the word thus; that is, it connects the promised high priestly sprinkling to whatever he received in Isa 52:14 that so altered His form beyond that of anyone else in history. Nothing other than someone's presuppositions indicate that Isa 52:14 is an exaggeration. The form and appearance of this One actually was marred vastly beyond that of any man who ever had lived or whoever will live. We do not know exactly when this transpired; it may have been a progression that terminated at His death. Accordingly, the appearance of Jesus differed immeasurably from that of the two men who were crucified on each side of Him. This would have been evident to all the onlookers who viewed them, including the thief on an adjacent cross who was ultimately saved, as well as the centurion and those on duty with him. These soldiers had never witnessed anything like the death of Jesus before—nor had anyone else, then or ever.

So many artists who paint a depiction of either the crucifixion or of Jesus after they had taken Him down from the cross fail miserably in their attempts to paint this scene accurately. From many paintings, which seem to get locked into people's perception as biblical truth, all things considered, Jesus did not look all that bad at His death. Tired and exhausted—and dead—but at least you could recognize who He was. That would not be true, however, for those who were present for the crucifixion. If the head of Jesus had not been connected to His body and had been discovered by someone in a field, the find could have raised questions as to whether it actually was a human head.

But still, why? Millions have been savagely beaten; multitudes have been scourged; hundreds of thousands have been crucified. History indicates that it was not unusual for those crucified to linger in agony on the cross for several days before they eventually succumbed. What was it about His relatively short six-hour crucifixion that vastly exceeded what none of Adam's seed had ever—or would ever—or could ever endure? Is there any way to know even remotely what or why?

In addition to this, one other point must be considered. In John 19:31–36 the Jewish officials approached Pilate asking that the legs of those crucified be broken so that they might die and be taken from the crosses before the Sabbath. The soldiers broke the legs of those crucified beside Jesus, but His they did not; He was already dead. The apostle John stated the importance of what he had witnessed: "And He who has seen has borne witness, and His witness is true; and He knows that He is telling the truth, so that you also may believe. For these things came to pass, that the Scripture might be fulfilled, 'Not a bone of Him shall be broken'" (John 19:35–36). This is a tremendously important revelatory nugget from God. Jesus was scourged (Matt 27:26; Mark 15:15), and yet not one of His ribs was broken. Matthew 27:30 states, "They spat on Him, and took the reed and began to beat Him on the head." Mark 15:19 puts the focus on the repetitive acts of violence against Him: "They kept beating His head with a reed, and spitting at Him, and kneeling and bowing before Him." If the reed had been a rod of iron, such as the one He will wield against the nations, it would not break one bone of this One who had set His face like flint (Isa 50:7). Regardless of the savagery against Him, His jawbone was not broken; neither was there the tiniest fracture of His cheekbones. Still, even without any broken bones, "His appearance was marred more than any man, and His form more than the sons of men" (Isa 52:14). Something beyond the normal physical trauma must have occurred.

With this background, consider this, from *The Darkness and the Glory* (p. 23):

Here then is the question before us: is there any way to know what the cup His Father had given Him contained? Or stated differently, is there any way to see—even in a mirror dimly—any of the elements that made Jesus drinking His cup so exceed all other cups combined?

Actually there is. God sets the answer before us in His Word. The Bible reveals that the cup that Jesus drank had at least three unique components that caused His death to be unlike any other and made His appearance to be marred more than any man. All three parts were hidden to humanity present at the crucifixion—and in many cases still remain hidden to modern readers of the Bible. All three items are the same type of behind the scenes spiritual truths (such as matters related to the birth of Jesus) that would not be known even to the elect unless God chose to reveal them in His Word. All three measures that made the cup Jesus drank so hideous are found within the pages of Scripture. We will identify each of them, but by no means will we even properly define nor describe them and by no means remotely exhaust their significance. In fact, it will take all eternity to understand the depths of what Jesus endured for us.

Come: let us observe—even as children, and from a distance—the cup that the Father had given to the Son.

And let us marvel at what He alone was able to do.

* * *

It is beyond dispute biblically how important a role Satan played in bringing about the crucifixion. Seven times John 13–17 and Luke 22 and parallel passages refer to Satan during this incredibly strategic time.

1. Luke 22:3–4: "And Satan entered into Judas who was called Iscariot, belonging to the number of the twelve. And he went away and discussed with the chief priests and officers how he might betray Him to them."
2. John 13:2: "During supper, the devil having already put into the heart of Judas Iscariot, the son of Simon, to betray Him."
3. Luke 22:31–32: "Simon, Simon, behold, Satan has demanded permission to sift you like wheat; but I have prayed for you, that your faith may not fail; and you, when once you have turned again, strengthen your brothers."
4. In the Upper Room Discourse, after Jesus has dismissed Judas/Satan, Jesus said in reference to Satan in John 14:30: "I will not speak much more with you, for the ruler of the world is coming, and he has nothing in Me.
5. And again in John 16:7–11 Jesus once more referred to Satan by saying, "But I tell you the truth, it is to your advantage that I go away; for if I do not go away, the Helper shall not come to you; but if I go, I will send Him to you. And He, when He comes, will convict the world concerning sin, and righteousness, and judgment; concerning sin, because they do not believe in Me; and concerning

righteousness, because I go to the Father, and you no longer behold Me; and concerning judgment, because the ruler of this world has been judged."

6. Luke 22:47–48: "While He was still speaking, behold, a multitude came, and the one called Judas, one of the twelve, was preceding them; and he approached Jesus to kiss Him. But Jesus said to him, 'Judas, are you betraying the Son of Man with a kiss?'" (Remember: Judas was indwelt by Satan, so when Judas approached, Satan approached as well.)

7. In Luke 22:52–53, at the arrest of Jesus, comes the seventh time that Jesus made reference in some way to Satan, which is incredibly important in understanding the severity of what awaited Him, because Jesus disclosed something unique was getting ready to happen: "Then Jesus said to the chief priests and officers of the temple and elders who had come against Him, 'Have you come out with swords and clubs as you would against a robber? While I was with you daily in the temple, you did not lay hands on Me; but this hour and the power of darkness are yours.'"

Literally in the Greek it is quite specific. Mark well also the definite articles: "But this is the hour of yours, the power [authority] of the darkness."

> **IMPORTANT:** The word translated *hour* can equal either (1) the same way we would use it, approximately sixty minutes, or (2) a designated period of time that unless otherwise indicated could last for years. Context is helpful to determine which is which as to how it is to be used. For instance, in John 2:4, at the wedding in Cana, where Mary came up to Jesus and informed Him that they had run out of wine, Jesus responded, "Woman, what does that have to do with us? My hour has not yet come." Jesus obviously was not referring here to only sixty minutes. Both uses of "hour" are used in the prayers in Gethsemane that would have already taken place. Viewing this in inverse order, Mark 14:37 states, "And He came and found them sleeping, and said to Peter, 'Simon, are you asleep? Could you not

> keep watch for one hour [approximately sixty minutes]?'" And a few
> verses earlier, the second usage occurs in Mark 14:35: "And He went
> a little beyond them, and fell to the ground and began to pray that if
> it were possible, the hour might pass Him by." Obviously this use of
> "hour" went beyond sixty minutes; this hour would last from the time
> of the arrest all the way through until He said, "It is finished." This is
> the same type of hour that Jesus revealed had been granted to Satan
> in Luke 22:53; it was a designated period of time granted to him.

We must observe what Satan was allowed and not allowed to do during the hour of the authority of the darkness. To begin with, it is quite clear in Scripture what Satan was not permitted to do to Jesus. John 10:17–18 reveals this crucial doctrine:

> *For this reason the Father loves Me, because I lay down My life so that I may take it again. No one has taken it away from Me, but I lay it down on My own initiative. I have authority to lay it down, and I have authority to take it up again. This commandment I received from My Father.*

MARK THIS WELL: There is a popular Christian song, which I and many other Christians love to sing, that contains a line about the death of Jesus. It says, "Light of the world by darkness slain." The composers of this song have greatly ministered to me and to many others. However, so often what people sing becomes deeply entrenched in their minds as doctrinal truth, and they conclude that what they sing is what the Bible teaches about how Jesus died. From what Jesus disclosed in John 10:18, no one—including Satan—could ever kill Him. So, when Jesus died, it was not darkness that slayed Him; it was His own deliberate choice to release His spirit as seen in Luke 23:46: "And Jesus, crying out with a loud voice, said, 'Father, INTO YOUR HANDS I COMMIT MY SPIRIT.' Having said this, He breathed His last." John 19:30 eternally records the last moments of Jesus's life this way: "When Jesus had received the sour wine, He said, 'It is finished!' And He bowed His head and gave up His spirit." The difficulty within the

> song I mention could be remedied by changing one simple word that
> would alter the entire concept: "Light of the world for darkness slain."
> This would include Jesus defeating Satan, redeeming the saved out
> of the domain of the darkness (Col 1:13–14), and fulfills Acts 26:18,
> as part of the gospel going forth "to open their eyes so that they may
> turn from darkness to light and from the dominion of Satan to God,
> that they may receive forgiveness of sins and an inheritance among
> those who have been sanctified by faith in [Jesus]." Finally, we would
> not just be removed from Satan's realm of darkness, but Eph 5:8
> describes us before salvation: "For you were formally darkness" [not
> just "in darkness"—utter darkness was our spiritual condition], but
> now you are Light in the Lord; walk as children of light." Thanks be to
> God for so great a salvation!

Scripture reveals another time when Satan was granted a designated period during which God placed limits on what Satan was permitted to do. Job 1 discloses that after Satan was permitted by God to take away Job's riches and to kill his children, Satan wrongly had claimed that Job would curse God to His face. Later, in Job 2, when God asked Satan about Job and how Job, in spite of the torment and sorrow, still stood firmly, came this account in verses 4–7:

> Satan answered the LORD and said, "Skin for skin! Yes, all that a man has he
> will give for his life. However, put forth Your hand, now, and touch his bone
> and his flesh; he will curse You to Your face." So the LORD said to Satan,
> "Behold, he is in your power, only spare his life." Then Satan went out from
> the presence of the LORD, and smote Job with sore boils from the sole of his
> foot to the crown of his head.

The above permission and limitations were hidden from Job and his friends, and these would have to stay hidden until the full disclosure of all things in heaven.

From The Darkness and the Glory (pp. 35–36):

So then, with the exception of his death, anything Satan's evil mind and nature could contrive, anything within his entire arsenal of perverse malevolence, could be fully and freely cast upon Jesus but only for a limited, designated period of time. This was an aspect of the cup the Father had given the Son to drink—and what Satan desired to do during his God-given hour is inconceivable on a human level.

For me, this is the part where God gives us a small window into some of what Satan was allowed to do, from the account of Jesus's arrest, immediately after Peter had accosted those who were getting ready to arrest Jesus, in Matt 26:52–53:

> *Then Jesus said to him, "Put your sword back into its place; for all those who take up the sword shall perish by the sword. Or do you think that I cannot appeal to My Father, and He will at once put at My disposal more than twelve legions of angels?"*

From The Darkness and the Glory (pp. 38–42):

The number of angels that Jesus revealed were available to Him further demonstrates His inner strength and composure. Jesus possessed more than sufficient numbers to end His ordeal if such had been His intention. A Roman legion consisted of 6,000 men. Twelve legions would thus contain 72,000 soldiers. Jesus said the Father would readily send more than twelve legions of angels, at bare minimum, over 72,000 angels to come to His aid, to rescue Him from His peril. However, escape was not Jesus's purpose, and He never summoned His attendant angelic multitudes. The very existence and readiness of warrior angels both willing and eager to help at a moment's notice only added to Jesus's temptation. It is one thing to be overwhelmed and helpless in a situation completely out of your control. It is quite another to have the means of escape readily available at your first call, but decline to use what is rightfully yours. Jesus possessed the Godhead's inner strength and composure encompassed in a frail human package—and Satan was about to deliver his full wrath against the designated Lamb of God.

We must note something important: while Jesus could call His angels, Satan could summon his angelic forces as well. Unlike his opponent, Satan had no hesitation whatsoever in calling his warriors into battle—and the numbers he brought against Jesus stagger us. But who are Satan's angels? How many are there? Where did they come from?

In order to answer this, we must examine various Scripture passages. Earlier in Matt 25:41 Jesus revealed that hell consists of "the eternal fire which has been prepared for the devil and his angels." So it is evident Satan does have angels—and has them in large quantities. In Luke 8, when Jesus asked demons their name, they answered "Legion," for many demons had entered the man (Luke 8:30). Within this one man was one of Satan's legions, which if the words mean the same thing, then there were approximately 6,000 demons within this man. How many more demons exist is beyond our scope of understanding, unless God chooses to reveal more.

Fortunately, to a degree He does. Revelation 12:4 reveals that when God cast Satan out of His heavenly abode, "his tail swept away a third of the stars from heaven." This is most likely a reference to the angels who followed Satan in his insurgence against God, especially since Rev 9:1 contains an account of a star descending from heaven who was shown to be an angel of God. So whatever the aggregate population of angels, one-third of them followed Satan in his rebellion and were instantly changed forever from angels of God to angels of the Devil, becoming his servants. The Bible usually refers to such fallen angels as demons. No earthly source knows exactly how many angels God created, but their numbers are overwhelming. Some Bible scholars think that at least as many angels exist as there are people born throughout history. Yet beyond human speculation, certain Scripture references indicate the innumerable multitudes of the angelic host. In a vision that God gave to Daniel, the prophet describes God's abode in Dan 7:9–10:

I kept looking

Until thrones were set up,

And the Ancient of Days took His seat;

His vesture was like white snow,

And the hair of His head like pure wool.

His throne was ablaze with flames,

Its wheels were a burning fire.

A river of fire was flowing

And coming out from before Him;

Thousands upon thousands were attending Him,

And myriads upon myriads were standing before Him;

The court sat,

And the books were opened.

The Hebrew could be translated as "ten thousand times ten thousands" or "hundreds of millions," angelic multitudes innumerable to Daniel but not to the omniscient Creator-God who made and knew each one.

In the same way, hundreds of years later, the apostle John was transported to heaven in a vision. There he records virtually the same description of the angelic host that surrounds God's throne in Rev 5:11–12:

> *Then I looked, and I heard the voice of many angels around the throne and the living creatures and the elders; and the number of them was myriads of myriads, and thousands of thousands, saying with a loud voice,*
>
> *"Worthy is the Lamb that was slain to receive power and riches and wisdom and might and honor and glory and blessing."*

The same phrases "myriads of myriads" and "thousands of thousands" that occurred in Daniel, although written in Greek in the book of Revelation instead of Hebrew, again show the innumerable number of God's heavenly host. So however many millions upon millions these myriads of myriads and thousands of thousands contain, one-third of the original number followed the deceiver and became his angels. One-third became the demonic hosts.

By simply restricting this to the number Jesus referred to at His arrest, at the very least more than twelve legions—over 72,000 angels—stood willingly ready to come to His immediate rescue. But the same math can likewise be applied to Satan's angels. The one-third who became demons would at the very least consist of over 36,000 demons (not one-third of 72,000 but the 72,000 equal the two-thirds that remained). As we saw, this is merely a fraction. While they do not equal God's numbers, the depth and design of Satan's demonic hosts are vastly beyond the comprehension and strength of the human world.

We do not know much about demons because God offers only glimpses of them in Scripture. Perhaps God intends for believers to focus more on Him and His truth rather than on the seductive allurements of the kingdom of darkness. Still, the Bible reveals certain aspects about demonic activities. Ephesians 6:12 presents Satan's angels as being organized into specified categories, stating that "our struggle is not against flesh and blood, but against the rulers, against the powers, against the world forces of this darkness, against the spiritual forces of wickedness in the heavenly places." The Bible does not give much information to distinguish between the four categories, such as what the difference is between a ruler and a power. But it does show rank, authority, and organization. These demonic hosts actively work throughout the entire world because, as 1 John 5:19 states that "the whole world lies in the power of the evil one." In other words, no part of the world is off-limits to their activity. Besides this, in some way, satanic activity occurs within the realm of the atmosphere because the Bible depicts Satan as "the prince of the power of the air" (Eph 2:2). We also know that demons are actively involved in disseminating false doctrine, especially inside what are considered Christian churches and institutions. First Timothy 4:1 states, "But the Spirit explicitly says that in later times some will fall away from the faith, paying attention to deceitful spirits and doctrines of demons." We will see in heaven how terribly effective these demonic beings were in propagating such false doctrines to so many.

We need to consider more doctrinal truths about demonic beings because this helps us understand better how they function. Demons continuously undertake only evil activities, being as completely evil and defiled as Satan. No good whatsoever exists in any of them. They have no mercy; their evil never becomes satiated. They have no conscience; they have no pity; they never repent. It should be especially noted that demons are immensely powerful. Daniel 10:11–13 gives the account of a holy angel commissioned by God to speak to the prophet Daniel. Yet even with God's instructions, an extremely mighty demon hindered this angel's mission for twenty-one days. Eventually, the archangel Michael had to be sent into battle against the demonic forces. Together they fought spiritual warfare completely devoid of human perception, a warfare that no human could have survived for even an instant—no one except the One headed for the cross.

Demons have one crucial capability that we must recognize. In the fifth trumpet judgment in the book of Revelation, God will unleash previously bound demons from the abyss and send them to the earth. Though spiritual beings will most likely be unobserved by those on earth, they will have the capacity to inflict severe pain upon human beings. Revelation 9:4–6 describes to a degree what they can do:

> *They were told not to hurt the grass of the earth, nor any green thing, nor any tree, but only the men who do not have the seal of God on their foreheads. And they were not permitted to kill anyone, but to torment for five months; and their torment was like the torment of a scorpion when it stings a man. And in those days men will seek death and will not find it; they will long to die and death flees from them.*

All of this will occur under the strict sovereignty of God. These select demons come only when summoned; they are restricted as to whom they can attack; they are restricted in how long they can attack: in this case, five months. By God's sovereign decree they will not be permitted to kill, but they will be permitted to torment "like the torment of a scorpion when it stings a man." The text does not say how they will accomplish this torment; it simply states that they will. In fact, the word torment occurs three times within these passages. What else God does or does not allow demons presently to do, we do not know very much. We see glimpses of what God at times permits in the sense of Job 1–2 and in spiritual warfare against Christians in Ephesians 6. Yet when authorized by God, demons can torment humans to the extent that death will be considered vastly better than life.

Interestingly, not only can demons torment others; they likewise can receive torment themselves. This was their great fear in encountering Jesus, as Luke 8:28 indicates: "Seeing Jesus, he [the demon possessed man] cried out and fell before Him, and said in a loud voice, 'What do I have to do with You, Jesus, Son of the Most High God? I beg You, do not torment me.'" In the parallel account of Matt 8:29, the demons clearly understand that a specified divine judgment awaits them, asking Jesus, "What business we have with each other, Son of God? Have You come here to torment us before the time?" Significantly, Satan's angels employ the same word for "torment" that is used to describe the demonic torment of Revelation 9. Demons have the capacity both to inflict and to receive torment.

From The Darkness and the Glory (pp. 42–43):

Thankfully, the events of Revelation 9 are still future. Thankfully, the time when Satan's realm will receive the proper judgment awaits the sovereign calendar of God. But the night Jesus was betrayed was different—immensely different from any other time in eternity past or present. It was their hour, and the power of the darkness was theirs.

Consider the evil magnitude of at the very least 36,000 demons, plus the added power of Satan himself. All would be summoned against Jesus. All would assemble over one hill in Jerusalem, all intent on one Individual. No other battle in the entirety of God's creation existed or mattered that morning. Calvary alone was the field of battle—Jesus was the lone Foe. The totality of Satan's strength and demonic forces would muster their collective power of evil against one beaten, weakened, and scourged Man. All of Jesus opened and exposed to all of them. With the exception of killing Him, Satan and his angels could employ all that was within their power to torment Jesus with no threat of Michael or anyone else coming to His aide. The legion that Jesus had cast out in Luke 8 most likely would be there too. Who currently knows other than the Godhead, but He may even have permitted the demons currently confined in the abyss of Revelation 9 to be temporarily released and added to the assault against Jesus. We will find out when we get to heaven. However, this much is abundantly clear: whatever the totality of the arsenal Satan had available to him, not one member would be absent. It was their God-given hour to assemble.

By the time the final battle began, Jesus was already in a depleted condition, both physically and spiritually. Gethsemane was many times more strenuous than the physical scourging and beating He would receive thereafter. The physical torture certainly added to the limitless burden. A lesser man's resolve would have ended long before this time. Jesus still stood—but He would face His battle alone, as He had previously informed His own the night before, "Where I am going, you cannot [are not able; do not have the capacity to] come" (John 13:33). Heavenly assistance would be given only if Jesus asked for it. But if He asked, if He cried out "Enough!" or "Stop!"—or simply stated it, if He stopped drinking His cup before it was empty—then the battle would have ended as soon as His Word left His mouth. Then Jesus and His angels would have returned to their rightful place with the Father in heaven—but they would have returned there alone. No one born of Adam's race would ever go there after them. Satan would maintain his worldwide dominion—and sin and death would continue to reign. All hope for future life would perish—and the apostle John would not be the only one weeping that no one was found worthy to take the scroll from God's hand and to open its seals (Rev 5:1–5).

From The Darkness and the Glory (pp. 44–45):

Here then, in reality, Satan still attempted to hinder Jesus from the cross or, stated better, from finishing His messianic course that culminated with His death on the cross. In the previous encounters Satan had slipped into his temptation the pleasant enticements related to Jesus's physical survival or His earthly reign. Now events exposed Satan's scheme for the ugly horror it had always been. Satan purposed to torture and torment Jesus beyond the capacity of all previous human suffering combined. All he had to do was to cause Jesus to resign before He finished the course—and the cup—the Father had designated He must take, and Satan would be the victor. We who have suffered or have been tempted have never suffered like this—God would not permit it (1 Cor 10:13). Even more to the point, we have long since disqualified ourselves from ever entering even the remotest confines of this restricted arena of battle. Furthermore, we who have suffered have never had the means or opportunity to remove ourselves from it as Jesus had. The question is, would He endure to the end?

Here was Satan's one God-granted hour of opportunity. He stood ready—as did his legions.

The wager had been placed—and literally the eternal destiny of both the human and spiritual worlds hung on its outcome.

This is the first of the three components of what Jesus meant in John 13 where He said, "Where I am going, you cannot come"; other than killing Jesus, the beyond-description wrath of Satan thrown upon Jesus during Satan's designated hour granted him by God.

Remembering that Jesus could have called more than 72,000 angels at any time, I find it noteworthy that God gives part of the reason of what He allowed in the crucifixion.

From The Darkness and the Glory, pp. 67–69:

We find out later in Scripture that, among other things, God had angels in view with what occurred on the cross and its subsequent ongoing results:

> *To me, the very least of all saints, this grace was given, to preach to the Gentiles the unfathomable riches of Christ, and to bring to light what is the administration of the mystery which for ages has been hidden in God, who created all things; so that the manifold wisdom of God might now be made known through the church to the rulers and the authorities in the heavenly places. This was in accordance with the eternal purpose which He carried out in Christ Jesus our Lord, in whom we have boldness and confident access through faith in Him. (Eph 3:8–12)*

Although we often like to think about salvation in terms of what we receive, Eph 3:10 reveals a totally different understanding of why God permitted the death of His Son: "so that the manifold wisdom of God might now be made known through the church to the rulers and the authorities in the heavenly places." We would not know this unless it was stated in Scripture: God specifically showed forth His wisdom that it might now be made known to—in this case not to humanity but, rather—"to the rulers and the authorities in the heavenly places" (3:10). Yet even beyond this, it was "in accordance with His eternal purpose which He carried out in Christ Jesus our Lord" (Eph 3:11). We are not even sure if "the rulers and authorities in the heavenly places" in this verse refer to the holy angels or the fallen angels. Many scholars conclude that it refers to both, which seems possible. This offers even more biblical support that with the death of Christ God was making known to the angelic world His manifold wisdom in accordance with His eternal purpose. Such angelic beings must have viewed the crucifixion in progress.

The attending angels had a mental comprehension of what God was doing, but they had no experiential base to connect it. Never before in all eternity had angels seen any member of the Godhead subjected to such brutal audacity from evil powers. It reasons that left to themselves God's angels would have instantly leapt into the battle, the same way a mother would leap in front of a speeding car to save her child caught in its path. But the Father did not permit them; they were divinely restrained from intervening. In their confirmed state of holiness, the angels had no temptation to disobey the Father's command. However, this very state of holiness would have caused them deep consternation as they stood witness to horrendous evil manifested in a way previously unknown to them. Similar to when the Lamb will eventually break the seventh seal during the future tribulation (Rev 8:1), there may very well have been complete silence in heaven as God the Son was dying.

From the holy angels' view, the death of Jesus would most likely seem to be an extremely long ordeal; the time would not go quickly. However, the angels did not simply stand by idly; they stood in active obedience to God, even standing against their own inclination to intercede. This was something Peter had not yet learned at the arrest of Jesus. The holy angels of God stood by without intervening as they watched Jesus suffer, but apart from the Father's command, it was not their very nature to do so.

Finally—with the beloved Son on the cross for hours, having endured what one fallen son of Adam was not able to endure for even a fraction of the speed of light—at the very height of Satan's wrath, the Father stirred to action. Even the human agents present at the crucifixion understood something tremendous and terrifying was about to transpire, but they did not exactly know what. Even less would they understand why.

God's attending angels would have noticed this movement immediately, such as seen throughout Ezekiel 1. Satan and his forces may or may not have readily taken note. Eventually they too understood that God Himself was approaching Calvary. Did the Father come to rescue His wounded Son? Was Satan's hour of authority over? Was this the end of the battle and the torment? Soon every spiritual entity, both holy and evil, realized that all the previous activities had been only the preliminary rounds. Now began the final assault in this epoch battle—and the next half would be so much more brutally horrible that the first half would forever pale in comparison to this new episode.

The totality of both the heavenly and demonic realm watched as God the Father approached God the Son.

Why the Darkness Was over the Cross

From The Darkness and the Glory (pp. 72–75):

Light shining in darkness also divides between that which is illumined and that which remains dark. However, such an advent of light in the midst of darkness is not always welcomed because its very presence forces one to choose with which sector one will align. Instead of relishing in the glory of the Light, some prefer darkness. John wrote of this in John 3:19–21:

> This is the judgment, that the Light has come into the world, and men loved the darkness rather than the Light, for their deeds were evil. For everyone who does evil hates the Light, and does not come to the Light for fear that his deeds will be exposed. But he who practices the truth comes to the Light, so that his deeds may be manifested as having been wrought in God.

The advent of the Light of Christ then becomes either the greatest truth one ever encounters—or the most horrendous. The Light remains the same for both; the response of the recipient to the Light becomes the core issue.

With so many scriptural analogies between light and darkness (and there are dozens more), a simple but confounding question stands before us: Why did darkness cover the land at Jesus's crucifixion? Three Gospels record this phenomenon, so it must be important theologically. But still, what does God intend for us to learn from this?

As with many issues of Scripture, by far the most repeated response by laity and scholars is, "Well, I don't know. I never really thought about it." For instance, many commentaries note that the darkness occurred but offer nothing regarding its significance. This may be appropriate. God certainly may choose to reveal matters in Scripture without giving any additional explanation, such as in Dan 12:1–9, where God's own prophet does not understand the meaning or significance of what has just been revealed to him.

However, after some thought, various attempts to explain the darkness at the crucifixion emerge. One answer identifies the darkness with the vast assemblage of satanic forces present. With Satan exercising his rule in the domain of the darkness (Col 1:13), especially during his God-granted hour of authority (Luke 22:53), it reasons that darkness would occur when he gathered his forces in an unprecedented manner. This would especially be true regarding his presence during the crucial activities at Calvary. Another view sees the darkness as God's testimony to individuals such as the attending Roman centurion. The darkness alerted those who had no known interest in the things of God that this was not merely another crucifixion of some condemned criminal. If those present did not understand what was transpiring or the claims of Jesus concerning Himself, God the Father bore witness to the gravity of the event by sending darkness over the land, perhaps extending over the entire world—such was the magnitude of Christ's death. Yet another approach places more emphasis on the presence of the Light at the cross. In other words, the darkness appeared because the Light of the world was dying. Jesus Himself bore witness to the multitude that the Light would not always be in their presence. Just a few days earlier, in John 12:35–36, Jesus warned, "For a little while longer the light is among you. Walk while you have the light, that darkness may not overtake you; he who walks in the darkness does not know where he goes. While you have the light, believe in the light, in order that you may become sons of light." The cross would be the departure of which Jesus cautioned. By using a simple analogy of nature, if the light is removed, darkness must manifest itself.

One answer has many advocates. Those who receive the Bible as God's truth understand that a divine separation transpired. The basis for this answer holds that a holy God cannot bear to look upon sin and must turn away His face. Therefore, as Jesus became sin for us (2 Cor 5:21), God turned away from the Son. The explanations for how God's turning away from His Son relates to the darkness over the cross (if it relates at all) vary considerably. Many see the turning away as occurring at the end of the crucifixion when Jesus cried out, "My God! My God! Why have You forsaken Me?" (Matt 27:46; Mark 15:34). Others, somewhat by default or by not addressing it, infer that the separation from the Father lasted the entire crucifixion. Galatians 3:13 is such a verse that views the crucifixion as a whole and how God viewed Jesus: "Christ redeemed us from the curse of the Law, having become a curse for us—for it is written, 'Cursed is everyone who hangs on a tree.'"

Obviously, something vastly significant occurred at the end of the crucifixion. We will get to this in the next chapter. But we need to consider other matters first. To begin with, no Scripture explicitly states that God cannot bear to look upon sin and therefore must turn His face from it, yet it is often quoted in sermons. The Bible contains many references to the judicial act of God turning His face away or hiding His face from people involved in blatant, rebellious sin but none that He cannot look on the sins they commit. Some people hold that Hab 1:13 supports the fact that God cannot look on sin: "Your eyes are too pure to approve [look at] evil." Yet the context indicates this verse deals with the idea of God looking on evil without responding to it—not that God must turn His face away from sin. Adam and Eve would not have made the same conclusion of God not being able to look at sin (Genesis 3). Consider also just a very small sampling of multiple biblical references of God's capacity to look on sin: Gen 6:5: "Then the Lord saw that the wickedness of man was great on the earth"; Exod 3:7: "The Lord said, 'I have surely seen the affliction of My people who are in Egypt, and have given heed to their cry because of their taskmasters, for I am aware of their sufferings'"; and centuries later in condemning the heinous sins that were done in His very own temple, God, by means of His prophet, both asks and answers: "'Has this house, which is called by My name, become a den of robbers in your sight? Behold, I, even I, have seen it,' declares the Lord" (Jer 7:11). These are just a few examples. After all, He truly is the God who sees (Gen 16:13).

Actually, just the opposite occurs. Instead of God not being able to look at sin, man cannot stand to see his own sinfulness in light of God's holiness. Isaiah saw the glory of God and concluded, "Woe is me, for I am ruined! Because I am a man of unclean lips, and I live among a people of unclean lips; for my eyes have seen the King, the Lord of hosts" (Isa 6:5). After Jesus taught the multitudes and then blessed Peter's fishing endeavor, a greatly convicted Peter pleaded, "Go away from me Lord, for I am a sinful man!" (Luke 5:3–8). When the apostle John beheld the glorified Christ, he described Him as the One whose "eyes were like a flame of fire," denoting the penetrating gaze of the all-knowing, all-powerful

God (Rev 1:14). Jesus did not look away from John. This beloved disciple who lovingly rested his head against Jesus during the last Passover (John 13:23) later fell as a dead man at the feet of One who looked upon him with the holy, fierce, flaming eyes of God (Rev 1:17). All these references describe the reactions of beloved servants of God. How much more would the turning away response be from someone like Judas, Nero, or Hitler?

God must retain the capacity to look at sin. After all, the Judge of this world needs a sense of reference in order to judge properly. Everyone must give an account to God for every word uttered (Matt 12:36). The great white throne judgment of Revelation 20 depicts the damned standing before Jesus as the divine accounting books will be opened, and they all will be judged "according to their deeds" (Rev 20:12–15). God certainly will not turn His face away from these sins. In addition to this, if God could not look upon sin, then He could never converse with Satan whenever He chose, especially since the Bible repeatedly depicts Satan as "the evil one" (John 17:15; Eph 6:16; 2 Thess 3:3). Scripture indicates that God has interacted with the evil one in the past (Job 1–2; Zechariah 3) and most likely continues doing so because at this present time Satan remains the accuser of the brethren (Rev 12:10). Nothing whatsoever in these accounts indicates that God has to turn His face away from this thoroughly evil one. Finally, if we take this logic to its extremity, God would never save anyone. The Good Shepherd would never seek the lost sheep because, after all, lost sheep are notoriously sinful. From these points it seems that we need to find a more substantial explanation for what occurred on the cross—especially at its conclusion. But before doing this, we need to address why darkness covered the land while Jesus hung on the cross.

From The Darkness and the Glory (pp. 75–76):

The Bible presents some information concerning Christ's death but not an abundance. The crucifixion of Jesus lasted approximately six hours, from 9:00 a.m. to 3:00 p.m. (Mark 15:25, 33). This was not an unusually long crucifixion. In fact, it was just the opposite. The relatively short time Jesus agonized on the cross before He died surprised Pilate (Mark 15:44–45). It is important to note that the six hours of Christ's crucifixion divide into two distinct three-hour segments, with the main division beginning with the advent of the darkness. Matthew, Mark, and Luke specifically place the darkness at about the sixth hour, that is, at noon (Matt 27:45; Mark 15:33; Luke 23:44). Luke gives additional details of how the sun was "obscured," literally translated "failing" (23:45), a point we will pick up later. So, the darkness arrived at noon and resided during the last three hours of Jesus's crucifixion. There is one important observation we must make: with the exception of the "My God!" cry of Ps 22:1 and a few brief statements at the end, all the recorded words of Jesus take place within the first three hours of the crucifixion—that is, before the advent of the darkness. Before the darkness, Jesus prayed, "Father, forgive them" (Luke 23:34), inter-acted with the thief on the cross who ultimately believed, and charged John to care for His mother. After the darkness arrived, Jesus spoke no more until only moments before His death.

We must further note that all three Gospel writers add a specific time marker in regard to the darkness. Matthew, Mark, and Luke each employ the same word "until" in describing the darkness. For instance, Matt 27:45 states, "Now from the sixth hour darkness fell upon all the land until the ninth hour." The darkness had a definitive beginning and a definitive end-ing. Also, it is significant to note that the "My God! My God! Why have You forsaken Me?" (Matt 27:46; Mark 15:34) scream occurred at the end of the darkness, not during it. So by means of eliminating possible solu-tions, the darkness could not have been present because the Father turned away from the Son; the darkness occurred for three hours before this final event took place.

So the darkness resided over the cross, and the Son became silent. Again, the simple question: why?

When God ratified the Abrahamic covenant in Genesis 15, He ap-peared in an unexpected means of ratification.

From The Darkness and the Glory (pp. 79–80):

So as Abram lay sleeping, God approached to ratify His covenant. Gene-sis 15:12 contains a most unusual description of God's presence. The phrase begins with the tiny word "behold," a word so often overlooked but nonetheless so crucial. Without exaggeration, one could translate the word, "Now, look! This is important! Pay attention!"—but we rarely do.

Perhaps the reason "behold" occurs within this verse is that the description of God's presence is so different from most of the other descriptions in Scripture. Genesis 15:12 states, "[B]ehold, terror and great *darkness* fell upon him [Abram]." A literal translation of the Hebrew is, "behold! a terror of great darkness," or "behold! a terror, even great darkness, falling upon him." In other words, two separate entities of terror and darkness did not occur—the terror *was* the darkness. So here, in this special pronouncement of God's presence, on the day when God ratified the eternally important Abrahamic covenant, He did so by means of darkness. God could have manifested Himself with light, such as when His glory filled His tabernacle and later His temple, but He chose not to do so. In this case God revealed Himself by means of darkness. This does not fit our understanding of God—and for good reason—but is true nonetheless. In fact, the Bible presents another instance where God's presence is accompanied by darkness, and it is almost as surprising as the Abrahamic covenant of Genesis 15.

In the ratification of the Mosaic covenant, the following description occurs.

From The Darkness and the Glory (pp. 81–82):

The account in Deuteronomy offers details omitted in the book of Exodus. After the retelling of Israel's history beginning with the sending out of the spies at Kadesh-barnea, Moses once more gathered the nation of Israel to remind them of their binding obligations stipulated in the Mosaic covenant of which the Jews had previously already entered. At the original giving of the Law, God had manifested Himself to the people. Though not limited to this, God once more employed darkness as an aspect of His presence before the people. Moses told how the people came near Mount Sinai, "and the mountain burned with fire to the very heart of the heavens: *darkness,* cloud, and thick gloom" (Deut 4:11). In the next chapter Moses again made note of the darkness, saying, "And it came about, when you heard the voice [of God] from the midst of the darkness . . ." (v. 23). Like Abram hundreds of years earlier, the entire nation responded to God's presence with terrible fear (Deut 5:26–27). In ratifying the Mosaic covenant, the standard by which God would judge His covenanted people Israel, God once more employed darkness as an aspect of His special presence. Darkness was not the only means recorded in Deuteronomy through which God chose to reveal Himself, nor was it the only venue available to Him. But in two Old Testament instances where God ratified eternally significant covenants, He did so surrounded by darkness.

The author of Hebrews likewise used this same description centuries later. In Heb 12:18–21 God's author reminded His readers how terrifying the advent of God at Mount Sinai had been:

> *For you have not come to a mountain that can be touched and to a blazing fire, and to darkness and gloom and whirlwind, and to the blast of a trumpet and the sound of words which sound was such that those who heard begged that no further word be spoken to them. For they could not bear the command, " IF EVEN A BEAST TOUCHES THE MOUNTAIN, IT WILL BE STONED." And so terrible was the sight, that Moses said, " I AM FULL OF FEAR and trembling."*

God displayed His presence at Sinai, but a major portion of it consisted of a terrible darkness, gloom, and fear.

From The Darkness and the Glory (pp. 85–86):

Never did the Christ refer to this eternally important promised covenant of God *until*—alone with His Eleven, shortly before Gethsemane—Jesus altered the sacred Passover ceremony. As Luke 22:20 unveils, having just partaken of the bread, He revealed a divine revelatory bombshell: "And in the same way He took the cup after they had eaten, saying, 'This cup which is poured out for you is the new covenant in My blood.'" Decades later the apostle Paul, in describing the account he received from the Lord about that night, wrote in 1 Cor 11:25, "In the same way He took the cup also, after supper, saying, 'This cup is the new covenant in My blood; do this, as often as you drink it, in remembrance of Me.'" We must note two important matters. First, both references have the definite article "the" in front of them: it is *the* new covenant—the specified, promised one by God, not merely some new covenant of God in a generic sense. Second, Jesus employed a present tense in describing this. Future references would no longer be fitting in awaiting the covenant. Simply put, the new covenant now becomes an "is" not a "will be."

The other covenants of God required ratification to become effective; God's new covenant did also. But it would not be during the Passover meal. The ratification of the new covenant did not transpire the night Jesus was betrayed. What Jesus stated would happen the next day with the slaying of the true Passover sacrifice from God (1 Cor 5:7). The blood of the new covenant would be poured out within hours; or stated differently, the ratification of the new covenant would occur the next day as Jesus offered the cup of the new covenant in His blood during the crucifixion.

God used darkness to manifest Himself when ratifying the Abrahamic and Mosaic covenants. Darkness is not required in order for a covenant of God to be ratified. For instance, when God ratified the covenant with Noah in Genesis 9, there is no mention of darkness. Yet, as we have noted, God may choose to have darkness with Him. Consequently, it should not surprise us to find darkness associated with the ratifying of the new covenant as well. After noting that the darkness fell upon the land, Luke wrote of the sun being "obscured" (Luke 23:45). This is a translator's attempt to harmonize this verse with either modern science or to attempt to convey it properly in English. Literally the phrase reads, "the sun failed," or "the sun utterly failed." The sun had good reason to fail. As the glory of God illumines any darkness, so would the darkness of God overcome any source of light—the sun or anything else. What occurred was not due to an absence of light; rather, it was because of the advent of the darkness of God's presence. This is the only recorded example in Scripture of darkness conquering light, and God intended that we mark its uniqueness. Something extraordinary occurred within the darkness at the cross, and that particular aspect would never happen that way again.

In answer as to why the darkness was over the cross comes this best biblical response: in the same manner by which the Abrahamic and Mosaic covenants had darkness when they were ratified, so too did God employ darkness as He ratified His new covenant in the blood of Jesus. This obviously requires God's presence at the cross. Could God possibly be absent from a covenant that He Himself ratifies?

From The Darkness and the Glory (pp. 88–89):

Stepping back to view the six-hour crucifixion, this scenario emerges. Satan and his forces assaulted Jesus for the first three hours. Then, in the very midst of their savagery, God the Father approached God the Son. Satan and his legions would not know exactly why the Father had come to the cross. If holy angels had a difficult time understanding what God was about to do (1 Pet 1:12), how much less the totally defiled demonic world would know. Having always feared the Son even in His humility, how much more would demons tremble in the presence of God Almighty? They may have concluded that the Father came to avenge His Son. Fearing God, they most likely would have rapidly dispersed in terror, even as they repeatedly had done when encountering the Son in His humility throughout the Gospel accounts.

It seems best to understand that Satan had completed his God-granted hour of authority at this point. He would no more play a major role in the crucifixion from this point onward; Scripture makes no more reference to him again regarding the crucifixion. What would transpire now lay only in the Father's hands. Jesus had endured so much by the midpoint of His crucifixion, yet the two most horrific aspects of His suffering were only now beginning. No one needed to explain to either the angelic or demonic realm the key question at hand: What would God the Father do once He approached His Son?

To the perplexed astonishment of the holy angelic world and to the utter disbelief of Satan and his angels, the Father began striking the Son with wrath—violent, divine wrath poured out in vengeance upon the only Guilt Offering worthy to receive it (Isa 53:10). Approximately two thousand years earlier in Genesis 22, God had instructed Abraham to sacrifice Isaac by his own hand. He did not instruct him to have someone else perform the offering. In a command that resonates of another Father and beloved Son later revealed in John 3:16, God commanded the father Abraham to "take now your son, your only son, whom you love, Isaac, and go to the land of Moriah, and offer him there as a burnt offering on one of the mountains of which I will tell you" (Gen 22:2). In the Genesis account the Angel of the Lord intervened to stop Abraham's sacrifice; later, with His own Son the Father would not stay the execution. In keeping with the prophetic picture established by Abraham and Isaac, God would raise His own hand against His Son, His only Son whom He loved.

* * *

Jesus remained silent during this phase of His suffering—the Lamb silent before the Chief Shearer (Isa 53:7). For three hours Jesus endured unspeakable torment, matched only by the Father's holy capacity to strike so severely the One He loved so infinitely.

From The Darkness and the Glory (pp. 88):

That God Himself poured out wrath on His own Son may seem either impossible or absurdly cruel to some when initially considered. After all, this hardly sounds like a loving God. Part of the reason this concept sounds so strange is that many churches and much of what is considered to be Christianity have virtually eradicated the wrath of God from their teachings. Natural man never understands such deep doctrinal truths nor properly appraises them (1 Cor 2:14) because such a concept originates in the person and mind of God—not in the mind of fallen man. The fact that God indeed does evoke holy wrath is quite often either purposely or ignorantly removed in Word-starved churches with a watered-down doctrine, but it never has been erased from the Person of God or His Word—and that is all that matters.

From The Darkness and the Glory (pp. 93–97):

Jesus bore our sins on the cross—not only at the end of the crucifixion when He died. All throughout His crucifixion He bore them, but in a unique capacity the last three hours of the cross were by far the heaviest. We must remember: "The wrath of God is revealed from heaven against all ungodliness and unrighteousness" (Rom 1:18). So how did the Holy God inflict His wrath on Jesus for all our ungodliness and unrighteousness? Scripture states it best with one sentence that will take us all eternity to fully grasp, if we ever can at all. The last sentence in 2 Corinthians 5 summarizes what Paul has been arguing. The reason that we are reconciled to God comes down to this one eternally sublime revelatory truth: "He made

Him who knew no sin to be sin on our behalf, so that we might become the righteousness of God in Him" (2 Cor 5:21).

We often casually sing songs or read about "the wrath of God completely satisfied" in Jesus, often without considering the magnitude of that statement. But we must pause and consider this because it is so vital to our reconciliation with God. Was the wrath of God actually completely satisfied through the blood of Jesus? Obviously this is true as is evident from the multiple references we have seen. But consider this: in order for Jesus to satisfy God's wrath, at some point He had to receive God's wrath. In order for Him to receive God's wrath, God had to pour out His wrath on His Son. So here is the question before us: When did Jesus receive God's wrath? By whom did He receive it? The wrath of God must come from God. This must be some direct act from God; it cannot be some subsidiary by-product. While God can use angels to administer His wrath (Rev 15:1), it is still His wrath. No other beings possess the wrath of God. Good angels cannot. Satan's wrath by no means equals God's wrath. Fallen humanity? Hardly. The wrath of God comes only from God.

Consider then the sheer absurdity of this question: Will those who ultimately receive the wrath of God notice it, feel it, or respond in any way when it occurs? Will those on whom the wrath of God currently abides (John 3:36), but do not yet have its full consequences, change in any way when they finally do fully receive it? Matthew 25:30 describes those who are tormented as enduring in a place where "there shall be weeping and gnashing of teeth." We saw in Rev 14:10–11 that the worshippers of the beast "will drink of the wine of the wrath of God, which is mixed in full strength in the cup of His anger; and he will be tormented with fire and brimstone in the presence of the holy angels and in the presence of the Lamb. And the smoke of their torment goes up forever and ever." Interestingly, the Revelation 14 passage uses the same terminology of drinking of God's wrath from a cup given them by God.

These individuals are fully alive and fully aware—and fully tormented when the wrath of God is poured out. Would it be any less true for Jesus? Would He notice it? Would He feel it? Eternally more than we have the capacity to comprehend would the Lamb of God know and feel when God poured out His wrath on Him.

Jesus bore our sins, but He also bore the wrath of God for all believers. The Bible does not disclose the exact means by which God poured out His wrath on His Son. We only know from the Word that He did because we see that the sacrifice of God's own Son was sufficient and accepted. The Son exhausted God's wrath for the redeemed. Whatever God required for His wrath to be received and satisfied, *He* had to pour out, just as He will in Revelation 14 and elsewhere. Whatever God required for His wrath to be received and satisfied, Jesus accomplished fully, wholly, completely in the cup of the new covenant in His blood—as part of the cup that He alone was able to drink.

God did not make Jesus a sinner; God did not treat Jesus as sinful. "**He** [God] made Him who knew no sin . . ."

> *We have such a high priest, holy, innocent, undefiled; separated from sinners and exalted above the heavens. (Heb 7:26)*
>
> *Tempted in all things as we are, yet without sin. (Heb 4:15)*
>
> *Who committed no sin, nor was any deceit found in His mouth. (1 Pet 2:22)*
>
> *And in Him there is no sin. (1 John 3:5)*

" . . . to be [or "become"] sin on our behalf. . ."

> *For the wrath of God is revealed from heaven against all ungodliness; against all unrighteousness. (Rom 1:18)*
>
> *For the wrath of God once abided—on Him—who became sin in our behalf. (John 3:36; 2 Cor 5:21)*

". . . that we might become the righteousness of God in Him."

God's wrath poured out on Jesus made Satan's previous tormenting minuscule in comparison. What Satan inflicted on Jesus in no way compares with what the Father could do—and, in fact, what the Father did do.

God required appeasement for sin—not Satan.

God alone has a divine standard of righteousness—not Satan.

God alone possessed the capacity to pour out divine wrath—not Satan.

God alone cared about the atonement for the sins of the redeemed—not Satan.

God laid the totality of the world's sin on His Son; Jesus bore the totality of the sin of the world (John 1:29). We know this concept in principle, but we must stop there. Our present limitations force us to wait until we get to heaven to have Jesus explain it to us personally because no one other than Jesus experientially knows what is required to appease the righteousness of God and absorb His wrath for even one of our own sins, much less for the accumulated sins of our lifetimes. We who are redeemed have had this done for us; angels have never experientially received grace and pardon; those who will endure eternal hell will be no step closer to appeasing that one sin they committed even after being there for a thousand years. Only Jesus experientially knows what is required.

The mere thought of the aggregate burden of one's own sin—let alone the weight of every sin ever committed for those saved from Adam onward—overwhelms us. At least the vilest offender who will receive God's wrath, perhaps with the exception of Satan, will not have the wrath deserved by others laid on him. For those who hold that the death of Jesus was only for the elect, still the magnitude of what He bore goes beyond our capacity to comprehend: "Worthy are You to take the book and to break its seals; for You were slain, and purchased for God with Your blood men from every tribe and tongue and people and nation" (Rev 5:9). We possess neither spiritual nor mental capacities to understand it completely. We could more easily fathom numbering the sands of all the beaches in the world, giving each granule a specific name, and then recalling each grain of sand by name. Multiply this by billions, and you will begin to understand some of the depth of God's love through Jesus Christ. We cannot even begin to seize it in thought—the magnitude of such a proposal rests only within the Godhead. No wonder angels fervently desire to look into the things related to salvation (1 Pet 1:12). No other event in history past or present even remotely compares to the divine love demonstrated that one dark day—as the Servant of Yahweh had His form altered and His appearance disfigured more than anyone who ever has or ever will live.

God did not look away from Jesus as the Lamb atoned for sins. During the darkness the Father looked fully on the Son. Each knew what the Other was doing during this unique second aspect of the cup that the Father had determined that His Son must drink. Is it any wonder that He was marred more than any Son of Adam ever had been (Isa 52:14)? How could He possibly not be?

For three hours—divine wrath inflicted and received by the One alone able to do so.

For three hours—silent, willful submission by the Lamb of God, the Servant of Yahweh.

For three hours—Jesus bore the full burden of sins past, present, and future.

For three hours—the Father smote the Son with the full wrath He alone could render.

And then—He stopped.

Summary and Conclusion

Among many other things, several main points were made in this important chapter. (1) Part of the cup that Jesus drank involved every day of His incarnation (Mark 10:38), and yet there was quite a specific future element to "the cup that [He was] about to drink" (Matt 20:22). The removal of this cup was the content of the threefold prayer that Jesus prayed (Mark 14:32–41). After this prayer He also stated His declarative acceptance of drinking the cup that the Father had given Him (John 18:10–11). Also, (2) because Satan had already entered into Judas by the time Jesus wrestled in prayer in Gethsemane, Satan was not present there; he was wherever Judas went.

(3) Everything about Matt 16:21–23 makes sense at an initial read. The last thing that Satan wanted was for Jesus to go to His cross, and yet in Luke 22:3–4, Satan entered into Judas in order to help bring about the crucifixion.

We also saw (4) that Isa 52:14 states that "so His appearance was marred more than any man / And His form more than the sons of men." His would be no ordinary crucifixion—and we saw that unfold in front of us. We saw (5) in John 13–17 and Luke 22 that Satan is referred to seven times in this section, with (6) Luke 22:52–53 revealing something that we would not know: God granted Satan a specific designated period of time, literally in the Greek text stating, "this is the hour of yours, and the power [authority] of the darkness is yours."

We learned (7) John 10:17–18 reveals the tremendously important doctrine that no one could ever kill Jesus—not even Satan. However, Job 1–2 shows some of the power that Satan can use if God allows him to do so. (8) From Matt 26:52–53, we learned that Jesus could have called for more than 72,000 angels to come and rescue Him, and God would have sent them as soon as the words left Jesus's lips. Having these angels readily available and still never calling for them only added to Jesus's burden. (9) Matthew 25:41 reveals that Satan has his angels, too, and Luke 8:30 and Rev 12:4 show the vast number of holy angels who fell when Satan fell.

Further, (10) demons are immensely powerful. In Rev 9:4–6, in a future judgment of the tribulation, three times it states that—when God allows—demons will torment people with a horrible torment. Luke 8:28 reveals demons can receive torment as well. So, (11) with the exception of killing Jesus, everything in Satan's arsenal could be cast on Jesus during the hour of the darkness. This is the first of three parts that made the cup that Jesus drank so much different from all others: enduring the wrath of Satan. Accordingly, (12) Satan wagered that he could bring such torment upon Jesus that He would readily call for His attending angels to rescue Him—and thus not redeem anyone nor crush Satan's head. Also, (13) Eph 3:8–12 beautifully reveals that part of the reason that God's plan was for Jesus to go to the cross was with the eternal purpose of making known "to the rulers and the authorities in the heavenly places." We know from this that demons watched what God exhibited—the holy angels of God witnessed this as well.

(14) The darkness over the cross has been explained in many different ways, with the most popular one being that God is too pure to look at sin, and thus He had to turn away from Jesus, but this has no biblical basis. Many Bible verses show God most certainly does look at sin. We noted (15) the Bible presents the duration of the crucifixion as six; the first three hours were in the light, and the next three hours were in the darkness. Everything Jesus said, He did in the light; when the darkness was present, He said nothing.

We saw (16) God used darkness to announce His presence in the ratification of the Abrahamic covenant (Gen 15:12) and later with the ratification of the Mosaic covenant (Deut 4:11; 5:23–24; Heb 12:18–21). (17) In Luke 22:20, Jesus revealed that the new covenant was going to be poured out in His blood at His cross. As with the Abrahamic and the Mosaic covenants, darkness was indicating God's presence—not His absence. (18) It was during the darkness that Jesus drank the cup of what He alone could endure: the wrath of God. This further contributed to marring His appearance, in keeping with Isa 52:14. (19) God's wrath being poured out on Jesus made Satan's wrath look miniscule in comparison.

Hopefully we came away from this chapter stunned at the depths that Jesus endured to save those whom He will save. What a wonderful Savior indeed is Jesus our Lord.

Deeper Walk Study Questions

1. Show biblically how "the cup" played such an important part of the overall life of Jesus (Mark 10:38), the future aspect that it had (Matt 20:22), in Gethsemane (Mark 14:32–41), and then at the arrest of Jesus (John 18:10–11). Write eight biblical truths we can learn from these accounts. Why are they important? Explain.

2. How do we know that Satan was not in Gethsemane tempting Jesus? Why is this important? Explain.

3. Name the quandary that comes from the initial reading of Matt 16:21–23 and Luke 22:3–4. Explain in detail why this is important.

4. What is the importance of Isa 52:13–15? Name five truths about the Messiah from these Scripture passages and explain why they are important, especially verse 14. How does this make Jesus's crucifixion differ from all others? Explain.

5. List seven times Satan is referred to in John 13–17 and Luke 22. What do these say, and why are they important? Also, Luke 22:53 is very important in understanding what is about to happen. How do we know this? What does it grant to Satan? Be specific in your answer.

6. How is the word *hour* used in different ways? How do you know? Which type of hour would it be for the events leading to the crucifixion, and why is this important? Explain and be specific in your answer.

7. Why is John 10:17–18 so important in understanding what was about to occur with the cross of Jesus? How do we know that Satan could not kill Jesus? Why is this important? Explain. Also, what can we learn from Job 1–2 about what Satan can do when permitted by God?

8. Why is Matt 26:52–53 so important to understanding what Jesus was doing in His willful submission to the Father? Why would having ready access to these angels make the situation that Jesus endured even harder than Job's situation? Explain with five biblical truths.

9. How do we know that Satan has his own angels, as seen in Matt 25:41? What can we learn about demons from Luke 8:30 and Rev 12:4? Why is this important? Explain.

10. From Rev 9:4–6, what can demons do when permitted by God? What do Luke 8:28 and Matt 8:29 reveal about them as well?

11. What was Satan allowed to do, and why did this make the cup that Jesus drank differ from anyone else's? Explain.

12. In Satan's designated hour of the darkness, what specifically did he wager? Why is this eternally important? List six biblical truths from this.

13. What does Eph 3:8–12 reveal as to why God allowed the events of Calvary to unfold the way they did? List eight biblical truths from this passage.

14. How do we know that the idea of God being so holy that He must turn away and not look at sin is not biblical, and that this cannot be the reason for the darkness over the cross? Explain with five biblical supports.

15. How long did the crucifixion of Jesus last? How is it divided? What does this have to do with the words of Jesus on the cross? Explain.

16. What is the significance of God's use of darkness in ratifying the Abrahamic covenant (Gen 15:12) and the Mosaic covenant (Deut 4:11; 5:23–24)? What does this mean, and why is it important theologically? Explain and be specific.

17. How does knowing God's presence at the ratification of two of His other covenants best explain the darkness at Calvary as being the ratification of the new covenant (Luke 22:20)? Why is this important theologically? Name four reasons.

18. List five biblical truths about the wrath of God in general. List five truths about the second part of the cup that Jesus drank—enduring the wrath of God. How is it so different from that of anyone else, and why does this marring of the visage and body of Jesus make much more sense now? Explain.

19. How can we compare the way that Jesus endured the wrath of God with how we not endure God's wrath, if we were still alive? Explain how we know biblically that Jesus really did bear the wrath of God for us on the cross. Give five biblical supports—and much praise to Jesus for doing so.

CHAPTER 23

In Christ Alone

W e who live this side of the cross are familiar with many verses in the New Testament containing "in Christ" and "in Christ Jesus" as well as the "in Him" Scripture passages that present the same doctrinal truths. Two popular and wonderfully crafted Christian songs entitled "In Christ Alone" make that term more familiar to many. Perhaps in hearing or singing that song, you have not considered why the biblical doctrine of "in Christ"—and all of the connective subsidiary biblical truths that flow from this—is so important.

Much about this eternal doctrine exists. In this chapter, we will follow the same format of tracing the astounding biblical trails that will teach beautiful truths about "in Christ"—and why this doctrine must be understood in order to understand the Godhead, especially Jesus, better and to respond in abject worship in spirit/Spirit and in truth that is due them.

A Few Biblical Presuppositions about "In Christ"

In the same way I used appropriate biblical presuppositions in the chapter in this *Handbook* about the glory of God, I do also with "in Christ."

1. Christ living within someone is doctrine that is totally and intentionally omitted from the Old Testament.
2. Wonderful Old Testament promises, such as "all who take refuge in Him" (Ps 2:12), "rejoices in Him" (33:21), or "hope in the LORD" (130:7), and many more—although eternally important—are not the focus of this current chapter. We will be dealing

with specific teachings from Jesus that are found later in the New Testament.

3. It is important to note that Christ and Messiah mean the same thing, denoting the office. John 1:41: "[Andrew] found first his own brother Simon and said to him, 'We have found the Messiah' (which translated means Christ)," which appropriately means "The Anointed One." So when we say "in Christ," we are actually saying (although it is not usually worded this way) "in Messiah." We will refer later to this biblical truth.

4. The Old Testament word/concept doctrine of "Messiah" in itself had nothing to do with a sacrificial death for atonement—only with Messiah's reigning as King of Israel and King over all the Gentiles/nations.

5. Many Old Testament prophecies show that the Messiah/Christ would reign, but *none* of these verses depict the Messiah as living within someone. "For unto us a child is born" (Isa 9:6, KJV) does not say, "into us a child is born." The Messiah/Christ will rule the nations "with a rod of iron" (Ps 2:9), and many verses show the Messiah as ruling and reigning on earth.

6. Thus, the "in Messiah/in Christ" doctrine was totally missing from any of the proclamations of John the Baptist because this beloved prophet of Yahweh had no theological basis for this concept/doctrine.

7. Also, during His incarnation, Jesus never spoke about nor taught on the doctrine of "in Messiah/in Christ"—with one major exception that I will show below.

8. "In Christ" is unquestionably a major New Testament doctrine/truth, but the first occurrence of this is not until Acts, long after the crucifixion, resurrection, and ascension of Jesus, and the birth of the church. It is written in the Epistles to the church.

A Few Biblical Presuppositions of What Being "In Christ" Does Not Mean

1. "In Christ" does not mean that there was no bodily resurrection of Jesus, as if only "the Spirit of Christ" was resurrected. In Luke 24:39 Jesus said, "Touch Me," which required a physical act. He ate fish and other meals among the disciples, and other such events prove His bodily resurrection.

2. "In Christ" does not mean that the reign of Jesus is only a spiritual reign within someone's heart. At the ascension of the resurrected Jesus into heaven, the following account is given in Acts 1:9–11:

   > And after He had said these things, He was lifted up while they were looking on, and a cloud received Him out of their sight. And as they were gazing intently into the sky while He was going, behold, two men in white clothing stood beside them. They also said, "Men of Galilee, why do you stand looking into the sky? This Jesus, who has been taken up from you into heaven, will come in just the same way as you have watched Him go into heaven."

3. "In Christ" does not mean that Jesus will always stay in His current spiritual form. When He returns, His feet will be on the Mount of Olives (Zech 14:3–4). Later in the chapter, Gentiles will come and worship Him in Jerusalem year by year (vv. 16–17).

The Origin of the "In Christ" Doctrine

To track this wondrous doctrine by using the biblical trail, we need to return to our fifth theological bombshell from Matthew 16, where it is promised that Jesus will return "in the glory of His Father with His angels" (v. 27). In this Scripture we observed that (1) this was the first time that Jesus ever had taught anything about the glory of God, and (2) Jesus places this demonstration of God's glory at His second coming—not during His incarnation.

Critics of the Bible who look for errors and contradictions in their attempts to besmirch the Word of God's credibility use a verse that many of us love: "I am the LORD, that is My name; / I will not give My glory to another" (Isa 42:8). "So who is right," they would sneer, "Jesus who promises to return in glory, or God in Isaiah 42 who says that He will not give His glory to another?"

But while critics of the Bible may condescendingly smirk at what seems an obvious contradiction to them, Scripture actually gives further support to the Person and Work—and Deity—of God's Messiah by using another example of the utter trustworthiness of God and His Word.

Isaiah 42:8 occurs within Isa 42:1–9, included below. It is what is considered the first of four Servant Songs in the book, and part of Isaiah 53 is the most famous.

"Behold, My Servant, whom I uphold;

My chosen one in whom My soul delights.

I have put My Spirit upon Him;

He will bring forth justice to the nations.

"He will not cry out or raise His voice,

Nor make His voice heard in the street.

"A bruised reed He will not break

And a dimly burning wick He will not extinguish;

He will faithfully bring forth justice.

"He will not be disheartened or crushed

Until He has established justice in the earth;

And the coastlands will wait expectantly for His law."

Thus says God the LORD,

Who created the heavens and stretched them out,

Who spread out the earth and its offspring,

Who gives breath to the people on it

And spirit to those who walk in it,

"I am the LORD, I have called You in righteousness,

I will also hold You by the hand and watch over You,

And I will appoint You as a covenant to the people,

As a light to the nations,

To open blind eyes,

To bring out prisoners from the dungeon

And those who dwell in darkness from the prison.

"I am the LORD, that is My name;

I will not give My glory to another,

Nor My praise to graven images.

"Behold, the former things have come to pass,

Now I declare new things;

Before they spring forth I proclaim them to you."

Remember that although the orthodox Jews do not believe in the deity of the Messiah—whom they believe is yet to come the first time—they do believe in God's Word (the Old Testament—that they refer to as the Hebrew Bible or Tanak). By answering critics of God's Word, I will show evidence of the Messiah and His deity with some wonderful biblical answers.

When Jesus spoke about His return in glory in Matthew 16, many references to this are actually Old Testament passages that support the belief of the Messiah as being God—and not only a man—and these verses are also connected with the glory of God.

A few sources will suffice. Psalm 24:7–10 reveals:

Lift up your heads, O gates,

And be lifted up, O ancient doors,

That the King of glory may come in!

Who is the King of glory?

The LORD strong and mighty,

The LORD mighty in battle.

Lift up your heads, O gates,

And lift them up, O ancient doors,

That the King of glory may come in!

Who is this King of glory?

> *The* Lord *of hosts,*
>
> *He is the King of glory. Selah.*

Isaiah 24:21–23 adds:

> *So it will happen in that day,*
>
> *That the* Lord *will punish the host of heaven on high,*
>
> *And the kings of the earth on earth.*
>
> *They will be gathered together*
>
> *Like prisoners in the dungeon,*
>
> *And will be confined in prison;*
>
> *And after many days they will be punished.*
>
> *Then the moon will be abashed and the sun ashamed,*
>
> *For the* Lord *of hosts will reign on Mount Zion and in Jerusalem,*
>
> *And His glory will be before His elders.*

Isaiah 60:1–3 concurs:

> *"Arise, shine; for your light has come,*
>
> *And the glory of the* Lord *has risen upon you.*
>
> *"For behold, darkness will cover the earth*
>
> *And deep darkness the peoples;*
>
> *But the* Lord *will rise upon you*
>
> *And His glory will appear upon you.*
>
> *"Nations will come to your light,*
>
> *And kings to the brightness of your rising."*

So when Jesus promises to return in the glory of His Father, He also testifies that these specific passages from the Old Testament, and many others, will be fulfilled in Him and by Him at His return.

NOTE: These verses are quite helpful to use in evangelizing Jews when the stumbling block is that the Messiah cannot be God. These verses argue the opposite. No mere man could fulfill any of the requirements about returning in the glory of God. Jews have no answer—because none exists—of how someone who is merely human can at the same time also claim the title of Yahweh.

This explanation will not satisfy critics of the Bible, but the truth is found in these deep wells of Scripture in John 10:22–30:

> *At that time the Feast of the Dedication took place at Jerusalem; it was winter, and Jesus was walking in the temple in the portico of Solomon. The Jews then gathered around Him, and were saying to Him, "How long will You keep us in suspense? If You are the Christ, tell us plainly." Jesus answered them, "I told you, and you do not believe; the works that I do in My Father's name, these testify of Me. But you do not believe because you are not of My sheep. My sheep hear My voice, and I know them, and they follow Me; and I give eternal life to them, and they will never perish; and no one will snatch them out of My hand. My Father, who has given them to Me, is greater than all; and no one is able to snatch them out of the Father's hand. I and the Father are one."*

So from the vantage point of this verse, God does not give His glory to another, but only to Jesus who is the One so uniquely interwoven in Himself and to Himself.

Another biblical doctrine is in a beautiful prayer that Jesus prays; it is called Jesus's High Priestly Prayer. He prays for specific items in the first part of His prayer in John 17:1–5:

> *Father, the hour has come; glorify Your Son, that the Son may glorify You, even as You gave Him authority over all flesh, that to all whom You have given Him, He may give eternal life. This is eternal life, that they may know You, the only true God, and Jesus Christ whom You have sent. I glorified You on the earth, having accomplished the work which You have given Me to do. Now, Father, glorify Me together with Yourself, with the glory which I had with You before the world was.*

In the second part of this prayer, Jesus prays for the Twelve, minus Judas, in verses 6–19. You can study this part on your own, if you like, because it does not relate to this chapter in the *Handbook*.

We definitely need to examine verses 20–26 that comprise the final part of this prayer of Jesus because it is eternally relevant. In this part, Jesus broadens His prayer to include His future disciples, which would include us who are saved, as seen in verses 20–21:

> *I do not ask on behalf of these alone, but for those also who believe in Me through their word; that they may all be one; even as You, Father, are in Me and I in You, that they also may be in Us, so that the world may believe that You sent Me.*

Whether or not Jesus had prayed that same prayer or parts of that prayer in His private prayers, we are not told, and we will have to wait until we get to heaven for the full disclosure. What we do have here is literally an eternity-changing doctrinal prayer request that Jesus had not previously prayed in public until that night for the Eleven: "I in You, that they also may be in Us."

And in verses 22–24, Jesus expands and expounds His prayer with worship-evoking truths from the Word of God:

> *The glory which You have given Me I have given to them, that they may be one, just as We are one; I in them and You in Me, that they may be perfected in unity, so that the world may know that You sent Me, and loved them, even as You have loved Me. Father, I desire that they also, whom You have given Me, be with Me where I am, so that they may see My glory which You have given Me, for You loved Me before the foundation of the world.*

If we had written this or if we claimed these truths for ourselves, we would be guilty of heretical blasphemy. But this is not blasphemy; these are awe-inspiring, never-then-heard-before doctrinal nuggets of gold that God gives to the redeemed. Concerning the idea that God will not give His glory to another, stated in Isa 42:8, Jesus offers this revelation: "The glory which You have given Me I have given to them, that they may be one, just as We are one" (John 17:22). This is an utterly astounding grace gift from God that we could meditate about for the remainder of our lives, and we could never fully comprehend the richness and beauty of this one verse in the Bible.

Now we will see the answer to what had seemed an enigma to many. Earlier in this chapter we saw the unique "Oneness" of the Godhead. Jesus now incorporates the redeemed into that Oneness: "I in them and You in Me" (v. 23). This is the first time in the Bible that Jesus reveals anything about His being inside anyone. It is from these John 17 verses that every "in Christ" verse later revealed in the New Testament will germinate, and all occur only after the death, burial, and resurrection of Jesus the Messiah—and all are given as promises to His true church.

In verse 24, Jesus makes this request of God the Father: "I desire that they also, whom You have given Me, be with Me where I am, so that they may see My glory which You have given Me, for You loved Me before the foundation of the world." This definitely fits into the category we saw in another chapter of the *Handbook* that "The Glory of God Changes Everything" proves the best six-word inclusive description of the entire Bible. Wonderful, beautiful, worship-evoking, eternal truths flow forth from this one section in Scripture. But then the Godhead expands and adds additional nuggets of truth in the remainder of the Bible.

The story gets better—and astoundingly so—with all that is revealed in the progressive revelation of God in the "in Christ" verses.

A Sampling of the Beauty of the "in Christ" Verses

Due to the limitations for the size of this *Handbook*, I had to be selective in the verses I chose to include. Approximately eighty times some form of an "in Christ" reference occurs in Scripture. You may want to use a concordance and go through and find and study the ones we omitted. Because variations exist in these verses, we will mark ours into the different ways in which these truths appear: "in Christ," "in Christ Jesus," and finally "in Him." The latter is used only in the cases where being "in Him" is used in the same way as "in Christ" is used elsewhere. All of the following verses mean the same thing as it relates to "in Christ." Further, we will follow the natural fourfold divisions of these that the Bible uses: (1) in Christ Jesus, (2) in Christ, (3) Christ in you, and (4) in Him. Also, we will let the beauty of the verses speak for themselves.

We will begin the use of each verse in mid-context, which is not the preferred study route to follow; nevertheless, you will find these to be wonderfully beneficial and encouraging verses for those of us "in Christ."

And remember, all of the verses used here are taken from the Epistles—written to the churches—and God gives all the "in Christ" verses to His beloved church.

"In Christ Jesus" (emphasis added)

- being justified as a gift by His grace through the redemption which is *in Christ Jesus* (Rom 3:24).
- Even so consider yourselves to be dead to sin, but alive to God *in Christ Jesus* (Rom 6:11).
- For the wages of sin is death, but the free gift of God is eternal life *in Christ Jesus* our Lord (Rom 6:23).
- Therefore there is now no condemnation for those who are *in Christ Jesus*. For the law of the Spirit of life *in Christ Jesus* has set you free from the law of sin and of death (Rom 8:1–2).
- nor height, nor depth, nor any other created thing, will be able to separate us from the love of God, which is *in Christ Jesus* our Lord (Rom 8:39).
- To the church of God which is at Corinth, to those who have been sanctified *in Christ Jesus,* saints by calling, with all who in every place call on the name of our Lord Jesus Christ, their Lord and ours (1 Cor 1:2).
- But by His doing you are *in Christ Jesus,* who became to us wisdom from God, and righteousness and sanctification, and redemption (1 Cor 1:30).
- There is neither Jew nor Greek, there is neither slave nor free man, there is neither male nor female; for you are all one *in Christ Jesus* (Gal 3:28).
- and raised us up with Him, and seated us with Him in the heavenly places, *in Christ Jesus,* so that in the ages to come He might show the surpassing riches of His grace in kindness toward us *in Christ Jesus* (Eph 2:6–7).
- For we are His workmanship, created *in Christ Jesus* for good works, which God prepared beforehand so that we would walk in them (Eph 2:10).
- But now *in Christ Jesus* you who formerly were far off have been brought near by the blood of Christ (Eph 2:13).

- to be specific, that the Gentiles are fellow heirs and fellow members of the body, and fellow partakers of the promise *in Christ Jesus* through the gospel (Eph 3:6).
- This was in accordance with the eternal purpose which He carried out *in Christ Jesus* our Lord (Eph 3:11).
- I press on toward the goal for the prize of the upward call of God *in Christ Jesus* (Phil 3:14).
- And the peace of God, which surpasses all comprehension, will guard your hearts and your minds *in Christ Jesus* (Phil 4:7).
- And my God will supply all your needs according to His riches in glory *in Christ Jesus* (Phil 4:19).
- in everything give thanks; for this is God's will for you *in Christ Jesus* (1 Thess 5:18).
- and the grace of our Lord was more than abundant, with the faith and love which are found *in Christ Jesus* (1 Tim 1:14).
- who has saved us and called us with a holy calling, not according to our works, but according to His own purpose and grace which was granted us *in Christ Jesus* from all eternity (2 Tim 1:9).
- You therefore, my son, be strong in the grace that is *in Christ Jesus* (2 Tim 2:1).
- For this reason I endure all things for the sake of those who are chosen, so that they also may obtain the salvation which is *in Christ Jesus* and with it eternal glory (2 Tim 2:10).

"In Christ" (emphasis added)
- so we, who are many, are one body *in Christ,* and individually members one of another (Rom 12:5).
- For as in Adam all die, so also *in Christ* all will be made alive (1 Cor 15:22).
- Now He who establishes us with you *in Christ* and anointed us is God (2 Cor 1:21).
- But thanks be to God, who always leads us in triumph *in Christ*, and manifests through us the sweet aroma of the knowledge of Him in every place (2 Cor 2:14).
- Therefore if anyone is *in Christ,* he is a new creature; the old things passed away; behold, new things have come (2 Cor 5:17).

- Blessed be the God and Father of our Lord Jesus Christ, who has blessed us with every spiritual blessing in the heavenly places *in Christ* (Eph 1:3).
- with a view to an administration suitable to the fullness of the times, that is, the summing up of all things *in Christ,* things in the heavens and things on the earth (Eph 1:10).
- to the end that we who were the first to hope *in Christ* would be to the praise of His glory (Eph 1:12).
- which He brought about *in Christ,* when He raised Him from the dead and seated Him at His right hand in the heavenly places (Eph 1:20).
- Be kind to one another, tender-hearted, forgiving each other, just as God *in Christ* also has forgiven you (Eph 4:32).
- For the Lord Himself will descend from heaven with a shout, with the voice of the archangel and with the trumpet of God, and the dead *in Christ* will rise first (1 Thess 4:16).

The last two references of "in Christ" I want to call special attention to because one of the verses I began with way back when I first started studying the glory of God:

- After you have suffered for a little while, the God of all grace, who called you to His eternal glory *in Christ,* will Himself perfect, confirm, strengthen and establish you (1 Pet 5:10).
- Greet one another with a kiss of love. Peace be to you all who are *in Christ* (1 Pet 5:14).

"Christ in you" (emphasis added)

Only one verse in the entire New Testament uses "Christ in you," but if you are a saved Gentile, this is an incredibly important one to know—and to thank God for:—to whom God willed to make known what is the riches of the glory of this mystery among the Gentiles, which is *Christ in you,* the hope of glory (Col 1:27).

Selected "in Him" Verses (from Acts onward; emphasis added)

The following verses are limited to the same concept as in "in Christ" and do not include the many verses about "believing in Him," such as Acts

10:43 ("Of Him all the prophets bear witness that through His name every-one who believes in Him receives forgiveness of sins").

> **CONSIDER:** Here is a good study point to keep in mind: if you used only your concordance for verses about "in Christ," the tool would not point out the verses that have "in Him." Be aware that there are times that just looking up a word or phrase will not suffice to cover the topic. Using a concordance may be a good start but may not be all that is needed for a broader understanding. Also, as before, we are not dealing here with verses such as Ps 34:8: "O taste and see that the Lord is good; / How blessed is the man who takes refuge in Him!" The verses we are dealing with are the ones in the New Testament that specifically teach of being "in Him."

- He made Him who knew no sin to be sin on our behalf, so that we might become the righteousness of God *in Him* (2 Cor 5:21).
- just as He chose us *in Him* before the foundation of the world, that we would be holy and blameless before Him (Eph 1:4).
- *In Him* we have redemption through His blood, the forgiveness of our trespasses, according to the riches of His grace (Eph 1:7).
- He made known to us the mystery of His will, according to His kind intention which He purposed *in Him* (Eph 1:9).
- *In Him,* you also, after listening to the message of truth, the gospel of your salvation
- having also believed, you were sealed *in Him* with the Holy Spirit of promise (Eph 1:13).
- and may be found *in Him,* not having a righteousness of my own derived from the Law, but that which is through faith in Christ, the righteousness which comes from God on the basis of faith (Phil 3:9).
- He is before all things, and *in Him* all things hold together (Col 1:17).
- For it was the Father's good pleasure for all the fullness to dwell *in Him* (Col 1:19).
- This is the message we have heard from Him and announce to you, that God is Light, and *in Him* there is no darkness at all (1 John 1:5).

- but whoever keeps His Word, in Him the love of God has truly been perfected. By this we know that we are *in Him:* the one who says he abides *in Him* ought himself to walk in the same manner as He walked (1 John 2:5–6).
- Now, little children, abide *in Him,* so that when He appears, we may have confidence and not shrink away from Him in shame at His coming (1 John 2:28).
- You know that He appeared in order to take away sins; and *in Him* there is no sin. No one who abides *in Him* sins; no one who sins has seen Him or knows Him (1 John 3:5–6).
- And we know that the Son of God has come, and has given us understanding so that we may know Him who is true; and we are *in Him* who is true, in His Son Jesus Christ. This is the true God and eternal life (1 John 5:20).

Summary and Conclusion

In this chapter we learned that (1) Christ or Messiah being within someone is doctrine that is totally and intentionally omitted from the Old Testament. (2) Many Old Testament verses exist for those "who take refuge in Him" (Ps 2:12) and "rejoice in Him" (33:21) or for those who "hope in the LORD" (130:7). Wonderful promises of God verses such as these and many more—although eternally important—were not the focus of this current chapter but will be wonderfully enhanced when the Messiah returns and reigns—and even more into the eternal state. (3) We saw in John 1:41 that the words "Christ" and "Messiah" are interchangeably used, and the words in themselves had nothing to do with a sacrificial death for atonement—only with Messiah's reigning as King of Israel and King over all the Gentiles/nations. (4) Many Old Testament prophecies show that the Messiah/Christ would reign, but *none* of these verses depict the Messiah as living within someone. (5) "In Christ" or "In Messiah" was totally lacking from the preaching of John the Baptist and also from Jesus—with one key exception. (6) We also saw that "in Christ" does not mean that there was no bodily resurrection of Jesus, as if only "the Spirit of Christ" was resurrected or that His reign on earth will be a spiritual one only.

We further learned, (7) in going back to our fifth theological bomb-shell from Matthew 16, that Jesus promised He will return "in the glory of His Father with His angels" (v. 27). Critics of the Bible look for errors and contradictions in their attempts to besmirch the Word of God's credibility, and they use a verse that many of us love: "I am the LORD, that is My name; / I will not give My glory to another" (Isa 42:8). But we saw that Isa 42:1–9 is actually from a messianic prophecy in Isaiah and harmonizes with other glory of God passages identified with the promised Messiah, such as Ps 24:7–10 and Isa 24:21–23 and 60:1–3. (8) So, actually contrary to the beliefs of orthodox Jews and many critics of the Bible, verses that Jesus gave, such as John 10:22–30 (especially v. 30, "I and the Father are one"), maintain the claim by God that He does not give His glory to another. In this case, He gives it—wondrously and appropriately—to His Son, the Messiah.

We also saw in this chapter (9) the beautiful prayer that Jesus prayed in John 17, just before going to Gethsemane: "The glory which You have given Me I have given to them, that they may be one, just as We are one" (v. 22). This is an utterly astounding grace gift from God that we could meditate about for the remainder of our lives, and we could never fully comprehend the richness and beauty of this one verse in the Bible. (10) In John 17:23, Jesus incorporated the redeemed into that same oneness that He and the Father share: "I in them and You in Me." This is the first time in the Bible that Jesus specifically reveals anything about His being inside anyone. (11) It is from these last verses that every "in Christ" verse later revealed in the New Testament will germinate—and all remaining New Testament statements occur only after the death, burial, and resurrection of Jesus the Messiah and are given as part of the blessings to His church. (12) In John 17:24, Jesus requested this from God the Father: "I desire that they also, whom You have given Me, be with Me where I am, so that they may see My glory which You have given Me, for You loved Me before the foundation of the world."

Further, (13) approximately eighty times in Scripture some form of "in Christ" appears in various ways: "in Christ," "in Christ Jesus," and finally "in Him." The latter we used only in the cases where being "in Him" is used in the same way as "in Christ" is used elsewhere. (14) We read some of the verses from the natural fourfold divisions of these that the Bible uses: "in Christ Jesus," "in Christ," "Christ in you," and "in Him"—where the intended meaning clearly meant the same as "in Christ"—and allowed the beauty of the verses to speak for themselves.

Deeper Walk Study Questions

1. Why is "in Christ" not a concept that the Jews would have been looking for? Also, why is the "in Christ" concept missing from the proclamation of John the Baptist? Show biblically how you know that the words "Messiah" and "Christ" are used interchangeably and explain why it matters theologically.

2. Based on the above answers, why would "in Christ" be such an absurd concept to people during the time of Jesus and, thus, was not a part of His public proclamation? Explain.

3. Why does the returning of Jesus in glory (Matt 16:27) and the Father not giving His glory to another seem to critics of the Bible to be another one of what they consider many contradictions? Also, from Ps 24:7–10 and Isa 24:21–23 and 60:1–3 write six biblical truths that associate the Messiah with God's glory.

4. Though not believed by critics of the Bible, how does John 10:22–30 (especially verse 30, "I and the Father are one") maintain the claim by God that He does not give His glory to another?

5. Based on what we have already studied in this chapter, why is what Jesus said in John 17:22 so staggering: "The glory which You have given Me I have given to them, that they may be one, just as We are one"? Give five biblical truths from this amazing verse.

6. Consider John 17:23. What is significant about Jesus incorporating the redeemed into that same oneness that He and the Father shared: "I in them and You in Me"? Why is this important theologically? Explain.

7. What does Jesus pray in John 17:24, and why is this important to what we have studied earlier in this chapter? Explain and support your answers biblically.

8. List ten of your favorite "in Christ" verses. Name three truths from each one and why these matter to us as Christians. Be specific.

CHAPTER 24

And How Shall They Hear
without a Preacher?

S imilarly to Isa 6:8, Rom 10:14–15 is frequently used in either commissioning services of pastors or missionaries or else as a call to expository preaching/teaching:

> How then will they call on Him in whom they have not believed? How will they believe in Him whom they have not heard? And how will they hear without a preacher? How will they preach unless they are sent? Just as it is written, "HOW BEAUTIFUL ARE THE FEET OF THOSE WHO BRING GOOD NEWS OF GOOD THINGS!"

We know God does send out people into the ministry, as Jesus explained in Luke 10:2: "The harvest is plentiful, but the laborers are few; therefore beseech the Lord of the harvest to send out laborers into His harvest." Also, while I certainly delight in biblically accurate Bible expository preaching/teaching, you cannot begin in Rom 10:14–15 and remotely hope to interpret these verses accurately. As we will clearly see, the context of these verses explicitly shows that God's usage has a totally different—and eternally profound and consequential—meaning for these verses in things past, present, and future.

A Broad Walk-Through of Romans

When Paul composed the epistle to the Romans, he wrote to the church(es) in Rome; he was not giving an evangelistic message to the city of Rome. Paul began in Rom 1:1–7:

> *Paul, a bond-servant of Christ Jesus, called as an apostle, set apart for the gospel of God, which He promised beforehand through His prophets in the holy Scriptures, concerning His Son, who was born of a descendant of David according to the flesh, who was declared the Son of God with power by the resurrection from the dead, according to the Spirit of holiness, Jesus Christ our Lord, through whom we have received grace and apostleship to bring about the obedience of faith among all the Gentiles for His name's sake, among whom you also are the called of Jesus Christ; to all who are beloved of God in Rome, called as saints: Grace to you and peace from God our Father and the Lord Jesus Christ.*

Paul wrote further in verse 15: *"So . . . I am eager to preach the gospel to you also who are in Rome."*

When Paul wrote the letter to the Romans, he wrote about how eager he was to preach the gospel to Christians in Rome—not only to the unsaved in Rome. Why would Christians who had already received the gospel need to hear the gospel that Paul preached? A major part of the answer was that Paul wanted to use Rome as his home base, especially in light of his desire to continue his missionary journeys to Spain, as seen in Rom 15:20–24:

> *And thus I aspired to preach the gospel, not where Christ was already named, that I might not build upon another man's foundation; but as it is written,*
>
> *"THEY WHO HAD NO NEWS OF HIM SHALL SEE,*
>
> *AND THEY WHO HAVE NOT HEARD SHALL UNDERSTAND."*
>
> *For this reason I have often been prevented from coming to you; but now, with no further place for me in these regions, and since I have had for many years a longing to come to you whenever I go to Spain—for I hope to see you in passing, and to be helped on my way there by you, when I have first enjoyed your company for a while*

Under the heading of the sovereignty of God, Paul had different reasons for writing the epistle to the Christians in Rome. First, it was a preventive/protective measure against false teachers/false apostles. Everywhere previously, whenever Paul departed from a church or churches, false teachers always crept in and attacked the church, causing much spiritual harm as shown in Galatians, 1 and 2 Thessalonians, and 1 and 2 Corinthians. Second, this gave Paul an opportunity to write ahead of time the biblical truths that he had taught/would be teaching. Paul did not found the church at Rome. In Acts 2:10, with the birth of the church and the pouring out of the Holy Spirit on Pentecost, the Romans are part of the people who attended that day: "Phrygia and Pamphylia, Egypt and the districts of Libya around Cyrene, and visitors from Rome [literally, "the sojourning Romans"], both Jews and proselytes [Gentile converts to Judaism]." These people most likely were the ones God used to found the church in Rome. So, without Paul's having met most of them, if the church in Rome was to be his missionary base, Paul must have his home church in agreement doctrinally before he could trust that false teachers would not come after he left and cause trouble in the church at Rome.

The third reason Paul wrote Romans was in view of the unsaved Roman mind-set and the roadblocks that could hinder many others from receiving the gospel. Two important questions specifically had to be dealt with: (1) How can anyone say that Jesus is the Christ/Messiah and the Son of God when His own people Israel rejected him? (2) How can anyone say the God of the Bible is actually the God who tells the truth because not only do most of the Jews today reject His Messiah, but also most of what is written in the Old Testament—especially the prophecies—has not come true?

So, in broadest terms these are the divisions of the book: Romans 1–11 is the doctrinal portion, and 12:1–15:13 is the section of application of the biblical truths in godly living. With these verses many are familiar. The section begins with 12:1–2:

Therefore I urge you, brethren, by the mercies of God, to present your bodies a living and holy sacrifice, acceptable to God, which is your spiritual service of worship. And do not be conformed to this world, but be

transformed by the renewing of your mind, so that you may prove what the
will of God is, that which is good and acceptable and perfect.

Paul followed this with many informative greetings to different people
(15:14–16:24) and concludes with a beautiful, doctrinally rich benediction, in Rom 16:25–27:

> *Now to Him who is able to establish you according to my gospel and the*
> *preaching of Jesus Christ, according to the revelation of the mystery which*
> *has been kept secret for long ages past, but now is manifested, and by the*
> *Scriptures of the prophets, according to the commandment of the eternal*
> *God, has been made known to all the nations, leading to obedience of faith;*
> *to the only wise God, through Jesus Christ, be the glory forever. Amen.*

The first major doctrinal portion in Rom is 1:18–5:21 presents the doctrine of justification by faith in the finished work of the Lord Jesus Christ.

KEY: It is not fitting just to say, "justification by faith." There must be
some object of that faith. It is not only faith alone; even demons have
that (Jas 2:19). Nor does just a broad belief in God suffice here. Such
saving faith is set solely on the person and the work of the Lord Jesus
Christ, His perfect life and perfect sacrifice, accepted by God in our
behalf.

Broadly speaking, Paul began with the bad news in Rom 1:18–3:20
that all humans (except Jesus) are condemned for every sin they have committed, which makes it fitting for the wrath of God to be poured out upon
them. There are no righteous individuals, people, or groups. That is true
for Gentiles, true for Jews, and true for all of us.

After establishing biblically the bad news of the total condemnation
of every natural-born person, Paul began building the argument for "the
good news," the gospel of the Lord Jesus Christ. To what degree this good
news means to us in our standing before God is answered—among other
places—in Rom 5:1–2: "Therefore, having been justified by faith, we have
peace with God through our Lord Jesus Christ, through whom also we
have obtained our introduction by faith into this grace in which we stand;

and we exult in hope of the glory of God." Romans 5:9–11 continues with other wonderful benefits of the salvation that God gives to the redeemed:

> *Much more then, having now been justified by His blood, we shall be saved from the wrath of God through Him. For if while we were enemies we were reconciled to God through the death of His Son, much more, having been reconciled, we shall be saved by His life. And not only this, but we also exult in God through our Lord Jesus Christ, through whom we have now received the reconciliation.*

The next major division of the doctrinal portion of the book of Romans is 6:1–8:17, presenting the doctrine of positional sanctification.

> **KEY:** Positional sanctification is a spiritual status granted to us by God; these are eternal truths that we have in Christ Jesus if we are saved. Paul's instruction about the Christian's progressive sanctification, living the Christian life, and growing in grace and knowledge of our Lord and Savior Jesus Christ does not begin until Rom 12:1 ("I urge you, brethren . . . present your bodies . . ."). In this doctrinal portion of Romans, Paul wrote about positional sanctification with few commands during this section; instead, Paul repeatedly used statements of facts that are true for every Christian.

In Rom 6:11, Paul wrote that those justified by Jesus Christ are—positionally—dead to sin as master over us: "Even so consider yourselves to be dead to sin, but alive to God in Christ Jesus." In Romans 7, Paul instructed that the believer is dead to law as the ruling master over the redeemed. However, he also recognized the present struggle that comes—and often wins—with the Christian who is living out these truths, as Rom 7:24–25 demonstrates: "Wretched man that I am! Who will set me free from the body of this death? Thanks be to God through Jesus Christ our Lord! So then, on the one hand I myself with my mind am serving the law of God, but on the other, with my flesh the law of sin."

In fact, so great and wonderful are these truths for the redeemed that we can rejoice over the following doctrinal truths in Rom 8:1–2: "Therefore there is now no condemnation for those who are in Christ Jesus. For the law of the Spirit of life in Christ Jesus has set you free from the law of sin and of death."

Romans 8:18–39 is the next part and is the future glorification of the redeemed and the earth, which not only relates to the present situation but also looks far into the future. Romans 8:18–21 show this to be true:

> *For I consider that the sufferings of this present time are not worthy to be compared with the glory that is to be revealed to us. For the anxious longing of the creation waits eagerly for the revealing of the sons of God. For the creation was subjected to futility, not willingly, but because of Him who subjected it, in hope that the creation itself also will be set free from its slavery to corruption into the freedom of the glory of the children of God.*

Remember that Rom 12:1 begins the application section of this epistle. Romans 9–11 begins the last part of the doctrinal portion of Romans about the Jewish people, their future, and how this relates to the promises and works of God.

KEY: This section about national Israel is just as much doctrine—not opinion, and not optional—if you are going to preach and teach God's Word accurately. Paul said in Rom 1:1 that he was set apart for the gospel of God, which includes Romans 9–11. If you remove this section from your theology or your teaching or preaching, you do this at your own peril in understanding God's Word. What will you tell Jesus when He asks you why you did not believe or preach/teach this part of the doctrinal section of Romans? If you followed the same unbelieving approach to its logical conclusion, then perhaps other doctrinal sections could/should be removed as well—which is the disastrous result of higher criticism of the Bible.

It is in this section of Romans that Paul addressed the critical questions of how Jesus could be God's Messiah if His own people rejected Him and how God can be God if His own Word has not come true. The latter question is asked because the Bible contains so many prophecies—especially in the Old Testament—that are yet to be fulfilled. Both are questions that skeptics and critics of God and His Word still currently use. We should also note that Romans 9–11 is one section in the book of Romans and must be treated as such: you cannot accurately read Romans 9 by itself or take a verse out of context from Romans 10 or begin or end your study of this section in Romans 11. You must have all three chapters, and you must study this section in the order in which God gave it. Moreover, you must also study the Holy Spirit-inspired logic that he used in these.

The Biblical Doctrine of Romans 9:1–29

Romans 9:1–5 begins this section by listing some of the incredible benefits/blessings that God had given to the Jewish people:

> *I am telling the truth in Christ, I am not lying, my conscience testifies with me in the Holy Spirit, that I have great sorrow and unceasing grief in my heart. For I could wish that I myself were accursed, separated from Christ for the sake of my brethren, my kinsmen according to the flesh, who are Israelites, to whom belongs the adoption as sons, and the glory and the covenants and the giving of the Law and the temple service and the promises, whose are the fathers, and from whom is the Christ according to the flesh, who is over all, God blessed forever. Amen.*

In writing about his fellow Jews, Paul states in verse 4, "They are Israelites, and to them belong the adoption, the glory, the covenants, the giving of the law, the temple service, and the promises." Look at all these privileges that belong—currently, not in past tense—to the Jewish people, although the temple services, which were functioning at that time, would soon end for an extended period beginning in AD 70.

> **KEY CONSIDERATION:** This obviously does not mean that every Jew is saved, but it does show, if we just wanted to limit it to this one doctrinal truth that "to them belong . . . the covenants"—plural. What covenants still belong to the Jewish people even at this time when the church has been established and the gospel is going to the Gentiles? Everyone born receives the benefit of the Noahic covenant. But God's promises in the Abrahamic covenant still belong to the Jewish people. The Mosaic covenant had passed by that time. So Paul would have

been referring as well to the Davidic covenant and the new covenant as still belonging to the Jewish people. This is clearly explained and easily understood; this is the biblical truth from God. Paul could have written only one sentence to say that "God's covenants used to belong to the Jewish people, but now they no longer have relevance nor benefits of these covenants—based on all the sins the Jewish people have done." But Paul did *not* write that; in fact, he wrote just the opposite.

Romans 9:6a sets forth the argumentation against one of the questions that we saw earlier ("But it is not as though the word of God has failed"), with either Israel rejecting the Messiah God had sent her or God's Word failing by not coming true in what He had promised. What follows in the remainder of Rom 9:6–29 is part of the Holy Spirit-inspired logic that God gives to answer these questions. To begin with, God in His sovereignty chose the Jewish people as a select people, in essence, because He wanted to. Verses 22–24 show that God did this in order to complete His divine purpose:

> *What if God, although willing to demonstrate His wrath and to make His power known, endured with much patience vessels of wrath prepared for destruction? And He did so to make known the riches of His glory upon vessels of mercy, which He prepared beforehand for glory, even us, whom He also called, not from among Jews only, but also from among Gentiles.*

While Romans 9 shows God choosing national Israel, before continuing our study in this section in Romans, we need to establish that other Scripture proves that God—in His sovereignty—has promised to save a remnant of the Jewish people. In the chapter where God commissioned Isaiah, Yahweh revealed His promises that He will save "a tenth portion" of national Israel (Isa 6:13). Later, and appropriately, from the Book of Immanuel section of Isaiah, which means it is tied in directly to the person and work of God's Messiah (chaps. 7–12), comes this promise of a future grace gift by God to a portion of the Jewish people at some undisclosed time in history future, as presented in 10:20–23:

Now in that day the remnant of Israel, and those of the house of Jacob who have escaped, will never again rely on the one who struck them, but will truly rely on the LORD, the Holy One of Israel.

A remnant will return, the remnant of Jacob, to the mighty God.

For though your people, O Israel, may be like the sand of the sea,

Only a remnant within them will return;

A destruction is determined, overflowing with righteousness.

For a complete destruction, one that is decreed, the Lord GOD of hosts will execute in the midst of the whole land.

IMPORTANT: Four times in the passage above, the word remnant occurs. Other than a strong theological bias against this doctrine, why would someone not accept that this is God's promise of what He would do at some point in the future, for a remnant of Jewish people whom He will redeem? Also, with this quote from the Book of Immanuel section, it will be directly tied in with God's promised Messiah. Further, if God did not mean that He would one day save a remnant of Jewish people, what exactly did God mean by what He repeatedly said, and how could you ever make sense of anything else God said?

Many centuries past the time of Isaiah, God promised in Zech 13:8–9 that in the times of the Gentiles during the tribulation, Yahweh will bring the one-third remnant of the Jewish people back to Him in full covenant obedience and restoration of fellowship with Him. Included is His full acceptance of that remnant by Him at that time:

"It will come about in all the land,"

Declares the LORD,

"That two parts in it will be cut off and perish;

But the third will be left in it.

"And I will bring the third part through the fire,

Refine them as silver is refined,

And test them as gold is tested.

They will call on My name,

And I will answer them;

I will say, 'They are My people,'

And they will say, 'The LORD is my God.'"

With the biblical doctrine of Yahweh's promise to save a Jewish remnant, one-third of them during the tribulation, Paul cited Isa 10:22–23 in Rom 9:27–28: "Isaiah cries out concerning Israel, 'THOUGH THE NUMBER OF THE SONS OF ISRAEL BE LIKE THE SAND OF THE SEA, IT IS THE REMNANT THAT WILL BE SAVED; FOR THE LORD WILL EXECUTE HIS WORD ON THE EARTH, THOROUGHLY AND QUICKLY.'" Continuing Paul's teaching about the Jewish remnant, instead of looking toward the future, Paul looked backward. He quoted from Isa 1:9, from the panoramic overview of the book of Isaiah (chaps. 1–5)—even with the depths of national Israel's sin, the utter faithfulness of God continues. In Rom 9:29 he wrote, "And just as Isaiah foretold, ' UNLESS THE LORD OF SABAOTH HAD LEFT TO US A POSTERITY, / WE WOULD HAVE BECOME AS SODOM, AND WOULD HAVE RESEMBLED GOMORRAH.'"

God promising and working to keep a remnant of the Jewish people, in the context of Isa 1:9, was in the midst of the magnitude of national Israel's sin before Him. If God wanted to destroy or reject the Jewish people, He had many opportunities to have done so. Sadly, in this section that decries that the sin of collective, national Israel was as great as or worse than the sin of Sodom and Gomorrah—which is staggering to think about—God still promised to faithfully fulfill His Word to preserve a remnant of the Jewish people. Doing this is totally by God's grace alone, and this is totally by God's faithfulness to His Word, and where God chooses to bind Himself by His own Scripture. Yahweh has to maintain national Israel all the way into the tribulation, and beyond, so that He can save a one-third remnant after two-thirds of the Jewish people will be destroyed during that time.

So in the logic of God in the first part of the four-part answer found in Romans 9–11, God, by means of the apostle Paul in Romans 9, after showing the wonderful promises and privileges that He had given to the

Jewish people, included that His covenants with them were still operative. Romans 9 shows how God had sovereignly formed and maintained the Jewish people as the Jewish nation, and yet God looked forward to "the last days"/end of the days where He would sovereignly work to remove two-thirds of the Jewish people and bring the one-third of the Jewish people "through the rod/under the rod" to Himself and accept them—bringing them into full covenant obedience and fellowship with Him.

Before continuing the section of Paul's logic and answers to questions people would ask about God and the Jews, one pertinent item is relevant to looking at the next part. In Rom 9:27 Paul used this unusual way of presenting an Old Testament verse, namely, "And Isaiah cries out" (emphasis added). This present tense usage is relatively rare in Scripture because usually the past tense is used (such as in Matt 4:14: "This was to fulfill what was spoken through Isaiah the prophet"). We should highlight these important truths: (1) This message from the book of Isaiah cries out similarly to the way Wisdom cries out in Proverbs, in a continuous manner. (2) The Isaiah quote Paul used is actually Yahweh crying out, not the person of Isaiah crying out. (3) It is important to understand that even in the use of these verses from Isaiah regarding national Israel, this portion of Isaiah cries out—present tense, not past tense; it is still crying out today concerning national Israel. (4) Further, we have already seen Isa 1:1 and 2:1–4 concerning Judah and Jerusalem and the end of the days/last days. And finally (5) the force and focus of these verses look to a future work that God will do—not to a past work that He has already accomplished. The past tense would have been expected if God was finished with national Israel, with the idea being that God had cried out to national Israel but had stopped doing so at some point in time. This is not at all what the text states.

The Theological Importance and Hinge of Romans 9:30–10:3

Remember that the chapter and verse divisions are manmade (and helpful) dividers that are for the most part accurate and wonderfully useful; nevertheless, these divisions are not inspired, and sometimes they could have been somewhat adjusted. Such is the case for the chapter divisions of Romans 9 and 10. The first part goes all the way down to Rom 9:29 about God sovereignly selecting the Jewish people by His desire to do so. In transitioning to the second part of the fourfold answer in Romans 9–11, the answer is, yes, God in His sovereignty chose national Israel; the second part, 9:30–10:3, explains national Israel's part in their present situation—including matters that pertain to the present day—all based on the majority of the Jewish people's sinful rejection of the Word of God. Paul was not referring to every member of the Jewish people such as to those who, like him, did eventually receive the Messiah Jesus as Savior and Lord. In this section he writes of the consequences of national Israel's rejection of Jesus, the Messiah, whom God had already sent to them. He specifically addresses the reason for the current spiritual lostness for most of the Jewish people and the four reasons for their current spiritual situation, as seen in Rom 9:30–10:3:

> *What shall we say then? That Gentiles, who did not pursue righteousness, attained righteousness, even the righteousness which is by faith; but Israel, pursuing a law of righteousness, did not arrive at that law. Why? Because they did not pursue it by faith, but as though it were by works. They stumbled over the stumbling stone, just as it is written,*
>
> "BEHOLD, I LAY IN ZION A STONE OF STUMBLING AND A ROCK OF OFFENSE, AND HE WHO BELIEVES IN HIM WILL NOT BE DISAPPOINTED."
>
> *Brethren, my heart's desire and my prayer to God for them is for their salvation. For I testify about them that they have a zeal for God, but not in accordance with knowledge. For not knowing about God's righteousness, and seeking to establish their own, they did not subject themselves to the righteousness of God.*

Four specific sins are listed here that they have nationally committed. First, unsaved Israel pursued works of the law—not faith—and yet with all of their works, they have not arrived, and they never will arrive, at the righteousness under the law for which they strive. "Why? Because they did not pursue it by faith, but as though it were by works" (Rom 9:32).

Second, the unsaved Jews tried or try to keep all the works of the law, but their most unforgivable sin was the rejection of the Messiah whom

God had already sent to them. God through Paul used two references to the Stone Prophecies about the Messiah (Rom 9:32b–33):

> They stumbled over the stumbling stone [from Isa 8:14; in "The Book of Immanuel" Section], just as it is written [Isa 28:16],
>
> "BEHOLD, I LAY IN ZION A STONE OF STUMBLING AND A ROCK OF OFFENSE, AND HE WHO BELIEVES IN HIM WILL NOT BE DISAPPOINTED."

So, in explaining the present spiritual status of unsaved national Israel, not only do they attempt justification by works instead of by faith; they collectively have sinned against God by rejecting the Messiah and now suffer the subsequent consequences of their not having received Jesus the Messiah whom God sent to them. Other than those who are saved or who will be saved, unbelieving national Israel collectively stumbles over the stumbling stone. God says in Isa 28:16 that He personally placed the stone in Zion. Jesus is therefore a rock to be tripped over, and there are only two options available when it comes to Him. People will either "believe on Him"—on Him, not on it—or those who will eternally trip over Him.

Third, by attempting salvation by works of the law instead of by faith but also by unsaved national Israel having rejected the One object of faith to whom they should look—Jesus, the Messiah—Paul added the third part of the explanation of the current spiritual status of unsaved national Israel in Rom 10:1–2: "Brethren, my heart's desire and my prayer to God for them is for their salvation. For I testify about them that they have a zeal for God, but not in accordance with knowledge." Now added to the list of actions that they currently perform are their own "works of righteousness," as they have established them. They have a zeal for God but not in accordance with true biblical knowledge, which would point to such passages as Isa 64:6 that reveals, "For all of us have become like one who is unclean, / And all our righteous deeds are like a filthy garment."

And fourth, in this section, Rom 10:3 explains, "For not knowing about God's righteousness and seeking to establish their own, they did not subject themselves to the righteousness of God." Unsaved national Israel collectively and wrongly believed that by keeping the law they would be able, on their own, to achieve the righteousness of God. This belief would have been true for the rich young ruler or Saul of Tarsus—the Pharisee

who later became Paul the Christian and later Paul the apostle—or orthodox Jews up to the present time—and ultimately for some—into the
tribulation.

Romans 10:4 shows the eternally different perception of biblical truth
for the saved: "For Christ is the end of the law for righteousness to everyone who believes."

And How Shall They Hear without a Preacher?

So, broadly speaking, one, God sovereignly chose and made national Israel (Romans 9), and, two, four specific sins exist for the current lostness
of most Jewish people (Rom 9:30–10:3).

Romans 10:4 starts the third part of God's fourfold answers that He
gives in chapters 9–11. Romans 10:4–10 was/is Paul's logic: If any of the
unsaved Jewish people claimed that the message of God's gospel is unattainable, such that it is concealed in heaven or in the abyss, and thus out
of reach,

> *For Christ is the end of the law for righteousness to everyone who believes.*
> *For Moses writes that the man who practices the righteousness which*
> *is based on law [that is, the Mosaic covenant] shall live by that righteous-*
> *ness. But the righteousness based on faith speaks as follows: "Do not*
> *say in your heart, 'Who will ascend into heaven?' (that is, to bring Christ*
> *down), or 'Who will descend into the abyss?' (that is, to bring Christ up*
> *from the dead)."*

Romans 10:8–10 begins with, "on the contrary":

> *But what does it say? "The word is near you, in your mouth and in your*
> *heart"—that is, the word of faith which we are preaching, that if you*
> *confess with your mouth Jesus as Lord, and believe in your heart that God*
> *raised Him from the dead, you will be saved; for with the heart a person*
> *believes, resulting in righteousness, and with the mouth he confesses, result-*
> *ing in salvation.*

The message of the gospel is not out of reach, neither is it unattainable
in their understanding. It is as near as their mouth and their heart, and it is
a message that they can confess with their mouth.

Paul further explained how the Gentiles are saved in the same manner and with the same message that God had given to national Israel, in Rom 10:11–13:

> For the Scripture says "WHOEVER BELIEVES IN HIM WILL NOT BE DISAP-
> POINTED." For there is no distinction between Jew and Greek; for the
> same Lord is Lord of all, abounding in riches for all who call on Him; for
> "WHOEVER WILL CALL ON THE NAME OF THE LORD WILL BE SAVED.

It is within this third part of Paul's four-part answer that we come to our famous phrase "And how can they hear without a preacher." It appears in Rom 10:14–15:

> How then will they call on Him in whom they have not believed? How will
> they believe in Him whom they have not heard? And how will they hear
> without a preacher? How will they preach unless they are sent? Just as it is
> written [in Isa 52:7], "HOW BEAUTIFUL ARE THE FEET OF THOSE WHO BRING GOOD
> NEWS OF GOOD THINGS!"

CORE TRUTH: Romans 10:14–15 is *not* a general call for Bible expositors nor for preachers to emerge. What we must address includes: (1) who the "they" are of whom Paul spoke when asking "and how can *they* hear?" and (2) what God does, by means of the apostle Paul, in this section of the epistle, as he answered any of those critics who might claim that national Israel did not receive the gospel of the Messiah because they were never told. The "they" in "and how can they hear?" is the unsaved national Israel, the Jewish people, to whom God had given many opportunities to hear His gospel. Some believed; most did not believe. They are the same ones in this section (Romans 9–11), the Jewish people, national Israel (9:1–5), whom Paul calls "my brethren, my kinsmen according to the flesh" (v. 3). These, who would certainly be Jewish in ethnicity, but they had not received Jesus nor the gospel.

We will continue to follow the logic of the biblical trail regarding the identity of "they" in "how can they hear without a preacher?" In this immediate context that we have seen, "they" are the ones who attempted—and many still do or will attempt later—works of righteousness in an effort to secure their salvation (Rom 9:30–32a); they are the ones who have stumbled over the stumbling Stone of Jesus the Messiah—the One God placed in Zion—and would not believe in Him (vv. 32b–33). They are the specific group that Paul associated with physically and culturally—but not spiritually—because they needed the salvation found in Jesus Christ (10:1); they have a zeal for God but not in accordance with knowledge (v. 2). All of these statements are specifically written about the unbelieving Jewish people.

Continuing with the same logic, "they" are also the unsaved national Israel who have neglected the righteousness of God and who, instead, have sought to establish their own righteousness; consequently, "they did not subject themselves to the righteousness of God," of which Christ is the end for everyone who believes, and they most assuredly did not believe—at least when Paul wrote Romans (10:3). They are the ones who were offered the simple gospel message as something that they could have comprehended or believed, if they had been willing to do so. Some of those who will stand before Jesus Messiah at the great white throne judgment as part of this group will argue that they never had an opportunity to hear. On the contrary, they have been told—repeatedly—and still are being told, such as we saw in Rom 9:27, "Isaiah cries out concerning Israel." (Remember and mark the present tense of cries out.) The book of Isaiah has been crying out to national Israel for almost three thousand years, and God through the book of Isaiah currently cries out to them—and will continue to cry out to Israel in the future.

They were the ones who would not believe or receive this wonderfully simplistic yet eternally profound gospel message, even though Paul further reminded them of how very close it was/is to them—and yet it is so far away to unregenerate Jewish hearts. In Rom 10:8–9 he asked:

But what does it say? "THE WORD IS NEAR YOU, IN YOUR MOUTH AND IN YOUR HEART"—that is, the word of faith which we are preaching, that if you confess with your mouth Jesus as Lord, and believe in your heart that God raised Him from the dead, you will be saved.

Paul, and others sent by God, had been preaching the word of faith and the gospel of salvation through the finished work of Jesus the Messiah to the Jewish people.

The above "they" are the unsaved Jewish people. They are those who have rejected (and died outside) of God's grace offer through Jesus the Messiah and are eternally damned. They are those who currently reject, or who will reject—even during the tribulation, God's offer of salvation through Jesus the Messiah. This now continues and connects God's answer to any of the Jews who would claim they never heard the gospel message nor had a chance to receive it. Beginning with the immediate context verse of Rom 10:13: "for 'WHOEVER WILL CALL ON THE NAME OF THE LORD WILL BE SAVED,'" comes Rom 10:14: "How then will they [meaning unsaved national Israel] call on Him in whom they have not believed? How will they [that is, unsaved Jewish people] believe in Him whom they have not heard? How will they [the unsaved Jewish people] hear without a preacher?"

The next verses continue the same argument: God Himself has sent prophets, preachers, and even Jesus the Messiah to give national Israel the good news of the gospel of Jesus Christ, as shown in Rom 10:15: "How will they preach unless they are sent? Just as it is written, 'HOW BEAUTIFUL ARE THE FEET OF THOSE WHO BRING GOOD NEWS OF GOOD THINGS!'"

What was the response by the Jewish people to the many different means that God used to get the gospel to them? Romans 10:16 further supports Paul's point and explains: "However, they [the unsaved Jewish people] did not all heed the good news; for Isaiah says, ' LORD, WHO HAS BELIEVED OUR REPORT?'" Mark this well: most of the unsaved Jewish people did not heed or receive the gospel, an act which at its core is a sin issue. As we have seen many times, rejection of God's Word is a sin issue—and one of the most serious ones. It is not an ignorance issue in that God had never sent anyone to the Jewish people to proclaim His salvation message. God had sent messengers to the Jewish people going all the way back to Isa 53:1: "Who has believed our message" (Isa 1:1; 2:1–2a); and in this context, the message was to those who were disobedient, nonbelievers who would not receive the person and the work of Jesus the Messiah. The remainder of Isaiah 53 so beautifully describes the Jewish people who will eventually, solely by God's grace and predetermined will, have their eyes opened to the person and work of Jesus the Messiah and be saved on the same basis that Gentiles are saved.

In Rom 10:17–18, Paul continued the same argumentation that we have seen repeatedly:

> *So faith comes from hearing, and hearing by the word of Christ. But I say, surely they [unsaved national Israel] have never heard [God's message of salvation], have they? Indeed they have;*
>
> *"THEIR VOICE HAS GONE OUT INTO ALL THE EARTH,*
>
> *AND THEIR WORDS TO THE END OF THE WORLD.*

Continuing the same logic in verse 19, he asks:

> *Surely Israel [that is, the unsaved Jewish people] did not know [understand], did they?*

First, Moses says:

> *"I will make you [the unsaved Jewish people] jealous by that which is not a nation;*
>
> *By a nation without understanding will I anger you."*

Continuing the same logic in verse 20, he speaks about national Israel's rejection of God and His Messiah:

> *And Isaiah [65:1] is very bold and says,*
>
> *"I WAS FOUND BY THOSE WHO DID NOT SEEK ME, [NAMELY, THE GENTILE BELIEVERS];*
>
> *I BECAME MANIFEST TO THOSE WHO DID NOT ASK FOR ME."*

To the foolishly naive unsaved Israelites who would protest that God never sent them any Word, and if He did send it, He only did it for a short time, Rom 10:21 quotes from Isa 65:2: "But as for Israel He says, 'ALL THE DAY LONG I HAVE STRETCHED OUT MY HANDS TO A DISOBEDIENT AND OBSTINATE PEOPLE.'"

Mark this well, beloved! Romans 10:20–21, quoting from Isa 65:1–2, is distinctly (in the context) for unsaved national Israel (the Jewish people) from the Old Testament days up to the present and into the future. God has spread out His hand to disobedient and defiant Jewish people over thousands of years; but, as before, we are not talking about saved Jews in Old Testament times, nor at the present time, nor even the Jewish remnant God will save in the tribulation.

> **CRUCIAL:** Remember that Romans 9–11 is one section in Romans; you cannot just go to Romans 9 by itself, nor to Romans 10 by itself, and you cannot start in Romans 11. They are one theological unit of *God's doctrine*—the application is not optional—and they must be viewed that way as a collective whole.

The Holy Beauty and Logic of Romans 11

To summarize briefly the logic of Romans 9–10: first, God sets forth that He sovereignly chose national Israel, in Rom 9:1–29; and second, Rom 9:30–10:3 explains the lostness of most of the Jewish people as the consequence for four specific sinful responses that led to their present state; and third, Rom 10:4–21 gives a strong, logical rationale for Israel's repeated and continued rejection of both God's Messiah and His message, even after the multiplicity of ways God chose to get His gospel to the Jewish people. So in spite of the many messengers, prophets, preachers—and eventually God's very own Son, the Messiah—most of the unsaved Jewish people/national Israel rejected God's Word, and as we saw in the chapter on parables, it is an exceedingly dangerous thing to reject the Word of God. Also, as we have stated, Romans 9–11 is a four-part answer that God gives. Romans 9 is the first part, and Romans 10 is the second and third parts. Now Romans 11 continues God's answer and is the fourth part and *must* be included in this doctrinal portion, and these three biblical chapters *must* be studied in the order by which they were given by God. Otherwise your understanding of God and His Word will be incomplete. In light of the sins and rejection of God and His messages and messengers, has God rejected national Israel for all the sins they have committed—including their part in the crucifixion of Jesus?

Romans 11:1–4 begins this last section in Romans and clearly gives the answer:

I say then, God has not rejected His people, has He? May it never be!
For I too am an Israelite, a descendant of Abraham, of the tribe of Benja-
min. God has not rejected His people whom He foreknew. Or do you not
know what the Scripture says in the passage about Elijah, how he pleads
with God against Israel? "Lord, THEY HAVE KILLED YOUR PROPHETS, THEY HAVE
TORN DOWN YOUR ALTARS, AND I ALONE AM LEFT, AND THEY ARE SEEKING MY LIFE."
But what is the divine response to him? "I HAVE KEPT FOR MYSELF SEVEN THOU-
SAND MEN WHO HAVE NOT BOWED THE KNEE TO BAAL."

In the time of collective national Israel's incredibly heinous sins, Elijah reasoned that he was the only follower of God left among the Jewish
people. The answer God gave to His weary and burdened prophet was
that Elijah was not the only faithful one—God had kept for Himself seven
thousand who had not bowed down to Baal. This was "the righteous remnant" of that day, chosen by the grace of God. Similarly, He has preserved
such a believing remnant of Jews out of the broader Jewish ethnicity, as
stated in Rom 11:5–6: "In the same way then, there has also come to be
at the present time a remnant according to God's gracious choice. But if
it is by grace, it is no longer on the basis of works, otherwise grace is no
longer grace."

In verses 7–10, the elect of Israel have found/will find what they are
seeking, but the rest of the unsaved Jewish people were hardened after
their rejection of God and His Word—and His Messiah—with some of the
disastrous consequences for their sin listed:

What then? What Israel is seeking, it has not obtained, but those who were
chosen obtained it, and the rest were hardened; just as it is written,

"GOD GAVE THEM A SPIRIT OF STUPOR,

EYES TO SEE NOT AND EARS TO HEAR NOT,

DOWN TO THIS VERY DAY."

And David says,

"LET THEIR TABLE BECOME A SNARE AND A TRAP,

AND A STUMBLING BLOCK AND A RETRIBUTION TO THEM.

"LET THEIR EYES BE DARKENED TO SEE NOT,

AND BEND THEIR BACKS FOREVER."

Romans 11:11–12 asks one pertinent question and gives God's answer concerning unbelieving national Israel, as well as part of the reason He has worked this way:

> *I say then, they did not stumble so as to fall, did they? May it never be! But by their transgression salvation has come to the Gentiles, to make them jealous. Now if their transgression is riches for the world and their failure is riches for the Gentiles, how much more will their fulfillment be!*

To the Gentiles, regarding this grace of God in their lives, Paul writes in verses 13–16:

> *But I am speaking to you who are Gentiles. Inasmuch then as I am an apostle of Gentiles, I magnify my ministry, if somehow I might move to jealousy my fellow countrymen and save some of them. For if their rejection is the reconciliation of the world, what will their acceptance be but life from the dead? If the first piece of dough is holy, the lump is also; and if the root is holy, the branches are too.*

To the Gentiles who may look at themselves boastfully, especially in looking down on the Jewish people, Paul strongly cautions in Rom 11:17–24:

> *But if some of the branches were broken off, and you, being a wild olive, were grafted in among them and became partaker with them of the rich root of the olive tree, do not be arrogant toward the branches; but if you are arrogant, remember that it is not you who supports the root, but the root supports you. You will say then, "Branches were broken off so that I might be grafted in." Quite right, they were broken off for their unbelief, but you stand by your faith. Do not be conceited, but fear; for if God did not spare the natural branches, He will not spare you, either. Behold then the kindness and severity of God; to those who fell, severity, but to you, God's kindness, if you continue in His kindness; otherwise you also will be cut off. And they also, if they do not continue in their unbelief, will be grafted in, for God is able to graft them in again. For if you were cut off from what is by nature a wild olive tree, and were grafted contrary to nature into a cultivated olive tree, how much more will these who are the natural branches be grafted into their own olive tree?*

From the logic of God's Word, whenever the Jewish people "do not remain in unbelief, [they] will be grafted in, because God has the power to graft them in again." In what becomes God-given hope for the Jewish people from the logic of God's argument is how much better it would be if "the broken off branches" (unsaved Jewish people) are collectively saved by God—they then become the Jewish believing remnant, accepting Jesus as their Savior and Redeemer and benefitting eternally through the fullness of the covenants that He has for them.

In Rom 11:25–27, this becomes more than a part of the logical conclusion; now it becomes—as we see in so many other places—the prophetic Word of God that must come true:

> *For I do not want you, brethren, to be uninformed of this mystery—so that you will not be wise in your own estimation—that a partial hardening has happened to Israel until the fullness of the Gentiles has come in; and so all Israel will be saved; just as it is written,*
>
> *"THE DELIVERER WILL COME FROM ZION,*
>
> *HE WILL REMOVE UNGODLINESS FROM JACOB."*
>
> *"THIS IS MY COVENANT WITH THEM,*
>
> *WHEN I TAKE AWAY THEIR SINS."*

In following the biblical logic, it is apparent that (1) this future work of God is presented as a biblical mystery; (2) that a partial hardening—not a total hardening—has happened to unbelieving national Israel, and God was the One who did this; (3) that this mystery has an ending point: it will not occur "until the fullness of the Gentiles has come in"; (4) that this time will end at the beginning of Jesus's reign as the Davidic covenant heir; (5) that all Israel will be saved, namely, the one-third righteous remnant of the Jewish people whom God will save; (6) that when the Deliverer will go to Zion in Jerusalem, He will remove ungodliness from the remaining Jewish people; and (7) that this is His covenant with them—the new covenant—resulting in "When I [He Himself personally] will take away their sin"—as only Jesus, their Redeemer and God could do, as He promised so many centuries earlier, as we saw earlier in Zech 13:8–9.

The Old Testament quotes that Paul used in Rom 11:26–27 are taken from Isa 59:20–21. These two important verses are found in the

eschatological section of Isaiah 58–66, and they are wondrously used because these become biblical prophecies—divine mandates—that must accompany the Messiah's return to earth to begin the fulfillment of all that
the Bible says will happen.

Romans 11:28–32 explains how saved Gentiles should view the unsaved Jewish people:

> *From the standpoint of the gospel they are enemies for your sake, but from
> the standpoint of God's choice they are beloved for the sake of the fa-
> thers; for the gifts and the calling of God are irrevocable. For just as you
> once were disobedient to God, but now have been shown mercy because of
> their disobedience, so these also now have been disobedient, that because
> of the mercy shown to you they also may now be shown mercy. For God has
> shut up all in disobedience so that He may show mercy to all.*

Romans 11:33–36 gives Paul's joyous responsive praise to this beautiful work of God that so appropriately concludes this wonderful section of
God's doctrine in Romans 9–11:

> *Oh, the depth of the riches both of the wisdom and knowledge of God! How
> unsearchable are His judgments and unfathomable His ways! For WHO HAS
> KNOWN THE MIND OF THE LORD, OR WHO BECAME HIS COUNSELOR? Or WHO HAS
> FIRST GIVEN TO HIM THAT IT MIGHT BE PAID BACK TO HIM AGAIN? For from Him and
> through Him and to Him are all things. To Him be the glory forever. Amen.*

Amen, indeed—and come soon Lord Jesus!

Appendix: Using the Stone Prophecies about the Messiah in Jewish Evangelism

Many times the Stone Prophecies about the Messiah as the Stone who
was rejected are explained by using negative examples as we have seen
Jesus do in Matt 21:33–42, Paul do in Rom 9:30–33, and Peter do in 1 Pet
2:4–8; they also appear in other references that could be used. Jesus most
definitely is the Stone, and He fulfills the stone-that-the-builders-rejected
prophecies from God. But not all of the uses of the Stone Prophecies are
explained in a negative way. Let me briefly tell you the story of how I first
came to this part of the study of the Bible.

When I wrote the third Glory book, *The Stone and the Glory*, the previous two books in this series were written. But they had not yet been published, and it would be years before they were. I kept writing these books as God led me, and I figured that He had something in mind for these somewhere, even if it were after my death. So in tracing a vein of the biblical trail for the Stone Prophecies, *The Stone and the Glory* was the result. And when I wrote this, I hoped that some people in the church would be ministered to in the same way that I was to study and to write this. Still, something within me wrote especially for people who will be in the tribulation. I realize that God is under no obligation to use the book that way, but there was a rightness for my doing this, and I included many Scripture references because many who endure the tribulation may have their Bibles or other sources confiscated.

I asked a friend, a choice vessel of God who has led many Jewish people to the Lord, to read *The Stone and the Glory*. I had the privilege of meeting with him on several occasions, and in one of our conversations, he said that he had many friends among the Jewish people to whom he would like to give a copy of *The Stone and the Glory*; they, however, would not read it if they saw anything Christian in the first two chapters. He asked if I would consider removing the Christian sections (such as in chap. 1 where we have the account of Jesus and the Samaritan woman of John 4) and rewrite the first two chapters using only the Old Testament.

Just a couple of quick disclaimers with this: anything that we took out, we put back in later in the book, and after the second chapter, we did not remove any references to Jesus, and we used the New Testament. Taking out the Christian part of the first two chapters is easy with a word processor; putting something back into a place that fits is a different proposition entirely. I prayed about what to do, and what follows shortly is where the Lord led me. Amazingly, as I went back and read it, I saw that by my changing only the first two chapters of *The Stone and the Glory*, an unexpected fourth Glory book had become a book unto itself.

After I sent the corrected version to the choice vessel of God, I was able to meet with him later. I was extremely interested in what he had to say about the revised edition. He thought it was fine and counseled me not to change anything else about it. I asked him, "What are we going to call this? We cannot call it *The Stone and the Glory—Jewish Evangelistic Version* (which it is). Right away he replied, "Let's call it *The Stone and the Glory of Israel.*" In response, I said, "Let's subtitle it *An Invitation For the Jewish People to Meet Their Messiah.*" The book is a long, biblical tract that you can use yourself, or you can just give it to some Jewish friends/contacts you know. You do not have to know any Jewish theology; you can just give them the book to read, if you like.

The following section is taken from "The Stone" chapter of *The Stone and the Glory of Israel*[1] (pp. 14–22):

When Jewish people name the prophets whom God gave them, most of them who read and believe their Bible would not consider Jacob to have been a prophet. That Jacob was one of the Fathers, they would give a wholehearted, most definite "yes," but that Jacob was a prophet of God is an entirely different matter. Yet Jacob certainly did prophesy, and, although not generally recognized as such, the prophecy that God gave him, in what would later be recorded in Genesis 49, is one of the most important chapters in the entire Bible. Hopefully, you also will eventually be convinced that Genesis 49 truly is utterly indispensable in understanding God and His work.

Genesis 49 begins with Jacob dying as an old man. As his father had done for him, he wanted to bequeath to his sons their proper portions. Because a father bequeathing to his children is a common occurrence, it is easy to see why this important event could be overlooked.

However, this bequest is different because it will become part of God's holy and unbreakable promises in Scripture. So in a very real sense, these are not solely Jacob's words or thoughts; these are God's words and thoughts given by Jacob.

Genesis 49:1 begins, "Then Jacob summoned his sons and said, 'Assemble yourselves that I may tell you what will befall you in the days to come.'" Although it is easy to miss their importance, two biblical nuggets of pure gold have already been exposed. For instance, "the days to come" can also be translated as "the end of the days," or "the last days," and Gen 49:1 is the first time that phrase appears in Scripture—but it will not be

---

[1] Greg Harris, *The Stone and the Glory of Israel: An Invitation for the Jewish People to Meet Their Messiah* (The Woodlands, TX: Kress Biblical Resources, 2016).

the last time. So God takes the original audience and all future readers throughout thousands of years from the original utterances to the people and events in the last days.

The second revelatory nugget from God is likewise easy to miss. In Genesis 49:1, God gave Jacob words regarding future specific events as Jacob proclaimed, "Assemble yourselves that I may tell you what will befall you in the days to come." God clearly reveals the "you" whom He has in mind. At the end of Jacob's blessing, Gen 49:28 summarizes: "All these are the twelve tribes of Israel, and this is what their father said to them when he blessed them. He blessed them, every one with the blessing appropriate to him." Genesis 49 makes it a biblical impossibility for the Jewish people to be eradicated by an enemy or by collective enemies. Genesis 49:1 and 28 require that the twelve tribes of Israel be living and functioning in the last days. Absolutely no one—from Haman to Hitler to anyone else—can eradicate the Jews from the face of the earth. It is a biblical impossibility because God's Word clearly shows that the twelve tribes will be present in the last days.

Those two verses in Genesis would be enough, but there is more—much, much more. Not only does Genesis 49 contain the first reference to the last days during which the twelve tribes of Israel will be present; Gen 49:8–12 gives one of the earliest prophecies of the coming Messiah and reveals new details that God had not yet disclosed elsewhere in Scripture:

Judah, your brothers shall praise you;

Your hand shall be on the neck of your enemies;

Your father's sons shall bow down to you.

Judah is a lion's whelp;

From the prey, my son, you have gone up.

He crouches, he lies down as a lion,

And as a lion, who dares rouse him up?

The scepter shall not depart from Judah,

Nor the ruler's staff from between his feet,

Until Shiloh comes,

And to him shall be the obedience of the peoples.

He ties his foal to the vine,

And his donkey's colt to the choice vine;

He washes his garments in wine,

And his robes in the blood of grapes.

His eyes are dull from wine,

And his teeth white from milk."

From this point forward, it becomes a biblical mandate that the Messiah, according to God's sovereign decree, must be from the tribe of Judah. So whoever the Messiah is, He must give clear documentation of His lineage—and it must be traced back to the tribe of Judah. Also, it should not be overlooked that the Messiah's reign will not be limited only to or over the nation of Israel. When God's Messiah reigns "to Him shall be the obedience of the peoples" (Gen 49:10), which is another way of saying that His kingdom will be a worldwide kingdom over all the earth; no people groups, kingdoms, nor individuals will be exempt from His reign and rule.

We could conclude here with what we have already seen and marvel at what God has already promised, but we have still more to glean from this wonderful revelation from God. In Genesis 49 comes this double blessing to Joseph and his lineage due to his faithful walk of holiness and obedience to God. Verse 28 states, "All these are the twelve tribes of Israel, and this is what their father said to them when he blessed them. He blessed them, each one with the blessing appropriate to him." So, in verses 22–26 God blesses Joseph this way:

Joseph is a fruitful bough,

A fruitful bough by a spring;

Its branches run over a wall.

The archers bitterly attacked him,

And shot at him and harassed him;

But his bow remained firm,

And his arms were agile,

From the hands of the Mighty One of Jacob

(From there is the Shepherd, the Stone of Israel),

From the God of your father who helps you,

And by the Almighty who blesses you

With blessings of heaven above,

Blessings of the deep that lies beneath,

Blessings of the breasts and of the womb.

The blessings of your father

Have surpassed the blessings of my ancestors

Up to the utmost bound of the everlasting hills;

May they be on the head of Joseph,

And on the crown of the head of the one distinguished among his brothers.

So much is contained in this wonderful blessing of the Lord that it would be understandable how one could miss some of its significance. But as with any other truth that God reveals in this chapter, we must have within this background before us "the last days," and "what shall befall you," the twelve tribes of Israel (Gen 49:1, 28). With the promise of the Lion of the tribe of Judah being the Messiah who will reign over the entire world, (Gen 49:8–12), comes these two further designations regarding God's future Messiah, in verse 24: "From the hands of the Mighty One of Jacob (From there is the Shepherd, the Stone of Israel)'" Two additional descriptions of the Messiah are given in this one verse. Whoever the Messiah is, He must do the work of God's sent Shepherd and God's sent Stone of Israel, and—this is important—he must do so in the last days (Gen 49:1), with the twelve tribes of Israel (v. 28). The promised Messiah sent by God must fulfill these prophecies, or else He is not the promised Messiah.

A few passages of Scripture that deal directly with the Messiah as being Shepherd to Israel in the last days are much later revealed by God in the books of Jeremiah and Ezekiel. In Jeremiah 1–29, after fourteen messages of mostly condemnation to the wicked Jewish generation, as Babylon was poised to destroy Jerusalem and God's temple, to rape, to murder many, and to carry others to exile, God gave a segment of future blessings that He will one day give to the same nation of Israel whom He was about to punish (Jeremiah 30–33). Contained in this section is God's

promise of shepherding—just as we would expect from Gen 49:24—as
seen in Jer 31:10:

> *Hear the word of the* Lord, *O nations,*
>
> *And declare in the coastlands afar off,*
>
> *And say, "He who scattered Israel will gather him,*
>
> *And keep him as a shepherd keeps his flock."*
>
> *For the* Lord *has ransomed Jacob,*
>
> *And redeemed him from the hand of him who was stronger than he. (emphasis added)*

Later, in reference to the Messiah who will eventually shepherd Israel
in the last days, Jer 33:14–15 promises,

> *"Behold, days are coming," declares the* Lord, *"when I will fulfill the good
> word which I have spoken concerning the house of Israel and the house
> of Judah. In those days and at that time I will cause a righteous Branch of
> David to spring forth; and He shall execute justice and righteousness on the
> earth."*

These are samples of dozens and dozens of such promises that God
has given throughout His Holy Word—and all align in perfect agreement
with what He had promised centuries before in Genesis 49.

One more example will suffice. Ezekiel was a fellow Jew who lived
in Jerusalem before he was exiled to Babylon. He and Jeremiah were
contemporaries who likely knew each other and may have become close
friends. Ezekiel was exiled to Babylon before Jerusalem fell, but later he
received word of the promised judgment, as Ezek 33:21 states, "Now in
the twelfth year of our exile, on the fifth of the tenth month, the refugees
from Jerusalem came to me, saying, 'The city has been taken.'" Yet, God,
in His sovereignty, had revealed this prophecy to Ezekiel the night before
the messengers arrived: "Now the hand of the Lord had been upon me in
the evening, before the refugees came. And He opened my mouth at the
time they came to me in the morning; so my mouth was opened, and I was
no longer speechless" (v. 22).

Similar to Jeremiah's prophecies, even before the judgment was announced, God had given Ezekiel much information regarding His promised

blessing on Israel in the future. Beginning in the very first part of this long section (Ezekiel 34–48), where God promises to regather Israel in the future and bless them with His own divine presence, God remembers His previous promises made in Genesis 49 and elsewhere. Beginning in Ezek 34:1–6 God condemned Israel's previous wicked shepherds who had turned from God and had helped lead the nation into sin, resulting ultimately in exile:

> Then the word of the LORD came to me saying, "Son of man, prophesy against the shepherds of Israel. Prophesy and say to those shepherds, 'Thus says the Lord GOD, "Woe, shepherds of Israel who have been feeding themselves! Should not the shepherds feed the flock? You eat the fat and clothe yourselves with the wool, you slaughter the fat sheep without feeding the flock. Those who are sickly you have not strengthened, the diseased you have not healed, the broken you have not bound up, the scattered you have not brought back, nor have you sought for the lost; but with force and with severity you have dominated them. They were scattered for lack of a shepherd, and they became food for every beast of the field and were scattered. My flock wandered through all the mountains and on every high hill; My flock was scattered over all the surface of the earth, and there was no one to search or seek for them."'"

Because of their wretched and prolonged wickedness, God pronounced judgment on the bad shepherds:

> Therefore, you shepherds, hear the word of the Lord: "As I live," declares the Lord GOD, "surely because My flock has become a prey, My flock has even become food for all the beasts of the field for lack of a shepherd, and My shepherds did not search for My flock, but rather the shepherds fed themselves and did not feed My flock; therefore, you shepherds, hear the word of the Lord: 'Thus says the Lord GOD, "Behold, I am against the shepherds, and I will demand My sheep from them and make them cease from feeding sheep. So the shepherds will not feed themselves anymore, but I will deliver My flock from their mouth, so that they will not be food for them."'" (Ezek 34:7-10)

In contrast to such wicked shepherds, God reveals His own future shepherding of national Israel in the future in Ezek 34:11–19:

*For thus says the Lord G*OD, *"Behold, I Myself will search for My sheep and
seek them out. As a shepherd cares for his herd in the day when he is among
his scattered sheep, so I will care for My sheep and will deliver them from
all the places to which they were scattered on a cloudy and gloomy day. I
will bring them out from the peoples and gather them from the countries
and bring them to their own land; and I will feed them on the mountains of
Israel, by the streams, and in all the inhabited places of the land. I will feed
them in a good pasture, and their grazing ground will be on the mountain
heights of Israel. There they will lie down on good grazing ground and
feed in rich pasture on the mountains of Israel. I will feed My flock and I
will lead them to rest," declares the Lord G*OD. *"I will seek the lost, bring
back the scattered, bind up the broken and strengthen the sick; but the fat
and the strong I will destroy. I will feed them with judgment.*

*"As for you, My flock, thus says the Lord G*OD, *'Behold, I will judge between
one sheep and another, between the rams and the male goats. Is it too slight
a thing for you that you should feed in the good pasture, that you must tread
down with your feet the rest of your pastures? Or that you should drink of
the clear waters, that you must foul the rest with your feet? As for My flock,
they must eat what you tread down with your feet and drink what you foul
with your feet!'"*

God once more shows that He will do this future shepherding of national Israel:

*Therefore, thus says the Lord G*OD *to them, "Behold, I, even I, will judge between the fat sheep and the lean sheep. Because you push with side and with
shoulder, and thrust at all the weak with your horns until you have scattered
them abroad, therefore, I will deliver My flock, and they will no longer be a
prey; and I will judge between one sheep and another. (Ezek 34:20-22)*

God then clearly discloses the means by which He will do this: "Then
I will set over them one shepherd, My servant David, and He will feed
them; He will feed them Himself and be their shepherd" (v. 23). We must
not miss this key component of God's theology: "My servant David" is a
reference to the future Messiah, the ultimate Son of David. David had been
dead for more than four hundred years by the time God granted this revelation to Ezekiel. God's Messiah is the means by which God will shepherd

the twelve tribes of Israel in the last days—all in precise fulfillment of what God had promised many centuries earlier in Genesis 49.

So finishing the context of this wonderful divine revelation from God, Ezek 34:23–31 continues:

> *"Then I will set over them one shepherd, My servant David, and He will feed them; He will feed them himself and be their shepherd. And I, the LORD, will be their God, and My servant David will be prince among them; I the LORD have spoken.*

> *"I will make a covenant of peace with them and eliminate harmful beasts from the land so that they may live securely in the wilderness and sleep in the woods. I will make them and the places around My hill a blessing. And I will cause showers to come down in their season; they will be showers of blessing. Also the tree of the field will yield its fruit and the earth will yield its increase, and they will be secure on their land. Then they will know that I am the Lord, when I have broken the bars of their yoke and have delivered them from the hand of those who enslaved them. They will no longer be a prey to the nations, and the beasts of the earth will not devour them; but they will live securely, and no one will make them afraid. I will establish for them a renowned planting place, and they will not again be victims of famine in the land, and they will not endure the insults of the nations anymore. Then they will know that I, the LORD their God, am with them, and that they, the house of Israel, are My people," declares the Lord GOD. "As for you, My sheep, the sheep of My pasture, you are men, and I am your God," declares the Lord GOD.*

We clearly see Messiah the Shepherd in Jeremiah and Ezekiel, plus in many other places, and all is in keeping with the same promises that God had already made in Genesis 49. And mark this core truth well, beloved: Messiah shepherding national Israel in the future during the last days is not something optional for Him; this is required of Him in order for Scripture to be fulfilled.

Some readers will see and understand the shepherding part of Messiah's work in the future, and may be thinking, "All right the shepherding part of Messiah's work in the future I see and understand. But, the Messiah as the Stone of Israel? It just doesn't make sense. But why would God foretell in His Word that the Messiah must function as the Stone of Israel with the twelve tribes of Israel in the last days in the same way that

God had said the Messiah must serve as Shepherd?" God did not leave us on our own to figure this out; throughout Scripture He has explained the Stone Prophecies about His Messiah equally as clearly as He foretold the prophecies about the Shepherding part of Messiah's ministry—but it is our responsibility to examine the scriptural trail that He has left in His Word.

We are on our way to Mount Zion, the city of the Great King. As with physical travelers over the centuries who would journey to Jerusalem three times yearly to the great national feasts of Israel, we too have begun our own journey. Before we see the vistas of Jerusalem that God so delights in showing His children, we have some land to traverse, but instead of walking miles up to Jerusalem, our pilgrimage is through the pages of Scripture—often through some dark passages and often through obscure books for most readers of the Bible. As with the earthly pilgrims, our journey promises to be worth more than any effort we exert.

How arduous it must have been during biblical times for mothers with small children or infants to travel up to one hundred miles or more on donkey or on foot. As the Jewish mothers no doubt used to encourage their weary and impatient children on their pilgrimage to Jerusalem, "Hush, child! We are not there yet. We have a ways to go. Settle down. Be patient. It will be worth it when we arrive. We are going to the Holy City of God!"—the same holds true for us. But we have work to do. We must drop down into the Word "to see with [our] eyes and hear with [our] ears" the events and truths that God reveals. As always, God's Word contains marvelous mysteries and markers that God Himself has set before us. But we must be good Bible detectives. Expressed in another way, we are mining for gold from God's gold mine—not only with divine permission but also with divine delight. Mining for riches, however, takes careful consideration and sifting. In order for us to properly worship God in spirit and truth, we need to know—and sift through—some biblical history and chronology and to recognize a gold nugget when we see one.

Behold! God has set forth His Stone all throughout Scripture for us to see.

So, come, let us find these Stone Prophecies that God had put in His Word. Beginning with the double blessing portion to Joseph in Genesis 49 and continuing from there, let us see what these mean, and why God calls us to read and receive these promises—and to receive Him—and His Shepherd, the Stone of Israel, sent from the Mighty One of Jacob to the twelve tribes in the last days, who will also rule over the entire world.

Summary and Conclusion

In this extremely important chapter, we learned, among other things that (1) God used the background events for the apostle Paul and the church at Rome, which Paul wanted to use as his missionary base for his evangelistic efforts in Spain. (2) Because Paul did not found the church at Rome, Paul wrote Romans to be proactive against false teachers who would come in later and try to undermine the gospel. He used it to send ahead biblical truths that he had taught/would be teaching, and what he wrote became the Holy Spirit inspired book of Romans. (3) Part of what Paul had to address in the book of Romans involved two specific questions: one, how can anyone say Jesus in the Christ/Messiah, the Son of God, when His own people Israel rejected Him? And two, how can anyone say the God of the Bible is actually God who tells the truth because not only do most of the Jews today reject His Messiah, most of what is written in the Old Testament—especially the prophecies—has not come true? (4) Broadly speaking, the book divides thusly: Romans 1–11 is the doctrinal portion, and Rom 12:1–15:13 is the section of application of the biblical truths in godly living. This section begins with verses you may be familiar with: "Therefore I urge you, brethren, by the mercies of God, to present your bodies a living and holy sacrifice, acceptable to God, which is your spiritual service of worship." (12:1–2). Paul concluded with many informative greetings to different people (15:14–16:24) and with a beautiful, doctrinally rich benediction (16:25–27).

(5) The doctrinal section of Romans (chaps. 1–11) includes 1:18–5:21: the doctrine of justification by faith in the finished work of the Lord Jesus Christ; 6:1–8:17: the doctrine of positional sanctification; and 8:18–39: the future glorification of the redeemed and the earth, which not only relates to the present situation but also looks far into the future. Remembering that the personal application section does not begin until 12:1, you can see that Romans 9–11 is as much part of the doctrinal section of Romans

as the other doctrinal section. This is God's doing by placing this section here, and you cannot be true to the Bible if you omit this section in your doctrinal understanding. (6) Also, Romans 9–11 is a single section in the letter; each chapter must be studied in the order it is given, without omitting any of the chapters, whether purposely omitting them or doing so by default in ignoring these chapters.

(7) Paul began (Rom 9:1–5) by addressing his fellow Jews and reminded them of the wonderful spiritual privileges that God gave to them, by which he specifically noted the covenants, which especially would include the Abrahamic, Davidic, and new covenants. Paul wrote nothing about the Jewish people once having these covenants given to them but that they no longer had any relevance for the Jewish people; in fact, Paul wrote just the opposite. (8) Romans 9:6–29 shows quite specifically that God's Word had not failed and shows how God in His sovereignty and grace chose national Israel. (9) Before continuing in Romans we saw examples from the Old Testament in which God specifically promises that He will save a remnant of the Jewish people at some time in the future (e.g., Isa 10:20–23; Zech 13:8–9). In Rom 9:27–28, Paul cited Isa 10:22–23, showing once more that God promises to save a remnant of Israel. He further wrote in Rom 9:27, and quoted from Isa 1:9, where national Israel's sins were so bad that the Jewish people would have been punished as Sodom and Gomorrah, which is a sad indication of the depth of national Israel's sin—and yet Yahweh remained faithfully true to His Word.

Next, (10) Romans 9:30–10:3 shifts the focus from God's sovereign choice of Israel in chapter 9 to Israel's sinful actions that led to their present spiritual condition. First, unsaved Israel pursued works of the law—not faith. Second, the unsaved Jews tried to keep all the works of the law, but their most unforgivable sin was the rejection of the Messiah whom God had already sent to them. God through Paul used two references to the Stone Prophecies about the Messiah (Rom 9:32b–33). So, in explaining the present spiritual status of unsaved national Israel, not only do they attempt justification by works instead of by faith; they collectively have sinned against God by having rejected the Messiah and now suffer the subsequent consequences of their sinful actions. Other than those who are saved or who will be saved, unbelieving national Israel collectively stumbles over the Stumbling Stone. God says in Isa 28:16 that He personally placed the Stone in Zion, leaving only two options available for dealing with Him, not it: there will be "the one who believes on Him" or those who will eternally trip over Him. Third, in Rom 10:1–2 Paul described unsaved national Israel, noting that they "have a zeal for God, but not in accordance with knowledge." And fourth, in this section, Rom 10:3 explains, "For not knowing about God's righteousness and seeking to establish their own, they did not subject themselves to the righteousness of God." They collectively and wrongly believed that by keeping the law they would be able, on their own, to achieve the righteousness of God.

Thus, (11) Paul argued in Rom 10:4–13 against anyone who claims the gospel message was purposely placed out of reach for national Israel; it was, and is, incredibly close to them. So (12) in coming to verses 14–15a, we now know that "How then will they call on Him in whom they have not believed? How will they believe in Him whom they have not heard? And how will they hear without a preacher? How will they preach unless they are sent?" is not a general call for Bible expositors nor preachers to emerge. The "they" in "and how will they hear?" is national Israel, the Jewish people, to whom God had given many opportunities to hear the gospel of God. Some believed; most did not believe. But these are the same ones in this section (Romans 9–11), the Jewish people, national Israel (Rom 9:1–5), "my brethren, my kinsmen according to the flesh" (v. 3), who would certainly be Jewish in ethnicity.

(13) The next verses continue the same argumentation: God Himself has sent prophets, preachers—and even Jesus the Messiah—to give to national Israel the good news of the gospel of Jesus Christ, as shown in Rom 10:15: "How will they preach unless they are sent? Just as it is written, "HOW BEAUTIFUL ARE THE FEET OF THOSE WHO BRING GOOD NEWS OF GOOD THINGS!" We also saw (14) the response by the Jewish people to the many different means that God used to get the gospel to them, as Rom 10:16 further supports and explains: "However, they [the unsaved Jewish people] did not all heed the good news; for Isaiah says, ' LORD, WHO HAS BELIEVED OUR REPORT?'" (15) We marked well that most of the Jewish people did not obey the gospel. As we have seen many times, rejection of God's Word is a sin issue—and one of the most serious ones—it is not an

ignorance issue as if God had never sent anyone to the Jewish people to proclaim His salvation message. The remainder of Romans 10 repeatedly shows—primarily using Old Testament quotes—that God repeatedly and persistently reached out to national Israel, but, for the most part, they collectively rejected Him, His Messiah, and the gospel.

Broadly speaking, arguing throughout Romans 9, God in His grace chose Israel, but Romans 10 speaks of Israel's sins (committed by the majority of the people), and their rejection of the Word of God is paramount. (16) We saw that Romans 11 continues the fourth part of Romans 9–11 and must be included in this doctrinal portion, and all three chapters must be studied in the order in which they were given by God. Otherwise one's understanding of God and His Word will be incomplete. In spite of the sins and rejection of God and His messages and messengers, including the people's role in the crucifixion of Jesus, God has not rejected national Israel. Romans 11:1–4 is clear:

> *I say then, God has not rejected His people, has He? May it never be! For I too am an Israelite, a descendant of Abraham, of the tribe of Benjamin. God has not rejected His people whom He foreknew. Or do you not know what the Scripture says in the passage about Elijah, how he pleads with God against Israel?* "Lord, THEY HAVE KILLED YOUR PROPHETS, THEY HAVE TORN DOWN YOUR ALTARS, AND I ALONE AM LEFT, AND THEY ARE SEEKING MY LIFE." *But what is the divine response to him?* "I HAVE KEPT FOR MYSELF SEVEN THOUSAND MEN WHO HAVE NOT BOWED THE KNEE TO BAAL."

Further, this was "the righteous remnant" of that day, chosen by the grace of God. He has preserved such a believing remnant of Jews out of the broader Jewish ethnicity, stating in Rom 11:5–6: "In the same way then, there has also been at the present time a remnant according to God's gracious choice. But if it is by grace, it is no longer on the basis of works, otherwise grace is no longer grace."

We finally saw (18) in Rom 11:25–27 that this becomes more than a part of the logical conclusion; now it becomes—as we see in so many other places—the prophetic Word of God which must come true:

> *For I do not want you, brethren, to be uninformed of this mystery—so that you will not be wise in your own estimation—that a partial hardening has*

happened to Israel until the fullness of the Gentiles has come in; and so all
Israel will be saved; just as it is written,

"THE DELIVERER WILL COME FROM ZION,

HE WILL REMOVE UNGODLINESS FROM JACOB."

"THIS IS MY COVENANT WITH THEM,

WHEN I TAKE AWAY THEIR SINS."

In following the biblical logic, it is apparent that (19) this future work of God is presented as a biblical mystery that a partial hardening—not a total hardening—has happened to unbelieving national Israel, and God was the One who did the hardening. (20) This mystery has an ending point that will not occur "until the fullness of the Gentiles has come in," and this will coincide with the beginning of Jesus's reign as the Davidic covenant heir.

(21) Thus, based on all we have seen—especially in the total context of Romans 9–11—all Israel will be saved, namely, the one-third who will be a righteous remnant of the Jewish people whom God will save when the Deliver will go to Zion in Jerusalem. He will remove ungodliness from the remaining Jewish people, and "this is My covenant with them"—the new covenant—resulting in "When I [He Himself personally] will take away their sin." Only Jesus could fill this role as Redeemer, thus allowing God to do just as He promised to do so many centuries earlier, as we saw in Zech 13:8–9. (22) Paul's joyous responsive praise to this beautiful work of God so appropriately concludes this wonderful section of God's doctrine in Romans 9–11:

Oh, the depth of the riches both of the wisdom and knowledge of God! How
unsearchable are His judgments and unfathomable His ways! For WHO HAS
KNOWN THE MIND OF THE LORD, OR WHO BECAME HIS COUNSELOR? Or WHO HAS
FIRST GIVEN TO HIM THAT IT MIGHT BE PAID BACK TO HIM AGAIN? For from Him and
through Him and to Him are all things. To Him be the glory forever. Amen.
(Rom 11:33–36)

In the section on using the Stone Prophecies about the Messiah in Jewish evangelism, we saw (1) Gen 49:1 and 49:28 are important because Jacob called his sons together and told them that he would tell them what would happen to their descendants—the twelve tribes of Israel. Also, verse

1 is the first time the words "end of the days," a literal translation of the original Hebrew, occur in Scripture. (2) Genesis 49:8–12 shows the Messiah being the Lion from the tribe of Judah. (3) In this section on the future blessings that would come to Joseph's descendants, God revealed two additional descriptive titles for the Messiah in verse 24, namely, "from there is the Shepherd, the Stone of Israel."

So (5) we should expect, in the last days, for the Messiah to shepherd Israel at some point then. (6) We saw passages such as Jer 31:10 and 33:14 show what it is that the Messiah will do. Further, (7) Ezekiel 34 gives quite a detailed account of Messiah coming to shepherd the Jewish believing remnant. (8) The biblical trail for the Stone Prophecies that can be used for Jewish evangelism can be found in *The Stone and the Glory of Israel.*

Deeper Walk Study Questions

1. Give a broad background for the occasion of Paul writing the book of Romans.

2. What two important questions did Paul have to address for the unsaved Roman mindset? Be specific and tell why these are important.

3. Broadly divide the book of Romans, and tell why it is important to know where you are in the book.

4. Why is it incorrect to say "justified by faith"? Explain and give a much more biblically accurate answer and be specific in doing so.

5. Romans 9–11 takes place in the doctrinal portion of Romans. Why is this important? Explain with four biblical truths concerning this.

6. Why must Romans 9–11 be studied as one entire section of the letter? What would you be leaving out if you stayed in chapter 9 or began at chapter 10 or omitted chapter 11? Give six reasons why this would be lacking, and support your answers biblically.

7. List six doctrinal truths from Rom 9:1–5. Why are these opening verses to this section so important? Explain. Especially note what the Holy Spirit inspires Paul to write about the covenants. Why is this important? Explain.

8. How does Rom 9:6–29 give part of the answer as to whether God's Word has failed? List ten biblical truths from these verses.

9. Very specifically, list the four sins that unsaved national Israel committed and continue to commit. List these and tell why each one is important theologically.

10. From Rom 10:4–13, list nine doctrinal truths, especially considering how they could be used in answering anyone who would claim that God had never sent His gospel message or messengers to the Jews.

11. How does Rom 10:13 connect with the answer that God gives in verses 14–15, especially in reference to God and His Word and the Jewish people? Give four biblical truths from these verses and tell why they are important.

12. From Rom 10:16, list eight doctrinal truths, noting especially how these answer the objection that God never sent anyone to the Jewish people to give the gospel to them.

13. Write two doctrinal truths each from Rom 11:1–4, 5–6, 7–10, 11–12, 13–16, and 24. After this, write a three- to four-sentence paraphrase about the doctrinal truths of Rom 11:1–24.

14. Write five biblical truths from Rom 11:25–27. Be specific. Also, what is the difference between a partial hardening of Israel versus a permanent complete hardening? Based on the context, what does "the fullness of the Gentiles" mean? Why would God put that here? Explain and be specific.

15. Write six biblical truths from Rom 11:28–32.

16. Write five biblical truths from Rom 11:33–36.

From the Appendix on Using "the Stone Prophecies" in Jewish Evangelism

1. Give five biblical truths from Gen 49:1 and 49:28. Why are these important? Explain and be specific.

2. Give three biblical truths from Gen 49:8–12 and explain why these are important.

3. In the section regarding Joseph's future blessing (Gen 49:22–26), in view of verses 1 and 28, why is verse 24 so important? What does this verse require of the Messiah? Be specific and tell why these doctrinal truths are important.

4. How does Jer 31:10 and 33:14 show the future work of the Messiah and national Israel? Give four biblical truths and explain why they are important.

5. What does God promise national Israel in Ezekiel 34 regarding who will shepherd them at some point in the future? List twelve biblical truths and explain why these are important, especially in view of the messianic requirements that we saw in Genesis 49.

CHAPTER 25

The Word of God or the Word of Man?[1]

A few years ago The Master's Seminary hosted a conference on the inerrancy of the Bible. One of the preliminary events associated with this was the Faculty Lecture Series done in the spring semester, and it tied in with the inerrancy conference. As part of this, I was assigned the text of 1 Thess 2:13: "For this reason we also constantly thank God that when you received the word of God which you heard from us, you accepted it not as the word of men, but for what it really is, the word of God, which also performs its work in you who believe."

This assignment was a little different in that (1) I was limited to forty-five minutes for the chapel message, (2) other professors also were speakers for the series on inerrancy, and (3) I was to write a journal article as part of my assignment. I had never done that before.

As always, I started with a Bible and a legal pad.

Introduction

The question of what is or what is not God's Word has instigated an age-old theological battle going all the way back to creation. Genesis 1 contains eleven verses with some form of "And God said":

3: "Then God said . . ."

---

[1] Gregory H. Harris, "The Word of God or the Word of Man?", *Master's Seminary Journal* 26, no. 2 (Fall 2015): 179–202. The Master's Seminary chapel video.: http://www.tms.edu/m/msj26.2.03.pdf.

6: "Then God said . . ."

9: "Then God said . . ."

11: "Then God said . . ."

14: "Then God said . . ."

20: "Then God said . . ."

22: "God blessed them, saying . . ."

24: "Then God said . . ."

26: "Then God said . . ."

28: "God said . . ."

29: "Then God said . . ."

Genesis 2 adds two more such references: "The LORD God commanded the man, saying" (v. 16), and "Then the LORD God said . . ." (v. 18). Thus, thirteen times in the first two chapters of Genesis present God as actively speaking, and this context also sets forth the mighty nature of God's spoken word. The Bible presents Him as God alone, who has no need outside of Himself to validate His speech, with creation itself validating and bearing witness to the effectiveness of His Word.

Genesis 3:1 abruptly changes things in two tremendously significant ways. First, this is the first question recorded in Scripture ("Indeed, has God said?"), and second, it is also the first temptation recorded in the Bible from the one who will soon be disclosed as an archenemy of God and humankind. When Eve did not properly respond to this deceptive temptation by saying, "God has indeed said," the initial question digresses to a statement: "You surely will not die!" (Gen 3:4). When the first questioning of whether or not God has spoken is not properly responded to, the scene digresses to include a formal denial of the truthfulness of God's Word. Now, for the first time in Scripture two statements stand in total opposition to each other; both statements cannot be true, and if one of them is found to be a true statement, the remaining statement must be a lie. Both of the serpent's approaches, then, call into doubt the trustworthiness of God, first by the doubting of His Word and, second, by doubting His Person. In both cases, the evil words spoken frame the focus of the attack, and they ultimately undermine the integrity of the one who speaks.

Later revelation given by God, such as John 8:44 and Rev 12:9, reveals that the enemy is an old and continuously active one. Jesus described Satan in John 8:44:

> *You are of your father the devil, and you want to do the desires of your father. He was a murderer from the beginning, and does not stand in the truth because there is no truth in him. Whenever he speaks a lie, he speaks from his own nature; for he is a liar and the father of lies.*

When the question of whether or not God had spoken is improperly answered, it always follows with the acceptance of a more brazen lie that God has not said, "You surely will not die." From the devastating fall of man and the subsequent curse, the broader/larger picture emerges:

THE TRUTH OF GOD

VS.

THE LIES [PLURAL] OF SATAN

This battle that began in Genesis 3 continues to the present time and ultimately goes to the final rebellion in Rev 20:7–10. First Timothy 4:1 reveals an important subset of this attack on God's truth: "But the Spirit explicitly says that in later times some will fall away from the faith, paying attention to deceitful spirits and doctrines of demons," clearly showing that religious lies, deceitful spirits, and doctrines of demons exist and are constantly active. However, it should also be noted that they are never presented by those who propagate such false doctrine for what they truly are; thus, they comprise a major component of the overall deception that continuously comes forth from Satan.

Obviously, with the overall battle being the truth of God versus the lies of Satan, two core questions result: (1) What is God's Word? And, (2) what is the ultimate source for what is presented as God's Word? These questions directly relate to both origin and authority, and these two concepts repeatedly occur in Scripture. Perhaps one of the best known examples of the source and effectiveness of God's Word is Isa 55:8–11, verses many are familiar with:

> *For My thoughts are not your thoughts,*
>
> *Nor are your ways My ways," declares the LORD.*
>
> *"For as the heavens are higher than the earth,*
>
> *So are My ways higher than yours,*
>
> *And My thoughts than your thoughts.*
>
> *"For as the rain and the snow come down from heaven,*
>
> *And do not return there without watering the earth,*
>
> *And making it bear and sprout,*
>
> *And furnishing seed to the sower and bread to the eater;*
>
> *So will My word be which goes forth from My mouth;*
>
> *It will not return to Me empty,*
>
> *Without accomplishing what I desire,*
>
> *And without succeeding in the matter for which I sent it.*

While the greater context ultimately deals with wayward Judah and Jerusalem (Isa 1:1; 2:1), the immediate context is God's offer of grace and forgiveness to national Israel: "Seek the LORD while He may be found; / Call upon Him while He is near" (55:6). Using the contrast between His thoughts and the highest heaven being higher than the collective thoughts of fallen humankind, God established the basis for His comparison and for His declarative statement: "So will My word be which goes forth from My mouth; / It will not return to Me empty, / Without accomplishing what I desire, / And without succeeding in the matter for which I sent it" (Isa 55:11). This last statement shows this is quite personal with God. He considers it "[His] word," going forth from "[His] mouth," and it will not return "to [Him]" empty, without accomplishing what "[He] desire[s]," for "[He] sent it." Only the most brazen of skeptics could come to a text such as this and not accept that God with ultimate authority views and presents this as His Word (its origin) and its divine power (its effectiveness). Also, one major deduction needs to be considered: verse 11 is either 100 percent true or 100 percent false. God offered no middle ground or third option; it is not "sort of God's word"; it is not "sort of higher than the heavens are above earth."

Jesus and the Word of God—A Brief Survey

Without time to address everything relating to Jesus and God's Word, I still must point out that particular verses directly apply to our study of 1 Thess 2:13. It should not be surprising that Jesus shared the same theology concerning the source and authority of the Word of God as found in Isaiah 55. For instance, centuries later than Isaiah's time, when He was tempted by the same evil one found in Genesis 3, Jesus responded perfectly, although Adam and Eve had not. He cited a verse similar in doctrine to Isa 55:11, by quoting Deut 8:3: "It is written, 'MAN SHALL NOT LIVE ON BREAD ALONE, BUT ON EVERY WORD THAT PROCEEDS OUT OF THE MOUTH OF GOD'" (Matt 4:4).

Later, after the parable of the Sower and the Soils (Mark 4:1–12), Jesus interpreted His own parable and explained it, starting in verse 14: "The sower sows the word [of God]." He further described the good soil as "the ones on whom seed was sown . . . ; and they hear the word [of God] and accept it, and bear fruit, thirty, sixty, and a hundredfold" (v. 20). Thus, those who are "good soil" must meet three requirements: (1) they hear the Word of God; (2) they accept the Word of God for what it is—the Word of God; and (3) instead of making some mere mental affirmation, they live in such a way that fruit is produced in their lives. All three components are required to meet the criteria set by Jesus of what composes "good soil."

Yet Scripture makes clear that not everyone has such a response as the good soil. When the Pharisees condemned Jesus by asking why His disciples did not "walk according to the tradition of the elders" (Mark 7:5), Jesus responded by strongly denouncing them. He quoted Isa 29:13 in reference to such ones, stating:

> *"Rightly did Isaiah prophesy of you hypocrites, as it is written,*
>
> *'This people honors Me with their lips,*
>
> *But their heart is far away from Me.*
>
> *'But in vain do they worship Me,*
>
> *Teaching as doctrines the precepts of men.'" (MARK 7:6–7)*

Jesus further denounced them by saying, "Neglecting the command-ment of God, you hold to the tradition of men" (v. 8), following this with the summary statement that they were "invalidating the word of God by [their] tradition which [they] have handed down; . . . [they] do many things such as that" (v. 13). Jesus clearly made a stark contrast between "the precepts of men" [the word of man] versus the Word of God. The people whom Jesus rebuked were repeatedly committing two different sins: first, they elevated the precepts of men (in their estimation only, not in reality) to the status of the Word of God; second, they lowered God's Word (in their minds and practice but not in reality) to be on the same level as their traditions, namely, the precepts of man. The sins of elevating fallen hu-manity's word to be equal with God's Word and the attempt at debasing God's holy Word to humanity's fallen level would not be limited only to the original audience; it is still just as sinful to do either or both today—and those who do so stand equally as guilty and convicted before Jesus as when such things first occurred.

Another passage of extreme significance regarding God's Word re-cords the words of Jesus in Mark 8:38, where Jesus forewarned, "For whoever is ashamed of Me and My words in this adulterous and sinful generation, the Son of Man will also be ashamed of him when He comes in the glory of His Father with the holy angels." The Person of Jesus can-not be eradicated or removed from the words of Jesus; they are insepara-ble; not to believe one is not to believe the other. Also, this sobering truth should not be neglected: everyone will believe someone or some thing, and eternal destinies literally depend on the reception or rejection of God's incarnate and spoken Word.

One final passage needs to be examined before we go to 1 Thess 2:13. After the mistakenly misnamed triumphal entry (Matt 21:1–11), the subse-quent cleansing of His own temple (vv. 12–17), and the cursing of the fig tree (vv. 18–22), the following encounter took place:

> *When He entered the temple, the chief priests and the elders of the people came to Him while He was teaching, and said, "By what authority are You doing these things, and who gave You this authority?" Jesus said to them, "I will also ask you one thing, which if you tell Me, I will also tell you by what authority I do these things. The baptism of John was from what source,*

> *from heaven or from men?" [Mark 11:30 adds the imperative, "Answer Me!"] And they began reasoning among themselves, saying, "If we say, 'From heaven,' He will say to us, 'Then why did you not believe him?' But if we say, 'From men,' we fear the people; for they all regard John as a prophet." And answering Jesus, they said, "We do not know." He also said to them, "Neither will I tell you by what authority I do these things." (Matt 21:23–27)*

Jesus gave them only two options—not twenty—as to the source of John the Baptist's ministry. Was the source of John the Baptist's ministry God or man? "Answer Me!" He said. Was John the Baptist a prophet of God, or did he present himself as a prophet of God without God's calling and approval? "Answer Me!" Did John the Baptist speak and teach the Word of God or merely the precepts of men? "Answer Me!"

Their reasoning in private shows that these religious leaders undoubtedly understood the core issue: "If we say, 'From heaven,' He will say to us, 'Then why did you not believe him?'" It is clearly evident they did not believe that John the Baptist originated from nor spoke for God. They had completely rejected the previous declaration that John the Baptist made in regard to himself as being the Messiah's biblically prophesied forerunner of Isa 40:2–3, as seen in John 1:19–23:

> *This is the testimony of John, when the Jews sent to him priests and Levites from Jerusalem to ask him, "Who are you?" And he confessed and did not deny, but confessed, "I am not the Christ." They asked him, "What then? Are you Elijah?" And he said, "I am not." "Are you the Prophet?" And he answered, "No." Then they said to him, "Who are you, so that we may give an answer to those who sent us? What do you say about yourself?" He said, "I am* A VOICE OF ONE CRYING IN THE WILDERNESS, 'MAKE STRAIGHT THE WAY OF THE LORD,' *as Isaiah the prophet said."*

None of these claims did the religious leaders believe, and so what should have been tremendously embarrassing to these Jewish academic elites was that after a lifetime of study, they could not collectively nor individually determine whether or not John the Baptist's baptism originated from God. Jesus appropriately would not answer their question concerning His own authority.

In summary, it should not be surprising that both God the Father and God the Son viewed God's Word the same way. Perhaps the best all-encompassing statement in all of the Bible regarding how Jesus viewed Scripture is His simple yet eternally profound declaration in His prayer in John 17:17: "Sanctify them in the truth; Your word is truth."

The Birth of the Thessalonian Church

In order to have a better understanding of Paul's letters to the Thessalonians, a few matters regarding his arrival and reception at Thessalonica should be noted, as seen in Acts 17:1–10a:

> *Now when they had traveled through Amphipolis and Apollonia, they came to Thessalonica, where there was a synagogue of the Jews. And according to Paul's custom, he went to them, and for three Sabbaths reasoned with them from the Scriptures, explaining and giving evidence that the Christ had to suffer and rise again from the dead, and saying, "This Jesus whom I am proclaiming to you is the Christ." And some of them were persuaded and joined Paul and Silas, along with a large number of the God-fearing Greeks and a number of the leading women. But the Jews, becoming jealous and taking along some wicked men from the market place, formed a mob and set the city in an uproar; and attacking the house of Jason, they were seeking to bring them out to the people. When they did not find them, they began dragging Jason and some brethren before the city authorities, shouting, "These men who have upset the world have come here also; and Jason has welcomed them, and they all act contrary to the decrees of Caesar, saying that there is another king, Jesus." They stirred up the crowd and the city authorities who heard these things. And when they had received a pledge from Jason and the others, they released them.*
>
> *The brethren immediately sent Paul and Silas away by night to Berea.*

In harmony with the previous texts we have seen in this chapter of the *Handbook,* God's Word—not humanity's word—lay at the heart of what Paul preached to the Thessalonians.

Six Substantial Truths from 1 Thessalonians 2:13

With this background we come to 1 Thess 2:13 and can consider its importance: "For this reason we also constantly thank God that when you received the word of God which you heard from us, you accepted it not as the word of men, but for what it really is, the word of God, which also performs its work in you who believe." When viewed with the previous information of this article, six substantial truths emerge.

Substantial Truth 1: *Strongly differentiating between the Word of God and the word of man is not a biblical mystery in the sense of some previously undisclosed biblical truth, such as the church (Eph 1:17; 3:2–10; Col 1:24–27) or the rapture (1 Cor 15:50–53); rather, it is a continuation of a doctrine that God has repeatedly revealed time after time—from Genesis 1 up to this point to the composure of 1 Thess 2:13.*

Paul fully knew and readily acknowledged the ultimate source as to what he had both preached and taught to the Thessalonians, and he knew the divine origin of what he preached. Concerning the boldness of the statement that Paul spoke the actual Word of God, that agrees with the previous disclosure of God's progressive divine revelation. Thus, the Word of God was central to Paul and all other teachers who truly wanted to honor God. With Paul presenting God's Word to the Thessalonians, he understood that he was simply continuing the succession of others whom God used over the centuries to reveal and present His holy Word.

Substantial Truth 2: *Closely connected to the previous truth is that 1 Thess 2:13 and other similar verses do not teach some minor, insignificant, inconsequential doctrine. Literally, the eternal destinies of the Thessalonians were contingent on them receiving, believing, and accepting God's Word as God's Word.*

This does not mean that those individuals who do not believe in inerrancy cannot be saved. However, they must at least receive the truth of the gospel message sent from God in order to be saved. If they continue this way, they will be, regardless of degrees granted, babes in Christ, and they will have to give an account to the Judge. Scripture reveals quite clearly that those who teach or preach to others will receive a greater condemnation (Jas 3:1).

Only a few samples of many other passages demonstrate the disastrous results of people not properly receiving or obeying the Word of God. For instance, God stated through the prophet Isaiah, in Isa 1:4, "Alas, sinful nation, / People weighed down with iniquity, / Offspring of evildoers, / Sons who act corruptly! / They have abandoned the LORD, / They have despised the Holy One of Israel, / They have turned away from Him." Later God pronounced judgment on His vineyard, saying in Isa 5:24, "Therefore, as a tongue of fire consumes stubble, / And dry grass collapses into the flame, / So their root will become like rot and their blossom blow / away as dust; / For they have rejected the law of the LORD of hosts, / And despised the word of the Holy One of Israel." The two passages go hand-in-hand and are similar to Jesus's words in Mark 8:38 ("Me and My words"). When Israel despised the Holy One of Israel (Isa 1:4), they also despised the Word of the Holy One of Israel (5:24).

The young Thessalonian church did not respond to God's Word the way that wayward Israel had responded. Rather, they took it for what it really is, the words of God, which are at work in believers (1 Thess 2:13).

Substantial Truth 3: *The manner by which the Thessalonians received God's Word showed them not to be "the rocky soil" that Jesus explained in His parable in Mark 4:16–17: "When they hear the word, [they] immediately receive it with joy; and they have no firm root in themselves, but are only temporary; then, when affliction or persecution arises because of the word, immediately they fall away."*

Having been forced out of town earlier than he hoped to have been, Paul wrote to the Thessalonian church to see how they were faring and to encourage this young church. All things considered, the church had fared well since his departure. Accordingly he wrote to them, "knowing, brethren beloved by God, His choice of you; for our gospel did not come to you in word only, but also in power and in the Holy Spirit and with full conviction" (1 Thess 1:4–5a).

That Paul placed the emphasis on the gospel itself—not the human messengers—is further evident from the fact that he says, "We came to you with the gospel." The messengers apart from the message would have been totally powerless to achieve such a result. Not only had the Thessalonians received the Word but had received the Word so resolutely that the entire area had heard of it: "For the word of the Lord has sounded forth from you, not only in Macedonia and Achaia, but also in every place your faith toward God has gone forth, so that we have no need to say anything" (1 Thess 1:8).

Paul also knew that "our exhortation does not come from error or impurity or by way of deceit" (1 Thess 2:3). Paul had written to them:

> *You are witnesses, and so is God, how devoutly and uprightly and blamelessly we behaved toward you believers; just as you know how we were exhorting and encouraging and imploring each one of you as a father would his own children, so that you would walk in a manner worthy of the God who calls you into His own kingdom and glory. (1 Thess 2:10–12)*

After writing our present text of 1 Thess 2:13 ("For this reason we also constantly thank God that when you received the word of God which you heard from us, you accepted it not as the word of men, but for what it really is, the word of God, which also performs its work in you who believe"), Paul additionally wrote, "For you, brethren, became imitators of the churches of God in Christ Jesus that are in Judea, for you also endured the same sufferings at the hands of your own countrymen, even as they did from the Jews" (v. 14). The "rocky soil" type of believer would have fallen away long before this time, but the Thessalonian church had not.

Substantial Truth 4: *The Thessalonian church's receiving and accepting God's Word as God's Word was not limited to the initial point of their salvation.*

The Word of God "also performs [present tense] its work in you who believe" (present tense). By God's Word producing good works within them, the Thessalonian Christians were again proving themselves to be "the good soil" (Mark 4:20) that Jesus described. (1) They heard God's Word ("received the word of God," 1 Thess 2:13); (2) they accepted it as God's Word ("you accepted it"); and (3) they bore spiritual fruit, thirty, sixty, and a hundredfold as 1 Thess 1:2–3 shows: "We give thanks to God always for all of you, making mention of you in our prayers; constantly bearing in mind your work of faith and labor of love and steadfastness of hope in our Lord Jesus Christ in the presence of our God and Father."

The Word of God was not only the basis for the salvation of the Thessalonians; it also became the basis for their sanctification, as God had indeed intended.

One quick note: not being "rocky soil" does not necessarily equate with being "good soil." Jesus gave a strong denunciation and rebuke of the most theologically correct but cold and loveless church in Ephesus in Rev 2:1–7; which sadly shows this to be true.

Substantial Truth 5: *Whereas 1 Thess 2:13 is not the origin of the biblical doctrine of starkly differentiating between the pure, holy Word of God versus the word of man, neither is it its terminus. Many correlating Scripture passages affirm this long past 1 Thess 2:13.*

As before, just a sampling of verses will show this. For example, Paul three times refers to His gospel as "the word of truth" (2 Cor 6:7; Col 1:5; 2 Tim 2:15). In Paul's death row epistle, Second Timothy, he writes, "Retain the standard of sound words which you have heard from me, in the faith and love which are in Christ Jesus. Guard, through the Holy Spirit who dwells in us, the treasure which has been entrusted to you" (2 Tim 1:13–14). Also, "Remember Jesus Christ, risen from the dead, descendant of David, according to my gospel, for which I suffer hardship even to imprisonment as a criminal; but the word of God is not imprisoned" (2:8–9). Paul further states:

> Remind them of these things, and solemnly charge them in the presence of God not to wrangle about words, which is useless, and leads to the ruin of the hearers. Be diligent to present yourself approved to God as a workman who does not need to be ashamed, accurately handling the word of truth. (2 Tim 2:14–15)

Paul continues:

> But realize this, that in the last days difficult times will come. For men will be lovers of self, lovers of money, boastful, arrogant, revilers, disobedient to parents, ungrateful, unholy, unloving, irreconcilable, malicious gossips, without self-control, brutal, haters of good, treacherous, reckless, conceited,

lovers of pleasure rather than lovers of God, holding to a form of godliness, although they have denied its power; Avoid such men as these. (3:1–5)

The all-important 2 Tim 3:12–17 comes from this same context:

Indeed, all who desire to live godly in Christ Jesus will be persecuted. But evil men and impostors will proceed from bad to worse, deceiving and being deceived. You, however, continue in the things you have learned and become convinced of, knowing from whom you have learned them, and that from childhood you have known the sacred writings which are able to give you the wisdom that leads to salvation through faith which is in Christ Jesus. All Scripture is inspired by God and profitable for teaching, for reproof, for correction, for training in righteousness; so that the man of God may be adequate, equipped for every good work.

Hebrews 4:12 describes God's Word as "living and active." In 1 Pet 1:22–2:3 Peter describes the Word of God in a similar but more detailed manner:

Since you have in obedience to the truth purified your souls for a sincere love of the brethren, fervently love one another from the heart, for you have been born again not of seed which is perishable but imperishable, that is, through the living and enduring word of God. For,

"ALL FLESH IS LIKE GRASS,

AND ALL ITS GLORY LIKE THE FLOWER OF GRASS.

THE GRASS WITHERS,

AND THE FLOWER FALLS OFF,

BUT THE WORD OF THE LORD ENDURES FOREVER."

And this is the word which was preached to you.

Therefore, putting aside all malice and all deceit and hypocrisy and envy and all slander, like newborn babes, long for the pure milk of the word, so that by it you may grow in respect to salvation, if you have tasted the kindness of the Lord.

Peter's death-row epistle, 2 Peter, is similar to Paul's death-row epistle in that both of them contain sections on God's Word and on future attacks against it. Second Peter 1:1–4 begins thusly:

Simon Peter, a bond-servant and apostle of Jesus Christ,

To those who have received a faith of the same kind as ours, by the righteousness of our God and Savior, Jesus Christ: Grace and peace be multiplied to you in the knowledge of God and of Jesus our Lord; seeing that His divine power has granted to us everything pertaining to life and godliness, through the true knowledge of Him who called us by His own glory and excellence. For by these He has granted to us His precious and magnificent promises, so that by them you may become partakers of the divine nature, having escaped the corruption that is in the world by lust.

In the last chapter of Scripture that Peter would ever write, he warns in 2 Pet 3:1–7:

This is now, beloved, the second letter I am writing to you in which I am stirring up your sincere mind by way of reminder, that you should remember the words spoken beforehand by the holy prophets and the commandment of the Lord and Savior spoken by your apostles. Know this first of all, that in the last days mockers will come with their mocking, following after their own lusts, and saying, "Where is the promise of His coming? For ever since the fathers fell asleep, all continues just as it was from the beginning of creation." For when they maintain this, it escapes their notice that by the word of God the heavens existed long ago and the earth was formed out of water and by water, through which the world at that time was destroyed, being flooded with water. But by His Word the present heavens and earth are being reserved for fire, kept for the day of judgment and destruction of ungodly men.

Substantial Truth 6: *Jesus demanded them, "Answer Me!" (Mark 11:30), regarding the source of the baptism of John the Baptist, and the demand for an answers is still just as much in force today as when Jesus first required it—and ultimately everyone must answer and give an account to Him concerning this.*

Differentiating between the source of John the Baptist's ministry and the source of other related passages is not limited to the Jews in Matthew 21 or to the Thessalonians in Acts 17. Jesus ultimately forces everyone to confess, one way or the other, "The baptism of John was from what source, God or man? Answer Me!"—and as before, eternal destinies are literally at stake.

We return to Matthew 21 to see this further expounded. In verse 23 the religious leaders questioned Jesus concerning His authority to disrupt the temple: "When He entered the temple, the chief priests and the elders of the people came to Him while He was teaching, and said, 'By what authority are You doing these things, and who gave You this authority?'"

> *Jesus said to them, "I will also ask you one thing, which if you tell Me, I will also tell you by what authority I do these things. The baptism of John was from what source, from heaven or from men?" And they began reasoning among themselves, saying, "If we say, 'From heaven,' He will say to us, 'Then why did you not believe him?' But if we say, 'From men,' we fear the people; for they all regard John as a prophet." And answering Jesus, they said, "We do not know." He also said to them, "Neither will I tell you by what authority I do these things. (vv. 24–27)*

Jesus then took the initiative from this point onward, as Matt 21:28–32 shows:

> *"But what do you think? A man had two sons, and he came to the first and said, 'Son, go work today in the vineyard.' And he answered, 'I will not'; but afterward he regretted it and went. The man came to the second and said the same thing; and he answered, 'I will, sir,' but he did not go. Which of the two did the will of his father?" They said, "The first." Jesus said to them, "Truly, I say to you that the tax collectors and prostitutes will get into the kingdom of God before you. For John came to you in the way of righteousness and you did not believe him; but the tax collectors and prostitutes did believe him; and you, seeing this, did not even feel remorse afterward so as to believe him."*

Verse 32 is the core issue—both then and now, with the word *believe* occurring three times in this one verse: "For John came to you in the way of righteousness, and you did not *believe* him, but the tax collectors and the prostitutes *believed* Him. And even when you saw it, you did not afterward change your minds and *believe* him" (emphasis added).

Two points are important here. First, Jesus substantiated the origin and authority of John the Baptist ("For John came to you in the way of righteousness"). Second, when the religious authorities had answered in Matt 21:27 that after a lifetime of study they could not determine the source/authority of the baptism of John the Baptist, they collectively lied before the Holy One of God. These men were not agnostics; they were firmly entrenched skeptics who would associate neither John the Baptist nor Jesus with God. They knew—or thought they knew—that the baptism of John the Baptist was not sent by God, but they were too afraid to say publicly at that time what they fully and completely did not believe.

It should also be emphasized that in earlier years, John the Baptist had refused to baptize them and many other religious leaders with whom Jesus was presently speaking. However, he reluctantly agreed to baptize Jesus. So, in reference to many of the same ones who were arguing with Jesus, John the Baptist had denounced them accordingly:

> *But when he saw many of the Pharisees and Sadducees coming for baptism, he said to them, "You brood of vipers, who warned you to flee from the wrath to come? Therefore bear fruit in keeping with repentance; and do not suppose that you can say to yourselves, 'We have Abraham for our father'; for I say to you that from these stones God is able to raise up children to Abraham. The axe is already laid at the root of the trees; therefore every tree that does not bear good fruit is cut down and thrown into the fire.*

> *"As for me, I baptize you with water for repentance, but He who is coming after me is mightier than I; and I am not fit to remove His sandals; He will baptize you with the Holy Spirit and fire. His winnowing fork is in His hand, and He will thoroughly clear His threshing floor; and He will gather His wheat into the barn, but He will burn up the chaff with unquenchable fire."* (Matt 3:7–12)

Yet when Jesus came to be baptized, John the Baptist freely accepted and (reluctantly) baptized Him:

> *Then Jesus arrived from Galilee at the Jordan coming to John, to be baptized by him. But John tried to prevent Him, saying, "I have need to be baptized by You, and do You come to me?" But Jesus answering said to him, "Permit it at this time; for in this way it is fitting for us to fulfill all righteousness." Then he permitted Him. After being baptized, Jesus came up immediately from the water; and behold, the heavens were opened, and he saw the Spirit of God descending as a dove and lighting on Him, and behold, a voice out of the heavens said, "This is My beloved Son, in whom I am well pleased." (Matt 3:13–17)*

In modern times and in the future, Jesus firmly poses the same question and He forces all eventually to answer as to the authority of the baptism of John the Baptist. This can be clearly understood by the cascading subsidiary questions and statements found in John 1.

First, Scripture presents John the Baptist twice saying that Jesus was pre-eternal: "John testified about Him [and still does] and cried out, saying, 'This was He of whom I said, "He who comes after me has a higher rank than I, for He existed before me"'" (John 1:15) and "This is He on behalf of whom I said, 'After me comes a Man who has a higher rank than I, for He existed before me'" (v. 30).

Is this true? Was Jesus pre-eternal? "Answer Me!"

Second, John the Baptist claimed to be the voice crying out in the wilderness and thus the fulfillment of Isa 40:3. Also, with this, he said not just "Make straight the way of Messiah," but "Make straight the way of the LORD":

> *This is the testimony of John, when the Jews sent to him priests and Levites from Jerusalem to ask him, "Who are you?" And he confessed, and did not deny, but confessed, "I am not the Christ." They asked him, "What then? Are you Elijah?" And he said, "I am not." "Are you the Prophet?" And he answered, "No." Then they said to him, "Who are you, so that we may give an answer to those who sent us? What do you say about yourself?" He said, "I am A VOICE OF ONE CRYING IN THE WILDERNESS, 'MAKE STRAIGHT THE WAY OF THE LORD,' as Isaiah the prophet said." (John 1:19–23)*

Is this true? "Answer Me!"

Third, John the Baptist instructed his followers about Jesus. At His approach John said, "Behold, the Lamb of God who takes away the sin of the world!" (v. 29).

Is this true? Is Jesus the means God uses to take away the sin of the world? "Answer Me!"

Fourth, simply stated, John 1:34 has John the Baptist refer to Jesus as the second member of the Godhead: "I myself have seen, and have testified that this is the Son of God"—not merely the Son of Man nor the Son of David.

Is this true? Is Jesus the Son of God? "Answer Me!"

Every one of these items points to Jesus; every one of these doctrines emerges from the preaching and baptism of John the Baptist; and for every one of these biblical truths Jesus still requires people to give Him an answer—in this life—that so factors in greatly to where they will spend eternity.

Summary and Conclusion

We did not start our study in 1 Thess 2:13 but walked there scripturally, and we did this because the core connective issues concerning what God's Word is and who speaks for God engage in an age-old battle, going back as far as Genesis 1–2. There, thirteen times in those chapters, some form of "and God said" is written, and in this context also sets forth the mighty efficacious nature of God's spoken word. The Bible presents Him as God alone who has no need outside of Himself to validate His speech, with creation itself validating and bearing witness to the effectiveness of God's word.

Genesis 3:1 abruptly changes things in two tremendously significant ways. First, this is the first question recorded in Scripture ("Indeed, has God said?"), and, second, it is also the first temptation recorded in the Bible from the one who will soon be disclosed as an archenemy of God and humankind. When Eve did not properly respond to this deceptive temptation by saying, "God has indeed said," the initial question digresses to a statement and a challenge: "You surely will not die!" (Gen 3:4). From at first, questioning whether God has indeed said, when the Bible repeatedly states that He has, leads to a formal denial of the truthfulness of God and His Word when not properly responded to. Now, for the first time in Scripture stand two statements in total opposition to each other; both statements cannot be true, and if one of them is found to be a true statement, the remaining statement must be a lie. Both of the serpent's approaches, then, call into doubt the trustworthiness of God, first by the doubting of His Word and, second, by doubting His Person. In both cases, the evil words spoken frame the focus of the attack, and they ultimately undermine the integrity of the One who speaks.

God later reveals, as in John 8:44 and Rev 12:9, that the enemy is an old and continuously active one. Jesus described Satan in John 8:44:

> *You are of your father the devil, and you want to do the desires of your father. He was a murderer from the beginning, and does not stand in the truth because there is no truth in him. Whenever he speaks a lie, he speaks from his own nature, for he is a liar and the father of lies.*

From the devastating fall of man and the subsequent curse, the broader/larger picture emerges:

THE TRUTH OF GOD

VS.

THE LIES [PLURAL] OF SATAN

This battle that began in Genesis 3 continues to the present time and ultimately will go to the final rebellion in Rev 20:7–10.

After these key introductory matters, we saw in the core of the chapter at least six substantial truths emerging from 1 Thess 2:13. (1) Strongly differentiating between the Word of God and the word of man is not a biblical mystery in the sense of some previously undisclosed biblical truth, such as the church (Eph 3:2–10; Col 1:24–27) or the rapture (1 Cor 15:50–53); it is a continuation of a doctrine that God has repeatedly revealed time after time—from Genesis 1 up [to this point] to 1 Thess 2:13. (2) First Thessalonians 2:13 and other similar verses are not some minor, inconsequential doctrine. Literally, eternal destinies were contingent on either receiving or rejecting God's Word as God's Word. (3) The manner by which the Thessalonians received God's Word showed they were not "rocky soil." (4) The Thessalonian church's receiving and accepting God's Word as God's Word was not limited to the initial point of salvation. The Word of God "performs its work in you" (present tense), "who believe" (present tense); thus, they showed themselves to be the "good soil" which Jesus described in Mark 4:20—they heard God's Word and accepted God's Word and bore fruit. (5) While 1 Thess 2:13 is not the origin of the biblical doctrine of starkly differentiating between the pure, holy Word of God versus the word of man, neither is it its terminus; many more Bible verses repeat this truth throughout the rest of Scripture. (6) Jesus demanded, "Answer Me!"

(Mark 11:30), regarding the source of the baptism of John the Baptist is still just as much in force today as when Jesus first required it—and ultimately everyone must give an account to Him concerning this. Thus, two sides emerge in Scripture: those who receive God's Word as God's Word and those who choose to reject it. These polar opposite sides transcend both time and culture; it still comes down to an issue of the heart in regard to both God and His Word.

It is fitting and appropriate to conclude by contrasting the first two psalms, which, as with so many other passages in Scripture, present two options and only two options. Let us begin with Ps 2:1–3 that first reveals such brazen wickedness being committed by so many today:

Why are the nations in an uproar

And the peoples devising a vain thing?

The kings of the earth take their stand,

And the rulers take counsel together

Against the LORD and against His Anointed, saying,

"Let us tear their fetters apart,

And cast away their cords from us!"

Contrast this with the serene beauty and promises of Psalm 1:

How blessed is the man who does not walk in the counsel of the wicked,

Nor stand in the path of sinners,

Nor sit in the seat scoffers!

But his delight is in the law of the LORD,

And in His law he meditates day and night.

He will be like a tree firmly planted by streams of water,

Which yields its fruit in its season,

And its leaf does not wither;

And in whatever he does, he prospers.

The wicked are not so,

But they are like chaff which the wind drives away.

Therefore the wicked will not stand in the judgment,

Nor sinners in the assembly of the righteous.

For the LORD knows the way of the righteous,

But the way of the wicked will perish.

While Psalm 2 begins with the nations attempting to tear apart "the fetters" and "cords" of God and His Messiah, the same psalm ends with an encompassing statement and an offer: "How blessed are all who take refuge in [the Lord's Anointed]!" (Ps 2:12). And thus, this likewise will be true and said about them: "For this reason we also constantly thank God that when you received the word of God which you heard from us, you accepted it not as the word of men, but for what it really is, the word of God, which also performs its work in you who believe"(1 Thess 2:13).

Deeper Walk Study Questions

1. How many times does some form of "and God said" occur in Genesis 1–2? Why is the large number important to understanding who was speaking? Explain.

2. What is the first question recorded in Scripture, and how is it used? Also, how did Satan's attack progress from the mere question he first asked? Be specific, and explain why this is important to know.

3. Write six substantial truths from the great spiritual battle from Genesis 3 to Revelation 20. Name four ways they potentially affect your own walk and/or your ministry. Name four ways you can stay on guard concerning these.

4. Write five truths from Isa 55:8–11 regarding God and His Word. Why are these important? Explain and be specific.

5. Basing your answer on Mark 4:1–12, what are three requirements for someone to be described as "good soil"? Why are these important? Explain. Also, give six reasons why good soil contrasts with the tradition of the elders as seen in Mark 7:5–13, especially as to how this relates to the Word of God.

6. What is the first substantial truth in this chapter? Explain five reasons why this is important.

7. What is the second substantial truth in this chapter? Explain five reasons why this is important.

8. What is the third substantial truth in this chapter? Explain five reasons why this is important.

9. What is the fourth substantial truth in this chapter? Explain five reasons why this is important.

10. What is the fifth substantial truth in this chapter? Explain five reasons why this is important.

11. What is the sixth substantial truth in this chapter? Explain five reasons why this is important.

12. Using the six substantial truths as a backdrop, tell six reasons why Matt 21:23–32 is so important. Also, in regard to the ministry of John the Baptist, why are Matt 3:7–12, 13–17, and John 1:15, 29–30 so important theologically? Write two substantial truths from each one of these and summarize why these are important.

CHAPTER 26

Seven Astounding Doctrinal Truths from 2 Thessalonians 2[1]

As we saw in the previous chapter of this *Handbook* ("The Word of God or the Word of Man?"), it appears based on the Acts 17:1–9 account that Paul had a relatively short time with the young Thessalonian church before he was forced to leave the city. God in His sovereignty used the events that led to Paul's having to depart to instigate his writing of the first epistle to the Thessalonians, which plays an important part for the divine revelation of new doctrine that God had not previously made known.

After writing the first epistle, Paul must have thought he had covered everything necessary in that letter to the Thessalonians. However, again in the sovereignty of God, He used the next unfolding events to cause Paul to write his second letter to them. In this epistle God uses chapter two to reveal incredible truths of eternal consequences; these include prophetic insights about the seven-year tribulation and the second coming of the Lord Jesus Christ. As you probably have already guessed, as we did in previous chapters of the *Handbook*, we cannot start our study in 2 Thessalonians 2 and hope to be remotely accurate in our study without first walking the biblical trail to get there.

---

[1] For free audio downloads of matters associated with this chapter: https://www
.sermonaudio.com/search.asp?sourceonly=true&currSection=sermonssource&key
word=gregharris&subsetcat=series&subsetitem=2+Thessalonians.

The Eschatological Vantage Point of 1 Thessalonians

One of the unique features of 1 Thessalonians is that every chapter ends with a verse or verses about the second coming of the Lord Jesus Christ.

The first eschatological ending occurs in 1 Thess 1:9–10: "For they themselves report about us what kind of a reception we had with you, and how you turned to God from idols to serve a living and true God, and to wait for His Son from heaven, whom He raised from the dead, that is Jesus, who rescues us from the wrath to come."

First Thessalonians 2:19–20 ends this way: "For who is our hope or joy or crown of exultation? Is it not even you, in the presence of our Lord Jesus at His coming? For you are our glory and joy."

First Thessalonians 3:11–13 adds this:

> Now may our God and Father Himself and Jesus our Lord direct our way
> to you; and may the Lord cause you to increase and abound in love for one
> another, and for all people, just as we also do for you; so that He may es-
> tablish your hearts without blame in holiness before our God and Father at
> the coming of our Lord Jesus with all His saints.

The Thessalonian church had questions about whether or not the Christians who had died before the Lord returned would lack or miss out on anything. In 1 Thess 4:13–18, Paul reassured them—and subsequent readers over the centuries—that they would not miss any of God's blessings when Jesus returns:

> But we do not want you to be uninformed, brethren, about those who are
> asleep, so that you will not grieve as do the rest who have no hope. For
> if we believe that Jesus died and rose again, even so God will bring with
> Him those who have fallen asleep in Jesus. For this we say to you by the
> word of the Lord, that we who are alive and remain until the coming of the
> Lord, will not precede those who have fallen asleep. For the Lord Him-
> self will descend from heaven with a shout, with the voice of the archangel
> and with the trumpet of God, and the dead in Christ will rise first. Then we
> who are alive and remain will be caught up together with them in the clouds
> to meet the Lord in the air, and so we shall always be with the Lord. There-
> fore comfort one another with these words.

Because this passage reveals what would later be called the rapture of the church, which will occur at some unrevealed time in the future, not only are they to "encourage [comfort] one another," but the Holy Spirit expressly commands they do so "with these words." That is, they are to remind each other that the dead in Christ will be raised first at the Lord's return (to the clouds, not to Earth at this return). Also, the remaining Christians who are still alive will be caught up together with them in the clouds; thus, they will always be with the Lord. Indeed, these are comforting words—as the Trinity intends. Sadly, many are not comforted by these sublime promises because they do not know them (their pastors, teachers, and/or disciplers did not teach them this section) or they simply have not read or do not believe them.

After promises that the church will be raptured at an undisclosed future date, God the Holy Spirit through the apostle Paul then revealed the immediate consequences of those who are not taken to heaven:

Now as to the times and the epochs, brethren, you have no need of anything to be written to you. For you yourselves know full well that the day of the Lord will come just like a thief in the night. While they are saying, "Peace and safety!" then destruction will come upon them suddenly like labor pains upon a woman with child, and they will not escape. (1 Thess 5:1–3)

It is evident from the above verses that the Thessalonian church knew "very well that the day of the Lord will come just like a thief in the night." Also—and this is important—sudden destruction would come "upon them." The fact that Paul gave no additional information regarding either "the day of the Lord" or who the "they" were to whom these verses refer, gives solid support that the apostle Paul was not revealing any new doctrine in his epistle to them. He fully expected the Thessalonian church not only to know about such things, because he had taught them when he was present with them, but also to know these biblical truths "very well."

A Biblical Walk-Through of Pertinent "Day of the Lord" Passages

The Bible is clear that the day of the Lord is not a New Testament teaching only. The Old Testament contains numerous passages/prophecies about the day of the Lord, and these were the passages that Paul either showed from the scrolls and the parchments to the Thessalonian church or quoted from memory. These passages show biblically what the day of the Lord entails. We will see that the phrase "the day of the Lord" has different component parts to it, and these parts will obviously include more than a twenty-four-hour period. We will look at what comprises the day of the Lord when it comes as well as the Scripture passages that support this:

1. The day of the Lord is a time of divine wrath of God's judgments due to great sins against Him.
2. The judgment part of the day of the Lord will be followed (in varying degrees) by a time of God's blessings to the faithful.
3. There have been other days of the Lord in the past, and sometimes when such prophecies were given by the prophet of God, it was considered a nearer day of the Lord because it was closer at hand. Once those prophecies were fulfilled, they became part of the subsequent judgment of sinners that God has already fulfilled.
4. However, many of the prophecies point to a time exceedingly beyond the situation at that present time and were directed toward the entire world in God's eschatological judgment(s) that He will yet pour out. In God's progressive revelation, we understand this time of judgment to be the seven-year tribulation period that will include the Antichrist's reign. Revelation 6–18 reveals many details about the judgment part of the eschatological Day of the Lord, as we will see in upcoming chapters in this *Handbook*.
5. As with the more temporal uses of other days of the Lord, the blessings that follow God's judgments of the tribulation will likewise be eschatological in nature and will include the return of the Messiah to earth (Revelation 19; Zechariah 14), and His kingdom rule (Revelation 20) that extends all the way into eternity (Revelation 21–22). The wonderful blessings associated with the Lord's return never end once they begin.

We will examine some pertinent biblical texts that show these truths. Obadiah, a neglected book for many Bible readers, begins with a nearer judgment against Edom in the first fourteen verses and then, in Obadiah 15–17, it switches to the eschatological judgment:

> *"For the day of the LORD draws near on all the nations.*
>
> *As you have done, it will be done to you.*
>
> *Your dealings will return on your own head.*
>
> *"Because just as you drank on My holy mountain,*
>
> *All the nations will drink continually.*
>
> *They will drink and swallow*
>
> *And become as if they had never existed.*
>
> *"But on Mount Zion there will be those who escape,*
>
> *And it will be holy.*
>
> *And the house of Jacob will possess their possessions.*

Obadiah 21 shows the kingdom's part of this blessing after God's judgment:

> *The deliverers will ascend Mount Zion*
>
> *To judge the mountain of Esau,*
>
> *And the kingdom will be the LORD's.*

Joel has nearer day-of-the-Lord judgments, beginning in Joel 1:14–15:

> *Consecrate a fast,*
>
> *Proclaim a solemn assembly;*
>
> *Gather the elders*
>
> *And all the inhabitants of the land*
>
> *To the house of the LORD your God,*
>
> *And cry out to the LORD.*
>
> *Alas for the day!*
>
> *For the day of the LORD is near,*
>
> *And it will come as destruction from the Almighty.*

Joel 2:1–2 continues:

> *Blow a trumpet in Zion,*
>
> *And sound an alarm on My holy mountain!*

Let all the inhabitants of the land tremble,

For the day of the LORD is coming;

Surely it is near,

A day of darkness and gloom,

A day of clouds and thick darkness.

As the dawn is spread over the mountains,

So there is a great and mighty people;

There has never been anything like it,

Nor will there be again after it

To the years of many generations.

Verse 11 adds:

The LORD utters His voice before His army;

Surely His camp is very great,

For strong is he who carries out His Word.

The day of the LORD is indeed great and very awesome,

And who can endure it?

From the immediate situation of Joel's time, he switched to a farther day of the Lord that will affect the entire world, such as we can see in verses 31–32:

The sun will be turned into darkness

And the moon into blood

Before the great and awesome day of the LORD comes.

"And it will come about that whoever calls on the name of the LORD

Will be delivered;

For on Mount Zion and in Jerusalem

There will be those who escape,

As the LORD has said,

Even among the survivors whom the LORD calls.

Joel 3:1–2 continues in this same context:

For behold, in those days and at that time,

When I restore the fortunes of Judah and Jerusalem,

I will gather all the nations

And bring them down to the valley of Jehoshaphat.

Then I will enter into judgment with them there

On behalf of My people and My inheritance, Israel,

Whom they have scattered among the nations;

And they have divided up My land.

Verses 11–16 speak of the wrath of God's judgments that will occur then:

Hasten and come, all you surrounding nations,

And gather yourselves there.

Bring down, O LORD, Your mighty ones.

Let the nations be aroused

And come up to the valley of Jehoshaphat,

For there I will sit to judge

All the surrounding nations.

Put in the sickle, for the harvest is ripe.

Come, tread, for the wine press is full;

The vats overflow, for their wickedness is great.

Multitudes, multitudes in the valley of decision!

For the day of the LORD is near in the valley of decision.

The sun and moon grow dark

And the stars lose their brightness.

The LORD roars from Zion

And utters His voice from Jerusalem,

And the heavens and the earth tremble.

But the LORD is a refuge for His people

And a stronghold to the sons of Israel.

Verse 17 adds not only the subsequent blessing part of the day of the Lord, but Joel also used that for proof that Yahweh is truly God. When He dwells in their very midst:

Then you will know that I am the LORD your God,

Dwelling in Zion, My holy mountain.

So Jerusalem will be holy,

And strangers will pass through it no more.

Amos 5:18–20 foretells a nearer judgment as part of a day-of-the-Lord judgment:

Alas, you who are longing for the day of the LORD,

For what purpose will the day of the LORD be to you?

It will be darkness and not light;

As when a man flees from a lion

And a bear meets him,

Or goes home, leans his hand against the wall

And a snake bites him.

Will not the day of the LORD be darkness instead of light,

Even gloom with no brightness in it?

A section in Isaiah gives instructions regarding God's judgments of the nations (Isaiah 13–23), and 13:6–8 includes the prophecy of a nearer day-of-the-Lord judgment for Babylon:

Wail, for the day of the LORD is near!

It will come as destruction from the Almighty.

Therefore all hands will fall limp,

And every man's heart will melt.

They will be terrified,

Pains and anguish will take hold of them;

They will writhe like a woman in labor,

They will look at one another in astonishment,

Their faces aflame.

And then Isaiah moves to a farther judgment that will affect the entire world, as seen with the cataclysmic events that will occur when this judgment comes, in 13:9–13:

Behold, the day of the LORD is coming,

Cruel, with fury and burning anger,

To make the land a desolation;

And He will exterminate its sinners from it.

For the stars of heaven and their constellations

Will not flash forth their light;

The sun will be dark when it rises

And the moon will not shed its light.

Thus I will punish the world for its evil

And the wicked for their iniquity;

I will also put an end to the arrogance of the proud

And abase the haughtiness of the ruthless.

I will make mortal man scarcer than pure gold

And mankind than the gold of Ophir.

Therefore I will make the heavens tremble,

And the earth will be shaken from its place

At the fury of the LORD of hosts

In the day of His burning anger.

Zephaniah 1:7 foretells of a nearer day-of-the-Lord judgment:

Be silent before the Lord GOD!

For the day of the LORD is near,

For the LORD has prepared a sacrifice,

He has consecrated His guests.

But then verses 14–18 give a graphic description of what comprises the future day-of-the-Lord judgment and the far-reaching global sweep of this judgment by God:

Near is the great day of the Lord,

Near and coming very quickly;

Listen, the day of the Lord!

In it the warrior cries out bitterly.

A day of wrath is that day,

A day of trouble and distress,

A day of destruction and desolation,

A day of darkness and gloom,

A day of clouds and thick darkness,

A day of trumpet and battle cry

Against the fortified cities

And the high corner towers.

I will bring distress on men

So that they will walk like the blind,

Because they have sinned against the Lord;

And their blood will be poured out like dust

And their flesh like dung.

Neither their silver nor their gold

Will be able to deliver them

On the day of the Lord's *wrath;*

And all the earth will be devoured

In the fire of His jealousy,

For He will make a complete end,

Indeed a terrifying one,

Of all the inhabitants of the earth.

Notice that sometimes the Bible refers to the day of the Lord in a short-ened form, such as "a day" or "the day." The context will show whether this is intended to be used for "the day of the Lord," especially the escha-tological one as seen in Isa 2:12–17:

For the LORD of hosts will have a day of reckoning

Against everyone who is proud and lofty

And against everyone who is lifted up,

That he may be abased.

And it will be against all the cedars of Lebanon that are lofty and lifted up,

Against all the oaks of Bashan,

Against all the lofty mountains,

Against all the hills that are lifted up,

Against every high tower,

Against every fortified wall,

Against all the ships of Tarshish

And against all the beautiful craft.

The pride of man will be humbled

And the loftiness of men will be abased;

And the LORD alone will be exalted in that day, ...

Jeremiah 30:7 describes it this way:

Alas! for that day is great,

There is none like it;

And it is the time of Jacob's distress,

But he will be saved from it.

Zechariah 14:1–3 prophesies:

Behold, a day is coming for the LORD when the spoil taken from you will be divided among you. For I will gather all the nations against Jerusalem to battle, and the city will be captured, the houses plundered, the women ravished and half of the city exiled, but the rest of the people will not be cut off from the city. Then the LORD will go forth and fight against those nations, as when He fights on a day of battle.

The final two occurrences of the day of the Lord prophecies are both found in Malachi 4.

The first one, in verses 1–3, uses the shortened form for the day:

"For behold, the day is coming, burning like a furnace; and all the arrogant and every evildoer will be chaff; and the day that is coming will set them ablaze," says the LORD of hosts, "so that it will leave them neither root nor branch." "But for you who fear My name, the sun of righteousness will rise with healing in its wings; and you will go forth and skip about like calves from the stall. You will tread down the wicked, for they will be ashes under the soles of your feet on the day which I am preparing," says the LORD of hosts.

The last reference in the Old Testament is in Mal 4:4–6, where the longer form is used. From its context it is evident that the Jewish people are specifically referenced in this last section:

Remember the law of Moses My servant, even the statutes and ordinances which I commanded him in Horeb for all Israel [the Mosaic covenant].

"Behold, I am going to send you Elijah the prophet before the coming of the great and terrible day of the LORD. He will restore the hearts of the fathers to their children and the hearts of the children to their fathers, so that I will not come and smite the land with a curse."

While the Hebrew Bible ends with 2 Chronicles, for the English (and many other translations), Mal 4:5 is not only the last reference to the day of the Lord in the Old Testament, but these are the last three verses of the entire Old Testament. Just that they are the last verses before the New Testament begins should make them noteworthy.

With this biblical backdrop established, we can continue exploring its relevance to the Thessalonian church. They have just been told that the church will be raptured at some undisclosed time in the future and that they are to encourage one another with these words (1 Thess 4:13–18). God the Holy Spirit, through Paul, revealed what the immediate response will be of those who will find themselves in the great eschatological day of the Lord in the tribulation:

Now as to the times and the epochs, brethren, you have no need of anything to be written to you. For you yourselves know full well that the day of the Lord [the judgment part/the tribulation] will come just like a thief in the night. While they are saying, "Peace and safety!" then destruction will come upon them suddenly like labor pains upon a woman with child, and they will not escape. (1 Thess 5:1–3)

Notice the switch to "they" in this passage. Paul wrote that the "brothers and sisters" do not have any need for anything to be written to them because, as just revealed by God in 1 Thess 4:13–18, all Christians alive at the time in view will be taken to heaven when the rapture takes place. This group of Christians is specifically differentiated from the latter group who are the unsaved people at the initial part of the tribulation. As we will see in an upcoming chapter in the *Handbook,* the ill-advised response of the world to claim "peace and security" will prove empty, except at the very early part of the tribulation. Instead, "sudden destruction will come upon them." This does not apply to the "us" who are saved. Rather, like the sudden labor pains of a pregnant woman, "they" who have not placed faith in Jesus and thus are not raptured "will not escape." The original Greek language, using a strongly intensified form, says they will "by no means escape."

In direct contrast to those who will not escape the horrendous judgments and events in the tribulation comes this exhortation to the saved, in 1 Thess 5:9–10: "For God has not destined us for wrath, but for obtaining salvation through our Lord Jesus Christ, who died for us, so that whether we are awake or asleep, we will live together with Him." After Paul instructed the Thessalonian Christians at the end of chapter 4 to "comfort one another with these words" (v. 18) comes God's exhortation through the apostle: "Therefore encourage one another and build up one another, just as you also are doing" (1 Thess 5:11). These are quite specific exhortations based on the biblical doctrines just revealed that those who are saved will escape the tribulation, and they have no need for anything else to be written to them about that period of time because "God has not destined us for wrath" but for salvation through our Lord Jesus Christ. Then, in inexpressible delightful words, comes the promise that we will live with Him forever.

The end of each chapter contains a verse(s) about the Second Coming, and chapter 5 is no exception, as we see in 1 Thess 5:23–24: "Now may the God of peace Himself sanctify you entirely; and may your spirit and soul and body be preserved complete, without blame at the coming of our Lord Jesus Christ. Faithful is He who calls you, and He also will bring it to pass." Paul instructed in verse 27, "I adjure you by the Lord to have this letter read to all the brethren." Not only did he instruct them, but he "charge(s) . . . by the Lord" (CSB) that they read this epistle to all the Christians there. This letter was not only intended to be God's/Paul's instruction and encouragement to the Thessalonian church members; it was also written as a protection for them to have this read—and believed.

CONSIDER: The way that each chapter in 1 Thessalonians ends proves those are wrong who think that eschatology (the doctrine of last things) is only for the seasoned, more mature Christian, and that it is a doctrine they will eventually come to in their studies when they will have to decide which interpretational side to align themselves with. For Paul—better still, for the Holy Spirit—eschatology is part of the core essentials of sound Christian doctrine. To remove this teaching from your teaching or preaching because it is controversial is to ignore not only beautiful truths from God's Word but also many explanations, warnings, and exhortations *from God.*

The Pressing Occasion for the Writing of 2 Thessalonians

When Paul composed the epistle of 1 Thessalonians, he added thoughtful instructions to what he had previously taught the church in his brief time with them after the inception of the Thessalonian church. He had grounded these young believers in God's truth so they would be able to stand firm; however, it soon became clear they were not able to accomplish that. After receiving Paul's letter, the young Thessalonian church came under massive persecution, causing them to believe they were in the midst of the judgment part of the dreaded day of the Lord, the tribulation. During that time, the Thessalonians were virtually isolated from other Christians because they had extremely limited means of correspondence as they endured the persecution without knowledge of whether or not other Christians, such as those in relatively nearby Berea, were also undergoing persecution.

Because of their being under such intense persecution, the young Thessalonian Christians erroneously concluded they were in the tribulation. From what we studied in Paul's first epistle, the belief of the Thessalonian church that they were in the tribulation created many cascading problems and great worries. First, if they were in the tribulation, perhaps they were not actually saved; maybe they had to do more to attain salvation other than receiving the gospel of grace of the Lord Jesus Christ. Second, if Paul was wrong in what he had clearly instructed them concerning the rapture and the tribulation, he could also be wrong about other doctrines that he taught them, such as justification by faith through the finished work of the Lord Jesus Christ. Third, if they were in the tribulation, it would greatly weaken their faith in God and His Word. This became the occasion for Paul to write the second epistle to the Thessalonians.

> **KEY:** It is evident through the text and through the response of the Thessalonians to their persecution that they were taught—and fully expected—that they would be raptured before the tribulation began. If they had been taught that they would not be raptured, they would have expected such persecution promised for the judgment part of the day of the Lord. If they had been taught that they would have to endure the tribulation, all they would have to do is survive to the end of the tribulation, knowing that each day they survived, they came a day closer to the tribulation ending and the Lord Jesus returning. But clearly they had *not* been taught that repeatedly by the apostle Paul.

Fully realizing that this young church was under strong persecution, Paul lovingly wrote to them (1) to correct their erroneous deductions based on their circumstances, (2) to further instruct them with additional new divine revelation, and (3) to further strengthen, comfort, and encourage them in the Lord. In 2 Thess 1:3–5 Paul wrote:

We ought always to give thanks to God for you, brethren, as is only fitting, because your faith is greatly enlarged, and the love of each one of you toward one another grows ever greater; therefore, we ourselves speak proudly of you among the churches of God for your perseverance and faith in the midst of all your persecutions and afflictions which you endure. This is a plain indication of God's righteous judgment so that you will be considered worthy of the kingdom of God, for which indeed you are suffering.

Also, in 2 Thess 1:9–10:

These will pay the penalty of eternal destruction, away from the presence
of the Lord and from the glory of His power, when He comes to be glori-
fied in His saints on that day, and to be marveled at among all who have
believed—for our testimony to you was believed.

With this background, we come to 2 Thessalonians 2, beginning with
the first two verses:

Now we request you, brethren, with regard to the coming of our Lord Jesus
Christ and our gathering together to Him, that you not be quickly shaken
from your composure or be disturbed either by a spirit or a message or
a letter as if from us, to the effect that [the judgment part of] the day of the
Lord has come.

Once Paul identified the core problems, he began in the same way that
Jesus had begun in Matthew 24–25, the section that gives many details
about the tribulation. In Matt 24:4, Jesus began: "See to it that no one misleads you." Paul likewise began his explanation about the erroneous belief
of the Thessalonians by giving the same warning in 2 Thess 2:3: "Let no
one in any way deceive you."

The Thessalonian church did not arrive at the conclusion that they
were in the judgment part of the day of the Lord by their own reasoning;
certain agents had actively worked to disseminate this false doctrine and
thus upset and trouble the Thessalonian faithful. These writings to them
were done in the early ministry of the apostle Paul. Bible-believing scholars usually say that either Galatians or 1 and 2 Thessalonians were the first
epistles that Paul wrote. Although it may be hard for some of us to understand, the early church obviously had few—and in some cases, perhaps
no—New Testament books. How could the church grow in the grace and
knowledge of our Lord and Savior, Jesus Christ, if they had no Bible to be
read in their assembly?

The answer is that, for the early church, God gave the following in
1 Cor 12:28:

And God has appointed in the church, first apostles, second prophets,
third teachers, then miracles, then gifts of healings, helps, administra-
tions, various kinds of tongues.

We know that these individuals in view are New Testament prophets (not Old Testament prophets) because they came after God gave apostles to the church, and there are no apostles in the Old Testament. As with the Old Testament prophets of God, the New Testament prophets would say, "Thus says the Lord." When this was legitimately done, it served the church of the Lord Jesus Christ wonderfully until God gave the full and closed canon of Scripture.

However, there was a problem: anyone could have claimed then—and many do today—"thus says the Lord" without being an actual prophet of God. In 1 John 4:1, John warned the church accordingly: "Beloved, do not believe every spirit, but test the spirits to see whether they are from God, because many false prophets have gone out into the world." So how was the early church to test the spirits? In 1 Corinthians 12–14 Paul gave the answer to this question in a section dealing with spiritual gifts and the early church's usage—or misusage. If a prophet stood up in the early church to give a prophecy, 1 Cor 14:29 states that the church was to "[l]et two or three prophets speak, and let the others pass judgment [that is, evaluate claims made]."

When Paul wrote to the Thessalonians that they should not believe "every spirit," this would not be a reference to some ephemeral spirits floating around; rather, it references anyone who stood up in the assembly and claimed to be a prophet and to have a spiritual source for his prophecies. In that church setting, that person would have claimed, "Thus says the Lord."

We see this same concept expanded in 2 Corinthians 11, in an epistle that Paul wrote soon after his epistles to the Thessalonians. In it Paul sarcastically mocks the foolish Corinthian church for their eagerness to receive anything labeled with "Thus says the Lord." In both Matthew 24–25 and 2 Thessalonians 2, which warned people to be careful and not to be deceived, the deception for the Corinthian church had already affected them, and—this is important—their deception was based on the same lies from the same source found in the earliest of the deceptions recorded in the Bible:

> *But I am afraid that, as the serpent deceived Eve by his craftiness, your minds will be led astray from the simplicity and purity of devotion to*

Christ. For if one comes and preaches another Jesus whom we have not preached, or you receive a different spirit which you have not received, or a different gospel which you have not accepted, you bear this beautifully. (2 Cor 11:3-4)

This occasion at Corinth gave God the opportunity through the apostle Paul to disclose doctrinal truths about false prophets because some of those at Corinth presented themselves as having the even higher New Testament office of an apostle. About this Paul wrote in 2 Cor 11:13–15:

For such men are false apostles, deceitful workers, disguising themselves as apostles of Christ. No wonder, for even Satan disguises himself as an angel of light. Therefore it is not surprising if his servants also disguise themselves as servants of righteousness, whose end will be according to their deeds.

These verses are vital for understanding spiritual deception, whether you are Eve, the Thessalonian faithful, the Corinthian church, anyone alive now, or—especially—anyone in the coming tribulation. The ultimate source of deception that stands contrary to God's truth is Satan. We should mark well the intentional verb uses in 2 Cor 11:14: "Satan disguises himself"—present tense—"as an angel of light." He will disguise himself only as long as God allows it. When we read that Paul wrote in 2 Thess 2:3 "Let no one in any way deceive you," and mentioned "a spirit" (someone saying in the assembly "Thus says the Lord"), we can know the ultimate source of that deception is Satan.

The next two means of deception that Paul warned of were "that you not be quickly shaken from your composure or be disturbed either by a spirit or a message [sermon] or a letter as if from us, to the effect that [the judgment part of] the day of the Lord has come." (2 Thess 2:2). These two means are revealing. Neither a false message nor a false epistle can create itself; someone went to great lengths to send these counterfeit doctrines to the Thessalonian church.

CONSIDER: Why would Satan go to such great measures to befuddle/baffle/battle this congregation? What Paul had already taught them in 1 Thessalonians and up to this chapter in 2 Thessalonians must be a *very* important matter for Satan. It is obvious from Satan's ongoing efforts to deceive that he does not want people to know the true doctrine that Paul taught in these books—then or now or in the future. We will see in our two chapters about Revelation in this *Handbook* why this would matter so much to Satan.

CONSIDER ALSO: Thanks be to God that He in His wise sovereignty used this background and setting to reveal astounding truths not previously revealed anywhere else in Scripture by the time this epistle was written.

Astounding Doctrinal Truth 1: *Second Thessalonians 2:3–4 explains what Jesus meant and what the Holy Spirit emphasized by warning about "the abomination of desolation."*

Jesus warned in Matt 24:15, "Therefore when you see the ABOMINATION OF DESOLATION which was spoken of through Daniel the prophet, standing in the holy place (let the reader understand)." We should mark that this refers to an actual event living people will see. The abomination of desolation is neither a spiritual condition nor a hidden event. Second Thessalonians 2:3–4 reveals exactly what the abomination of desolation will be:

> *Let no one in any way deceive you, for it [the judgment part of the day of the Lord] will not come unless the apostasy comes first, and the man of lawlessness is revealed, the son of destruction, who opposes and exalts himself above every so-called god or object of worship, so that he takes his seat in the temple of God, displaying himself as being God.*

Everything in 2 Thessalonians 2 is religious in nature. Paul warned that *the* judgment part of the day of the Lord cannot come "unless *the* apostasy comes first" (emphasis added). Having the definite article the before apostasy distinguishes it from a general type of apostasy and from any apostasy that had occurred historically. God does not disclose in this verse all that the apostasy will entail, but He will reveal some details in subsequent verses in this chapter, and He will reveal complete details in the book of Revelation.

The next part adds some detail and gives us the answer that God intends: "and the man of lawlessness is revealed, the son of destruction," which is the Antichrist. Fitting for him, the term translated "is revealed" is taken from the verb form from which the word revelation comes, and it is from the same form that the title "The Revelation of Jesus Christ" is based. Using both a comparison and a contrast, we know that just as Jesus lived His life in relative obscurity for thirty or more years before His being presented to Israel, the Antichrist will have lived in obscurity until he will be uncovered/unveiled/revealed. However, this revealing of the Antichrist will not be at his birth, but this will happen at his ascension to worldwide status. God will reveal much more in detail about this in Revelation 13. The most important role that the Antichrist will assume is described by Jesus and the Holy Spirit as the abomination of desolation: "who opposes and exalts himself above every so-called god or object of worship, so that he takes his seat in the temple of God, displaying himself as being God" (2 Thess 2:4).

Revelation 13 gives more information about the Antichrist, but we should not lose sight of the original reason that 2 Thess 2:3–4 was written: to explain and encourage the Thessalonian Christians that without "the apostasy," and without the Antichrist having seated himself in God's temple, they cannot be in the judgment part of the day of the Lord. Stated in the simplest form, no revealing of the Antichrist means no being in the tribulation—period. The Antichrist and the tribulation go hand in hand. One cannot exist without the other.

> **CRUCIAL:** Paul mildly rebukes the Thessalonian church in 2 Thess 2:5: "Do you not remember that while I was still with you, I was telling you these things?" Paul used the imperfect tense in the Greek for "I was telling," which denotes repeated action. Not only had Paul taught the Thessalonians that they would not be in the judgment part of the day of the Lord (the tribulation), but also that there will be no tribulation unless the Antichrist is first revealed, who will take his seat in the temple of God displaying himself as God. From the text it is evident that Paul had also taught them a pretribulation rapture. You cannot look for Jesus Christ to appear and the Antichrist to appear at the

same time. Nowhere is the church told to look for the Antichrist, only for Jesus Christ.

Astounding Doctrinal Truth 2: *Second Thessalonians 2:6–7 reveals the identity and the ministry of the Blessed Restrainer: "And you know what restrains him now, so that in his time he will be revealed. For the mystery of lawlessness is already at work; only he who now restrains will do so until he is taken out of the way."*

Many debates have occurred over the millennia about the identity of the Restrainer. These crucial truths should be kept in mind: (1) We could not know until 2 Thessalonians 2 that the Restrainer existed, and (2) the existence of the Restrainer must be viewed in keeping with the ascent of the Antichrist to worldwide dominion and all of the evil that his reign will include, as Revelation later discloses. We see biblically that the Restrainer (1) cannot be human because no person qualifies as being strong enough to restrain, and (2) it cannot be any high-ranking holy angel. Jude 9, a verse that gives us a surprising disclosure about Satan and the body of Moses, also shows the present respect that a high-ranking angel of God has for Satan's current authority: "But Michael the archangel, when he disputed with the devil and argued about the body of Moses, did not dare pronounce against him a railing judgment, but said, 'The Lord rebuke you.'"

This leads only to a Godhead member being strong enough to keep satanic forces at bay—and this must be the Holy Spirit. Under God's chronology, because Jesus has already ascended to heaven, it has to be the Holy Spirit who serves in this wonderful ministry, and that is why I refer to Him as "the Blessed Restrainer" who restrains. For as long as He restrains, no matter how horrible the conditions become in our society or in the world, the satanic forces that lead to the advent and unveiling of the Antichrist will be restrained and will never be able to bring him forth until the time of God's choosing.

Some people believe that He who restrains cannot be the Holy Spirit because He is omnipresent, and to say that He is removed is to limit an attribute of God from a Godhead member. While agreeing that the Holy Spirit is omnipresent, if you were to take that argument to its logical end, then it also means that the Holy Spirit could never have been sent by Jesus, even though Scripture requires that the Holy Spirit be sent by Him. In the Upper Room Discourse, in some of the last teaching given before Jesus began His journey to Gethsemane, Jesus encouraged His Eleven with the following promise in John 15:26: "When the Helper comes, whom I will send to you from the Father, that is the Spirit of truth who proceeds from the Father, He will testify about Me, and you will testify also, because you have been with Me from the beginning." Shortly thereafter, Jesus promises again in John 16:7, "But I tell you the truth, it is to your advantage that I go away; for if I do not go away, the Helper will not come to you; but if I go, I will send Him to you."

Having already demonstrated and concluded that the Restrainer must be a member of the Godhead—not a human or an angel, I believe it is evident from these texts (1) that Jesus promises to send One who has to be the Holy Spirit because Jesus repeatedly refers to Him as "He" and, (2) accordingly, that the Holy Spirit had not at that time been sent by Jesus; yet (3) that the Holy Spirit would have a special advent at some point in the future by no means diminishes or removes His omnipresence, even though He had not yet been sent. Acts 2 clearly bears witness to the fulfillment of Jesus's ministry.

When the Blessed Restrainer ceases His restraining, it does not mean that He will go out of existence, nor does it mean that He will play no part in the unfolding of prophetic events.

What it does mean is that He will be removed so that evil can manifest itself to the fullest extent—and this part is important—under God's sovereign control. For a designated time in the future, the Antichrist and his forces will be allowed to commit unbelievably heinous sins that no one has ever done nor ever will do again in the future; but, as we will see in Revelation, such sins will be permitted only because the Godhead permits them. They are measured, restrained, temporary in nature, and they will meet a certain demise at the return of Jesus. Before Jesus returns, what will be allowed to take place is a major aspect of what makes the tribulation the tribulation.

Astounding Doctrinal Truth 3: *Second Thessalonians 2:7 reveals "the mystery of lawlessness is already at work."*

The mystery of lawlessness is not a generic lawlessness that began after Genesis 3 and occurred in varying degrees up to this present time; this is "the mystery of lawlessness," and, as with any such mystery, it is only being revealed by God to whatever degree of uncovering He wishes. Also, this mystery of lawlessness "is already at work," which helps explain some of the present world situations—as well as the current ministry of the Restrainer.

We return to the verse we saw earlier in this chapter and now add some support verses in 1 John 4:1–3:

> *Beloved, do not believe every spirit, but test the spirits to see whether they are from God, because many false prophets have gone out into the world. By this you know the Spirit of God: every spirit that confesses that Jesus Christ has come in the flesh is from God; and every spirit that does not confess Jesus is not from God; this is the spirit of the antichrist, of which you have heard that it is coming, and now it is already in the world.*

The last part of verse 3 gives us the understanding: "this is the spirit of the antichrist, of which you have heard that it is coming, and now it [that is, the spirit of the antichrist] is already in the world." These verses reveal important doctrines that harmonize with the revelation of 2 Thessalonians 2. First, the spirit of the Antichrist, as with the mystery of lawlessness, is already in the world. This refers to satanic spiritual forces that will culminate in the Antichrist's reign. The Antichrist does not just mysteriously arrive, but spiritual forces intervene to cause him to rise to his God-ordained pinnacle of evil. Second, the closer we get to the advent of the Antichrist, the more we can expect evil to grow in our society and around the world. Third—and praise God for this—no matter how much all spiritual forces attempt to usher in the worldwide dominion of the Antichrist, they will never be able to do so until after the Restrainer is taken out of the way. Connected with what God has revealed in His Word, the Antichrist can come only after the rapture has occurred, and this doctrine was part of the repeated teaching of Paul to the Thessalonian believers (2 Thess 2:5) and is part of God's teaching from His Word to all of those who will accept it. This also magnifies the past and current ministry of the Restrainer whose removal allows events to progress from "the spirit of the antichrist" to the actual advent of the person of the Antichrist and all the wickedness that goes with it. The Holy Spirit did not begin His restraining in 2 Thessalonians 2; He began from before Genesis with the fall of Satan; He restrained all the way through history past; He still restrains today.

Astounding Doctrinal Truth 4: *Second Thessalonians 2:8–9 are the first verses in Scripture that connect Satan to the Antichrist:*

> *Then [after the Restrainer is removed] that lawless one will be revealed whom the Lord will slay with the breath of His mouth and bring to an end by the appearance of His coming; that is, the one whose coming is in accord with the activity of Satan, with all power and signs and false wonders.*

The book of Revelation will give details in regard to how close that association will be between Satan and the Antichrist, and we will study this in more detail in two upcoming chapters in the *Handbook*.

Astounding Doctrinal Truth 5: *Second Thessalonians 2:9–10 harmonizes with, expands on, and then restricts what Jesus had earlier warned about regarding miracles being performed during the tribulation.*

In Matt 24:24–25, in describing some of what will make the tribulation unique, Jesus warns accordingly, "For false Christs and false prophets will arise and will show great signs and wonders, so as to mislead, if possible, even the elect. Behold, I have told you in advance." In the information that Jesus reveals here, He instructs people to pay attention to this. The word "behold" should have an exclamation point after it each time it occurs in Scripture ("Behold!"); it should be understood as "Mark this!" Even though Satan's name is not used, it is evident that false Christs and false prophets will show "great signs and wonders" and will do so to such an extent that, if it were possible, even the elect would be deceived. These events must be of tremendous magnitude if they could possibly deceive the elect. That such things do not presently occur is probably one of the side benefits of the Restrainer currently restraining.

In 2 Thess 2:9–10 comes this connection: "that is, the one whose coming is in accord with the activity of Satan, with all power and signs and false wonders, and with all the deception of wickedness for those who perish, because they did not receive the love of the truth so as to be saved." In Matthew 24 Jesus used the plural with false Christs and false prophets; in 2 Thess 2:9–10a, this work is specifically limited to the Antichrist—singular—and will be one of the main means that the Antichrist will use to try to prove to the world that he is God. Based on the words of Jesus, these "signs and false wonders" will be—during the tribulation and with the Restrainer no longer restraining—authentic miracles. In this one place, they are called "false wonders" because the people will have the wrong reaction as to the source of these miracles and their significance. All of the other words used for these miracles are the exact same words used for the miracles of Jesus and the apostles. In fact, there are no words used for the miracles of Jesus and the apostles that are not also used for false Christs and false prophets—and ultimately—for the Antichrist.

Notice how quickly and easily unsaved people will be deceived by Satan and the Antichrist, as explained in the last part of 2 Thess 2:10: "because they did not receive the love of the truth so as to be saved." From the perspective that all of the events of the tribulation already have transpired, Paul wrote that those who were deceived did not receive "the love of the truth so as to be saved." He could have written only "they did not receive the truth"—that would be accurate; this account is much more in keeping with the John 3:16 love of God.

Astounding Doctrinal Truth 6: *Second Thessalonians 2:11–12 reveals that God will send an energized deception on certain ones among the lost in the tribulation: "For this reason God will send upon them a deluding influence [that is, literally "an energized deception"] so that they will believe what is false [literally, "the lie"], in order that they all may be judged who did not believe the truth, but took pleasure in wickedness."*

During the tribulation, after the gospel of God has gone out to the entire world, after God has given people many opportunities to repent and to receive the love of the truth so they might be saved, God will then actively work to secure the unsaved people in the disbelief that they will have already chosen for themselves. There will be no deathbed conversions at that point.

Astounding Doctrinal Truth 7: *As we saw earlier, and maybe now we can appreciate more, it is in this same chapter in which God reveals so much about Satan and the Antichrist that He also includes the redeemed receiving portions of His glory, as seen in 2 Thess 2:13–14:*

> *But we should always give thanks to God for you, brethren beloved by the Lord, because God has chosen you from the beginning for salvation through*

sanctification by the Spirit and faith in the truth. It was for this He called you through our gospel, that you may gain the glory of our Lord Jesus Christ.

In this eternally stark contrast with those who will not receive the love of the truth so as to be saved, God intentionally makes the promise of giving portions of His glory to the redeemed. We know from our studies that this will begin at the return of the Lord Jesus Christ to earth (the fifth theological bombshell from Matthew 16), as 2 Thess 1:9–10 so wonderfully shows:

These will pay the penalty of eternal destruction, away from the presence of the Lord and from the glory of His power, when He comes to be glorified in His saints on that day, and to be marveled at among all who have believed—for our testimony to you was believed.

This also means that Jesus "will slay [the Antichrist] with the breath of His mouth and bring [him] to an end by the appearance of His coming" (2 Thess 2:8). This also means that the first part of the promises of Isa 24:21–23 will take place:

So it will happen in that day,

That the LORD will punish the host of heaven on high,

And the kings of the earth on earth.

They will be gathered together

Like prisoners in the dungeon,

And will be confined in prison;

And after many days they will be punished.

Then the moon will be abashed and the sun ashamed,

For the LORD of hosts will reign on Mount Zion and in Jerusalem,

And His glory will be before His elders.

Appropriately, the Holy Spirit by means of the apostle Paul concludes with this warm and instructive exhortation and benediction, in 2 Thess 2:15–18, which is suitable for modern-day Christians as well:

So then, brethren, stand firm and hold to the traditions which you were taught, whether by word of mouth or by letter from us. Now may our Lord Jesus Christ Himself and God our Father, who has loved us and given us eternal comfort and good hope by grace, comfort and strengthen your hearts in every good work and word.

Summary and Conclusion

We learned many important biblical truths in this chapter. (1) One of the unique features of 1 Thessalonians is that every chapter ends with a verse or verses about the second coming of the Lord Jesus Christ. (2) The Bible is clear that "the day of the Lord" is not a New Testament teaching only. The Old Testament contains numerous passages/prophecies about the day of the Lord, and these are the passages Paul either showed from the scrolls and the parchments to the Thessalonian church or quoted from memory. (3) Passages such as Joel 2–3, Isa 13:9–13, and Zech 14:1–3 show the eschatological, worldwide aspect of the future day of the Lord.

With this biblical backdrop established, (4) we saw the relevance of the day of the Lord to the Thessalonian church. They had just been told that the church would be raptured at some undisclosed time in the future and that they were to encourage one another with these words (1 Thess 4:13–18). In the very next verses, God the Holy Spirit through Paul revealed what the immediate response will be of those who will find themselves in the great eschatological day of the Lord in the tribulation. So (5) we noted the switch to "they" in 1 Thess 5:1–3 after Paul had written that the "brethren and sisters" do not have any need for anything to be written to them because, as just revealed by God in 4:13–18, all Christians alive at that time will be taken to heaven when the rapture takes place. This previous group of Christians is specifically differentiated from the latter group who are the unsaved people at the initial part of the tribulation. (6) As we will see in an upcoming chapter in the *Handbook*, this ill-advised response of world "peace and safety" that is noted in 1 Thess 5:1–3 will not be anything like that, except at the early part of the tribulation. Instead, sudden "destruction will come upon them"—much like the labor pains of a pregnant woman. This will fall not on "us" who are saved; instead, "they"—the ones who are not raptured—"will not escape." The strongly intensified form used in the Greek means they will "by no means escape." We further noted (7) the way each chapter in 1 Thessalonians ends proves people are wrong who think that eschatology (the doctrine of last things) is only for the seasoned, more mature Christian, and that it is a doctrine they will eventually come to in their studies when they will have to decide which interpretational side to align themselves with. For Paul—better still, for the Holy Spirit—eschatology is part of the core essentials of sound Christian doctrine.

So, in actually coming to 2 Thess 2:1–2, we saw (8):

> Now we request you, brethren, with regard to the coming of our Lord Jesus Christ and our gathering together to Him, that you not be quickly shaken from your composure or be disturbed either by a spirit [prophecy in the CSB] or a message or a letter as if from us, to the effect that [judgment part of] the day of the Lord has come.

(9) Once Paul identified the core problems, he began in the same way that Jesus had begun in Matthew 24–25, the section that gives many details of the tribulation. In Matt 24:4, Jesus began: "See to it that no one misleads you." Paul likewise begins his explanation about the erroneous belief of the Thessalonians with the same warning, in 2 Thess 2:3: "Let no one in any way deceive you." So, (10) the Thessalonian church did not arrive at the conclusion that they were in the judgment part of the day of the Lord by their own reasoning. Certain agents had actively worked to disseminate this false doctrine and thus "upset" and "trouble" the Thessalonian faithful. (11) God used New Testament prophets to give His church His Words, and He also provided the means of detecting between a true prophet of God and a false one. In 1 Corinthians 12–14 Paul gave the answer to this question in a section dealing with spiritual gifts and the early church's usage—or misusage of them. If a prophet stood up in the early church to give a prophecy, 1 Cor 14:29 states, the believers were to "[l]et two or three prophets speak, and let the others pass judgment." That is, they were to evaluate what was said. When Paul wrote to the Thessalonians in 2 Thess 2:2 that they should not be concerned "by a spirit," He did not refer to some ephemeral spirit floating around; rather, He referred to a person who stood up in the assembly and claimed to be a prophet with a spiritual source for

His prophecies. In a church setting, such a person would have claimed, "Thus says the Lord." Also, (12) this occasion at Corinth gave God the opportunity through the apostle Paul to disclose doctrinal truths about false prophets because some of those at Corinth presented themselves as having the even higher New Testament office of an apostle. These are the ones about whom Paul wrote in 2 Cor 11:13–15:

> For such men are false apostles, deceitful workers, disguising themselves as apostles of Christ. No wonder, for even Satan disguises himself as an angel of light. Therefore it is not surprising if his servants also disguise themselves as servants of righteousness, whose end will be according to their deeds.

These verses are vital for understanding spiritual deception, whether you are Eve, the Thessalonian faithful, the Corinthian church, anyone alive now, or—especially—anyone in the coming tribulation. The ultimate source of deception in the spiritual realm that runs contrary to God's truth is Satan. We should mark well the intentional verb uses in 2 Cor 11:14: "Satan disguises himself"—present tense—"as an angel of light." He will disguise himself only as long as God allows it. When Paul wrote in 2 Thess 2:3, "Let no one in any way deceive you," he referenced those prophesying in the assembly and claiming, "Thus says the Lord." We know the ultimate source of deception is Satan.

We further saw seven astounding doctrinal truths that emerge from this context in 2 Thessalonians 2. Astounding Doctrinal Truth 1: Second Thessalonians 2:3–4 explains what Jesus meant and what the Holy Spirit emphasized by warning about "THE ABOMINATION OF DESOLATION" in Matt 24:15. We saw that he "who opposes and exalts himself above every so-called god or object of worship, so that he takes his seat in the temple of God, displaying himself as being God" is the Antichrist. Also, Paul mildly rebuked the Thessalonian church in verse 5: "Do you not remember that while I was still with you, I was telling you these things?" Paul used the imperfect tense in the Greek for "I was telling," which denotes repeated action. Not only had Paul taught the Thessalonians that they would not be in the judgment part of the day of the Lord (the tribulation), but he also repeatedly taught that there will be no tribulation unless the Antichrist is first revealed; he will take his seat in the temple of God, displaying himself

as God. From the text it is evident that Paul had also taught them a pretrib-
ulational rapture. You cannot look for Jesus Christ and the Antichrist to
appear at the same time. Nowhere is the church told to look for the Antichrist, only for Jesus Christ.

Astounding Doctrinal Truth 2: Second Thessalonians 2:6–7 reveals
the identity and the ministry of the Blessed Restrainer. It is evident from
these texts that (1) Jesus promises to send the One who has to be the Holy
Spirit because Jesus repeatedly refers to Him as "He" and, (2) accordingly,
that the Holy Spirit had not at that time been sent by Jesus. Yet (3) that
the Holy Spirit would have a special advent at some point in the future by
no means diminishes or removes His omnipresence, even though He had
not yet been sent. Acts 2 clearly bears witness to the fulfillment of Jesus's
ministry. We also saw biblically that the Restrainer (1) cannot be human
because no person qualifies as being strong enough to restrain, and (2)
it cannot be any high-ranking holy angel. Jude 9, a verse that gives us a
surprising disclosure about Satan and the body of Moses, also shows the
present respect that a high-ranking angel of God has for Satan's current
authority: "But Michael the archangel, when he disputed with the devil
and argued about the body of Moses, did not dare pronounce against him
a railing judgment, but said, 'The Lord rebuke you.'"

When the Blessed Restrainer ceases His restraining, He will not go out
of existence or play no part in the unfolding of prophetic events. What it
does mean is that He will be removed so that evil can manifest itself to the
fullest extent—and this part is important—under God's sovereign control.
For a designated time in the future, the Antichrist and his forces will be
allowed to commit unbelievably heinous sins as no one has ever done nor
ever will do again in the future. But as we will see in Revelation, such sins
will be permitted only because the Godhead permits them, and they are
measured, restrained, temporary in nature, and will meet a certain demise
at the return of Jesus. Before Jesus returns, what will be allowed to take
place is a major aspect of what makes the tribulation the tribulation.

Astounding Doctrinal Truth 3: Second Thessalonians 2:7 reveals "the
mystery of lawlessness is already at work." The mystery of lawlessness
is not a generic lawlessness that began after Genesis 3 and occurred in
varying degrees up to this present time; this is the mystery of lawlessness.

And, as with any such mystery, it is only being revealed by God to whatever degree of uncovering He wishes. Also, this mystery of lawlessness "is already at work," a fact that helps explain some of the present world situations, as well as the current ministry of the Restrainer. We further saw that the last part of 1 John 4:3 gives us this understanding: "This is the spirit of the antichrist, of which you have heard that [the antichrist] is coming, and now [the spirit of the antichrist] is already in the world." These verses reveal important doctrines that harmonize with the revelation of 2 Thessalonians 2. First, the spirit of the Antichrist, as with the mystery of lawlessness, is already in the world. This consists of the satanic spiritual forces that will culminate in the Antichrist's reign. The Antichrist does not just mysteriously arrive, but spiritual forces intervene to cause him to rise to his God-ordained pinnacle of evil. Second, the closer we get to the advent of the Antichrist, the more we can expect evil to grow in our society and around the world. Third—and praise God for this—no matter how much all spiritual forces attempt to usher in the worldwide dominion of the Antichrist, they will not be able to do so until after the Restrainer is taken out of the way.

Also, Astounding Doctrinal Truth 4: Second Thessalonians 2:8–9 are the first verses in Scripture that connect Satan to the Antichrist. The book of Revelation will give details of how close that association will be between Satan and the Antichrist, and we will study this in more detail in two upcoming chapters in the *Handbook.*

Astounding Doctrinal Truth 5: Second Thessalonians 2:9–10 harmonizes with, expands on, and then restricts what Jesus had earlier warned about regarding miracles being performed during the tribulation and makes this connection: "that is, the one whose coming is in accord with the activity of Satan, with all power and signs and false wonders, and with all the deception of wickedness for those who perish, because they did not receive the love of the truth so as to be saved."

In Matt 24:24–25, while describing some of what will make the tribulation unique, Jesus warns accordingly, "For false Christs and false prophets will arise and will show great signs and wonders, so as to mislead, if possible, even the elect. Behold, I have told you in advance." In the information that Jesus reveals here, He instructs people to pay attention to this. The word "behold" should have an exclamation point after it each time it occurs in Scripture and should be interpreted to mean, "Mark this!" Even though Satan's name is not used, it is evident that false Christs and false prophets will show "great signs and wonders" and will do so to such an extent that, if it were possible, even the elect would be deceived. These events must be of tremendous magnitude if they could possibly deceive the elect. That such things do not presently occur is probably one of the side benefits of the Restrainer currently restraining.

We further noted how quickly and easily nonbelievers will be deceived by Satan and the Antichrist, as explained in the last part of 2 Thess 2:10: "because they did not receive the love of the truth so as to be saved." Writing this from the perspective that all of the events of the tribulation will have already have transpired, Paul said those who were deceived did not receive "the love of the truth so as to be saved." He could have written only "they did not receive the truth"—that would be accurate; this account is much more in keeping with the John 3:16 love of God.

Astounding Doctrinal Truth 6: Second Thessalonians 2:11–12 reveals that God will send an energized deception on certain ones of the lost in the tribulation: "For this reason God will send upon them a deluding influence [that is, an energized deception] so that they will believe what is false [literally, "the lie"], in order that they all may be judged who did not believe the truth, but took pleasure in wickedness."

During the tribulation, after the gospel of God has gone out to the entire world, after God has given people many opportunities to repent and to receive the love of the truth so as they would be saved, God will then actively work to secure the unsaved people in the disbelief that they have already chosen for themselves. There will be no deathbed conversions at that point.

Astounding Doctrinal Truth 7: As we saw earlier, and maybe now can appreciate more, it is in this same chapter in which God reveals so much about Satan and the Antichrist that He also includes mention of the redeemed receiving portions of His glory, as seen in 2 Thess 2:13–14:

> But we should always give thanks to God for you, brethren beloved by the
> Lord, because God has chosen you from the beginning for salvation through
> sanctification by the Spirit and faith in the truth. It was for this He called

you through our gospel, that you may gain the glory of our Lord Jesus Christ.

In this eternally stark contrast with those who will not receive the love of the truth so as to be saved, God intentionally makes the promise of giving portions of His glory to the redeemed. We know from our studies that this will begin at the return of the Lord Jesus Christ to earth (the fifth theological bombshell from Matthew 16), as 2 Thess 1:9–10 so wonderfully shows:

> *These will pay the penalty of eternal destruction, away from the presence of the Lord and from the glory of His power, when He comes to be glorified in His saints on that day, and to be marveled at among all who have believed—for our testimony to you was believed.*

This also means that Jesus "will slay [the Antichrist] with the breath of His mouth and bring [him] to an end by the appearance of His coming" (2 Thess 2:8), and the first part of the promises of Isa 24:21–23 will take place also.

Appropriately, the Holy Spirit by means of the apostle Paul, concludes with this warm and instructive exhortation and benediction in 2 Thess 2:15–18. It is suitable for modern-day Christians as well:

> *So then, brethren, stand firm and hold to the traditions which you were taught, whether by word of mouth or by letter from us. Now may our Lord Jesus Christ Himself and God our Father, who has loved us and given us eternal comfort and good hope by grace, comfort and strengthen your hearts in every good work and word.*

Deeper Walk Study Questions

1. What is unique about the way 1 Thessalonians ends each chapter? Why is this important? Make four cogent biblical deductions.

2. What was the basis for Paul writing 1 Thess 4:13–18? What does he write, and why is this important? Give five reasons.

3. How do we know from 1 Thess 5:1–3 that the young Thessalonian church knew very well about events associated with the day of the Lord? Give three reasons why this is important, and be specific.

4. Give five biblical characteristics of "the day of the Lord," as shown in this chapter, and tell why these are important.

5. From Joel 2–3, write eight important biblical truths and tell briefly why these are important.

6. Using the shortened term "the day," write eight important biblical truths from Isa 2:12–17; Zech 14:1–3; and Mal 4:1–3.

7. Name five cogent differences between 1 Thess 4:13–18 and 5:1–3. Explain. What does 1 Thess 5:8–9 teach? Give three reasons this is important.

8. What was the pressing occasion for Paul to write 2 Thessalonians? Give three reasons why the thought of being in the judgment part of the day of the Lord would be such a theological peril for the young church.

9. How does 2 Thess 2:1–2 show that evil agents were at work against this young church? Why does this matter? Why is this important? Give three reasons.

10. How did God use legitimate New Testament prophets for the early church before believers had the completed Bible? How did this pave the way for the advent of false teachers or false prophets? What was the Bible's answer that God gave to protect His church?

11. Name six profound biblical truths from 2 Cor 11:11–13 and, specifically, tell why these biblical truths are so important to know.

12. What is the first of the seven astounding truths of 2 Thessalonians 2? Specifically, what does it mean? Carefully tell why that meaning is important.

13. What was the mild rebuke that Paul gave to the Thessalonian church? What did this mean regarding what Paul had taught them both in content and during multiple teaching times? Why does this matter theologically? Explain two reasons and be specific.

14. What is the second of the seven astounding truths of 2 Thessalonians 2? Specifically, what does it mean? Carefully tell why this is important.

15. What is the third of the seven astounding truths of 2 Thessalonians 2? Specifically, what does it mean? Carefully tell why this is important.

16. What is the fourth of the seven astounding truths of 2 Thessalonians 2? Specifically, what does it mean? Carefully tell why this is important.

17. What is the fifth of the seven astounding truths of 2 Thessalonians 2? Specifically, what does it mean? Carefully tell why this is important.

18. What is the sixth of the seven astounding truths of 2 Thessalonians 2? Specifically, what does it mean? Carefully tell why this is important.

19. What is the seventh of the seven astounding truths of 2 Thessalonians 2? Specifically, what does it mean? Carefully tell why this is important.

CHAPTER 27

A Biblical Theology of the Ages of God

Although many people do not recognize this, one of the more controversial theological debates—sometimes initiating intensely hot dialogue—has to do with the ages of God. All of those who believe in God's Word and who study it already have ages built into their studies, whether or not they have previously considered the word age as part of their knowledge of the Bible. For instance, if we divide the Bible into only the Old Testament and the New Testament, we have two different ages.

So all who believe God's Word have ages as part of their theology; the question then becomes: How many ages are there? Part of the reason for so many diverse interpretations of the ages of God is that no single verse answers the question of how many ages God has ordained. For instance, are Adam and Eve pre-fall and Adam and Eve post-fall two ages? Or if we limited the discussion to the life of Jesus, would before the cross, after the cross to His ascension, and His return to earth constitute three distinct ages?

While no single Bible verse answers the question about the exact number of the ages of God, the Bible does give much information regarding those ages. In this chapter, we will formulate a biblical theology of the ages of God using Scripture, as we have done with every other subject in our study. After all, we must study what the Bible reveals (that is, follow the biblical trail) about the ages of God before considering or quoting theologians' arguments.

Eight Biblical Doctrines Concerning the Ages of God

I will present eight doctrines taken *from the Bible* on the ages of God. Sadly, this is by no means the approach taken by everyone producing his or her views on the ages of God.

Biblical Doctrine 1: *By God's design and doing, there are different ages.*
Paul instructed the Corinthians in 1 Cor 2:6–7:

> *We do, however, speak a wisdom among the mature, but not a wisdom of this age, or of the rulers of this age, who are coming to nothing [The NASB says they are "passing away."] On the contrary, we speak God's hidden wisdom in a mystery, a wisdom God predestined before the ages for our glory. (CSB)*

VERY IMPORTANT: "Predestined before the ages" requires that there be at least two ages in the past that no longer function as ages in order to have the plural usage. If your theology or biblical understanding does not have at least two ages, your belief does not match what the Bible clearly discloses.

Biblical Doctrine 2: *Biblically speaking, with ages (plural) there have been/will be change from one age to another age.*
Later, we will connect this with another biblical truth. Often there are major events associated with changing from one age to another. However, not every major event necessarily means the changing from one age to another age. A great example is the birth of God's Messiah—an incredibly important theological event; it did not end one age and begin another one. How do we know this? Galatians 4:4 says that Jesus was "born of a woman, born under the Law [that is, under the Mosaic covenant]," and the temple veil separating the holy place from the holy of holies was not torn in two but remained in place. It was not the birth of Jesus, but the death of Jesus, that would be the changing of the age.

Biblical Doctrine 3: *The Bible likewise discloses that this present age will also come to an end with the return of the Lord Jesus Christ.*

In interpreting the parable of the Weeds among the Wheat, Jesus explained this in Matt 13:39–40: "and the enemy who sowed them is the devil, and the harvest is the end of the age; and the reapers are angels. So just as the tares are gathered up and burned with fire, so shall it be at the end of the age." Notice the instructions that Jesus gave in what is called the Great Commission and how He ended what He said in Matt 28:18–20:

> And Jesus came up and spoke to them, saying, "All authority has been given to Me in heaven and on earth. Go therefore and make disciples of all the nations, baptizing them in the name of the Father and the Son and the Holy Spirit, teaching them to observe all that I commanded you; and lo, I am with you always, even to the end of the age."

Obviously, this particular age of which Jesus spoke has not ended. How do we know? The harvest will be the end of this age. The angels must be sent out to harvest, the return of the Lord Jesus must occur, and the separation and burning of "the weeds" must take place. If these things have not yet been accomplished—and they have not—this particular age has not ended. The ending of this present age must be accompanied by the fulfillment of these prophesied, worldwide events.

Biblical Doctrine 4: *The completion of this present age will be followed by the coming of another age.*

In the section explaining the unpardonable sin, Jesus warned in Matt 12:32, "Whoever speaks a word against the Son of Man, it shall be forgiven him; but whoever speaks against the Holy Spirit, it shall not be forgiven him, either in this age or in the age to come." As it is used here, "the age to come" is singular; however, Scripture plainly teaches that when this present age ends, the age to come will immediately follow.

Biblical Doctrine 5: *Actually, there is not only one age to come, but there are ages—plural—to come after this present age ends.*

When Paul wrote to the Ephesians about anyone's pre-salvation spiritual condition, he gave this condemning assessment in Eph 2:1–3:

> And you were dead in your trespasses and sins, in which you formerly walked according to the course of this world, according to the prince of the power of the air, of the spirit that is now working in the sons of disobedience. Among

498 The Bible Expositor's Handbook

them we too all formerly lived in the lusts of our flesh, indulging the desires of the flesh and of the mind, and were by nature children of wrath, even as the rest.

Then, in verses 4–6, Paul wrote about the incredibly gracious, amazing—and eternal—work of God brought about in Christ Jesus for the redeemed:

But God, being rich in mercy, because of His great love with which He loved us, even when we were dead in our transgressions, made us alive together with Christ (by grace you have been saved), and raised us up with Him, and seated us with Him in the heavenly places in Christ Jesus,

Not only did God, through Paul, reveal what He has done in redeeming us out of our spiritual deadness and making us alive with Jesus the Messiah, but God also reveals the reason He did this. Verse 7 states, "so that in the coming ages [NASB says "in the ages to come"] he might display the immeasurable riches of his grace through his kindness to us in Christ Jesus" (CSB).

CORE TRUTH: In order for your biblical theology to be accurate, you must have ages to come—plural—not just an age to come past this present age.

KEY CONSIDERATION: So what are the ages to come? Whatever your eschatological (the doctrine of last things) belief is, in order for it to match Scripture, it must have at least two ages. While this by itself does not prove the case, two ages that certainly fit from other biblical revelation of God are (1) the millennial kingdom (Revelation 20) and (2) the eternal state, with the new heavens, new earth, and new Jerusalem (Revelation 21–22).

CONSIDER ALSO: Why would you accept ages (plural) such as in 1 Cor 2:7 ("the hidden wisdom which God predestined before the ages to our glory"), which we would only know about because God revealed it in Scripture, and yet not accept from the same God through the same

> apostle "the ages to come" (plural) in Eph 2:7, which we also know
> about only because God revealed it in Scripture?

Often the reasoning against this plain teaching from Scripture is troublesome. As a starting point, why would you approach Scripture to see if you could change it or to make it say something other than what it plainly states—which is the approach liberal theologians use? Also, for those who say that ages (plural) is used only once in Scripture (Eph 2:7), it is not the number of times that God's Word says something that makes it true; it is true the moment it is God's Word (John 17:17). Furthermore, if some insist that Paul wrote only to generalize in Eph 2:7, what other components in our state of being lost would you consider generalized in all of the items mentioned in verses 1–3 or, even more to the point, in the eternal benefits of our salvation as detailed in verses 4–6? If Paul wrote only to generalize concepts, maybe we are not alive in Christ/Messiah Jesus, nor are we seated in the heavenly places with and in Christ Jesus. It is a dangerous rationale to take such an approach to God's Word because once this methodology is used, you have already determined your means of approaching virtually any passage in Scripture.

> **CAUTION:** Beware of taking away any part of Scripture to make it fit
> your theological system. Instead, adjust your theological system to
> harmonize with Scripture. Remember the sober warning in Jas 3:1
> regarding how seriously God takes the words of those who teach.

Biblical Doctrine 6: *When this present age ends, there will not be just a changing of the age that many people will not recognize (such as was the case at the end of the Mosaic covenant when the new covenant was ratified with the temple veil being torn from top to bottom); the changing of the present age to the next age will bring about the changing of the entire world.*

In Rom 8:18–23 Paul described the future glory that would be revealed:

> *For I consider that the sufferings of this present time are not worthy to be compared with the glory that is to be revealed to us. For the anxious longing*

of the creation waits eagerly for the revealing of the sons of God. For the creation was subjected to futility, not willingly, but because of Him who subjected it, in hope that the creation itself also will be set free from its slavery to corruption into the freedom of the glory of the children of God. For we know that the whole creation groans and suffers the pains of childbirth together until now. And not only this, but also we ourselves, having the first fruits of the Spirit, even we ourselves groan within ourselves, waiting eagerly for our adoption as sons, the redemption of our body.

Although the word age is not used here, the passage shows these same concepts. There was a brief time when creation was not subjected to futility (Genesis 1–2). That was an age. But with the same line of reasoning, there is coming a time when the entire world—and all who are in it—will eventually be changed. So, in other words, the present age (creation subjected to futility groans) will definitely be changed (not be subjected to futility) at some undisclosed time in the future already established by God. You could not have all three ages operative at the same time: pre-fall, post-fall, and the glory to be revealed.

Biblical Doctrine 7: *The ending of the present age is not only New Testament theology; the Old Testament includes this theology as well, even though the literal phrase "end of the age" does not occur. Many of the same concepts are found there, although obviously God will give more and clearer divine revelation as Scripture is unfolded.*

As we saw in previous verses about the day of the Lord that did not include that actual phrase, so it is for the end of the age in the Old Testament. We know this from the eschatological events unveiled in Scripture regarding those events specifically connected with "the end of the age."

Just limiting this to a few examples from the book of Daniel, we can see that God sent forth an angelic messenger with divine revelation about the last times, as Dan 8:17–19 reveals:

So he came near to where I was standing, and when he came I was frightened and fell on my face; but he said to me, "Son of man, understand that the vision pertains to the time of the end."

Now while he was talking with me, I sank into a deep sleep with my face to the ground; but he touched me and made me stand upright. He said, "Be-

hold, I am going to let you know what will occur at the final period of the indignation, for it pertains to the appointed time of the end."

Daniel 12:1 gives us a look behind the scenes of the prophetic events God has planned for national Israel:

Now at that time Michael, the great prince who stands guard over the sons of your people, will arise. And there will be a time of distress such as never occurred since there was a nation until that time; and at that time your people, everyone who is found written in the book, will be rescued.

Michael the prince is actually a high-ranking angel God revealed to us through Scripture. Jude 9 describes this choice angelic servant as "Michael the archangel," whom God specifically tasked with watching over national Israel (Dan 12:1). This verse tells of a time unlike any other time in history because of its designated utter horror. More details will be forthcoming in the book of Revelation.

After the events of those days, a resurrection is promised, as seen in Dan 12:2–3:

Many of those who sleep in the dust of the ground will awake, these to everlasting life, but the others to disgrace and everlasting contempt. Those who have insight will shine brightly like the brightness of the expanse of heaven, and those who lead the many to righteousness, like the stars forever and ever.

In 12:9, the angel instructs Daniel: "Go your way, Daniel, for these words are concealed and sealed up until the end time." Daniel 12:13, the final verse in the book, instructs God's prophet about what will ultimately transpire: "But as for you, go your way to the end; then you will enter into rest and rise again for your allotted portion at the end of the age" [literally, at the "end of the days"]. After the tribulation the Old Testament saints will be resurrected, at which time they will receive their rewards. All of these events will be connected with "the end of the age" verses elsewhere in the New Testament.

Biblical Doctrine 8: *Jesus used "the end of the age" three times when He was teaching about the kingdom of heaven in the Matthew 13 in the*

"Weeds among the Wheat" parable. Each time He connected "the end of the age" with events associated with His second coming to earth.

In verses 24–30, Jesus taught thusly in the parable:

> *Jesus presented another parable to them, saying, "The kingdom of heaven may be compared to a man who sowed good seed in his field. But while his men were sleeping, his enemy came and sowed tares among the wheat, and went away. But when the wheat sprouted and bore grain, then the tares became evident also. The slaves of the landowner came and said to him, 'Sir, did you not sow good seed in your field? How then does it have tares?' And he said to them, 'An enemy has done this!' The slaves said to him, 'Do you want us, then, to go and gather them up?' But he said, 'No; for while you are gathering up the tares, you may uproot the wheat with them. Allow both to grow together until the harvest; and in the time of the harvest I will say to the reapers, "First gather up the tares and bind them in bundles to burn them up; but gather the wheat into my barn."'"*

Fortunately, in Matthew 13:37–43 Jesus explains the parable, so we have no question about what He meant by this parable.

> *And He said, "The one who sows the good seed is the Son of Man, and the field is the world; and as for the good seed, these are the sons of the kingdom; and the tares are the sons of the evil one; and the enemy who sowed them is the devil, and the harvest is the end of the age; and the reapers are angels. So just as the tares are gathered up and burned with fire, so shall it be at the end of the age. The Son of Man will send forth His angels, and they will gather out of His kingdom all stumbling blocks, and those who commit lawlessness, and will throw them into the furnace of fire; in that place there will be weeping and gnashing of teeth. Then* THE RIGHTEOUS WILL SHINE FORTH AS THE SUN *in the kingdom of their Father. He who has ears, let him hear.*

Three times the term "end of the age" occurs in Matthew 13. The first two are "the harvest is the end of the age" (v. 39) and the initial punishment of the gathered "weeds" to be burned "at the end of the age" (v. 40). The weeds represent those who are the children of the evil one, the devil (v. 38). For the harvest at the end of the age "[t]he Son of Man will send out His angels, and they will gather out of His kingdom all stumbling blocks, and those who commit lawlessness" (v. 41), and the gathered will begin their eternal torment (v. 42).

Having previously noted two specific times in Matthew where "the end of the age" is used, we are ready to see that Matt 13:43 connects with this and more fully expounds the result: "Then THE RIGHTEOUS WILL SHINE AS THE SUN in the kingdom of their Father." Here Jesus makes direct reference/quotes from Dan 12:3 and, thus, connects it to the events of Daniel 12. At that time Michael the guardian of Israel will stand during the tribulation; it will be a time unlike any other time in the history of the world. Remember that Daniel 12 ends with the rewarding of the Old Testament saints—such as Daniel—who will receive their allotted portion, now biblically connected with some of the other events at the end of the age.

The third use of "the end of the age" in Matthew 13 shows another aspect of what will happen then:

> *Again, the kingdom of heaven is like a dragnet cast into the sea, and gathering fish of every kind; and when it was filled, they drew it up on the beach; and they sat down and gathered the good fish into containers, but the bad they threw away. So it will be at the end of the age; the angels will come forth and take out the wicked from among the righteous, and will throw them into the furnace of fire; in that place there will be weeping and gnashing of teeth. (vv. 47–50)*

So, the return of the King is wonderful news only if you are rightly related to Him as part of the sons of the kingdom (vv. 37–38), who have received the Good Seed/Word of God given to them. All others, "the weeds," "are the sons of the evil one; and the enemy who sowed them is the devil" (vv. 38–39). As is often the case in Scripture, God gives two options and two options only.

Succinctly stated, the changing from this present age to the next age occurs at the return of the Lord Jesus Messiah/Christ to establish the kingdom of God on earth. What began in Matt 3:1–2 with John the Baptist and later with Jesus Himself (4:17) included sending out the Twelve only to the lost sheep of the house of Israel (10:5–7). It also included the telling of the kingdom parables to reveal what will happen until the King returns. Thus, at His return those things will all be past tense. No more saying, "The kingdom of God is at hand," or no more, "wait until the harvest," because the harvest occurs at the end of the age.

And no longer will we need this final "end of the age" usage in Matthew's Gospel: "and lo, I [Christ] am with you always, even to the end of the age" (28:20). This verse will no longer be needed, for the King Messiah Himself—Immanuel—will be among us.

Come soon, Lord Jesus!

Summary and Conclusion

In this chapter we learned that (1) one of the more controversial theological debates has to do with the ages of God. All of those who believe in God's Word and who study it already have ages built into their studies, whether or not they have previously considered the word age as part of their knowledge of the Bible. (2) Because all who believe God's Word have ages as part of their theology, the question then becomes, How many ages are there? Part of the reason for so many diverse interpretations of the ages of God is that there is no single verse that answers the question of how many ages God has ordained. (3) Still, the Bible does give much information regarding those ages.

We also learned eight biblical doctrines taken from the Bible on the ages of God, which is not always the case with regard to how people obtain their doctrine. (1) By God's design and doing, there are different ages (1 Cor 2:6–7). "Predestined before the ages" requires that there be at least two ages; otherwise the plural usage would be incorrect. If your theology or biblical understanding does not have at least two ages, your belief does not match what the Bible clearly discloses. (2) It reasons that with ages (plural) there have been/will be changes from one age to another age. Often there are major events associated with the changing from one age to another. However, not every major event necessarily means the changing from one age to another. It was not at the birth of Jesus but at the death of Jesus that the changing of an age occurred. (3) The Bible likewise discloses that this present age will also come to an end with the return of the Lord Jesus Christ (Matt 13:39–40; 28:18–20). (4) The completion of this present age will be followed by the coming of another age (12:32).

We further saw that the Bible reveals that (5), actually, there is not only one age to come, but there are ages—plural—to come after this present age ends (Eph 2:1–7). In order for your biblical theology to be accurate, you must affirm ages to come—plural—not just an age to come. We also asked why you would accept ages (plural) such as in 1 Cor 2:7 ("the hidden wisdom which God predestined before the ages for our glory"), which we would only know about because God revealed it in Scripture, and yet not accept from the same God through the same apostle "the ages to come" (plural) in Eph 2:7, which we would also only know about because God revealed it in Scripture.

We saw that (6) when this present age ends there will not be just a changing of the age that many people will not recognize (such as the end of the Mosaic covenant and the new covenant that was ratified with the temple veil being torn from top to bottom). The changing of the present age to the next age will bring about the changing of the entire world (Rom 8:18–23).

(7) The ending of the present age is not only New Testament theology; the Old Testament includes this theology. Although the exact phrase "end of the age" does not occur in the Old Testament, events clearly associated elsewhere in Scripture with the return of the Lord and the end of the age help us know these are connected. For instance, (8) the actual term "end of the age" does not occur in the Bible until Matthew 13, as part of the kingdom parables that Jesus gave (Matt 13:24–30, 36–43). Two of the three times the phrase "end of the age" occurs in Matthew are in chapter 13: "the harvest is the end of the age" (v. 39) and the initial punishment of the gathered "weeds" to be burned "at the end of the age" (v. 40). The weeds represent those who are the children of the evil one, the devil (v. 38). The harvest at the end of the age includes "[t]he Son of Man [sending] forth His angels, and they will gather out of His kingdom all stumbling blocks, and those who commit lawlessness" (v. 41) and their eternal torment will begin (v. 42). Also, (9) Dan 12:3 used by Jesus in Matt 13:43 connects these events with those of Daniel 12. Additionally, we saw that Matt 13:47–50 includes the third use of "the end of the age" to show another aspect of what will occur then, namely, the angels will separate the evil people from the righteous and throw them into the blazing furnace. In that place there will be weeping and gnashing of teeth. Succinctly stated,

the changing from this present age to the next age occurs at the return of the Lord Jesus Messiah/Christ to establish the kingdom of God on earth.

Finally, (10) once Jesus Christ returns, no longer will we need this final "the end of the age" usage in Matthew's Gospel: "and lo, I am with you always, even to the end of the age" (28:20). This verse will no longer be necessary, for the King Messiah Himself—Immanuel—will be among us.

Come soon, Lord Jesus!

Deeper Walk Study Questions

1. Why is understanding the ages of God so important theologically? Why are there so many diverse interpretations about the ages of God? Explain and be specific.

2. How do we know different ages of God exist? Support your answer biblically and tell why this is important theologically.

3. How do we know there have been changes from one age to another? How do we know that not necessarily every major event—even a biblically important one—means the ages have changed? Support your answer biblically.

4. How do we know this present age has not yet ended? Support your answer biblically.

5. How do we know the completion of this present age will be followed by another age? Support your answer biblically.

6. How do we know that this present age will not be replaced by another age (singular) but by ages (plural)? Support your answer biblically.

7. Why *must* your eschatological system contain at least two more ages beyond the present one in order to be biblically correct?

8. Why is it biblically illogical to accept ages (plural), such as in 1 Cor 2:7 ("the hidden wisdom which God predestined before the ages to our glory"), which we would only know about because God revealed it in Scripture, and yet not accept from the same God through the same apostle "the ages to come" (plural) reference in Eph 2:7, which we would also only know about because God revealed it in Scripture? Explain and be specific.

9. How will creation be affected with the changing of the next age? Support your answer biblically.

10. What does Daniel 12 teach regarding the end of the age and events associated with that? Support your answer biblically. Be specific.

11. What can we learn about the end of the age from the parable of the Weeds among the Wheat (Matt 13:24–30), especially from Jesus's explanation of His parable? Write six cogent biblical truths from this.

CHAPTER 28

Twelve Things Most People Do Not Know about the Book of Hebrews

The book of Hebrews is a treasure God gave almost two thousand years ago. Many Christians enjoy reading and memorizing certain verses from it, and they realize its value. And yet, the book of Hebrews seems strange to many of us, especially to those of us who are of the Gentile culture since the language and customs of Jewish people during the first century are so alien to our understanding.

This chapter will address twelve things that most people do not know about the book of Hebrews. It will not answer every question about this sublime book, but it will make Hebrews more enjoyable, and it will make God's holy logic more understandable. So, I am not trying to make the book of Hebrews say anything; you and I are following the biblical trail that God has set before us.

1. The Book of Hebrews Is a Sermon

In the last chapter of Hebrews, the author made a request of those who had read or who would read the epistle: "Brothers and sisters, I urge you to receive this message of exhortation [the NASB says, "this Word of exhortation"], for I have written to you briefly" (13:22 CSB). We see in another section of Scripture what this message of exhortation entailed. In Acts 13:13–15, during Paul's first missionary journey, the following occurred:

Paul and his companions set sail from Paphos and came to Perga in Pamphylia, but John left them and went back to Jerusalem. They continued their journey from Perga and reached Pisidian Antioch. On the Sabbath day they went into the synagogue and sat down. After the reading of the Law and the Prophets, the leaders of the synagogue sent word to them, saying, "Brothers, if you have any word of encouragement [the NASB says, "word of exhortation"] for the people, you can speak." (CSB)

What follows in verses 16–41 is the sermon/message of encouragement the apostle Paul preached in that setting. When we realize that the book of Hebrews was written in the same manner as a message of exhortation, it adds to our understanding of what it is and why it is written and helps us navigate through the book more easily.

For instance, every preacher should readily note the time restraint the author/Author of Hebrews felt in his sermon, as seen in Heb 11:32: "And what more shall I say? For time will fail me if I tell of Gideon, Barak, Samson, Jephthah, of David and Samuel and the prophets."

2. The Book of Hebrews Is a Holy Spirit-Inspired Sermon

If you have ever wondered how God the Holy Spirit would preach, the book of Hebrews is that sermon. Some appropriately see eight different sermons, or other divisions, within this overall sermon from which we can find so much biblical gold. While by no means taking anything away from this, for this chapter of the *Handbook,* I limit the description of the book of Hebrews as one unified sermon because (1) this is how the author of Hebrews refers to it in Heb 13:22 ("this Word of exhortation"—singular—not "these words of exhortation"—plural); this also matches the Acts 13:15 singular usage as well; (2) the entire book can be read in one sitting and was probably how the original church audience heard it; and (3) it allows for the logic of the book as a whole to unfold before us. No doubt the church received *so* many wonderful truths that they could use in their later studies for decades to come, as we can—and as we should.

Because Hebrews is a Holy Spirit-inspired revelation from God, we will sometimes refer to the author of Hebrews—the unknown human vessel used for its composition—and the Author of Hebrews—the Godhead member who is the ultimate Author of the book. The first word out of the Holy Spirit's mouth in Heb 1:1 is "God." Hebrews begins with and stays with God, and, in keeping with the Holy Spirit's role to exalt Jesus, we will see that exaltation in the book of Hebrews.

3. The Book of Hebrews Is Not an Evangelistic Book Written to the Jewish People

The original recipients of the book of Hebrews were Jewish people who had already named the name of Christ/Messiah, had been baptized in His name, and were church going people. So Hebrews is not a "come forward and meet and receive the gospel" message because the original audience, as a collective group, had already received the gospel.

However, depending on the group and circumstances, among most assemblies—including those of today—there are those people who are truly saved and those who have made a profession of receiving Jesus as their Lord and Savior but who are not actually saved. This should not be surprising. In the Sermon on the Mount, Jesus warned in Matt 7:21–23,

> *"Not everyone who says to Me, 'Lord, Lord,' will enter the kingdom of heaven, but he who does the will of My Father who is in heaven will enter. Many will say to Me on that day, 'Lord, Lord, did we not prophesy in Your name, and in Your name cast out demons, and in Your name perform many miracles?' And then I will declare to them, 'I never knew you; depart from Me, you who practice lawlessness.'"*

The apostle Paul, in Gal 2:4, explained a situation that he had to deal with: "It was because of the false brethren secretly brought in, who had sneaked in to spy out our liberty which we have in Christ Jesus, in order to bring us into bondage." Years later, when Paul had to contrast his own life with the lives of false apostles (2 Cor 11:13–15), he wrote about the hardships that he endured in the ministry in verses 23–26. Note especially the last item in this long list:

> *Are they [the false apostles] servants of Christ?—I speak as if insane—I more so; in far more labors, in far more imprisonments, beaten times without number, often in danger of death. Five times I received from the Jews thirty-nine lashes. Three times I was beaten with rods, once I was stoned, three times I was shipwrecked, a night and a day I have spent in the deep. I have been on frequent journeys, in dangers from rivers, dangers*

from robbers, dangers from my countrymen, dangers from the Gentiles, dangers in the city, dangers in the wilderness, dangers on the sea, dangers among false brethren; ... [emphasis added].

IMPORTANT: False brethren never introduce themselves as false brethren; they always introduce themselves as being saved. Judas Iscariot, as Bible events show, is a great example of someone who claimed to be a follower of Jesus, and yet he never truly was one.

Within the congregations who were the original recipients of the book of Hebrews were those accepted as a part of their assemblies (excluding guests/visitors), who were genuinely saved and others who had only made a profession of faith. Without naming names, both groups will be addressed in the Holy Spirit-inspired word of exhortation book of Hebrews.

4. The Jewish Professing Believers Were under Persecution from Fellow Jews

The author/Author of Hebrews acknowledged some of the hardships the people had endured for the name of Messiah Jesus, such as in Heb 10:32–35:

> *But remember the former days, when, after being enlightened, you endured a great conflict of sufferings, partly by being made a public spectacle through reproaches and tribulations, and partly by becoming sharers with those who were so treated. For you showed sympathy to the prisoners and accepted joyfully the seizure of your property, knowing that you have for yourselves a better possession and a lasting one. Therefore, do not throw away your confidence, which has a great reward.*

The unsaved Jews reasoned that they could oppose the professing Jewish Christians because God, in His sovereignty, had allowed the temple sacrifices and the Levitical priesthood and high priesthood to function for almost forty years. Even though the new covenant was inaugurated and operative (in parts), the sacrifices under the Mosaic covenant still functioned. Jewish opponents would have asked the Jewish Christians how

Jesus could be the Messiah if the temple of Yahweh still functioned. We know the Romans destroyed the temple in AD 70, and that affects part of the times of the Gentiles—up to this day. But, when the original recipients received the book of Hebrews, the temple had not yet fallen. All they had to do to stop the persecution was to return to the temple sacrifices—but only after renouncing Christianity and the claims Jesus made regarding Himself.

Because the people who had received the book of Hebrews were still assembled together as believers, they had not yet apostatized. This renunciation of Jesus would not be the same as the temporary slippage of Peter who denied the Lord he loved three times the night of Jesus's arrest. This would have to involve the full renouncement—before the Sanhedrin, or a subset of it, who would ask them specific questions about their rejection of Jesus as God's Messiah and their returning to Judaism under the Mosaic covenant.

Furthermore, this apostasy would not be just stepping from one system (Christianity) to another system (Judaism). The author/Author of Hebrews warned them about what falling away would entail in Heb 3:12. As with so many other temptations, it begins in the heart before it shows in the actions: "Take care, brethren, that there not be in any one of you an evil, unbelieving heart that falls away from the living God."

In the same manner, Jesus, in explaining the parable of the Soils, addressed this falling away as well, in Luke 8:11–13:

> *Now the parable is this: the seed is the word of God. Those beside the road are those who have heard; then the devil comes and takes away the word from their heart, so that they will not believe and be saved. Those on the rocky soil are those who, when they hear, receive the word with joy; and these have no firm root; they believe for a while, and in time of temptation fall away.*

Those who "believe for a while, and in time of temptation fall away"/ apostatize, who never come back to obedience in Christ, do not lose their salvation. They were never saved to begin with, in spite of their previously held professions.

Remember, different people can be addressed within the same sermon: the truly saved and those who claimed to be saved but who were not saved.

In this Holy Spirit-inspired sermon, not every verse in Hebrews is intended for both sets of people.

For instance, for the false brethren who were thinking in their hearts of abandoning Jesus in order to stop their persecution, Heb 10:26–31 strongly warns,

> *For if we go on sinning willfully after receiving the knowledge of the truth, there no longer remains a sacrifice for sins, but a terrifying expectation of judgment and the fury of a fire which will consume the adversaries. Anyone who has set aside the Law of Moses [the Mosaic covenant] dies without mercy on the testimony of two or three witnesses. How much severer punishment do you think he will deserve who has trampled underfoot the Son of God, and has regarded as unclean the blood of the covenant by which he was sanctified, and has insulted the Spirit of grace? For we know Him who said, "Vengeance is Mine, I will repay." And again, "The Lord will judge His people." It is a terrifying thing to fall into the hands of the living God.*

Those who were truly saved had no need for the previous warning in Hebrews—they were not thinking of abandoning the faith. They needed, among many other exhortations, this one in Heb 10:36: "For you have need of endurance, so that when you have done the will of God, you may receive what was promised." Notice how both groups are included in Heb 10:39: "But we are not of those who shrink back to destruction, but of those who have faith to the preserving of the soul." As so many other times in Scripture, two options and two options only are available: those who shrink back to eternal destruction or those who exercise by faith the true gospel and with it the preserving of the soul. Everyone will be in one category or the other, and one cannot be in both categories at the same time.

CONSIDER: A good way of viewing these categories of professing believers—the true and the false—is to see how this applies to Judas as contrasted with someone such as Peter or John. Judas, in his spiritual lostness—in spite of his previous confession of faith and ministry activities—did not have need of endurance; he had need of receiving the only true remedy for the "terrifying expectation of judgment and THE FURY OF A FIRE WHICH WILL CONSUME THE ADVERSARIES" and falling "into the hands of the living God." In the same way, for someone who is truly saved (such as Peter or John) and who is walking in fellowship with Him, the warnings of Heb 10:26–31 do not apply. In fact, they don't apply to anyone else ever saved. Neither does the description fit them of going on "sinning willfully" or "trampling under foot the Son of God"; they will not fall eternally into the hands of an angry God. What they need, as did the truly saved original recipients of Hebrews, and as we now who are saved need, among other things in our temporary alien and stranger status, is encouragement and admonishment. The need that is applicable to all true believers in the past and in the present is the need for endurance to run the race that God has set before us. We must fix our eyes on Jesus, the Author and Perfecter of faith (Heb 12:1–2), or, as verse 3 admonishes, "Consider Him who has endured such hostility by sinners against Himself, so that [we] will not grow weary and lose heart."

5. The First Major Section of Hebrews Presents Primarily the Davidic Covenant and the Second Coming of the Lord Jesus Christ

Many commentators and students of the Bible know that Hebrews can be divided according to the superior person of Jesus Christ, His superior priesthood, and His superior sacrifice—and all of these are in the text and have their eternal relevancy. Still, not noted usually is that the author/Author of Hebrews emphasizes the Davidic covenant and the second coming of the Lord Jesus Christ to earth in the first major section of the book (1:1–4:13). Remember, this is entirely fitting because most of the promises of the Davidic covenant are currently unfulfilled prophecies that will be fulfilled when Jesus returns and reigns.

The Davidic covenant emphasis in Heb 1:1–4:13 is readily seen. Hebrews 1:5 includes Old Testament quotes such as "YOU ARE MY SON; TODAY I HAVE BEGOTTEN YOU." This is taken from Ps 2:7, a messianic psalm about the Messiah's reign and His unique relationship with God the Father. The quote "I will be His Father, and he will be My Son," to borrow from the wording in the CSB, is from 2 Sam 7:14—the chapter that first gives the details about what will later be called the Davidic covenant. Hebrews 1:6 adds, "When He again brings the firstborn into the world." This statement refers to the Second Coming; God's Messiah will again come into the world. "The firstborn" is a title of honor, usually given to the physical lineage firstborn, but sometimes—such as in the case of Joseph son of Jacob—one's behavior has warranted the special blessing of the firstborn. Hebrews 1:6 comes from Ps 89:27–29, a psalm specifically describing the eternal nature of the Davidic covenant:

> *"I also shall make him My firstborn,*
> *The highest of the kings of the earth.*
> *"My lovingkindness I will keep for him forever,*
> *And My covenant shall be confirmed to him.*
> *"So I will establish his descendants forever*
> *And his throne as the days of heaven."*

Hebrews 1:8—quoted from Ps 45:6—concerns the throne and scepter:

> *But of the Son He says,*
> *"YOUR THRONE, O GOD, IS FOREVER AND EVER,*
> *AND THE RIGHTEOUS SCEPTER IS THE SCEPTER OF HIS KINGDOM."*

You can read Heb 1:1–4:13 and find other Davidic covenant/Second Coming references, but already you should be convinced of the validity of this approach to the book of Hebrews. Perhaps you will read this section in a different way now and appreciate how lacking our understanding of the book of Hebrews would be if we left out the importance of the Davidic covenant.

One more verse, though, will support this approach to this section: Heb 2:5: "For He did not subject to angels the world to come, concerning which we are speaking." The author/Author of Hebrews has been talking about "the world to come" that, as we have seen in other verses, directly relates to the promises God has made and will fulfill at the second coming of Jesus Christ to earth. Also, you must read this section of Hebrews concerning the world to come, if you are reading it as God intends it, as "the world to come that we are"—not were—talking about. So not only has the author/Author of Hebrews been talking (because it is a sermon) of the world to come; he still is talking about the world to come in the remaining portion of Heb 1:1–4:13.

6. Hebrews 2:12 Has a Unique Usage of Psalm 22

Following this biblical trail will take just a bit longer, but I think you will find it worth the effort.

Hebrews 2:11–12 states, "For both He who sanctifies and those who are sanctified are all from one Father; for which reason He is not ashamed to call them brethren, saying: 'I WILL PROCLAIM YOUR NAME TO MY BRETHREN, / IN THE MIDST OF THE CONGREGATION I WILL SING YOUR PRAISE.'" The Old Testament verse cited is Ps 22:22, which I will refer to later.

If you are a Christian who has read your Bible, you are familiar with Psalm 22, whether or not you realize it. In Matt 27:46, Jesus's last cry forever connects Him—and His death—to the question He screamed from Ps 22:1: "ELI, ELI, LAMA SABACHTHANI? that is, 'My God, My God, why have You forsaken Me?'" Although this Ps 22:1 usage may be familiar, you may not have noted that Matthew 27 contains three other quotations/allusions to specific items connected with the crucifixion of Jesus, and all are taken from Psalm 22. The first use in Matt 27:35 ("And when they had crucified Him, they divided up His garments among themselves by casting lots") comes from Ps 22:18. The second use in Matt 27:39 ("And those passing by were hurling abuse at Him, wagging their heads)" is from Ps 22:7. The third use in Matt 27:43 ("HE TRUSTS IN GOD; LET GOD RESCUE Him now, IF HE DELIGHTS IN HIM; for He said, 'I am the Son of God'") is taken from Ps 22:8.

Using four quotations/allusions sequentially taken from one psalm is highly unusual in Scripture. It is obvious that the Holy Spirit—if we are judging by His fourfold quotes taken from Psalm 22—emphasizes the need for careful attention to that psalm. So, let's investigate.

Psalm 22 actually divides into three distinct parts. The initial part, verses 1–18, speaks of the horrible events that will occur with the crucifixion of Messiah Jesus. Appropriately, all the quotes cited in Matthew's Gospel come from this first section of Psalm 22:

My God, my God, why have You forsaken me?

Far from my deliverance are the words of my groaning.

O my God, I cry by day, but You do not answer;

And by night, but I have no rest.

Yet You are holy,

O You who are enthroned upon the praises of Israel.

In You our fathers trusted;

They trusted and You delivered them.

To You they cried out and were delivered;

In You they trusted and were not disappointed.

But I am a worm and not a man,

A reproach of men and despised by the people.

All who see me sneer at me;

They separate with the lip, they wag the head, saying,

"Commit yourself to the LORD; let Him deliver him;

Let Him rescue him, because He delights in him."

Yet You are He who brought me forth from the womb;

You made me trust when upon my mother's breasts.

Upon You I was cast from birth;

You have been my God from my mother's womb.

Be not far from me, for trouble is near;

For there is none to help.

Many bulls have surrounded me;

Strong bulls of Bashan have encircled me.

They open wide their mouth at me,

As a ravening and a roaring lion.

I am poured out like water,

And all my bones are out of joint;

My heart is like wax;

It is melted within me.

My strength is dried up like a potsherd,

And my tongue cleaves to my jaws;

And You lay me in the dust of death.

For dogs have surrounded me;

A band of evildoers has encompassed me;

They pierced my hands and my feet.

I can count all my bones.

They look, they stare at me;

They divide my garments among them,

And for my clothing they cast lots.

The second part, Ps 22:19–21, is a prayer by the same one who endured what was described in the initial section of the psalm:

But You, O LORD, be not far off;

O You my help, hasten to my assistance.

Deliver my soul from the sword,

My only life from the power of the dog.

Save me from the lion's mouth;

From the horns of the wild oxen You answer me.

But Psalm 22 also has a third and final section unfamiliar to many Christians. Look how beautifully God displays this: For One who endured what only He could endure (vv. 1–18), His story does not end there. He prays to the Lord to deliver and rescue Him (vv. 19–21). God chose not to answer His Son's prayer at that time during the crucifixion, but He definitely will answer—at some point in the future—and this requires a resurrection of the One who was killed in order to receive the blessings that Yahweh will give to Him. Psalm 22:22 is the first verse of the third section (vv. 22–31), and this verse is cited in Heb 2:12: "I WILL PROCLAIM YOUR NAME TO MY BRETHREN; / IN THE MIDST OF THE CONGREGATION I WILL SING YOUR PRAISE."

Mark well that this is the first time the future tense is used in Psalm 22, and future tenses are used for the remainder of this psalm that will show what else God promises:

> *I will tell of Your name to my brethren;*
>
> *In the midst of the assembly I will praise You.*
>
> *You who fear the LORD, praise Him;*
>
> *All you descendants of Jacob, glorify Him,*
>
> *And stand in awe of Him, all you descendants of Israel.*
>
> *For He has not despised nor abhorred the affliction of the afflicted;*
>
> *Nor has He hidden His face from him;*
>
> *But when he cried to Him for help, He heard.*
>
> *From You comes my praise in the great assembly;*
>
> *I shall pay my vows before those who fear Him.*
>
> *The afflicted will eat and be satisfied;*
>
> *Those who seek Him will praise the LORD.*
>
> *Let your heart live forever! (vv. 22–26)*

This third part (vv. 27–31) of the threefold division of Psalm 22 contains appropriately Davidic covenant promises and blessings:

> *All the ends of the earth will remember and turn to the LORD,*
>
> *And all the families of the nations will worship before You.*
>
> *For the kingdom is the LORD'S*
>
> *And He rules over the nations.*
>
> *All the prosperous of the earth will eat and worship,*
>
> *All those who go down to the dust will bow before Him,*
>
> *Even he who cannot keep his soul alive.*
>
> *Posterity will serve Him;*
>
> *It will be told of the LORD to the coming generation.*
>
> *They will come and will declare His righteousness*
>
> *To a people who will be born, that He has performed it.*

But as we saw earlier in Psalm 22, the One who will receive these blessings from Yahweh must have endured the unfathomable misery of the first part; all of the parts go together. Because Jesus at His crucifixion has already fulfilled in minute detail the first part of Psalm 22, the remaining part of Psalm 22 must also be fulfilled by the Lord Jesus Christ.

How fitting that the author/Author of Hebrews would quote from Ps 22:22–31 in Heb 1:1–4:13, which speaks primarily of the Davidic covenant and the second coming of the Lord Jesus Christ, with future tense promises that must be and will be fulfilled so that—among many other things—Jesus will praise God in the very midst of the redeemed, as revealed in Heb 2:12 and Ps 22:22: "I will tell Your name to my brethren; / In the midst of the assembly I will praise You."

7. The Second Major Section in Hebrews (4:14– 10:18) Deals Primarily with the New Covenant and the First Advent/Incarnation of Jesus

Earlier in *The Bible Expositor's Handbook—New Testament Edition,* we noted that the birth of Jesus did not end an age. He lived His entire life under the Mosaic covenant (Gal 4:4), and the new covenant would not be ratified and the initial part inaugurated until His death. We see glimpses of the effects of the new covenant earlier in Hebrews, such as in the last part of 1:3: "When He had made purification of sins [*completed work*], He sat down at the right hand of the Majesty on high [*accepted work*]." And in the Bible book's second major division, we get our first glimpse of another covenant in 7:22: "Jesus has become the guarantee of a better covenant." And then Heb 8:6 says, "But now He has obtained a more excellent ministry, by as much as He is also the mediator of a better covenant, which has been enacted on better promises." The better covenant is the new covenant, and notice that the past tense is used to describe its ratification ("which has been established").

In Heb 8:7 the logical explanation continues: "For if that first covenant had been faultless, there would have been no occasion sought for a second."

> **CRUCIAL IMPORTANCE:** In Hebrews, especially in this context, the
> contrast is made only between the new covenant and the Mosaic
> covenant—not between the new covenant and the first covenant of
> God, the Noahic covenant, and *not* the other covenants of God nor the
> divine promises contained within them. You would err substantially
> if you interpreted this Scripture differently and removed all of God's
> eternal covenant promises.

So in the continued logical progression from Scripture, long after God
had inaugurated the Mosaic covenant, He promised in His Word that He
would one day—at some undisclosed time from when it was first given—
establish a new covenant. If the question were asked, Does the Bible state
that another covenant will eventually come to replace the Mosaic covenant?, the answer is most assuredly yes. In the context of Heb 8:7–12, Jer
31:31–34 is quoted to show this promise in the Old Testament of what
would come one day:

*For if that first covenant [the Mosaic covenant] had been faultless, there would
have been no occasion sought for a second [the new covenant]. For finding fault
with them, He says,*

"BEHOLD, DAYS ARE COMING, SAYS THE LORD,

WHEN I WILL EFFECT A NEW COVENANT

WITH THE HOUSE OF ISRAEL AND WITH THE HOUSE OF JUDAH;

NOT LIKE THE COVENANT WHICH I MADE WITH THEIR FATHERS

ON THE DAY WHEN I TOOK THEM BY THE HAND

TO LEAD THEM OUT OF THE LAND OF EGYPT;

FOR THEY DID NOT CONTINUE IN MY COVENANT,

AND I DID NOT CARE FOR THEM, SAYS THE LORD.

"FOR THIS IS THE COVENANT THAT I WILL MAKE WITH THE HOUSE OF ISRAEL

AFTER THOSE DAYS, SAYS THE LORD:

I WILL PUT MY LAWS INTO THEIR MINDS,

AND I WILL WRITE THEM ON THEIR HEARTS.

AND I WILL BE THEIR GOD,

AND THEY SHALL BE MY PEOPLE.

"AND THEY SHALL NOT TEACH EVERYONE HIS FELLOW CITIZEN,

AND EVERYONE HIS BROTHER, SAYING, 'KNOW THE LORD,'

FOR ALL WILL KNOW ME,

FROM THE LEAST TO THE GREATEST OF THEM.

"FOR I WILL BE MERCIFUL TO THEIR INIQUITIES,

AND I WILL REMEMBER THEIR SINS NO MORE."

To summarize the holy logic of this argument, Heb 8:13 states, "When He said, 'A new covenant,' He has made the first covenant [the Mosaic covenant] obsolete. But whatever is becoming obsolete and growing old is ready to disappear." When God's temple in Jerusalem was destroyed, the sacrificial system under the Mosaic covenant ceased.

> **REMEMBER:** As we saw previously in *The Bible Expositor's Handbook— Old Testament Edition,* in Jeremiah 31, not only did God make the promises regarding the forgiveness of sin based on the wonderful benefits of the coming new covenant, but in this same chapter He also promised that if the fixed order of the sun, moon, and stars be shaken, then God would cast off national Israel for all the sins they have committed (Jer 31:35–37). Further, "Behold, days are coming" when Jerusalem will be rebuilt for the Lord, and when this happens the city "shall be holy to the LORD; it will not be plucked up or overthrown anymore forever" (vv. 38–40). These two promised sections of Jeremiah 31 are just as much a part of God's Word—and His promises—as are those in verses 31–34, and they must come true in the future.

8. The Book of Hebrews Uses God's Holy Logic to Show That the Biblical Necessity of Changing the Priesthood Also Requires Changing the Covenant

Hebrews 9:1–4 shows what those who know their Old Testament know: the Mosaic covenant is the basis for the tabernacle first and the temple later:

> Now even the first covenant [the Mosaic covenant] had regulations of divine worship and the earthly sanctuary. For there was a tabernacle prepared, the outer one, in which were the lampstand and the table and the sacred bread; this is called the holy place. Behind the second veil there was a tabernacle which is called the Holy of Holies, having a golden altar of incense and the ark of the covenant covered on all sides with gold, in which was a golden jar holding the manna, and Aaron's rod which budded, and the tables of the [Mosaic] covenant.

However, it was not just the outer structure for which the design was commanded, but also there were requirements for the priesthood and its order, with what was called the Levitical priesthood that must come by Aaron's descendants. Numbers 3:10 not only specifies these requirements but also demonstrates God's seriousness about them and about anyone who would attempt to fraudulently attain priesthood who was not from God's designated order under the Mosaic covenant: "So you shall appoint Aaron and his sons that they may keep their priesthood, but the layman who comes near shall be put to death." Not long afterward, during Korah's rebellion (Numbers 16), Yahweh showed Himself true to His own Word again by punishing 250 sinners who presented themselves as priests though they did not qualify, as seen in Num 16:35–40:

> Fire also came forth from the Lord and consumed the two hundred and fifty men who were offering the incense.

> Then the Lord spoke to Moses, saying, "Say to Eleazar, the son of Aaron the priest, that he shall take up the censers out of the midst of the blaze, for they are holy; and you scatter the burning coals abroad. As for the censers of these men who have sinned at the cost of their lives, let them be made into hammered sheets for a plating of the altar, since they did present them before the Lord and they are holy; and they shall be for a sign to the sons

of Israel." So Eleazar the priest took the bronze censers which the men who were burned had offered, and they hammered them out as a plating for the altar, as a reminder to the sons of Israel that no layman who is not of the descendants of Aaron should come near to burn incense before the LORD; so that he will not become like Korah and his company—just as the LORD had spoken to him through Moses.

Numbers 18:7, in which God was reaffirming Aaron and his descendants for the priesthood under the Mosaic covenant, states, "But you and your sons with you shall attend to your priesthood for everything concerning the altar and inside the veil, and you are to perform service. I am giving you the priesthood as a bestowed service, but the outsider who comes near shall be put to death."

As the author/Author of Hebrews has said, so it would be here: "time does not permit me to speak" in any detail about the priesthood of Melchizedek, as seen in Heb 7:11–14:

Now if perfection [completion] was through the Levitical priesthood (for on the basis of it the people received the [Mosaic covenant] Law), what further need was there for another priest to arise according to the order of Melchizedek, and not be designated according to the order of Aaron? For when the priesthood is changed, of necessity there takes place a change of law also. For the one concerning whom these things are spoken belongs to another tribe, from which no one has officiated at the altar. For it is evident that our LORD was descended from Judah, a tribe with reference to which Moses spoke nothing concerning priests.

Note these crucial matters in this section. Initially, not only does the Old Testament reveal that another covenant would come at some undisclosed time in the future—the new covenant—it also tells of another priesthood outside of Aaron and his descendants and beyond the parameters of the Mosaic covenant. Secondly, this part is so important that I must emphasize it:

KEY: As long as the Mosaic covenant functioned, you *must* have only Aaron and his descendants as priests. Hebrews 7:12 states, "For when the priesthood is changed, of necessity there takes place a change of law also." If the priesthood is changed, then

> the covenant from which it originates must be changed. And the reverse is true: change the covenant [the Mosaic covenant], then the priesthood *must* change as well. So, with Jesus the covenant becomes the new covenant, and the old priesthood of the Mosaic covenant is eradicated.

Notice another important point. Many priests operated under the Mosaic covenant, but there was only one high priest—who was originally Aaron—at a time. But under the new covenant, a new high priest serves, as Heb 4:14–16 initially explains:

> *Therefore, since we have a great high priest who has passed through the heavens, Jesus the Son of God, let us hold fast our confession. For we do not have a high priest who cannot sympathize with our weaknesses, but One who has been tempted in all things as we are, yet without sin. Therefore let us draw near with confidence to the throne of grace, so that we may receive mercy and find grace to help in time of need.*

The concept of Jesus being our high priest—that is, the high priest of those who are saved—and the qualifying requirements He meets are beautifully developed in Heb 7:26–28:

> *For it was fitting for us to have such a high priest, holy, innocent, undefiled, separated from sinners and exalted above the heavens; who does not need daily, like those high priests [under the Mosaic covenant], to offer up sacrifices, first for His own sins and then for the sins of the people, because this He did once for all when He offered up Himself. For the Law [the Mosaic covenant] appoints men as high priests who are weak, but the word of the oath [which tells of the Melchizedekian priesthood], which came after the [Mosaic covenant] Law, appoints a Son, made perfect forever.*

To emphasize this, the author/Author of Hebrews specifically calls our attention to the main point in Heb 8:1–2:

> *Now the main point in what has been said is this: we have [present tense] such a high priest, who has taken His seat at the right hand of the throne of the Majesty in the heavens, a minister in the sanctuary and in the true tabernacle, which the LORD pitched, not man.*

CRUCIAL CONCEPT TO USE: God permits only one high priest at a time. Key questions to ask the original audience for Hebrews also offer incredibly simple—but powerful—doctrinal truths. These connected evangelistic questions can be used with others, especially with those who think they are saved automatically and do not need to be born again:

Who is your high priest? (Mine is Jesus Messiah. He is yours, too, if you are saved.)

What covenant does He minister under? (the new covenant)

When did that begin for you? (at the moment I received Him by faith, on the reception of the finished work that He did for my salvation)

---

9. The Book of Hebrews Logically Tells Us That Jesus Would Have Sinned If He Had Offered a Sacrifice in Either the Holy Place or the Holy of Holies

This may initially seem like a radical question: Are there things that God cannot do? Yes, there are—and we are eternally grateful for this. For instance, God cannot lie. God cannot sin. God cannot be defeated by evil. The things that God cannot do are for our good, and the Bible substantiates these answers to the question.

During His incarnation, Jesus Christ was God in the flesh; He was born of a woman, born under the Mosaic covenant (Gal 4:4). With Jesus being from the tribe of Judah and from the direct lineage of David—and from what we have seen in our verses from Numbers about who could perform any of the priestly functions—consider the great-great . . . grandfather of Jesus, King Uzziah. After a list of acts of faithfulness that the Davidic covenant King Uzziah did (2 Chr 26:1–15) comes this sad and sobering account from 2 Chr 26:16–21:

> *But when he became strong, his heart was so proud that he acted corruptly, and he was unfaithful to the Lord his God, for he entered the temple of the Lord to burn incense on the altar of incense. Then Azariah the priest*

entered after him and with him eighty priests of the Lord, *valiant men. They opposed Uzziah the king and said to him, "It is not for you, Uzziah, to burn incense to the* Lord, *but for the priests, the sons of Aaron who are consecrated to burn incense. Get out of the sanctuary, for you have been unfaithful and will have no honor from the* Lord *God." But Uzziah, with a censer in his hand for burning incense, was enraged; and while he was enraged with the priests, the leprosy broke out on his forehead before the priests in the house of the* Lord, *beside the altar of incense. Azariah the chief priest and all the priests looked at him, and behold, he was leprous on his forehead; and they hurried him out of there, and he himself also hastened to get out because the* Lord *had smitten him. King Uzziah was a leper to the day of his death; and he lived in a separate house, being a leper, for he was cut off from the house of the* Lord. *And Jotham his son was over the king's house judging the people of the land.*

In giving the royal lineage of the descendants of Jesus, Matt 1:8–9 shows King Uzziah as being one of the forefathers of Jesus: "Asa was the father of Jehoshaphat, Jehoshaphat the father of Joram, and Joram the father of Uzziah. Uzziah was the father of Jotham, Jotham the father of Ahaz, and Ahaz the father of Hezekiah." Jesus was born and lived just as much under the Mosaic covenant as did His Davidic covenant ancestor, King Uzziah.

So, in the passage we have already seen, look at God's logic in Heb 7:11–14:

Now if perfection was through the Levitical priesthood (for on the basis of it the people received the Law), what further need was there for another priest to arise according to the order of Melchizedek, and not be designated according to the order of Aaron? For when the priesthood is changed, of necessity there takes place a change of law also. For the one concerning whom these things are spoken belongs to another tribe, from which no one has officiated at the altar. For it is evident that our Lord *was descended from Judah, a tribe with reference to which Moses spoke nothing concerning priests.*

With this, add 8:4: "Now if He were on earth, He would not be a priest at all, since there are those who offer the gifts according to the [Mosaic covenant] Law."

Under these circumstances of the law, if Jesus had offered a sacrifice, even as His direct ancestor Uzziah had, Jesus would have been just as sinful. If Jesus had offered a sacrifice, He would not have been able to have answered His critics as He did in John 8:42–46:

> *Jesus said to them, "If God were your Father, you would love Me, for I proceeded forth and have come from God, for I have not even come on My own initiative, but He sent Me. Why do you not understand what I am saying? It is because you cannot hear My word. You are of your father the devil, and you want to do the desires of your father. He was a murderer from the beginning, and does not stand in the truth because there is no truth in him. Whenever he speaks a lie, he speaks from his own nature, for he is a liar and the father of lies. But because I speak the truth, you do not believe Me. Which one of you convicts Me of sin? If I speak truth, why do you not believe Me?*

If Jesus had done what His ancestor Uzziah had done, His critics would have pointed that out before or during His trial.

And even more tragic—horribly and eternally so for us—Jesus no longer would have been qualified to fit the description in 1 Pet 1:17–19:

> *If you address as Father the One who impartially judges according to each one's work, conduct yourselves in fear during the time of your stay on earth; knowing that you were not redeemed with perishable things like silver or gold from your futile way of life inherited from your forefathers, but with precious blood, as of a lamb unblemished and spotless, the blood of Christ.*

He would have been blemished; He would not have been spotless—and we would have no one to shed His blood for us. But instead He was spotless; He did shed His blood for us; and we graciously thank God for Him. "For He was foreknown before the foundation of the world, but has appeared in these last times for the sake of [us]" (1 Pet 1:20).

10. Hebrews 9:27 ("And as it is appointed unto men once to die, but after this comes judgment," KJV) Does Not Teach That It Is Appointed for Everyone to Die

This is not a blasphemous statement! Let me affirm that death is certainly the normal flow for almost everyone, but there have been, and will be, some exceptions. Elijah the prophet did not die; God took him to heaven without death (2 Kgs 2:11). Even the book of Hebrews bears witness to this truth that not everyone will die, as is shown also in the account of Gen 5:21–24. Hebrews 11:5 says, "By faith Enoch was taken up so that he would not see death; AND HE WAS NOT FOUND BECAUSE GOD TOOK HIM UP; for he obtained the witness that before his being taken up he was pleasing to God." The author/Author of Hebrews is not going to contradict himself nor forget what he had written in 9:27 by the time he gets to Hebrews 11. Furthermore, another generation of Christians also has the same prom-ise from God regarding their not dying—those who will go to heaven by means of the rapture, as discussed in 1 Cor 15:50–53:

> Now I say this, brethren, that flesh and blood cannot inherit the kingdom of God; nor does the perishable inherit the imperishable. Behold, I tell you a mystery; we will not all sleep [the sleep of death], but we will all be changed, in a moment, in the twinkling of an eye, at the last trumpet; for the trumpet will sound, and the dead will be raised imperishable, and we will be changed. For this perishable must put on the imperishable, and this mortal must put on immortality.

Actually, a few people literally died twice. For instance, Jairus's daughter (Mark 5:35–43) and Lazarus, whose story is recorded in John 11:11–15:

> This He said, and after that He said to them, "Our friend Lazarus has fallen asleep; but I go, so that I may awaken him out of sleep." The disciples then said to Him, "Lord, if he has fallen asleep, he will recover." Now Jesus had spoken of His death, but they thought that He was speaking of literal sleep. So Jesus then said to them plainly, "Lazarus is dead, and I am glad for your sakes that I was not there, so that you may believe; but let us go to him."

The remainder of the account is in John 11. Note John 12:9: "The large crowd of the Jews then learned that He was there; and they came, not for

Jesus' sake only, but that they might also see Lazarus, whom He raised from the dead." At some future time, however, both Jairus's daughter and Lazarus each died a second time.

So what does Heb 9:27 teach? The immediate context in Heb 9:24–26 places emphasis on Jesus being our high priest and on His singular sacrifice of Himself, contrasted with the functions of the high priests who had to perform the same procedure each year for the Jewish people under the Mosaic covenant's statutes for Yom Kippur (the Day of Atonement, from Leviticus 16):

> *For Christ did not enter a holy place made with hands, a mere copy of the true one, but into heaven itself, now to appear in the presence of God for us; nor was it that He would offer Himself often, as the high priest enters the holy place year by year with blood that is not His own. Otherwise, He would have needed to suffer often since the foundation of the world; but now once at the consummation of the ages He has been manifested to put away sin by the sacrifice of Himself.*

The Jewish Christians would recognize the language and concepts they were already familiar with—the normal, threefold procedure of high priests on the Day of Atonement, as seen in Heb 9:27–28: "And inasmuch as it is appointed for men to die once and after this comes judgment, so Christ also, having been offered once to bear the sins of many, will appear a second time for salvation without reference to sin, to those who eagerly await Him." Using the simplified threefold division of the procedure of the Day of Atonement, the high priest of Israel, under the Mosaic covenant, would (1) appear before the people gathered at the temple, (2) minister/intercede for them in the holy place and then enter into the holy of holies (when the high priest performed this service, he was not in view of those awaiting his return), and (3) reappear again before the people, after he had finished serving as their high priest in the presence of God.

Jesus completed the first part: He appeared before the people, during His entire incarnation—even if His appearing was limited to having been brought before the people by Pilate. Second, Jesus currently serves as our high priest in heaven for us. Just as the high priest under the Mosaic covenant was out of view when He performed this service, so Jesus is currently out of our vision. The third part of the Day of Atonement procedure He has yet to do: He has to reappear before the people, which will be accomplished as He returns in the glory of His Father to rule and reign over what is rightfully His.

11. Hebrews 10:1–4 Gives Us a Wonderful Contrast for the Significance of the Lord's Table

Hebrews 10:1–3 states:

> *For the Law [that is, the Mosaic covenant], since it has only a shadow of the good things to come and not the very form of things, can never, by the same sacrifices which they offer continually year by year, make perfect those who draw near. Otherwise, would they not have ceased to be offered, because the worshipers, having once been cleansed, would no longer have had consciousness of sins? But in those sacrifices there is a reminder of sins year by year.*

As long as the Mosaic covenant was operative, it required national Israel to appear before Yahweh on the Day of Atonement, each year at the designated time and with the designated procedure. Hebrews 10:3 states that "in those sacrifices there is a reminder of sins year by year." And that was part of the major reason to observe annually the Day of Atonement. The national sins of Israel were to be confessed and atoned for, but the rituals used that day did not stop in any way on their own. Until God stopped them, national Israel was required under the law to meet the next year at the exact time and to perform the exact ritual again.

In 1 Cor 11:23–26, Paul explained God's instruction concerning His Table:

> *For I received from the Lord that which I also delivered to you, that the Lord Jesus in the night in which He was betrayed took bread; and when He had given thanks, He broke it and said, "This is My body, which is for you; do this in remembrance of Me." In the same way He took the cup also after supper, saying, "This cup is the new covenant in My blood; do this, as often as you drink it, in remembrance of Me." For as often as you eat this bread and drink the cup, you proclaim the Lord's death until He comes.*

Perhaps you will have a better appreciation of what Jesus has done the next time you partake of the elements of the Lord's Table:

Do this—the Day of Atonement—in remembrance of you, Jewish people under the Mosaic covenant, as a reminder of sins year after year (Heb 10:3).

Do this—the Lord's Table—"in remembrance of Me," says Jesus to His church (1 Cor 11:24). The beautiful sacrifice of Jesus as the cup of the new covenant in His blood, we are to partake of in remembrance of Him—and in thankfulness to Him.

For as often as we eat of this bread and drink of the cup, we proclaim the Lord's death until He comes—still having Davidic covenant promises to keep, as well as the returning to our sight after He has performed His high priestly function on our behalf.

12. Hebrews 13:20–21 Is a Wonderfully Rich Benediction That We Should More Greatly Appreciate

Based on what we have seen earlier in our study of Heb 13:20–21 is so fitting as part of the end of this Bible book:

Now the God of peace, who brought up from the dead the great Shepherd of the sheep through the blood of the eternal covenant, even Jesus our Lord, equip you in every good thing to do His will, working in us that which is pleasing in His sight, through Jesus Christ, to whom be the glory forever and ever. Amen.

"The God of peace, who brought up from the dead the great Shepherd of the sheep" is a wonderful line. The resurrection of Jesus shows the basis on which God will accept those of us who are saved: "through the blood of the eternal [new] covenant." Notice that the wording is in the singular; Christ's blood is all anyone needs, and God offers no other means of salvation. The new covenant blood of Jesus vastly exceeds the entirety of all the restricted and repeated sacrifices under the Mosaic covenant because we know from Heb 10:4 that "it is impossible for the blood of bulls and goats to take away sins."

"Thanks be to God for His indescribable gift!" (2 Cor 9:15).

Summary and Conclusion

In this chapter, we learned twelve things about the book of Hebrews:

(1) Using its own singular designation, the book of Hebrews is a "word of exhortation," namely, a sermon (Heb 13:22; Acts 13:13–15). (2) Not only is the book of Hebrews a sermon, but it is a Holy Spirit-inspired sermon. (3) The book of Hebrews is not an evangelistic book written to the Jewish people; the original recipients of the book of Hebrews were Jewish people who had already named the name of Christ/Messiah. (4) The Jewish professing believers were under persecution not from Gentiles but from fellow Jews (Heb 10:32–35). Because the people who had received the book of Hebrews were still assembled together as believers, they had not yet apostatized. All they had to do to stop the persecution was to renounce Jesus as the Messiah and return to the Mosaic covenant. Furthermore, this apostasy would not be just stepping from one system (Christianity) to another system (Judaism). In Heb 3:12 the author/Author of Hebrews warns them about what falling away would entail, and, as with so many other temptations, it begins in the heart before it shows in the actions: "Take care, brethren, that there not be in any one of you an evil, unbelieving heart that falls away from the living God."

(5) The first major portion of Hebrews (1:1–4:13) presents primarily the Davidic covenant and the second coming of the Lord Jesus Christ. (6) Hebrews 2:12 has a unique usage of Psalm 22. How fitting that the author/Author of Hebrews quoted from Ps 22:22–31 in the first section of Hebrews (1:1–4:13). Presentation of those topics uses future tense promises that must be and will be fulfilled so that—among many other things—Jesus will praise God in the very midst of the redeemed, as revealed in Heb 2:12/Ps 22:22: "I will tell of Your name to my brethren; / In the midst of the assembly I will praise You." Also, (7) the second major division in Hebrews (4:14–10:18) is primarily the new covenant with the First Advent/incarnation of Jesus. (8) The book of Hebrews uses the holy logic of God to show the biblical necessity that changing the priesthood requires changing the covenant. As long as the Mosaic covenant functioned, you must have only Aaron and his descendants as priests. Hebrews 7:12 states, "For when the priesthood is changed, of necessity there takes place a change of law also." If the priesthood is changed, then the covenant from which it originates

must be changed. And the reverse is true: change the covenant [that is, the Mosaic covenant], then the priesthood must change as well. So, with Jesus the covenant becomes the new one, and the old priesthood of the Mosaic covenant is eradicated. The temple and the Levitical priesthood existed for forty years or so after the death of Jesus, but that did not mean that God accepted any of the sacrifices offered under that system. (9) The book of Hebrews logically discloses that even though Jesus Christ was God in the flesh, during His incarnation, He was born under the Mosaic covenant (Gal 4:4), and He would have sinned if He had offered a sacrifice either in the holy place or in the holy of holies. Jesus would have sinned the same sin that His ancestor King Uzziah did (2 Chron 26:16–21; Matt 1:8–9).

(10) Hebrews 9:27 does not actually teach that it is appointed for everyone to die (cp. Heb 11:5). Using the simplified threefold division of the procedure of the Day of Atonement, the high priest of Israel, under the Mosaic covenant, would . . .

1. *appear before the people gathered at the temple,*

2. *minister/intercede for them in the holy place and then go into the holy of holies (when the high priest performed this service, he was not in view by those awaiting his return), and*

3. *reappear again before the people, after he had finished serving as their high priest in the presence of God.*

Jesus has performed two of the three requirements, and we are awaiting the third and last part: His return to earth. (11) Hebrews 10:1–4 offers a wonderful contrast for the significance of the Lord's Table. Finally, (12) Heb 13:20–21 is a wonderfully rich benediction that (hopefully) we appreciate more at this point based on the other biblical truths we have previously seen in Hebrews.

Deeper Walk Study Questions

1. How do we know that the book of Hebrews is a sermon? Support your answer biblically.

2. What is the significance of Hebrews being a Holy Spirit-inspired sermon? Name three truths from this.

3. What is the significance of Hebrews being written to professing Jewish Christians rather than being penned as an evangelistic message sent to the Jewish people at large? How do we know false brethren exist? Give three biblical supports for your answer and identify why this is important for understanding the original audience who received this epistle.

4. Describe the biblical setting surrounding the original recipients of Hebrews and the pressures they were under. Also, how would their falling away from the faith differ from Peter's threefold denial of Jesus? Explain.

5. How do we know that Heb 1:1–4:13 is primarily about the Davidic covenant and the second coming of Jesus to earth? Give five biblical supports and explain why these are important.

6. Hebrews 2:11–12 contains a quote from Psalm 22. Name the four citations of Psalm 22 in Matthew 27. What are the three divisions in Psalm 22? How does the first division of Psalm 22 relate to Matthew 27? What is the second division of Psalm 22? What is the third division of Psalm 22, and how does it specifically relate to Heb 2:12? Finally, name six doctrinal truths from Ps 22:22–31 and tell why these are important.

7. Give five biblical reasons why Heb 4:14–10:18 is primarily addressing the new covenant and the First Advent/incarnation of Jesus. Explain why knowing this is important for understanding both the book of Hebrews and the ministry of Jesus.

8. How does the book of Hebrews demonstrate that the changing of the priesthood established as part of the Mosaic covenant requires a change of covenant? Give five biblical supports for this, and tell why this is important doctrinally.

9. How do we know biblically that Jesus would have sinned if He had offered a sacrifice in the temple during His incarnation? Give five biblical supports and explain why these are important to know.

10. How do we know that Heb 9:27, "it is appointed unto men once to die," does not teach a strict application to every single individual? Give four biblical reasons. Also, from the context, what does Heb 9:24–28 teach, and why is this biblically important? Explain.

11. How does Heb 10:1–3 contrast with the Lord's Table as explained by Paul in 1 Cor 11:23–26? Write six profound biblical truths from these passages and explain why they are important.

12. Write six doctrinal truths found in Heb 13:20–21 and tell why each one is
    important—especially in light of what we have seen in the book of Hebrews.

CHAPTER 29

A Broad Theological Walk through the Book of Revelation[1]

T he *entirety* of the book of Revelation is so important that many articles, sermons, and books have been written using its contents as
subjects. We realize that one chapter of this *Handbook* certainly will not
cover everything; nonetheless, we will proceed to study Revelation. Many
Bible readers, teachers, and preachers completely avoid the book of Revelation, even though one of the unique features of it is that God specifically
promises His blessing on this final—and irreplaceable—portion of His
progressive revelation: "Blessed is he who reads and those who hear the
words of the prophecy, and heed the things which are written in it; for the
time is near" (Rev 1:3).

I cannot cover all of the verses in Revelation, so you will need to do
that on your own. But one thing we can do together is to walk through
broadly and to feel more at home in this book that mystifies so many yet
contains truths that Jesus wants His churches to know (Rev 22:16).

The Introductory Material in Revelation

The preamble part of Revelation (1:1–8) includes John's greeting to the
churches, his pronouncement that includes references to God, and his immediate focus on the return of the Lord:

---

[1] For free audio downloads about related matters in this chapter: https://www.sermon
audio.com/search.asp?sourceonly=true&currSection=sermonssource&keyword=gregharris
&subsetcat=series&subsetitem=The+Book+of+Revelation.

John to the seven churches that are in Asia: Grace to you and peace, from Him who is and who was and who is to come; and from the seven Spirits who are before His throne; and from Jesus Christ, the faithful witness, the firstborn of the dead, and the ruler of the kings of the earth. To Him who loves us and released us from our sins by His blood—and He has made us to be a kingdom, priests to His God and Father—to Him be the glory and the dominion forever and ever. Amen. BEHOLD, He is coming with the clouds, and every eye will see Him, even those who pierced Him; and all the tribes of the earth will mourn over Him. So it is to be. Amen.

"I am the Alpha and the Omega," says the Lord God, "who is and who was and who is to come, the Almighty."

After the preamble, the introduction of the material is in Rev 1:9–11:

I, John, your brother and fellow partaker in the tribulation and kingdom and perseverance which are in Jesus, was on the island called Patmos because of the word of God and the testimony of Jesus. I was in the Spirit on the Lord's day, and I heard behind me a loud voice like the sound of a trumpet, saying, "Write in a book what you see, and send it to the seven churches: to Ephesus and to Smyrna and to Pergamum and to Thyatira and to Sardis and to Philadelphia and to Laodicea."

John was the last of the apostles still living and was probably in his nineties at that time. When he turned to see who had spoken to him, this is what he saw according to Rev 1:12–16:

Then I turned to see the voice that was speaking with me. And having turned I saw seven golden lampstands; and in the middle of the lampstands I saw one like a son of man, clothed in a robe reaching to the feet, and girded across His chest with a golden sash. His head and His hair were white like white wool, like snow; and His eyes were like a flame of fire. His feet were like burnished bronze, when it has been made to glow in a furnace, and His voice was like the sound of many waters. In His right hand He held seven stars, and out of His mouth came a sharp two-edged sword; and His face was like the sun shining in its strength.

One of the reasons that Revelation is so difficult for people to understand is that in this book Jesus appears so different from the beloved Jesus whom we read about in the Gospels. Maybe these two concepts will help: In Revelation 1, Jesus displayed Himself (1) in judgment mode and (2) with the attributes of God. His incarnation mode (cp. Phil 2:5–8) has ended, and Jesus will never be seen that way by the world again. Even the beloved apostle John, who had leaned against the chest of Jesus at the Last Supper, now saw Jesus in a capacity that was utterly new to him: "When I saw Him, I fell at His feet like a dead man" (Rev 1:17a). Jesus therefore responded, "He placed His right hand on [John], saying, "Do not be afraid; I am the first and the last, and the living One; and I was dead, and behold, I am alive forevermore, and I have the keys of death and of Hades" (vv. 17b–18).

Revelation 1:19 is crucial in understanding what follows: "Therefore write the things which you have seen, and the things which are, and the things which will take place after these things." In His mentioning "the things which you have seen" (past tense), it is evident that Jesus had changed His appearance from the manner in which He had just displayed it to the apostle John. We are not told exactly how Jesus then appeared to John, but it was no longer in the previous judgment mode.

IMPORTANT: Revelation 1:19 gives the threefold outline of Revelation:

1. "Therefore write the things which you have seen" (past tense) refers to the content of Revelation 1.

2. "The things which are" would be (present tense at that time) the letters to the seven churches as recorded in Revelation 2–3.

3. *"The things which will take place* after these things" refers to the bulk of the book, beginning with Rev 4:1: "After these things I looked, and behold, a door standing open in heaven, and the first voice which I had heard, like the sound of a trumpet speaking with me, said, 'Come up here, and I will show you *what must take place after these things'"* (namely, after the things that are at that time, Revelation 2–3). This goes all the way to Rev 22:6: "And he said to me, 'These words are faithful and true'; and

the Lord, the God of the spirits of the prophets, sent His angel
to show to His bond-servants *the things which must soon take
place.*" Even the opening verse of Revelation pointed to the
importance of what must take place: "The Revelation of Jesus
Christ, which God gave Him to show to His bond-servants, *the
things which must soon take place*" (emphasis added). So the
third part of the outline is the bulk of the book, covering Rev
4:1–22:6. Revelation 22:8–21 contains closing declarations/
commands/affirmations.

In the second division of the book of Revelation (chaps. 2–3), Jesus
addresses seven of His churches in Asia Minor. He begins each letter with
some of His attributes (displayed in Revelation 1), each attribute fitting
for that particular church. Most of the churches received warnings from
Jesus. Two churches received no such warnings: the church at Smyrna
(Rev 2:8–11) and Philadelphia, which is in modern Turkey (Rev 3:7–13).
Each of the seven letters closes with admonitions and encouragements by
means of promises to the overcomer, who ultimately is each genuinely
redeemed Christian.

CONSIDER: An encouraging devotional is to go through every promise
that Jesus has given to the overcomer and make all of them into one
unit. If you are walking in obedience to the Lord, this can be (1) a
great encouragement to you personally, especially if you are going
through a difficult time, and (2) an encouragement to others whom
you disciple or have contact with. Also, (3) especially the closer we
get to the Lord's return when it seems that evil is winning, God's
promises to the overcomer are a reminder that the story is by no
means over—Jesus will be the victor, and He will give the overcomer
the fullness of each of these wonderful promises. Most of the
overcomer promises will be fulfilled at His return.

The Beginning of the Third Major Division in Revelation

The third division of the book (Rev 4:1–22:6), begins thusly:

> *After these things I looked, and behold, a door standing open in heaven, and the first voice which I had heard, like the sound of a trumpet speaking with me, said, "Come up here, and I will show you what must take place after these things." Immediately I was in the Spirit; and behold, a throne was standing in heaven, and One sitting on the throne. (4:1–2)*

Note well the number of times that the word throne appears in Revelation 4–5. In this vision, John was transported into the very throne room of God. Revelation 4:2–4 is how God manifested Himself in the vision, and verses 5–8 show other beings in His presence in heaven in this vision.

CONSIDER: In our fallen nature and from the vantage point of earth, the descriptions of these beings may be hard for us to understand, but we should note this important doctrine: these are not hideous creatures. In both the tabernacle and later in the temple of God, the closer one came to God—such as the holy of holies—the purer the materials and the more beautiful these beings were. The closer anything gets to God, the more beautiful it is. For those of us who are saved, if God allowed us to see these beautiful creatures in His presence, we would be so overwhelmed that it would influence most of our thoughts for the remainder of our lives on earth.

CONSIDER ALSO: The reverse of the above is true as well: the farther removed one is from God, beginning on earth and continuing into eternal hell, the more hideous these beings either are or become— whether human or satanic beings—and their on-going activities become more sinful and uglier.

Revelation 4:8–11 shows this from the throne room of God the Creator:

> *And the four living creatures [a type of angel], each one of them having six wings, are full of eyes around and within; and day and night they do not cease to say,*

"Holy, holy, holy, is the Lord God, the Almighty, who
was and who is and who is to come."

*And when the living creatures give glory and honor and thanks to Him who
sits on the throne, to Him who lives forever and ever, the twenty-four elders
will fall down before Him who sits on the throne, and will worship Him who
lives forever and ever, and will cast their crowns before the throne, saying,*

> *"Worthy are You, our Lord and our God, to receive glory and
> honor and power; for You created all things, and because of
> Your will they existed, and were created."*

God's creation—be it the spiritual part or the physical part—will play
a tremendously important role in the book all the way through Revelation 22. We will study more about that later. The point of the book of Revelation at this section is not specifically to show the beauties of God; that
will follow later with the brief description of heaven/New Jerusalem in
Revelation 21–22. Revelation 5:1–3 shows the vantage point originating
from the throne room of the holy God, the Judge:

> *I saw in the right hand of Him who sat on the throne a book written inside
> and on the back, sealed up with seven seals. And I saw a strong angel pro-
> claiming with a loud voice, "Who is worthy to open the book and to break
> its seals?" And no one in heaven or on the earth or under the earth was
> able to open the book or to look into it.*

John's response in Rev 5:4 shows that he somehow understood that
if no one steps forward to take the scroll from the hand (in this vision) of
God the Father, the curse of the world would never be removed, and the
blessed kingdom of God would never come: "Then I began to weep greatly
because no one was found worthy to open the book or to look into it." John
is admonished and encouraged by one of the elders in the vision. The elder
says, "Stop weeping; behold, the Lion that is from the tribe of Judah, the
Root of David, has overcome so as to open the book and its seven seals"
(Rev 5:5).

> **CRUCIAL TRUTH:** The answer for John's fear that no one will come—as well as the answer to what the book of Revelation is about to reveal—comes directly from the messianic prophecies in Gen 49:8–12, about the Lion from the tribe of Judah. Remember that Gen 49:1 began this way: "Then Jacob summoned his sons and said, 'Assemble yourselves that I may tell you what will befall you in the days to come,'" or "in the end of the days." We also know whom Jacob referred to from Gen 49:28: "All these are the twelve tribes of Israel, and this is what their father said to them when he blessed them. He blessed them, every one with the blessing appropriate to him." What follows are not random acts; they are righteous acts at "the end of the days," by the Lion from the tribe of Judah, Jesus the Messiah.

John turned to see a Lion and instead saw a Lamb, in Rev 5:6–7:

I saw between the throne (with the four living creatures) and the elders a Lamb standing, as if slain, having seven horns and seven eyes, which are the seven Spirits of God, sent out into all the earth. And He came and He took the book out of the right hand of Him who sat on the throne.

> **CORE TRUTHS:** In John 5:22 Jesus discloses what we would not know otherwise: "For not even the Father judges anyone, but He has given all judgment to the Son." So, in Revelation 5, Jesus appears in judgment mode—though not in the full display of judgment mode that He displayed briefly in Revelation 1. It is now required biblically that anytime a divine judgment of some kind is to occur Jesus will be the Godhead member who does the judging. We see this, fittingly, at "the judgment seat of Christ" (2 Cor 5:9–10), where the redeemed will receive their rewards. Also, we should not be surprised when Jesus is the One present and active when we come to the great white throne judgment of Revelation 20.

Revelation 5:8–10 shows the reactionary worship that occurs because of what the Lamb did:

When He had taken the book, the four living creatures and the twenty-four elders fell down before the Lamb, each one holding a harp and golden bowls full of incense, which are the prayers of the saints. And they sang a new song, saying,

"Worthy are You to take the book and to break its seals; for You were slain, and purchased for God with Your blood men from every tribe and tongue and people and nation.

"You have made them to be a kingdom and priests to our God; and they will reign upon the earth.

CONSIDER: From Rev 5:10 we see that (1) the reigning is future tense (we do not presently reign as Christians), and (2) it specifically states that the redeemed will reign on the earth. Other than an outright predisposition to reject this biblical truth, why would we not take this promise exactly as it is stated? Also, if it does not mean that the redeemed will one day reign on the earth, then the question must be answered as to what God was attempting to communicate by the promise of Rev 5:10. But how would you know what He means? All God had to do was add the word "not": "And they will not reign on the earth." Instead, He chose language that specifically denotes the earth. And remember that it is part of His creation, as we saw in Revelation 4.

The worship in heaven continues in Revelation 5:11–12:

Then I looked, and I heard the voice of many angels around the throne and the living creatures and the elders; and the number of them was myriads of myriads, and thousands of thousands, saying with a loud voice,

"Worthy is the Lamb that was slain to receive power and riches and wisdom and might and honor and glory and blessing."

Revelation 5:13–14 is a preview of what will happen when, as Phil 2:9–11 reveals,

"every knee will bow":

> *And every created thing which is in heaven and on the earth and under the earth and on the sea, and all things in them, I heard saying,*
>
> *"To Him who sits on the throne, and to the Lamb, be blessing and honor and glory and dominion forever and ever."*
>
> *And the four living creatures kept saying, "Amen." And the elders fell down and worshiped.*

We understand several things by looking back at Revelation 4–5 together. (1) Much like the spiritual realities in Luke 1 that made preparations for Luke 2 to occur, Revelation 4–5 reveals the spiritual realities for the events that will unfold on earth from Revelation 6 onward. (2) These spiritual realities will be reasons why things occur on earth, but these reasons will be completely hidden from the unsaved; and (3) for those who will be redeemed during the tribulation, these truths—plus many others—will be a light and a lamp to those who will receive and believe them.

The Early Part of the Tribulation

Revelation 6–18 is the broad section that covers the tribulation, ending with the return of Jesus to earth in Revelation 19. After the rapture occurs, the tribulation begins, but we are not told whether or not there will be a time lapse between the rapture and the beginning of the tribulation. But whenever the tribulation begins, *everyone* entering it will initially be lost; only the unsaved will enter the tribulation.

Revelation 3:10 helps us with two major answers that add to our overall biblical understanding. First, it tells what the tribulation will be: "that hour which is about to come upon the whole world, to test those who dwell on the earth." Sometimes the word hour can be used for an approximate sixty-minute time span, such as the amount of time that Jesus spent in His first segment of praying at Gethsemane (Mark 14:37 states, "And He came and found them sleeping, and said to Peter, 'Simon, are you asleep? Could you not keep watch for one hour?'"). It can also mean a designated period of time, such as in the prayer of Jesus in Gethsemane—as in Mark 14:35: "And He went a little beyond them, and fell to the ground and began to pray that if it were possible, the hour might pass Him by." Obviously, Jesus was not referring to sixty minutes here. So, from Rev 3:10 we know that the tribulation is a designated period of time. From other Scriptures, as we will see, we know this to be a seven-year period that will be divided in half; the last three and a half years are often called "the great tribulation." We will see why that is an appropriate name for that time period.

Included in this section is Jesus promising to the faithful overcomer in Rev 3:10. He describes the Christian faithfulness that they demonstrated in verse 8: "I know your deeds. Behold, I have put before you an open door which no one can shut, because you have a little power, and have kept My word, and have not denied My name." And accordingly, He gives promises to His faithful in His church, based on their faithfulness, and in verse 10 He promises them a wonderful preliminary reward: "Because you have kept the word of My perseverance, I also will keep you from the hour of testing, that hour which is about to come upon the whole world, to test those who dwell on the earth." This promise currently remains unfulfilled prophecy; the saved that belonged to the original church at Philadelphia have gone home to be with the Lord. So, this prophecy is for some generation of Christians who will be kept from what is about to transpire on earth.

We know from Rev 15:1 what the tribulation will be: "Then I saw another sign in heaven, great and marvelous, seven angels who had seven plagues, which are the last, because in them the wrath of God is finished." The tribulation will be a designated period of time when Jesus Christ will pour out—in very measured doses—the wrath of God's judgments on the earth that He created. The judgments will intensify in severity, especially as we get closer to the Lord's return in Revelation 19.

Thus, the biblical description of the tribulation begins with breaking the seven seals of the scroll that we saw in Revelation 5, and each breaking of a seal will be the spiritual reality behind a judgmental event that will occur on earth, as 6:1–2 shows:

> Then I saw when the Lamb broke one of the seven seals, and I heard one of the four living creatures saying as with a voice of thunder, "Come." I looked, and behold, a white horse, and he who sat on it had a bow; and a crown was given to him, and he went out conquering and to conquer.

Many people who study either Revelation or related prophecies fail to view the tribulation in its uniqueness. We should remember the warnings by Jesus, such as in Matt 24:21–22:

For then there will be a great tribulation, such as has not occurred since the beginning of the world until now, nor ever will. Unless those days had been cut short, no life would have been saved; but for the sake of the elect those days will be cut short.

Likewise, in Mark 13:19 Jesus described the coming uniqueness of the tribulation: "For those days will be a time of tribulation such as has not occurred since the beginning of the creation which God created until now, and never will." Many people do not consider that during the tribulation, the Blessed Restrainer (2 Thess 2:6–7) will no longer be restraining evil under God's strict sovereignty. As we will see, the removal of the Restrainer will allow Satan and the Antichrist every opportunity to take evil to unfathomable depths—more so than has occurred at any other time in history.

After the rapture of the church, and for a relatively short while, the unsaved world at large will think that they have peace and that all is well, as we saw earlier in 1 Thess 5:1–3:

Now as to the times and the epochs, brethren, you have no need of anything to be written to you. For you yourselves know full well that the day of the Lord will come just like a thief in the night. While they are saying, "Peace and safety!" then destruction will come upon them suddenly like labor pains upon a woman with child, and they will not escape.

In remembering the spiritual realities behind the world events, Jesus instead breaks the second seal in Rev 6:3–4: "When He broke the second seal, I heard the second living creature saying, 'Come.' And another, a red horse, went out; and to him who sat on it, it was granted to take peace from the earth, and that men would slay one another; and a great sword was given to him."

MARK THIS WELL: During the tribulation, massive world warfare will arise. This is directly due to the second seal judgment broken by

Jesus in which He will remove world peace and bring about incredibly devastating wars.

From the fourth seal judgment come these staggering disastrous effects in Rev 6:7–8:

> When the Lamb broke the fourth seal, I heard the voice of the fourth living creature saying, "Come." I looked, and behold, an ashen horse; and he who sat on it had the name Death; and Hades was following with him. Authority was given to them over a fourth of the earth, to kill with sword and with famine and with pestilence and by the wild beasts of the earth.

This seal judgment alone means that one-fourth of the entire world's population will be killed. We are not given the total number, but if there are six billion alive on earth, this would mean one and a half billion people will be killed during this one seal judgment—and we are not yet even to one-third of the wrath-of-God judgments in the tribulation.

The fifth seal judgment in Rev 6:9–11 is different:

> When the Lamb broke the fifth seal, I saw underneath the altar the souls of those who had been slain because of the word of God, and because of the testimony which they had maintained; and they cried out with a loud voice, saying, "How long, O Lord, holy and true, will You refrain from judging and avenging our blood on those who dwell on the earth?" And there was given to each of them a white robe; and they were told that they should rest for a little while longer, until the number of their fellow servants and their brethren who were to be killed even as they had been, would be completed also.

CONSIDER: As we will see in Revelation, there will be a redemptive aspect during the tribulation because it will be a time of massive and unparalleled worldwide evangelism, as Jesus promised in Matt 24:14: "This gospel of the kingdom shall be preached in the whole world as a testimony to all the nations, and then the end will come." And although obviously not everyone in the tribulation will be saved, Rev 6:9–11 gives the first indication that a large number of people will already have been be saved—and martyred—by this early part of the tribulation.

CORE TRUTH: Once the tribulation begins, no one who is saved during that time can claim the promise Jesus made in Rev 3:10: "Because you have kept the word of My perseverance, I also will keep you from the hour of testing, that hour which is about to come upon the whole world, to test those who dwell on the earth." These redeemed ones who will be saved during the tribulation will already be in "the hour of testing," and God will give them different promises and admonitions at various points in the book of Revelation.

The sixth seal judgment occurs in Rev 6:12–14:

I looked when He broke the sixth seal, and there was a great earthquake; and the sun became black as sackcloth made of hair, and the whole moon became like blood; and the stars of the sky fell to the earth, as a fig tree casts its unripe figs when shaken by a great wind. The sky was split apart like a scroll when it is rolled up, and every mountain and island were moved out of their places.

Notice the reaction, even at this relatively early part of the tribulation, that shows many of the unsaved are no longer saying, "Peace and safety," as they will have originally responded (1 Thess 5:1–3). Instead, their response will be as Rev 6:15–17 reveals:

Then the kings of the earth and the great men and the commanders and the rich and the strong and every slave and free man hid themselves in the caves and among the rocks of the mountains; and they said to the mountains and to the rocks, "Fall on us and hide us from the presence of Him who sits on the throne, and from the wrath of the Lamb; for the great day of their wrath has come, and who is able to stand?"

Those who are unsaved in the tribulation know what is happening and from whom these judgments are coming. Many of them will know, even at this early part of the tribulation, that it is "the great day of their wrath"—and there is much more still to occur.

The seventh seal judgment will not occur until Rev 8:1. Revelation 6 ends with the question, "And who is able to stand?" Revelation 7 is a heavenly interlude that, among other things, gives a preliminary answer about who is able to stand. Appropriately, verse 1 starts this chapter by revealing: "After this I saw four angels standing at the four corners of the earth, holding back the four winds of the earth, so that no wind would blow on the earth or on the sea or on any tree." The four angels are instructed in verses 2–3:

> And I saw another angel ascending from the rising of the sun, having the seal of the living God; and he cried out with a loud voice to the four angels to whom it was granted to harm the earth and the sea, saying, "Do not harm the earth or the sea or the trees until we have sealed the bond-servants of our God on their foreheads."

Revelation 7:4–8 discloses who these special bond-servants of the Lord will be:

> And I heard the number of those who were sealed, one hundred and forty-four thousand sealed from every tribe of the sons of Israel: from the tribe of Judah, twelve thousand were sealed, from the tribe of Reuben twelve thousand, from the tribe of Gad twelve thousand, from the tribe of Asher twelve thousand, from the tribe of Naphtali twelve thousand, from the tribe of Manasseh twelve thousand, from the tribe of Simeon twelve thousand, from the tribe of Levi twelve thousand, from the tribe of Issachar twelve thousand, from the tribe of Zebulun twelve thousand, from the tribe of Joseph twelve thousand, from the tribe of Benjamin, twelve thousand were sealed.

But What about the Tribe of Dan?

Many skeptics of the Bible and many who are only curious point to Rev 7:4–8 as proof that a literal-grammatical interpretation should not be made about these people because the tribe of Dan is omitted from this list. One cannot start in Revelation 7 as a point of beginning (or stay there) to get the answer regarding what is happening in this passage. God has given a wonderful biblical trail that clearly answers this.

First, one hundred and forty-four thousand is not a complete number of all the Jewish people whom God will save in the tribulation. Zechariah 13:8–9 informs us about the remnant of Jewish people that God will save during the tribulation:

"It will come about in all the land,"

Declares the LORD,

"That two parts in it will be cut off and perish;

But the third will be left in it.

"And I will bring the third part through the fire,

Refine them as silver is refined,

And test them as gold is tested.

They will call on My name,

And I will answer them;

I will say, 'They are My people,'

And they will say, 'The LORD is my God.'"

The tribe of Dan will be part of the one-third of the Jewish people who are saved during the tribulation. We will clearly see this in our studies.

Second, the one hundred and forty-four thousand are introduced in Revelation 7, but no further explanation is given about them until Rev 14:1–5:

Then I looked, and behold, the Lamb was standing on Mount Zion, and with Him one hundred and forty-four thousand, having His name and the name of His Father written on their foreheads. And I heard a voice from heaven, like the sound of many waters and like the sound of loud thunder, and the voice which I heard was like the sound of harpists playing on their harps. And they sang a new song before the throne and before the four living creatures and the elders; and no one could learn the song except the one hundred and forty-four thousand who had been purchased from the earth. These are the ones who have not been defiled with women, for they have kept themselves chaste. These are the ones who follow the Lamb wherever He goes. These have been purchased from among men as first fruits to God and to the Lamb. And no lie was found in their mouth; they are blameless.

During the tribulation, these will be one hundred and forty-four thousand choice Jewish vessels who will most likely be involved in massive evangelism, especially to the Jewish people, and they will play a major role in getting the gospel to the one-third of the Jewish remnant whom God will save at that time. These will be choice, sanctified vessels, similar to Daniel and his three friends, who, in Daniel 1, consecrated themselves to serve the Lord. Also, as part of the answer to the question that Revelation 6:17 asked about who will be able to stand in the great day of God and the Lamb's wrath, Revelation 14 begins this way: "Then I looked, and behold, the Lamb was standing on Mount Zion, and with Him one hundred and forty-four thousand."

Third, we need to return to our "old friend" chapter that we have turned to so many times in this *Handbook* to see God's answer. Genesis 49:1 begins this way: "Then Jacob summoned his sons and said, 'Assemble yourselves that I may tell you what will befall you in the days to come [literally, in "end of the days"].'" Genesis 49:28 specifically notes who is involved in this chapter of prophecies at the end of the days: "All these are the twelve tribes of Israel, and this is what their father said to them when he blessed them. He blessed them, every one with the blessing appropriate to him." We have already seen "the Lion from the tribe of Judah" in Revelation 5, coming directly from the prophecies made about Him in Gen 49:8–12.

On the basis of blessing each son with the blessing appropriate to him, and in answering the question that God knew would eventually be asked, the three-verse prophecy about the tribe of Dan begins this way: "Dan shall judge his people, / As one of the tribes of Israel" (Gen 49:16). The disastrous harm that Dan will do in the sinful behavior of his tribe is depicted in Gen 49:17:

> *"Dan shall be a serpent in the way,*
>
> *A horned snake in the path,*
>
> *That bites the horse's heels,*
>
> *So that his rider falls backward."*

Scripture has many references to the tribe of Dan as being involved in sinful behavior, and here is the short version.

In Judg 1:34, Dan is among the tribes who did not take their rightful portion of the land God had promised them: "Then the Amorites forced the sons of Dan into the hill country, for they did not allow them to come down to the valley." Later, in Judg 18:1–2, the tribe of Dan begins to look for a long-term place to live:

> *In those days there was no king of Israel; and in those days the tribe of the Danites was seeking an inheritance for themselves to live in, for until that day an inheritance had not been allotted to them as a possession among the tribes of Israel. So the sons of Dan sent from their family five men out of their whole number, valiant men from Zorah and Eshtaol, to spy out the land and to search it; and they said to them, "Go, search the land." And they came to the hill country of Ephraim, to the house of Micah, and lodged there.*

You can read the rest of Judges 18 on your own, if you like, but the tribe of Dan took by force what was not theirs and were described thusly, in Judg 18:27–30:

> *Then they took what Micah had made and the priest who had belonged to him, and came to Laish, to a people quiet and secure, and struck them with the edge of the sword; and they burned the city with fire. And there was no one to deliver them, because it was far from Sidon and they had no dealings with anyone, and it was in the valley which is near Beth-rehob. And they rebuilt the city and lived in it. They called the name of the city Dan, after the name of Dan their father who was born in Israel; however, the name of the city formerly was Laish. The sons of Dan set up for themselves the graven image; and Jonathan, the son of Gershom, the son of Manasseh, he and his sons were priests to the tribe of the Danites until the day of the captivity of the land.*

Another important Scripture notation regarding the tribe of Dan's continued wickedness involves King Jeroboam and the start of his reign over the ten northern tribes in 1 Kgs 12:28–30:

> *So the king consulted, and made two golden calves, and he said to them, "It is too much for you to go up to Jerusalem; behold your gods, O Israel, that brought you up from the land of Egypt." He set one in Bethel, and the other he put in Dan. Now this thing became a sin, for the people went to worship before the one as far as Dan.*

The omission of the tribe of Dan from Revelation 7 would seem to be a part of the punishment that God appropriately rendered based on their behavior.

However, in Gen 49:18, in spite of the sin that the tribe of Dan committed, a prayer is made to God, looking to Him to be gracious: "For Your salvation I wait, O LORD."

So, fourth, in view of God promising that the tribe of Dan would judge his people as one of the tribes of Israel and in spite of the blatant sinfulness of that tribe, when eventually a prayer to Yahweh will be prayed, comes God's answer. After the return of the Lord in glory to begin His reign (Ezek 43:1–5) comes the distribution of the land promises to be given to the twelve tribes. Appropriately, Ezek 48:1–2 promises,

> *Now these are the names of the tribes: from the northern extremity, beside the way of Hethlon to Lebo-hamath, as far as Hazar-enan at the border of Damascus, toward the north beside Hamath, running from east to west, Dan, one portion. Beside the border of Dan, from the east side to the west side, Asher, one portion.*

Ezekiel 48:29–35 concludes and reaffirms:

> *"This is the land which you shall divide by lot to the tribes of Israel for an inheritance, and these are their several portions," declares the Lord GOD.*

> *"These are the exits of the city: on the north side, 4,500 cubits by measurement, shall be the gates of the city, named for the tribes of Israel, three gates toward the north: the gate of Reuben, one; the gate of Judah, one; the gate of Levi, one. On the east side, 4,500 cubits, shall be three gates: the gate of Joseph, one; the gate of Benjamin, one; the gate of Dan, one. On the south side, 4,500 cubits by measurement, shall be three gates: the gate of Simeon, one; the gate of Issachar, one; the gate of Zebulun, one. On the west side, 4,500 cubits, shall be three gates: the gate of Gad, one; the gate of Asher, one; the gate of Naphtali, one. The city shall be 18,000 cubits round about; and the name of the city from that day shall be, 'The Lord is there.'"*

CRUCIAL: That the tribe of Dan is not listed as part of the twelve tribes of Israel in Revelation 7 does not weaken the literal-grammatical "normative" use of interpretation. Rather, it strengthens it because

> God has clearly declared that Dan would have a tribe to judge, and God's Word expressly names him three times in Ezekiel 48 when the land boundaries are given and established. This is another one of the many times where Isa 25:1 is so fittingly again appropriate: "Plans formed long ago, with perfect faithfulness."

Having introduced the one hundred and forty-four thousand special Jewish bond-servants of God, He at this point introduces another part of the "who is able to stand" answer, in Rev 7:9–10:

After these things I looked, and behold, a great multitude which no one could count, from every nation and all tribes and peoples and tongues, standing before the throne and before the Lamb, clothed in white robes, and palm branches were in their hands; and they cry out with a loud voice, saying,

> *"Salvation to our God who sits on the throne, and to the Lamb."*

One more answer as to who is able to stand occurs in Rev 7:11–12:

And all the angels were standing around the throne and around the elders and the four living creatures; and they fell on their faces before the throne and worshiped God, saying,

> *"Amen, blessing and glory and wisdom and thanksgiving and honor and power and might, be to our God forever and ever. Amen."*

Revelation 7:13–17 reveals more details and gives the basis of salvation for these people:

Then one of the elders answered, saying to me, "These who are clothed in the white robes, who are they, and where have they come from?" I said to him, "My lord, you know." And he said to me, "These are the ones who come out of the great tribulation, and they have washed their robes and made them white in the blood of the Lamb. For this reason, they are before the throne of God; and they serve Him day and night in His temple; and He who sits on the throne will spread His tabernacle over them. They will hunger no longer, nor thirst anymore; nor will the sun beat down on them, nor any heat; for the Lamb in the center of the throne will be their shepherd, and will guide them to springs of the water of life; and God will wipe every tear from their eyes.

> **AN ENCOURAGEMENT:** All of us have loved ones or friends who are currently unsaved. Many of them have no interest in Jesus or the gospel. When the tribulation occurs, *everyone who is unsaved* when it begins will at that time be lost and will be living in disobedience before God. While we would not wish anyone we know or love to go through the tribulation, do not give up hope. Some of our family members/friends may be among those saved during the massive evangelism at that time. Those of us who are saved already will get to hear their testimonies in heaven—and rejoice before the Lord forever.

Returning to Revelation to the Next Wrath-of-God Judgments

Revelation 8 returns again to the intensifying wrath-of-God judgments from the Lamb, and with the seventh seal broken, seven more intensive judgments will emerge—seven trumpet judgments—and seven angels will stand before God. In verses 1 and 2 we read, "When the Lamb broke the seventh seal, there was silence in heaven for about half an hour. And I saw the seven angels who stand before God, and seven trumpets were given to them."

> **MARK THIS:** In Revelation 4 we observed from the throne room of God the Creator. In Revelation 8, God will use part of His creation in many of these judgments; in some of these He will begin taking back part of His creation that most people have taken for granted, as we will see.

Jesus sends the first two trumpet judgments in Rev 8:7–8:

The first sounded, and there came hail and fire, mixed with blood, and they were thrown to the earth; and a third of the earth was burned up, and a third of the trees were burned up, and all the green grass was burned up.

The second angel sounded, and something like a great mountain burning with fire was thrown into the sea; and a third of the sea became blood;

Revelation 8:10–12 shows the third and fourth trumpet judgments:

The third angel sounded, and a great star fell from heaven, burning like a torch, and it fell on a third of the rivers and on the springs of waters. The name of the star is called Wormwood; and a third of the waters became wormwood, and many men died from the waters, because they were made bitter.

The fourth angel sounded, and a third of the sun and a third of the moon and a third of the stars were struck, so that a third of them would be darkened and the day would not shine for a third of it, and the night in the same way.

As you know, this is a continuing vision, and Rev 8:13 concludes the chapter with this warning: "Then I looked, and I heard an eagle flying in midheaven, saying with a loud voice, 'Woe, woe, woe to those who dwell on the earth, because of the remaining blasts of the trumpet of the three angels who are about to sound!'" The threefold use of "woe" calls our attention to the intensified wrath of God's judgments that are to follow with the last three trumpet judgments.

Revelation 9 reveals a depiction that occurs nowhere else in Scripture: it gives a description of what demons look like. God in His gracious care does not let us see demons. (We might go insane if we saw them.) However, in the tribulation, many demons will be used as the first "woe" and the fifth trumpet judgment.

Revelation 9:1–6 introduces this demonic hoard and gives the boundaries of what they are permitted to do, how long, and to whom—all of which is under the strict sovereignty of God:

Then the fifth angel sounded, and I saw a star from heaven which had fallen to the earth; and the key of the bottomless pit was given to him. He opened the bottomless pit, and smoke went up out of the pit, like the smoke of a great furnace; and the sun and the air were darkened by the smoke of the pit. Then out of the smoke came locusts upon the earth, and power was given them, as the scorpions of the earth have power. They were told not to hurt the grass of the earth, nor any green thing, nor any tree, but only the men who do not have the seal of God on their foreheads. And they were not permitted to kill anyone, but to torment for five months; and their torment was like the torment of a scorpion when it stings a man. And in those days men will seek death and will not find it; they will long to die, and death flees from them.

Revelation 9:7–10 reveals details about the appearance of these creatures:

The appearance of the locusts was like horses prepared for battle; and on their heads appeared to be crowns like gold, and their faces were like the faces of men. They had hair like the hair of women, and their teeth were like the teeth of lions. They had breastplates like breastplates of iron; and the sound of their wings was like the sound of chariots, of many horses rushing to battle. They have tails like scorpions, and stings; and in their tails is their power to hurt men for five months.

Revelation 9:12 offers this summary and gives a forewarning: "The first woe is past; behold, two woes are still coming after these things."

The sixth trumpet judgment, quite specific and staggering, is introduced in Rev 9:13–15:

Then the sixth angel sounded, and I heard a voice from the four horns of the golden altar which is before God, one saying to the sixth angel who had the trumpet, "Release the four angels who are bound at the great river Euphrates." And the four angels, who had been prepared for the hour and day and month and year, were released, so that they would kill a third of mankind.

Revelation 9:18 tells how incredibly destructive this sixth trumpet judgment will be: "A third of mankind was killed by these three plagues, by the fire and the smoke and the brimstone which proceeded out of their mouths."

Whereas Revelation 7 gave a "good fruit report," 9:20–21 gives a bad report of those that we saw in 2 Thess 2:10. These are the people who during the tribulation will "not receive the love of the truth so as to be saved":

The rest of mankind, who were not killed by these plagues, did not repent of the works of their hands, so as not to worship demons, and the idols of gold and of silver and of brass and of stone and of wood, which can neither see nor hear nor walk; and they did not repent of their murders nor of their sorceries nor of their immorality nor of their thefts.

The Next Interlude in the Book of Revelation

The seventh trumpet will not sound until Rev 11:15. Revelation 10:1–11:14 is another interlude from the action and calls attention to certain matters. Another strong angel comes down from heaven, and 10:6–7 discloses this pronouncement:

> *[The strong angel] swore by Him who lives forever and ever,* WHO CREATED HEAVEN AND THE THINGS IN IT, AND THE EARTH AND THE THINGS IN IT, AND THE SEA AND THE THINGS IN IT, *that there will be delay no longer, but in the days of the voice of the seventh angel, when he is about to sound, then the mystery of God is finished, as He preached to His servants the prophets.*

In the vision, John is told to take the scroll and eat it, and this action resembles God's command for Ezekiel to eat the scroll in Ezek 2:7–3:3:

> *But you shall speak My words to them whether they listen or not, for they are rebellious.*

> *"Now you, son of man, listen to what I am speaking to you; do not be rebellious like that rebellious house. Open your mouth and eat what I am giving you." Then I looked, and behold, a hand was extended to me; and lo, a scroll was in it. When He spread it out before me, it was written on the front and back, and written on it were lamentations, mourning and woe.*

> *Then He said to me, "Son of man, eat what you find; eat this scroll, and go, speak to the house of Israel." So I opened my mouth, and He fed me this scroll. He said to me, "Son of man, feed your stomach and fill your body with this scroll which I am giving you." Then I ate it, and it was sweet as honey in my mouth.*

Instructions are given to the apostle John in Rev 10:8–10:

> *Then the voice which I heard from heaven, I heard again speaking with me, and saying, "Go, take the book which is open in the hand of the angel who stands on the sea and on the land." So I went to the angel, telling him to give me the little book. And he said to me, "Take it and eat it; it will make your stomach bitter, but in your mouth it will be sweet as honey." I took the little book out of the angel's hand and ate it, and in my mouth it was sweet as honey; and when I had eaten it, my stomach was made bitter.*

The sweetness would be all of the blessings of God, especially as they are related to the Lord's return and reign; the bitterness would be the utter horror of what was to come in the last part of the tribulation.

John's eating of the scroll was done expressly for the purpose of Rev 10:11: "And they said to me, 'You must prophesy again concerning many peoples and nations and tongues and kings.'" The emphasis in this section is specifically on the explicit details given with the individuals involved—both of good and evil.

Revelation 11:1–2, which will transpire during the great tribulation, gives very important details concerning Jerusalem:

> *Then there was given me a measuring rod like a staff; and someone said, "Get up and measure the temple of God and the altar, and those who worship in it. Leave out the court which is outside the temple and do not measure it, for it has been given to the nations; and they will tread under foot the holy city for forty-two months."*

Remember what Jesus said in Luke 21:24: "Jerusalem will be trampled under foot by the Gentiles until the times of the Gentiles be fulfilled." This agrees with the abomination of desolation we have seen already in Matt 24:15 and 2 Thess 2:3–4.

However, in the midst of this unparalleled evil, God raises up two witnesses whom He empowers to do the miraculous in Rev 11:3–6. These may be Moses (see Jude 9) and Elijah (Mal 4:5–6). Revelation 11:7–10 is important because it is the first reference to the Antichrist, although it does not call him by that name:

> *When they [that is, the two special witnesses of God] have finished their testimony, the beast that comes up out of the abyss will make war with them, and overcome them and kill them. And their dead bodies will lie in the street of the great city which mystically is called Sodom and Egypt, where also their Lord was crucified. Those from the peoples and tribes and tongues and nations will look at their dead bodies for three and a half days, and will not permit their dead bodies to be laid in a tomb. And those who dwell on the earth will rejoice over them and celebrate; and they will send gifts to one another, because these two prophets tormented those who dwell on the earth.*

> *Verses 11–12 will change things considerably:*

But after the three and a half days, the breath of life from God came into them, and they stood on their feet; and great fear fell upon those who were watching them. And they heard a loud voice from heaven saying to them, "Come up here." Then they went up into heaven in the cloud, and their enemies watched them.

Verses 13–14 tell what will happen next and give the chronology of the events concerning the tribulation judgments:

And in that hour there was a great earthquake, and a tenth of the city fell; seven thousand people were killed in the earthquake, and the rest were terrified and gave glory to the God of heaven.

The second woe is past; behold, the third woe is coming quickly.

In Rev 11:15 the seventh trumpet sounds: "Then the seventh angel sounded; and there were loud voices in heaven, saying, 'The kingdom of the world has become the kingdom of our Lord and of His Christ; and He will reign forever and ever.'" This gives a preview of what is to come in verse 18:

And the nations were enraged, and Your wrath came, and the time came for the dead to be judged, and the time to reward Your bond-servants the prophets and the saints and those who fear Your name, the small and the great, and to destroy those who destroy the earth.

The Crucial Recognition of Revelation 12–14 As One Unit

Many people like to open their Bibles directly to Revelation 13 because it tells of the Antichrist, and that is the chapter that reveals his biblical number 666. But in order to understand this section of Scripture, you cannot begin in Revelation without (ideally) having read chapters 1–11 first and (ideally) having a broad grasp of the entire Bible up to that point. But what many readers of the Bible do not know about this section is that Revelation 12–14 is one unit in Scripture. You cannot begin in chapter 13, nor can you stay in that chapter; both Revelation 12 and 14 give important parts of God's revelation.

Revelation 12 contains the spiritual realities that are behind the scenes for the events in chapter 13 that those on earth will see. These spiritual realities are important because they describe a series of preliminary defeats of Satan. Revelation 12:1–2 says, "A great sign appeared in heaven: a woman clothed with the sun, and the moon under her feet, and on her head a crown of twelve stars; and she was with child; and she cried out, being in labor and in pain to give birth." This is called "a great sign," which means we should pay attention to it; yet, sadly, few do. We need to identify the woman in this sign, who is not Mary, but the Jewish people. In Gen 37:9–11 we read of Joseph's dream:

> *Now he had still another dream, and related it to his brothers, and said, "Lo, I have had still another dream; and behold, the sun and the moon and eleven stars were bowing down to me." He related it to his father and to his brothers; and his father rebuked him and said to him, "What is this dream that you have had? Shall I and your mother and your brothers actually come to bow ourselves down before you to the ground?" His brothers were jealous of him, but his father kept the saying in mind.*

In Joseph's dream the sun and the moon depicted Jacob and his brothers, and the eleven stars were those of the twelve tribes of Israel—especially because Joseph considered himself one of the stars in this dream.

Revelation 12:3–5 tells of another great sign in heaven and gives a broad sweep of one of Satan's preliminary defeats:

> *Then another sign appeared in heaven: and behold, a great red dragon having seven heads and ten horns, and on his heads were seven diadems. And his tail swept away a third of the stars of heaven and threw them to the earth. And the dragon stood before the woman who was about to give birth, so that when she gave birth he might devour her child. And she gave birth to a son, a male child, who is to rule all the nations with a rod of iron; and her child was caught up to God and to His throne.*

In this vast swath of time represented, Satan failed to kill the child whom he could not devour; this would include efforts made in the Matthew 2 account. Instead, the child grew to manhood, has ascended to God and to His throne, and is the One who will rule the nations with a rod of iron.

This continuation of the vision in Rev 12:6 explains what the Jewish remnant will do during the tribulation: "The woman fled into the wilderness where she had a place prepared by God, so that there she would be nourished for one thousand two hundred and sixty days." We will need to examine a few other Scripture passages to better understand what is about to happen biblically in this section.

In Dan 12:1, this prophecy is made about Michael during the tribulation:

Now at that time Michael, the great prince who stands guard over the sons of your people, will arise. And there will be a time of distress such as never occurred since there was a nation until that time; and at that time your people, everyone who is found written in the book, will be rescued.

The explanation and significance of this prophecy are not given until the account of this second preliminary defeat of Satan in Rev 12:7–9:

And there was war in heaven, Michael and his angels waging war with the dragon. The dragon and his angels waged war, and they were not strong enough, and there was no longer a place found for them in heaven. And the great dragon was thrown down, the serpent of old who is called the devil and Satan, who deceives the whole world; he was thrown down to the earth, and his angels were thrown down with him.

> **CONSIDER:** We are not specifically told why Satan's having no future access to heaven will hinder him, but in Eph 2:2 he is called "the prince of the power of the air." Maybe the demonic hierarchy revealed in Eph 6:12 will no longer be structured that way. When Michael and his angels defeat Satan and his angels, Satan and his demons will be thrown down to earth. They still will be very powerful, but their movements will be much more cumbersome at that time.

Revelation 12:10–11 gives the worshipful response that will occur after Satan and his angels have been thrown down:

Then I heard a loud voice in heaven, saying,

"Now the salvation, and the power, and the kingdom of our God and the authority of His Christ have come, for the accuser of our brethren has been

thrown down, he who accuses them before our God day and night. And they
overcame him because of the blood of the Lamb and because of the word of
their testimony, and they did not love their life even when faced with death."

Verse 12 reminds people on earth that the battle is far from over: "For this reason, rejoice, O heavens and you who dwell in them. Woe to the earth and the sea, because the devil has come down to you, having great wrath, knowing that he has only a short time."

Remember that this is a continuing vision that shows Satan's attempt to destroy the Jewish remnant, but God will use His creation to protect that remnant, as Rev 12:13–16 shows:

And when the dragon saw that he was thrown down to the earth, he perse-
cuted the woman who gave birth to the male child. But the two wings of the
great eagle were given to the woman, so that she could fly into the wilder-
ness to her place, where she was nourished for a time and times and half
a time, from the presence of the serpent. And the serpent poured water like
a river out of his mouth after the woman, so that he might cause her to be
swept away with the flood. But the earth helped the woman, and the earth
opened its mouth and drank up the river which the dragon poured out of his
mouth.

After this third preliminary defeat, verse 17 forebodes the following: "So the dragon was enraged with the woman, and went off to make war with the rest of her children, who keep the commandments of God and hold to the testimony of Jesus." This resulting wrath of Satan helps explain the massive number of martyrs seen in the fifth seal judgment of Rev 6:9–11.

It is extremely significant to note that in the chapter that gives details of the rise of the Antichrist (Revelation 13), Satan will not disclose to the world his three preliminary defeats in Revelation 12, nor that he has only a short time left. Revelation 13 reveals the highest peak of evil activity of Satan and the Antichrist. More about certain crucial matters in Revelation 13 will be in the last chapter of this *Handbook*.

The spiritual realities that were shown in Revelation 12 will be the basis for what the world will see, and Rev 13:3–4 shows Satan relinquishing his power, throne, and great authority to the Antichrist:

I saw one of his heads as if it had been slain, and his fatal wound was healed. And the whole earth was amazed and followed after the beast; they worshiped the dragon because he gave his authority to the beast; and they worshiped the beast, saying, "Who is like the beast, and who is able to wage war with him?"

KEY: Satan's ultimate goal is to be worshipped (see his temptation of Jesus in Matthew 4). In that same temptation, after Satan had shown Jesus all the kingdoms of the world in a moment of time, Satan told Jesus, "I will give You all this domain and its glory; for it has been handed over to me, and I give it to whomever I wish" (Luke 4:5–6). Jesus rejected the offer; the Antichrist will gladly take it during the tribulation.

Revelation 13:5–8 shows the pinnacle of Satan's evil:

There was given to him a mouth speaking arrogant words and blasphemies, and authority to act for forty-two months was given to him. And he opened his mouth in blasphemies against God, to blaspheme His name and His tabernacle, that is, those who dwell in heaven. It was also given to him to make war with the saints and to overcome them, and authority over every tribe and people and tongue and nation was given to him. All who dwell on the earth will worship him, everyone whose name has not been written from the foundation of the world in the book of life of the Lamb who has been slain.

Notice how the promise to the overcomer in Rev 3:10 differs from the sobering admonition in Rev 13:9–10: "If anyone has an ear, let him hear. If anyone is destined for captivity, to captivity he goes; if anyone kills with the sword, with the sword he must be killed. Here is the perseverance and the faith of the saints." Notice, as well, how this differs from the earlier sevenfold usage in Revelation 2–3, such as in 2:29: "He who has an ear, let him hear what the Spirit says to the churches." Revelation 13:9–10 is expressly for those who are saved during the tribulation.

Verses 11–18 disclose that another beast, who will be called "the false prophet," will arise also and will play a major role in the Antichrist gaining his God-ordained conquest:

Then I saw another beast coming up out of the earth; and he had two horns like a lamb and he spoke as a dragon. He exercises all the authority of the first beast in his presence. And he makes the earth and those who dwell in it to worship the first beast, whose fatal wound was healed. He performs great signs, so that he even makes fire come down out of heaven to the earth in the presence of men. And he deceives those who dwell on the earth because of the signs which it was given him to perform in the presence of the beast, telling those who dwell on the earth to make an image to the beast who had the wound of the sword and has come to life. And it was given to him to give breath to the image of the beast, so that the image of the beast would even speak and cause as many as do not worship the image of the beast to be killed. And he causes all, the small and the great, and the rich and the poor, and the free men and the slaves, to be given a mark on their right hand or on their forehead, and he provides that no one will be able to buy or to sell, except the one who has the mark, either the name of the beast or the number of his name. Here is wisdom. Let him who has understanding calculate the number of the beast, for the number is that of a man; and his number is six hundred and sixty-six.

Remember that Revelation 12–14 is one unit. So in the chapter immediately following the pinnacle of Satan's evil (Revelation 13) comes the victory of the one hundred and forty-four thousand choice Jewish vessels standing with the Lamb (Rev 14:1–5). This looks past Satan's temporary reign to Jesus's return to His earth—and the guaranteed ultimate victory. Revelation 14:6–7 reveals,

And I saw another angel flying in midheaven, having an eternal gospel to preach to those who live on the earth, and to every nation and tribe and tongue and people; and he said with a loud voice, "Fear God, and give Him glory, because the hour of His judgment has come; worship Him who made the heaven and the earth and sea and springs of waters."

CRUCIAL: The last part of the tribulation will ultimately conclude with only two choices: Jesus Christ or the Antichrist. No other options, no other rivals will be present then. Everyone alive will eventually have to choose which one to serve, and this choice has eternal consequences—and temporary ones as well.

Revelation 14:8 states, "And another angel, a second one, followed, saying, 'Fallen, fallen is Babylon the great, she who has made all the nations drink of the wine of the passion of her immorality.'"

Revelation 14:9–11 shows:

> *Then another angel, a third one, followed them, saying with a loud voice, "If anyone worships the beast and his image, and receives a mark on his forehead or on his hand, he also will drink of the wine of the wrath of God, which is mixed in full strength in the cup of His anger; and he will be tormented with fire and brimstone in the presence of the holy angels and in the presence of the Lamb. And the smoke of their torment goes up forever and ever; they have no rest day and night, those who worship the beast and his image, and whoever receives the mark of his name."*

KEY: People living in the tribulation will not be physically forced to be branded with the mark of the beast. It must be received by those who willfully accept it. However, Scripture clearly states that once they make the choice to receive the mark of the beast, their eternal destinies are sealed. There will be no hope for salvation.

Revelation 14:12–13 is another admonition for the faithful during the tribulation:

> *Here is the perseverance of the saints who keep the commandments of God and their faith in Jesus.*

> *And I heard a voice from heaven, saying, "Write, 'Blessed are the dead who die in the Lord from now on!'" "Yes," says the Spirit, "so that they may rest from their labors, for their deeds follow with them."*

Revelation 14:14–20 concludes with a vision of an angel about to put his sickle (in this vision) into all the earth, thus setting the stage for the final judgments. Verses 19–20 reiterate that these are wrath-of-God judgments that are promised:

> *So the angel swung his sickle to the earth and gathered the clusters from the vine of the earth, and threw them into the great wine press of the wrath of God. And the wine press was trodden outside the city, and blood came out*

from the wine press, up to the horses' bridles, for a distance of two hundred miles.

Revelation 15:1 continues the judgments that will come in rapid succession: "Then I saw another sign in heaven, great and marvelous, seven angels who had seven plagues, which are the last, because in them the wrath of God is finished." Coming from the temple of God in heaven, verses 7–8 reveal:

Then one of the four living creatures gave to the seven angels seven golden bowls full of the wrath of God, who lives forever and ever. And the temple was filled with smoke from the glory of God and from His power; and no one was able to enter the temple until the seven plagues of the seven angels were finished.

Revelation 16:1 gives the command for these final judgments to begin: "Then I heard a loud voice from the temple, saying to the seven angels, 'Go and pour out on the earth the seven bowls of the wrath of God.'" Verses 2–4 are the first three bowl judgments:

So the first angel went and poured out his bowl on the earth; and it became a loathsome and malignant sore on the people who had the mark of the beast and who worshiped his image.

The second angel poured out his bowl into the sea, and it became blood like that of a dead man; and every living thing in the sea died.

Then the third angel poured out his bowl into the rivers and the springs of waters; and they became blood.

Revelation 16:6–7 gives a brief interlude and an answer to one who might ask how God can be so cruel:

[F]or they poured out the blood of saints and prophets, and You have given them blood to drink. They deserve it." And I heard the altar saying, "Yes, O Lord God, the Almighty, true and righteous are Your judgments."

In Rev 16:8–11, the fourth and fifth bowl judgments show the vast-reaching sphere of these judgments, and these verses prove that Antichrist certainly is not God because he will also be a recipient of these judgments:

The fourth angel poured out his bowl upon the sun, and it was given to it to scorch men with fire. Men were scorched with fierce heat; and they blasphemed the name of God who has the power over these plagues, and they did not repent so as to give Him glory.

Then the fifth angel poured out his bowl on the throne of the beast, and his kingdom became darkened; and they gnawed their tongues because of pain, and they blasphemed the God of heaven because of their pains and their sores; and they did not repent of their deeds.

Revelation 16:12–14 begins gathering nations for the final battle:

The sixth angel poured out his bowl on the great river, the Euphrates; and its water was dried up, so that the way would be prepared for the kings from the east.

And I saw coming out of the mouth of the dragon and out of the mouth of the beast and out of the mouth of the false prophet, three unclean spirits like frogs; for they are spirits of demons, performing signs, which go out to the kings of the whole world, to gather them together for the war of the great day of God, the Almighty.

Jesus interjects an admonition to the faithful in Rev 16:15: "Behold, I am coming like a thief. Blessed is the one who stays awake and keeps his clothes, so that he will not walk about naked and men will not see his shame." When God dries the Euphrates River, it will become a conduit for gathering armies from the east to assemble. The resulting effect of the sixth bowl judgment is seen in verse 16: "And they gathered them together to the place which in Hebrew is called Har-Magedon."

In Rev 16:17–21, the final bowl judgment is poured out:

Then the seventh angel poured out his bowl upon the air, and a loud voice came out of the temple from the throne, saying, "It is done." And there were flashes of lightning and sounds and peals of thunder; and there was a great earthquake, such as there had not been since man came to be upon the earth, so great an earthquake was it, and so mighty. The great city was split into three parts, and the cities of the nations fell. Babylon the great was remembered before God, to give her the cup of the wine of His fierce wrath. And every island fled away, and the mountains were not found. And huge hailstones, about one hundred pounds each, came down from heaven upon men; and men blasphemed God because of the plague of the hail, because its plague was extremely severe.

How fitting it is that part of this judgment will be one-hundred-pound hailstones. In Genesis 1, God created absolutely everything He would need for His creation, and then He rested, which means that He would do no more creating. How awe-inspiring that God, when speaking to Job in some of the earliest Scriptures written, gave us a glimpse of storehouses of hail. After much hardship and sorrow, Job blames God for the many tragic circumstances and demands an answer from Him. God responds, beginning in Job 38:1–4, by asking Job a series of questions that he must answer correctly if he is to receive an explanation from God.

Then the LORD answered Job out of the whirlwind and said,

"Who is this that darkens counsel

By words without knowledge?

"Now gird up your loins like a man,

And I will ask you, and you instruct Me!

"Where were you when I laid the foundation of the earth?

Tell Me, if you have understanding,"

God lovingly chastises Job with questions about His heavenly storehouses. Especially notice what is stored in one of them and the specific time and way that it will be used, according to Job 38:22–23:

"Have you entered the storehouses of the snow,

Or have you seen the storehouses of the hail,

Which I have reserved for the time of distress,

For the day of war and battle?"

In the last bowl judgment in Rev 16:21, God will gather these hailstones that He has previously created and that He has stored somewhere in His creation, and He will use them against the Antichrist and his kingdom. This is another use of the Isa 25:1 praise passage, we find "plans formed long ago, with perfect faithfulness."

Revelation 17 reveals the doom of religious Babylon, which the Antichrist and his underlings will tolerate for a while in the tribulation. In verses 12–14, this part of the vision shows ten kings whose alignment with the Antichrist also means their eternal doom:

The ten horns which you saw are ten kings who have not yet received a kingdom, but they receive authority as kings with the beast for one hour. These have one purpose, and they give their power and authority to the beast.

These will wage war against the Lamb, and the Lamb will overcome them, because He is Lord of lords and King of kings, and those who are with Him are the called and chosen and faithful."

In another great sovereignty of God passage, Rev 17:16–17 discloses this:

And the ten horns which you saw, and the beast, these will hate the harlot and will make her desolate and naked, and will eat her flesh and will burn her up with fire. For God has put it in their hearts to execute His purpose by having a common purpose, and by giving their kingdom to the beast, until the words of God will be fulfilled.

For a while, economic Babylon will flourish. Eventually God will bring it to its sudden end. Two different reactions are seen in 18:19–21:

And they threw dust on their heads and were crying out, weeping and mourning, saying, "Woe, woe, the great city, in which all who had ships at sea became rich by her wealth, for in one hour she has been laid waste!' Rejoice over her, O heaven, and you saints and apostles and prophets, because God has pronounced judgment for you against her."

Then a strong angel took up a stone like a great millstone and threw it into the sea, saying, "So will Babylon, the great city, be thrown down with violence, and will not be found any longer."

With this final judgment, the judgments of the tribulation end, and the true Triumphal Entry is about to ensue. It too will include a series of judgments.

Events Leading Up to the Return and
Reign of the King to Earth

After the end of the wrath of God judgments in the tribulation, the focus shifts with a fourfold "Hallelujah!" beginning in Rev 19:1–2:

After these things I heard something like a loud voice of a great multitude in heaven, saying,

> *"Hallelujah! Salvation and glory and power belong to our God; BECAUSE HIS JUDGMENTS ARE TRUE AND RIGHTEOUS; for He has judged the great harlot who was corrupting the earth with her immorality, and HE HAS AVENGED THE BLOOD OF HIS BOND-SERVANTS ON HER."*

> Revelation 19:6 adds, *"Then I heard something like the voice of a great multitude and like the sound of many waters and like the sound of mighty peals of thunder, saying, 'Hallelujah! For the Lord our God, the Almighty, reigns.'"*

While the tribulation has been taking place on earth, the marriage supper of the Lamb has begun in heaven and will eventually broaden out to include all of the redeemed, beginning its description in Rev 19:7–10:

> *"Let us rejoice and be glad and give the glory to Him, for the marriage of the Lamb has come and His bride has made herself ready." It was given to her to clothe herself in fine linen, bright and clean; for the fine linen is the righteous acts of the saints.*

> *Then he said to me, "Write, 'Blessed are those who are invited to the marriage supper of the Lamb.'" And he said to me, "These are true words of God." Then I fell at his feet to worship him. And he said to me, "Do not do that; I am a fellow servant of yours and your brethren who hold the testimony of Jesus; worship God. For the testimony of Jesus is the spirit of prophecy."*

In verses 11–16, the real Triumphal Entry will transpire, and Jesus will return in judgment mode—and with the attributes of God:

> *And I saw heaven opened, and behold, a white horse, and He who sat on it is called Faithful and True; and in righteousness He judges and wages war. His eyes are a flame of fire, and on His head are many diadems; and He has a name written on Him which no one knows except Himself. He is clothed with a robe dipped in blood, and His name is called The Word of God. And*

the armies which are in heaven, clothed in fine linen, white and clean, were following Him on white horses. From His mouth comes a sharp sword, so that with it He may strike down the nations, and He will rule them with a rod of iron; and He treads the wine press of the fierce wrath of God, the Almighty. And on His robe and on His thigh He has a name written, "KING OF KINGS, AND LORD OF LORDS."

Revelation 19:17–18 contains an angelic invitation to all of the birds in midair to come to eat of the carnage that will result from the coming war. The enemies of Jesus assemble themselves against Him and are judged appropriately, as Rev 19:19–21 reveals:

And I saw the beast and the kings of the earth and their armies assembled to make war against Him who sat on the horse and against His army.

And the beast was seized, and with him the false prophet who performed the signs in his presence, by which he deceived those who had received the mark of the beast and those who worshiped his image; these two were thrown alive [literally "living'"] into the lake of fire which burns with brimstone. And the rest were killed with the sword which came from the mouth of Him who sat on the horse, and all the birds were filled with their flesh.

Much more about these and related matters will be in the final chapter of the *Handbook.* In harmony with what God has already promised (see Isa 24:21–22), Satan is captured and secured for a temporary judgment:

Then I saw an angel coming down from heaven, holding the key of the abyss and a great chain in his hand. And he laid hold of the dragon, the serpent of old, who is the devil and Satan, and bound him for a thousand years; and he threw him into the abyss, and shut it and sealed it over him, so that he would not deceive the nations any longer, until the thousand years were completed; after these things he must be released for a short time. (Rev 20:1–3)

The redeemed of the tribulation will rise at this time and receive their resurrected bodies, and they will reign with Jesus for a thousand years, as Rev 20:4–6 indicates:

Then I saw thrones, and they sat on them, and judgment was given to them. And I saw the souls of those who had been beheaded because of their testimony of Jesus and because of the word of God, and those who had not worshiped the beast or his image, and had not received the mark on their forehead and on their hand; and they came to life and reigned with Christ for a thousand years. The rest of the dead did not come to life until the thousand years were completed. This is the first resurrection. Blessed and holy is the one who has a part in the first resurrection; over these the second death has no power, but they will be priests of God and of Christ and will reign with Him for a thousand years.

Verses 7–10 describe the final rebellion that Satan will lead and its outcome:

When the thousand years are completed, Satan will be released from his prison, and will come out to deceive the nations which are in the four corners of the earth, Gog and Magog, to gather them together for the war; the number of them is like the sand of the seashore. And they came up on the broad plain of the earth and surrounded the camp of the saints and the beloved city, and fire came down from heaven and devoured them. And the devil who deceived them was thrown into the lake of fire and brimstone, where the beast and the false prophet are also; and they will be tormented day and night forever and ever.

Revelation 20:7–10 records the last sinful act mentioned in the Bible. Remember to whom the complete authority to instigate judgments has been given as stated in John 5:22. In accordance with that pronouncement of authority, Jesus judges the eternally damned at the great white throne judgment described in verses 11–15:

Then I saw a great white throne and Him who sat upon it, from whose presence earth and heaven fled away, and no place was found for them. And I saw the dead, the great and the small, standing before the throne, and books were opened; and another book was opened, which is the book of life; and the dead were judged from the things which were written in the books, according to their deeds. And the sea gave up the dead which were in it, and death and Hades gave up the dead which were in them; and they were judged, every one of them according to their deeds. Then death and Hades were thrown into the lake of fire. This is the second death, the lake of fire. And if anyone's name was not found written in the book of life, he was thrown into the lake of fire.

> **USE THIS IN WITNESSING:** Should people say to you that they only want from God what they deserve for what they have done, point them to Rev 20:11–15. There everyone at the white throne judgment will have the books of their lives opened and will be judged by the works they have done. Tragically, each will receive from God exactly what they deserve. No one who appears at this judgment will be saved. We who are saved do not want from God what we deserve; we want—and thankfully receive—grace upon grace.

Whereas Rev 20:7–10 portrays Satan in his final efforts at deceiving and seducing people to commit the last sins listed in Scripture, the great white throne judgment gives a vivid description of how this is the last time that anyone who is lost will ever be heard of—forever.

The Preferred Name

The Bible is explicit in matters regarding the end. Initially, in answering what happens at the end of the millennial kingdom, 1 Cor 15:20–24 foretells what will occur:

> *But now Christ has been raised from the dead, the first fruits of those who are asleep. For since by a man came death, by a man also came the resurrection of the dead. For as in Adam all die, so also in Christ all will be made alive. But each in his own order: Christ the first fruits, after that those who are Christ's at His coming, then comes the end, when He hands over the kingdom to the God and Father, when He has abolished all rule and all authority and power.*

Fittingly, Christ/Messiah is a title for Jesus—but not His name. It is a title that one day He will fulfill completely. Revelation 20:6 is the last time the word Christ is found in the Bible: "Blessed and holy is the one who shares in the first resurrection! The second death has no power over them, but they will be priests of God and of Christ, and they will reign with Him for a thousand years."

So in this section, Revelation 21–22, where God gives us quite a small preview of heaven (also called the eternal state) and because only the

Godhead, the redeemed of all time, and the holy angels will be present and active, Jesus has chosen for us to call Him by His preferred name among His family: the Lamb. We will see that this name is used frequently in this section on heaven.

Revelation 21:1–4 begins:

Then I saw a new heaven and a new earth; for the first heaven and the first earth passed away, and there is no longer any sea. And I saw the holy city, new Jerusalem, coming down out of heaven from God, made ready as a bride adorned for her husband. And I heard a loud voice from the throne, saying, "Behold, the tabernacle of God is among men, and He will dwell among them, and they shall be His people, and God Himself will be among them, and He will wipe away every tear from their eyes; and there will no longer be any death; there will no longer be any mourning, or crying, or pain; the first things have passed away."

Verses 5-7 continues:

And He who sits on the throne said, "Behold, I am making all things new." And He said, "Write, for these words are faithful and true." Then He said to me, "It is done. I am the Alpha and the Omega, the beginning and the end. I will give to the one who thirsts from the spring of the water of life without cost. He who overcomes will inherit these things, and I will be his God and he will be My son."

In Rev 21:9–14, John gets to see a preview of new Jerusalem:

Then one of the seven angels who had the seven bowls full of the seven last plagues came and spoke with me, saying, "Come here, I will show you the bride, the wife of the Lamb" [note the first usage of "the Lamb" throughout this section.] And he carried me away in the Spirit to a great and high mountain, and showed me the holy city, Jerusalem, coming down out of heaven from God, having the glory of God. Her brilliance was like a very costly stone, as a stone of crystal-clear jasper. It had a great and high wall, with twelve gates, and at the gates twelve angels; and names were written on them, which are the names of the twelve tribes of the sons of Israel. There were three gates on the east and three gates on the north and three gates on the south and three gates on the west. And the wall of the city had twelve foundation stones, and on them were the twelve names of the twelve apostles of the Lamb.

Very fittingly, verse 11 uses the phrase "arrayed with God's glory," and as we know, the glory of God changes everything—including eternity.

Revelation 21:22–23 reveals these incredibly warming and encouraging verses for the faithful:

> *I saw no temple in it, for the Lord God the Almighty and the Lamb are its temple. And the city has no need of the sun or of the moon to shine on it, for the glory of God has illumined it, and its lamp is the Lamb.*

Revelation 22:1–5 continues:

> *Then he showed me a river of the water of life, clear as crystal, coming from the throne of God and of the Lamb, in the middle of its street. On either side of the river was the tree of life, bearing twelve kinds of fruit, yielding its fruit every month; and the leaves of the tree were for the healing of the nations. There will no longer be any curse; and the throne of God and of the Lamb will be in it, and His bond-servants will serve Him; they will see His face, and His name will be on their foreheads. And there will no longer be any night; and they will not have need of the light of a lamp nor the light of the sun, because the Lord God will illumine them; and they will reign forever and ever.*

Verse 6 ends the apostle John's—and our—very broad preview of heaven: "And he said to me, 'These words are faithful and true'; and the Lord, the God of the spirits of the prophets, sent His angel to show to His bond-servants the things which must soon take place." God closes the book on—so to speak—and will not give us any more details about our future dwelling place until we go home to be with Him, or until He comes back for us to be with Him.

Final Words and Admonitions in Revelation 22:7–21

Appropriately, Jesus begins this final section in Rev 22:7 this way: "And behold, I am coming quickly. Blessed is he who heeds the words of the prophecy of this book." John's attestation and interaction with the angel are shown in Rev 22:8–10:

> *I, John, am the one who heard and saw these things. And when I heard and saw, I fell down to worship at the feet of the angel who showed me these*

> things. But he said to me, "Do not do that. I am a fellow servant of yours
> and of your brethren the prophets and of those who heed the words of this
> book. Worship God."

> And he said to me, "Do not seal up the words of the prophecy of this book,
> for the time is near."

We should note that if this angel somehow had been Satan—which, of
course it could not be at this point—he would gladly have received John's
worship and never would have corrected him.

In Rev 22:12–16 comes some of the last admonitions and warnings
by Jesus:

> "Behold, I am coming quickly, and My reward is with Me, to render to every
> man according to what he has done. I am the Alpha and the Omega, the first
> and the last, the beginning and the end."

> Blessed are those who wash their robes, so that they may have the right
> to the tree of life, and may enter by the gates into the city. Outside are the
> dogs and the sorcerers and the immoral persons and the murderers and the
> idolaters, and everyone who loves and practices lying.

> "I, Jesus, have sent My angel to testify to you these things for the churches.
> I am the root and the descendant of David, the bright morning star."

The Holy Spirit adds His affirmation in verse 17: "The Spirit and the
bride say, 'Come.' And let the one who hears say, 'Come.' And let the one
who is thirsty come; let the one who wishes take the water of life without
cost." We are not told who speaks Rev 22:18–19, but because it has such
an authoritative manner, many believe that this is Jesus speaking:

> I testify to everyone who hears the words of the prophecy of this book: if
> anyone adds to them, God will add to him the plagues which are written
> in this book; and if anyone takes away from the words of the book of this
> prophecy, God will take away his part from the tree of life and from the holy
> city, which are written in this book.

Revelation 22:20 records the last words of Jesus in Scripture: "Yes, I
am coming quickly." This concludes with this short prayer of praise and
affirmation: "Amen. Come, Lord Jesus." Revelation 22:21 gives the last
sentence in the book of Revelation and thereby ends the entire closed

canon of God from Genesis through Revelation: "The grace of the Lord Jesus be with all. Amen."

Summary and Conclusion

Among many other things, in this chapter we learned that (1) Jesus appeared to the apostle John in judgment mode in Revelation 1. (2) Revelation 1:19 contains the God-given, three-part outline for Revelation as a whole. John was to "write the things which [he had] seen" (past tense)—things up to that point in Revelation 1; "the things which are"—that is, those things that happened in John's lifetime—with regard to the seven churches in Revelation 2–3; and about "the things which will take place after these things"—that is, the material now comprising the bulk of the book, Rev 4:1–22:6. (3) Revelation 4:1 concludes with the words "what must take place after these things." In Revelation 4, John is transported in a vision into the very throne room of God the Creator. (4) Revelation 5 is crucial for understanding the rest of Revelation. In the vision, only One is found worthy to take the scroll from the right hand of God the Father—the Lion from the tribe of Judah (see Gen 48:8–12). When John turns, instead of seeing Jesus as a Lion, he sees Him as "a Lamb standing, as if slain" (Rev 5:6). (5) Revelation 4–5 presents the spiritual realities behind the events that will take place in the tribulation (chaps. 6–18). (6) Revelation 3:10 is an important, presently unfulfilled promise to the overcomer, whom Jesus will keep out of the tribulation. This verse also helps explain what the tribulation (Revelation 6–18) will be: "[it is] the hour of testing, that hour which is about to come upon the whole world, to test those who dwell on the earth." Revelation 15:1 explains that "the wrath of God" judgments will take place in the tribulation, and they will be meted out in very measured doses. (7) We were reminded again of the biblical promises as to the uniqueness of the tribulation; it cannot properly be compared to any other time in the history of the world.

We also learned that, (8) far from offering "peace and safety" (1 Thess 5:3), the first six seals and the judgments that follow mean that more than one-fourth of the world's population will be killed by the end of that time. (9) The fifth seal judgment (Rev 6:9–11) is different from the other seal judgments and shows an early fruit report of the gospel going out into all the nations during the tribulation (Matt 24:14). The mass martyrdom also shows the strong opposition and perils many of these redeemed ones will receive during the tribulation. (10) Revelation 7 is a divine interlude between the tribulation judgments. This chapter reveals the sealing of the one hundred and forty-four thousand from the twelve tribes of Israel (vv. 1–8) and gives a disclosure of the vast number of Gentiles who will be saved during the tribulation (vv. 9–17). (11) The description of the one hundred and forty-four thousand sealed from the twelve tribes of Israel occurs in Rev 14:1–5. These individuals will be used greatly in Jewish evangelism. For those who use the absence of the tribe of Dan as proof against any normative reading of the book of Revelation, the Bible offers more than enough substantial answers to resolve this seeming (to some) dilemma (Gen 49:1, 16–18, 28; Ezek 43:1–5; 48:1–2, 29–32; Zech 13:8–9). (12) In Rev 8:1, Jesus breaks the seventh seal, which leads to the intensified severity in trumpet judgments, four of which occur in Revelation 8; the fifth and sixth trumpet judgments are in Revelation 9. Cumulatively, approximately two-thirds of the entire earth's population—or more—will have been killed by the end of this time in the tribulation.

In this chapter we also learned that (13) Revelation 10 is the next interlude in the book of Revelation. Similar to instructions given to Ezekiel in Ezek 2:7–3:3, the apostle John was commanded to eat a little scroll (in this vision). Eating the scroll was commanded expressly for the purpose stated in Rev 10:11: "And they said to me, 'You must prophesy again concerning many peoples and nations and tongues and kings.'" The emphasis in this section is specifically on the explicit details given with the individuals involved—both of good and evil. (14) In Rev 11:1–2 the temple of God and Jerusalem is given over to the Gentiles to trample underfoot for forty-two months. In the midst of this, God raises up two witnesses and grants to them supernatural abilities (vv. 3–6) and uses this context to give the first reference to the Antichrist in Revelation (vv. 7–10). That individual kills the two witnesses, but later God grants them a resurrection and ascension (vv. 11–12).

We learned also that (15) Revelation 12–14 is one section in Revelation. You cannot begin your studies in chapter 13 and hope to understand it correctly. Chapter 12 reveals the spiritual realities behind the events that the world will see, especially with the rise of the Antichrist and the false prophet in Revelation 13. (16) Revelation 12 is a series of preliminary defeats, including Michael and his angels casting Satan and his angels out of heaven and restricting them to earth (vv. 10–12). Satan will then try some means to devour the Jewish remnant, but God will miraculously intervene to rescue and protect them (vv. 13–16). At that time Satan turns his wrath to the rest of the redeemed who remain on earth. (17) With the ascendency of the Antichrist and given what the world will see (Revelation 13), Satan is not about to admit he is there that day only because of multiple preliminary defeats he has experienced (chap. 12) and knows "that he has only a short time" (v. 12). Satan relinquishes his power to the Antichrist whereby both he and the Antichrist will be worshiped. Revelation 13:5–8 shows the pinnacle of Satan's power. (18) With Revelation 12–14 being one unit, the story by no means ends there. Chapter 14 shows preliminary victories, such as the Lamb and His one hundred and forty-four thousand standing on Mount Zion (vv. 1–5), and an eagle (in this vision) giving the eternal gospel to those on earth. Revelation 14 also contains the warning that anyone who receives the mark of the beast seals his or her eternal damnation (v. 8).

We further learned that (19) Revelation 15–16 give the seven rapid-fire last wrath-of-God bowl judgments, each of which will increase in intensity as God starts preparing the world for Armageddon. (20) Revelation 17 is the doom of religious Babylon, who will initially help the Antichrist and his kings rise to dominance, though they will turn against and devour Babylon eventually. Revelation 18 shows the fall of economic Babylon; she will never rise again.

We saw also that (21) Revelation 19 is the true Triumphal Entry, and this begins with the vantage point of heaven (vv. 1–6), the marriage supper of the Lamb (vv. 7–10), and the return of Jesus in judgment mode and bearing the attributes of God (vv. 11–16). (22) Jesus defeats His spiritual enemies, throwing the Antichrist and the false prophet into the lake of fire alive. He kills those who remain of His early enemies (Rev 19:19–21), and a strong angel casts Satan into the abyss, seals it, and holds him there a thousand years. We are told that after the thousand years, Satan must

be released for a short time. (23) Revelation 20:4–6 discloses that the redeemed of the tribulation come to life and reign with Jesus the Messiah
for a thousand years. (24) Verses 7–10 describe Satan's promised release
for the short time and the final rebellion and its outcome, and Revelation
20:11–15 presents the great white throne judgment. After this judgment,
never again will there be either sin or sinner.

We additionally learned in this chapter that (25) Rev 20:6 is the last
time the word "Christ" is used in the book of Revelation and in the Bible as
a whole. The preferred name that Jesus will go by from Revelation 21 and
throughout eternity is "the Lamb." (26) God gave John a preview of new
Jerusalem, a city which will be quite an important part of the eternal state
but by no means all of heaven. Revelation 21:1–22:6 gives the description
for which many of us so zealously long. It gives a foretaste of what it will
be like to live in the midst of the Trinity and the redeemed and angelic
realm—with the glory of God—and in full fellowship with them—forever.
(27) The final section (Rev 22:7–21) concludes with words of exhortation,
warning, and praise.

Deeper Walk Study Questions

1. What is the significance of how Jesus first revealed Himself to John in Revelation 1?
   Why is this important? Explain.

2. Why is Rev 1:19 so important for understanding not only Revelation 1 but also the
   remainder of the book of Revelation? Explain with four biblical truths.

3. What is the importance of the throne room of God in Revelation 4–5? Name six
   important biblical truths from these two chapters.

4. Revelation 5 is crucial for understanding the rest of the book of Revelation. Name nine important biblical truths from this chapter.

5. What does John 5:22 ("For not even the Father judges anyone, but He has given all judgment to the Son") have to do with the remaining events from Revelation 5 onward, as well as with other prophesied events? Explain and give four biblical supports for your answers.

6. What does Rev 5:10 teach regarding the future reign of the redeemed? Does this actually mean the redeemed are promised that one day they will reign on earth? Why or why not? Support your answer biblically.

7. Why is Rev 3:10 important to understanding events before and during the tribulation? Explain your answer biblically. Also, what does Rev 15:1 teach regarding what the tribulation judgments will be? Why is that important to know?

8. Give five biblically sound reasons for the utter uniqueness of the tribulation. Be specific.

9. Identify the amount of life to be killed in the first six seal judgments of Revelation 6. Be specific in giving your answers. How is the fifth seal judgment different? Explain.

10. What is the significance of Rev 7:1–8 as it relates to the whole book? Also, many use the absence of the tribe of Dan as proof that the book of Revelation should not be read in a normative use of the language. Framing your answer biblically, give four ways the Bible answers this seeming dilemma in the text. Then show how these answers actually strengthen the literal-grammatical normative use of the language. Be specific.

11. Summarize the events of Revelation 8–9. Be specific and show the intensifying tribulation judgments biblically. Also, note cumulatively about how many people will have been killed in the tribulation by the end of this time.

12. How does Revelation 10 connect with Ezek 2:7–3:3? What does Rev 10:11 explain about the writing of the next part of Revelation? Explain and be specific.

13. Name six biblical prophecies in Revelation 11 and tell why these are important to know. Support your answer biblically.

14. Why must Revelation 12–14 be studied as one section of Scripture? What are the preliminary defeats of Satan stated in Chapter 12? Tell what Rev 12:12 reveals and why this is very important to know. How do these relate to Revelation 13? Explain and be specific.

15. Go through Revelation 13 and put down eight important biblical truths from this chapter. Be specific.

16. Write seven cogent biblical truths from Revelation 14.

17. Give the sequence of events in Revelation 15–16. Be specific and tell why these are important and how they connect with the previous chapters of Revelation.

18. Give six truths from Revelation 17 and another six from chapter 18. Why are these important to know in relation to Revelation and the rest of the Bible? Explain and support your answer biblically.

19. Give twelve biblical truths from Rev 19:1–16 and explain why these are important to know.

20. Give a detailed account of Jesus's victory in Rev 19:21–20:3. Be specific.

21. What does Rev 20:4–6 present as occurring then? Give five biblical truths and tell why each one is important.

22. Give a broad account of Rev 21:1–22:6. Name eight biblical truths from these verses and tell why they are important.

23. Write six biblical truths from Rev 22:7–21 and tell why these are important.

CHAPTER 30

Will the Antichrist Actually Rise from the Dead? And, Why Satan Must Be Released[1]

Preliminary Interpretational Issues Considered

For those who accept the Bible as the holy Word of God, two positions exist between two diametrically opposing explanations concerning Rev 13:3–4. Regarding the fatal wound of the beast and his subsequent return to life, John wrote,

> I saw one of his heads as if it had been slain, and his fatal wound was healed. And the whole earth was amazed and followed after the beast; they worshiped the dragon because he gave his authority to the beast; and they worshiped the beast, saying, "Who is like the beast, and who is able to wage war with him?"

Multiple questions have arisen about these verses throughout the centuries and continue to arise even from those who hold to a futuristic understanding of the book of Revelation. Is this actually the death and return to life of a future individual, or is it a reference to the return and revitalization of the future worldwide Roman Empire? Furthermore, if Rev 13:3–4 does, in fact, refer to an individual, one core issue must be considered: who brings the beast back to life, Satan or God? This is a pertinent question

---

[1] For much more information on this, see the full article by Gregory H. Harris, "Can Satan Raise the Dead? Toward a Biblical View of the Beast's Wound," *Master's Seminary Journal* 18, no. 1 (Spring 2007:) 23-41 (https://www.tms.edu/m/tmsj18b.pdf).

because, as will be shown, often the interpretation of who or what comes back to life is based on an assessment of what Satan can or cannot actually perform.

Those who hold that the beast returns to life by means of Satan present this as part of the uniqueness of what will transpire during the tribulation. Because the power of the Antichrist will be the pinnacle of Satan's power and deception, it is held that Satan is the one who brings his beast, the Antichrist, back from the grave. However, if the above statement is true, multiple questions and concerns have been raised about whether or not John did witness a return to life of one who actually died—especially a return to life wrought by Satan. In rebuking this position, some respond with their own inferences, from which they have arrived at their interpretation of Rev 13:3–4, that this event could have come only in the realm of God.

Both positions raise valid points to consider; both have issues of their own to address. People express legitimate concerns about anyone other than God being the Author of life. Jesus affirmed as much, such as in John 5:21: "For just as the Father raises the dead and gives them life, even so the Son also gives life to whom He wishes." As seen in this verse, the Father raises the dead; in the same verse, Jesus asserts that He has the authority to give life to whomever He wishes.

Because of verses such as these, it is valid to question the supposition that Satan could at anytime possess and exercise the creative power of God, which is what will transpire if Satan brings his Antichrist back from the grave. Yet those who hold the futurist position of the Antichrist being brought back from the dead at least allow the text to speak for itself and seek to explain the wound of the beast. Plus, this harmonizes with other references within the book of Revelation, including the amazement of the entire unbelieving world and the worship of the beast and of Satan that will result. Others note that it is the exact phrase used in Rev 5:6 where John "saw between the throne (with the four living creatures) and the elders a Lamb standing, as if slain." These are the same words used to describe Jesus who died and returned to life, and we would not nor could not weaken that miraculous occurrence in any way as not being a legitimate death and return to life.

One of the more popular views is that all the events surrounding the Antichrist (Rev 13:1–8) already occurred during the reign of Nero. Sometimes part of the rationale for those who have this belief is that if the Bible would be literally interpreted this would mean that two-thirds of the Jews who go into the tribulation would be promised death, something many conclude would never happen. However, as we have previously seen in Zech 13:8–9, God does indeed promise such a judgment for the Jews in the tribulation:

"It will come about in all the land,"

Declares the LORD,

"That two parts in it will be cut off and perish;

But the third will be left in it.

"And I will bring the third part through the fire,

Refine them as silver is refined,

And test them as gold is tested.

They will call on My name,

And I will answer them;

I will say, 'They are My people,'

And they will say, 'The LORD is my God.'"

God Himself promises to bring about such a refining judgment to some particular remnant of the Jewish people. The only interpretive options for those who believe the Bible is that this would have either already occurred historically (and shown that it did, in fact, transpire), or it awaits future fulfillment; no other options exist. Regardless of whether one understands this to have been an event in past history or thinks it awaits future fulfillment, the promised perishing of the two-thirds is God's own Word—not the word or invention of humans.

If all of the events surrounding the Antichrist happened in Nero's lifetime, it would mean that the Blessed Restrainer would already have been removed and could no longer be restraining sin. It also means that the world at large would have experienced and endured the wrath of Satan in Revelation, as we saw in 12:12: "Woe to the earth and the sea, because the devil has come down to you, having great wrath, knowing that he has only a short time." Also, Rev 15:1 and 16:1 would have to be fulfilled:

> *Then I saw another sign in heaven, great and marvelous, seven angels who had seven plagues, which are the last, because in them the wrath of God is finished. . . . Then I heard a loud voice from the temple, saying to the seven angels, "Go and pour out on the earth the seven bowls of the wrath of God."*

The idea that these things have already occurred historically is beyond incredible, for one would have to believe not only that people lived through all these things but that the world at large did not even notice "the woe to the earth" warning regarding the wrath of Satan, and then later God Himself poured out His finished wrath in judgment. The righteous are told to live by faith (Hab 2:4), yet to accept that the life or death of Nero and the events of the first century in any way remotely match these Scriptural requirements—plus dozens more—goes vastly beyond living and accepting by faith.

For Those with a Futuristic Understanding of Revelation 13

The concerns about the raising of the beast as a resurrection of an individual are not restricted to opponents of a futuristic understanding of the book of Revelation. Numerous scholars who look for the future reign of Jesus on earth have also raised many of the same questions and concerns and have wrestled with some of the same basic problems adherents to the previous position have raised—especially if the Antichrist is indeed killed and then brought back to life by Satan. Because of such concerns, many such scholars do not see that the raising of the Antichrist from the dead refers to an individual, but rather, restoring to life "the beast" as symbolizing the revived final and worldwide Roman Empire. Based on the promise that the dead are brought out of the grave by the Son of God's voice (John 5:28–29), they believe that the beast's return in Rev 13:3–4 cannot refer to an individual. Therefore, they argue that (1) Satan does not have the power to give life; (2) because Christ alone has the power of the resurrection, (3) Satan could not bring one back to life; and (4) since all the references to this individual present him as a man—not as a supernatural being—it is impossible that this would be a resurrected individual brought back from the dead.

Others have wrestled with the dilemma of attempting to allow the text to speak for itself, while at the same time struggling with many of the same ramifications that such an interpretation might entail. Usually they conclude that a future resurrection of an individual will transpire in the tribulation, at least in appearance, but leave the means of his return to life undecided. Many note that the language used in Rev 13:14 of "the beast who had the wound of the sword and has come to life," is quite strong, denoting a definitive act that will occur. Others argue that the language of the Bible clearly presents a return to life but presents no conclusion as to how this might happen, acknowledging that God will somehow do this for His own purposes. And still others highlight the counterfeit nature of what the world will see: it will be a fake death; it will be a fake resurrection.

The purpose of this part of the chapter is to present a third position between the two opposing positions. It will address the concerns of those who consider it a biblical impossibility for the Antichrist to die and return to life. It will also offer an alternative proposal and solution for those who hold that the return of the beast will, in fact, be an authentic death and return to life of the Antichrist himself performed by Satan, and this part of the chapter will attempt to support the third position biblically.

Preliminary Considerations from the Text

As an initial consideration in addressing the various positions, note that John wrote what he saw in the vision on Patmos (e.g., Rev 1:2; 13:3), as he had earlier been instructed by the Lord (Rev 1:11, 19). Scripture does not disclose who brought the beast back to life in Revelation 13. God revealed this future event to John, who recorded what God had made known to him; neither God nor the apostle explained the means of the beast's return or its significance. John himself may not have understood at the time how the fatal wounding of the beast and his subsequent return to life transpired, as when he later marveled about the great harlot of Rev 17:6–7. Identification of the source of the beast's return—if it is identifiable at all—must come from consideration of related passages, especially those found within the book of Revelation.

Furthermore, Revelation 13 is not an isolated event. Whatever position one takes about the wound of the beast (v. 3) will reflect on other matters related to the beast, particularly his ascent out of the abyss, which is actually mentioned before his advent to the world in chapter 13. For instance, the first reference to the beast in Revelation occurs in 11:7, where he is described as "the beast that comes up out of the abyss" who will make war against God's two witnesses. This verse simply states that the beast will emerge out of the abyss, and it gives no additional information or explanation. More details about this ascent will be revealed later in Revelation 13 and 17. Further, the first reference (11:7) by itself gives no time frame for his ascent out of the abyss. By some means that same beast must first be in the abyss and then must ascend out of it, as shown in Rev 17:8:

> *The beast that you saw was, and is not, and is about to come up out of the abyss and go to destruction. And those who dwell on the earth, whose name has not been written in the book of life from the foundation of the world, will wonder when they see the beast, that he was and is not and will come.*

Ultimately, how one interprets these passages directly relates to how one understands the resurrection of the beast in Revelation 13: Are the death of the beast, his descent into the abyss, and subsequent return out of it references to a future individual, or do they refer to the beast as a revived world empire? Obviously, if the beast (the individual) is never killed, he will never descend into the abyss. Furthermore, if the beast (the individual) never descended into the abyss, he will never emerge from it.

Much has been written that has dealt with the issues that are raised against any supernatural view of understanding the signs and wonders repeatedly predicted for the tribulation. This includes both the return to life of the beast of Rev 13:3 and the authenticity of the satanic miracles during the tribulation. Again, although not the primary purpose of this chapter of the *Handbook,* many oppose any futuristic concept that agents of Satan would actually be allowed to perform authentic miracles in the tribulation. Some make sweeping claims that if an agent of Satan were actually permitted to do authentic miracles, this would virtually dissolve a Christian worldview. Thus, they conclude that Satan will be able only to parody the miracles of Christ in the tribulation.

But against this view, one of many points needs to be considered: Did Judas actually do miraculous works, or were they only parodies of miracles? This is important because of the implications of how this relates to Matt 10:1: "Jesus summoned His twelve disciples and gave them authority over unclean spirits, to cast them out, and to heal every kind of disease and every kind of sickness." Matthew 10:4 presents Judas as one of the Twelve to whom Jesus gave such power to do miracles. Nothing within the biblical texts presents Judas as not doing the same authentic miracles that the other apostles did. Here then was an unbeliever, who ultimately became a tool of Satan, who was temporarily granted authority—by Jesus—to perform authentic miracles. This did not create any dualistic worldview in the mind of Jesus, or He never would have done it this way. Also, if Jesus granted to one "son of perdition" (John 17:12) the temporary authority to perform authentic miracles, it should not be totally surprising if He grants another son of perdition (that is, destruction), using identical language as we saw earlier in 2 Thess 2:3, likewise to perform authentic miracles—if such is God's holy design.

Even though we have repeatedly cited many Scripture passages in this *Handbook* about the uniqueness of what God will allow to occur, one statement should not be lightly overlooked or set aside as unimportant: The tribulation will be a unique time in history, and it will be unparalleled in satanic evil, power, and worldwide deception. Matthew 24:24–25 says, "For false Christs and false prophets will arise and will show great signs and wonders, so as to mislead, if possible, even the elect. Behold, I have told you in advance." The Bible not only repeatedly presents statements with very specific details about the unprecedented deception that will occur during the tribulation; it also presents multiple strong warnings regarding the coming deception as well as offering the means to avoid it. The worldwide magnitude of the promised deception rather than mere pockets of isolated deception, must be kept in the forefront of studying matters related to the tribulation, and that deception is something that has no historical fulfillment we can look to as already having been fulfilled.

The Judgments of God's Enemies at Christ's Return

Since the ultimate fate of the beast is not an object of contention among those looking for a futuristic Antichrist to appear, the particulars relating to his demise will be useful in addressing other matters and events associated with his life. The return to earth of Jesus Christ begins a series of judgments and blessings that culminate with the great white throne judgment, followed by the new heavens and new earth, also called the eternal state. That the judgments commence at the Lord's return should not be surprising because Jesus had taught as much in John 5:22, stating, "For not even the Father judges anyone, but He has given all judgment to the Son." The Greek text was written in a way that shows the permanency of the Son's right to execute "all judgment," which in this verse alone is quite close to being a claim of deity by Jesus.

Revelation 19:19–21 describes the first judgment Jesus will perform after His return to earth:

> *And I saw the beast and the kings of the earth and their armies assembled to make war against Him who sat on the horse and against His army. And the beast was seized, and with him the false prophet who performed the signs in his presence, by which he deceived those who had received the mark of the beast and those who worshiped his image; these two were thrown alive [literally "living"] into the lake of fire which burns with brimstone. And the rest were killed with the sword which came from the mouth of Him who sat on the horse, and all the birds were filled with their flesh.*

Only the beast, the Antichrist, and the false prophet receive immediate eternal judgment at Christ's return as they are cast alive into the lake of fire. This is the first biblical occurrence of the phrase "lake of fire" used in reference to hell. The Bible presents those who die without accepting the Lord as awaiting the final judgment by being confined in the Sheol referred to by the Old Testament, which is generally considered synonymous with the New Testament use of Hades. As far as we can tell from the biblical texts, the Antichrist and the false prophet will be the first inhabitants of hell, and they will precede Satan by one thousand years. The final judgment of Satan occurs later, one thousand years after hell receives its first two occupants, at the end of the millennial kingdom, and after Satan's final rebellion. Revelation 20:10 states, "And the devil who deceived them was thrown into the lake of fire and brimstone, where the beast and the false prophet are also; and they will be tormented day and night forever and ever." For those who do not impose their already established theology or philosophical presuppositions and who will allow the text to speak for itself, Rev 19:20 clearly shows that the Antichrist and the false prophet are thrown alive (literally "living") into the lake of fire. One thousand years later, they are still alive (20:10). That they were "tormented day and night forever" indicates that their previous tormented experience, which had initially been for a millennium, will continue throughout eternity.

The final judgment depicting all of the remaining lost will be the great white throne judgment of Rev 20:11–15:

> *Then I saw a great white throne and Him who sat upon it, from whose presence earth and heaven fled away, and no place was found for them. And I saw the dead, the great and the small, standing before the throne, and books were opened; and another book was opened, which is the book of life; and the dead were judged from the things which were written in the books, according to their deeds. And the sea gave up the dead which were in it, and death and Hades gave up the dead which were in them; and they were judged, every one of them according to their deeds. Then death and Hades were thrown into the lake of fire. This is the second death, the lake of fire. And if anyone's name was not found written in the book of life, he was thrown into the lake of fire.*

Here is the final judgment of the eternally damned, as they too are thrown into the lake of fire.

It is generally concluded among most Bible-believing Christian scholars (and Bible-believing Christians in general) that all the wicked dead will face Jesus at the great white throne judgment. It is evident that with death and Hades emptied of all inhabitants there will be no place for the unredeemed to escape their final judgment, and it is generally held that in order to tolerate the tortures of hell, all unsaved people must receive a resurrected body—not only the redeemed. Without giving any additional details or information, Jesus had alluded to the body aspect of the final judgment in Matt 10:28: "Do not fear those who kill the body but are unable to kill the soul; but rather fear Him who is able to destroy both soul and body in hell." As we saw in the previous chapter of the *Handbook*, the great white throne judgment concludes the totality of God's judgments against Satan and his angels and unredeemed mankind.

EXTREMELY IMPORTANT: For bodies to be able to endure the lake of fire necessitates having bodies that are fit to endure such punishment, and those bodies must meet supernatural requirements that surpass those of present human frailties. However, in agreement with what has previously been written in reference to the unsaved receiving bodies fit for eternal damnation, the same thing must equally be true for the Antichrist and the false prophet. In order for the Antichrist and the false prophet to be two genuine human beings, at some time—either before or at Rev 19:20—these two individuals *must* likewise receive bodies fit to endure the everlasting torment that God has promised. At some time, the two beasts must change in bodily form from a human to a superhuman capacity, having their resurrected bodies. This must occur, or else their bodies could never withstand the lake of fire for a fraction of a second; certainly they could never still be alive there one thousand years later when Satan is also cast into hell, "where the beast and the false prophet are also; and they will be tormented day and night forever and ever" (Rev 20:10).

Significance of Revelation 19 on Understanding Revelation 13

Because the Antichrist and false prophet will be cast alive ["living"] into the lake of fire and still are alive when Satan is thrown in, that makes the restoring to life of the slain beast in Revelation 13 much more plausible. That these two designated agents of Satan must ultimately receive a supernatural transformation from their earthly bodies to their resurrected bodies and that they must be transformed prior to the transformation of all of the remainder of the damned from all time is fully supported biblically in Revelation 13.

I agree with those who adhere to the doctrine of a future resurrection of the Antichrist. However, there is one point where I differ with those who say that we cannot know with certainty the source of their future resurrection. We will see that we can prove biblically whether God or Satan will restore the beast to life. While claiming that we can prove the source for this future resurrection may seem to be an extremely ambitious undertaking, I think we will see biblical references that clearly indicate whether or not this resurrection is authentic and who will accomplish it.

CRUCIAL: Even beyond what has already been examined, one tremendously significant deduction warrants consideration: *The Antichrist and the false prophet are the only two unsaved human beings in all history who will be permitted—by God—to bypass the great white throne judgment* (Rev 20:11–15). In keeping with the divine promise that *all* judgment has been given to the Son (John 5:22), we must note that these two beings are exempt from the great white throne judgment solely by God's doing—especially by the work and doing of Jesus—not Satan's work.

The devil has absolutely no willful part in the performance of any of the judgments of God, other than enduring what God has prepared for him and his angels (Matt 25:41). Furthermore, Satan will already be in the lake of fire, joining the two previous inhabitants, before this final great white throne judgment begins. Because all judgment has been given to the Son, this obviously is the Son's ultimate will and accomplishment. He Himself will seize the Antichrist and the false prophet and cast them alive into the lake of fire (Rev 19:20). He Himself has already determined that unlike the remainder of the unredeemed, the Antichrist and the false prophet—although these two will be authentic human beings—will not stand before Him in judgment at the promised great white throne when He judges all of the other unsaved human beings from all the ages. Satan has no part in any aspect of this; only the Godhead does—with, again, Jesus being the second Member of the Godhead who does all judging. Certainly this passage does not support a dualistic worldview in which God and Satan are pitted as equal and opposite rivals who fight each other for dominance, as some claim would be the case.

At some time before being cast into the lake of fire in Rev 19:20, an event which occurs before the inauguration of the millennial kingdom in Revelation 20, the two beasts must receive from God bodies fit for enduring eternal torment, as will be true for anyone else who eventually will be thrown into the lake of fire. We know the necessity of those destined for eternal torment receiving such resurrected bodies in order to endure must also be true for the Antichrist and the false prophet. We know from Scripture that these two future enemies of God already will have received their resurrected bodies at some point during the tribulation because Scripture gives no indication that there is any transformation of the two beasts' bodies at the Lord's return in Revelation 19.

That the two beasts must receive supernatural bodies one thousand years before the rest of the lost will receive theirs must factor into the interpretation of related verses regarding the beast. For instance, some use the rationale of the chronology of the judgments given in Scripture to conclude that the wound of the beast and his return to life cannot be that of an individual. They also reason that a resurrection in Revelation 13 could not be a return to life of a human being because the wicked are not resurrected until the great white throne judgment (Rev 20:11–15), and they consider that if a wicked one were resurrected before this final judgment, it would set aside God's divinely ordained program of resurrection. However, a proper understanding of the timings of the different resurrections would not disrupt God's chronology. Only a slight altering of what is considered the standard chronology of God's judgment among those looking for a future fulfillment of the events of Revelation 19–20 will be necessary to include the unique judgment of the two beasts. However, the specified judgment of the two beasts in Rev 19:20 often fails to be included when the future judgments of God are listed. Revelation 19:20 is a disclosure from God of part of the greater mystery about end-time events that were not revealed earlier in Scripture. The Son uniquely judges the Antichrist and the false prophet at His return in Revelation 19, one thousand years before the judgment of any other humans. Indeed these two beasts are living, functioning, actual human beings, as is indicated by their fate.

The best biblical option for the timing of this required change from human to superhuman condition is Rev 13:3–4, which shows that change will have occurred three and one-half years earlier than Rev 19:20:

> *I saw one of his heads as if it had been slain, and his fatal wound was healed. And the whole earth was amazed and followed after the beast; they worshiped the dragon because he gave his authority to the beast; and they worshiped the beast, saying, "Who is like the beast, and who is able to wage war with him?"*

Revelation 19:20 as It Pertains to the Ascent Out of the Abyss

With the ultimate supernatural status of the Antichrist and false prophet having been established, at least by Rev 19:20, the ascent of the beast out of the abyss in 17:8 should be reconsidered. This is particularly true because many of the arguments used for the beast as being an empire instead of a person apply here. In other words, often the interpretation of Rev 13:3–4 influences the understanding of 17:8 (and vice versa), as well as the interpretation of 9:11 and 11:7. Since Revelation 9 contains the first reference to the abyss/bottomless pit in Revelation, who or what one determines to have come out of it likewise affects their interpretations elsewhere in related passages. We also know about passages that necessitate the interchangeable use of the head with the whole beast, that is, the king with his kingdom. In Dan 2:37–38, in the explanation of Nebuchadnezzar's dreams about the Gentile world kingdoms and the end of time, Daniel says this about the statue:

> *You, O king, are the king of kings, to whom the God of heaven has given the kingdom, the power, the strength and the glory; and wherever the sons of men dwell, or the beasts of the field, or the birds of the sky, He has given them into your hand and has caused you to rule over them all. You are the head of gold.*

Because of the interchangeability of the terms used, sometimes the beast in Revelation is the worldwide kingdom of the Antichrist, and sometimes the beast refers to the actual Antichrist and not to his kingdom. So, therefore, the part of the rationale for those who interpret verses about the abyss with the inference that no human could ever be in the abyss should be reconsidered. For instance, their proposal that the beast of Rev 13:3 is a future empire instead of an individual is often based on the conclusion that 17:8 does not teach that this future beast is human, and instead sees this Scripture referring to Satan. Thus, the world government that he promotes is entirely satanic in its power and to this extent is identified with him. So those who hold this view would see the beast as the world government that is to be revived in the tribulation that will cause the world to wonder, especially with regard to the rise to power of an absolute worldwide leader over the ten-kingdom federation who will wield absolute power. Their reasoning for this position is that all relevant verses from Revelation 9, 13, and 17 about the beast returning to life cannot be a resurrection in chapter 13 because no human being could come out of the abyss (17:8), and in their understanding, only Satan can come out of the abyss (9:11).

However, there are problems with the above approach that need to be addressed. Part of the difficulty with the above position involves explaining how the totality of the unsaved world during the tribulation, who will have strongly rejected God's Word as truth, will know that the abyss exists or be cognizant of any activities related to it. Even if the beast is a reference to the final worldwide empire, one would not know that the empire beast descended into the abyss or that it arises out of it without divine revelation. Humans will not witness anything related to this; such is only a divinely revealed truth that will not be revealed to anyone who rejects the revelatory truth of God. Yet the unsaved of the tribulation will not only know about the beast coming out of the abyss but will respond in utter amazement after they witness this, as Rev 17:8 reveals:

> *The beast that you saw was, and is not, and is about to come up out of the abyss and go to destruction. And those who dwell on the earth, whose name has not been written in the book of life from the foundation of the world, will wonder when they see the beast, that he was and is not and will come.*

CONSIDER: One item that needs to be explored by those who hold that Satan is current sovereign of the abyss is the response of the demons in Luke 8:31. When the legion of demons quaked before Jesus, "They were imploring Him not to command them to go away into the abyss." If Satan were the current master of the abyss, it seems improbable that the demons would be fearful of going there. Besides, if Satan ruled the abyss, he could simply unlock the abyss and send the released demons back out into another field of endeavor somewhere on earth.

Because it is shown that the Antichrist and false prophet will have supernatural bodies at the very least by Revelation 19, and most likely in chapter 13, the same could be argued about who is entering and leaving the abyss in chapter 17, which states that the beast will ascend from the abyss. The text does not require that Satan be the one uniquely linked with the abyss. It is true that no normal human could ever go to the abyss; no normal human could survive the abyss; no normal human could escape from there—and yet the beast does just that in Rev 17:8. Ordinary men do not come out of the abyss; any being who comes out of the abyss either has to be Satan or some man who will go there. The resurrected bodies the Antichrist and the false prophet will have—at least by Rev 19:20—made them suitable for enduring the abyss. If one can endure the final lake of fire, one can endure the abyss. God alone in His sovereignty accomplishes this—not Satan. Since the beast and the false prophet have to receive resurrected bodies at some point so that their bodies can endure the lake of fire throughout eternity, this is the most feasible option from the information disclosed in Scripture.

Still one important item needs addressing: Rev 19:20 discloses that "these two were thrown alive into the lake of fire." Yet it is the beast singular who has the fatal wound in Rev 13:14, and it is the beast singular who comes out of the abyss in Rev 11:7: "When they [the two special witnesses of God] have finished their testimony, the beast that comes up out of the abyss will make war with them, and overcome them and kill them." And then later in Rev 17:8,

> The beast that you saw was, and is not, and is about to come up out of the abyss and go to destruction. And those who dwell on the earth, whose name has not been written in the book of life from the foundation of the world, will wonder when they see the beast, that he was and is not and will come.

Connected with this is one final matter that should be addressed but is often overlooked. Although not specifically stated in the text, somehow the other beast that John saw, the false prophet of Rev 13:11, must be included in a supernatural status because the text does not say the beasts (plural) come out of the abyss but rather only the beast (singular). Yet the two are thrown alive into the lake of fire.

As we have previously seen in the *Handbook,* it is important to remember that the Bible often presents the spiritual realities behind what takes place on earth. Those on earth, especially those who do not accept the Bible as the Word of God, will only see the physical events, yet the spiritual side is the real reason that the events occur. As we saw in the previous chapter of the *Handbook,* so it is with Revelation 13 because chapters 12—14 are a unique segment within the book of Revelation. In chapter 12 God discloses the spiritual realities, totally hidden from the lost world, before the visible events of Revelation 13 occur. So, before the pinnacle of the power of Satan's man of sin emerges in chapter 13, God discloses the spiritual truths from which the events will emerge in chapter 12, which reveals a series of preliminary defeats of Satan. To summarize, Revelation 12 includes (1) Satan being cast down out of heaven, (2) the pronouncement of the pending kingdom of Christ, (3) the victory of the overcomers by the blood of the Lamb, (4) the woe to the earth because of Satan's great wrath, and (5) Satan's realization that his time is short. The lost ones of the tribulation will not know of any of these preliminary defeats of Satan, and this preeminent liar will not disclose these defeats to the lost world (John 8:44). The world will see only the physical beings and events before them; people will not ascertain the spiritual realities that make the events proceed, and they especially will not grasp their significance. Stated succinctly, the unsaved world alive at that time will marvel at the Antichrist and will be amazed by the signs and wonders performed by the false prophet, as the predicted worldwide deception will occur.

Accompanying this is a distinct possibility to consider: It is possible that the false prophet is killed, perhaps at the same time the first beast receives his mortal wound, and that the Antichrist brings the false prophet back to life—that is, again, taking this from the perspective of those on earth who will witness this. It is God who will grant these two their resurrected bodies, but it will seem to the thoroughly deceived world that the beast performs this by his own divine power. This harmonizes with the uniqueness of the tribulation as well as with the multiple warnings by Jesus Himself and the apostle Paul regarding the deception of that period. All of this deception suits Satan's design, as his ultimate desire is not that of world dominion, which he will give to the Antichrist (Rev 13:4, 7). Ultimately, the beast and Satan both desire to be worshiped as God, as seen in the temptation of Jesus (Matt 4:9), the worship of the beast and the dragon (Rev 13:4), and in the Antichrist's presentation of himself to the world as being God (2 Thess 2:4).

Those who are deceived during the tribulation will respond to the Antichrist in worshipful adoration, as Rev 13:8 shows: "All who dwell on the earth will worship him, everyone whose name has not been written from the foundation of the world in the book of life of the Lamb who has been slain." Anyone who will persuade the entirety of the world's unsaved population that he himself is God must support his claims by overwhelmingly convincing means. The tribulation will eventually be devoid of atheists and agnostics. Since the Antichrist will present himself as greater than Jesus, he must claim at least to be the equal of what the Bible claimed about Jesus. For instance, when John the Baptist questioned Jesus as to whether He was the promised One or if they should look for another, part of Jesus's answer involved the dead being raised: "Go and report to John what you hear and see: the BLIND RECEIVE SIGHT and the lame walk, the lepers are cleansed and the deaf hear, the dead are raised up, and the POOR HAVE THE GOSPEL PREACHED TO THEM" (Matt 11:4–5). For the Antichrist to present himself as God and to be thusly believed by the collective lost, it would not be unexpected that he would bring someone back to life—at least from the world's perspective.

Many have noticed that with Satan, the Antichrist, and the false prophet, a Satanic trinity emerges. This satanic trinity—which will not emerge until the tribulation—should not be taken lightly, nor should their capacities be automatically diminished, especially given the parameters under which they will operate during the last three and a half years before the Lord's return to earth. If the Antichrist is supposed to be God in the flesh and is to be exalted above Jesus, who the Bible repeatedly presents as raising the dead, it should not be unexpected that the Antichrist will also raise the dead at some time. The raising of the false prophet from the dead would accomplish this. It would also explain the latter's supernatural status shown in Rev 19:20. In further explanation, it would answer another matter that must be noted: only Satan and the Antichrist are worshipped during the tribulation—not the false prophet. Yet he, too, will have a resurrected body when he is cast alive into the lake of fire. That another heals him would also explain why the world will worship the first beast and worship the dragon (Rev 13:4) but not the false prophet. It would also harmonize with the previously noted Satanic trinity. One returns from the abyss, and one is returned to life in a supernatural form, giving worldwide witness and credit to the one who raised him from the dead and leading the entire lost world to worship him as God.

All of this ultimately originates from God. From the world's perspective, the Antichrist and the dragon will have accomplished these divine acts and are worthy of worship and praise. From the biblical perspective, God alone performs these divine acts and is alone worthy of worship and praise. In fact, the rise of the Antichrist in Revelation 13 comes only after the preliminary defeat of Satan in chapter 12. No true dualism exists—only the erroneous perception of dualism by those who are the lost during the tribulation.

Conclusion and Significance

The realization that the Antichrist and the false prophet will be judged uniquely and exclusively by the Son in Rev 19:20 and be mandated by the Godhead to bypass the great white throne judgment of Revelation 20 has many far-reaching elements. First, it permits a much more natural understanding of the language of the book of Revelation, something that those who hold to the premillennial reign of Jesus Christ frequently emphasize. Realizing that a change from the human to the supernatural must occur for the Antichrist and the false prophet by this time certainly adds to the possibility that it may be sooner, such as Rev 13:3 and 17:8. It further explains the worshipful adulation and marveling by the unbelieving masses that is predicted for the tribulation and explains the manner in which they will respond in worship-evoking amazement. Since those who are lost will respond with abject wonder at the return of the beast from the abyss, it is also evident that they will not be expecting his return from the dead. Having brazenly rejected the truth of God, the deceived of the tribulation will embrace the lie when the Antichrist returns from the grave:

> . . . *with all the deception of wickedness for those who perish, because they did not receive the love of the truth so as to be saved. For this reason God will send upon them a deluding influence so that they will believe what is false, in order that they all may be judged who did not believe the truth, but took pleasure in wickedness. (2 Thess 2:10–12)*

This underscores the absolute sovereignty of God in all areas, including even a supernatural return from the dead of the Antichrist. Even at the pinnacle of Satan's reign on earth, God remains fully in control. Although Satan and the Antichrist will initially take credit for it, this supernatural return from the dead can come about only by God's sovereign design, something, of course, which the deceived world will not in any way acknowledge at that time, and they will be allowed to do their collective evil for a relatively short three and a half years.

Second, we who look for a future fulfillment of these events should slightly amend our theology concerning the final judgments of God, especially in reference to Rev 20:11–15. It is almost universally presented by Bible-believing scholars that all unredeemed humans will appear before Jesus at the great white throne judgment. We need to amend that to say that all except two—the Antichrist and the false prophet—will be there, and this only by God's sovereign design and disclosure. This in no way undermines a premillennial understanding of God's judgments. It actually strengthens it because it allows the text to speak for itself, as the Trinity has revealed a unique judgment reserved for two of His unique earthly adversaries.

Third, God being the ultimate source of the beast's return and of the two resurrected bodies in Rev 19:20 refutes every criticism and concern that critics raise regarding the return to life of the beast. Only God has the power to raise the dead, not Satan. The Antichrist does not raise himself; God raises him. Satan does not possess creative power; God alone has creative power, although Satan will lie to the entire world about this in the future so that he will receive worship that is not properly due him (Rev 13:4). While it will appear to the unbelieving world during the tribulation that Satan has no equal, Scripture clearly proves that it is God who never had and never will have an equal. Satan operates only when God allows and only to the degree that God allows. Never in any interpretation of Scripture could such a view be considered a dualism between God and Satan, whereby they exist as competing equals. They are not equals; they never have been; they never will be—not even at the height of the tribulation and the accompanying predicted deception.

When the unsaved masses respond in bewildered adoration at the return of the beast from death, asking in Rev 13:4, "Who is like the beast, and who is able to wage war with him?," God has already provided the answer in His Word. The One who is able to wage war with the beast is the One whose attributes have already been delineated in detail in Revelation 1–5, such as where Jesus is presented as "the ruler of the kings of the earth" (v. 5), which, of course, includes even the Antichrist. To be more emphatic, the One who is able to wage war with the beast is also the One to whom all judgment is given (John 5:22). He is also the One who declares, "I have [present tense] the keys of death and of Hades" (Rev 1:18), which, by the way, is further evidence that return of the beast from death is not Satan's doing but solely God's.

Must Satan Be Released in Revelation 20:3? Indeed He Must[2]

Many statements within Scripture contain the word *must*. Perhaps the most famous occurrence is the declaration by Jesus to Nicodemus in John 3:7, "You must be born again." The word *must* is most commonly used in the Greek to convey the idea of the necessity of an event. It does not convey the sense as something that will happen, such as would be expected in a normal future tense, but rather as something being necessary or used in the sense of a divine destiny or unavoidable fate.

---

[2] For much more information on this, see the full article by Gregory H. Harris, "Must Satan Be Released? Indeed He Must Be: Toward a Biblical Understanding of Revelation 20:3," *Master's Seminary Journal* 25, no. 1 (Spring 2014): 11–27 (https://www.tms.edu/m/msj25b.pdf).

If John 3:7 is the most famous "must" statement in the Bible, perhaps the most unexpected use is its next-to-the-last occurrence in Scripture, namely, Rev 20:1–3. These verses reveal specific events that will transpire and specifically note one event that must occur:

> *Then I saw an angel coming down from heaven, holding the key of the abyss and a great chain in his hand. And he laid hold of the dragon, the serpent of old, who is the devil and Satan, and bound him for a thousand years; and he threw him into the abyss, and shut it and sealed it over him, so that he would not deceive the nations any longer, until the thousand years were completed; after these things he must be released for a short time.*

As with all previous "must" statements, it is not only that Satan will be released, as seen with the future tense in Rev 20:7 ("When the thousand years are completed, Satan will be released from his prison"), but also Scripture plainly states that after the thousand years are over Satan "must be" released for a short time. Many scholars consider this verse to be a tremendous mystery, its meaning hidden in the deep mind of the Godhead; they assume it is futile and foolish to try to find out why Satan must be released. Based on the normal use of "must" in other Scriptures, many scholars also mark its use in Rev 20:3, in regard to Satan's release, so that the last part of the verse could be read this way: "after these things he [that is, Satan] must [of a divine necessity] be released for a short time," and just leave it as that, and do not comment beyond this statement.

However, many students may not realize that these are some of the most controversial Scripture verses in the entire Bible, and the massive theological divide that emerges from these prophecies has been the subject of endless debates and disputes because the whole controversy between premillennialists and amillennialists hangs upon it. Should these verses be interpreted in the normative sense of what the text presents, or are these verses only allegorical lessons to be learned?

Obviously, Rev 20:3 is a verse that must not be interpreted in isolation from the rest of the text. Consequently, the way one approaches the events from Rev 19:11–20:10 greatly factors into its interpretation and has usually been determined in one's theology long before one comes to the specifics of Revelation 20.

From those who agree that Scripture is God's Word, two distinct interpretations of this prophecy emerge: (1) the events given in Rev 20:1–6 will occur before the return of Jesus Christ to the earth, as most amillennialists would teach. In this view the binding of Satan is seen as occurring at the crucifixion of Jesus, and it is sometimes explained that the binding of Satan at that time makes it possible for the Gentiles to receive the gospel. And (2) the alternate position—essentially the premillennial position—is the view that the events in Rev 20:1–6 follow the second coming of Christ as given in 19:11–21. This view sees the Bible presenting a chronological progression between the two passages. By simply adhering to the text of Scripture, God reveals the following events: (1) Satan will be bound in the future when Christ returns to earth. (2) Christ will reign for a literal one thousand years on earth from Jerusalem and with His people during millennial kingdom. (3) Satan will be loosed for a brief period at the end of the millennium, and this will be followed by the resurrection and judgment of the wicked at the great white throne judgment. (4) God will create the new heavens and the new earth after the millennium, that is, a thousand years after Christ's second coming to earth. Revelation 20:1–10 continues the events of chapter 19 and does not reproduce or duplicate them. Also, it is recognized that Satan is not presently in the abyss, and he currently blinds/deceives the nations, but when he is imprisoned in the abyss in chapter 20, he will have no contact with earth/humanity until the end of the one-thousand-year reign of Jesus on earth. At that time Satan must be released for a brief period of time.

The purpose of this final part of the *Handbook* and of this chapter is to determine whether or not there is a biblical rationale for the absolute necessity that Satan must be released (Rev 20:3). This will be determined by (1) briefly examining different approaches to Rev 20:3, (2) briefly examining different approaches to the covenant promises God made to Israel to see if a literal hermeneutic has basis, and (3) implementing these promises into the text to see if these covenant promises fit a normative understanding of what Rev 20:1–10 states will happen.

A Brief Examination of Various Approaches to Revelation 20:3

Generally, the responses regarding why Satan must be released fall into three categories. The first approach is that one should not attempt to understand why Satan must be released. Among those holding this view you will find comments such as, "*It is futile to speculate and vain to speculate* why there needs to be this final battle in Revelation 20." However, the perception that it is "futile" or "vain" to speculate often closes the door on any further biblical investigation to see if God has given us any information in His Word that would help explain the text. While being in full agreement that speculation cannot be equated with "thus says the Lord," I believe that at least biblical texts should be investigated before anyone arrives at such broad and encompassing conclusions.

The second approach is taken by those who believe the Bible to be the inspired text and look for a future fulfillment, but they do not address the use of "must" in Rev 20:3; instead, they deal with Satan's actual release that will transpire in verses 7–10, beginning in verse 7: "When the thousand years are completed, Satan will be released from his prison." This does not mean that such scholars do not believe or recognize these verses nor deem them unimportant; it is rather that they shift their focus to the more descriptive account of the actual events in verses 7–10. This is helpful, but it neither answers nor addresses the use and the significance of the "must" behind Satan's release.

In the third category are many adherents who do note the use of "must" in Rev 20:3, mark its theological significance based on the normative use of "must" elsewhere, and look for future events to transpire in Revelation 20 but often leave it as some sovereign work of God whose explanation is completely hidden from humankind. Other scholars deduce reasons why Satan must be released: (1) to demonstrate the innate spiritual deadness of fallen humanity, to demonstrate again that, if left alone, one will always choose sin, even when the Messiah is reigning on earth; (2) to demonstrate God's foreknowledge of all humanity's actions as well as to reveal ultimately His knowledge, which He will reveal in His disclosure of all things; (3) to demonstrate the totally incurable evil and wickedness of Satan; and (4) to give justification for the eternal hell and unrelenting torment for the unredeemed.

While in agreement with much of what has been written about God's sovereignty, humanity's depravity, and Satan's unchanging evil, I will give an additional and corroborative biblical rationale for why Satan must be released (Rev 20:3).

A Brief Examination of God's Covenant of Promises to Israel

Many scholars or students of the Bible do not acknowledge any connection between Israel and God's future work, and that viewpoint affects one's understanding of God and what He has already promised. Obviously, I cannot cover every item in matters related to the covenants of God, but I will note some important features. For much more information, read the appropriate chapters in *The Bible Expositor's Handbook—Old Testament*.

In giving the Abrahamic covenant, God made promises for the future to those who would become the nation of Israel: they would be a distinct people, would have their own land, and would be used by God to be a source of blessing to all the families of the earth (Gen 12:1–3, 7). As part of the Abrahamic covenant, Yahweh further promised what would become national Israel that He would curse the ones who curse them; this was initially given in Gen 12:3 and reiterated and developed in subsequent Scripture. For example, as we saw in Numbers 22–24, a section rich with wonderful and multiple messianic promises, God used Balaam to respond to Balak's request to have Balaam curse national Israel. God's command and declaration to Balaam was, "You shall not curse the people, for they are blessed" (Num 22:12); this was based on the promises of God from the Abrahamic covenant and not on the disobedience of the Jewish people under the Mosaic covenant. Then in the midst of multiple prophecies about the coming Messiah who will rule the nations, Yahweh repeated in Num 24:9 what He had previously promised in Gen 12:3: "Blessed is everyone who blesses you, / And cursed is everyone who curses you." Consequently, in the millennial kingdom when Messiah reigns, not only will the land promises be fulfilled and all the nations of the earth be blessed through the Messiah, but God's promise to curse the ones who curse Israel and the Messiah will still be operative.

The promises Yahweh made through the Davidic covenant are numerous as well (2 Samuel 7; Psalm 89) and are so important for understanding the book of Revelation that the fulfillment of the Davidic covenant promise is one of the major themes of Revelation from its start until its end. When Messiah reigns on David's throne, the entire earth will receive benefits. In particular, Scripture presents multiple promises that relate to earthly Jerusalem—and the re-gathered nation of Israel—and reveals numerous characteristics associated with the Lord's return both to judge and to rule. Even a small sampling of important verses shows that when Messiah reigns on David's throne, the promises that God made will factor into interpreting the final release of Satan in Revelation 20. For example, Mic 5:2 promises the Jewish people, "But as for you, Bethlehem Ephrathah, / Too little to be among the clans of Judah, / From you One will go forth for Me to be ruler in Israel. / His goings forth are from long ago, / from the days of eternity." Micah 5:5 concludes this section with another promise from Yahweh: "This One will be our peace." So when Messiah reigns, God's promise of peace is a major component of His reign.

In the same manner, we saw earlier in this *Handbook* that Isa 9:6 contains prophecies about Messiah's birth and a tremendously important pronouncement that He will both judge and rule: "For a child will be born to us, a son will be given to us; / And the government will rest on His shoulders; / And His name will be called Wonderful Counselor, Mighty God, Eternal Father, Prince of Peace." However, in Isa 9:7 the same God offers additional promises that never were fulfilled during the first advent of Jesus: "*There will be no end* to the increase of His government or *of peace*, / On the throne of David and over his kingdom, / To establish it and to uphold it with justice and righteousness / From then on and forevermore. / The zeal of the LORD of hosts will accomplish this" (emphasis added). Isaiah 9:7 is as much a part of the "Scripture cannot be broken" principle as is any other part (see John 10:35). When Messiah reigns on David's throne in fulfillment of the Davidic covenant promises of God, one of the characteristics will be that "there will be no end to the increase of His government or of peace."

Similarly, when God revealed that He would at some point in the future establish the new covenant, as with the Davidic covenant earlier,

Yahweh again made promises for peace in another everlasting covenant, and as a part of that covenant, everlasting peace will occur. This prophecy is especially striking when one studies the book of Jeremiah as a whole because it is the descendants of this disobedient nation in chapters 2–29 who receives the future promises, especially in Jeremiah 30–33, which is commonly called "The Book of Consolation." These four chapters are even more striking in that national Israel was just about to go into the Babylonian exile, and Jerusalem and God's temple would be destroyed. When the book of Jeremiah is considered as a whole, these four chapters of promised renewal and glory radiate with divine hope compared to the mainly condemnatory tone of the remainder of the book. The whole context of the Book of Consolation specifically connects the new covenant with a literal restoration of the Jewish nation, as do many parallel passages. As with the Abrahamic and Davidic covenants, the new covenant contains many promises of essential events that must transpire in order for Scripture to be fulfilled. In the same way, the new covenant also presents God's multiple promised blessings that must come true as part of His holy Word, that once stated cannot be broken.

The immediate context of the new covenant begins with the phrase "Behold, days are coming" (Jer 31:31), which occurs five times within the Book of Consolation section (chaps. 30–33). Emerging in the midst of pending judgment by God (chaps. 1–29) comes the promise of wonderful blessings for the future. The first use is in Jer 30:3: "'For behold, days are coming,' declares the LORD, 'when I will restore the fortunes of My people Israel and Judah.' The LORD says, 'I will also bring them back to the land that I gave to their forefathers and they shall possess it.'" Three times in the immediate context occurs the phrase "behold, days are coming" (31:27, 31, 38), which serves to produce a threefold division of what God promises is this very important chapter. The first use of "behold, days are coming" in this section is Jer 31:27–30 where God promised this: "'Behold, days are coming,' declares the LORD, 'when I will sow the house of Israel and the house of Judah with the seed of man and with the seed of beast'" (v. 27). The same God who promised to destroy also promises that at some time in the future He will restore fully to the same land the same people that He Himself already will have punished. The second use of "Behold, days are coming" in Jeremiah 31 begins the section on the new covenant. Verses 31–34 promised:

> *"Behold, days are coming," declares the LORD, "when I will make a new covenant with the house of Israel and with the house of Judah, not like the covenant which I made with their fathers in the day I took them by the hand to bring them out of the land of Egypt [the Mosaic covenant], My covenant which they broke, although I was a husband to them."*

Before giving additional revelation, Yahweh interjects the absolute certainty that He will fulfill His Word based on His upholding His own created order (Jer 31:35–37). The third and final "behold, days are coming" use in this chapter, verses 38–40, contains divine promises that are just as truthful and binding as are the previous two used in Jeremiah 31:

> *"Behold, days are coming," declares the LORD, "when the city will be rebuilt for the LORD from the Tower of Hananel to the Corner Gate. The measuring line will go out farther straight ahead to the hill Gareb; then it will turn to Goah. And the whole valley of the dead bodies and of the ashes, and all the fields as far as the brook Kidron, to the corner of the Horse Gate toward the east, shall be holy to the LORD; it will not be plucked up or overthrown anymore forever."*

It must be noted that the same God who promised the forgiveness of sin with the making of a new covenant gives further promises that, at some undisclosed time, Jerusalem will be rebuilt for Himself, and from that time onward, it will never be plucked up or overthrown again. What Yahweh reveals in this section is the actual city of Jerusalem and not the new Jerusalem, which will not appear until all the biblical prophecies and events up to the end of Revelation 20 have occurred.

To briefly summarize God's covenant promises to Israel when Messiah reigns, God promises that (1) Jerusalem will be rebuilt for the Lord (Jer 31:38), and (2) at that time will become "holy to the LORD" (v. 40); (3) there shall be no end to peace or the increase of Messiah's government (Isa 9:6–7); (4) Jerusalem will not "be plucked up any more or overthrown forever" (Jer 31:40); and, (5) the fully operative blessings of the Abrahamic covenant contain and continue God's promise to curse the ones who curse Abraham's descendants, specifically Israel (Gen 12:3; Num 24:9).

An Examination of the Final Revolt in View
of God's Covenant Promises to Israel

With these divine promises that must be fulfilled because Scripture cannot be broken, Rev 20:7–10 can now be considered:

> *When the thousand years are completed, Satan will be released from his prison, and will come out to deceive the nations which are in the four corners of the earth, Gog and Magog, to gather them together for the war; the number of them is like the sand of the seashore. And they came up on the broad plain of the earth and surrounded the camp of the saints and the beloved city, and fire came down from heaven and devoured them. And the devil who deceived them was thrown into the lake of fire and brimstone, where the beast and the false prophet are also; and they will be tormented day and night forever and ever.*

So how would these verses be interpreted in a normative understanding if one expected God to be true to His Word? God's subsequent actions should be expected because He has repeatedly given them in His Word, especially as seen in His covenant promises to Israel and to the rest of the world. As part of the Abrahamic covenant promises, God's promise to curse the ones who curse Israel would also include this final Gentile rebellion since Messiah will have previously dealt with the rebellion of the tribulation in Revelation 19 and will have already established His kingdom on earth in 20:1–6.

As a major problem against this view, it is often taught that this would have to allow physical death and sin to occur after Jesus returns. Included in this is whether Jesus returns to earth to reign or whether this is the beginning part of eternity with new Jerusalem present.

While the above view considers it folly that there could be sin and death when the Messiah reigns, verses from the Bible teach that there will be. Isaiah 65:20 shows a longevity of life but also of death when the Messiah reigns:

> *No longer will there be in it an infant who lives but a few days,*
>
> *Or an old man who does not live out his days;*
>
> *For the youth will die at the age of one hundred*
>
> *And the one who does not reach the age of one hundred*
>
> *Will be thought accursed.*

Isaiah 65:20 not only shows that there will be an increased longevity of life, but—even when the Messiah reigns—there will also be the presence of sin and death. Many scholars note that never has such a condition existed in history past and argue against it being in the eternal state of Revelation 21–22, where sin will not exist. Consequently, these events must transpire in the millennial kingdom.

Many hold that the nations will have been destroyed in Rev 19:21; therefore, it would not be logical to speak of protecting the nations from Satan's deception in 20:1–3. Yet we know that the nations that are destroyed in Rev 19:21 can—and will—be reconstituted later when the Messiah reigns (Isa 2:4; 11:10–16; Zech 14:16–21).

Zechariah 14:1–4 declares that the Messiah will return to earth:

> *Behold, a day is coming for the LORD when the spoil taken from you will be divided among you. For I will gather all the nations against Jerusalem to battle, and the city will be captured, the houses plundered, the women ravished and half of the city exiled, but the rest of the people will not be cut off from the city. Then the LORD will go forth and fight against those nations, as when He fights on a day of battle. In that day His feet will stand on the Mount of Olives, which is in front of Jerusalem on the east; and the Mount of Olives will be split in its middle from east to west by a very large valley, so that half of the mountain will move toward the north and the other half toward the south.*

The last part of Zech 14:5 adds, "Then the LORD, my God, will come, and all the holy ones with Him!"

Zechariah 14:9 shows the full extent of Messiah's reign: "And the LORD will be king over all the earth; in that day the LORD will be the only one, and His name the only one." And yet—even now with Satan bound in the abyss and Jesus reigning on earth—the Bible clearly teaches that there will still exist sin and punishment, as verses 16–19 so clearly show:

> *Then it will come about that any who are left of all the nations that went against Jerusalem will go up from year to year to worship the King, the LORD of hosts, and to celebrate the Feast of Booths. And it will be that whichever of the families of the earth does not go up to Jerusalem to worship the King, the LORD of hosts, there will be no rain on them. If the family of Egypt does not go up or enter, then no rain will fall on them; it will be the*

plague with which the LORD smites the nations who do not go up to celebrate the Feast of Booths. This will be the punishment of Egypt, and the punishment of all the nations who do not go up to celebrate the Feast of Booths.

These things must occur—and they will—because there cannot be even one sin on earth after the great white throne judgment occurs, which immediately is followed by the eternal state.

The events of Zechariah 14 do not fit the present age, for the Lord Messiah has not yet returned and started reigning as King over all the earth. But neither does Zechariah 14 fit the eternal state with the new heavens and earth/new Jerusalem (Revelation 21–22) because of the willful disobedience and sin against the Lord that is clearly present in the passage, even with Jesus reigning over all the earth. But with the fullness of the Davidic covenant, God clearly promises there will be "no end to . . . peace" (Isa 9:6–7). Consequently, in Rev 20:7–9a only an assemblage for battle will transpire in this final rebellion but not a battle itself, for even one singular battle would go against the promised word that Messiah's reign would experience no end of peace.

Yet even without the promise of never-ending peace in Isa 9:7, Yahweh long before determined and revealed the outcome of any such rebellion when Messiah reigns. Once Jerusalem is rebuilt for the Lord it will never "be plucked up or overthrown . . . forever" (Jer 31:40). When God fulfills His promises when the new covenant comes in its fullness (vv. 31–34), Jerusalem being rebuilt for the Lord (vv. 38–40), and He promises it will never face destruction again. Satan will indeed come up against Messiah with massive Gentile forces (Rev 20:7–8), but that will not remove the peace of Jerusalem—even though the forces come up and surround "the camp of the saints and the beloved city" (v. 9a). Add to this a promise in the last part of Luke 21:24: "Jerusalem will be trampled under foot by the Gentiles until the times of the Gentiles are fulfilled." The times of the Gentiles will have been fulfilled with the Messiah's return to earth and reign, and thus—as a specifically stated declaration by the Messiah Jesus—never again will Jerusalem be trampled underfoot by the Gentiles—not even once.

Although the method by which God will accomplish this judgment of the final rebellion is not given until Revelation 20, God's actions to accomplish what He has revealed He will do should not be surprising because they harmonize perfectly with His previous promises that there will be no disturbance of Messiah's peace. Consequently, fire from heaven will come down and devour Satan's assembled masses (v. 9b). Further, God's promise to curse the ones who curse Israel (Gen 12:3; Num 24:9) is not limited only until Christ's return to earth but extends even to the last part of His millennial reign and will be just as operative in this final Gentile rebellion as it was when God first gave it in Genesis 12.

Significantly, even before the eternal state with the new heavens and the new earth, even in the midst of Jesus's kingdom reign, evil has not run its course until the very end. First Corinthians 15:20–26 corroborates this and offers a glimpse of what will eventually be described in more detail in Rev 20:7–10:

> But now Christ has been raised from the dead, the first fruits of those who are asleep. For since by a man came death, by a man also came the resurrection of the dead. For as in Adam all die, so also in Christ all will be made alive. But each in his own order: Christ the first fruits, after that those who are Christ's at His coming, then comes the end, when He hands over the kingdom to the God and Father, when He has abolished all rule and all authority and power. For He must reign until He has put all His enemies under His feet. The last enemy that will be abolished is death.

Finally, Jesus must reign until He has abolished all rule and all authority—the last enemy He will abolish is death. Then He will deliver up the kingdom to the Father, which is the transition from Revelation 20 to the eternal state of Revelation 21–22.

In addition to the other reasons, Satan must be released to deceive the nations and bring about not only the final rebellion but also the final deaths of all humans who reject the Messiah. Further, God's promise to Israel to curse the ones who curse them actually relates to all enemies of Israel and not only to the Gentile nations. In keeping with God's Word, Satan has repeatedly cursed Israel. God thus curses Satan, and while not depicted in Revelation 20, this would include his angels, the demons, also (see Matt 8:29 and Jas 2:19), and throws them all into the lake of fire (Rev 20:10). Then when death has been abolished forever and after the great white throne judgment of the eternally damned are thrown into the lake of fire (vv. 11–15), when all evil will have been divinely eradicated, then the new heavens and new earth—and new Jerusalem—will arrive.

* * *

In Revelation 20 God will act precisely as one would expect Him to if one reads His covenant promises with a literal, normative understanding. There is nothing bizarre or abnormal in anything that God will do in chapter 20, for He has repeatedly promised to do these things. Revelation 20 is merely the final setting of God's faithfulness and the summing up of all things in Christ, which He has been so faithfully doing from Genesis 1 onward until ushering in the eternal state.

Simply stated, while in full agreement with other reasons including the sovereignty of God, the depravity of man, and Satan's utter wickedness, another extremely important reason exists for Satan's release: it allows God to demonstrate to Israel and to the world the utter veracity of His covenant promises, as He completely and precisely will fulfill in minute and specific detail—all the way to the arrival of the eternal state. During the millennial kingdom, with the Abrahamic covenant promises still in effect, God will still curse the ones who curse Israel and His Messiah (Gen 12:3; Num 24:9). As part of the Davidic covenant and Messiah's reign, "there will be no end to . . . peace" (Isa 9:7); consequently, no final battle occurs in Rev 20:7–9, only the assemblage for battle because an actual battle would disturb Messiah's peace. With the fullness of the new covenant in force, Jerusalem will again be rebuilt for the Lord and will be holy to the Lord, and Jerusalem "will not be plucked up or overthrown" ever again (Jer 31:38–40). Add to this the promise of Jesus in Luke 21:24 that the trampling underfoot of Jerusalem ends the previous "times of the Gentiles." After this final rebellion when God has completed all of His covenant promises, God will vanquish the assembled enemies before the battle begins—just as would be expected based on his previous promises. "Then comes the end, when He hands over the kingdom to the God and Father, when He has abolished all rule and all authority and power" (1 Cor 15:24). For indeed "He must reign until He has put all His enemies under His feet" (v. 25), a time that includes the last human deaths ever recorded in Scripture (Rev 20:8-9), for "the last enemy that will be abolished is death" (1 Cor 15:26). Finally, Jesus will judge Satan and his legions, the last spiritual enemies who likewise cursed Israel (Rev 20:10). Once this transpires, no enemies of God play any future role. After the great white throne judgment (Rev 20:11–15) comes the wonderful perfection of the new heavens and earth, and New Jerusalem (chaps. 21–22).

Reading the text in this normative way makes perfect sense unless one has a theological predisposition against God doing what He said He will do. After all, "God is not a man that He should lie, / Nor a son of man, that He should repent; / Has He said, and will He not do it? / Or has He spoken, and will He not make it good?" (Num 23:19). Plus, how fitting and appropriate that we can once more make another—and final—use of Isa 25:1: "Plans formed long ago, with perfect faithfulness."

Summary and Significance

In this very important chapter we learned among many other things that (1) the two major interpretational divisions for those who hold that Rev 13:3–4 involves a future event in the tribulation is whether that is a return to life of a king (the Antichrist) or a kingdom (the final worldwide empire). (2) For Rev 13:1–8 to have occurred historically—as many claim—would mean that the Blessed Restrainer no longer restrains and has not restrained sin from the first century onward (see 2 Thess 2:6–7). Satan would already have had to be cast to earth, having great wrath and knowing that he has but a little time (Rev 12:12); moreover, the wrath of God's judgments would have been poured out by this time also (Rev 15:1; 16:1)—without anyone noticing. Such is not possible. (3) Part of the rationale for those who argue that the fatal wound healed involves their concept of a futuristic return of the final world empire, which will uniquely be Satan's kingdom, because Satan does not have the power to restore life, only God does. Others argue that the normal reading of the text shows that an individual, not a kingdom, is returned to life; and they usually leave this as God's doing, or else consider it to be a fake death and a fake resurrection. (4) Others say the Christian worldview would be weakened if legitimate miracles occur during the tribulation by Satan's agents; however—if God permits such things to occur—it in no way weakens the Christian worldview because

Judas performed the miraculous, and this by no means weakened God's control over all things. Also, (5) the Bible not only repeatedly presents statements with specific details about the unprecedented deception that will occur during the tribulation, but it also presents multiple strong warnings regarding the coming deception as well as the means to avoid it. The *worldwide* magnitude of the promised deception—rather than the idea that there will be mere pockets of isolated deception—must be kept in the forefront of the thoughts of those studying matters related to the tribulation; moreover, the deception in view is something that has no historical fulfilment we can look to as already having been fulfilled, or with which to make a comparison.

In this chapter we also learned that (6) the Antichrist and the false prophet will be the first inhabitants of the lake of fire (hell), being thrown alive there by Jesus (Rev 19:20). Those two will precede Satan by one thousand years but will still be alive when he himself is cast into hell (Rev 20:10). (7) Everyone ever born—whether saved or lost—will eventually receive a resurrected body with which to either enjoy heaven or to endure hell. This includes the Antichrist and the false prophet, who will receive their resurrected bodies at least one thousand years before anyone else will. (8) The Antichrist and the false prophet are the only two unsaved human beings in all history who will be permitted—by God—to bypass the great white throne judgment (Rev 20:11–15). In keeping with the divine promise that all judgment has been given to the Son (John 5:22), that these two are exempt from the great white throne judgment is solely God's doing—especially Jesus's doing—not Satan's. (9) At some time before being cast into the lake of fire in Rev 19:20, which occurs before the inauguration of the millennium, the two beasts must receive from God bodies fit to endure eternal torment—as will be true for anyone else who eventually will be thrown into the lake of fire. The necessity of those destined for eternal torment to receive such resurrected bodies in order to endure must also be true for the Antichrist and the false prophet. (10) The best biblical option for the timing of this required change from human to superhuman condition is Rev 13:3–4, which shows that change will have occurred three and a half years earlier than 19:20.

Therefore, (11) knowing that the Antichrist and the false prophet will have received their resurrected bodies by Rev 19:20, I reason that it is much more biblically plausible that the beast—the human being—will come out of the abyss in 11:7 and 17:8, which would explain the worldwide wonder and astonishment at his return to life. (12) The resurrected bodies the Antichrist and the false prophet will have—at least by Rev 19:20—make them suitable for enduring the abyss. If one can endure the final lake of fire, one can endure the abyss. God alone in His sovereignty does this—not Satan. Since the beast and the false prophet have to receive resurrected bodies at some point so that their bodies can endure the lake of fire throughout eternity, this is the most feasible option from the information disclosed in Scripture. (13) The raising of the false prophet from the dead by the Antichrist (from the unsaved world's perspective)—all of which happens by God's doing—would explain the latter's supernatural status shown in Rev 19:20, and it would answer another matter that must be noted: only Satan and the Antichrist are worshipped during the tribulation—but never the false prophet. Yet he, too, will have a supernatural body when he is cast alive into the lake of fire. Finally, (14) because those who are lost will respond with abject wonder at the return of the beast from the abyss, it is also evident that they will not be expecting his return from the dead. Having brazenly rejected the truth of God, the deceived of the tribulation will embrace the lie when the Antichrist returns from the grave:

> . . . with all the deception of wickedness for those who perish, because they did not receive the love of the truth so as to be saved. For this reason God will send upon them a deluding influence so that they will believe what is false, in order that they all may be judged who did not believe the truth, but took pleasure in wickedness. (2 Thess 2:10–12)

From the part of the chapter on why Satan must be released from the abyss, we learned that (1) a major theological divide exists for understanding Rev 20:1–6 to occur before the return of Jesus Christ or after it. (2) As part of the Abrahamic covenant provisions, God promised to curse the one who curses Israel (Gen 12:3); later in Num 24:9, Yahweh broadened this promise in the midst of a section that specifically speaks of the Messiah's reign. (3) The Davidic covenant promises include Isa 9:6–7, which promises that once the Messiah sits on David's throne, "there will be no end to the increase of His government or of peace." (4) In Jeremiah 30–33, the Book of Consolation, God makes a series of promises of future blessing, especially when the Messiah reigns. (5) In the same chapter in which God first calls the new covenant by name (Jer 31:31–34), He also promises that Jerusalem will one day be rebuilt for Himself, and once it is done, it shall be holy to the Lord and never again "be plucked up or overthrown" (vv. 38–40). (6) Passages such as Zechariah 14 and Isa 65:20 show that sin, punishment, and death will occur on earth even after the Lord returns to earth to reign.

Accordingly, then, we learned that (7) as part of the benefits of the Davidic covenant, God promises there will be "no end to . . . peace" (Isa 9:6–7). Therefore, in Rev 20:7–9a only an assemblage for battle will transpire in this final rebellion rather than a battle itself, for a battle would go against the promised word that Messiah's reign would experience no end of peace. (8) When Satan comes up against Messiah with massive Gentile forces (Rev 20:7–8), so that "they came up on the broad plain of the earth and surrounded the camp of the saints and the beloved city" (v. 9a), Yahweh has long before determined and revealed the outcome of any such rebellion because Jerusalem, once rebuilt for the Lord, will never "be plucked up or overthrown" (Jer 31:40). (9) Further, God's promise to curse the ones who curse Israel (Gen 12:3; Num 23:9) is not limited only until Christ's return to earth but includes even the last part of His millennial reign and will be just as operative in this final Gentile rebellion as it was when God first gave it in Genesis 12. (10) Also, Jesus must reign until He has abolished all rule and all authority—with the last enemy He will abolish being death. Then He will deliver up the kingdom to the Father, which is the transition from Revelation 20 to 21–22. (11) Finally, God's promise to Israel to curse the ones who curse them actually relates to all enemies of Israel and not only to the Gentile nations. In keeping with God's Word, God curses Satan and the demons, and throws them into the lake of fire (Rev 20:10, Matt 8:29, and Jas 2:19).

Deeper Walk Study Questions

1. What are the two major theological divisions in understanding Rev 13:3–4? Be specific.

2. What are the problems if Rev 13:1–8 has already occurred in history past, with someone like Nero? Name three reasons and support your answer biblically.

3. Name the four reasons why many with a futuristic understanding of the return to life of the beast cannot view this beast as an individual. Name the reasons why they would say it must be the return of the final world empire.

4. Give three biblical rebuttals against those who say that if an agent of Satan (such as the Antichrist) could actually perform miracles in the tribulation, it would warp any biblical worldview for the uniqueness of God. Explain and be specific.

5. Who are the first two inhabitants of the lake of fire? What does Rev 19:20 reveal about this, and why is it important? Also, what does Rev 20:10 show concerning the Antichrist and the false prophet? Why is this important? Explain.

6. Why is it incorrect to say all of the unsaved will appear before Jesus at the great white throne judgment? Explain and support your answer biblically.

7. What is the significance of the Antichrist and the false prophet bypassing the great white throne judgment? What does this indicate, and why is this important? Explain and support your answer biblically.

8. How does knowing that the Antichrist and the false prophet will not be killed at the return of Jesus (Rev 19:20) but already at some point will have received their resurrected bodies allow more credibility for the idea that the Antichrist will truly receive a fatal wound in Rev 13:3–4 and actually return to life? Explain and be specific.

9. How does knowing that the Antichrist will have a resurrected body by Rev 19:20 make it more feasible that the beast who will come out of the abyss will be an individual and not an empire, especially since the *entire* lost world will marvel over this? Explain.

10. What is the significance of Revelation 12 as it relates to what will happen in Revelation 13? Explain and support your answer biblically.

11. What is the significance of the false prophet not being worshipped in the tribulation? Explain and be specific.

12. What is the basis for how Rev 20:1–6 is explained in totally different ways? Present both positions of how these verses are interpreted.

13. What are the three general categories of how Rev 20:3 is viewed? Explain.

14. What are the promises God made in Gen 12:3 and Num 24:9, and why are these significant? Explain and be specific.

15. What does Isa 9:6–7 promise will happen? Be specific with this, and explain why this is important theologically.

16. What is the significance of Jeremiah 30–33 in the context of Jeremiah? Explain and be specific. What does God promise in Jer 31:31–34, 38–40? Be specific and tell why both passages are significant theologically.

17. What does Zechariah 14 state in regard to the return of the Lord to earth and the sin and punishment that will occur even at that time? Explain and be specific, and tell why this is important theologically.

18. Why is there no actual battle, but only an assemblage for battle, in Rev 20:7–9a? Answer by using the covenant promise God has given concerning Jerusalem and the peace that will accompany the Messiah's reign. Be specific and tell why this matters theologically.

For Further Reading by Greg Harris

The Cup and the Glory: Lessons on Suffering and the Glory of God (The Woodlands, TX: Kress Christian Publications, 2006) (Study guide available).

The Darkness and the Glory: His Cup and the Glory from Gethsemane to the Ascension (The Woodlands, TX: Kress Christian Publications, 2008) (Study guide available).

The Stone and the Glory: Lessons on the Temple Presence and the Glory of God (The Woodlands, TX: Kress Christian Publications, 2010) (Study guide available).

The Stone and the Glory of Israel: An Invitation for the Jewish People to Meet Their Messiah (The Woodlands, TX: Kress Christian Publications, 2016).

The Bible Expositor's Handbook: Digital Old Testament (Nashville: B&H Academic, 2018) (With videos, audio and video, and journal links).

The Bible Expositor's Handbook: Digital New Testament (Nashville: B&H Academic, 2019) (With videos, audio and video, and journal links).

The Face and the Glory: Lessons on the Invisible and Visible God and His Glory (The Woodlands, TX: Kress Christian Publications, 2019).

Subject Index

Scripture Index